P9-CRI-462

Distributed Computing: Implementation and Management Strategies

Raman Khanna
Editor

P T R Prentice Hall
Englewood Cliffs, New Jersey 07632

Editorial/production supervision
and interior design: *Dit and Dominick Mosco*
Cover design: *Lundgren Graphics*
Manufacturing buyer: *Mary E. McCartney*
Acquisitions editor: *Mary Franz*

Prentice-Hall, Inc.
A Paramount Communications Company
Englewood Cliffs, New Jersey 07632

The publisher offers discounts on this book when ordered in bulk quantities. For more information, contact:

Corporate Sales Department
PTR Prentice Hall
113 Sylvan Avenue
Englewood Cliffs, NJ 07632

Phone: 201-592-2863
Fax: 201-592-2249

Printed in the United States of America
10 9 8 7 6 5 4 3 2 1

ISBN 0-13-220138-0

Prentice-Hall International (UK) Limited, *London*
Prentice-Hall of Australia Pty. Limited, *Sydney*
Prentice-Hall Canada Inc., *Toronto*
Prentice-Hall Hispanoamericana, S.A., *Mexico*
Prentice-Hall of India Private Limited, *New Delhi*
Prentice-Hall of Japan, Inc., *Tokyo*
Simon & Schuster Asia Pte. Ltd., *Singapore*
Editora Prentice-Hall do Brasil, Ltda., *Rio de Janeiro*

Contents

Foreword

During the mid-1990s, distributed computing will take wing. All major users of information technology are moving from computing models that feature a central processor and dependent resources to models that distribute the display, data, and data-processing tasks associated with an application onto many computers connected by a network.

The shift from centralized to distributed computing is already having a profound effect on the way we use computers to support business operations. Most organizations are building and deploying client/server applications, and realizing greater openness, functionality, and user productivity as a result. However, these organizations are also encountering a number of technical, economic, and organizational issues as they move to client/server architectures. As more and more corporate applications are built on distributed architectures, the impact will become greater. *Distributed Computing: Implementation and Management Strategies* is required reading for information systems architects, managers, and developers seeking to master the transition from centralized to distributed computing.

The evolution from centralized to distributed computing has been under way since the first end-user terminals were attached to IBM mainframe databases some 20 years ago. Terminals made accessible data stored in large central computers to large numbers of business users by distributing the display of those data. The next step in the evolution, taken during the 1980s, was to break up the big central computers–scattering display, functional logic, and data across a variety of workstations and servers. The 1980s left us with a legacy of *decentralized* resources. During the 1990s, we have begun coordinating these decentralized resources. Coordination of resources on a network is the essence of distributed computing.

Although it is logical to coordinate decentralized systems to attain greater value, the movement to distributed computing is being driven by more than technological evolution. Distributed computing is being driven by powerful business forces. The corporate downsizing movement of the late 1980s and early 1990s yielded radically restructured business organizations. The most visible result of this restructuring was the elimination of middle-tier managers, who had been responsible for synthesizing and filtering information obtained from the field for top management and communicating top management's directives to the field. The typical corporation no longer pushes most business issues up large management hierarchies for resolution. Rather, decisions are being made by managers closest to the end customer. There is still a need for top management to guide decision-making by managers and employees on the front lines, but without middle managers, how?

Few corporations have mastered the answer to this question yet. The answer undoubtedly will involve organizational procedures and structures as well as new information systems. Those information systems will rely on a distributed computing foundation. Distributed computing leverages the flexibility and cost-effectiveness of networks to distribute applications and data to the point of greatest customer effectiveness, to promote collaboration between co-workers, customers, and partners, and to give end-users unprecedented access to data.

As the early users of distributed computing technology attest, the transition from centralized computing architectures will not be easy. As it turns out, Sun Microsystems' famous marketing tagline, "the network is the computer," was all too glib. It has not been easy to duplicate the data-integrity, manageability, and security features of mature centralized architectures (particularly mainframes) on distributed computing platforms. Nor has it been easy for systems architects and builders to master the new operating-system software required by distributed platforms. They must learn new tools and development techniques.

Distributed Computing: Implementation and Management Strategies presents an excellent survey of developments in both of these areas. It shows that we have made real progress toward robust and complete distributed computing platforms and tools, and points toward future advances in distributed computing.

John R. Rymer
Editor
Distributed Computing Monitor

Preface

In today's demanding business climate, information systems have become a critical resource. Large organizations are investing hundreds of millions of dollars every year on their information systems. In order to maximize returns on their investment, these organizations are evolving their information systems to achieve lower operating cost, increased productivity, and competitive advantage. In most cases, this evolution means implementation of a cohesive distributed information and computing environment. In order to build this environment, an organization needs to create a distributed computing infrastructure that provides global information access and support services, such as distributed data management service, distributed file management service, messaging service, and directory service.

To end-users, the term distributed computing environment signifies a seamless information and computing environment that can be accessed from a customized graphical user interface. To systems administrators, a distributed computing environment means a changing technology, increased complexity, and the lack of management tools. To applications developers, a distributed computing environment provides supporting services and a framework that offers reduced complexity, interoperability, portability, and the ability to reuse code. Organizations expect to obtain flexibility, scalability, real-time access to information, and faster development and deployment of business solutions.

During the last five years, the rapid proliferation of personal computers and affordable workstations and pervasive data communication networks have changed the way organizations support computing. Most large organizations have already implemented networked computing environments comprised of mainframes, UNIX-based servers, and personal computers. These organizations are faced with the challenge of integrating disparate environments into a scalable, reliable, secure, and manageable distributed computing environment. Distributed computing frameworks such as Open Software Foundation's Distributed Computing Environment (OSF/DCE) and SunSoft's ONC+ were created in response to the challenges faced by these organizations.

Objectives

The purpose of this book is to provide an overview of distributed computing technologies, describe the experiences of early implementors of distributed computing environments, and present implementation and management strategies to benefit organizations that are planning to migrate to a distributed computing environment. This book is intended for information systems professionals who are planning to be involved with design, implementation, or management of distributed computing environments at a departmental or institutional level. Computer science and information science students who have taken classes in networking and distributed systems can use this book to understand issues related to the implementation and management of distributed computing environments.

The contributors to this book are all experienced information systems professionals who have been involved in the design, implementation, and management of distributed computing environments. At the time of this writing, most of the contributors are involved in designing or implementing second-generation distributed computing environments for their institutions. This process includes a close examination of the first-generation distributed computing environments in order to make the second-generation more reliable and manageable. End-users at these institutions are involved in providing feedback regarding the usefulness of various services, the responsiveness and reliability of the system, and the user interface. What makes this book unique among others on distributed systems and computing environments is that the main emphasis is on implementation and management. This book is written from the perspective of people who have to support large numbers of end-users in a distributed computing environment. This book is not a collection of previously published articles. All the chapters were written after a detailed outline was finalized; it took over six months of discussions with more than 25 people to finalize the outline. My biggest contribution to this book was identifying key issues, identifying people who had dealt extensively with those issues, and getting them interested in this project. Most of the contributors to this volume have played key roles in the design and implementation of successful distributed computing environments. Readers will notice that a significant amount of information in this book is based on the actual experiences of people who not only design and implement systems but are also responsible for managing distributed computing environments used by thousands of users on daily basis.

Organization and Contents

This book is intended to provide a tutorial on distributed computing technology and to help the reader understand what is involved in implementing and managing a distributed computing environment. I have assumed that the reader understands the concepts underlying basic data communication, operating systems, and computer architecture. Although each chapter on a specific topic can stand by itself, the reader will benefit more by reading the chapters in sequence.

The first chapter describes the framework of the book. It introduces the issues and challenges involved in implementing and managing a distributed computing environment; provides definitions of commonly used terms such as downsizing, rightsizing, client/server; and summarizes the process for migrating from a centralized, timesharing, computing environment to a distributed computing model.

Part I: Technology and Standards

Part I is an overview of distributed computing technology and standards. It includes tutorials on: distributed file systems; distributed database management; security in distributed computing environments; distributed systems management; Sun Microsystems' Open Network Computing Plus (ONC+) environment; and the Open Software Foundation's Distributed Computing Environment (OSF/DCE).

Part II: Case Studies

Part II includes five case studies of institutional distributed computing environments. The studies focus on lessons learned by professionals responsible for design, implementation, and management of these environments. The case studies are: the Project Andrew at Carnegie Mellon University; Project Athena at MIT; the Institutional File System project at the University of Michigan; Hewlett Packard's migration to client/server architecture; and Eastman Kodak's distributed computing architecture.

Part III: Implementation and Management Strategies

Part III focuses on design, implementation, and management strategies for creating an institutional distributed computing environment. Based on the information presented in parts I and II, this part presents a cohesive strategy for migrating to a distributed computing environment. It includes: distributed computing strategies of major computer systems vendors; distributed systems management strategies; strategies for migration to distributed computing environments; and organizational issues related to the migration process.

Appendices

This book also includes four appendices on topics that are likely to have significant influence on distributed computing environments. Appendix A provides a brief overview of Open Software Foundation's Distributed Management Environment (OSF/DME). Appendix B provides a brief description of Object Management Group's Common Object Resource Broker Architecture (CORBA) and the role of object technology in distributed computing. Appendix C describes Apple Open Collaboration Environment (AOCE), a framework for developing collaborative applications. Appendix D provides a tutorial on Simple Network Management Protocol (SNMP), and the increasingly important role SNMP is playing in distributed systems management.

Acknowledgments

I want to thank all the contributors: authors for taking time out of their busy schedules and providing superb material; Mary Franz of Prentice Hall for her continued support; Dit Mosco of Prentice Hall for overseeing the production of the book; and Dominick Mosco for copyediting the material. Special thanks are due to my wife Indu for her indefatigable support, and to my children Sonal and Sahil for letting me do my "homework" on weekends.

From the beginning, I treated this book as a collaborative project in which I played the role of project manager. I am very proud of the result; this project is a good example of using information technology for collaboration. To complete this book, I exchanged over 400 messages with contributors, and many more were exchanged among contributors. I want to thank all the people who run the reliable Internet, which allowed us to share information and ideas, review each others work, and move documents around quickly.

Raman Khanna
Stanford University

Chapter 1

Introduction

Raman Khanna
Stanford University

1.1 Background

Over the past 15 years, the computing environment at most large organizations has evolved considerably from one comprised of dumb terminals connected to expensive mainframes in glass houses to one comprised of networked personal workstations[1] and servers (see figures 1.1a through 1.1c). The next step in this evolution is known by many names, but I like the term *distributed computing environment.* Many organizations have been using networked personal computers for over a decade now. Companies like Novell have thrived on the business of connecting personal computers over networks to allow resource and data sharing. Distributed file systems, like Sun's Network File System (NFS), have been around since 1985. It is generally agreed that for the last ten years the industry has focused on networking, and for the next ten years the focus will be on distributed computing. Of course, advances in networking technology will continue to be critical for the success of multimedia and distributed applications.

What is it that distinguishes a *distributed computing environment* (see figure 1.1d) from a *networked computing environment*? Networked computing environments allow users: to share peripherals, data, and programs; to access information; and to communicate with others through electronic mail and conferencing, but lack system management and the infrastructure for providing integration across various applications running on multiple platforms. The distributed computing infrastructure and distributed services blocks shown in figure 1.2 will be absent in a similar block diagram for a networked computing environment.

In just a few years, most enterprises have become complex webs of computers of various sizes, attempting (and often failing) to interoperate through a plethora of networking technologies. Information technology vendors are quick to offer solutions for the global networked

[1] The term personal workstation is used to represent personal computers and workstations.

computing that users require. However, they have been slower to address the more difficult problem of integrating these solutions to create a cohesive distributed computing environment. Computers are still too hard for people to use. Graphical user interfaces (GUIs) and the conventions that they provide have done much to improve some of the worst aspects of using computers, but little has yet been done at the level of system services, particularly distributed services, to make computers act the way humans would expect.

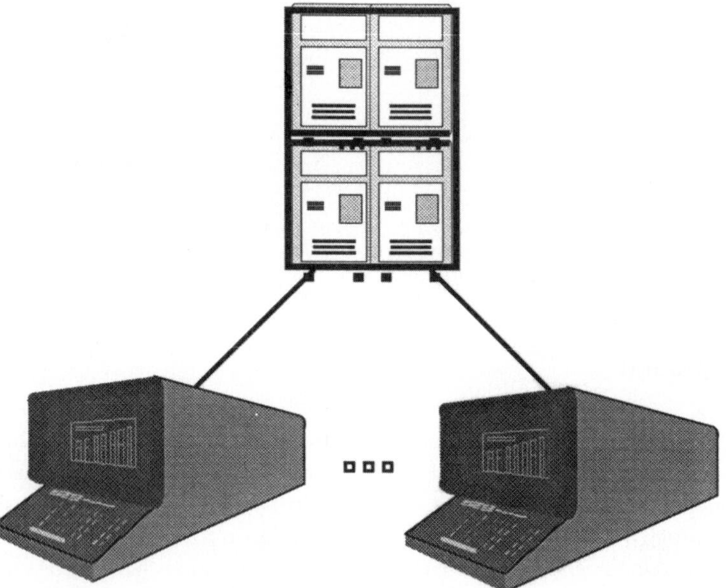

Figure 1.1a Terminals connected to mainframe.

Today's networked computing environments, which have made an enormous amount of information available through global networks, present users with a rather hard paradox: you must know where information is before you can find it. For example, let's consider the things you will have to do if you want to know the amount your company spent on airline travel last year. First you must know how to find the expense accounting system; then you must figure out how to find the appropriate database tables; and then you must use a database-specific query tool (that you may never have used before) to search for the information you want. So, with any luck, if you already know where it is, you just might find it. Now you might want to find the phone number of a colleague in a distant office. Where do you look? What querying and browsing tools do you use for that database? Even if you find her telephone number, will you then need to use a third set of tools to find her e-mail address and send her an electronic message? Then a fourth set of tools to create a group memory database so that the two of you can share information and documents on a common project? A fifth set of tools to content-index, query, retrieve, and manage versions of a set of documents that you create as part of the project? And a sixth set of tools to set her access permissions on a group of confidential spreadsheet files stored on your local file server?

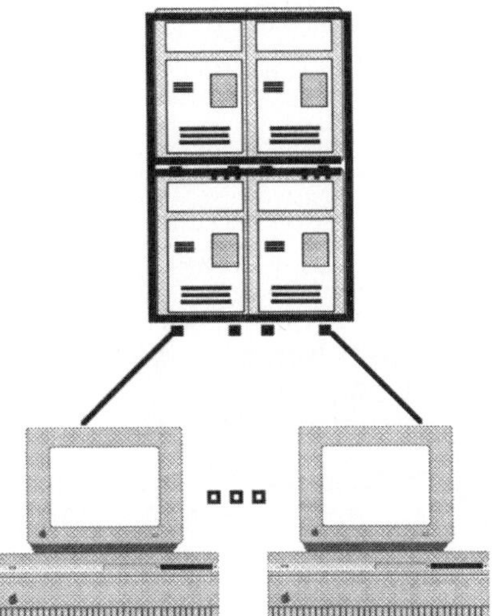

Figure 1.1b Stand-alone PCs connected to mainframe.

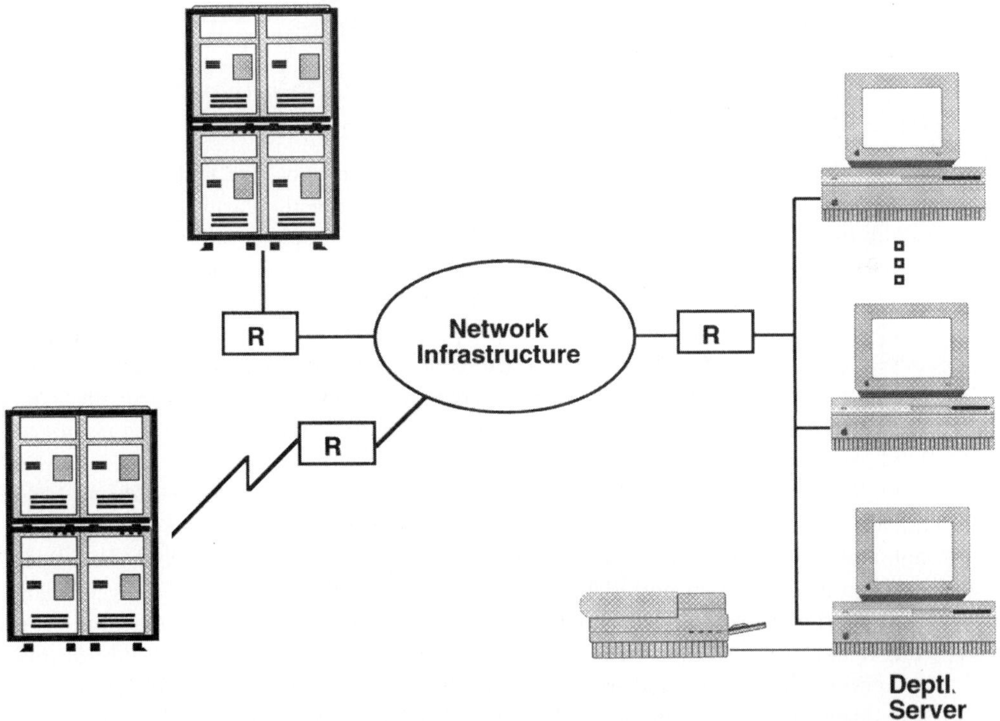

Figure 1.1c Networked PCs connected to mainframe(s).

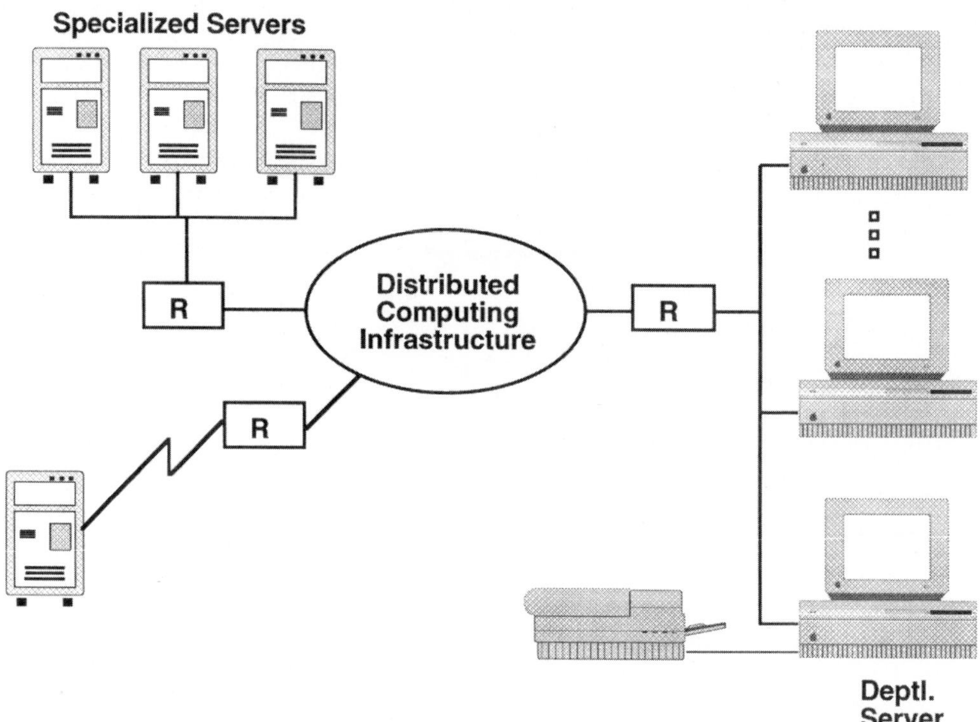

Figure 1.1d Distributed computing environment.

What's the solution? Integrated distributed applications that look and feel alike and allow users to perform a set of activities seamlessly might be the obvious answer. Distributed applications require supporting services such as inter-application communication protocols, directory service, time service, file- and print-sharing protocols, security service, messaging service, systems management service, structured query language (SQL) database programming models, groupware, or unstructured replicated database services. The problem is that there are too many *open standards* for these services. Distributed applications built on top of one "open" infrastructure will not interoperate with some other *open* infrastructure standard. It is discouraging to see many standards for distributed computing infrastructure just in the UNIX domain alone.

What should organizations do? They can either sit on the sidelines and wait for some miracle to happen, or they can start with pilot projects to gain experience with implementation and management of distributed computing applications. Organizations should participate in the user forums and lobby vendors to provide solutions that allow organizations to implement and manage cohesive distributed computing environments. Organizations planning to implement distributed computing environments need to follow closely the distributed computing plans of key systems vendors like Apple Computer, Digital Equipment Corporation, Hewlett-Packard, International Business Machines, Microsoft, Novell, and Sun Microsystems.

Some organizations feel that rather than making a huge investment to build integrated applications at this time, its better to only make the investment in implementing a reliable and manageable distributed computing infrastructure. This approach is based on the notion that ultimately the integration of information from different applications must be made in the user's mind. Rather than implementing truly integrated distributed applications, an organization can achieve integration by providing a convenient way for users to simultaneously access and move information among multiple applications. One implementation of this model might use X terminal (or Windows on personal computers) with different windows providing access to different applications, both old and new, and cut/paste to move data among applications. This is a cost-effective way of dramatically increasing productivity, while waiting for better distributed application development tools to become available.

Implementing and managing distributed computing environments is an enormous task. There are three key components of a distributed computing environment:

- •Distributed computing infrastructure
- •Systems management
- •Distributed applications

Figure 1.2 shows a distributed computing environment from a user's perspective. From his or her personalized computing environment on the desktop, a user may access departmental systems, enterprise systems, or on-line information resources. These business systems are built on top of a distributed services running over a distributed computing infrastructure that is running on top of computing platforms and a data communication infrastructure. It should be noted that a user may occasionally access distributed computing services directly.

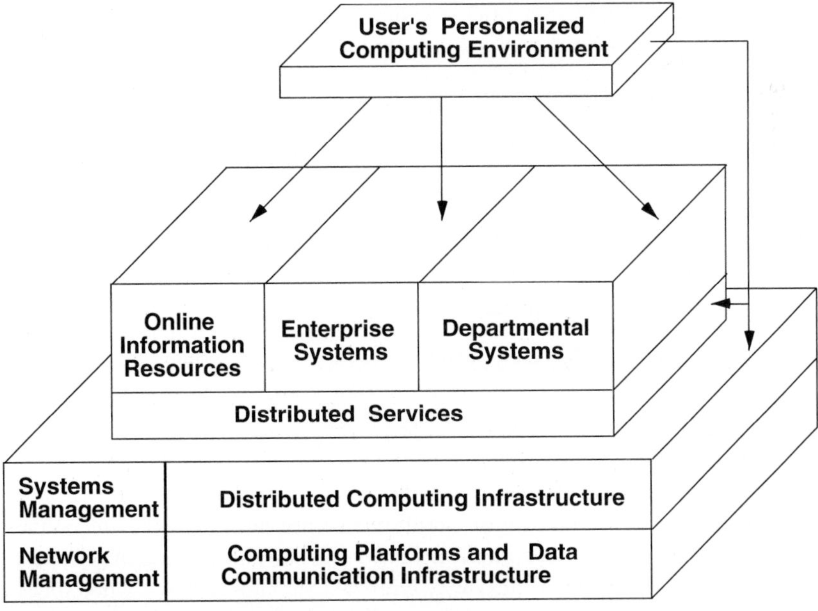

Figure 1.2 Distributed computing environment.

This book provides a tutorial on technologies, standards, and strategies related to the first two components. Distributed applications development, especially that which is based on an object-oriented paradigm, will certainly be addressed by many other books. Even though most issues discussed in this book should be applicable to all platforms, readers will notice that mainly UNIX platforms are considered as server platforms. I am fully aware of the fact that all UNIX platforms combined have only 9 percent of the desktop market. However, most large-scale distributed computing projects I am familiar with have used UNIX as the server platform and provided mechanisms to integrate non-UNIX personal computers. For example, the Institutional File System (IFS) described in Chapter 10 supports UNIX, MacOS, and DOS/Windows clients. There have been some very interesting, small-scale distributed computing projects involving homogeneous personal computers and interconnect technology. Non-UNIX platforms dominate the desktop and the LAN environment, but I think that UNIX will continue to dominate the server market.

In the computing platform arena, three developments worth watching are: 1) the result of Novell's acquisition of UNIX Systems Laboratories (USL); 2) availability of Microsoft's Windows NT on RISC platforms like DEC's Alpha; and 3) impact of Apple-IBM joint venture, Taligent, on personal computer industry. Moreover, vendors dominating the personal computer market are providing interoperability with OSF/DCE. For example, Microsoft is using elements of OSF's DCE technology, including RPC, Kerberos, and SMB file and print connectivity. Apple has announced that AOCE will interoperate with OSF's DCE. Integration of non-UNIX personal computers into a distributed computing environment is an important issue and should be addressed in a separate book. The strategies described in this book will be most suitable for medium- to large-size organizations that already have a networked computing environment.

This chapter provides a brief overview of various aspects of distributed computing. I have attempted to answer the following questions:

- Why are large organizations adopting a distributed computing model?
- What is the meaning of terms such as distributed computing, client/server computing, and downsizing?
- What are the key drivers, enablers, and challenges of distributed computing?
- What are the main components of the total cost of migration to a distributed computing environment?
- What issues are addressed in this book?

1.2 Definitions

Before describing the advantages of distributed computing environments and associated phenomena, such as client/server computing and cooperative processing, it is important to understand what these terms mean. It is very clear that the industry as a whole does not agree on these definitions. The following definitions illustrate this problem. In a volume like this with multiple contributors, it is even more important to understand that all authors might not be working with the same definitions.

1.2.1 Open Systems Environment

As we all know, all vendors in the world now provide products that are *open* and *standards-based!* When was the last time anyone heard a computer vendor advertising its products as *closed* and *proprietary*? The basic idea of open systems is to provide integration, interoperability, and portability of applications and data.

In a single vendor environment, this can be accomplished with proprietary solutions that are not open. As a matter of fact, the terms *open* and *proprietary* are not mutually exclusive. Various flavors of UNIX, Netware, and Microsoft Windows are all proprietary technologies. However, interfaces to these platforms are published and widely available.

In his book "Open Systems," Gary Nutt (Nutt, 1992) states:

> *"An open system is one in which the components and their composition are specified in a non-proprietary environment, enabling competing organizations to use these standard components to build competitive systems."*

The concept of Open Systems allows users to select solutions from different vendors. However, the problem is that there are too many open system standards. A vendor can come up with a completely new architecture, make specifications for various application programming interfaces (APIs) public, and claim that they support open systems. Many users relate open systems to UNIX as historically it has been easy to port applications across various UNIX platforms.

The Institute of Electrical and Electronics Engineers (IEEE) Technical Committee on Open Systems (TCOS) emphasizes international standards in its definition of open systems. TCOS defines open systems as:

> *"A comprehensive and consistent set of international information technology standards and functional standards profiles that specify interfaces, services, and supporting formats to accomplish interoperability and portability of applications, data, and people."*

IEEE TCOS also defined a portable operating system interface (POSIX). Other organizations, like X/Open, International Organization for Standardization (ISO), OSF, and Object Management Group (OMG), play important roles in defining open systems. In March 1993, six major UNIX vendors (Hewlett Packard Company, IBM Corp., The Santa Cruz Operation, Inc., Sun Microsystems, Inc., Univel, and UNIX Systems Laboratories) announced their intent to deliver a *common open software environment* (cose) across their UNIX platforms. Their intention is to define a specification for a common desktop environment that gives end users a consistent look and feel. On June 8, DEC announced its endorsement of the *cose* process. By the time this book is published, more details will be available. In the white paper on open system process acceleration [published by UniForum on June 8, 1993], *cose* members describe *open system process* as the process in which "ample opportunity exists for every voice to be heard" and define a technology to be *industry standard open technology* only if "there is available a detailed written specification that governs correct behavior, and if implementation of complying software is unrestricted."

According to *cose* definition for *open standard technology*, technologies such as OSF/Motif, NetWare, and Microsoft Windows API are not open systems. However, one has to pay attention to the market as well. Independent software vendors (ISVs) are interested in the installed base and continue to build their applications on interfaces like Windows API.

1.2.2 Cooperative Processing

Shaku Atre (Atre, 1992) defines a cooperative processing environment as one in which "portions of an application run on different computers, and data may be at various installations." Cooperative processing also assumes the presence of a distributed computing infrastructure that allows transparent access to resources. Cooperative processing can use a client/server model, peer-to-peer processing, or some other model. John Gantz (Gantz, 1991) describes some of the main features of cooperative processing as:

- Client/Server or similar architecture to allow processing of a program across two or more processors;
- Heterogeneous networks;
- Open systems, with a qualification on the meaning of *open*;
- Common user interfaces, generally graphical and windows-based;
- Distributed application development tools and integrating subroutines;
- Lots of middleware, or software programs that aid in distributed system, network, and storage management;
- Distributed database management; and
- Object management technology.

Of course, multi-protocol networks and heterogeneous computing platforms are not necessary for cooperative processing. Many system administrators will claim that heterogeneity is the main source of complexity. Cooperative processing can be implemented and managed more easily in an environment where homogenous computing platforms are interconnected by a network with common mechanisms for accessing services.

1.2.3 Client/Server Computing

Client/server computing allocates application processing between the client and server processes. A typical application has three basic components:

- Presentation logic
- Application logic
- Data management logic

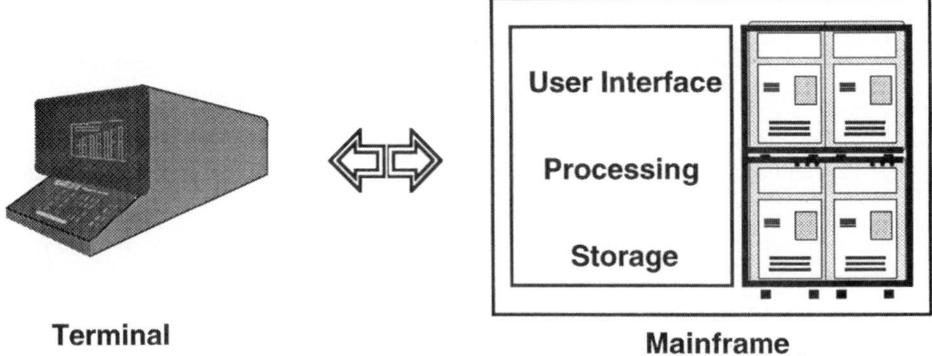

Figure 1.3a Mainframe environment.

As shown in figure 1.3a, in the traditional mainframe environment, a user interacts with an application via a dumb terminal that has a keyboard for entering commands and a display to see the results. The terminal does not have any processing ability, and all three components of an application run on the mainframe. In the client/server computing model shown in figure 1.3b, these components run on two or more systems. There are at least three different models for distributing these functions in a distributed computing model:

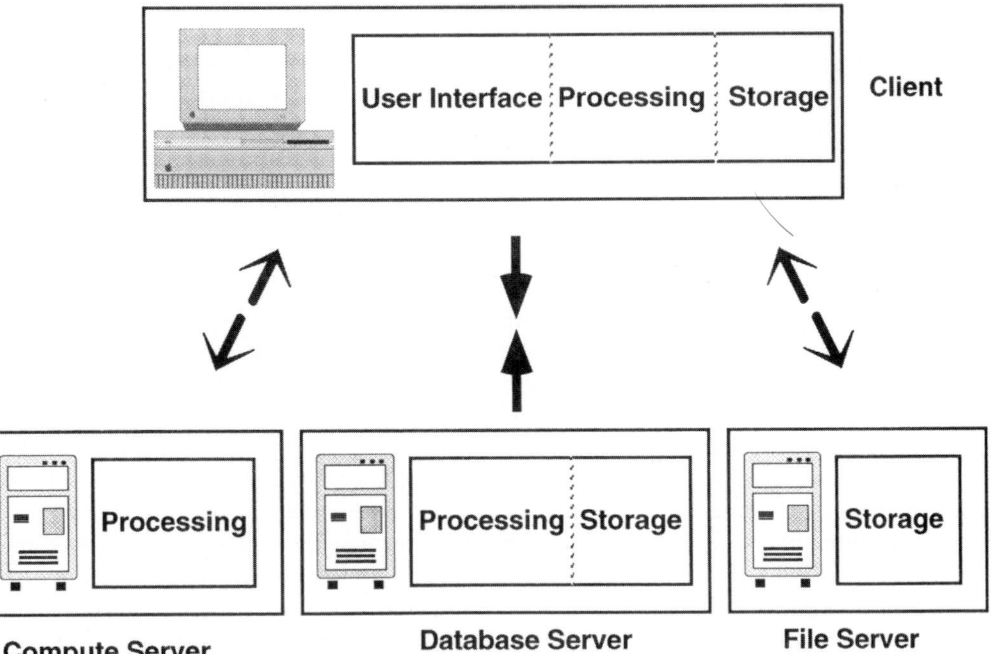

Figure 1.3b Client/server environment.

- Presentation logic module running on the client system and the other two modules running on one or more servers.
- Presentation logic and application logic modules running on the client system and the data management logic module running on one or more servers (file server model).
- Presentation logic and a part of application logic module running on the client system and the other part(s) of the application logic module and data management module running on one or more servers.

Of course, in any of the above cases, it is possible that part or all of the data is local to the client system.

In his book "Client/Server *Architecture*" Alex Berson (Berson, 1992) provides an excellent description of client/server architecture and its relationship to cooperative processing and distributed computing. According to him, cooperative processing is a necessary but not sufficient condition for the creation of the client/server architecture. An example of a scenario that would not be considered a client/server mode of operation would have two application processes cooperating in requestor/responder mode for a small duration on the same system. Hardware specialization of client and server platforms and ease-of-use gains associated with the advent of graphical user interfaces have played important roles in the popularity of the client/server paradigm. In the client/server environment, clients and servers communicate via a well defined set of APIs and/or remote procedure call (RPC).

It should be noted that in the client/server model, user presentation logic need not run on the client. For example, in the X terminal environment, the definition of client is somewhat blurred. The X window system model has three components: *display*, *X server*, and *X client*. Display is the X terminal itself, X server controls the display, and X client runs the presentation logic. What we intuitively consider the client (X terminal) runs the X server and display functions, while X client runs on a compute server.

Chapter 11 describes the reasons for and process, challenges, and benefits of Hewlett-Packard's migration to a client/server architecture for its internal business applications.

1.2.4 Downsizing

According to Atre, (Atre, 1992) "downsizing is the process of migrating complete applications, or some functions of the applications, from centralized mainframes to networks of smaller decentralized systems. It's also implementing the latest technologies, resulting in reduced costs, improved user access, and greater flexibility."

Downsizing involves distributing local processing tasks to various organizational units. The reasons for downsizing are cost effectiveness, flexibility, and more accurate reflection of organizational structures. Since downsizing involves re-implementing applications on smaller platforms, it offers organizations an opportunity to revise the architecture of business applications and eliminate some costly functions. A two-tier environment with specialized servers allows organizations the flexibility to allocate separate servers for critical functions, both to avoid problems of unintended interference, and for easier capacity planning. Capacity planning with specialized servers is easier because the impact on performance of each function can be examined in isolation.

1.2.5 Rightsizing

According to Morse, (Morse, 1993) "rightsizing is the process of choosing among available hardware, software, and connectivity options so the actual needs of a given application are served correctly and the underlying business considerations are given their due." Morse argues that downsizing is not always the right thing to do. In some cases, it makes perfect sense to migrate a large application that once served a department on a small server to a large server, which can be a mainframe. Many people use the better price/performance of PCs and RISC based systems to justify *downsizing*. However, one has to look at the overall cost of developing and supporting an application, the availability of development tools, and the scalability of platforms.

1.2.6 Distributed Computing Environments

The term distributed systems has been used to describe loosely coupled multiprocessor systems, clusters of computers, and cooperating multiple computer systems. I decided to use the term distributed computing environment to describe the information technology infrastructure and distributed applications that are being developed and deployed by large organizations. As shown in figure 1.4, to end-users, the term distributed computing environment

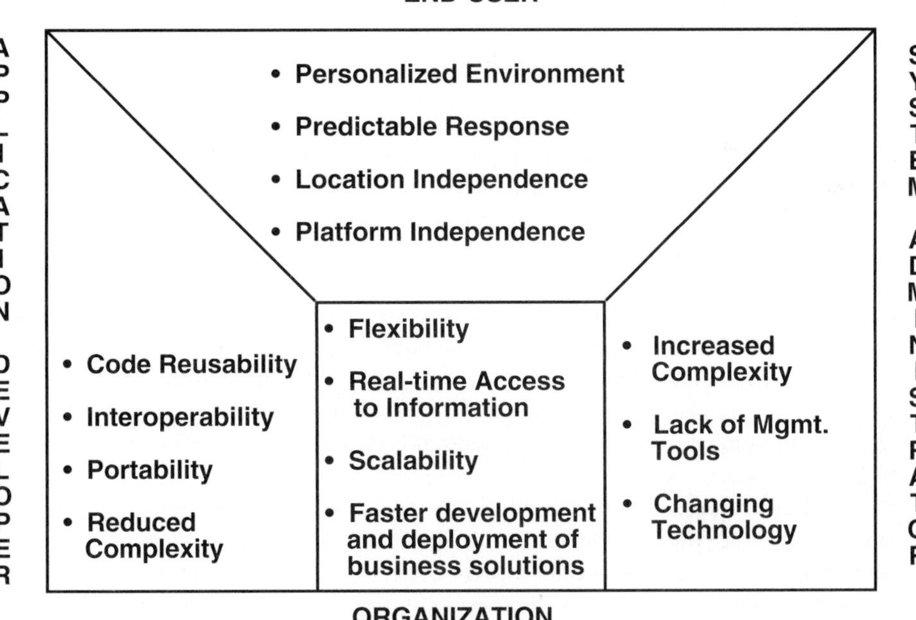

Figure 1.4 Different views of distributed computing.

signifies a seamless information and computing environment that can be accessed from a customized GUI. To systems administrators, a distributed computing environment means changing technology, increased complexity, and lack of management tools. To applications developers, distributed computing environments provides supporting services and a framework that offers reduced complexity, interoperability, portability, and provides them with the ability to reuse code. Organizations expect to obtain flexibility, scalability, real-time access to information, and faster development and deployment of business solutions.

In his book on distributed computing, Amjad Umar (Umar, 1993) states:

> *"A Distributed Computing System (DCS) is a collection of autonomous computers interconnected through a communication network to achieve business functions. Technically, the computers do not share main memory so that the information cannot be transferred through global variables. The information (knowledge) between the computers is exchanged only through messages over a network."*

A distributed computing environment is much broader than a distributed computing system; the former includes applications, enterprise systems, and management facilities. Organizations want to implement a manageable vendor-neutral distributed computing infrastructure that provides all services needed by distributed applications. Among the services needed are support for remote messaging, RPC, a directory service, time synchronization, security services, and a distributed file service. Taken together, these services provide something analogous to an operating system for distributed applications.

Eastman Kodak's vision study and two pilot projects to identify and develop a mid-range distributed computing environment are described in Chapter 12.

1.3 Overview

Large organizations throughout the world are proactively seeking innovative ways to use information technology to gain competitive advantage and/or improve the productivity of knowledge workers. Traditional hierarchical organizational structures are getting replaced by networked organizations with emphasis on personal and organizational communication, flexibility, responsiveness, collaboration, and decentralized decision-making. On-line transaction processing and decision support systems are becoming important tools as organizations need to capture transactions at the source, and managers need to make quick decisions. As a result, organizations are planning to transform their information technology infrastructure to reflect their organizational structure. In most cases, this means a migration to a distributed computing environment.

Most large organizations already have organization-wide data communication networks and local area networks at the departmental level. Information technology infrastructure at these organizations is comprised of three tiers: personal workstations used as personal productivity applications; client/server computing at the departmental or workgroup level; and mainframe-based computing for mission critical applications. This means that these organizations have a truly heterogeneous environment with at least three flavors of operating systems and many flavors of other important technologies such as databases and file systems. Users are fully aware of the environment they are operating in. Personal computing and workgroup computing generally involve GUIs and mainframe computing involves traditional command-line or transaction interfaces. These organizations have to manage different technologies and staff with very different skills, and users have to deal with at least two very different computing environments.

Since the mainframe environment is expensive and inflexible, and the users like the personal workstation environment, the obvious solution is to replace mainframes with clusters of specialized servers that support client/server interaction and GUIs. Many people think that the main purpose of implementing distributed computing environments is to downsize. A distributed computing environment does not preclude mainframes. An IBM mainframe running MVS and DB2 can be a database server in a distributed computing environment. The University of Michigan is using IBM ES/9000 running MVS/ESA as an institutional file server for its IFS project. However, organizations are looking at replacing mainframes as a way to reduce costs as they make additional investments in distributed computing technology. It seems natural that organizations want to reduce the number of hardware and software platforms they support.

Organizations planning to downsize or migrate their mission-critical applications from mainframes to a collection of networked servers are faced with many challenges. MIS staff have valid concerns about the complexity, reliability, security, and manageability of decentralized computing environments. Many people believe that before migrating mission critical applications from mainframes, organizations should first implement a distributed computing infrastructure and prove that the existing decentralized computing environment can be managed. It is hard to argue with this position. For many of the Fortune 500 corporations, the cost of failure is too high to take any risks. In many ways, this migration is like replacing the engine of your car with a more powerful one while competing in a cross-country race–one mistake and your competition will overtake you.

Information technology journals are publishing numerous case studies describing how organizations are replacing or supplementing large, monolithic mainframes with clusters of networked personal computers, workstations, and servers. A common theme among these case studies describing migration to distributed computing environments is that there are no cost savings, at least in the short term, and issues concerning people and organizational culture are as important as technical issues. MIS professionals who have been running reliable production environments for mission critical applications might not be enthusiastic about emerging technologies. On the other hand, programmers and analysts who understand the new technologies might not have the background in operating a production environment in which even small mistakes can be catastrophic. It is not surprising that universities that were pioneers in the development and deployment of distributed computing environments are still running their administrative applications on mainframes.

As adoption of distributed computing environments is accelerating, so is the availability of tools to manage these complex, decentralized environments. At this stage, organizations are implementing a distributed computing infrastructure and migrating non-critical and/or new applications to understand the challenges of supporting the new computing model. Central MIS organizations are forming partnerships with MIS support personnel within departments to support a decentralized computing model. In general, users like the flexibility of the new environment. The real challenge is to migrate mission critical applications from mainframes to the emerging distributed computing environment. Before plunging into the new environment, organizations are evaluating costs, benefits, and the challenges of migrating to a distributed computing environment.

Why are organizations planning to migrate to distributed computing environments when there are serious concerns about their ability to manage these environments? Why are organizations pursuing *downsizing* when it is not clear that there will be any savings associated with these projects? An analysis of the costs and benefits of delivering services in a distributed computing environment is provided in Chapter 16. Real benefits will be realized by end-users, but those benefits might be harder to document. Distributed computing environments have not become popular over night. The key driving forces, such as the demand for personalized computing environments, radical changes in organizational structure, and the cost-effectiveness of personal workstations are described in section 1.4. Some people believe that advances in information systems technology have allowed organizations to create a more decentralized and distributed organizational structure; others argue that new developments in information systems technology are in response to the changes in the organizational structures. However, there is no disagreement about the fact that distributed computing has arrived and is here to stay.

Overall information systems costs fall in three categories: desktops, LANs, and associated support costs for various organizational units; the central MIS organization; and the organization-wide networking and distributed computing infrastructure. Assuming that organizational units have already invested in desktops, LANs, and local support, organizations need to reduce central MIS costs so that they can invest in the distributed computing infrastructure. Due to migration costs described in section 1.7, an organization planning to migrate to a distributed computing model will have to invest more on information systems, at least in the short-term. Organizations should base their investment in distributed computing infrastructure on benefits such as flexibility, additional capabilities, increase in productivity, and competitive advantage. Once the distributed computing environment is stable and manageable, organizations will be able to reduce central MIS costs by taking advantage of cost-effective mid-range systems.

Buzzwords used to describe distributed computing environments include terms such as open systems, downsizing, rightsizing, client/server, distributed processing, collaborative processing, cooperative processing, distributed knowledge, and distributed computing. No matter what buzzwords are used, the goal is to take advantage of recent developments in information technology to create a flexible environment that allows users to access information and manipulate it regardless of the location of the information and processors.

1.4 Drivers

He that will not apply new remedies must expect new evils.
Francis Block

The move to distributed computing environments is driven by business imperatives as well as technology. Organizations are realizing that information is their most critical resource, and in order to compete effectively, they must create an environment that allows them to move information around the world efficiently. Most global organizations have already created global data communication networks. This section describes some of the key factors driving the acceptance of distributed computing.

1.4.1 The Demand for a Personalized Computing Environment

The rapid proliferation of personal computers in the 1980s has resulted in the automation of individual tasks. Most users have learned how to use word processors, spreadsheets, and databases. Personal workstations have become popular because users like the consistent response time and the ability to customize environments. As a result, personal workstations have become useful as personal productivity enhancement tools. In the mid-eighties, cost-effective networks and open systems became available, and by the end of the decade, most of the personal workstations were connected to corporate networks. It sounds too trivial, but it is important to note that peripheral sharing continues to be an important aspect of networked and distributed computing environments. It is no accident that every successful network operating system includes support for printer and disk sharing.

Personal workstations provide GUIs and the ability to support multiple, concurrent windows so that users can easily manage increasing volumes of information. Object technology and application development environments provide visual programming tools. The goal of *Visual Computing*, a concept described by Jim Manzi in the article "Working Together," (Manzi, 1992) is to enable end users to develop sophisticated, fully integrated applications using the point-and-click technique.

In the networked computing environment, significant work has been done to allow users to take advantage of specialized servers without leaving their local environments. For example, the post office protocol (POP) allows users to compose and read mail on their personal workstations while taking advantage of UNIX-based mail servers for mail transport and storage. However, there continues to be a dichotomy between the *personal* computing environment and the mainframe computing environment. For example, a personal workstation user will use Microsoft Word to do most of local document editing, while having to use a completely different interface for placing a purchase order through the organization's on-line system running on a mainframe. Users want to access various resources on corporate and global networks without having to leave their customized local environments. This drives the need for integrated applications with common user interfaces.

1.4.2 Radical Changes in Organizational Structure

In order to stay competitive, organizations are becoming flatter, decentralized, and loosely coupled global entities. Many organizations are now relying on information technology to improve internal and external coordination, and to provide centralized control and distributed decision making. In order to facilitate decision making and reduce the time it takes to complete projects, organizations need to make all types of enterprise-wide data accessible (with appropriate access control) to their employees. In their book Paradigm Shift, Don Tapscott and Art Caston (Trapscott and Caston, 1993) describe three fundamental shifts in organizational computing:

- Shift from personal to workgroup computing, allowing organizations to form high-performance teams.
- Shift from information islands to integrated systems, allowing loosely coupled teams to function better as cohesive organizations.
- Shift from internal to inter-enterprise computing to create better links between suppliers and consumers of products and services.

1.4.3 Location Independence

"No matter where you go, there you are."
Buckaroo Banzai

It is amazing to see how many people are carrying their favorite portable personal computers everywhere. It all started with non-networked portable computers. People copied some files from their networked computers at their offices so that they could finish work while traveling. I am sure that a good part of this book was written on portable computers. When these people came back to their home bases, they had to copy diskettes on to the hard disks of their computers at work. Some of them ran into version control problems as they started working with four different copies of the same document.

The next step was to buy built-in data modems for these portables so that people could connect to their home base from a hotel or home to upload and download files, read their e-mail, send e-mail, and so on. That solved some problems but a created desire for connecting portables like any other node on an organization's network. As higher speed modems (9600 to 19,200 bps) became affordable, serial line IP (SLIP) and point-to-point protocol (PPP) were used to connect portables as full functionality nodes. As wireless networks become viable, the need to connect to a wall outlet will also disappear. Companies like RadioMail are already offering services over wireless networks.

Terms such as *nomadic computing*, *mobile computing*, *virtual office*, and *location-independent computing* are becoming common place. Organizations are building project teams without regard to the geographical locations of team members. Distributed computing environments are essential to support distributed teams. In addition, organizations are providing personal computers and modems (and even ISDN links) to their employees so that they can access the computing environments from their homes. For example, at Stanford, rather than having engineers on duty during off-hours, we have provided network management stations to key engineers.

Whoever is on call can diagnose a problem from home and, in many cases, even resolve the problem from home.

1.4.4 Cost Effectiveness of Personal Workstations

One of the advantages of microprocessor based personal computers and workstations is that they offer much better price/performance than mainframes. Berson (Berson, 1992) compares the cost of transaction per second (TPS) for an IBM mainframe running DB2 (approximately $100,000 to $200,000 per TPS) with that of a similar capacity IBM RS/6000-520 or Sun SparcServer 40 (approximately $1,000 to $4,000 per TPS). Maintenance costs are also much lower because large organizations can afford to keep spare workstations. Workstations are also getting very reliable, and annual maintenance costs can be less than 1 percent of the purchase price. These days, disk drives come with five year warranties and the prices have come down so much that it is more economical to stock spares and discard malfunctioning components and devices than to purchase maintenance contracts.

1.4.5 Need for Real-Time Access to Information

In mainframe based applications, most data is embedded within the application and not easily accessible from other applications. In today's business environment, employees need real-time access to information. According to Grenier and Metes, (Grenier and Metes, 1992) "an organization's ability to deliver products and services depends on how well it continues to build its knowledge, and on the data and information upon which that knowledge is based." Many vendors have started using electronic mail to provide customer support. If customer engineers have real-time access to bug-fixes made by engineering departments, they can do a much better job of supporting their customers. Also, by having a distribution list for customer service, various clients are able to help each other.

1.5 Enablers

Distributed computing involves running integrated distributed applications over a distributed computing infrastructure. These applications need to run on multiple processors and require support from system software running on a collection of machines rather than an operating system running on one machine. A reliable and coherent distributed computing environment requires many pieces of technology working reliably. This section describes some of the key enablers that have made distributed computing environments viable.

1.5.1 Reliable and Pervasive Data Communication Networks

During the past ten years, significant improvements in the reliability and performance of data communication networks have been made.

Most organizations consider a data communication networks to be a utility like electricity and telephone service. For new buildings, the cost of activating a network connection in each room is considered part of the building cost. Most computer vendors have started including network interfaces on the *mother boards*. As a result, it is safe to assume that all computers owned by an organization will be connected to the corporate network.

1.5.2 Availability of Distributed File Systems and Databases

One of the key motivations for moving to a distributed computing environment is to provide, transparently, a structure for managing and accessing information from geographically dispersed file systems, shared resources, and databases. Before distributed file systems became available, users had to transfer files from servers to their local workstations, work with the files, and then transfer the modified files back to the server. Network File System (NFS) from Sun Microsystems and the Andrew File System (AFS) from Transarc corporation have simplified data sharing in a distributed computing environment. On the personal computer side, NetWare and other network operating systems have provided excellent environments for sharing resources. Organizations are looking at the integration of LAN operating systems like NetWare with OSF/DCE. Similarly, major database vendors are releasing distributed databases that provide access to multiple sources of data as if they were all part of a single database. A database application might store, retrieve, and update information in transactions that span databases without violating any database consistency and integrity.

1.5.3 Messaging

Electronic mail continues to be the most popular application in networked environments. Messaging, on the other hand, is part of the distributed computing infrastructure that supports electronic mail and other applications. Large organizations consider messaging to be one of the key elements of distributed computing infrastructure. Systems vendors have realized the importance of establishing standard APIs for accessing the messaging infrastructure. Groups like X.400 API Association (XAPIA) are working on common mail calls to allow a wide range of applications to interoperate. Messaging provides a store-and-forward transport of electronic objects, and the ability to address objects, applications, and people. Messaging infrastructure is being used for interpersonal communication (electronic mail), inter-application communication (electronic data exchange), and information distribution.

1.5.4 Distributed Object Computing

According to Christopher Stone, President of the Object Management Group (OMG), "Object technology will do for the software industry what Ford's model-T did for the automotive industry." An object-oriented software paradigm is enabling faster software development by promoting code reusability, interoperability, and portability. C++ and SmallTalk are the two dominant object-oriented languages. In addition to enhancing the productivity of applications developers, object frameworks are being used for data management, enterprise modeling, and systems and network management. Objects can contain complex information and data types, such as sounds and images. Each object has a unique identifier that allows applications to access the object without knowing specifics of the object's location or implementations. Computer networks have allowed organizations to link together islands of information. Object technology will play a key role in application development and the management of distributed computing environments by reducing complexity and providing high-level interfaces. A discussion of the role of object technology in distributed computing is provided in Appendix B.

1.5.5 Network and Systems Management Platforms

Effective network and system management tools are critical for reliable operation of distributed computing environments. During the past four years, the networking industry has made significant progress in building useful network management platforms. Protocol wars are over, and the whole industry is consolidating around a small number of management platforms.

Management platform vendors have finally realized that they cannot develop all the tools required by users, and they are encouraging independent software vendors (ISVs) to develop management tools on their platforms. Appendix D provides an overview of the simple network management protocol (SNMP) and the its role in network and distributed systems management.

Many management platform vendors have also realized that what users really need are management tools that can be used to manage the distributed computing environment that includes the network, clients, servers, and so on. OSF's Distributed Management Environment (DME) emphasizes the need for tools that take advantage of the object technology. It is too early to predict the future of DME, but it is clear that DME has helped focus attention on the need for management tools for distributed computing environments. An overview of DME is provided in Appendix A.

1.6 Challenges

Integration of all corporate computing platforms and applications into a distributed computing environment is a daunting task.

MIS professionals who have been managing centralized, mainframe-based computing environments understand how hard it is to manage the environment and keep tabs on performance. Systems management, security, and performance monitoring in a distributed environment are much more complex. This section identifies some of the key challenges of implementing and managing a distributed computing infrastructure. Chapter 9 describes some of the lessons learned from MIT's project Athena. Chapter 14 provides a detailed discussion of distributed computing management strategies and some of the approaches used in Project Andrew at Carnegie Mellon University.

1.6.1 Complexity

As described in Chapter 5, systems management is a complicated task, even for a single system. In distributed computing environments, the complexity increases significantly due to the large scale, heterogeneity, security, distribution, naming, and synchronization. This complexity is caused by a combination of a distributed model as well as heterogeneity. One might argue that a distributed computing environment does not have to be heterogeneous. At Stanford, we support four different UNIX platforms in our academic computing environment. Managing this environment requires that systems administrators become familiar with system administration tools for four different UNIX platforms. There are also other incompatibilities between these systems that make operating this environment much harder than managing a homogeneous environment of the same size. Good systems management tools for heterogeneous environments are not available at this time. Systems management tools comprise one of the key areas mentioned in the *cose* announcement. Chapters 5 and 9 describe various issues related to managing distributed resources.

In distributed computing environments, the responsibility of users can increase tremendously as users must manage desktop computers rather than a dumb terminals. Many organizations are using the X Terminal model, dataless workstation model, and other techniques to solve this problem. Chapter 9 describes MIT's solution. Better tools are needed for remote installation and management of various computing platforms.

1.6.2 Data Integrity and Security

As described in Chapter 4, security is perhaps the most important aspect of distributed computing environments. In the course of a day, a typical user might have to access as many as 50 different services. In the absence of an organization-wide authentication system, a user will have to be authenticated and authorized for each service request. Maintaining information for a requisite audit trail is also very important. Security mechanisms such as authentication, access control, encryption, and audit trail must be designed and implemented as an integral part of an organization's distributed computing environment. These mechanisms are a combination of technology and policies that are agreeable to all organizational units. A distributed computing environment is as secure as its weakest link.

1.6.3 Performance

How does one measure the performance of a distributed computing environment? Is it in the transactions or queries per minute (TPC rating), response time for interactive traffic, throughput when accessing a remote file, or something else? Is it the SPECmark rating of the server platform? It is very important to manage expectations regarding reliability and performance, but who decides when to increase network bandwidth, processing capacity of the clients, servers, or the number of servers?

1.6.4 Organizational Changes

Distributed computing results in savings in certain areas and additional expenses in others. For example, hardware savings for servers will accrue to the systems division, but end-user departments incur new costs for desktop hardware, software, and training. Organizations need to shift savings from the systems division to fund end-user departments that incur new costs. Because distributed computing environments are more flexible than mainframe-based environments, they are often more complex. Various IS functions might have to be reorganized in order to support this more complex environment.

In a distributed computing environment, it is very important to have a highly skilled central staff that is responsible for strategic planning. In many cases, a transition to a distributed computing is also coupled with a transition to distributed support model. As a result, MIS professionals who were doing institutional planning are sometimes eliminated. This is a big mistake; in a distributed computing environment, it is even more important to coordinate computing activities of individual units and plan for infrastructure.

1.6.5 Training

Even though distributed applications using GUIs are easier to use, there is an increased need to train end-users when the first set of applications are made available. If an organization makes sure that different applications follow a consistent user interface standard, users need only learn about new business processes.

Training requirements for technical staff, both central and at the organizational unit level, increase significantly. In order to diagnose problems, systems administrators need to be familiar with networking concepts as well as operating systems. A performance problem could be caused by an overloaded network, overloaded server(s), or some problem in the client machine. Network and systems management tools provide a good snapshot of traffic and statistics on a particular LAN or backbone. However, there is nothing that can analyze the complete path from the client module of an application to the server and data access modules of the same application running on various servers.

1.7 Migration

Migration to a distributed computing environment must be analyzed in terms of return on investment. An organization may choose to call it rightsizing, downsizing, or whatever the latest term in vogue is. Some organizations make this decision on an application by application basis. For example, if the life of an application is expected to be short (less than two years), it makes sense to leave it running in the existing environment.

In his article on "Rightsizing," Morse (Morse, 1993) provides an excellent summary of potential expense items. This section is based largely on that article and my interpretation of the issues it covers. Chapter 15 describes some strategies for large organizations planning a migration to distributed computing environments.

Hardware costs: This is perhaps the easiest component of the overall cost to calculate. Organizations need to determine server platforms, number of servers, amount of storage required, increased investment in the data communication infrastructure to improve reliability and manageability, cost of maintenance contracts, and an estimate of additional hardware required in subsequent years.

Software acquisition costs: This is perhaps the major component of the overall cost. While the hardware is getting cheaper, software costs have been going up steadily. Software costs will include systems software for the infrastructure, systems management and administration tools, and applications. Application costs seem small on a per machine basis. However, aggregated over thousands of workstations, the numbers add up to millions of dollars. Any scheme involving administrative tracking of individual copies will have very high costs. As a result, organizations are pressuring vendors to offer more aggressive volume discounts so that they can justify making central purchase decisions. Network based, concurrent use licenses are becoming popular and can be very useful in distributed environments. Many vendors are offering volume discounts if organizations agree to provide support and documentation internally. This increases support costs for organizations. Maintenance costs for applications is also becoming a significant part of ongoing costs.

Application development costs: Depending on the nature of a need, an organization might choose to develop an application rather than purchase an existing one. Costs will include staff time and software development tools. In addition to the development costs, there will be significant retraining costs to bring the development team up to speed on the latest programming techniques.

Data conversion: During the transition to distributed computing, many organizations make the mistake of addressing data conversion after applications have been ported. Data organization and verification are important aspects of the migration strategy. Data structures that were suitable for mainframe applications might not be suitable for distributed applications running on smaller platforms. Also, current business needs might be very different from the business needs at the time the existing data organization model was selected. In his article on data conversion, Doug Van Kirk (Van Kirk, 1992) recommends that data organization must be in place before new applications are written. According to him, the five key elements of successful data conversion are:

- Careful examination of data before commitment to a table structure;
- Allowing plenty of time and resources for a clean-up effort;
- Developing a company-wide data architecture;
- Recognizing that a new platform could require a different data structure;
- Elimination of outmoded business processes that produce useless data.

It is important to develop a high-level data model that represents an organization's data requirements first and then address application design and data conversion.

Parallel operation: Despite careful testing before an application is migrated from a mainframe environment to a distributed computing environment, it is important to run two systems in parallel for a few months to make sure that there are no problems. Also, organizations don't migrate all their applications on the same day. It is not unreasonable to expect a five year period for migrating all applications. Organizations typically migrate older applications that were designed 10 or more years ago and might not be suitable for current business needs. This means that in the short-term, total costs will increase as both systems will have to be run in parallel.

Retraining: Any time there is a major change in the computing environment, retraining users and support personnel becomes very important. If the organization standardizes on GUIs and application conventions, learning new applications becomes easier. Organizations are considering the use of multimedia technology to reduce training costs. Another factor to be kept in mind is that many users and data center employees will resist change.

Support: Most organizations choose a decentralized model to support a distributed computing environment. In the terminal-to-mainframe computing model, there is no need to have local support, as all the complexity is on the mainframe. In the distributed computing model supporting end users becomes complex; it is very hard for a central organization to support end users. When problems crop up, they could be with personal workstations, LANs, bridges, routers, servers. In many cases, a peer-support model emerges in which users who have become experts help their co-workers. Many organizations realize this and fund at least one *local expert* per 50 users. It is important to realize that support costs will shift from central MIS organizations to individual departments as institutions migrate to distributed computing environments.

It should be noted that a distributing computing model does not necessarily require a distributed support model. Many people will argue that a distributed computing infrastructure allows them to implement an effective centralized support model. As described in Chapter 12, Eastman Kodak is using a centralized support model for the system administration of their distributed computing environment.

1.8 Summary

Medium- to large-size organizations are planning to transform their information technology infrastructure to reflect their organizational structure. Organizations have been running individual and workgroup productivity applications on a networked personal workstation and specialized server environment. Now organizations are looking at ways to save MIS costs by migrating mission critical applications from mainframes to UNIX and other mid-range server platforms. In order to provide effective system integration, many organizations are planning to invest in a cohesive, distributed computing infrastructure. The real benefits to end users are realized through integrated applications with common user interfaces.

This book is focused primarily on the implementation and management of distributed computing infrastructures for large organizations. Chapters following this one provide: an overview of key distributed computing technologies, such as distributed file systems, distributed database management, distributed systems security, distributed systems management, and distributed computing frameworks (Sun's ONC+ and OSF's DCE); case studies of distributed computing projects at three universities and two corporations with emphasis on the lessons learned from these projects; the distributed computing strategies of the Hewlett-Packard Company, IBM Corporation, Microsoft Corporation, and SunSoft, Inc.; strategies for migration to and management of distributed systems; an overview of organizational issues; and appendices on OSF/DME, the role of object technology in distributed computing, Apple's Open Collaboration Environment (AOCE), and a description of Simple Network Management Protocol (SNMP) and the role it is playing in distributed systems management.

This book will provide readers with an understanding of key technologies and an insight into the process of implementing and managing a distributed computing infrastructure.

1.9 Acknowledgments

The author gratefully acknowledges Mark Ryland of Microsoft for his contribution to the first section of this chapter, JQ Johnson of University of Oregon and Terry Gray of the University of Washington for their insightful comments, and Rosalind HaLevi of Stanford University for the final review.

1.10 References

Atre, S., 1992. *Distributed Databases, Cooperative Processing, and Networking.* McGraw Hill.

Berson, A., 1992. *Client/Server Architecture.* McGraw-Hill.

Gantz, J., 1991. Cooperative Processing and the Enterprise Network, *Networking Management*, Jan., pp 25–40.

Grenier, R. and Metes, G., *1992. Enterprise Networking: Working Together Apart,* Digital Press.

Manzi, J.,, *1992.* Working Together, Proceedings of Groupware '92, Morgan Kaufman, pp3–9.

Morse, S.,, 1993. Rightsizing: Tailoring the Applications and the Platforms. *Network Computing,* Feb, pp 63–77.

Nutt, G.,, 1992. *Open Systems.* Prentice Hall.

Tapscott, D. and Caston A.,, !993. *Paradigm Shift.* McGraw Hill.

Umar, A.,, 1993. *Distributed Computing: A Practical Synthesis.* Prentice Hall.

Van Kirk, D., *1992.* Downsizing host applications; data conversion is often the last but most critical step in re-engineering. *InfoWorld,* Dec 28, p39.

Raman Khanna is the director of Networking Systems at Stanford University. He is responsible for the design, implementation, and management of a campus-wide data communication network, distributed computing infrastructure, and academic computing environment on Stanford campus. Raman has special interest in the integration of personal workstations in distributed computing environments.

Raman holds a BS in Electrical Engineering, an MS in Computer Science, and an MBA in High Technology Management. He has been working, consulting, and lecturing in computing and data communication fields since 1980. Raman is contributing editor of a recent book on FDDI published by John Wiley and one of the contributors to the Internet System Handbook published by Addison Wesley. Raman also teaches courses on Computer Networks and Distributed Computing at the UC Berkeley Extension program.

Part I

Technology and Standards

Chapter 2

Distributed File Systems

Peter Honeyman
University of Michigan

2.1 Introduction

The ability to store permanent data has always been fundamental to information technology. The part of an operating system that offers long-term storage is called the file system. For files to be shared and reused, the file system arranges stored objects in such a way that they can referred to with names. The file system is obliged to guarantee that a file and its name will exist from the time that it is created until the time that it is destroyed.

A local file system is one that resides entirely on one computer and is inaccessible from other computers. Local file systems using magnetic disk are fast, inexpensive, and reliable. Technology advances are expected to make tens or hundreds of megabytes available on credit card-sized devices, so that one's personal files can be carried in a shirt pocket.

Notwithstanding their advantages, there are drawbacks to entrusting all of one's storage to local file systems. A major concern must be the security and integrity of data. A file system carried in a shirt pocket is subject to loss or corruption. Important data must be backed up onto archival media at regular intervals to ensure against its loss, and the fact is that most individuals do not care to be saddled with system administration responsibilities.

Another problem with local file systems is the clumsiness associated with sharing. Back when many users time-shared a single computer, file sharing was easy and natural. With computers now personal, sharing files frequently entails exchanging diskettes, or explicitly transferring copies of files among users on a network. With the proliferation of copies, it can become a challenging problem to determine which among the copies is the current version.

In this chapter, we describe trends in distributed file systems, which support transparent access from disparate, interconnected computers. We touch on the communications technology that interconnects client and server, but in general that is too low-level a topic for this chapter.

2.2 Fundamentals and Terminology

Over the last decade, the UNIX operating system has achieved prominence as the vehicle for operating systems research and development. As such, most distributed file systems owe an intellectual debt to the UNIX file system, emulating it to varying degrees, and most of the concepts of distributed file systems are best seen by comparison to the UNIX file system.

Distributed file systems are based on client/server technology. One or more file servers cooperate with clients of the file system so that the clients can access the files managed by the servers. With the locus of control distributed among clients and servers, some of the goals of file systems that are easy to maintain on centralized systems become quite complicated. We examine some of these goals in the remainder of this section.

2.2.1 Sharing

The UNIX file system, typical of native file systems running on a single computer, offers a kind of shared memory to applications: file changes are immediately visible to all at arbitrarily fine granularity. Such fine-grained sharing can be maintained in a distributed system, but at substantial complexity and cost, so distributed file systems make compromises on the single-site UNIX model. One direction is open/close semantics, where updates are visible only when a file is opened, and changes propagated only when the file is closed. Open/close semantics eliminates many of the file reads and writes by clustering operations on very large buffers, often as large as the whole file. Client caching naturally goes hand-in-hand with open/close semantics.

Concurrency control in a local file system is usually straightforward, as all of the action occurs in one place. For example, UNIX serializes file system access through a cache of buffers in the kernel: the last writer wins any race. Of course, lock support is available to applications that require strict concurrency control. Distributed file systems complicate matters by decentralizing the problem of maintaining a consistent copy of the file.

Of course, concurrency control is necessary only when files are shared. We can categorize sharing into three modes: read sharing, sequential write sharing, and concurrent write sharing (see figure 2.1). Read sharing, in which all of the accesses to a shared file are read accesses, imposes no special constraint on file system semantics. When there is a single writer and one or more readers, we have sequential write sharing. Here the challenge is to make all of the users of the shared file have a consistent view of the contents. Concurrent write sharing takes place when there are multiple, simultaneous writers. This adds to the challenge of sequential write sharing by forcing consideration of interleaved updates.

Write sharing in distributed file systems is especially troublesome when more than one copy of the shared file exists, for example, when clients cache file contents for lengthy periods or when servers replicate files. Were there no caching or replication, clients would go to the file server on every request, and could rely on the sharing semantics native to the file server.

Not incidentally, along with its semantic role in sharing, the UNIX buffer cache also greatly speeds access to files. In distributed file systems, client caching serves similar purposes: both consistency and performance are addressed.

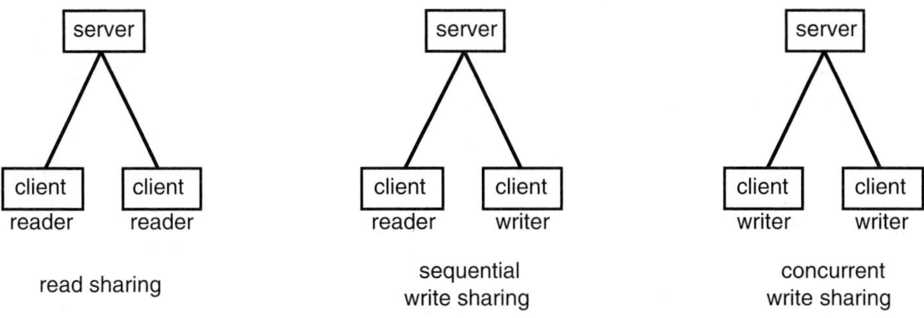

Figure 2.1 Types of sharing. In read sharing, all of the clients sharing a file are readers. Here there is no potential for conflict. If write sharing is sequential, that is, exactly one client is writing at a time, consistency is assured, but caching readers may not see the most current data. In concurrent write sharing, two or more clients are writing a file. If their writes are interleaved, the final state of the file is unpredictable.

In later sections, we shall see a number of techniques that balance sharing and caching in distributed file systems. Some emulate precisely the single-site UNIX sharing model, while others make compromises in the direction of more effective caching to reduce communication and processing overhead.

2.2.2 Failure and Availability

Availability is at odds with concurrency control. The principal approach to increasing availability is replication: if one server is unavailable, a replicated server picks up the slack. But when writers are competing, that is, when concurrency control is needed the most, the existence of multiple storage sites leads to complicated and expensive algorithms and extra delays.

The mechanisms for maintaining consistency in replicated servers depend on the sort of failures that are anticipated. It is possible, but very costly, to accommodate the most general sort of failures, in which failed servers continue to respond to requests, albeit incorrectly. This model is often relaxed, so that failed servers are assumed to crash. With the crash model, restarting a failed server necessitates providing it with any file system updates that it missed while it was unavailable. This is frequently implemented by designating a master site for each file, with updates flowing through the master site to the slaves holding copies (see figure 2.2).

A further restriction, one that is quite common, is read-only replication. Of course, eliminating writers vastly reduces problems with concurrency control!

Another class of failure specific to distributed systems is network partition. It is impossible to tell if a remote system is unavailable because it has crashed or because it is on the other side of a partitioned network. Techniques useful for server crash recovery are also used here.

Whether or not replication is featured, all distributed file systems have some sort of recovery procedure to handle failure, although few offer the sort of transactional guarantees prominent in database systems. Client failure is usually easily detected and accommodated. Most recovery protocols focus on server failure; the most common approach is for clients to await the server restart and then patch matters.

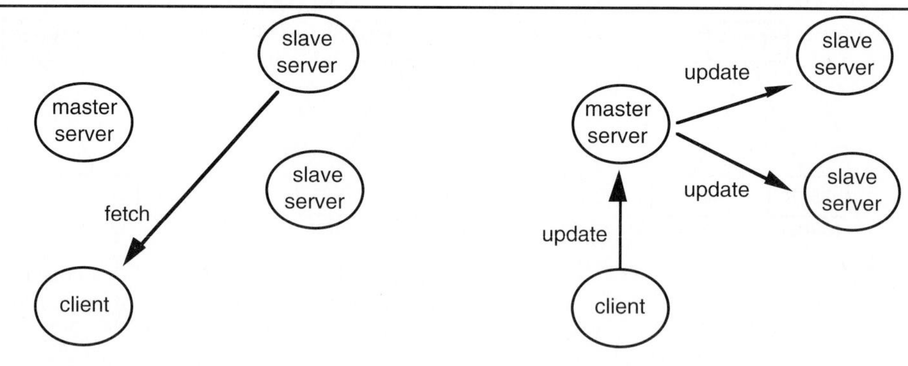

Figure 2.2 Master–slave replicated file servers. A client may read from any server, in this case from a slave server, but updates are required to go through the master server. In some systems, there is exactly one master server for a given file, while in others, each client can determine its own master server. Client updates are sent to the master server, which is then responsible for notifying the slaves. If a slave server is unavailable, it must be updated after repair.

Whether or not replication is featured, all distributed file systems have some sort of recovery procedure to handle failure, although few offer the sort of transactional guarantees prominent in database systems. Client failure is usually easily detected and accommodated. Most recovery protocols focus on server failure; the most common approach is for clients to await the server restart and then patch matters.

2.2.3 Scalability

When considering the scalability of a distributed file system, the major concern is the effect of increased scale on client performance. Of course, if increased scale has an effect on server performance, that will become visible to clients in the form of extra delay; really both concerns must be kept in mind. For a distributed file system to scale well, it must exploit the resources of clients. There are presumably far more clients than servers, so the bulk of the computing resources are with the clients.

For this reason, distributed systems that scale well try to make servers as simple as possible and delegate a portion of the responsibility of system management to client machines. In the context of distributed file systems, this is evident in the way cache consistency is managed, as we shall see.

Just as replication complicates concurrency control, it can affect scalability. Additional storage sites increase the amount of work servers must do to maintain a consistent state of the file system. Similarly, clients in a replicated file system may have more work to do when they make file updates.

It is difficult to capture the characteristics of an ideal scalable system, but a few things are clear. A system that scales well should degrade gracefully as saturation is reached, while remaining fair in the servicing of requests. In addition, it should be possible to grow the service base incrementally, bringing additional resources to bear as they are needed. But this must not adversely affect the other parts of the system: if each piece of a system must know about every other piece, the complexity of the system becomes overwhelming as it becomes large-scale.

2.2.4 Location Transparency

Distributed computing environments enable greater user mobility; with ubiquitous access to computers, it is difficult to anticipate a user's physical location. Yet, access to personal files is among the most important pieces of a computing environment. To achieve the goal of location transparency, it is necessary to offer a file system that looks the same in numerous places. While a shirt pocket file system, mentioned earlier, offers one solution, it has numerous disadvantages. Distributed file systems offer a different approach to location transparency: they offer a uniform view of the distributed filing environment by offering a common service to dispersed clients, users, and applications.

Another aspect of location transparency pertains to naming: a naming scheme should insulate clients from having to know the location or identity of servers. This eases application development, as transient host names need not be embedded in software or supporting services. It also makes system administration easier, as files and directories can be moved among servers to help balance the load without the concern that this would break applications.

The distributed file systems we will consider in detail support the needs of location transparency to varying degrees. In some cases, careful system administration is required to present a uniform name space to all clients.

2.2.5 Naming

Naming is the process of associating logical structures, such as character strings, with physical objects, such as files. The UNIX file system provides a simple naming structure built out of directories that contain files and other directories. UNIX prohibits a directory from being contained in more than one parent directory; accordingly, the structure formed by a collection of UNIX directories is a strict hierarchy. One distinguished directory, the root, is designated "/". File and directory names are constructed by traversing the hierarchy, composing names with the "/" character (see figure 2.3).

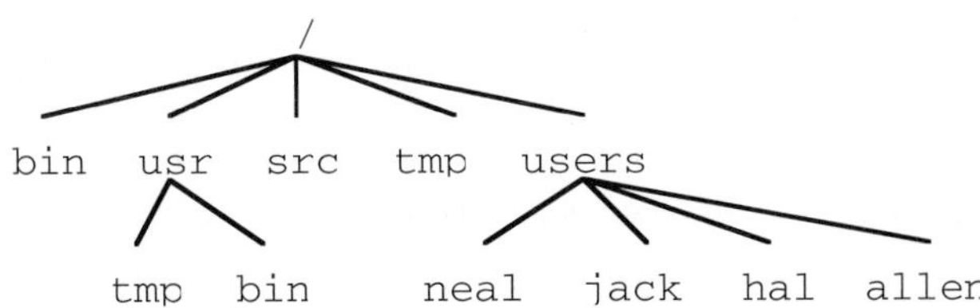

Figure 2.3 UNIX directory hierarchy. Names depicted here include `/usr/bin` and `/users/neal`.

For transparency, distributed file systems try to emulate the naming practices of native file systems as closely as possible. Hierarchical naming is prevalent, so the same holds for distributed name spaces. Constructing hierarchies entails grafting, or mounting subtrees onto one another (see figure 2.4). Names are mapped into files by traversing the name hierarchy component by component.

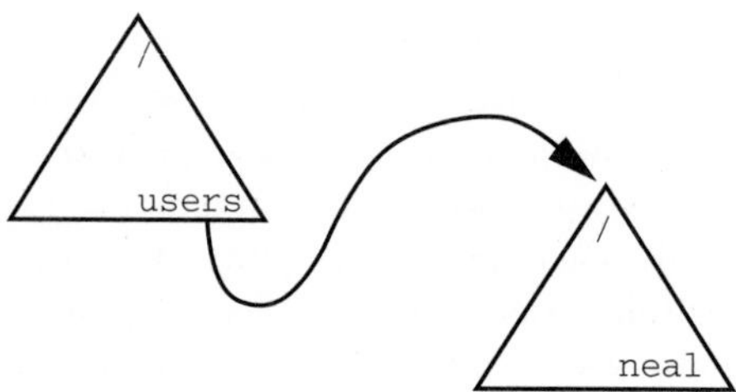

Figure 2.4 Mount points. The figure shows two logical file systems, one containing `/users`, the other containing `/neal`. Mounting the latter onto the former's `/users` produces the name `/users/neal`.

The handling of mount points varies among different distributed file systems. On some systems, mount points are built on the clients as part of an initialization procedure, while on others, mount points are among the data stored on file servers. In the latter case, clients of the file system all see exactly the same names. But when mount points are stored only on clients, two clients can mount the same object in different places, resulting in different names for the same files.

2.2.6 Access Control

As with the name space, transparency dictates that distributed file systems try to support access control mechanisms comparable to those on native file systems. This mandates external agents or services for user identification and authentication. These topics are taken up in Chapter 4; here we will give some instances of the way identities are manipulated by distributed file systems.

In operating systems that support multiple users, the granularity with which operations such as read, delete, and so on, can be permitted to others varies widely. Because UNIX groups are difficult to administer, UNIX offers limited control over sharing. Distributed file systems exacerbate the problem, where world-read capability can take on literal meaning.

Group management more directly under the control of users is critical to large-scale file systems. But the ability to create and manage groups depends directly on the ability of users to specify other identities in the system, which returns us to the question of authentication and directory services.

2.3 *De Facto* Standards

In this section, we look at examples of popular distributed file systems. The first two, Sun Microsystems' NFS and Transarc's AFS, are highly successful, commercially available distributed file systems. We also consider the Open Software Foundation's DFS, which promises to play a major role in distributed computing environments of the 90s.

2.3.1 NFS

One of the first commercial distributed file systems, and certainly one with broad appeal, is Sun Microsystems' Network File System. NFS has several architectural features, now standard among open distributed file systems, that showed great innovation. First, NFS is an open system: the protocol is specified in publicly available documents in sufficient detail that it can be implemented from the description. Second, in designing NFS, Sun defined the Virtual File System, or VFS, an abstract interface between the operating system and the file system. VFS allows multiple underlying implementations to coexist and has been used to support a broad range of local and distributed file systems. Third, NFS is defined in terms of a remote procedure call (RPC) abstraction, and is implemented in a freely available RPC software package. Finally, the NFS RPC package includes an external data definition language called XDR that supports passing structured information among computer systems built from heterogeneous hardware and software.

Now commonplace, these four characteristics were wildly innovative when NFS was new. Being early allowed Sun the luxury of defining the standards that would guide practice for years to come. A detailed description of NFS is provided in Chapter 6.

2.3.1.1 NFS Implementation

The raw interface between applications and file systems consists of directives such as open, close, read, write, and so on, and most file systems have direct analogs for these operations. The VFS interface abstracts these file system operations into a brief list of generic operations:

open	open a file and return a descriptor
close	close a file
rdwr	read or write a file
ioctl	perform a special, file system specific operation on a file
select	wait for activity on a file
getattr	fetch attributes of a file
setattr	set attributes of a file
access	test access rights of a file or directory
lookup	read a directory entry
create	create a file

remove	destroy a file
link	give a file an alternate name
rename	change the name of a file
mkdir	create a directory
rmdir	destroy a directory
readdir	read the contents of a directory
symlink	create a symbolic link
readlink	examine a symbolic link
fsync	make permanent any changes to a file

These operations serve as the interface between applications and the underlying file system. There is some variability among operating systems regarding additional VFS operations, addressing such concerns as local virtual memory, but the above list forms the core set of file system interfaces.

The implementation of a VFS-based file system is straightforward: each VFS operation is implemented as a procedure call to an underlying file system implementation. In NFS, this procedure call is implemented as an RPC from the file system client to the NFS server (see figure 2.5). The file server processes the request by executing calls to the local file system and returns the status and data associated with the operation to the client that issued the request. For structured data, such as binary integers, Sun's RPC uses XDR, a standard external data representation that provides for a common representation among clients and servers of most architectures.

2.3.1.2 Client and Server Issues

The NFS protocol has been carefully designed so that every request can be processed independently of the requests that preceded it. This allows the server to be stateless: no information is maintained on behalf of the NFS clients. The major advantage of a stateless server is the simplicity of its failure recovery procedures. As each client request can be serviced without regard to previous requests, requests following a server restart can be processed as though nothing untoward has happened. NFS clients are generally implemented in a way that lets them be extremely patient in the face of an unresponsive server; if an NFS server crashes, the client simply retries its request forever until the server responds to it. That is all there is to NFS server crash recovery. And because an NFS server is stateless, there is nothing special to be done about client failure either. There are no data structures or other information for the server to clean up.

However, a stateless server makes client caching difficult to get right. Being stateless, the server is unaware of any client caching going on. If a client caches a file, it must check with the server before each use to ensure that the file remains current. Checking with the server requires an RPC, but processing this RPC is nearly as expensive to both client and server as a request for a fresh copy of the cached data. These potential performance problems undermine the benefits of NFS client caching.

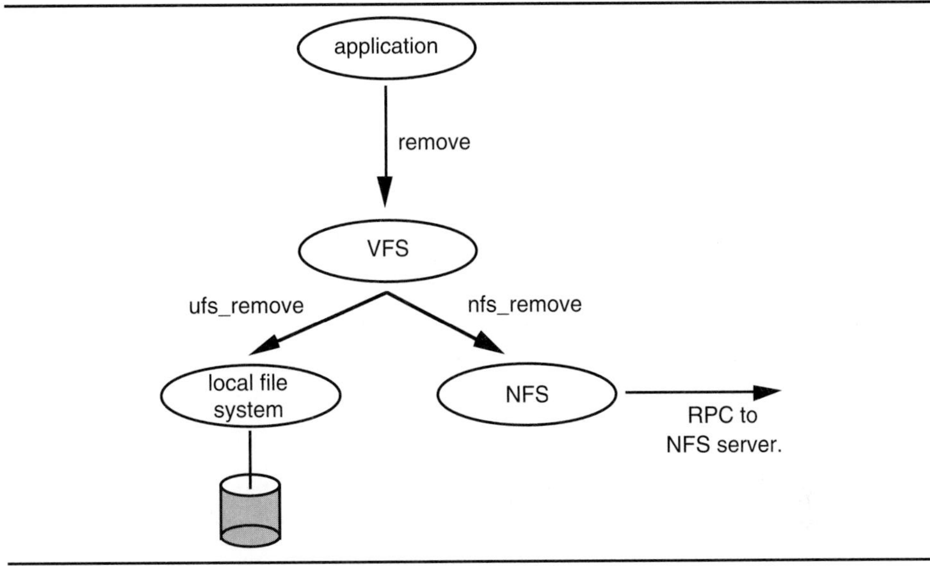

Figure 2.5 Virtual file system. An application requests that a file be removed. If the file is on the local disk, the VFS layer issues a ufs_remove call to the local file system. If an NFS file is being removed, the VFS issues an nfs_remove call to the NFS layer, which performs a remote procedure call with the NFS server.

Consequently, NFS clients take steps to improve performance by optimistically assuming that cached data are valid for a brief period of time. It is common to see NFS client implementations that decline to check for file changes if the file was checked within the last three seconds, or for directory changes if the directory was examined in the last thirty seconds. These implementation details can have grave consequences if the optimism inherent in the implementation is unwarranted, but the performance gains realized seem to outweigh the possibility of inconsistent access to files. Later, we will look at Spritely NFS, a research distributed file system that addresses precisely these concerns.

The NFS protocol offers no explicit support for sharing either, and as we just saw, client caching of shared files can cause incorrect views of file contents. Sun Microsystems offers a separate protocol for locking files over a network, but it has not really caught on in multivendor NFS environments.

An NFS server exports portions of a hierarchical name space. These hierarchies are then grafted together by an NFS client into a single hierarchy. For example, a collection of NFS servers might export some set of file systems, but an NFS client may mount them together in any way it sees fit, including mounting one hierarchy within the other. NFS does not provide for remote mounts on the server's file system; all such name space manipulation is left to the clients. As a result, it is possible for clients to have access to identical files, but have completely different names for them, which inhibits location transparency (see figure 2.6).

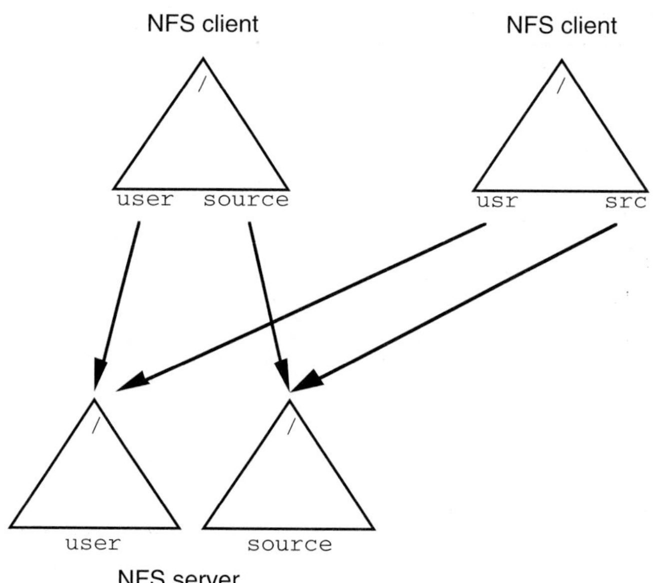

Figure 2.6 NFS client mounts. In this figure, an NFS server is exporting two file systems, which it calls `/user` and `/source`. The NFS client on the left mounts the exported file systems with corresponding names, `/user` and `/source`. But the NFS client on the right mounts the file systems on `/usr` and `/src`, respectively. Thus, even though the two clients have access to identical file systems, they have different path names for the files.

The NFS protocol offers no support for server replication. An application called the *automounter* can be used to associate a mount point with a set of NFS servers rather than a single server. Absent any systematic means to assure that this set of servers maintains identical file system images, automounter is rarely used to distribute rapidly changing exported file systems, such as home directories. However, it is useful for replicating read-only files, such as system binaries.

The NFS protocol does not specify any particular form of access control, but Sun's RPC does support a handful of methods. Usually, NFS installations elect to deploy UNIX-style authentication, in which each client provides a numeric identifier of the user who issued the file system request. As a consequence, it is important that there be agreement among clients and servers on the mapping between users and their numeric identities. Chapter 6 visits these issues.

2.3.2 AFS

At about the same time that Sun MicroSystems was preparing NFS for the marketplace, the Information Technology Center (ITC) at Carnegie Mellon University formed to develop an academic distributed computing environment called Andrew, named after Messrs. Mellon and Carnegie. The file system that grew out of this effort, called Vice, was later renamed AFS.

Subsequently, many of the ITC technical staff departed to form the Transarc Corporation, which continues to develop and market AFS.

Architecturally, AFS has much in common with NFS: clients use the VFS interface to access AFS files, AFS is based on a remote procedure call paradigm, and AFS uses the same external data representation format as NFS. The major difference that AFS introduced to the marketplace is broad support for client caching. AFS client caches are big, usually dozens of megabytes of disk. The AFS client is a VFS file system, but because AFS uses the local file system for its cache, it subcontracts to the local file system after performing any necessary RPCs (see figure 2.7).

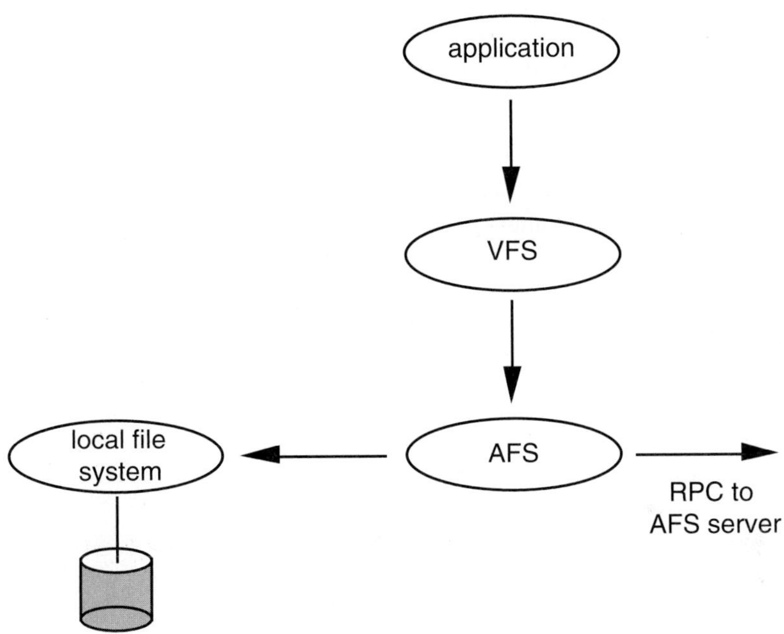

Figure 2.7 AFS client architecture. AFS requests come through the VFS interface to the AFS client cache manager, which processes the request out of the local cache if possible. If necessary, the cache manager first issues an RPC to the AFS server and caches the result.

Early on, ITC engineers discovered that Vice file servers spent a substantial amount of time servicing client cache validation requests. NFS tries to avoid such requests by optimistically assuming that cached information remains valid for a certain period after it has been validated. AFS designers were looking for more concrete guarantees.

The solution they came up with is the callback promise. When an AFS client fetches information from a file server, the information comes with a promise that the server will contact the client if the information changes. When a client updates a file on a server, the server informs all other clients caching the file that their copies are no longer valid. In this way, the server revokes callback promises when cached information is modified.

Before an AFS client uses a cached file, it checks to see whether there is a callback promise for the file. If so, the client is assured that the file contents are current, and it may use the information without communicating with the server. If the callback promise has been broken or if it has expired, the client requests the version number of the cached file from the server. If this reveals that the cached version is stale, the client refreshes its cache.

Obviously, an AFS server can not be stateless: it keeps track of client cache contents so that callback promises can be kept. To avoid becoming overwhelmed by the volume of information, an AFS server attaches an expiry to each callback promise. Furthermore, an AFS server is free to revoke callback promises at any time, should the overhead of maintaining a large amount of state information exhaust server resources.

Failure recovery is complicated by the AFS cache invalidation mechanisms. Callback promises are stored in volatile memory; when an AFS server restarts, it has no record of the callback promises it issued before the crash. This introduces the possibility of inconsistency: callback promises issued before a crash are lost, so they can not be revoked. If a client updates a file after a server restart, any client holding a callback promise for the file might use the old, stale data. To prevent this, AFS clients contact their servers periodically to inspect the server restart times. If a client sees that a server has restarted, or if a server does not respond, the client discards all callback promises offered by that server.

The AFS name space is constructed out of volumes, which can be thought of as UNIX partitions: a volume is a file system hierarchy that can be mounted into an existing AFS hierarchy. Although the mount procedure is initiated from a client, the mount lives in the file server, and is visible to all. This way, AFS provides a common name hierarchy to all clients (see figure 2.8).

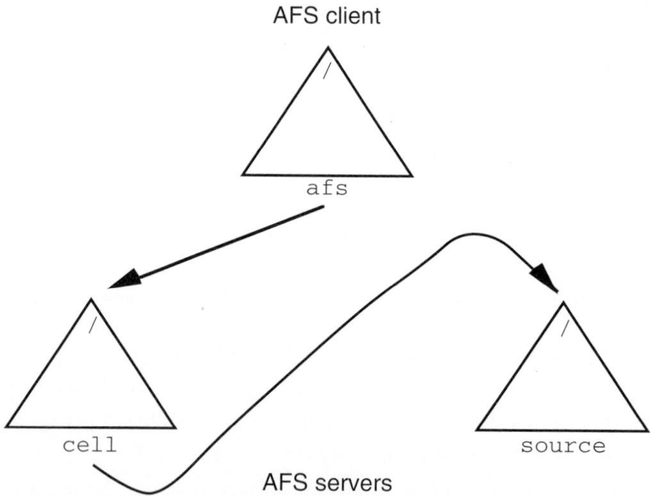

Figure 2.8 AFS volume mounts. Conventional AFS clients mount the root volume on /afs. Thereafter, remote mounts are links to other volumes. The path depicted here is /afs/cell/source.

Because remote mounts refer to low-level volume identifiers, volumes can be physically moved from one server to another without having to change any mount points. AFS keeps track of volume locations in a distributed database that is consulted by clients. The mapping between volume and server is cached by clients as a hint. Volumes can also be replicated, but replicated volumes are read-only. The volume abstraction serves the needs of location transparency and load balancing well.

Access control in AFS is governed by access control lists attached to each directory. The kinds of access gated by AFS are read, write, and lock access to files; lookup, insert, delete, and administer access to directories. Administration access to a directory allows a user to modify its access control list. Access control lists offer more flexibility than UNIX groups, yet something is lost by applying them solely to directories. In addition, access control conventions local to the client continue to pertain, which can lead to some confusion on the part of users.

2.3.3 OSF/DCE DFS

Because DFS, the distributed file system in the Open Software Foundation's Distributed Computing Environment (OSF/DCE), grew out of AFS, the two are very similar. The principal difference lies in more accurate single-site UNIX semantics in DFS. For example, where AFS uses open/close semantics on file updates, DFS makes updates visible at arbitrarily small levels of granularity. DFS supports client cache invalidation with access tokens, instead of callback promises. One type of token grants a client access to modify data in a specific range of a DFS file. With such a token in hand, a client is assured exclusive access to the range.

Access tokens admit concurrent writes with essentially no overhead if the writers' ranges do not overlap. If a client seeks a write token that overlaps with another, the server revokes the outstanding token, demands any updates, and re-issues the token. Other DFS tokens act similarly to provide single-site UNIX semantics at low cost.

In most other respects, DFS provides the same kind of services as AFS: client caching, uniform name space, read-only replication, and so on. The major difference visible to users is that while AFS brings a suite of distributed services to a client operating system, DFS is itself a client of a distributed computing environment. As a result, DFS is more effectively integrated with its distributed service base. More detail on DFS can be found in Chapter 7.

2.3.4 Comparison

The following table summarizes the external characteristics of the distributed file systems in common practice.

	Sharing	Availability	Caching	Naming	Protection
NFS	Potentially inconsistent if clients cache.	Read-only replication with automounter.	Negligible client caches.	Client-controlled mount points. Naming may not be location transparent.	UNIX identities, UNIX mode bits.

AFS	Consistent open/close sessions.	Read-only replication.	Large, coarse-grained client caches.	Name space controlled by server through remote mounts.	Kerberos identities, access control lists on directories.
DFS	Single-site UNIX semantics.	Read-only replication.	Large, fine-grained client caches.	Name space controlled by server through remote mounts.	Kerberos identities, full access control lists.

One dimension we have not explored is the ability of the various protocols to interoperate in heterogeneous environments. The protocols we have examined are harmonious in that all three can be run simultaneously on a single client. Furthermore, AFS and DFS go to some lengths to interoperate with NFS.

But problems arise when a protocol that offers UNIX-like semantics interoperates with non-UNIX clients. Even among UNIX clients there are differing standards for file name length or admissible characters in names. Extending distributed file systems to DOS or Macintosh clients, whose naming conventions are utterly foreign to a UNIX-based protocol, exacerbates these problem. Authentication and identification also present difficult challenges in environments designed without multiple users in mind. These issues are taken up in Chapter 10.

2.4 Research Systems

In this section, we look at some distributed file systems under development in research labs and universities. These systems build on what has been learned from existing distributed file systems, taking them in new directions for performance, reliability, and scalability.

2.4.1 Sprite

Sprite is an operating system for large memory, diskless workstations designed at the University of California in the late 1980s. The Sprite file system displays great innovation in two areas: naming and caching.

The Sprite name space, like all we have seen so far, is a hierarchy of directories, with name space grafting used to construct large hierarchies from small ones. The grafting is accomplished with remote links embedded in the file system of Sprite servers. A remote link points to a file or directory on another Sprite server.

Sprite has a novel approach for resolving path names. A Sprite file server associates an exported hierarchy with a path name prefix and advertises the association. Each Sprite client maintains a table that maps file name prefixes back to the server that advertised the resource. Given a path name to be resolved, a Sprite client scans the table looking for the longest matching prefix. Using the longest prefix allows Sprite file servers to export hierarchies underneath other servers' mount points.

Upon finding the longest matching prefix in the table, a client issues the file system request to the server indicated. Sprite treats the prefix table values as a hint: if the prefix table is wrong, for example, if the file being requested has been moved to another server, then the client discards the invalid prefix mapping from its table and attempts once again to resolve the name.

Initially, each client has an empty prefix table, so the first step is to broadcast a request for a root server. The broadcast protocol is also used when the prefix table is incomplete, for example, if a remote link is encountered and the table lacks a matching prefix. In this case, the Sprite client broadcasts the file name it seeks and waits for a server to respond with the appropriate prefix information. The client updates its prefix table with this information and continues.

The prefix table acts as a cache of path name lookups, which greatly reduces the network lookup traffic that would otherwise ensue. But because it uses broadcast, Sprite does not scale well beyond a single local area network.

Sprite supports client caching comparable to AFS: the server keeps track of the clients that have an open copy of a given file, and invalidates their caches should the file change. If there is exactly one client with a file open, that client is permitted cache its write operations. If a server sees write sharing among a set of clients, it instructs those clients to refrain from caching the file. With caching disabled, all read and write operations become RPCs from client to server. In short, Sprite obeys single-site UNIX file system semantics to the letter.

Sprite also allows a writer to hold onto its changes briefly after closing a file. This way, if a file is discarded soon after its creation, which is common for many output files, the data written are never transferred to the server. But if a client is holding on to its updates and another client becomes interested in the same file, the Sprite server demands the cached changes.

It may seem that Sprite would perform poorly in the face of write-shared files, and in fact it does, requiring network communication for every request. But write-sharing is rare, so overall system performance is unaffected. Sprite's caching policies also have the advantage that absent write-sharing, the client uses asynchronous writes, which decouples client write operations from network and server performance.

2.4.2 Spritely NFS

Spritely NFS, a distributed file system devised at Digital Equipment Corporation's Western Research Laboratory, combines the best features of NFS and Sprite. From NFS, it takes the complete protocol and underlying support. This provides a huge installed base of compatible systems. From Sprite, Spritely NFS borrows the cache-consistency policies and algorithms. By explicitly addressing cache consistency, Spritely NFS offers single-site UNIX sharing semantics, while its aggressive caching promises better client throughput and server performance. Naturally, a Spritely NFS server must be statefull, which complicates server failure recovery.

Spritely NFS adapts NFS by adding three RPCs: open, close, and callback. The open and close RPCs allow the server to keep track of client use of files, and are coordinated with callback promises. The callback RPC is unusual for an NFS-like system, in that it is an RPC from the server to the client. The callback RPC is used to revoke the right to cache a file, as well as to demand that cached client file changes be returned to the server.

Although statefull, Spritely NFS has lacked failure recovery mechanisms. However, such mechanisms were recently proposed and a prototype Spritely NFS system is under construction. The recovery mechanisms under development place much of the burden for server recovery on the clients. They require a small amount of stable storage on each server, to keep track of the set of clients with open files taken from that server. After a server restart, the clients listed in the server's stable storage are notified that server recovery is starting. The clients then inform the server which files they have open, and server state is reconstructed.

There are some wrinkles in the recovery protocol, such as clients that do not respond to the server's request to initiate recovery; these are handled as a special case. Client crash recovery is simple: when a client restarts, its servers are notified as part of the initial mount procedure. The servers use this information to clean up any stored state regarding that client.

Spritely NFS can simulate NFS, so it can match the performance of NFS. But Spritely NFS clients can be much more aggressive in the way they cache data, so they have the potential to show great improvement in system performance. It is too early to tell whether Spritely NFS can achieve these objectives, as an implementation is still under way.

2.4.3 Coda

The Coda distributed file system, under development at Carnegie-Mellon University, has much in common with AFS, as both systems were based on the earlier Vice distributed file system. Coda adds two features to AFS: full server replication and support for disconnected clients.

Coda implements server replication by providing that each server track the update history for each of its files. Servers that have files in common exchange version information among themselves and maintain the information in a vector of version numbers. In the quiescent state, all of the servers in common for a given file have the same file contents and the same version vectors. When a client updates a file, it sends its changes to each of the servers that maintain the file. The servers return their version vectors to the client, which compares them, looking for stale or inconsistent data. If a server has missed an update, the client arranges for the server to repair the inconsistency.

Should a server crash, it discovers after restart that it has missed some updates and recovers gracefully. The difficulty that can arise is if servers lose contact with one another because of network partition. Coda optimistically permits concurrent updates in the partitioned subnets. After network repair, servers may discover that their copies of a replicated file are inconsistent. In this rare instance, the file is made inaccessible, and manual intervention is required to repair the inconsistency.

Coda also supports disconnected operation for its clients. With Coda, mobile computers can disconnect from the network and continue to use their cached files. While disconnected, a client logs the operations it performs on its cached files. After reconnection, the client replays the log. Any inconsistency that arose during disconnection is apparent when the log is replayed; again manual techniques are employed to repair inconsistency.

2.5 Summary

Distributed filing, a routine part of everyday computing environments, continues to evolve. Even the NFS protocol, the granddaddy of them all, undergoes revision. The original goals of location transparency and sharing are met well by today's systems. Tomorrow's systems will offer vast scale and high availability. But many needs are not yet met by these distributed file systems.

One pressing need in large-scale systems lies above the file system. Global file systems will truly span the world, encompassing a huge name space. Today's file systems lack special tools to support such a broad scale. For users to find the information they are looking for, future information repositories will require the development of powerful directory servers, browsers, and search assistants.

Another direction for exploration is enterprise-scale file systems. Integration of distributed file systems and mass storage devices is clumsy. While backup tools have become increasingly sophisticated, they may be inadequate for terabyte capacity and require marriage of file servers with archival systems. Fresh ideas are needed here.

Also prevalent in the approaches we've looked at is weak support for very large files, such as still and moving images. Today's systems flush the entire cache when confronted with huge files. Specialized cache replacement policies will be among the requirements of future systems.

2.6 Further Reading

For further general information on distributed file systems, see the excellent surveys:

Levy, E. and Silberschatz, A., 1990. Distributed File Systems: Concepts and Examples. *Computing Surveys*, 22(4) Dec.

Satyanarayanan, M., 1989. A Survey of Distributed File Systems. *Annual Review of Computer Science*, Vol. 4.

2.6.1 *De facto* Standards

Howard, J.H., 1988. An Overview of the Andrew File System. *Winter USENIX Conference Proceedings*, Dallas.

Howard, J.H., Kazar, M.L., Menees, S.G.,Nichols, D.A., Satyanarayanan, M., Sidebotham, R.N., and West, M.J., 1988. Scale and Performance in a Distributed File System. *ACM Transactions on Computer Systems*, 6(1) Feb.

Kazar, M.L., Leverett, B.W. , Anderson, O.T., Apostolides, V., Bottos, B.A., Chutani, S., Everhart, C.F., Mason, W.A., Tu, S.T., and Zayas, E.R., 1990. Decorum File System Architectural Overview. *Summer USENIX Conference Proceedings*, Anaheim.

Kleiman, S., 1986. Vnodes: An Architecture for Multiple File System Types in Sun UNIX. *Summer USENIX Conference Proceedings*, Atlanta.

Sandberg, R., Goldberg, D., Kleiman, S., Walsh, D., and Lyon, B., 1985. Design and Implementation of the Sun Network Filesystem. *Summer USENIX Conference Proceedings*, Portland.

Satyanarayanan, M., Howard, J.H., Nichols, D.A., Sidebotham, R.N., Spector, A.Z., and West, M.J., 1985. The ITC Distributed File System: Principles and Design. *Proceedings of the 10th ACM Symposium on Operating Systems Principles*, Orcas Island, Dec.

Walsh, D., Lyon, B., Sager, G., Chang, J.M., Goldberg, D., Kleiman, S., Lyon, T., Sandberg, R., and Weiss, P., 1985. Overview of the Sun Network Filesystem. *Winter USENIX Conference Proceedings*, Dallas.

2.6.2 Research Systems

Kistler, J. and Satyanarayanan, M., 1992. Disconnected Operation in the Coda File System. *ACM Transactions on Computer Systems*, 10(1) Feb.

Mogul, J.C., 1992. A Recovery Protocol for Spritely NFS. *Proceedings of the USENIX File Systems Workshop*, Ann Arbor, May.

Nelson, M.N., Welch, B.B., and Ousterhout, J.K., 1988. Caching in the Sprite Network File System. *ACM Transactions on Computer Systems*, 6(1) Feb.

Satyanarayanan, M., Kistler, J.J., Kumar, P., Okasaki, M.E., Siegel, E.H., and Steere, D.C., 1990. Coda: A Highly Available File System for a Distributed Workstation Environment. *IEEE Transactions on Computers*, 39(4) Apr.

Srinivasan, V. and Mogul, J.C., 1989. Spritely NFS: Experiments with Cache-Consistency Protocols. *Proceedings of the 12th ACM Symposium on Operating Systems Principles*, Litchfield Park, Arizona, Dec.

After completing undergraduate studies at the University of Michigan, **Peter Honeyman** was awarded the Ph.D. by Princeton University for research in relational database theory. He has been a Member of Technical Staff at Bell Labs and Assistant Professor of Computer Science at Princeton University. He is currently Associate Research Scientist at the University of Michigan's Center for Information Technology Integration.

Chapter 3

Distributed Database Management

Harvinder Singh
Oracle Corporation

3.1 Introduction

Rapid advances in computer network technology have made it possible for disparate computers and database management systems to transparently share data and applications at more than one sites on the network. Proliferation of intelligent and high speed networks and desktop computers connected to powerful minis and mainframes have created a demand for sophisticated network wide database services. Due to the increased complexity and multidimensionality of distributed database management systems the issues, theories, and implementations are quite diverse and vast. To fully describe the issues, theories, strategies, and implementations is beyond the scope of this chapter. This chapter only attempts to provide an overview of the topic and sets a stage for relevancy of distributed database management systems within the broader subject of computer networking or distributed computing discussed throughout this volume.

This chapter defines distributed database and its justification. It explores the multiple dimensions and concepts concerning distributed data, its processing, and management.

Remote data access or database service is frequently discussed within the scope of client/server technology. In client/server architecture, data and query processing logic reside in one or more designated servers. Multiple clients locally process data needed by applications by sending queries to one or more servers. The notion and features of client/database-server technology are discussed with respect to the new trends of cooperative processing, rightsizing, and downsizing trends.

Finally, the chapter explores examples of commercial implementations, pitfalls, and the future directions in the evolving field of distributed database management systems.

3.2 What is a Distributed Database?

First, what is a database? Very loosely described, a database is a collection of data which may include structured organization such as a spreadsheet or unstructured organization such a text document. As the collection of data increases in volume and complexity, the need for a database management system (DBMS) becomes more and more important. An industrial strength DBMS supports multiple users, manages simultaneous access to shared data, and serves different purposes or interests. A DBMS is primarily achieved through software and it provides a multitude of services to assist application developers and end-users to store, retrieve, organize, and maintain the data stored. The most common interface to the database is implemented in the form of a database query language.

A database management system is organized around a data model which is ideally independent of a particular application. In the 1960s, database systems such as the IBM's IMS and Honeywell's IDS were respectively based on the hierarchical model (in which data items are stored in a tree structure) and network model (in which data can be interconnected more freely than a tree structure). The 1970s and 1980s saw the evolution and pervasion of the relational model which provides increased data independence (application is not dependent on the underlying storage or file structure of the data), mathematical foundation for data access and manipulation, and organizational simplicity from the user perspective. The database management systems in the 90s are evolving toward more semantically rich data model known as the object data model and support for multimedia data types such as text, sound, animation, and video.

Along with the richness of data models and support for newer and more complex data types, database management systems are also evolving to support a higher level of distribution. This leads to the question: what is a distributed database? Most simply stated, *distributed database* implies that data from more than one site is accessed in an application. A distributed database management system can be contrasted with a *centralized database* in which the database is centrally maintained and controlled at one site.

A distributed database management system can be measured along various dimensions:

- Distribution of sites: how physically dispersed are the database sites? The sites can be from different databases on the same machine to different databases on machines which are across the globe connected by a wide area network. In distributed database, typically a site means a remote machine accessible on the computer network. The site is often called a *node*.

- Degree of node autonomy: How independent are the database nodes? In one extreme, the access to distributed data depends on a single designated central site. On the other extreme, each database is maintained in such a way that failure of any other nodes does not prevent data access; that is, the node is autonomously able to resolve the query without contacting other nodes.

- Degree of site administration autonomy: how much control does the local site administrator have over the organization, maintenance, and coordination of the database service? The responsibility of managing the distribution of the data and coordination of database transactions can be completely determined by a central administrator or shared between central and local site administrator. An absolute site autonomy implies that the local database site is managed by a local database administrator or local staff.

- Hardware platform variety: what is the level of diversity in hardware platforms? The data can reside on different machines which have same hardware configuration or totally different hardware platforms such as mainframes and desktop PCs.
- Network variety: How many different types of network configurations and protocols are supported? Typically, a large network of computers includes different types of networks such as local area networks (LANs) and wide area networks (WANs) and interconnects subnetworks running different network protocols such TCP/IP, Netware, DecNet, and so on.
- Degree of heterogeneity: How heterogeneous are the database management services? Homogeneous database management system implies that all the data resides on same type (e.g., relational database management system) of database management system supplied by the same vendor, which can be considered as a single product. Heterogeneity may include addition of database management software from different vendors and each system may store data according to a totally different data model. An interesting heterogeneous distributed database management system may include a client application on a PC accessing a local Paradox database and also accessing Oracle relational database server remotely over the network.
- Degree of distribution in processing: How distributed is the application itself? The previous sections talked about the data being accessed at remote sites. But with the proliferation of PCs on the network a much greater processing power is available and more and more applications are being off loaded from traditional mainframes to PCs. In client/server and cooperative processing architectures, as discussed later in the chapter, the processing of the data may be shared between more than one node.

In an ideal situation, the primary goal of the database management system is to provide access to multiple sources of data and make it appear as a single local database. A database application may store, retrieve, and update information in transactions that span multiple databases on the network just as it would carry out the transaction if all the data were stored locally. The system has to be sophisticated enough to coordinate the transaction between multiple sites without violating any database consistency and integrity rules.

In practice, however, achieving location transparency especially in a heterogeneous world is a monumental task and is far from being realized in commercial systems.

3.3 The Need for Distributed Database Management

Distribution is a natural outcome of the business practices, therefore the need for distributed databases is inevitable. Corporate locations are distributed and so is corporate data. Different departments or divisions maintain different aspects of corporate data however, many applications need to access data maintained by multiple departments. For example, an inventory applications may need to access data from all the individual departments or locations which may be geographically dispersed.

Most business organizations have invested heavily in information systems to run their businesses. However, newer technologies such as networks, hardware, and software are constantly emerging to provide better solutions. Distributed services allow deployment of newer technologies in co-existence with the previous systems. For example, in the more traditional settings a mainframe served as a central repository for the corporate data. But with the advent of workstations and PCs some of the presentation and application processing was off loaded to the smaller systems without completing replacing the mainframes. The PCs and the mainframe are networked together to provide an evolutionary enterprise wide solution.

A centralized database management system is limited in performance. One database server may be limited in its power to support all the users at the same time and may lack data storage capacity to contain all the data. In a distributed system such as client/server architecture, the end-users initiate the database applications at their workstations or PCs. The applications obtain connection to one or more remote database servers and process the data locally. Much of the immediate data needed by the application can be cached locally to improve the response time. Distributed and decentralized database management may be a more cost-effective vehicle for delivering information in a highly competitive and responsive business environment.

In many mission critical applications, the data must always be available on demand. In a centralized database, a single failure can bring the entire system down. To achieve a higher degree of availability, data replication is desired. For example, in a point-of-sale operation, the terminals request price lookup from the back-end database server. In case of a disk crash, the terminals can access the same data from a secondary source.

3.4 Concepts in Distributed Data

The concepts of data distribution apply to any data model (hierarchical, network, relational, or object) supported by the database management system. However, the concepts are best illustrated within the context of a relational data model. Furthermore, most recent implementations and advancements in distributed database management systems are situated in the context of relational technology.

3.4.1 The Relational Data Model–a Brief Introduction

The data in a relational model is perceived as distinct set of *tables*, or *relations*. Each table is presented as an unordered set of rows with the same set of attributes or columns. A row is equivalent to the definition of record in the more traditional data models. The tables in the data model are conceptually related to one another by common values in the corresponding columns. For example, as shown in figure 3.1a, if the database contains a department and employee table, the department number (Dept. No.) in the department table can be linked to the department number (Dept. No.) in the employee table as shown.

Department	
Dept. No.	**Name**
1001	Tools group
1002	Systems group
1003	Support group

Employee		
Emp No.	**Name**	**Dept. No.**
2100	Joe Maloney	1001
2133	Fa Oros	1001
6200	Jay Sipp	1003
2203	Cathy Ross	1002

Figure 3.1a Department and employee tables.

Simplicity of data representation is the main strength of the relation model. The *physical structures* of the data are entirely hidden from the end-user who perceives information in *logical structures,* namely tables. The separation of the logical and physical structures is commonly referred to as *data independence.* Relational databases also offer an industry standard Structured Query Language, SQL, (pronounced sequel) which has been adopted by nearly all relational database vendors. SQL provides a simple declarative approach to database querying, avoiding complex procedural coding required to achieve the same goal in the older data models such as a hierarchical model. More importantly, the burden is placed on the system to translate simple query statements which specify *what* is needed in a lower level optimized scheme for *how* to compute the results. For example, to fetch the names of the employees working in the tools group one could simply state:

```
SELECT EMPLOYEE.NAME
FROM EMPLOYEE, DEPARTMENT
WHERE EMPLOYEE.DEPT# = DEPARTMENT.DEPT#
AND DEPARTMENT.NAME = 'TOOLS GROUP';
```

Notice, the first line of the where clause: EMPLOYEE.DEPT# = DEPARTMENT.DEPT# *joins* the department table with the employee table (joins can be flexibly performed between any columns with matching data types) and produces a tabular result as shown in figure 3.1b.

Employee.Name
Joe Maloney
Fa Oros

Figure 3.1b Tabular result.

Tabular results can be queried the same way as the base tables allowing for arbitrarily complex queries. Other advantages of a relational model include a firm set theory basis for data manipulation and the ability to flexibly execute ad hoc queries without being limited by the underlying physical data layer. The older models like hierarchical data model constrain the navigation to a strict hierarchy of records.

Levels of abstraction and security are provided in relational database through the use of views. *Views* are virtual tables which provide a window into the underlying base table(s). Only the view definition is stored in the database and the view is materialized when queried. For example, a view Tools_Employee can be created on the employee table which hides all the employee but the ones who work in the tools group:

```
CREATE VIEW TOOLS_EMPLOYEE
AS SELECT EMP#, NAME, DEPT#
FROM EMPLOYEE
WHERE DEPT# = 1001;
```

3.4.2 Fragmentation

Recall that theoretically, a distributed database should appear to the user as one centralized and local database. The data can be distributed in various ways. A common but not so convenient method of distribution of data is *fragmentation.* The data in a relation can be partitioned into non overlapping segments or fragments which are distributed at different sites where they will be accessed the most. The fragments are joined together in a global query when needed. The original relation that is fragmented is known as the *global relation.*

Some rules must be followed when defining fragmentation (Ceri, 1987): The *completeness condition* states that all the data in a relation must map to one of the fragments. Second, the global relation can be completely recreated from its fragments following the *reconstruction condition.* Finally, the *disjointness condition* states that the fragments must be non-overlapping. This condition is sometimes violated in vertical fragmentation in which a common attribute may be used to bring the fragments together into a global relation as explained below.

There are two ways in which data in a table may be fragmented–horizontal and vertical. In vertical fragmentation, columns in a table are split into different fragments and each col-

Fragment 1			Fragment 2		
Item No.	Price	Quantity	Item No.	Stock	Supplier
1001	25.00	1	1001	25	5600
1002	10.99	1	1002	97	5600
1003	1.87	2	1003	22	7643
1123	11.99	1	1123	5	5600
1255	100.50	1	1255	23	7643
Site A: Price Lookup			Site B: Inventory Control		

Figure 3.2 Vertical fragmentation.

umn or attribute must map into at least one fragment. For example, in a point-of-sale database the item and its prices may be placed on a local store and the stock and supplier information may be placed at site local to purchasing department. Notice in figure 3.2 that the item number is duplicated in both the fragments to facilitate joining the two fragments in a query.

Horizontal fragmentation divides the table along the rows. For example, as shown in figure 3.3, items sold be individual departments may be placed in the local department databases.

Fragment 1

Item No.	Price	Quantity	Stock	Supplier No.
1001	25.00	1	25	5600
1002	10.99	1	97	5600
1003	1.87	2	104	7643
1011	9.98	1	32	5600

Site A: Department X

Fragment 2

Item No.	Price	Quantity	Stock	Supplier No.
1123	11.99	1	5	5600
1255	100.50	1	23	7643
1290	23.99	1	43	7643

Site B: Department Y

Figure 3.3 Horizontal fragmentation.

3.4.3 Snapshots and Replication

To provide more efficient access, data may be extracted from a central database and copied to multiple local sites. Many database management systems provide an automatic snapshot mechanism specified using a declarative query statement. A *snapshot* is a recent copy of a remote table or sub-table stored locally. The table which is copied is known as the *master* table. Typically, snapshots are used for read-only access and can be created by specifying a declarative statement or a query which extracts the data from a remote database at some specified interval of time. Depending on the need, the interval may vary between a few hours to a few days.

Local snapshots of remote data can improve the query performance especially if a particular table is read frequently. Placing snapshots of critical data can also prevent heavy traffic to a single site and problems associated with single point of failure.

Replication, a more dynamic mechanism than snapshots is needed for distributed updates involving updates at multiple sites. To efficiently access the data and to avoid single point of failure, copies of a relational table or its fragments may be replicated at several sites. The trade-off for increased efficiency and availability is the overhead to synchronize the multiple replicas of the data scattered throughout the distributed database. In a *synchronous update propagation,* the replicas are updated immediately after a copy changes and in an *asynchronous update propagation*, the changes are propagated to the replicas at a specified interval of time. Synchronous update is not only very costly in terms of network traffic but also, in many cases, not a strict requirement.

3.4.4 Data Dictionary

Data dictionary in a distributed database management system must have centralized knowledge about all the nodes and databases. A global dictionary of databases helps manage and track information. A partial list of services supported by a data dictionary includes:

- Locate schema objects and data on different sites.
- Provide information about the properties and structure of the objects like files, tables, views, tables, columns, procedures, and their replicas.
- Provide information about the resource usage to detect deadlocks (contentions between multiple processes in accessing the same data or resources).
- Assist in distributed query optimization by providing information such as the speed of links to compute the shortest path to the data and volume of data in a database to decide which database to choose.

The data dictionary can be stored centrally on one machine, or it can be distributed on multiple sites. The disadvantages of storing the dictionary on one site are that all the distributed queries must pass through a single site resulting in a possible bottleneck situation and risk loosing critical information if the central site fails. Distributed database dictionary can be implemented by placing copies of all the local data dictionaries at all the nodes. So each node has a *global data dictionary.* The disadvantages of a distributed data dictionary include the overhead of ensuring that the dictionary information remains synchronized at all the nodes.

3.4.5 Schema Objects and Global Naming

Tables, views (a virtual table which does not exist in physical storage and is materialized upon query), and stored procedures (shared executable modules stored in the database) are *schema objects.* In a Distributed Database Management System (DDBMS), the schema objects are defined and named locally but are accessible to all the nodes. *Global naming* ensures that names of databases, tables, views, and procedures within the databases are uniquely defined across the distributed database. A global name includes user/object creator identifier, object name, and the database name (including the network address). To avoid using long global names, synonyms are sometimes used locally to access remote objects.

3.5 Concepts in Distributed Data Processing

3.5.1 Remote Access and Distributed Queries

Remote Access implies that the data is accessed at a site other than the site where the query originated. The access can be controlled locally where each physical access occurs over the network. In a logical access, the requesting application (client) executes a query which is transparently processed by a database server and the results are returned to the client. Even in client/server query processing, the data is not necessarily distributed at multiple sites; all the data may reside on a single server machine. In fact, most vendors provide remote read and update access but the access is limited to one database per transaction. A distributed query is more complicated than remote query since it involves coordination of data access at multiple sites.

A *distributed query* can read or update data that may be stored at multiple sites. For example, a query could join two tables that are stored at two separate locations. In a *distributed update,* the table fragments may be stored on more than one site.

3.5.2 Distributed Locking

Data locking is an important feature in a multi-user/multi-process database management system. To maintain the consistency of the database it is necessary that a record which is being updated be locked so that no other application reads an inconsistent state of the record. In a distributed database environment the locks have to be placed on data that may not all reside at one site. In some cases, the data may be replicated at multiple sites and all the replicas have to be locked simultaneously even if only one replica is updated. Coordinating the locking activity between multiple sites in a network environment is a complex problem and one that is seldom achieved in commercial implementations.

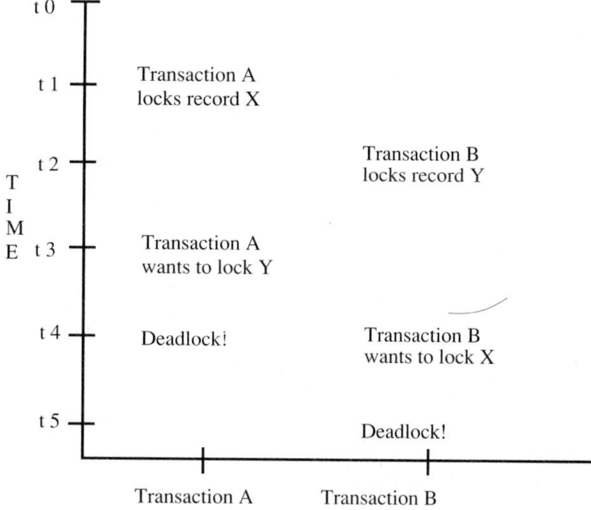

Figure 3.4 Transactions in deadlock.

As shown in figure 3.4, another complication arises when two or more transactions are waiting for one another for resources. In a distributed database management system, again, because of data locks placed at remote sites managing, avoiding, and detecting deadlocks is a more complex problem than in a centralized database system. Distributed data locking and deadlock detection are beyond the scope of this chapter.

3.5.3 Distributed Query Optimization

A distributed query requires the data to be fetched from multiple sites. Furthermore, the same data may be replicated on multiple sites. For best results, a global optimization scheme must be used which takes into account the network speed, expected size of the results, and the type of computers on different sites involved in the query.

Query optimizer can make significant improvement in query response time. For example, the optimizer could help in transferring the least amount of data necessary over the network. Rather than transmitting the entire table, for instance, only the required rows could be transmitted.

Improving query processing may involve, replicating most frequently used data and informing the controlling software about the replications. Automatic replication procedures may be used to reduce management overhead.

Typically, query optimization takes place under the covers and the user or querying application need not specify any detail on how to fetch the data across the network or from the physical storage structures. Different types of query optimization schemes are used in different database management systems. Some of the more commonly known strategies include rule-based and cost-based optimization schemes. In rule-based optimization, the data is accessed based on some predefined set of rules. Cost-based optimization schemes take into account information such as the amount of data transmitted over the network.

3.5.4 Distributed Transactions and Two-Phase Commit

Conceptually speaking, a transaction is a logical unit of work (Date, 1986), which may be subdivided into multiple database actions such as updates. The goal of any transaction processing system is to ensure that either all the subcomponents of the transaction complete successfully *(commit)* or none of them commit. The reason is very simple, consider a banking example where a customer transfers money from a savings account to a checking account. If the checking account and savings accounts are registered in two separate databases at different sites or *nodes,* both the update of the savings account (withdraw money) and the update of the checking account (deposit money) must commit together. If either of the databases crashes, or the network failure occurs while the transaction is proceeding, then the system must be able to *recover* from it. In the recovery procedure, the transaction must be *rolled back,* that is, both the updates must be stopped or *aborted* and the state of both the databases reverted back the state before the transaction began.

The primary concern of the transaction processing system is to maintain the integrity of the database, that is the accuracy or correctness of the data in the database (Date, 1986). *Two-*

phase commit protocol is sometimes used in a distributed database environment to ensure the integrity of data at multiple sites.

A two-phase commit transaction is distributed into multiple subtransactions at multiple sites. All the sites involved in a two-phase commit must come to a common understanding with respect to committing or aborting all the local subtransactions. The goal of the first phase of the protocol is to reach a common decision and the goal of the second phase is to implement this decision (Ceri, 1987). One node serves as a *coordinator* and the other nodes involved in a two-phase commit transaction are called *participants.*

Phase one of the protocol is also called the *prepare phase* in which the coordinator node sends a message to each participant node to prepare for commitment. As shown in figure 3.5, the coordinator decides to commit the transaction if *all* participants respond with a ready message within a particular interval of time set by the coordinator otherwise the transaction must be aborted.

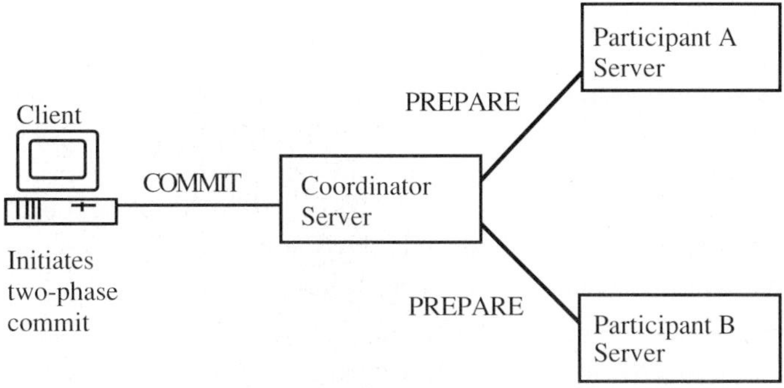

Figure 3.5 Phase 1, prepare phase of two-phase commit.

In the second phase of the protocol (see figure 3.6), also referred to as the *commit phase,* the coordinator sends either an abort or commit message to all the participants depending on the responses from all the participants. Finally, all the participants respond by carrying out the action and sending an acknowledgment message.

Two-phase commit is an expensive operation. If the remote sites are distributed over a wide area network the response time could suffer further. Two-phase commit is also very sensitive to availability of all sites at the time of update and even a single point of failure could jeopardize the entire transaction. A two-phase commit can be avoided by placing all the data involved in transaction at one site. Reexamining the above scenario, if all the accounts of customers are placed at a single site, the transactions involving transfer of money can be carried out at the same site. Obviously, such decisions would be based on the business needs and trade off between the cost of maintaining the data on a single site and cost of two-phase commit when the data is distributed at multiple sites. Two-phase commit can also be avoided if real-time synchronization and consistency is not required. In many cases, the data can be brought to a consistent state at periodic intervals rather than in real-time.

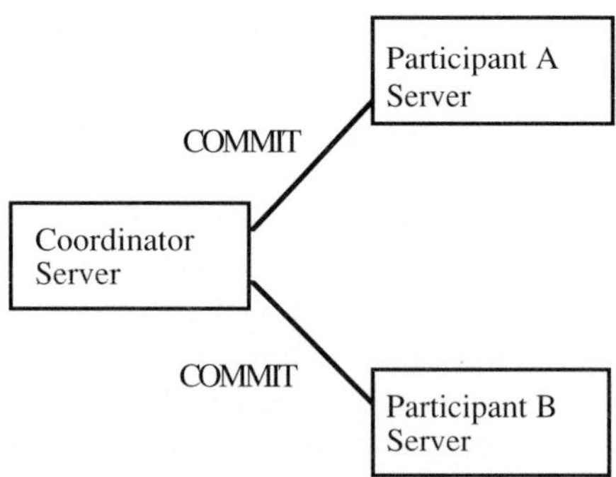

Figure 3.6 Phase 2, commit phase of two-phase commit.

Even though less than one percent of all database users have implemented two-phase commit, the need is growing (Lawton, 1993). Two-phase commit protocol is often thought of as a prerequisite feature in a distributed database management system. Many vendors are responding by providing a transparent or automatic implementation of two-phase commit which used to be implemented by manual coding of the protocol at the application level.

Ingres, Informix and Oracle manage data distribution transparently. A client issues the query to one server, which then sends off requests to other servers and coordinates two-phase commit of distributed updates (Anderson, 1992).

3.5.5 Replication as an Alternative to Two-Phase Commit

Although two-phase commit has been studied and experimented as an important component of DDBMS, it is not widely implemented. Due to two-phase commit's impact on performance, database administrators consider replicated databases as an alternative to updating the data at multiple sites. In *replicated databases,* copies of the data are stored at more than one node and not necessarily synchronized at real-time as in two-phase commit.

Using replication service, applications are not forced into all-or-nothing updating, which can lead to problems for large organizations (Korzeniowski, 1993). Unreliable network could cause one or more database servers to be out of service forcing two-phase commit to abort the transaction. Furthermore, two-phase commit does not work very well when a large number of nodes are participating in the transaction. The cost of coordinating an update and rolling back every single subtransaction may not be justifiable in all situations.

Updating replicated databases avoids costly instant updating. The database administrator can set a schedule for updating the replicated databases on the network. Updates can be done at periodic intervals, such as when the communication is reestablished (if a node was previously down), or can be based on some external event, such as a change of data. During the update, if one of the many participants in the update is temporarily not available the transaction is not rolled back. Instead the missing participant is notified of the update during the next update.

Obviously, replicated databases do not ensure an immediate synchronization at all the sites and this may not be acceptable for certain time critical data. Therefore, a combination of two-phase commit and replicated services may be more desirable.

3.6 Desired Characteristics

The multiple facets and interpretations of a distributed database management system make it hard to explain and easy to misunderstand. Different vendors provide an array of different implementations of a distributed management system and there are no clear cut guidelines or standards concerning the design requisites of distributed database management systems.

C.J. Date's (one of the first designers of relational databases) rules or objectives are now widely accepted as the working definition of distributed databases (Alex Berson, 1992). Although none of the commercial implementations of distributed database management systems fully comply with all the objectives outlined in the following sections, vendors are providing distributed database features which are slowly approaching these criteria.

3.6.1 Local Autonomy

The database management system at each site should be autonomous, that is, it must be maintained at the local site independent of the other sites. This rule allows the applications to access one database server even if the others are not available.

3.6.2 Avoid Reliance on a Central Site

This rule stipulates that all the database sites are equally important and no one site is critical in completing a transaction. Therefore, failure at one central site does not necessarily prevent the completion of the transaction. A site may coordinate a transaction involving multiple sites but the coordination function may not necessarily always be designated to a central site.

3.6.3 Continuous Operation

One of the major advantages of a distributed database is the availability of data at multiple sites. In order to satisfy the data requests made by applications, a distributed database management system must always be operational. Some site(s) must always be accessible even if one of more sites are down due to maintenance or failure. In some point-of-sale environments the price lookup database is mirrored on a second node which can take over if the first one is recovering from a crash. Shut down can also be avoided by on-line operation of common functions such as backup. They are multi-tasked with the regular business transaction processing.

3.6.4 Data Location Independence

The end-user benefits the most from location independence or transparency in which the users and the applications perceive the data to be available locally and do not need to know that it is distributed and where it is. The users and their applications use logical references to the database objects and the distributed databases management system maps the logical references to the network and physical occurrences. The mappings between the logical and physical constructs are maintained in a data dictionary.

3.6.5 Data Fragmentation Independence

Data fragmentation independence or transparency implies that the end-user and applications need not specify how a relational table might be split–horizontal or vertical. Furthermore, the location of each fragment is tracked by the DDBMS and not specified by the user. Fragmentation may result in efficient access to the data when the most frequently accessed fragments are placed closest to the accessing site. But the user perceives the entire table as a unified whole. Fragmentation transparency places an additional burden on the DDBMS since a transaction may access multiple tables and one or more of those tables may be fragmented.

3.6.6 Data Replication Independence

The user or application must be oblivious of how the data is replicated, whether the updates propagate synchronously or asynchronously, and where the replicas are stored. The DDBMS figures out the shortest path to the data on demand, again, reemphasizing that the user specifies *what* is needed and the system figures out *how* to get it. The data synchronization takes place under the covers, without user intervention. More importantly, the system must simultaneously place exclusive locks on all the replicas if an update request is made to one of them. Managing synchronization and distributed locking is a very costly operation in a distributed database management system, therefore, most vendors provide only a partial replication independence by offering, for example, a snapshot mechanism without updates.

3.6.7 Distributed Query Processing

A distributed database management system must allow the applications to execute distributed queries which fetch or update data at more than one database site on the network. This characteristic requires that the DDBMS include distributed query optimization schemes which use the distributed data dictionary.

3.6.8 Distributed Transaction Management

Distributed database transactions management requires support for consistency, integrity, concurrency, and recovery in a distributed database management system. A distributed transaction must maintain *atomicity,* that is all the subtransactions affecting data at multiple sites must execute as a single unit in order to keep the data at all sites consistent. Two-phase commit or replication methods may be deployed to keep the data consistent. Concurrency control must be supported in DDBMS whereby multiple transactions maintain the capability to serialize, that is, they execute without interfering with one another and the results are the same if they were to be executed in some serial order. In order to maintain atomicity, a distributed transaction must also be able to recover (undoing the partial work at different sites) when the transaction aborts or network fails.

3.6.9 Hardware Independence

The hardware independence objective stipulates that the distributed database management must be able to run on multiple hardware platforms. Most leading database vendors supply their database products on multiple platforms and allow network connections between those platforms. Hardware independence is a critical requirement in most client/server systems where the clients are implemented on workstations or PCs and server machines may be mainframes.

3.6.10 Operating System Independence

The distributed database management system must not be limited to a particular operating system. Indeed, many leading database vendors provide their solutions on multiple operating systems. A client workstation, for example, could get data from a database on UNIX and a second database running on MVS.

3.6.11 Network Independence

In addition to variety of hardware platforms and operating systems, most large information systems use a variety of network services and protocols within the same interconnected network. Therefore, the distributed database management system must be independent of a particular network system or protocol. Many database vendors support multiple protocols. For example, Oracle implements transparent network substrate (TNS), a common interface to multiple protocols in order to transparently access the heterogeneous network.

3.6.12 DBMS Independence

There are two interpretations to the DBMS independence objective. At one level, a distributed database management system must be able to transparently operate in an environment where database products from more than one vendor have been installed. However, the data model supported by the different vendors is common. This has been achieved to some extent with relational model and SQL as the access language. However, differences in each vendor's implementation of SQL make the interoperability harder to achieve.

At the second level, a truly heterogeneous distributed database management system requires that not only the system support multiple vendors products but also different data models. Compromising data access between a relational model and a hierarchical or network model, for instance, is a non-trivial task. A fully heterogeneous DDBMS is far from being achieved in reality.

3.7 Cooperative Processing and Client/Server Computing

3.7.1 What is Cooperative Processing?

With the proliferation in the personal computers and workstations, organizations are increasingly taking advantage of the increased processing power and ease-of-use offered by the workstations/PCs to increase productivity. More workstations on the network mean more distributed processing between the PCs and existing mainframe installed base. An application may involve cooperation of multiple programs on different machines accessing multiple databases and sending messages back and forth to achieve the results. Cooperative processing can be implemented in many ways (Atre, 1992):

- *Front-end processing*; in which typically a mainframe program runs as before and the PC is used for display and user interaction. For example, a terminal emulation 3270-based communication API is used to map the data from the PC to the mainframe application.
- *Peer-to-peer processing:* in which more than one processor shares the responsibility of executing parts of an application for which they are best suited. For example, a high-end SGI Iris workstation may display three dimensional graphics and a powerful Sequent parallel machine may handle the database intensive function of the application. Peer-to-peer processing is implemented as LU 6.2/APPC, remote procedural call, or client/server architecture.
- *LU 6.2/APPC:* which is IBM's systems network architecture (SNA) based communication protocol and API for processing cooperation. LU 6.2 (logical unit) is the low-level protocol and APPC is the application program interface (API). APPC is being replaced with a newer API called common programming interface: communications (CPI-C), which is superset of APPC.

Another mechanism to implement the cooperative processing which has been popularized with rise of UNIX and internetwork is known as remote procedure call (RPC). Using RPC, a program can transparently invoke procedures or executable modules on a remote machine giving the impression of a single local program.

Client/server technology is the most popular form of cooperative processing which is gaining center stage in recent architectures.

3.7.2 What is Client/Server Technology?

A network of computers can be viewed as distributed information service resource. In the network some computers are designated as service providers, known as *servers* or sometimes back-end servers. They may provide a variety of services including communications, mail, file, database, and so on. The discussion in this chapter focuses on the database service. The computers or applications that receive the services are known as *clients* or front-end clients. The clients may access the servers over a LAN or remotely over WANs. In client/server computing, the database application processing is distributed among multiple clients and server machines. An example of client/server setup is shown in figure 3.7.

More importantly, from the end-user's perspective, the client/server database services are synonymous to on demand services in which users can access the information they need to get their work done. The client/server applications provide the infrastructure to transparently and most efficiently access the information the user requires from a network of resources.

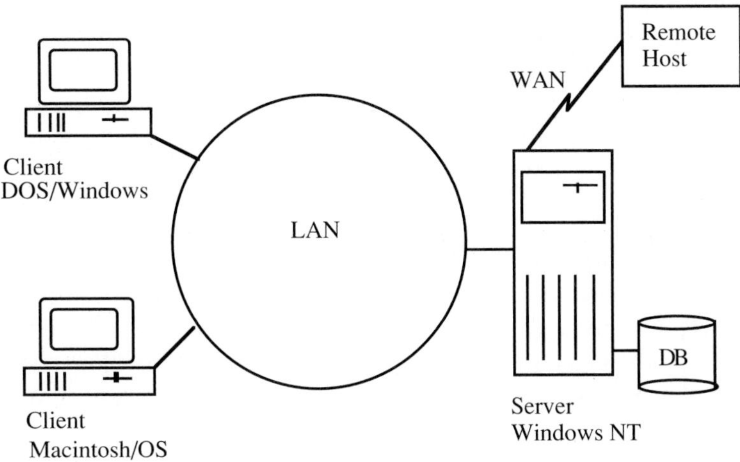

Figure 3.7 An example of a client/server setup.

Client machines like workstations/PCs handle the user interaction and presentation function. Client applications are evolving from character-mode presentation to graphical user interfaces (GUIs). GUIs are characterized by events triggered by user action, bit-mapped graphics which include support for multiple windows, point-and-click selections, and pop-down menus. X Windows system from MIT and Microsoft Windows are examples of graphical user interface systems.

In a typical client/server system, the number of clients will far exceed the number of database servers. Server machines are specially designed for high performance support for multiple client requests, very large disk spaces for large databases, and significant processing power. For example, a Unix server from Sequent Computer Systems, Inc. may run a very large Oracle database.

3.7.3 Downsizing and Rightsizing with Client/Server Model

Organizations are constantly updating their distributed database services to keep up with the changes and trends in technology to meet their evolving business needs. The model offers the advantage of mixing and matching hardware and software components to achieve higher levels of cost-effectiveness, productivity, and efficiency.

The client/server computing has been pushed to the front line in computer information services because of the proliferation of reliable and high-speed computer networks and high-end personal computers or workstations. Client applications usually reside on the PCs or workstations which may lack very large disks for storing high volume enterprise data which resides on the servers but possess the processing power to further process or manipulate the data retrieved from the servers. The client processing off loads the computing from the server and allows it to efficiently service multiple clients. Additionally, the PCs enhance the display and user interaction functionality of the applications with graphical user interfaces. The move to replace or off load some of the traditional mainframe applications down to smaller machines like PCs is called *downsizing*.

Despite the trend toward workstations and PCs, most of corporate data resides on the traditional mainframes (Finkelstein, 1993). Mainframes typically store and handle very large databases and support very high transaction rates for database access. Many corporations, in the past, have invested heavily into mainframe applications which include data management, administration, and security components. Mainframes, therefore, serve as an important resource for enterprise wide data and it is necessary to provide gateways to that data from PCs and workstations which are scattered and connected throughout the enterprise via LANs or WANs. The ability to leverage the strengths of both the newer workstation and PC technology and the existing mainframe technology is often termed as *rightsizing*. Rightsizing is viewed as a design strategy which promotes cost-effective means of providing business solutions.

3.7.4 Issues in Client/Server Data Services

3.7.4.1 Asynchronous Data Access

The goal of client/server computing is to make the entire system very responsive to the end-user. With the decrease in price per mips (processing speed), users have more and more client machine processing power at their disposal. Client machines typically run operating systems which support multiple windows such as Microsoft Windows which can initiate multiple applications in different windows. A database application running on a client machine must be able to asynchronously access the data from the server so that the user does not have to be put on hold while the data is being accessed over the network. Depending on the network speed and server throughput, delay in data access could be very annoying for the end-user. In an asynchronous data access, the user may switch to another window and initiate other requests while a previously executed query returns results.

3.7.4.2 Data Processing and Caching at the Client Site

The main motivation for client/server model is the efficient use of resources. Traditionally the data processing and query processing functions were handled solely by the server using the *query shipping* model in which the client sends a query (SQL query in relational databases) to the database server which in return processes the query and sends the specific results back to the client. This approach places the burden of data manipulation primarily on the servers (Franklin, 1993). To off load the computing at the server and reduce the network traffic, it is necessary to explore alternatives. The newer object-oriented database management systems use the *data shipping* model in which a client requests large chunks of data (e.g., in the form of pages) and maintains a local cache (in main memory or hard disk) of the data. Most of the data manipulation is then performed at the client site where multiple transactions may be serviced by the local cache itself thereby eliminating server-induced performance and scalability bottlenecks by exploiting the resources of the client machines (Franklin, 1993).

Maintaining local cache at multiple sites involves overhead. The data has to be kept up to date and consistent with the changes made elsewhere. Other issues pertaining to local cache include maintaining global schema of the data and efficient use of memory. The analysis of these issues is beyond the scope of this chapter.

3.7.4.3 Multi-Platform Client/Server Applications

Networks and computer services evolve over a period of time. Ongoing introduction of new technologies inevitably needs to be seamlessly integrated with the existing technologies. The technologies may range from new network technologies to computer hardware and from new operating systems to end-user applications. Compatibility and interoperability between different graphical user interfaces, network protocols, operating systems, database management systems, and hardware platforms is necessary but difficult in practice for true multi-platform applications.

3.8 The Rise of Middleware and Database Gateways

The cost of implementing a corporate wide homogeneous distributed database in which the data is stored in the same format on all sites, for example relational, is prohibitive and does not mirror the corporate reality. Corporate data sources more resemble a federation of databases, a conglomeration of different types of autonomous databases which may be organized according to relational, object-based, sequential, or hierarchical data models. It is necessary to enable applications running on workstations or PCs to access data from a variety of databases.

Since most of the corporate data still resides on the traditional mainframes, the emerging database gateway or middleware technology enables PCs and workstations to access data on the databases servers (primarily mainframes).

3.8.1 Advantages of Middleware

Many applications can use middleware to access data from multiple and disparate data sources. The database services can be administered autonomously at each site without trying to create massive infrastructures to seamlessly integrate them. Middleware promotes adaptability; new technologies, applications, and data services can easily be added to existing services without limiting the newer models to fit the older ones. Furthermore, some middleware offers access to common database services from within popular applications such as spreadsheets using macro or very high-level, English-like syntax.

3.8.2 Limitations of Middleware

Because middleware supports heterogeneous data sources including relational and non-relational databases, and indexed files, the access to the data is not as transparent as in a homogeneous distributed database. For the same reason, middleware can not combine results from multiple sites which are normally accomplished through optimization algorithms in homogeneous data structures; for example, multi-site table joins in a relational world. Middleware can only support single site updates since multi-site updates require two-phase commit and other mechanisms supported in a homogeneous distributed database.

3.8.3 Examples of Middleware

Realizing the emergence and importance of multi-platform applications many vendors are responding by providing application programming interfaces (API) to their products which allow other vendors' products to access their services. An API is essentially a procedural call based mechanism used within the application logic to communicate with a database management system on the network. There are no universally established standards in API design.

Typically, as shown in figure 3.8, a client application uses an API to access the middleware software which uses the client query converter (converts the client request or query to server understandable format) and the network link management software to access the database server. The server, typically a mainframe accesses the database and responds to the client.

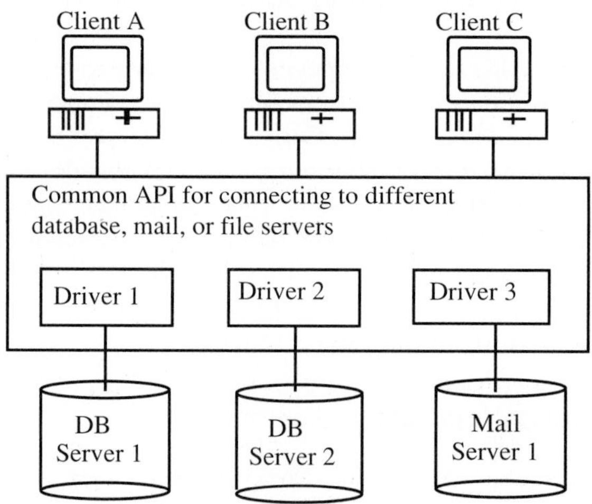

Figure 3.8 Middleware–API and drivers.

3.8.3.1 Oracle Glue

Oracle Corporation's Oracle Glue, a general purpose API, provides common commands and language for clients to connect with multiple databases (Oracle, DB2, SQL Server, etc.), file (DBASE, Paradox, etc.), and mail services (Oracle*Mail, cc:Mail, etc.). Intended as a portable API, different versions of Oracle Glue will run under multiple platforms like Microsoft Windows, Macintosh System 7, UNIX operating systems, PenPoint, and others.

Oracle glue is high level API which can be used within many end-user applications such as Apple Computer Inc.'s HyperCard and Microsoft Corp's Visual Basic, and Excel to access back-end database servers. From Excel, for example, you may use macro commands to access the data and in Visual Basic you may use function calls.

In the Microsoft Windows environment, Oracle Glue is implemented as a series of dynamic link libraries (DLLs), executable code modules which can be loaded in the memory and dynamically used by multiple applications.

3.8.3.2 Open Data Base Connectivity

Microsoft Corp. provides open database connectivity (ODBC) API and messaging API (MAPI) for applications on Microsoft Windows and other platforms. ODBC builds on the call-level interface (CLI) specification developed by the SQL access group (SAG), a consortium of over 40 leaders in the database and systems industry (Kernighan, 1992). ODBC is a superset of CLI designed to enable interoperability between different relational database management system (RDBMS) products and applications.

Using ODBC API, an application can execute SQL calls, send, receive data, and interface with RDBMSs as long as the interfacing RDBMS's middleware or gateway implements an ODBC driver which maps middleware API to ODBC API. Applications which used multiple DBMS specific APIs can use a single ODBC API to access multiple database products. The success of the ODBC would depend on the availability of ODBC drivers for different RDBMSs.

3.9 Examples of Distributed Database Management Systems

The next two sections examine the distributed database management solutions offered by two different vendors.

3.9.1 Distributed Database Features of ORACLE 7 (Version 7)

Oracle 7 is termed as a *cooperative server* technology which creates an illusion of a single database by providing seamless connectivity between database applications running on heterogeneous platforms and networks. Its key distributed database management features include two-phase commit, distributed query optimization, and heterogeneous connectivity. The following paragraphs outline some of salient distributed database management features of Oracle 7:

Oracle application uses global object names to reference the schema objects: <schema name>.<object name>@database name. In a distributed database environment, the database name must be globally unique. The global database name includes database name and network domain specification which follows the internet conventions. For example, a database named *mydb* could be written as mydb.uk.europe.mycompany.com.

Local views, synonyms, and procedures can be used in Oracle to provide location transparency (make a remote object appear local). A local view can provide a window over a remote table. A synonym is an alias for a database object which can hide the location of the remote object. A procedure may refer to a remote object and local reference to the procedure hides the location of the remote object.

Oracle 7 provides automatic distributed updates with two-phase commit protocol which ensures that in a distributed transaction either all the nodes involved in the transaction commit or all nodes roll back the transaction.

Oracle 7 allows database table replication capability in which multiple read-only *snapshots* of a table can be placed at different nodes of a distributed database. Only the master table may be updated and its copies or snapshots are not updatable. Oracle also supports triggers which can be used to synchronously update the snapshot data whenever the corresponding master data changes.

Oracle's gateway architecture: SQL*Connect supports access to many non-Oracle databases on variety of platforms like DB2 on IBM mainframes in the MVS environment. The architecture provides complete data transparency and translates the standard Oracle queries and instructions into equivalent DB2 commands.

The distributed applications running on multiple and scattered platforms and networks need to communicate and exchange data with one another. Differences in protocols present a formidable barrier to interoperability. SQL*Net V2 is Oracle's solution to interoperability problem. SQL*Net provides client/server or server/server communication using any combination of a variety of network protocols like IBM's APPC/LU 6.2 under OS/2, DECnet under VMS, or TCP/IP under UNIX. SQL*Net uses Oracles transparent network substrate (TNS) technology which provides a common interface to all industry-standard protocols and handles multi-protocol interchange, internetwork connectivity, routing, and data transfers.

3.9.2 IBM's Distributed Database and Gateway Implementation

Within the systems application architecture (SAA), IBM provides DB2 in MVS and SQL/DS in VM environments which allow distributed data access.

In order to provide access to data stored in mainframes from PCs or workstations, there are two kinds of gateway schemes. In the first case, a wide area network router is added to the users client/server configuration. The router intercepts client requests to the database server and reroutes them to the mainframe database using a communications protocol (advanced program-to-program–APPC for IBM DB2) supported by both the workstation and mainframe databases. Somewhere in the gateway, either in the workstation portion or the mainframe portion the request is converted so that it can be submitted to the mainframe database SQL API. The mainframe portion of the gateway receives the client request as a transaction to the mainframe database SQL API. Results received back from the mainframe database similarly go through a conversion within the gateway before they are presented back to the client on the workstation.

As shown in figure 3.9, all IBM SAA compatible databases have made the gateway connection transparent and more functional for connections between databases supporting IBM's distributed relational database architecture (DRDA). This type of connection is made by IBM's distributed database connection services (DDCS). The DDCS in turn uses the DRDA architecture to complete the connection.

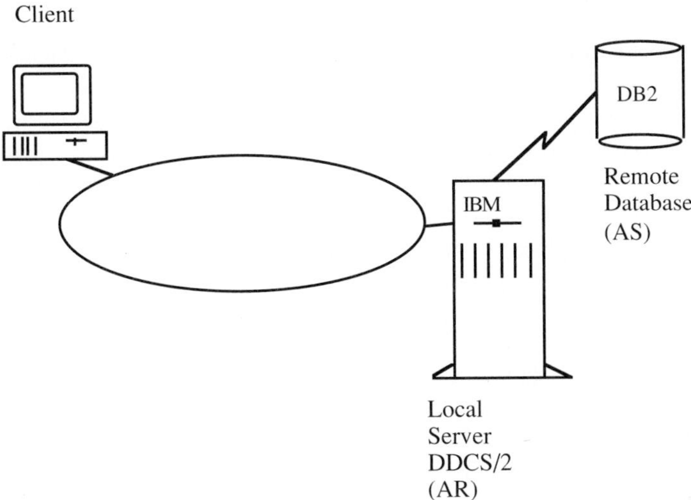

Figure 3.9 IBM's distributed database connection services (DDCS/2).

In the DDCS connection, the database client program on any SAA compatible workstation (e.g., DB2/6000, OS2/DBM) can directly connect with a SAA compatible host database (e.g., DB2, SQL/DS OS/400). In this connection, DRDA application requestor (AR) communicates with an application server (AS) at the database server (McKelly, 1983). All clients in this environment present SQL queries to the DRDA application requestor which does all necessary conversions required for the query to be sent to the host database. Note that in this case the gateway does not send the SQL query to the SQL API of the host database, but interacts directly with the DRDA application server of the host database.

The specialized knowledge of the target host database allows the DDCS connection many advantages. Some of the advantages are listed below. A complete discussion of the advantages is beyond the scope of this chapter.

- The DDCS connection is more transparent to the application program. The application programmer does not need to code any special instructions.
- Data Stream conversion is done only when required.
- DB2 Static SQL is supported. All traditional gateways cannot do a remote BIND and therefore can handle only dynamic queries.

3.10 Trends and Future Directions

The distributed database management systems are rapidly evolving to incorporate new trends in hardware and software technology. Few of these future directions are especially challenging and worth noting:

3.10.1 Mediators

Advancement in computer network technology and distributed database management systems has lead to availability of a wide variety of information resources. However, it is not the quantity or diversity of data but the quality and extrapolation that matters most to high-level decision makers in finance, marketing, planning, or other areas in organizations. There is an increasing need to provide computer-based information systems which address the needs of the decision makers, knowledge workers, or end-users.

The technical challenges in providing meaningful information involve dealing with extrapolation or abstraction of useful information from a large collection of data. For example, the data pertaining to buying habits of customers for the past several months has to be translated into decisions about planning for the subsequent months in a department store. Certain aggregation functions can be applied to provide summary of sales and inventory. Moreover, the information collected from various data sources may not match on the basis of data types, storage representation, format, or meaning. For instance, the branch office of a bank may store account summary data on a daily basis and the central office may store the same data on a weekly basis.

Wiederhold, suggests mediator layer between the end-user applications and the multiple databases as a solution to the information system need. A *mediator* is a software module that exploits encoded knowledge about some sets or subsets of data to create information for a higher layer of applications (Wiederhold, 1990). Mediator acts as a human expert who manages a variety of knowledge (information abstraction needed for decision making) which may be derived out of multiple sources of data. A mediator may compute, extrapolate, derive, merge, transform the data from multiple databases keeping the applications independent of the underlying databases. Multiple sharable and autonomous mediators can be made available on the network to provide specialized services as shown in figure 3.10.

3.10.2 Multimedia Objects

The changing role of the computer from a data crunching and information access device to a communication and empowerment tool is creating a demand for richer graphical user interfaces and support for new media which includes graphics, animation, sound, and video in addition to text. The workstation technology is rapidly advancing to support new multimedia data types. The database technology is also maturing to support multimedia objects in binary large object (BLOB) data types. The traditional data models and querying schemes do not easily lend themselves to manipulating multimedia objects. Furthermore, multimedia data poses special challenges for distributed databases and applications.

Performance is the primary problem with distributed access to multimedia data which is orders of magnitude greater in size and complexity compared to the simple text data type. The storage space and disk access time are critical problems in multimedia databases. For example, according to (Besser, 1992), a single full megapel workstation screen (SUN or Next) color digital image is between one third to one megabyte after compression. One gigabyte of storage can only store between 1,000 to 3,000 such images. Retrieving an image from the disk could cost from two thirds of a second to mote than a second. Multiple user database system further delays the access. The transmission time for a 1 megabyte image is between 139 minutes on a 1,200 bps modem line to 1 second on a 10 Mb/sec Ethernet to 0.1 second on 100 Mb/sec on FDDI link.

In a distributed environment high speed network, replication of data, and caching the data at a site closest to the client workstation, and accessing it could significantly improve the performance of multi-user multimedia databases.

3.10.3 Object-Based Database Management Systems

The complexity of information and volume of data maintained by organizations are constantly increasing. More efficient, maintainable, reusable, scalable, timely, and cost-effective methods are needed to solve the problems faced by information systems organizations. The software industry is increasingly adopting object-oriented technology to address the problems in software design, development, and maintenance.

The main features of object-oriented technology include the ability to define *abstract data types* or classes which are created by combining existing data types in new ways. Abstract data types encapsulate or package together the data and the procedures which manipulate that data. *Encapsulation* promotes information hiding in which independent software units protect themselves by hiding the internal details from the outside world. Information hiding leads to easily maintainable programs. *Inheritance,* another important ingredient of object-oriented systems, allows creating type or class hierarchies in which a more general abstract data type or class may serve as a superclass of a more specialized one. A specialized class is created by inheriting the properties of a generalized class and by overriding or adding certain specific properties. Inheritance leads to reusability of older software structures. Objects are instances of some class (a type definition or template) within the class hierarchy. An object-oriented system comes to life when objects get instantiated, start mimicking real world entities like invoice statements and customers, interact with one another, and get destroyed when no longer needed.

Objects interact with one another through message passing. Each message invokes an associated procedure in the receiving object. Through polymorphism, a key concept in object-oriented technology, different objects can respond to a same message differently. For example, a print procedure in both professor and student object is referenced with the same name but performs a different operation depending on which object is referenced. The ability to *overload* the names of the operations this way allows new object types or classes to be created without impacting the existing software structure. The object sending the message can be oblivious of the intricacies or nuances of the other object's behavior. For example, a payroll object may send the same deposit paycheck message to both professor and staff objects and each receiving object may handle the details differently.

In an object-oriented program, the behavior of the whole program is a result of the cooperative behavior of a network of objects, with each object's behavior resulting from the activation of its operations (Daniels and Cook, 1993). The objects are interconnected and contain references to other objects by storing their object identity (OID) which is a system generated number used to uniquely reference an object.

One necessary condition in an object-oriented system is the need for *persistent objects.* Marriage of object-oriented paradigm and database technology enables objects to be stored, retrieved, and manipulated in a multi-user environment. Several schemes have been proposed to achieve object persistence. One strategy is provide an interface layer which maps objects on a relational database and back. Another approach is to extend the existing relational technology by using complex data-structures and stored procedures or triggers to imitate object-oriented characteristics.

The next step in a scalable and enterprise wide system is the ability to access objects in a distributed environment over the computer network. Many of the issues considered previously in this chapter pertaining to distributed database management apply to distributed object-based databases as well, however object-based databases pose some additional issues. For example, an object referencing scheme has to be devised to access objects stored on different databases on the network. If the object types are different on two databases, then a mapping from one type to the other needs to be provided.

Message passing between objects in a distributed object-oriented system readily blends into client/server computing. The client sends a request or a message to the server and the server responds by executing the associated methods and providing the requested service. Enterprise modeling is another new direction which harnesses the object-oriented approach. Object databases store the procedures and corporate policies with the data and allow for sharing large scale corporate models. These models directly mirror the structure and operation of the company (Taylor, 1992).

Object-oriented technology and object-based databases or extensions to relational databases are likely to gain prominence in the next few years.

3.10.4 Wireless Access to Data

In computer networking, wireless communications is one of the most rapidly advancing technology in the 90s. Wireless communication using radio waves affords mobile computing which has powerful application in distance learning, sales, inventory control, and other on-the-field jobs. For example, K-Mart Corp. is using a wireless data-transmission system that uses a new radio frequency-optimized version of Informix-4GL (LaPlante, 1992).

Performance, reliability, and network speed are important considerations in wireless communication which is considerably slower than wired networks. For example, maximum wireless transmission speed ranges between 2 Mbps to 10 Mbps compared with Ethernet speed of 10 Mbps to FDDI transmission speed which reaches 100 Mbps. Therefore, a wireless network is deployed to complement a wired network (Baran, 1992). Most of the queries over a wireless network typically result in transmission of small chunks of data. Furthermore, special provisions need to be made in the software to account for interruption in data transmission so the communication can be seamlessly suspended and resumed.

FCC regulation and allocation of radio frequencies for data communication is another hurdle in the proliferation of wireless data networks. FCC allows unlicensed use of ISM bands (three frequency ranges) for data communication using spread-spectrum modulation which distributes the signal over a wide frequency domain to reduce interference. But ISM faces many contentions with other devices. Many computer vendors including Apple Computer are petitioning for allocation of a dedicated frequency band for data communication.

Wireless or mobile computing offers one of the most exciting advancements in computer networking. Mobile computing affords a true *any place and any time* model of information access.

3.11 Conclusion

To meet the growing needs of organizations, databases are evolving from centralized monolithic systems to distributed resources of information. However, the acceptance of distributed databases has been slow because of the cost associated with reliable networks, application development and redesign to support client/server architecture. Lack of tools to manage distributed database and client/server systems is further slowing the deployment of distributed DBMS.

The distributed database vendors are constantly adding new features to meet the business needs and the technology is expected to evolve rapidly in the 90s. The general trends in evolution of distributed databases include more transparent access to the distributed data, increased support for accessing heterogeneous sources of data, better response time, better administration, and support for enterprise wide distributed solutions.

3.12 Acknowledgments

The author gratefully acknowledges Raman Khanna for instigating the writing of this chapter and providing very useful directions throughout its development, Satya Yenigalla of Oracle for reviewing the chapter and giving helpful comments, and Virinder Batra of IBM for reviewing the chapter and writing about IBM's distributed database management system solutions. Tom Cox's prompt help in reviewing the chapter and pointing out potential overstatements is greatly appreciated.

3.13 References

Anderson, J., 1992. DBMSes Head For The Same Destination. *Open Systems Today* Oct.

Baran, N., 1992. Wireless Networking. *Byte* Apr.

Besser, H., 1992. Adding An Image to an Existing Library and Computer Environment: Design and Technical Considerations. *Studies in Multimedia,* S. Stone and M. Buckland, eds.

Daniels, J., and Cook, S., 1993. Strategies for sharing objects in distributed systems. *Journal of Object-oriented programming,* Jan.

Date, C.J., 1986. An Introduction to Database Systems, vol 1, Fourth Edition.

Finkelstein, R., 1993. Client/Server Middleware: Making Connections Across the Enterprise. *DBMS Magazine,* Jan. vol. 6 no. 1.

Franklin, M., 1993. University of Wisconsin-Madison, abstract for the talk at Database seminar at Stanford University, Mar.

Kernighan, R.L., 1992. Are you ready for ODBC?. *DBMS Magazine*, Oct.

Korzeniowski, P., 1993. Replicating Gains in Distributed DBMS. *Software Magazine*, Apr.

LaPlante, A., 1992. K-Mart's Client/Server Special. *DBMS* Dec. vol 5, number 13.

Lawton, G., 1993. Protecting Integrity of Distributed Data. *Software Magazine*, Jan.

McKelly Jr., C.R., 1993. IBM's SAA Database Workstation Connection. *DBMS,* Mar.

Taylor, D.A.., 1992. *Object-Oriented Technology: A Manager's Guide,* Sep.

Wiederhold, G., 1990. Mediators in the Architecture of Future Information Systems, Nov.

Harvinder Singh received his BSCS at North Carolina State University and MSCS from Stanford University. He is currently working at Oracle Corporation in the Advanced Product Division developing system tools for administering distributed databases. His interests include database design, object-based and client/server database technology, and graphical user interfaces.

Chapter 4

Distributed System Security

Jeffrey Schiller
Massachusetts Institute of Technology

4.1 Introduction

An important aspect of distributed systems, is their security. Some say it is *the* most important aspect. Yet providing security in a distributed environment is very different then in other environments.

Perhaps the key difference is that it is easy in more traditional computing environments to define the perimeter, the boundary around that which you are protecting and that which is the outside world. In a traditional time-sharing system, the terminal represents the boundary. In order to gain access to the system, the user logs in, proves his or her identity to the system and is assigned a name by the system along with various access attributes. Among the physical components of the system, the disk storage, the CPU and the main memory, there are no security boundaries (see figure 4.1).

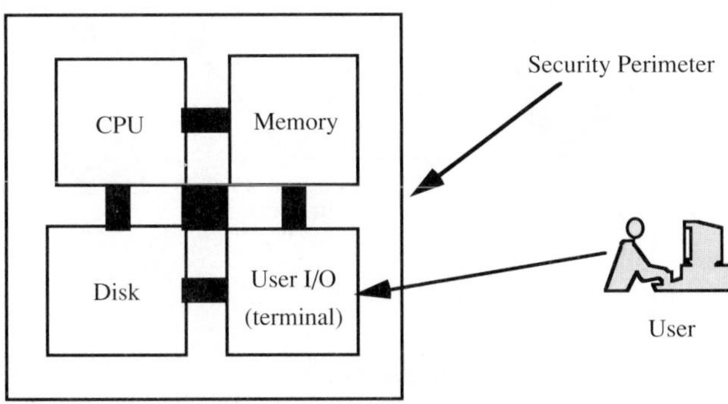

Figure 4.1 Traditional time-sharing security perimeter

However distributing a system is much like taking a time-sharing system apart, separating disk from CPU for example, and placing an untrusted interface between them. An interface where *outsiders* might be able to read all the information and modify it at will. This untrusted interface is in fact the network. For it is the separation of a system's components by a network that creates a distributed system (see figure 4.2).

What follows in this chapter is a framework of how to view a network from a security standpoint. We will first define some terms, which are not distributed system specific, and then move on to the various real world security problems that appear on networks. We will then discuss solutions, how they work and what they really accomplish. If you are looking for a solution to a particular distributed system problem, there may well be a solution for you. However no single solution will meet all needs, and careful thought and analysis needs to be given to decide what the problem is that you are really trying to solve!

Another important point to keep in mind is that security is not an absolute. It is easy to build the world's most secure computer system, that does nothing! It is often the case that security needs to be traded off with other goals of the system, like performance or ease of use. The key is coming up with the right set of trade-offs that take into account the likelihood that a system will be compromised with the cost of providing the security, both in terms of dollars and personnel experience.

It is always important to understand the value of the information being protected, or the cost to the organization for its compromise or loss. Providing security comes at a cost, it is important that this cost be commensurate with the value of the protected information. It is also important to understand other approaches that an attacker (read: bad guy) might take to compromise the system. For example, physically breaking in and stealing the system, kidnapping the systems administrator's family (!) and so on. When speaking with people I like to say "It makes no sense to put a bank vault door on a cardboard house to guard an orange!"

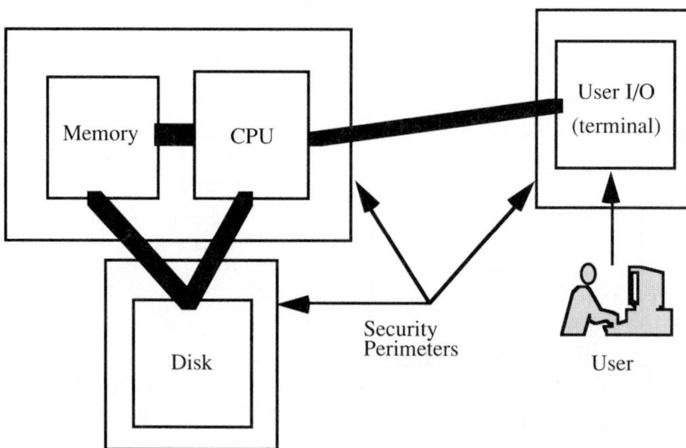

Figure 4.2 Distributed system security perimeters

4.2 Security Definitions

The following definitions layout the basic problem of security. It is sometimes important to have a clear understanding of the differences between them, in order to understand a particular security problem.

4.2.1 Vulnerability

A Security *vulnerability* is a flaw or design consideration in a system that leaves it vulnerable to exploitation. For example having public dial up modems on a system makes it vulnerable to access from unauthorized persons outside of the physical location where the system resides.

It is important to understand that a vulnerability is not necessarily a bad thing. Like the example above, it may be the result of a conscious decision to meet other goals of the system.

4.2.2 Threat

A *threat* to a system is a person or organization with the ways and means to attempt to compromise the system.

4.2.3 Attack

An *Attack* is what happens when a threat attempts to take advantage of a vulnerability. Attacks themselves fall roughly into two categories.

Active attacks are attacks where the threat makes an overt change or modification to the system in an attempt to take advantage of a vulnerability. For example a person attempting to log in to someone else's account and guessing passwords is an active attack.

A *passive* attack is an attack where the threat merely watches information move across the system. However no attempt is made to introduce information in order to exploit a vulnerability. For example, if someone monitors a network cable watching for when someone logs in, in order to read their password when they type it, they are mounting a passive attack.

A passive attacker may take active means to facilitate a passive attack, for example they may actively install a wire tap on a network cable. However the nature of the attack itself, once the tap is in place is fundamentally a passive attack.

4.2.4 Countermeasure

A *countermeasure* is an action taken to counter a specific attack (or class of attacks) against a particular vulnerability. For example on some dial up systems, if you attempt to log in too many times with an incorrect password, the system will hang up on you. The hanging up is a countermeasure designed to make password guessing more difficult. Often when it is impossible to remove a vulnerability, it may be possible to come up with effective countermeasures against the most probable kinds of attacks.

4.3 The Network Security Problem

Most distributed systems operate over local area networks (LANs), so it makes sense to discuss different kinds of LANs from a security perspective.

4.3.1 Disconnected LANs

Many systems operate over what I call *disconnected* LANs. These LANs are characterized as being physically available to only a limited set of people, usually an organization's employees. Disconnected LANs, obviously, normally have fewer security concerns that non-disconnected LANs because the potential threats are much reduced.

The primary threat to a disconnected LAN are an organization's employees themselves. As only these people have physical access, only these people may be threats. However an organizations own people, or *insiders* as we call them, are often the hardest to protect against. For the most part they are people with a good understanding of how the system works, and are therefore probably aware of all (or most) of its vulnerabilities. If a vendor's system is used, the insiders may not have a complete understanding of how it works, but they will probably have a good understanding of how the organization enforces security, or more to the point, how the organization fails to enforce or use the security tools that the vendor provides.

Probably one of the most insidious of vulnerabilities of disconnected LANs has to do with when they unknowingly become connected! You may assume that your LAN is safe, because it only connects the computers in your workgroup, all of which belong to trusted people. Then someone puts a modem on one computer. Suddenly, and usually without anyone being aware, the LAN is no longer disconnected, but is available to anyone in the world who stumbles across the telephone number of the modem!

Therefore when evaluating the security of a disconnected LAN, it is wise to consider security precautions that might normally apply only to a more connected LAN, as a countermeasure against the LAN being inadvertently connected.

4.3.2 Connected LANs

Connected LANs are networks which are connected in some fashion with other networks beyond the control of the owning organization. The primary security difference with connected LANs is that the list of potential threats to the network are much greater. In addition to the traditional insider threats to a disconnected LAN, connected LANs need to be worried about outsiders who can access the LAN through its interconnections.

Connected LANs fall into two categories. Fully connected LANs are LANs that form a seamless part of the larger networks that they connect to. Partially connected LANs are those which are available beyond the local organization, but through means or technology different from the LANs native technology. The example given above, where a person connects a modem to a computer on a disconnected LAN, the result created is a partially connected LAN. The connection is partial because the telephone network (using the modem) may well involve only limited access to the network. On the other hand, when an Internet Protocol LAN joins the global Internet, it is fully connected.

Perhaps the most important thing to understand about connected LANs is that they are vulnerable to threats from just about anywhere in the world. The *world* network is an uninhibited beast, there are no policies and no rules about who can access it (though some may think so!). Some organizations have been attacked by threats operating in countries where their activities were not even against the law! The point is that the first commandment of LAN (and distributed system) security is "Defend Thyself." Do not depend on the outside world behaving in any well defined way!

4.4 Vulnerabilities of Networks

4.4.1 Passive Attacks

As defined above, passive attacks are attacks where information is being siphoned off the network. The traditional passive attack is the password listener. However the most important aspect of a passive attack is that any information that is sent over the network is potentially available to the passive attacker.

Passive attacks can be prevented. Prevention may be as simple as physically securing all points where the network cable and components reside, or may involve sophisticated encryption schemes to render network data unreadable to an attacker.

4.4.2 Active Attacks

Active attacks are by their definition non-preventable. However they are detectable. Detection of an active attack naturally leads to the development of a countermeasure (or apprehension of the attacker).

4.5 Some Background

Security systems provide three basic services, authentication, authorization and auditing.

4.5.1 Authentication

Authentication has to do with determining who is making a request (or on whose behalf). Authentication involves determining that a request originates with a particular person or process and that it is an authentic, non-modified request. An important thing to understand is that authentication is *not* authorization. However most systems that perform authentication today have an implicit authorization component. Namely whether or not an individual is authorized to receive an authenticated identity on a given system or not. Put another way, outsiders to a closed system are typically not authenticated, they exist outside the system. However separating the world into those who are identifiable and those who are not is itself an authorization decision.

I dwell on this simply because proposed authentication systems in the future may permit *anyone* to have an authenticated identity, regardless of whether or not they customarily use a particular system.

Authentication in any system starts with the authentication of its human users. In this context, people can identify themselves and prove that identity via one of three different techniques.

4.5.1.1 What You Are

One obvious way of identifying an individual is to use some biological characteristic of them. This is the way that people usually authenticate others, namely by recognizing their physical characteristics. However it is the least used technique in computerized systems.

Systems do exist to read finger prints, voice prints and so on, however the technology is still developing and their use is rare.

4.5.1.2 What You Have

Anyone who has ever used a credit card (or a key) is familiar with this technique. You prove your identification by presenting a physical credential. The obvious problem with this type of authentication is that the physical object is easily transferable (and in some cases pretty easy to copy as well) from one person to another.

4.5.1.3 What You Know

The third way of identifying an individual is by something that they (and only they) know. The traditional login password is an example of this type of authentication technology. With computer systems, this is the most frequent type of identification. It is also one of the more problematical because people tend to choose extremely poor passwords on average.

4.5.1.4 Combining Them

One way of strengthening these authentication techniques is to combine them. The most common combination found involves mixing *what you have* with *what you know.* A bank ATM card that is only useful with a secret Personal Identification Number (PIN) is a good example of this combining of techniques.

4.5.2 Authorization

Once a system has identified an individual (or process) and a request is made, the next important function has to do with authorizing that request. The most common form of authorization in computer systems is that of *Access Control Lists* or (ACLs). ACLs typically reside on objects such as files and list the names of authenticated entities along with a list of which operations are permitted.

4.5.3 Auditing

One of the more overlooked security technologies is auditing. The goal of authentication and authorization systems are to ensure that only authorized actions are performed. However in any environment, bad things will happen. Auditing is the process of maintaining detailed records of who did what to whom in order to determine how an attack was performed and what information was compromised.

Auditing also acts as a deterrent. By increasing the likelihood that an attacker will be caught, an auditing system may in fact prevent some attacks from ever being launched.

Of course it is not enough to maintain audit records, usually you need to actually check them over to ensure that illicit activity has not taken place. This motivates an interesting trade off in the design of auditing systems. On the one hand you want to audit as much detailed information as possible and on the other hand you need to limit the amount of information that you present a human peruser to prevent them from becoming inundated with information that they cannot hope to process.

A good audit system will not only record as much detail as is possible, but will also have facilities to help a person review the information for illicit activities without requiring them to view vast quantities of data.

4.5.4 Auditing of Configuration

So far I have spoken of auditing from the standpoint of recording events as they take place on a running system. There is another important aspect of security auditing that is almost as important. That is configuration auditing.

In most (if not all) computer systems (distributed or otherwise) there are usually system configuration files that control how the system operates and even may control how security is enforced. A configuration auditing system will check over these files to ensure that the current configuration is both secure and in conformance with a predetermined configuration (which has been safely stored in a fashion that an attacker is unlikely to be able to modify).

4.6 Supporting Technology

Before we continue onto specific security systems and how they work, it is a good idea to have a basic understanding of some of the technology employed by these systems. In essence an understanding of the *tools* of the trade.

4.6.1 Cryptography and its Importance

Perhaps one of the most important distributed security tools is cryptography. Cryptographic systems permit us to take information and send it across hardware that we do not trust and be able to receive that information and know, depending on what cryptographic services we used, that the information was not tampered with or disclosed on its journey. Without cryptographic technology, distributed computer security would be impossible without physically securing every computer, modem and wire in a system.

In short, without cryptographic technology, it is simply not possible to build large enterprise wide distributed systems that have a prayer of being secure!

4.6.2 Cryptographic Services

Cryptographic services can be divided into three basic services they are:

4.6.2.1 Confidentiality

Confidentiality is perhaps the first thing people think of when they think of encryption. Confidentiality service is that cryptographic service that ensures that information is not readable to unauthorized parties as it traverses an information system.

4.6.2.2 Authentication

Authentication service is that service which permits us to know that a particular piece of information was authored by a particular entity.

4.6.2.3 Integrity

Finally *Integrity* service permits us to determine that a piece of information has not been modified as it traversed an information system.

4.6.3 Encryption Systems

Central to cryptographic service provision, are the cryptographic algorithms and methods themselves. There are several different kinds of encryption systems and we will discuss some of the more interesting ones here.

Designing encryption algorithms is an art, and a particularly subtle art at that. There are no publicly known design rules that you may apply to help build an encryption algorithm. In fact the way you learn to build encryption systems is to first learn how to break them. With enough experience breaking encryption systems, you can design systems that are resistant to the attacks that you have become familiar with. Of course other attacks unknown to you may exist. This is what makes designing encryption algorithms hard.

Another important way encryption systems are demonstrated to be secure is the *test of time.* If a system is published and in use for a significant amount of time (measured in years), then if no known successful attacks exist, the cipher is probably pretty good.

The computer professional is best off using publicly available and documented algorithms, particularly algorithms that have been around for a while and have been in use in other systems (thus assuring that someone has cared to attack it or otherwise attempt to determine its strength as an encryption algorithm).

Cipher (encryption) systems can be classified into two distinct types. *Symmetric Ciphers* also called *Conventional Ciphers* use the same key to encrypt data and decrypt data. *Asymmetric Ciphers* also called *Public Key Ciphers*, are a relatively new type of cipher. They use different keys for encryption and decryption.

4.6.4 Symmetric Ciphers

Symmetric Ciphers have been known for centuries. In a typical symmetric cipher, information is algorithmically transformed from its readable form, called *plaintext*, to an unreadable form, called *ciphertext.* The exact transformation is a function of a *key,* which is usually maintained as a secret. With symmetric cryptography, the same key that is used to encrypt information is also employed in the algorithm that decrypts ciphertext back into the original plaintext.

Many symmetric ciphers have been developed over the years, and many have been broken. Probably the most widely used encryption system is the U.S. *Data Encryption Standard (DES).* DES (National Bureau of Standards, 1977) is a U.S. national standard, documented in FIPS 46 (NBS, 1977). The DES was developed by the IBM corporation during the mid

70s and submitted to the National Bureau of Standards (NBS)[1] as a candidate national encryption standard. NBS reviewed it with the help of the National Security Agency (NSA) which recommended some changes in the cipher and eventually published it as a national standard.

Although there is controversy around the changes the NSA made to the DES that continues to this day, no one has demonstrated a serious weakness in the DES. The fact that it has not been broken in over 15 years is a positive sign, particularly given that the algorithm is published and no doubt seriously attacked.[2]

Perhaps the largest drawback to the use of DES in distributed systems is the time consuming nature of the algorithm. Originally designed to be implemented in hardware, the DES is not the fastest encryption algorithm when it comes to implementation in software. However most distributed systems make use of software based security systems, so software performance is important.

Some software vendors that make use of encryption in their products use proprietary algorithms that are significantly faster then the DES (though many also offer the DES as an option). However because these algorithms are proprietary, it is very hard to make an independent assessment of their cryptographic strength. More importantly, the only way possible to examine these systems is to disassemble the products that they are embedded in. This is a task that few user organizations are typically willing to do (not to mention that product disassembly is often prohibited by licensing arrangements). However a motivated attacker may be willing to undertake such a task, and probably will not be deterred by licensing arrangements!

The bottom line on symmetric ciphers is that if you use DES, you will probably be fine. If you use proprietary algorithms, then you are depending on the competence of the software vendor to protect your interests.

4.6.5 The Problem of Key Management

One of the biggest problems that a security system that uses cryptography has to face is the distribution of the secret encryption keys. In order to be useful, in a distributed system, an encryption based system needs to be able to securely disseminate the necessary encryption keys to all parties that need them *and* ensure that the key distribution mechanism is not easily compromised.

If you hear that an encryption based system has been *broken*, it is almost always the case that the key distribution mechanism was what was broken. If an attacker can learn the secret encryption keys, no encryption algorithm will do you any good!

In many systems that use symmetric cryptography, the keys need to be distributed by manual means that are *outside* the normal functioning of the system. Often the manual mechanism will require that individuals actually transport and install keys. However if these individuals are not aware of their responsibility to keep the keys confidential, or are simply not trustworthy, then the whole system may be compromised.

---

[1]The NBS has since been renamed the National Institute of Standards and Technology (NIST).

[2]Recent work by Eli Biham and Adi Shamir have shown some weaknesses in the DES, but this author does not consider them to be of significance.

4.6.6 Asymmetric Ciphers (Public Key)

The first asymmetric cipher was described by Whitfield Diffie and Martin Hellman in 1976 (Diffie and Hellman, 1976).

Asymmetric, or Public Key, ciphers differ from symmetric ciphers in that instead of having one key that is used to control both the encryption operation and the decryption operation, two keys are employed. Furthermore, one of these keys may be made public without endangering the other key.

Of course the obvious question is "Why is this interesting?" The answer is simple. It makes the key distribution problem discussed earlier much easier to solve.

Consider a simple situation involving two people who wish to communicate securely. With only a symmetric encryption algorithm, they would first need to exchange a shared key without anyone else being able to see the key. However because they do not yet have a shared key between them, the only way to do this is in person (or through some trusted communications channel).

Now consider the same situation but using an asymmetric algorithm. Each person tells the other person their public key, out in the open, because it does not matter whether or not anyone else can see these Public keys. Once they have exchanged public keys, they can communicate secretly to encrypting messages to each other encrypted with the other persons public key.

In fact, there is no reason to limit the situation to just two people. A directory of public keys can be published and anyone can then communicate secretly with anyone listed in the directory, without ever needing to pre-establish a shared secret key.

The best known of the asymmetric ciphers is the RSA cipher developed at MIT by Ron Rivest, Adi Shamir and Leonard Adleman (1978) (the R, S and A of RSA). Encryption in RSA is accomplished by taking the information and raising it to a power modulo a large number such:

$$C = P^e \bmod M \tag{1}$$

Where P is the plaintext and C is the Ciphertext. The values e and M are the public key. e is typically a value that is used by many users, the values 3 and 65537 (the 4th format number) are popular choices. M is a very large number that is usually at least 155 digits long. P is required to be a value less then M, so that RSA is a block cipher that works on blocks of data that can be represented as numbers in the range $2 < M$-1. Thinking in bits, A 155 digit M is 512 bits long (wonder where the 155 came from did you?), so P is typically broken down into 512 bit quantities. However most messages that are enciphered with RSA are less then 512 bits (I will explain why a little later).

Decryption is accomplished by the following equation:

$$P = C^d \bmod M \tag{2}$$

The parameter d is the secret key which is not published or disclosed. You will note that the format of the decryption equation is almost identical to that of the encryption equation. The only difference is that the encryption exponent e is replaced by the decryption exponent d. Whereas e tends to be a small value (compared to M), d tends to be as large as M.

The strength of the RSA cipher is that *d* cannot be trivially computed by only knowing *M* and *e*.

One big disadvantage of asymmetric cipher systems, RSA included, is that they tend to be significantly slower then their symmetric counterparts. In fact, they are usually orders of magnitude slower. However in practice this is not usually a problem. To get around the slow speed of asymmetric ciphers, they are often used to exchange a key for a symmetric cipher.

For example, you want to send a secret message to someone for whom you have their RSA public key (their *e* and *M*), rather then break the message up into *M* sized pieces you can use RSA to encrypt a randomly chosen key. First you chose a random DES key (say if you are going to use DES for symmetric encryption) and use this key to encrypt the message itself. You then encrypt this DES key using the RSA public key of the message's recipient. You then send the encrypted message and the encrypted key to the recipient.

The recipient decrypts the DES key (using their private RSA key) and can then decrypt the message itself. An intruder cannot intercept and decrypt the message because the intruder does not have the recipients RSA private key and cannot therefore recover the DES key which was used to encrypt the message.

This technique offers all of the speed of the symmetric encryption system (which is used to encrypt the bulk of the message) while the advantages of asymmetric cryptography are also realized. Because DES keys are 56 bits and most *M* s in use with RSA are at least 512 bits, only one RSA operation is required to encrypt (and decrypt) the DES key.

4.6.7 Common Authentication and Integrity Checks

Authentication and Integrity services are often provided by a single mechanism. Two mechanisms are *Message Authentication Codes (MACs)* and *Digital Signatures*. The goal of a MAC or digital signature is to make it possible for information to be communicated from one party to another with the recipient being able to demonstrate that the information in fact came from the claimed sender and that it had not been tampered with in transit.

Many people often confuse a MAC with a data checksum. In fact both are an attempt to provide the same basic service, namely ensuring that the conveyed information has not been changed in transit from sender to recipient. The difference between the two has to do with the threats that are out to change the information.

A typical checksum is designed to catch errors that are the result of noise or other more *natural* or non-intentional sources. An important property for a checksum algorithm is to accurately detect bit errors that occur in bursts, as this is a common phenomenon in real world networks.

On the other hand a MAC is a cryptographic checksum which is designed to be hard to attack by a knowledgeable attacker, not a *natural* source. For example with many checksum and Cyclic Redundancy Checks (CRCs) it is relatively easy to make a change in a piece of information and then compute another, second change, that has the effect of causing the checksum or CRC value to be the same as the original completely unmodified information. It should not be computationally feasible to do this with a MAC.

4.6.7.1 MACs

MACs are generally used with symmetric encryption systems such as the Data Encryption Standard. A common MAC is to use the DES in Cipher Block Chaining mode. This mode of encrypting information will yield a 64- bit *leftover* value when run over a piece of data. Even if the encrypted data is not retained, this residue can serve as a MAC of the document.

If two parties share a symmetric key, it is possible for one, the sender, to compute a MAC by running the DES over the data and taking the leftover 64- bit residue and sending it as the MAC to go along with the data. The recipient then performs the same encryption over the received data and should obtain the same value. If the data is tampered with in any way, the receiver will not obtain a residue that matches the transmitted MAC.

Of course an attacker can usually tamper with a piece of data's MAC value just as readily as the data itself. However without knowledge of the key used to create the MAC, it is not possible for an attacker to be able to generate a piece of data and then compute a corresponding MAC that will be accepted by the recipient.

4.6.7.2 Digital Signatures

A Digital Signature is a special type of MAC that results when asymmetric encryption systems, particularly RSA, are used to protect information. As in the case of bulk data encryption, an asymmetric algorithm such as RSA is rarely used to MAC an entire message. Instead a one-way cryptographic hash function is used to reduce a piece of data to a smaller (typically 128 or 160 bits) piece of data that will fit into one RSA block (512 bits or more).

One-way cryptographic hash functions are much like CRCs or checksums in that they do not take a key as part of their input. You feed the data to be hashed to the hash algorithm and a 128 (or 160 bits, depending on algorithm) hash results. However cryptographic hashes are significantly different then checksums in that it should not be computationally feasible, with a good cryptographic hash, to generate two pieces of different data that hash to the same value.

Once you compute a cryptographic hash of a piece of information, you encrypt this hash with a private RSA key. The resulting value is called the digital signature of the original information.

Given a document (or other information) and its digital signature, you can verify it by first computing the cryptographic hash value of the document (using the same hash algorithm that was used to compute the signature) and then decrypting the digital signature value with the signer's public key. The decrypted digital signature should yield the same value as the cryptographic hash (sometimes referred to as a message digest or MD) of the document. If these values fail to match, then the document (or the signature) have been altered.

In order for an attacker to tamper with a signed piece of data undetected, they either have to make an alteration that does not effect the hash of the information (which by the definition of a good hash algorithm, should be too hard to do) or they have to generate the signature that corresponds to the encryption of the hash of the altered document (which they cannot do without the signer's private RSA key).

What makes digital signatures different then MACs is that while MACs require a secret key to verify, digital signatures are verifiable with a public key, a published value. Whereas

MACs are used to exchange information between two parties, where both have knowledge of a secret value (the key). A digital signature does not require any secret information in order to be verified. This implies that if many people have my public key, I can publish information (data packets or whole documents, even this book!) and then publish its digital signature. Anyone who has my public key can then demonstrate that the information they received from me (or is claimed to have been published by me) is in fact from me.

The digital signature is also very valuable because it can have significance over a long period of time. Information stored in a computer system can be digitally signed and then later proven to be authentic, regardless of the security of the system used to store it (as long as the RSA private key used to generate the signature remains secret). See figure 4.3.

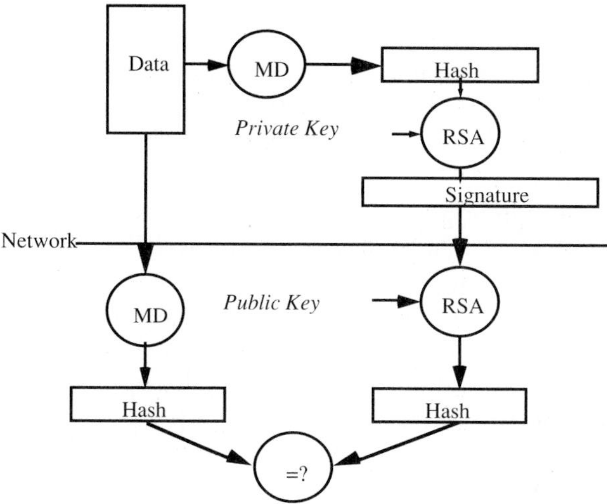

Figure 4.3 Digital signature generation and verification.

4.6.8 Cards

Perhaps one of the largest vulnerabilities of most authentication systems is the way that users initially authenticate themselves to the systems that they use. Traditionally this is accomplished via the use of passwords. A user will indicate their login name and then provide a password which in theory is known only to the system and to them.

The problem with passwords, in a nutshell, is that most passwords can be classified into two basic categories, easy to remember *and* easy to guess and hard to guess, but also hard to remember. People who choose easy to remember passwords are usually victims of having their passwords stolen or guessed. People who choose hard to guess password may either forget them, or worse, write them down someplace for reference. A common, dumb, place that people write down passwords is usually on the terminal itself.

In general, passwords can be made secure in an environment consisting of security knowledgeable users. However, few environments have this property. Other alternatives are therefore needed if you wish to provide security in a distributed environment, with a mere mortal user community.

The most common solution is to use some form of machine readable identification card. These fall into two basic categories, those which are passive and contain data (dumb) and those which may contain active memory or even processing power (smart).

4.6.8.1 Dumb Cards

Bank Automated Teller Cards are good examples of dumb cards. They contain a magnetic stripe which is read by the ATM machine when they are used. To ensure that the card has not been stolen, the user is required to supply a Personal Identification Number (PIN). This is a good example of combining "something you have" with "something you know."

4.6.8.2 Memory Cards

Memory cards are basically similar to dumb cards, however information is stored in the cards' Electrically Erasable Prom (EEPROM) memory instead of on a magnetic stripe. The primary advantage of memory cards over dumb cards is that they can store a significant amount of information on the card.

The primary disadvantage of memory cards is that they require a direct electrical connection between the card and the equipment that queries it.

Memory cards are not only used in authentication applications but are also targeted at other applications which require that the user carry around significant amount of information. For example, it has been proposed that people carry medical history information with them in such a card so that it would be available to any health care professional who may be called upon to provide care in an emergency.

4.6.8.3 Challenge Cards

Challenge/Response cards are smart cards that not only contain memory, but also have processing capabilities. They are typically initialized with a secret key which is used to encrypt challenges to the card. For example to prove that you have the correct card, the system will send a random number to the card and expect the card to algorithmically transform the number (typically via a data encryption algorithm) into a *response* number. The system performing the authentication then can determine if the card has the correct key.

The advantage of this approach is that the key is never disclosed during the challenge/response dialog. An attacker listening to the exchange does not learn any information that permits him to determine the secret key stored in the card.

Challenge/response type of smart cards need to provide a pathway for getting information both in and out of the card. This can be accomplished either via an electrical interface or via a keyboard and mini-display if the amount of information to be exchanged is small enough that it is reasonable to have the human act as the go between from the card to the challenging system.[3]

---

[3]In fact smart cards can be used not only to respond to challenges from a computer system, but also to challenge the computer system so that the card's user can authenticate the system.

4.6.8.4 Time Based Cards (SecureID)

Another approach to smart card design is to use a time based card. Time based cards have an on-board clock. They display a time varying number which is used by the user when they need to authenticate themselves. The computer system can compute the proper value that the card should be displaying and therefore can determine whether or not a legitimate card is being used. In essence, the card uses the current time as an implicit challenge and generates an appropriate response automatically. Because the challenge is implicit, the user does not need to type it to the card. The card can be manufactured without a keypad (or electrical interface) and is in general pretty easy to actually use.

4.7 Mechanisms to Provide Network Security

There are many approaches to network security. Below we will go into some detail on the more popular techniques.

4.7.1 Firewalls

A popular network security technique is the use of *firewalls*. Building a firewall is accomplished by putting in packet filtering in the routers that connect an organization with the outside world. Only certain packets are permitted to flow from the *inside* to the outside world.

To understand firewalls you need to understand a little of the protocols that underlie the network itself.

In the TCP/IP world, there are two primary transport protocols. TCP, for Transmission Control Protocol and UDP for User Datagram Protocol. TCP is the basic reliable stream protocol and UDP is used for simple query response protocols. Both of these protocols make use of *port* numbers. A *port* is a unique number that is assigned to one end of a network communication. A connection (be it TCP or UDP) is fully specified by the two host addresses and the ports at those addresses.

Services are reached by contacting them at *well known* ports. For example, TELNET (remote login) always *listens* on port 23 while file transfer listens on port 21.

The key to firewalling is controlling access between pairs of ports. For example a router can be instructed to drop all packets from the outside world that are attempting to reach an internal host via port 23. Doing so will effectively shut out incoming TELNETs.

Most major router vendors support features that allow network administrators to establish a list of permitted and denied ports. Many will also permit you to establish port filters on a per host or subnet basis, allowing the network administrator to control access on a finer grained basis then just the whole organization.

The primary advantage to using firewalls is that it is something that a network administrator can do to increase security to a whole organization without having any access to individual host computers within the organization. In other words, people who configure hosts within the organization can be as careless as they wish, the firewall will protect them.

However, firewalls bring plenty of liabilities. After all, the best firewall is synonymous with simply making the internal network unreachable. Yet, presumably, there is a reason why the organization is connected to the network or it would not be in the first place! One of the primary reasons for having a network connection to the outside world is to facilitate the exchange of information. Yet, by their very nature, firewalls do not help you exchange information, they prohibit it!

When configuring firewalls it is also very important to ensure that network support protocols are permitted through the firewall. The most important of these is the Domain Name System (DNS) protocol which uses UDP and TCP port 53. You need to permit this traffic to flow across any firewall so that hosts within the organization can resolve the names of hosts outside the organization. Similarly if you wish to permit any communication between hosts outside the organization and hosts internal, you need to ensure that outside hosts can reach the necessary DNS servers within the organization so that they can resolve the names of hosts within the organization.

The most common way that firewalls are implemented is to prevent most outsiders from making connections into the organization accept through specially designated (and presumably securely managed) systems.

Great care must be exercised about limiting access for people inside the organization to make outgoing connections. It is important to always understand who and what your threats are. Not permitting connections from within the organization implies that insiders are part of the threat potential that you are concerned with. However a motivated and knowledgeable insider can usually penetrate any firewall, if the firewall allows any protocol to cross it.

For example, a knowledgeable insider can conspire with a friend outside the organization to configure a virtual network link between a selected internal host and an external host. It is pretty easy to configure such a link so that the traffic encapsulated within it appears to be using UDP port 53, the DNS system port. The firewall would naturally let this pass, because blocking DNS traffic, as was mentioned earlier, can cause legitimate connectivity to fail.

Another cost of firewalls in many organizations is the cost of opportunity. Most firewalls only permit specific predetermined types of protocols (usually electronic mail) to cross while forbidding others. Yet this has as a side effect, locking the organization and its employees out from any new, interesting and potentially useful uses of the network that may develop. This effect can easily stifle innovative uses of the network, one of its traditional features.

4.7.2 Application Gateways

Application gateways are a mechanism that is used often in conjunction with a firewall. The idea is to have a firewall that blocks most packet level traffic from crossing into an organization accept traffic to designated application gateways.

For example instead of permitting electronic mail traffic (TCP port 25) to arbitrarily cross the firewall, traffic is only permitted to a particular host. This host is then configured to accept mail for the whole organization and forward it accordingly within the organization's internal network. Similarly TELNET connections may be permitted to a specific host (which is managed securely) and then once logged in there, users can connect to other hosts on the *inside* of the firewall.

Applications gateways exist for mail, remote login (TELNET) and file transfer. Creating some is merely a matter of properly configuring software, while others are commercial products.

In summary, firewalls along with applications gateways can provide a measure of security, at the cost of convenience and innovation. They are most appropriate when an organization's network is insecurely run internally and the network administrators are held responsible for security, but have no authority to set security policy for hosts within the network. However, an important thing to keep in mind is that they are not perfect. The Internet Worm of 1988 (which infected hosts via the *sendmail* program) is in some network manager's view the vision of disaster. Yet, it would have no trouble climbing through most of today's firewalls!

4.7.3 Virtual Private Networks

Some organizations connect to the Internet as a way to communicate with geographically separate locations, but have no interest in communicating with other organizations on the Internet at large. One secure way to accomplish this is to configure a virtual private network *through* the Internet. This can be accomplished by defining a firewall that prohibits all traffic except traffic between a particular set of systems (which are usually routers), one at each location. Between these routers a *virtual link* is configured. The virtual link is configured to look like a dedicated leased circuit between the offices, however instead of an actual virtual link being in place, traffic is instead encapsulated (wrapped) in IP packets and sent to the peer router. In fact for confidentiality, the wrapping routers can encrypt the traffic prior to sending it on the outside Internet.

4.7.4 Kerberos

Kerberos is a cryptographic based network authentication system developed at MIT for Project Athena (Steiner, Neuman, and Schiller, 1988). The goal of Kerberos is to provide a mechanism for client/server computing authentication. It permits client programs and server programs, operating across a network, to authenticate each other without any information going over the network *in the clear* where it can be intercepted.

Although developed primary for client/server systems, it can also be used for more traditional authentication problems, like TELNET and Berkeley *rlogin.*

Kerberos also arranges for the secure exchange of session encryption keys between client and server. This enables application developers to not only authenticate all transactions between client and server, but to encrypt those which are sensitive and should not be disclosed to network eavesdroppers.

4.7.4.1 Kerberos Design Goals

Kerberos was designed to operate in MIT's Project Athena distributed computing environment. In this environment, client workstations are located in public places and are used serially by different users. Client workstations contain no *private* data or in fact any information that cannot be quickly regenerated from the network. In essence they are *portals* for the user to obtain network services.

All personal files as well as all programs reside over the network and must be accessed only via Kerberos authenticated transactions.

Server systems are centrally managed and are located in moderately secure computer rooms.

The Kerberos Key Distribution Centers (KDCs) are located in much more secure physical locations and are closely guarded.

Because servers are located in only *moderately* secure computer rooms, an important goal of Kerberos is to ensure that a compromise of one server does not compromise another server.

Workstations are located in effectively *public* places where their consoles are available to whatever user happens to be physically in front of them. Therefore they are completely untrusted. Workstations cannot simply assert a user's identity to a server.

Because users are generally unsophisticated when it comes to computer security precautions, no long term encryption keys (like those which may be a function of a user's password) may be stored on a public workstation. A user could easily be tricked into leaving their workstation unattended and an attacker can obtain any encryption keys that the workstation may store.

Finally the last goal is that Kerberos must operate securely, even when the network is under constant surveillance by potential attackers.

4.7.4.2 Kerberos Design

Every Kerberos server and user is registered in the Kerberos KDC database. For each user their name is stored along with a secret DES key known only to them (and the database). Other administrative information is stored as well, but need not concern us here. Figure 4.4 shows the fields in a Kerberos KDC database.

name	instance	attributes	key	key version	expiration	last modified	last modified by
jis		0	0xf46723892 3129056	2	12/31/99	04/16/93	jis

Figure 4.4 Kerberos database entry.

Because humans are not particularly good at remembering 64 bit random numbers, user's keys are known to them as a password. Part of the MIT Kerberos software is a function which translates a password into a 64 bit DES key.

Whereas users *store* their key by remembering a password, servers must store their key in a file which is read protected against unauthorized perusal.

The Kerberos protocol is shown graphically in figure 4.5. The basic idea is that when a user *c* wishes to use a service *s* the user obtains a *ticket* by sending a request to the Kerberos server detailing her own name and the name of the desired service.

The Kerberos service constructs a *ticket* (we will explain the contents of tickets in a moment) and a corresponding session DES key. Both of these are then encrypted in the user's DES key and returned to the requesting workstation.

The workstation will then prompt the user for her password which will be translated into a DES key and used to decrypt the returned ticket and DES session key. If the password is entered incorrectly, then a proper decryption cannot result.

Assuming that the Ticket and DES session key are properly decrypted, then the user can construct an *Authenticator* to send to service *s* along with the ticket.

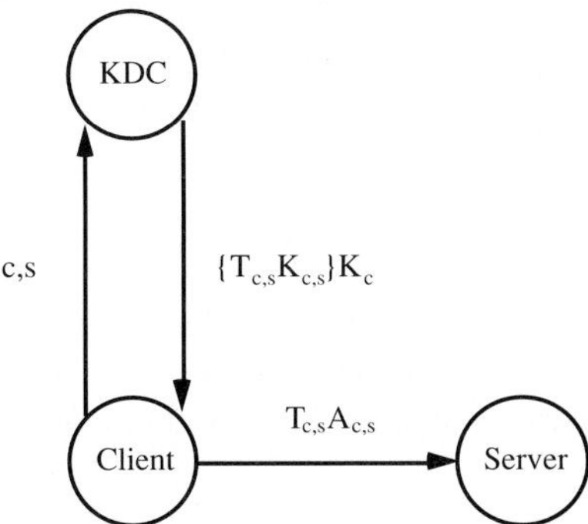

Figure 4.5 Kerberos protocol.

Let's look now at the contents of a ticket:

$$T = \{c, s, addrto, e; K_{c,s}\}_{K_s} \quad (3)$$

The Ticket T contains the name of the user c, the name of the desired service, s, the workstation's transport address (an IP address at MIT), the time it was created by the Kerberos server and a lifetime. This information is then encrypted in K_S the secret DES key of the service s (by enclosing terms within {}s with a subscript I indicate that the terms are encrypted under the subscripted key). Note that the contents of the ticket are unreadable to the user which receives it, because the user does not have the server's key K_S.

The ticket also contains a $K_{C,S}$ which is a randomly chosen session DES key. It is returned to the user (encrypted) directly along with the ticket itself. So the user receives from the Kerberos server:

$$\{T, K_{c,s}\}_{K_c} \quad (4)$$

You will note that this information is encrypted in K_C which is the users DES key and which is derived from their password. Therefore $K_{C,S}$ is available to the user and is locked away inside the ticket T.

After receiving a ticket from the Kerberos server, a user authenticates a transaction to the service s by sending it a copy of the ticket along with an authenticator A:

$$A = \{c, s, time, addr\}_{K_{c,s}} \quad (5)$$

Note that the authenticator is encrypted in $K_{C,S}$, the session DES key. Unlike the ticket, which is generated by the Kerberos server, the authenticator is generated by the user's workstation. It contains the name of the user, the name of the service being desired and the current time.

When a server receives a ticket and an authenticator, it first decrypts the ticket using its secret DES key, K_S. After decryption (if it was successful) it knows that c is attempting to make an authenticated request. It then looks to see if its own name s appears in the ticket (its an error if it does not) and then verifies that the ticket is valid (it has not expired) and was delivered from the *addr* specified in the ticket. Finally if the ticket appears correct, the session DES key $K_{C,S}$ is removed and used to decrypt the authenticator. If the authenticator decrypts properly, then the clients name is compared between the authenticator and the ticket, it better match. Similar the name of the service needs to match as well as the transport address being proper. Finally the timestamp within the authenticator needs to be within a few minutes of *now.* If all these conditions are met, then the transaction can be assumed to have originated with the user *c* and appropriate action may be taken.

The strength of Kerberos is that without the user's key K_c an intruder can not accomplish this exchange. Similarly if an intruder records a series of transactions, nothing is disclosed that permits the intruder to attempt a similar transaction. Even if the identical data is sent by the intruder, it will be rejected because the timestamp in the authenticator will likely be too old.

A careful reader will notice at this point that to complete a Kerberos authenticated transaction, the user's key K_c is required to decrypt the first response from the Kerberos server. This implies that either the workstation stores K_c in memory for reference when needed, or the workstation continually prompts the user to provide her password. Neither are desirable situations.

To solve this problem, we invented the ticket granting service (TGS). The TGS runs on the same system as the Kerberos server and has access to the Kerberos KDC database.[4]

When a user first logs in to a workstation, they use the *normal* Kerberos protocol to obtain a ticket for the TGS service (this step requires their password be entered, which is usual at login time). However when additional tickets are required, rather then using the *normal* Kerberos service, the client workstation makes a Kerberos authenticated request to the TGS requesting additional tickets (and corresponding DES session keys). Rather then being returned to the user's workstation encrypted in K_c they are instead encrypted in the session key of the TGS ticket. Therefore the only *secret* that the workstation needs to store is the session key $K_{c,tgs}$ which is needed to use the TGS. The MIT implementation in fact stores all the tickets obtained during a login session, along with their session keys in a ticket cache file. Although this information needs to be protected, it does not need to be protected forever. This is because the TGS has a finite lifetime, measured in hours, after which it and its corresponding session key become void and useless.

4.7.4.3 What Kerberos Looks Like to the User

At MIT Kerberos is in daily use, yet most users are not aware of it. When a user approaches a workstation she sees the normal login greeting requesting a user name and password. However instead of using the password for a traditional password file lookup, the username is used to fetch a ticket for the TGS and the password is converted into K_c for decrypting it. Applications which fetch Kerberos tickets do so with little direct knowledge of the end user. The point is that Kerberos and other encryption based authentication systems need not interfere with apparent normal application processing. In fact the overhead of performing encryption operations for purposes of transactional authentication is hardly noticeable.

---

[4]In fact in the MIT implementation the KDC and TGS are implemented within the same process.

4.7.4.4 Managing a Kerberos Realm

An administrative domain which makes use of a common Kerberos KDC is called a *realm.* Typical administrative operations such as adding new users and changing the passwords of existing users are accomplished via a Kerberos authenticated (and fully encrypted) protocol via the *admin* client. The KDC maintains a list of Kerberos usernames (this list is maintained locally on the KDC) which are permitted to add users and change the passwords of users.

The Kerberos KDC must be secured. We recommend that it be on physically protected machines and ideally the KDC system should provide no other service. In other words it should not be a time sharing system or support other services which may prove insecure, providing a path for an attacker to obtain access to the KDC database. We also recommend that only a limited number of trusted individuals have direct access to the KDC database. Staff who need to perform administrative operations such as adding users do *not* need direct access but can use the Kerberos authenticated *admin* client. This is much safer, for although an administrator can change any password, they cannot obtain the password of any user.

This advice is motivated by the fact that the DES keys of all users and servers reside on the KDC. If an unauthorized copy of the KDC database is made, then in essence all user passwords have been compromised and need to be changed. Needless to say this would be an embarrassing disaster in just about any environment.

To ensure reliability of the KDC, Kerberos supports replication of the Kerberos KDC function. One KDC is designated the *master* KDC and all changes are made only to it. Periodically (daily at MIT) changes on the master KDC are propagated to slave KDC servers. Because the slave KDCs have copies of all the sensitive keys in the master KDC database, they too have to be carefully protected. The master to slave update protocol is (of course) Kerberos authenticated and encrypted.

Because each slave is as vulnerable as the master KDC, a trade-off exists between having many KDC slaves for reliability and having but a few because fewer machines are easier to ensure security on.

4.7.4.5 Kerberos Availability

Kerberos has been in daily use at MIT since 1987 and the MIT software implementation is distributed via anonymous FTP from MIT. Since its creation, many institutions have received copies of it. Kerberos is also the authentication system used by Transarc's AFS file system and is the underlying component of the Open Software Foundations Distributed Computing Environment's security server.

4.7.5 Kerberos Variants and Similar Systems

4.7.5.1 X.509

X.509 identifies the CCITT X.500 directory authentication framework standard. X.509 defines two basic authentication schemes. One labeled *simple* is based on using passwords and is therefore uninteresting. The other mechanism is called *strong* authentication. Strong authentication has as its primary goal providing proof of authentication (and data integrity) without disclosing over a network any information that would enable an intruder to obtain unauthorized access either immediately or in the future.

X.509 is based on the use of Public Key cryptography. Although the formal standard does not identify a particular algorithm, the RSA system is identified in an annex to the standard. Each entity (be they user, server, or other object) has a key pair, public and private. The entity has to maintain the private key securely, but the public key is stored in the directory.

Authentication is proved by signing requests (generating a digital signature) using the private key. An entity receiving a signed request may then fetch the entity's public key and use it to verify the signature.

An important feature of X.509 is the definition of a certificate structure (see figure 4.6). The certificate mechanism is how X.509 *binds* a particular user name (expressed in the syntax of the X.500 standard) with a particular public key. Because public keys are stored in directories available over the network, it is essential that a mechanism be used to ensure that a public key is indeed affiliated with a particular user. Public Key technology comes to the rescue here. A certificate is protected because it itself is a digitally signed document.

```
Certificate = {
   version,        // Version number of certificate structure v1988
= 0 (default)
                   // v1992 = 1
   serial number,// For uniquely identifying this certificate
   name,           // X.500 name of the certificate's user
   public key,     // the Public Key of the certificate user
   validity = {    // timeframe when this certificate is valid
       notbefore,// timestamp
       notafter, // timestamp
   issuer name,    // Name of the entity that signs this certificate
   signature,      // The signature of this certificate as supplied
   by the issuer
}
```

Figure 4.6 Definition of a certificate structure.

A certificate contains a user name, a public key, the name of the entity which has signed it and other bookkeeping information.

You will note from figure 4.6 that a certificate contains a *validity* which defines the certificate lifetime. Although this implies that a certificate needs to be reissued periodically, it is envisioned that most certificates will have lifetimes measured in years (or at least months).

When a transaction needs to be verified, the public key of the user is fetched by fetching the appropriate certificate structure from a directory. The certificate is verified by recursively fetching the public key of the certificate signer (called the issuer) until a public key is obtained (and corresponding name) that is trusted implicitly by the transaction verifier.

It makes the most sense to arrange certificates in a hierarchy. At the top of the hierarchy is a well known trusted public key, sometimes referred to as the *root* key. This key is installed in all entities that need to verify transactions. The private key of the *root* is then used to sign certificates for major subdivisions of the directory tree (maybe countries, or states, or large corporations[5]). These subordinate certifying authorities can then sign certificates for others.

When a transaction is verified, the tree is walked from the public key of the transaction issuer up to the root of the tree.

Of course in the real world there will no doubt be multiple such hierarchies. However this is not a problem as long as entities which need to interact can find a common key, or set of keys, that they can implicitly trust.

4.7.5.2 SPX

SPX is an experimental authentication system developed by the Digital Equipment Corporation. It performs a function very similar to Kerberos, but uses RSA Public Key encryption at several steps both to increase security and scalability.

Each user and server has an RSA key pair as opposed to a DES key in Kerberos.

In place of a KDC, SPX has a server called the *Certificate Distribution Center* (CDC). However unlike Kerberos, instead of storing the association between users and their DES keys, it stores each user's certificate (using the same format as X.509 certificates) and the user's private RSA key encrypted with a DES key which is derived from the user's password.

Because the user's password is not stored on the CDC in any form and because their RSA private key is only stored in an encrypted form, a CDC does not have to be as secured as a Kerberos KDC.[6]

Describing the SPX transactions requires a little more symbology. Whereas I enclose encrypted information in { }s, here I also enclose digitally signed (but not encrypted) data with []s. Whereas I use *Ks* to represent DES keys, here I also use *Ps* to represent RSA Public Keys and *Rs* to represent RSA Private Keys. So K_C would be a DES key belonging to *c*, and P_C would be a RSA PublicKey belonging to *c* (which is not confidential because it is *public*) and R_C would be the corresponding RSA Private Key, which *is* confidential.

By using Public Key Encryption only the end-user ever needs to access R_C. However because RSA keys are both large and have structure (i.e. not any bit pattern can be used as an RSA private key), it is not convenient to derive them directly from a typed password. Instead they tend to be stored in files (or in servers such as a CDC) encrypted in a DES key which is a function of a typed password.

SPX makes use of two types of certificates. Normal certificates, where a certifying authority (CA) issues a certificate for an end-user and *Trusted Authority Certificates* (TA) where the end-user signs a certificate binding the CA's name to its key. TAs may be thought of as upside down certificates. Rather then having a *higher level* entity certifying its user's, each user also has a TA certifying the CA (the higher level) using its own key to generate the signature. Although SPX uses a hierarchy of certificates (like most applications of X.509) the root of the hierarchy does not need to have it's key widely known and trusted. Instead each CA below the

[5]In the X.500 directory, many entities are identified besides users and servers. Organizations themselves are entities which appear in the directory as well as provinces, states and countries.

[6]Even though user's private RSA keys are stored encrypted, the CDC contents should be considered sensitive and protected. However a compromise of the CDC contents (for reading) is not a disaster as it is with Kerberos.

root maintains a TA certificate that binds the root's key with its name. Similarly users (and subordinate CAs) below a given CA have TA certificates that certify it.

For the purposes of the explanation below, we will assume that *the world* only has one CA under which all users and servers are registered. Of course this is not a real example, but it makes the explanation much easier to understand. I leave it as an exercise of the reader to extend the example to include an arbitrary hierarchy!

I will use the symbol $C_{i\text{->}c}$ to represent a certificate issued by i which certifies c's RSA Public Key. in essence a certificate is:

$$C_{i \rightarrow c} = [i, c, P_c, serial, lifetime]_{R_i} \tag{6}$$

I will use the symbol $T_{c\text{->}i}$ to denote a trusted authority certificate where c is binding i's key to its name.

For each SPX user the CDC stores:

$$C_{i \rightarrow c} T_{c \rightarrow i} \{R_c\} K_c \tag{7}$$

Although the user's RSA private key is stored in the CDC, it is encrypted in K_c which is derived from the user's password. K_c is stored nowhere! No other person (besides the user), including the system administrators need know K_c and therefore do not have access to R_c. This is why the CDC does not have to be as secure as a Kerberos KDC.

Furthermore the SPX protocol itself does not require that the CDC store the user's private keys. For example it can just as easily be stored in a file on the user's workstation (encrypted of course) or on a floppy disk that they carry with them!

When a user logs into a workstation using the SPX system a random RSA key pair is generated for them. I will refer to this random RSA key as R_{cLogin} (and P_{cLogin}). The workstation sends a request to the CDC indicating that it wants the information that the CDC has stored for the user. The CDC returns: $C_{i\text{->}c}$, $T_{c\text{->}i}$, $\{R_c\}K_c$. The user is prompted for a password which is converted to K_c in much the same fashion as kerberos. With K_c, R_c is decrypted and used to create a *Login Ticket* (L_{cLogin}). This *ticket* is a virtual certificate which has a lifetime equal to the length of the session. It is typically measured in hours. It contains:

$$L_{cLogin} = [c, P_{cLogin}, lifetime]\, R_c \tag{8}$$

Note that it contains the Public RSA Key P_{cLogin} but is signed using R_c, the user's permanent RSA private key. Once L_{cLogin} is generated at login time, a workstation no longer needs R_c for the duration of the login session. This is done for much the same reason that Kerberos uses the Ticket Granting Ticket, to avoid storing very sensitive secrets on end-user workstations for any length of time.

Once the workstation creates the Login Ticket, it uses the user's Public RSA key to verify $T_{c\text{->}i}$ from which it obtains i's Public RSA key. In our example i is the *root* of the certification tree.

When a user wishes to use a service, say s, the workstation generates a random DES session key, $K_{c,s}$ which will be used only to talk to s. The service's Public RSA key is then obtained by requesting a chain of certificates leading from the root (i in our example) to the service s from the CDC. In our example the CDC would return $C_{i\text{->}s}$, the certificate of s.

The service, s, is then sent:

$$L_{cLogin}, [\{K_{c,s}\} P_s] R_{cLogin}, \{time\} K_{c,s} \quad (9)$$

The service, when it receives this request, will fetch P_C from the CDC by obtaining *c's* certificate ($C_{i->c}$), verifying it and extracting the RSA Public Key. Using P_c, the service verifies the authenticity of L_{cLogin} (remember it is signed using R_c, so is verified using P_c). From L_{cLogin} the service obtains P_{cLogin} which it uses to verify the signature on $\{K_{c,s}\}P_S$. Assuming this succeeds (authentication fails if any step here fails), then the service decrypts $\{K_{c,s}\}P_s$ using its own permanent private RSA key R_S. This yields $K_{c,s}$ which is then used to decrypt the supplied timestamp which is tested to see if it is current.

At the conclusion of these computations the service knows that the client is authentic *and* the service has been provided the random DES key $K_{c,s}$ which may then be used to encrypt any information (with the DES) the application wishes to pass from server to client. This key may also be used for a simple challenge response to prove to the client that the correct service has been reached.

4.7.5.2.1 Advantages of SPX

The primary advantage of SPX is that it makes good use of Public Key Cryptography. This allows some of the advantages of Public Key to be realized. Perhaps the most important of these is the removal of the absolute confidentiality requirement from the CDC (the CDC in fact can be run completely in the open if only the user's private keys were not stored on it at all!). Because CDCs do not have to contain a lot of confidential information they can be replicated *and* certificates from foreign CDCs can be cached locally because their authenticity does not depend on where they are stored, but on the integrity of their signatures!

A related advantage is that user's private RSA keys are never disclosed to anyone, including system administrators. Privacy is much easier to ensure when few people (or no people!) have the technical ability to violate it.

4.7.5.2.2 Drawbacks of SPX

Perhaps the largest drawback of SPX at this time is that it remains an experimental system that has not been widely adopted nor deployed. Some of the cryptographic operations (the RSA private key operations) are extremely computation intensive and how this will effect the overall performance of large distributed systems in a production environment is not known. For example today an Andrew File System server, which uses Kerberos for authentication, can have over 2,000 simultaneous connections. If it fails, these connections need to be renegotiated when the server restarts. Performing the necessary 2,000 DES operations is known to not be a problem (by experience!). However performing 2,000 RSA private key operations may require several minutes without hardware encryption support. Would an AFS file server using SPX be able to restart in a usable period of time? Questions like these need answers!

4.7.5.3 Kerberos and SPX, the Future

Although SPX remains an experimental prototype, the Kerberos system enjoys popularity and is continuing to evolve. One direction that MIT will likely take with Kerberos is to incorporate Public Key encryption technology, perhaps borrowing heavily from the SPX system.

Already the Kerberos and SPX developers have agreed to a standard applications programming interface called Generic Security Services Application Programming Interface (GSSAPI) and have proposed that it become an Internet standard (the first API standard for the Internet) to the Internet Engineering Task Force (IETF).

Programmers who write their applications to conform to the GSSAPI will be able to compile them either with SPX or with Kerberos (both present and future versions) with minimal programming changes required to switch from one system to another. At the time of this writing (April 1993), the GSSAPI standard was an Internet Draft (available in the standard places where Internet drafts are stored) and may well be an RFC at the time you are reading this.

4.7.6 One Time Password Schemes

One of the primary problems with the traditional password approach to authentication is that on a network, a password may be intercepted by any workstation on the LAN. Kerberos, SPX and other cryptographically based systems offer a viable alternative to passwords for client/server applications, or any application where there is *smarts* on the client side.

However very often we are faced with the situation of having a *dumb* terminal interface to our distributed system. With such an interface we cannot engage in the complicated transactions that are required by Kerberos and friends. Furthermore even if we have a local PC with us to perform the computations, the bulk of the data that would need to be transcribed from PC to terminal is prohibitive.

One time password systems offer a solution in this problem space. As there name implies, the idea is to use a password but once after which it is no longer considered valid.

4.7.6.1 Manual Schemes

The most obvious way to build a one time password scheme is to store a file of passwords on the host system and carry a copy on a sheet of paper (with the passwords sorted by the order they will be used in).

This suffers from two main drawbacks. The first is that carrying around a piece of paper is both inconvenient, and of course what do you do when you run out of passwords but are still physically separated from the location where you can generate new ones![7] The second problem is that the list of passwords on the host is available for anyone who can read compromise the host system. This is not a show stopper, but does require some careful file access permission management!

4.7.6.2 Time Varying Passwords (Using Smart Card)

One important approach to one time passwords is to take advantage of a time varying smart card. These cards display a number, typically six to eight digits long, that changes every minute or two. The host computer understands the algorithm that the card uses (or has access

[7]You can only generate the password list when connected to the host via a secure connection. Otherwise an intruder can obtain your password list when you are setting it up initially!

to a server which does) and knows what number is displayed at any point in time. To login the user types in the number displayed on the card.

This is generally an expensive approach for it requires that all users purchase cards. However it has the advantage that once set up, it is fairly easy to administer (as opposed to a manual password list which requires frequent updating for all users). It is also fairly easy for the user to use and for support personnel to explain!

4.7.6.3 ChallenGe Schemes (Using Smart Cards)

Another type of smart card is used for challenge response. This type of card was described earlier. In essence, this type of smart card engages in a very Kerberos like dialog. However the messages are much shorter, necessitated by the fact that the end-user is likely typing them in!

4.7.6.4 S/Key, A Clever Approach from Bellcore

S/Key is an interesting approach to providing one time passwords. It is composed of two basic algorithms. The first is an algorithm that converts arbitrary 64-bit values into a pass phrase.[8] The second is a method of using a hash function (S/Key actually uses the RSA Data Security MD4 [Rivest, 1992] algorithm) to provide one time passwords.

A good way to understand S/Key is to think of how the system is initialized and then used.

To initialize S/Key a user, via a secure connection, chooses a secret pass phrase and short *seed* value. The pass phrase shall remain a secret, the seed will not. Choose a value *n,* typically 100. Now take the pass phrase and concatenate it with the seed and crank it through the MD4 function *n* times.[9]

Take the value *n,* the seed and the final MD4 value and store them in a system database associated with the user's login name. Now again take the seed and pass phrase and crank it through MD4 *n* times. However at each step take the MD4 result, and translate it to a string and output this string along with the value of *n* at that step. This becomes the user's password list which they print and carry with them.

Now when a user wishes to log in, the system login program looks them up in the S/Key database. It then prompt them with the string:

```
s/key (n-1) (seed)
```

where *n-1* is the actual value of *n-1* and the *seed* is the original user supplied seed. The user then looks up the n-1th password and supplies it to the login program. The login program converts this value into a 64-bit number and saves it in a temporary variable. It then runs MD4 over it and compares the result to the value stored in the database. If they match then

[8]Kerberos and SPX use mechanisms to convert an arbitrary phrase or word into a 64 bit value, but not the other way around as is the case with S/Key.

[9]MD4 generates a 128 bit value. For simplicity we only want 64 bits so at each step we take the 128 bit output, separate it into two 64 bit halves and xor them together to get one final 64 bit value. For all the S/Key steps, whenever I refer to MD4 I really mean this modified version.

login is successful and the database is updated so that "n" is decremented and the saved 64 bit value replaces the value stored in the database.

One of the beauties of S/Key is that the user does not necessarily have to use a paper password list. Instead the user can run a program on a laptop computer (versions are available for DOS and Macintosh systems as well as most UNIX systems) that takes their original pass phrase, the seed and the value of *n* (from the challenge string) and performs the same calculation as the initialization program in order to compute the necessary one time password.

Eventually *n* will reach 0, at which point the user will be unable to login unless they have reinitialized s/key. However reinitialization does not require a secure connection if the user has a local laptop. With a laptop (or any trusted local computing) the user can generate a new seed and passphrase and crank it through MD4 *n* times locally and only supply the host based initialization program with the final result along with the seed and *n* value. This permits the password list to be regenerated, even when the user does not have a secure connection.

Why bother with all this? Well the interesting feature of s/key is that with a local laptop, most of the operations can be automated. Another important feature is that none of the information stored on the host computer is confidential. The values stored on the host are the values from the previous login session, which will never be accepted again. Instead at login what is required is a value that when put through MD4 yields the stored values. The only way to take advantage of the value stored would require that an attacker run MD4 backwards. However if MD4 is a good cryptographic hash function (and we believe it is) then running it backwards is not computationally feasible!

4.7.7 Privacy Enhanced Mail (PEM)

One of the first secure applications available on the Internet is Privacy Enhanced Mail (PEM) (Linn, Kent, Balenson, and Kaliski, 1993). PEM represents an approach where the network infrastructure is not considered trusted, but that each user of PEM can trust their own local computing system.

PEM is an enhancement to normal Internet mail that provides for digital signatures on individual messages which in turn provide both integrity and authentication of origination. In addition PEM can be asked to encrypt a message for a particular set of identified recipients so that only they can read the message.

PEM is intended to be able to offer seriously strong security for electronic mail. Specifically its authentication and integrity features are intended to provide a mechanism whereby the Internet can be used to provide business correspondence such as purchase orders and invoices. The confidentiality features are intended to supply sufficient trust that the general Internet user population will feel comfortable sending messages that contain sensitive information about themselves. For example PEM might be used by an electronic catalogue store to permit Internet users to send in orders accompanied by their credit card numbers.

The PEM standard is designed to be able to utilize symmetric encryption (DES) as well as asymmetric encryption (RSA). However most implementations of PEM only support the asymmetric version, so only that version will be discussed here.

PEM (in asymmetric mode) uses certificates as defined by X.509 to associate Public RSA keys with individual users. Interoperable PEM communities share a common trusted *root* RSA public key which is used as the base of a tree of certificates where the end-user's certificates form the leaves.

PEM is completely implemented by end systems. Network routers and mail relays treat PEM messages as any ordinary piece of mail.

A PEM message consists of two basic parts. A PEM header (which is separate from any mail routing header) and a PEM body. The PEM body contains the actual message which is protected. The PEM header contains the information necessary to process the PEM body. The PEM header contains the identity of the sender of the message and optionally a copy of their certificate. A PEM header field identifies the version of the PEM protocol (current version is 4 as of this writing) along with how the message should be processed (specifically whether or not it is encrypted for a particular set of recipients are merely only signed).

A PEM header contains the digital signature of the PEM body. In essence this header is the *key* to PEM.

Header fields are defined that also permit the sender to supply a list of issuer certificates which define all the necessary RSA public keys to trace their certificate to the root. This is available in case the sender is concerned that some recipients may not have access to all the necessary certificates to verify the signature on the message, the sender can send them along.[10]

If the message is encrypted, then the PEM message will include a series of *Recipient-ID* headers and associated *Key-Info* headers. The recipient-id headers identify a particular recipient and the key-info contains the keying information that the particular recipient needs to decrypt the message.

Because not every system uses the same native character set, yet PEM needs to interoperate between heterogeneous systems, messages are converted to ASCII (even if originating on a EBCDIC system) prior to signature generation and encryption (if the message will be encrypted). This step is referred to as canonicalization and is required to ensure that signatures can always be verified. Also not every mail system can transport binary objects, and many of the items handled by PEM are binary (like certificates and encrypted messages). Therefore the PEM standards define a translation that converts 8-bit binary data into *printable* ASCII. This technique, similar to *unencode* in the UNIX world or BinHex in the Macintosh world, converts 3 eight bit bytes into 4 six bit bytes which are represented with one of 64 ASCII characters (the IA5 alphabet) chosen to best survive translation through various and sundry mail gateways.

How is a PEM message created?

First we will consider the creation of a signed only (not encrypted) message.

Start with the message text to be signed. Convert it to RFC1421 canonical form (which usually only involves representing the end of line character in a standard way). Take the canonical form of the message and feed it to an MD2 or MD5 message digest routine (both algorithms are supported by the standard, though of course you need to indicate which was used). Take your RSA private key (which you may need to extract from an encrypted file) and encrypt the message digest. The encrypted message digest (the message's digital signature)

[10]This is safe from a security standpoint because the sender cannot tamper with any certificate. Because every certificate is digitally signed, any tampering will be detected when a signature verification is performed.

along with an identifier of which algorithms were used, forms the *MIC-INFO* field of the PEM message.

Format a message header which indicates that this message is only signed (and not encrypted) along with information to identify you (so the recipient can find your public RSA key) which might include your certificate (depending on implementation). Include the MIC-Info computed above and finally output the unencrypted message. This message might be encoded into the IA5 character set, or not depending on whether or not it is likely to go through mail gateways that will disturb its format sufficient to *break* the digital signature. Figure 4.7 shows a sample unencrypted PEM message.

```
-----BEGIN PRIVACY-ENHANCED MESSAGE-----
Proc-Type: 4,MIC-CLEAR
Content-Domain: RFC822
Originator-Certificate: MIIBvzCCAWkCAQIwDQYJKoZIhvcNAQECBQAwXTELM
 AkGA1UEBhMCVVMxCzAJBgNVBAgTAk1BMS4wLAYDVQQKEyVNYXNzYWNodXNldHRzI
 Eluc3RpdHV0ZSBvZiBUZWNobm9sb2d5MREwDwYDVQQLEwhUZXN0aW5nMjAeFw05M
 jA4MjExOTU5NTVaFw05NDA4MjExOTU5NTVaMHsxCzAJBgNVBAYTAlVTMQswCQYDV
 QQIEwJNQTEuMCwGA1UEChMlTWFzc2FjaHVzZXR0cyBJbnN0aXR1dGUgb2YgVGVja
 G5vbG9neTERMA8GA1UECxMIVGVzdGluZzIxHDAaBgNVBAMTE0plZmZyZXkgSS4gU
 2NoaWxsZXIwWTAKBgRVCAEBAgICAANLADBIAkEAvZBFIDh5hHVXuefXXzrjSnVAC
 8PAvnXi+uRnjR6icg8hPFfoBKF5kav0vFSnS6KbBiQFc6wwPCYsH7YoIHMDGQIDA
 QABMA0GCSqGSIb3DQEBAgUAA0EAbF9kEYtmQ34EZILyhmFrer5lyEhhwhLctoaXz
 r3RunX4CQURjlAa9T08FAgMGZjXWtLB4S7G76YAZcVT5dutwQ==
Issuer-Certificate: MIIBezCCASUCAQYwDQYJKoZIhvcNAQECBQAwNzELMAkGA
 1UEBhMCVVMxKDAmBgNVBAoTH1RydXN0ZWQgSW5mb3JtYXRpb24gU3lzdGVtcyBQQ
 0EwHhcNOTIwODI1MTMzMTIzWhcNOTQwODI1MTMzMTIzWjBdMQswCQYDVQQGEwJVU
 zELMAkGA1UECBMCTUExLjAsBgNVBAoTJU1hc3NhY2h1c2V0dHMgSW5zdGl0dXRlI
 G9mIFRlY2hub2xvZ3kxETAPBgNVBAsTCFRlc3RpbmcyMFkwCgYEVQgBAQICAgADS
 wAwSAJBAL26CuUzF3lkV6ZB/WYPiqEmnQm0OP4rTli/5qouOvn85UupUwQ89LesS
 XaQbu+tQfGPMPG+6sKs/M8JfcoWhRsCAwEAATANBgkqhkiG9w0BAQIFAANBACuu8
 On2Dh4RYMmwSUksZ4Pw4J/m0i/oji69BSf20KT8SaZk1frBgjKn5eRlBHXnfNJ8B
 A7r4E2kj4FIE5cDIMQ=
MIC-Info: RSA-MD5,RSA,reDTjDaJMKyRmdV583k2booAE1pXihT7MJCpNLaknJ5
 ndrk/O/qhuVTZoi/5Zvfm64djk/5zoD5u6+5c6dsFuw==

This is a sample message. This message is not IA5 encoded so you can
read it quite simply.
-----END PRIVACY-ENHANCED MESSAGE-----
```

Figure 4.7 Sample signed only PEM message

Note: To create a signed-only PEM message does not require knowing anything about the recipients during PEM processing. In fact, the PEM signing mechanism can be used to sign documents intending to be published where there is no way to know up front who will receive the document or wish to verify it's signature.

Creating an encrypted message requires having the certificates (and thus the RSA public keys) of all the message's recipients. You proceed in the same manner as for a signed only message. However once the message contents are complete, namely the sender is identified and the digital signature computed, you process the message for confidentiality. This involves first generating a random DES session key, or a key for whatever algorithm will be used to encrypt the message, today the PEM specifications only include DES as a message confidentiality algorithm, but others may be added in the future. This DES key is used to encrypt the canonicalized message body. Because the resulting encrypted data is non-ASCII, it must be processed through the RFC1421 IA5 encoding algorithm to yield a 7-bit-ASCII message which can safely travel across the mostly ASCII-only mail forwarding system of the Internet.

In addition to the message body being encrypted, the contents of the MIC-Info field (the digital signature itself) is also encrypted in the DES session key.[11]

When formatting the message header, for each intended recipient you output a Recipient-ID header identifying them followed immediately by a Key-Info header which contains the random DES session key encrypted with their RSA public key. Figure 4.8 shows an encrypted PEM message (which of course the reader will be unable to decrypt because we have not provided the recipients RSA private key with this book!).

```
-----BEGIN PRIVACY-ENHANCED MESSAGE-----
Proc-Type: 4,ENCRYPTED
Content-Domain: RFC822
DEK-Info: DES-CBC,A1486541637439F3
Originator-Certificate: MIIBvzCCAWkCAQIwDQYJKoZIhvcNAQECBQAwXTELM
 AkGA1UEBhMCVVMxCzAJBgNVBAgTAk1BMS4wLAYDVQQKEyVNYXNzYWNodXNldHRzI
 Eluc3RpdHV0ZSBvZiBUZWNobm9sb2d5MREwDwYDVQQLEwhUZXN0aW5nMjAeFw05M
 jA4MjExOTU5NTVaFw05NDA4MjExOTU5NTVaMHsxCzAJBgNVBAYTAlVTMQswCQYDV
 QQIEwJNQTEuMCwGA1UEChMlTWFzc2FjaHVzZXR0cyBJbnN0aXR1dGUgb2YgVGVja
 G5vbG9neTERMA8GA1UECxMIVGVzdGluZzIxHDAaBgNVBAMTE0plZmZyZXkgSS4gU
 2NoaWxsZXIwWTAKBgRVCAEBAgICAANLADBIAkEAvZBFIDh5hHVXuefXXzrjSnVAC
 8PAvnXi+uRnjR6icg8hPFfoBKF5kav0vFSnS6KbBiQFc6wwPCYsH7YoIHMDGQIDA
 QABMA0GCSqGSIb3DQEBAgUAA0EAbF9kEYtmQ34EZILyhmFrer5lyEhhwhLctoaXz
 r3RunX4CQURjlAa9T08FAgMGZjXWtLB4S7G76YAZcVT5dutwQ==
Key-Info: RSA,nL1UulOU6iUcAr+1W+5TRmoRL+EMFX+WMacISoVpBepYonxemDl
 MHziRJzabEHpXj+uO3mhKWpArV4xIBPhiGg==
Issuer-Certificate: MIIBezCCASUCAQYwDQYJKoZIhvcNAQECBQAwNzELMAkGA
 1UEBhMCVVMxKDAmBgNVBAoTH1RydXN0ZWQgSW5mb3JtYXRpb24gU3lzdGVtcyBQQ
 0EwHhcNOTIwODI1MTMzMTIzWhcNOTQwODI1MTMzMTIzWjBdMQswCQYDVQQGEwJVU
 zELMAkGA1UECBMCTUExLjAsBgNVBAoTJU1hc3NhY2h1c2V0dHMgSW5zdGl0dXRlI
 G9mIFRlY2hub2xvZ3kxETAPBgNVBAsTCFRlc3RpbmcyMFkwCgYEVQgBAQICAgADS
 wAwSAJBAL26CuUzF3lkV6ZB/WYPiqEmnQm0OP4rTli/5qouOvn85UupUwQ89LesS
```

[11]Encrypting the MIC-INFO field was a change made to the PEM standards relatively late in their development cycle due to a potential security problem with leaving it unencrypted. I leave it as an exercise for the reader to determine why this is important. Hint: What if an attacker knew that the message body contained only the word *yes* or *no*.

```
 XaQbu+tQfGPMPG+6sKs/M8JfcoWhRsCAwEAATANBgkqhkiG9w0BAQIFAANBACuu8
 On2Dh4RYMmwSUksZ4Pw4J/m0i/oji69BSf20KT8SaZk1frBgjKn5eRlBHXnfNJ8B
 A7r4E2kj4FIE5cDIMQ=
MIC-Info: RSA-MD5,RSA,TzxA7PBZCM7OQpk+uF/Xi7l2wGSPQ8gWKP3ZTr7WUDE
 zQXw/5Or++QEZWp4siRJ73LDyEU2XfORvjtC/M9GZ/h4pJXD/LcD/
Recipient-ID-Asymmetric: MF0xCzAJBgNVBAYTAlVTMQswCQYDVQQIEwJNQTEu
 MCwGA1UEChMlTWFzc2FjaHVzZXR0cyBJbnN0aXR1dGUgb2YgVGVjaG5vbG9neTER
 MA8GA1UECxMIVGVzdGluZzI=,05
Key-Info: RSA,Q1r2dW9OUfI8qEzN8ELqnN2Z7Qy1AqlitNGpwLn8nujYMFeArMJ
 17lgLPxYRYoHStvVQflyLk3u4roNpKNk23Q==

ViIWsKj1hhTnGjmqJB38MCrekQAcfxnb8LO956B6N3ba7fh55uMFMHE4SVPlhx/T
DT8GvZB/wEIS6s6PxgIhqMmnubm1rvsiGm4FR+ls6rzKGjAE7bb8jvzyNJ9qGcVS
PV0rvFtflpu/D+EDwo96F3Jdgv/TV09de2AfP7Z9o2ytgtVwlc7/zLxkPOI0WAwJ
WuOuvOMeQdTgBOTAmRPINX4g5FIF1ryA4MeM6k5EfIVvkIoO2lsEQ1jLXeJWQA3H
tJsNE9aKOcyE4nAId2zy5YFvpRjOFKZdJkxcVUpjUETV4+tRHOiojFbpY3Gw4VQe
giJ+ZxR1rxxBx6/br6XPQGMFX1lhsFct8Cxnv/QNP7sT0+f7ey6jAaDCbQ2E5gfo
-----END PRIVACY-ENHANCED MESSAGE-----
```


Figure 4.8 An encrypted PEM message.

4.7.8 PEM-Like Possibilities for Other Systems

PEM technology does not need to be limited in application simply to electronic mail. Many applications use the *store and forward* paradigm common to electronic mail, and many of these are good candidates for the use of PEM technology.

For example, it is not too hard to envision an electronic requisitioning system where requisitions are structured ASCII documents that include all the necessary fields to specify a purchasing transaction. Many systems do this securely by requiring all requisitioners to use the same (supposedly secure) time-sharing system for typing in requisitions. If this system is accessed over a network, then all keystrokes (including passwords if a system like Kerberos is not being used) are subject to interception.

However this type of application is a good candidate for a client server system where the client workstations format the requisition document (perhaps doing some syntactic errors checking etc.) and then submit it via electronic mail. Such a system, however, is only as secure as the underlying electronic mail system. Most of these systems are not very secure. However if the requisition is PEM processed, then significant security is gained.

The message can be authenticated, because PEM processing requires an identifiable sender to sign the message with their private key. The message's integrity is ensured by the digital signature, which will break if the message is tampered with in any way. If confidentiality is required (which it may not be in many systems) then the requisition message can be encrypted for the requisitioning system (the requisitioning system in this case will have a private key known to the processing system and a certificate available to the submitting clients).

Another potential application for PEM technology is in electronic documents. For example the electronic dissemination of standards documents introduces the risk that someone may modify a standard document and then pass it on as the authentic original.[12] However a standards document could easily be electronically distributed in the form of a signed-only (MIC-Clear) PEM document signed by a recognized authorized representative of the standards body. Any modified version of the document could be detected by performing a PEM signature verification.[13]

4.8 The "Social" Dimension

Before closing off this discussion of distributed systems security, it is appropriate to discuss briefly what I call the *social* dimension. The use of any security system requires some knowledge on the part of system users. Security systems can only provide mechanisms, it is up to users to use them and system managers to educate their users in their use.

My favorite example of an attacker taking advantage of the social dimension involves the guy who sent electronic mail to his victims identifying himself as the system manager and instructing them to change their password to a supplied value "for security reasons." Most users who receive such a message (see figure 4.9) will simply follow its advice not realizing that system management should never have a reason to give them such instruction.

```
From: System Management <attacker@somehost>
To: [supply user name here]
Subject: System Security

For reasons of system security, please change your password to "sys-
test5" so we may correct a security flaw.

Thank you,
System Management
```

Figure 4.9 Example social attack message

The moral of the story: Have a good security system. Have a good security policy. The security policy should explain not only how the users should behave, but should also explain how system management can be expected to behave. This should include what system management will never do, like tell you what your password should be! Users should be aware of the need for security, and educated in how to achieve it with the tools provided.

[12]This risk is present with paper documents as well, but such forgery is much easier to accomplish in the electronic realm that it is a much more likely scenario.

[13]The verification procedure will not tell you how the document was modified, only that it was.

4.9 References

National Bureau of Standards, 1977. Data Encryption Standard. Federal Information Processing Standards Publication 46.

Balenson, D., 1993. Privacy Enhancement for Internet Electronic Mail: Part III: Algorithms, Modes, and Identifiers. *Internet RFC1423.*

Diffie, W., and Hellman, M.E., 1976. New directions in cryptography. *IEEE Transactions on Information Theory,* IT-22(6):644–654.

Kaliski, B.S., 1993. Privacy Enhancement for Internet Electronic Mail: Part IV: Key Certification and Related Services. *Internet RFC1424.*

Kent, S.T., 1993. Privacy Enhancement for Internet Electronic Mail: Part II: Certificate-Based Key Management. *Internet RFC1422.*

Linn, J., 1993. Privacy Enhancement for Internet Electronic Mail: Part I: Message Encryption and Authentication Procedures. *Internet RFC1421.*

Rivest, R.L., 1992. MD4 Message-Digest algorithm. *Internet RFC1320.*

Rivest, R.L., Shamir, A., and Adleman, L.M., 1978. A Method for Obtaining Digital Signatures and Public-key Cryptosystems. *Communications of the ACM,* 21(2):120–126.

Steiner, J.G., Neuman, B.C., and Schiller, J. I., 1988. Kerberos: An Authentication Service for Open Network Systems., *Usenix Conference Proceedings.* Feb. pp. 191–202.

Jeffrey I. Schiller received his S.B. in Electrical Engineering (1979) from the Massachusetts Institute of Technology. As MIT Network Manager he has managed the MIT Campus Computer Network since its inception in 1984. Prior to his work in the Network Group he maintained MIT's Multics timesharing system during the time frame of the ArpaNet TCP/IP conversion. He is an author of MIT's Kerberos Authentication system. Mr. Schiller is an active member of the Security Area Advisory Committee of the Internet Engineering Task Force as well as a member of the Privacy and Security Research Group of the Internet Research Task Force. His recent efforts have involved work on the Internet Privacy Enhanced Mail standards (and implementation). Mr. Schiller is also a founding member of the Steering Group of the New England Academic and Research Network (NEARnet). NEARnet provides Internet Access to institutions in New England.

Chapter 5

Managing Distributed Systems

Wallace Colyer
Walter Wong
Carnegie Mellon University

5.1 Introduction

System management, though clouded with mystery and confusion, has a very straightforward goal: keep machines running so that work can get done. Similarly, the goal of distributed system management is to facilitate work in an environment where machines are connected to each other. In the ideal system, there is a painless process of installing, updating, and maintaining a machine or set of machines in a usable and consistent state.

It sounds simple, but keeping the machines and their users working is a difficult task. A component of good system management practice is planning. Over time the usage patterns on computing systems tend to change. For proper planning, system resources must be monitored and trends tracked. A good understanding of the capacities of the system and where improvements can be made is needed. Problems with the system must be identified and corrected. As hardware and software change the management system may have to be modified. The need for resource management, tracking and access control requires constant attention. For most systems, in order to keep the machines usable they must pay for themselves or at least justify their existence through the use of these accounting systems.

It is very easy to neglect system management tasks. Under many circumstances, bad systems management is merely inefficient systems management. The system manager is performing the necessary tasks but a great deal of unnecessary work is done. Aside from wasting the system manager's time, this often prevents the system manager from providing new services or improving upon the current situation. On the other hand, if the system manager is simply negligent, the negligence may not be noticed until a critical failure has occurred and it becomes very difficult for the system to be restored to a working state.

What makes system management so difficult? First, managing single systems is still not a well-defined task. Things are often done in a haphazard manner and change may only occur as a reaction to problems that arise, rather than as a result of planning. Second, as distributed computing becomes more and more prevalent, increasing numbers of machines need to be managed. While sheer numbers of different systems pose a problem, distributed system management introduces new issues that the system manager must be aware of and it also invalidates many assumptions that were once valid for single-system management. Finally, a number of *total system management* packages and *total distributed system management* packages have emerged which unfortunately perform only a limited set of the necessary tasks, or do not work well in many heterogenous environments.

This chapter begins the discussion of distributed systems management by examining the issues involved with system management of a single system. It then proceeds to examine how distributed systems management complicates and expands upon the problem. The discussion of systems management is at a high level. Details on how to perform backups or how to check quotas better in a distributed environment will not be discussed. We will also not concentrate on the problem as a strictly management problem, as many Management Information System (MIS) documents do. Instead, we hope to provide a foundation for our discussion, and describe some of the key problems in distributed system management. Chapter 14 discusses strategies and provide a case study of the management of the Andrew system.

Some discussion of network management is included in this chapter for the sake of completeness. Simple Network Management Protocol (SNMP) and the role it plays in network and distributed system's management are described in Appendix D.

5.2 Single System Management

Even on a single machine, system management can be a time consuming process. Configuration files need to be customized and updated. Software must be installed, configured, upgraded, possibly reconfigured, and removed. Access to resources must not only be granted, removed, and modified, but also recorded and potentially charged for. Log files need to be examined and corrective measures taken when necessary. Performance characteristics have to be evaluated and the system optimized where necessary. Peripherals have to be added and removed. Along with all those tasks, many others must be performed such as making backups, mounting tapes, running accounting jobs and replenishing consumed items such as paper or toner for printers.

Depending on the system and organization, this list may not even begin to describe the jobs of the system manager.[1] In other instances, the system manager may perform none of the tasks above, or perform only a subset of those tasks. This disparity in duties led Rob Kolstad to ask "What do system administrators really do?" Kolstad first tried to answer the question by examining job postings for "system managers." This tact was not very successful as the job descriptions asked for individual expertise in a multitude of different software packages, different networking technologies, different operating systems and hardware platforms, in addition to programming and managerial skills. In one example, a job description listed over 20

[1]The term "system manager" can also be applied to a group of people acting as system managers. We also consider the terms "system manager" and "system administrator" to be equivalent, but we will use the term "system manager" for the sake of consistency. The same applies to the two terms: system management and system administration.

different non-trivial responsibilities, which would be allocated no more than two hours a week, on the average, for each one. Not succeeding there, Kolstad offers an analysis of the field. His categories include dealing with software and hardware, acting as a human interface between the system and the users, taking preventive measures against possible disasters, and ensuring that the *scarce* resources of CPU, disk, memory, and so on, get allocated properly. There is, however, a catch-all category of *standard administration* which includes stuff as network management, ordering supplies, rebooting machines, naming machines, security issues, and other similar items (Kolstad, 1991).

Recently, there has standards activity to define the scope of systems management. The IEEE POSIX effort on systems management (P1003.7) divides the field into the following management components: configuration management, performance management, fault management, accounting management, and security management. In this case, "configuration management" is the catch-all category. Configuration management, in this context, refers "to the management of information which defines a machine's function." Initially, this category included password file management, and printing (Smith, 1989). Now, the POSIX effort is divided into printing administration, software administration, and user and group administration.

As a result of all this confusion, we will propose our own definition of systems management that is a synthesis of many of the other management definitions. First, we separate the categories from the tasks. Our categories are defined as:

- user management
- task management
- software management
- hardware management
- network management

Within each category, there are tasks that need to be performed. The tasks can be divided, as follows:

- configuration management
- performance management
- fault management
- security management
- resource management

These classifications attempt to create abstractions and to compartmentalize the domain. Nevertheless, these classifications are far from absolute as all the categories and all the tasks have interdependencies. In many ways, these classifications and tasks are, as figure 5.1 shows, just labels of certain aspects of the domain. These interdependencies make the problem domain difficult to decompose and quantify and hence the confusion that exists today is not so surprising.

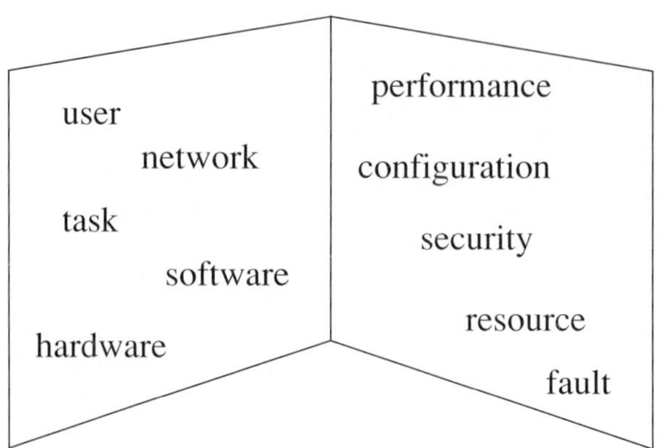

Figure 5.1 Labels of certain aspects of the domain.

To help flesh out these categories, the management categories and the typical tasks that fall under each task classification in a single system environment will be described. Later we will describe the differences with distributed systems.

While the categories are relatively straightforward, let us define the tasks better. Configuration management (CM) is the most complex and thus has the longest definition. Even though Peter Feller defines CM in the context of software engineering, his definition applies quite well to system management, as well:

> (CM) is a discipline that provides stability (...) by controlling the product evolution, i.e., continued and concurrent change. As a management discipline, CM controls the evolution of a product through identification of product components and changes through initiation, evolution, authorization, and control of change, and by recording and reporting the history and status of the product and its changes. As a development support function, CM maintains the actual components of a product, records the history of the component as well as the whole product, provides a stable working context for changing the product, supports the manufacture of the product from its components, and coordinates concurrent changes (Feller, 1991).

The goal of resource management is gathering of data of resource usage in order to plan for the future and for performance management tasks. Performance management is comprised of tasks that are necessary to optimize each category. Fault management deals with handling any problem that arise and the preventive measures to avoid problems from arising. Security management, in essence, is a part of fault management, however, security management concentrates on faults that are initiated or a result of users.

These task and category descriptions should not be considered a definitive list, but rather a guide to help classify arbitrary tasks and provide a structure for our discussion. Also, some of the management tasks do not apply to all systems. For example, there is no need to worry about multiprocessing issues on a system capable of only running a single process.

5.2.1 User Management

The users are the most important part of the system, but they are one of the most ill defined parts. The users are the most variable component of system management. They come in many categories and have greatly varying skill levels, usage patterns, goals, expectations and attitudes. The group makeup may constantly change in both membership and experience.

The primary responsibility of user management is to take care of the people who use this system. This includes consulting support for the users as well as managing their access to the system, such as creation of *userids* for obtaining access to multi-user systems.

Configuration management: This category oversees creation and deletion of user accounts. It installs and customizes the default files used by those accounts. Configuration management may also include configuring system resources to allow the users access.

Performance management: While this may seem to be an unlikely classification, consulting, educating and training for the user can be placed into this category. Performance management also deals with identifying if the users have the right software and tools necessary to do their work. Performance management tries to optimize a managed resource. With respect to user management, it optimizes their use of the system.

Fault management: The tasks in this section are primarily concentrated with backups of users' personal data both through automatic means and through user education. Some systems run periodic jobs that look for problems in user accounts and either correct those problems or notify the user. One could also argue that making users aware of health risks (e.g., carpal tunnel) associated with computing should also be included in the list.

Security management: These tasks protect the users from external and internal influences, and from each other. The security system is also used to enforce restriction on the use of system resources.

Resource management: Tasks associated with resource management for the user include; determining how many resources have been used, what resources the user should have access to, and billing for resources used. The resource management components work with the configuration management and security systems to get resource limitations installed, and supplies the configuration performance and fault management system with data.

5.2.2 Task Management

It was previously stated that the main goal of systems management was to help the users of a computer system get work done.To achieve this goal the users must be able to perform tasks usually in the form of running processes.

Task management is the management of these user processes, system processes needed to support users' processes, and those carrying out system management tasks. This includes scheduling tasks to be performed, verifying that they were performed, and managing the resources used by each task. A task is the equivalent to control of the CPU. In UNIX it is usually a process, while in other systems, it may be a thread of execution or something more exotic.

Configuration management: Systems must be configured to ensure the continual execution of critical system processes. Many processes must be scheduled and started automatically. System services must be started and configured to run properly. User processes must often be scheduled and the system must be configured to determine which users are allowed to run which processes.

Performance management: Since the main task of the system is to run these processes, their performance has a strong impact on the ability of work to get done. The performance of the processes may have to be constantly examined. In the examination of the processes, many questions are asked. Are the running processes actually performing an acceptable amount of work? Is the scheduling performing adequately? Can more processes run, or should fewer? Performance management helps to determine if an adequate amount of resources is dedicated to the given tasks.

Fault management: The fault management system of task management ensures that tasks are running properly. It must determine if running jobs are executing properly, if jobs have exited abnormally, and whether those jobs should be restarted. The fault management system must notify the user or system manager of abnormal conditions that affect the execution of jobs. An important aspect of fault management is the oversight of system processes. Many system processes are integral to the functionality of the system and need to be restarted if they quit or immediate notification of the problem is needed so that it can be resolved manually.

Security management: Most modern operating systems perform the majority of the security management of tasks. They ensure that processes belonging to different users do not interfere with each other and that they do not access system resources to which they are not privileged. The system manager sets up the majority of the security system while configuring the users account during user management. Some systems have batch or other systems for job submission that need attention to setup security requirements.

Resource management: Any process or task performed by a computing system uses resources. Some examples of resources are CPU seconds, pages printed, disk accesses and other I/O characteristics. While the configuration management system sets up which tasks should have access to which system resources and the security management system enforces the decision, the resource management system determines the criteria for resource allocation. It also must track the use of system resources for accounting purposes. The resource management system produces data that can be used by the performance and fault management systems. Many resource management systems make resources that are limited or effect system performance more expensive to use than ones that are more available or have less of an effect.

The types of limitations placed on resource usage vary greatly. In some cases charges are incurred directly for resource usage. Some allocate limited amounts of resources then deny usage. Others rely on gently prodding users to not exceed acceptable resource usage. Finally, some rely on the system to limit resource usage through limited availability. Those final systems limit usage by the natural constraints on the number of pages per minute the printer can print or the total CPU bandwidth available on the system.

5.2.3 Software Management

We classify software management as the management of files on the system that are not *user files.* Software management deals with system configuration files, the operating system, locally developed and vendor software, software configuration files, compilation, testing, object and source areas, and the tools for managing the software.

Software is what the users run on a system to get their work done. If it does not work the system is unusable. Software, on a system, generally progresses through the cycle of being be installed, configured, tested, upgraded, re-configured, and removed. Many software packages interact with each other and most systems have single installation areas which many software packages share. These interdependencies make the process of software management difficult because changes in one area have an often unpredictable effect on other areas.

In many ways, software management is the most complicated task. It is the area of the system where the largest numbers of people are involved. The system managers usually set up the framework for software installation, the developers produce software and work with the system managers to get it installed, and external software providers make a large number of assumptions of the environment. These frameworks setup by the system managers often break because of interactions with software packages that must be installed or unforeseen changes in the environment.

The planning of the software management environment is one of the most difficult tasks. With all the different people involved it is important that the system be flexible. If the system is made too flexible, it may not be manageable. Total anarchy in a software management system will lead to a situation down the road where there is no knowledge of what exactly exists on the system and where it came from. If the system is too rigid, the system may be circumvented or compromised to the state where anarchy is once again present.

Configuration management: The configuration management part of software management may be the largest and most complicated single component of software management. The configuration management component takes care of software installation, configuration, reconfiguration upgrading and deletion. The state of the software licenses must also be tracked.

Initially it must be determined what software will be installed on the system. This can be a long and involved processes including finding funds to pay for the software or resources to develop it, potentially running a relatively long term project to develop, test, configure, and install the software.

It must be determined whether the software can run on the system it will be installed on and what users it will affect. New versions must be tested and differences between previous versions must be understood. The installation must be timed to be the least disruptive to the system and its users. Often once software is installed problems are encountered. In critical cases, the previous version of the software must be reinstalled. The software management system should be able to easily reinstall old versions.

Some software packages have mechanisms for restricting usage to particular users or times. Those mechanisms must be configured. Almost all packages have a variety of configuration options. The correct configuration options for the environment the package is going to be run on must be chosen. In some cases, a great number of customizations are available. The default look and feel for the package can be greatly varied. Some sites choose to keep the defaults that the vendor supplied, while others make a great deal of changes.

Performance management: The effect of applications on system performance is an important aspect of software management. New packages can sometimes have unexpected results on the performance of the entire system. Even just installing a new version of a software package can change the performance characteristics of a system a great deal because of different usage characteristics and changes in the performance profile of the application. It does not have to be a change in the application itself. Sometimes a great deal of changes come from changes in usage patterns.

The performance management task is not merely protecting the system from an application. Often the machine or program must be tuned so that the one application performs well.

Fault management: Software is far from perfect. There are constantly new problems reported with software packages because they are used in new ways or aspects of the environment they run are changed. Fault management deals with identifying if there are problems in a software package, how critical they are, whether they can be fixed, or whether the software should be *backed out* to a previous version or removed entirely.

Sometimes problems are identified through testing or automatic checks for problems, but in most systems the majority of problems are reported by the users through one of the user support mechanisms discussed in the section on user management.

Resource Management: Software packages consume resources through their usage and installation. When users run applications they consume machine resources. Those resources must be accounted for. Most systems provide accounting systems that will measure how many resources are consumed by each invocation of each application. In addition some applications have limited run time licenses that determine the number of active copies that can run on a system at any one time. In this case, the application itself is a limited resource and its usage must be monitored and accounted for.

5.2.4 Hardware Management

Computer systems are made of a variety of components. Each component is connected and needs to be configured and managed. Many components have finite resources that must be managed. Still other components use resources of other components and that resource usage must also be managed. Hardware breaks and broken parts must be identified and removed or replaced.

Configuration management: When new hardware is placed on a machine the machine must be configured to recognize the hardware. This often includes both a hardware and software components. The machine's hardware must be configured to recognize the new hardware and often the operating system must be configured to recognize and utilize the component. This configuration of software is sometimes just changing a configuration file or loading a device driver, but sometimes the entire operating system needs to be re-installed. Adding hardware devices often requires the machine to be taken down. This *downtime* must be scheduled to reduce inconveniencing the user. Often records of the serial number and devices attached to machines must be recorded to make them work or simply to satisfy internal property management requirements.

Since use of much equipment has real costs or because resources are often limited, it is important to configure the resources so that their use is limited to users and times that are acceptable. In systems that allow these types of restrictions, lists of allowed users, times, and devices are kept.

Performance management: Hardware devices have different performance characteristics associated with each one. The performance of each device and the impact devices have on each other must be monitored. Often hardware resources and system activities must be reassigned to best existing hardware. The usage patterns of hardware devices over time must be examined to determine growth of usage and help to determine when more or less powerful devices are needed. A great deal of performance management must go into trend analysis to determine future needs.

Fault management: The first aspect of fault management is, when something ceases to function properly, to quickly determine which component is at fault and get the situation under control. Most hardware errors are detectable by the operating system, but most of the difficult hardware errors result in bizarre software behavior.

To help reduce downtime, it is necessary to have spare equipment available or maintenance plans that promise good turn around. When the hardware is not working either a part of the system or the entire system is not available to the users of the system and it is important to get as much of the system up and running as soon as possible. It is important to maintain good backups of all the data on the system in case of disk failures. Many sites require data and spare machines be kept off site so that the system can be brought up in case there is an event which destroys or disables the site.

Fault management also includes monitoring resource usage of limited resources to help identify when they run out, and notification of the condition to the responsible authorities. The fault management system may be able to correct the problems in some cases. An example of a limited resource which must be monitored is disk space. When disks fill up it is important to notify the system manager to remedy the situation. In some systems, when the usage of disk space passes a certain threshold, an automatic migration will move the data to other disks, other media, or compress data to relieve the problem with exhaustion of system resources.

Security Management: The security management system enforces the restrictions placed on resource usage by the configuration management system. Many operating systems have security systems which help restrict, allow, and control resource usage.

Security management is also concerned with the physical safety of the system. Single systems were generally placed in environmentally controlled machine rooms with secure access.

Resource Management: The system hardware makes up the majority of resources on the system. These resources are limited and often have real hard costs associated with their use. For example, a modem dialing out has the cost of the phone call associated with it or a printer has the cost of paper and toner. In addition to these *real* costs the cost of purchasing, and maintaining must be recovered or justified. The usage of system resources must be monitored and data about the usage must be kept to plan for future needs, charge for usage, and justify the equipment.

5.2.5 Network Management

In the single system scenario, network management is straightforward and simple. One mainly concerned with the connectivity of your system to the rest of the network. Generally, you are given a network address and a cable for your system. It also may be the case that the single system has no network connectivity and this management category can be ignored.

5.2.6 Single System Management Example

The tasks to be performed often have a large number of components. All the components must be performed in order for the task to be complete. Often the components must be performed in a specific order. If there are errors during the tasks, the system must be returned to a consistent state. In order to return the system to this consistent state, many times changes made in previous steps must be backed out. In other cases, when an error is encountered it is not possible to return the system to its previous state and it is better to continue despite the error.

On a UNIX system the simple task of adding a user often requires a large number of tasks to be performed. Some of these tasks are decisions that must be made and others are changes made to the system. On a typical UNIX system, the following may be performed:

- choose a user name and verify that the user name is not already used
- determine the UID (unique number associated with the user)
- determine on which disk to place the user's home directory
- determine the path to the user's home directory
- determine what group the user should be in
- choose an initial password for the user
- update password file
- update group file
- create home directory
- place prototype files in home directory
- change ownership of home directory and files
- create mail spool area

A mistake made in any of these components may make the user's new account unusable or may cause problems which are difficult to identify and track down sometime in the future. This is a good example of a routine task that should be automated. Automation would reduce the chance of simple errors such as typographical errors made because of the repetitiveness of the task. Imagine having to repeat this task by hand to add 20 users to a system. Automated systems can also better handle error conditions and deal with problems that arise. Finally, if an error is made, it will be the same error and recovery is thereby much simpler.

Many vendors provide tools for managing much of this information. These tools drastically simplify the system administration process, but they tend to be too specifically tailored for the vendor environment or so general as to require the system administrator to significantly customize it. Unfortunately, most of them do not meet many of the more complex needs of more complicated environments They often break easily when non-standard configurations are adopted. In the worst cases the operating systems and system utilities are intricately tied to the use of these management systems and can not be disabled. Automated tools for managing single systems have become common in most UNIX systems.

5.3 Distributed System Management

Even with all the issues involved with single system management, there was very little interest in developing comprehensive, generalizable solutions. At best, a management system tailored to the machine was developed. Considering the amount of money required to just maintain many mainframe systems, the cost of such a system would be quite minor.

Distributed systems have changed this. Distributed systems management has become almost universally recognized as a significant problem. All the issues of managing a single system are carried over to distributed systems, and many new problems are introduced. The benefits of distributed computing are often limited and may even be offset by the problems introduced by distributed systems. The new problems introduced by distributed systems and the wide variety of potential environments create an enhanced need for careful planning of the distributed management system for growth and flexibility. Distributed management systems can make or break the success of a distributed system. It takes a great deal of good planning and careful implementation to make a successful system.

5.3.1 Issues

As with single systems management, distributed systems management will be examined by looking at each management category and tasks. Before doing so, we will present some of the problems which are applicable to all of the management categories. These issues include: scalability, heterogeneity, security, distribution, and synchronization.

5.3.1.1 Scalability

Distributed systems can achieve scalability by allowing more units to be added to the system. In this instance, the larger the problem, the larger you make your system for solving it. The gain of adding more units would ideally lead to an linear gain in performance, as shown in figure 6.2a. However, as with any endeavor which requires multiple units, it soon becomes the case where the overhead of coordinating all the units starts to limit, and possibly even degrade performance, as shown in figure 6.2b.

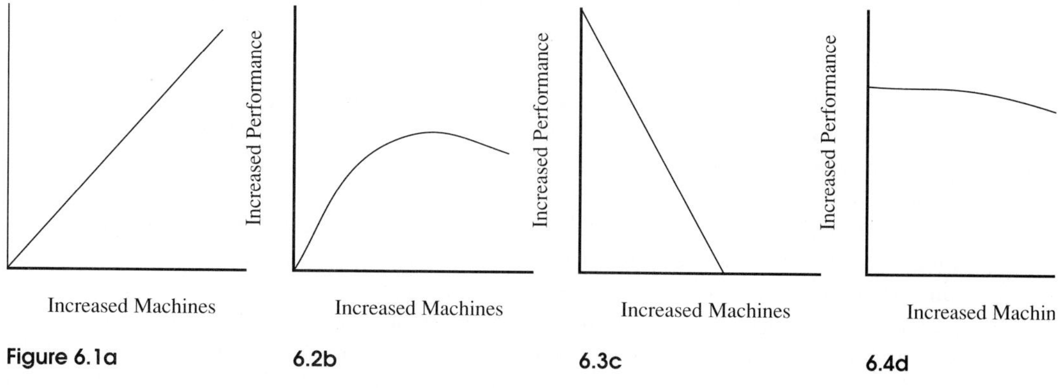

Figure 6.1a **6.2b** **6.3c** **6.4d**

With managing distributed systems, it is the unfortunate case that the result of adding each unit is the inverse performance relationship, as shown in figure 6.2c. The fewer the machines that exist, the better the overall management performance. As more and more machines need to be managed, the more difficult the process becomes. This degradation continues until a certain point is reached, beyond which no more machines can be effectively managed. However, there are distributed management techniques and strategies that can reduce the effect of scale. These techniques and strategies generally have a higher start-up cost so they may not be feasible in small sites, but these do allow a significantly larger number of machines to be managed. Theoretically, there may be no limits to the number of machines that can be supported, but in reality there are usually bottlenecks and constraints that limit the number of machines that can be managed. Hopefully, this limit is beyond the possible growth of the organization.

5.3.1.2 Distribution and Synchronization

Distribution and synchronization are *standard* problems of a distributed system. Once a change is made to any part of the distributed system, it is necessary to propagate that change out to all the participating systems. Synchronization tries to solve the problem of how to distribute such that each machine picks up changes at the same time.

For single systems, changes could be made once and forgotten about, or merely noted in case they had to be applied again at a later date. With a distributed system, changes often must be distributed to different machines soon after they are made. Many times these machines run different operating systems and have different configurations. The configuration files must also be tailored to fit the particular system. Data which will be distributed to heterogeneous systems must be initially entered in a way which will ease the process of customizing it for multiple systems. In cases where that is not done, systems are developed to massage data into formats acceptable on different systems. Markets have been created for gateway and translator products which help to transfer data between these heterogeneous systems.

The process of distribution often takes time on a distributed system. A process, which on a single system, took place immediately may take days on a distributed system to fully propagate. Distribution is also often not guaranteed if machines are unavailable due to various failure conditions. The time it will take to propagate important information to distributed sites must be taken into consideration when designing a distributed management system.

5.3.1.3 Security

Whole new concepts of security are introduced with distributed systems. By their nature, distributed systems require machines to communicate with each other and, at times, it is critical that the machines are able to identify each other. Jeff Schiller discussed this issue in depth in Chapter 4.

Security is often the greatest failing of management solutions. Distributed systems, like single systems can be installed in environments where the network community is not hostile and security is not a problem. In hostile environments and even moderately hostile environments where users may want to break system security just for the sake of it, the security issues take on a great deal of importance. The management system deals very sensitive parts of the distributed system, and by definition requires access to the entire system. A security hole in the management system may compromise the overall security of a system. Often security holes in management systems are simply oversights in the design. For example, many management systems make the incorrect assumption that the systems can trust hosts.

5.3.1.4 Heterogeneity

Some vendors make this distribution process particularly difficult because of methods setup to maintain their workstation configurations in both single system and distributed system configurations. The vendor systems often make it much easier to maintain homogeneous environments including only machines and operating systems of their choosing. They often do not adequately handle issues of scaling, security or configurability.

Intricately tied vendor management systems which can not be modified or turned off make it difficult to integrate systems in a heterogeneous environment. When the management system breaks because of scale, heterogeneity of the environment, or other causes and can not be turned off machines often lie unused or are forced to be excluded from much of the rich networked computing environments they live in.

Even if everyone ended up running the same operating system on the same hardware platform, heterogeneity would still be a problem as the configuration of each machine in the distributed system may differ and probably should differ as to suit the needs of the owner of the workstations. Also, by the fact that management systems were not incorporated with all operating systems, many sites have developed their own way of doing things and now integration between locally developed systems and distributed system environments must be done.

5.3.2 Management Categories in Distributed Systems

5.3.2.1 User Management

In distributed systems, the idea of a user is extended from the user of a machine to a network user. A network user is an entity existing at a location or variety of locations on the network which has an identity or set of identities associated with it and a set of characteristics. The identity and characteristics are used to determine which network resources the user has access to and where the users resources exist in the network.

In single systems, although the activity of the users were often unknown, the user was usually using a very finite set of methods of accessing the system. In most systems, the user was either on a terminal hooked up by phone line, serial line or something similar, or working directly on the console of the machine. In distributed systems, the user can be anywhere. Since the user is merely a network entity they may also be coming in from Macintoshes, PCs, UNIX workstations of a variety of flavors, terminals, X terminals, or any of a number of other network devices. Often users will use a variety of these environments in the course of getting their work done. The machines they are coming in may be just acting as terminals or that may be directly accessing server processes by using network protocols.

This introduces additional problems for managing the user. In order to provide some degree of consistency between platforms, information about the user must be synchronized between platforms. In the best cases, all platforms use common directory and security services for storing and verifying user information. Unfortunately, this is often not the case because of limitations in hardware, software, and vendor systems. Where it is not possible to maintain one system for storing this information, gateways and translators must be developed for passing information between heterogeneous environments.

In some cases, it has been possible to produce multi-protocol servers which can serve the same information to these different worlds. A good example of this type of server Novell Netware. Netware allows and supports multiple protocol stacks operating on the same server.

Configuration management: As has been discussed, distributed systems extend the need for configuration management from editing files on individual machines to maintaining configuration files, distributing them, and customizing them for heterogeneous locations. Configuration information about users may exist on one central information server, on multiple servers, or each individual network server may contain information about the server.

In heterogeneous systems with gateways between worlds of information from one system must be sent through the gateways, translated to the format use at the other end and stored in the native format used by those machines for use by a native network server. Translator machines act in real time to translate requests from one environment to those used in a different environment. Rather than shipping the data through a gateway to a network service on the other end, the data is all kept in one environment and machines in the other environment must access the data through translators.

Distributed systems are composed of a variety of network based services. Each service may have to have user information stored locally. The configuration management system needs to distribute information needed to remote services about new users, changes in user information, or deletions of users. In addition to adding the users account to machines which the user will login to or the central directory service, mail systems may need mailboxes created for forwarding information set for the user, remote file systems need to have directories created for the user and need to be informed of the user existence and privileges, and a variety of other services may need to know about the users existence.

Still other systems do not need to be informed of the user's existence, they will create the proper configuration information for the user the first time he uses the service. An example of this is the first time a user receives mail or uses the mail system a mailbox will be created, a set of default configuration options will be installed, and the user will be given a default set of privileges. The mail system may need to verify with a central security or directory service whether the user is a valid user.

Performance management: We discussed earlier that the performance management aspect of user management is consulting, training, and other facilities for helping the user. Now the user is less defined and is potentially using the distributed system from a variety of platforms. Different platforms have different behavior characteristics and often the users must use drastically different interfaces to do the same thing on different platforms. This greatly increases the amount of help the users need.

Distributed systems tend to be used by larger numbers of users than regular systems. These users often perform a much more varied set of tasks. Thus, the complexity of helping those users is increased. Therefore, methods of getting users to help themselves are used more often in distributed systems. Rather than the central system providing all the software, often users are encouraged to submit software to special user contributed areas which make them available to all users of the distributed system. Many times the contributing users even provide support for the software. In addition, notification systems like Zephyr from MIT have turned out to be excellent real time advice systems for getting help from volunteer helpers who happen to be subscribed to special help notification instances.

Resources in distributed systems exist in different parts of the network and are often native to different environments. Performance is usually better when working with resources closer on the network and which run and use native technology rather than lowest performance translator technology. In order to increase performance for the user primary resources for the user should be allocated to optimize performance based on their usage patterns.

Fault management: Distributed systems contain data about users all over the network. Distributed fault management systems perform integrity checks on the remote information to ensure that the data is consistent throughout the network. For systems that do not utilize central directory services which are queried by remote services for user information, these integrity checks are very important.

Like in the single system, fault management includes backing up of user data. The new problem introduced in distributed systems is that user data may exist all over the network. This remote data exists in network services and on the local hard disks of client machines. Some distributed systems limit backups to services and distributed file systems. In these systems, the user must backup data kept on client machines or copy the data periodically to a distributed file system which is backed up. Other systems try to backup all client machines.

There are an increasing numbers of products for doing backups of client machines. Many of these products backup heterogeneous clients. Increasingly, the DOS and Macintosh backup products include virus detection components to help identify and eliminate viruses installed on client machines.

Security management: User security management includes protecting the user from external and internal influences, and from each other. They also enforce restrictions on use of system resources. Distributed systems add complexity in carrying out these tasks, but in some cases security management gets more powerful and manageable.

Traditionally, there has been a lack of security for individual users on Macintoshes and DOS machines since they were designed to be single user systems and the natural assumption is that access to the machine would be direct, for example, sitting down in front of it. As a result, anyone who sits down in front of the machine is all powerful, and can do anything on the machine. The data kept on the machine is accessible for all users of the machine. When these same machines use a remote distributed file system there are usually security systems in place. Files and directories can usually be protected per user or by groups of users.

An additional issue which distributed systems address is that often because of the distributed nature of these systems resources which must be restricted by the security management system, portions of the security system need to be managed by users or departmental administrators not part of the central distributed system administration. Thus, the security system must allow for distributed administration.

The user security management task with distributed systems controls access to remote distributed services based on the network identity of the user. For more information on how security works in distributed systems, Chapter 4 on distributed security should be consulted.

Finally, in large distributed systems it is often impossible to know all your users. In the event of a major security break, one is forced to perform draconian measures in order to maintain any degree of security. For example, users may be forced to go and present a picture id in order for their account to be reactivated.

Resource management: Resources in distributed systems are no longer housed and controlled from one central location. These resources are often owned and maintained by different groups using the distributed system. These groups want to have some degree of control over the usage of their resources.

Distributed resource management has to tackle the problem of gathering data from a variety of locations on usage of resources. Since the diversity and amount of resources tend to be greatly increased in distributed systems, system which charge for resource usage must have more sophisticated methods of gathering data and deciding different charging algorithms.

5.3.2.2 Task Management

Tasks in distributed systems can be performed in a variety of locations on the network. In fact, a single task may consist of a variety of subtasks which are performed in several different locations. This separation may be desirable for several reasons. The data or resources may exist in different locations on the network. Parts of the task may perform better on some machines than other parts of the task. A quicker result may be obtained by distributing parts of the tasks to run in parallel amongst unused resources on the network.

A large number of tasks are performed by remote servers using traditional client/server configurations. Each server must be configured, monitored, and maintained. Sometimes a single machine performs one server task while other times a single machine will perform a variety of tasks. The server and client machines are often made up of a variety of hard and operating system platforms.

Configuration management: Each system that server processes run on must be configured to run the processes. The servers themselves have a variety of configuration parameters which determine how they should run, what users are allowed to use them, what network ports to listen on, and a variety of other options. Since the servers may be heterogeneous, their differences must be taken into consideration when configuring them.

The clients need to be configured to find the servers. Directory services which list the locations and configurations of both clients and servers help this process substantially. Otherwise the client needs to either have the name of the server hard coded or files containing the names and locations of the servers must be distributed to the clients. Sometimes the domain name system (DNS) is used in place of a standard directory service. An alias with the service name is entered into the DNS. Then when a service moves the alias is changed in DNS and clients can find the service.

The number of remote servers and clients accessing them are often very large in distributed system. It is important that the process of setting up and configuring remote services be an easy one.

Performance management: Distributed systems often do not have very good performance monitoring built in. Most of the early systems almost completely ignored the need to perform performance management. There was relatively little instrumentation of server processes. Since these processes run on multiple machines and clients often have very intricate dependencies on different services running on different machines, it becomes very quickly unwieldy to run standard utilities which monitor the activity of a single machine.

A great deal of network management has evolved toward management of services on the network and standards for gathering data have emerged. This process is very helpful, but services which are not instrumented can provide very little data to remote monitoring tools. In these cases, a variety of methods are used to monitor services with no built in instrumentation. The most often used method is to make a request of the service from a monitoring location and record the amount of time it takes for an action to be performed. When a service is having problems, it is often true that a cascading effect is causing problems with other dependent services as well. With an understanding of these dependencies, problems with services which can not be easily monitored can be identified by problems in other services once the patterns have been identified. The I/O and CPU load of the server machines themselves can be examined as well.

There are a variety of ways services which have instrumentation built in provide data. The most flexible methods are via network monitoring protocols such as SNMP which do both real time data delivery and notification on faults. Sometimes the servers are configured to record the times it takes on the server to perform each task and review the data at a later date. In these cases, each task of the task is recorded. This greatly aids in profiling system utilization by people not involved in it's development or who do not have access to the sources.

Performance management, even in single user systems, has been a difficult process. With distributed systems, the interaction between multiple components makes the process even more difficult. It is also the case where hardware upgrades to faster systems may result in performance degradations. For example, the Andrew system did a major systems upgrade where Sun3 AFS fileservers were replaced with Sparc IIs with twice the physical memory and faster disks. Clients were upgraded from RTs and VAXstations to DECstation 5000, again with more memory and faster disks. Overall, there was a minimum of two times increase in sheer CPU power. However, instead of providing a faster system, the resulting configuration resulted in extremely poor performance. Eventually, the major problem was determined to be that the replication fileservers were being overloaded and more replication sites had to be added.

Fault Management: Many of the same tools used for performance management double as tools for fault management. SNMP allows for services to broadcast a fault to a host or set of hosts. Faults are determined because some resource has been or is about to be exhausted or some task is not running or responding properly. Constant polling to determine the state is the most flexible method because the agent doing the polling can determine what set of events constitutes a fault, but this often requires more activity than a system which will send a message upon failure and can be delayed by whatever the poll interval is and with some failures the message may never be sent. Good fault management systems use a combination of both of these methods.

Fault management also includes what you need to do to rectify the fault. Distributed systems often have system services cloned to provide better availability and load balancing. When it is detected that one of these cloned units has failed, the others will take over its activities. For critical services, it is imperative that they can cloned and that clients can hand off to active servers when there are problems. Many services are not cloned and even worse single machines often provide multiple servers. A failure of the machine, or of a service on that machine which requires or causes the machine to be unavailable will effect the other services as well. The dependencies between services need to be understood and kept to an absolute minimum. Sites often keep hot spares around which can replace machines which fail. If machines providing different services are kept as similar as possible, often a hot spare can be available to replace the machine used in a number of services.

5.3.2.3 Software Management

On a single system, there are only sources, objects and binaries for one system type and operating system. Distributed systems in heterogeneous environments introduce multiple system types and operating system combinations. Software must be distributed and configured on these different systems which also may have different combinations of software installed on them. When software is released and distributed to different systems, problems with that software can have a much more drastic effect than on a single system. It is important that installation and distribution systems not be one way. In some cases when they need to be one way, like installing new kernels on remote machines, they must check to see if there are enough resources to do the installation to completion and verify that everything worked. Releasing a bad operating system to 1,000 machines can have an immediately catastrophic effect.

Often a much larger group of people, or at least people from different groups with looser controls, are developing, installing, and testing software. This means that the environments they work in must be more robust and have better control. Most systems incorporate the use of version numbers and version control throughout to help in identifying differences and backing them out when needed.

One important aspect of distributed system management is that the system not require an actual visit to every machine for any of its actions (except possibly the initial software installation). In order to be scalable, it must be possible for the systems personnel to install, monitor, and configure software remotely.

Configuration management: Machines in distributed environments can be found in endless varieties. They have different configurations, different system architectures, the are on different networks, have different operating systems, and do different things. It is often not possible to have a single configuration management system for these possible configurations, though some information must be shared in common amongst them all. This often necessitates a strong framework for system management which can serve as the central repository for system information. That information is then converted and distributed to the various management systems.

Distributed configuration management systems must deal with this varied world. When installing software remotely it needs to install and configure the right software for the right operating system/architecture combination. Since some machines have different sets of software installed, the software installation and configuration must properly take that into consideration.

Performance management: Previously, we defined performance management in software management as finding the optimal software package for the user. In the distributed arena, a compromise between usability and manageability comes into play. Since there are potentially more people with different needs, it becomes more difficult for a central group to provide the software needs of each department, let alone each individual user.

Fault management: In distributed systems, not only is fault recovery more difficult but so is testing. With the variety of different configurations available, it is impossible, or, at least, impractical, to test every combination that exists. This also makes it easy for software to be configured to a single class of machines, such as the machines the mangers have direct access to, and not work for a different class of machines. When software that does not work is released and then distributed, it becomes difficult to restore the previous software, especially if the release has damaged the system such that it can no longer participate in the software distribution scheme. Finally, because of the distributed nature, errors may not be quickly noticed by the managers and it is only when the users start complaining that the managers even start to solve the problems.

Security management: With security management, the manager now has a much greater concern of the software being compromised by an attack or by the case where an attacker is pretending to be one of the software distribution servers. Also, software may not be site licensed and so access to the software must be regulated either to specific hosts or to specific users.

Resource management: If software were free or site licenses more common, resource management would not be as much of an issue. One would still have to account for what software exists on what machines out there, but one would not have to deal with enforcing licenses or dealing with software vendors that still have a single system approach. For example, at Carnegie Mellon University, machines come and go and network addresses are often reused without notification of the network database maintainers. So, when it comes time to renew the AT&T source license, it becomes a real pain to try to get serial numbers for all the machines.

5.3.2.4 Hardware Management

Hardware management may be one of the most difficult aspects to manage in a distributed system as there are a limited number of things that one can automate. If the hardware breaks, someone has to go out and fix it. If a new peripheral needs to be added, someone qualified needs to add it.

Configuration management: In a distributed system, keeping track of the hardware becomes more difficult. Users may be have special requirements for hardware and there needs to be a way for users to find the configuration or the system that they need to get to. Also, in a distributed system, one needs to make the software generic enough to handle the hardware so that the central support staff does not have to constantly tweak the software to work with the hardware.

Performance management: In distributed systems, performance problems may not matter as much as the work of a single user and his use of resources may not effect others in the system. Then again, there could be really strange interactions that cause performance problems. Monitoring becomes more difficult as there are more machines to take care of.

Fault management: Some degree of remote fault detection can be done via SNMP and other such monitoring tools, but often the machine is up and running but the services are not. Often times, there is no real good way of detecting if the service is actually running and so fault detection is the result of people complaining.

Security management: Hardware with distributed systems is generally not hidden away in secure locations with 24-hour surveillance. Hardware is often located in hostile locations where it may be possible for people to walk away with the hardware or anything not tied down.

Resource management: Again because of the distributed nature and by the fact that is not always possible to remotely query what is on the machine, it becomes hard to keep track of all the hardware components.

5.3.2.5 Network Management

Network management ensures that the network connecting the various systems is functioning properly. According to our functional definition of systems management, network management is a component of it. However, one can see that the network manager also has to deal with similar issues, such as task, hardware, and software management since the network manager is responsible for the systems that drive the network, such as routers, bridges, and so on. Luckily for the network manager, the scope of the management is more specific and there are less issues in each category for the network manager to worry about.

In the single system case, network management concentrates on the connectivity of the system to the rest of the network. In distributed systems, the network is the entity that makes a system distributed. So, the network itself becomes a primary concern.

5.3.3 Distributed System Management Example

Taking the example from the previous section of adding a users account and extending it to adding a user to a distributed system adds a much larger number of tasks. Since distributed systems vary so much, it is difficult to give a typical example. The following is a list of steps to add a user to the Andrew environment at Carnegie Mellon University (see the Andrew chapter):

- select and set a user name that is not already used
- determine the UID (unique number associated with the user);
- determine on which file server and disk to place the user's home directory
- determine the path to the user's home directory
- select and an initial password for the user
- create entry in protection server
- create entry in authentication server
- create volume for home directory
- mount volume in file system
- place prototype files in home directory
- change ownership of home directory and files
- create the standard directories
- give user and system services access to proper directories

- update password file
- update white pages user directory service
- distribute new white pages to service machines
- distribute new password file to client machines

The creation and distribution of new users on the Andrew system is all automated. However, even though no mistakes are made in the process, there is still the case where a user may not be able to use his account as synchronization of the password file on public machines only occurs when the machine goes to update software, and in our case, that is when the machine reboots.

There are a number of other possible failures in the process which would lead to the account not being created. Within each task, like creating an AFS volume for the users home directory, there are several steps that must be performed. In any of these steps there could potentially be a failure. The creation of an AFS volume requires a entry be created with the volume location database (VLDB), the VLDB must be queried for the volume number to use when creating the volume, the entry must then be locked, a server is then selected to house the volume, the server must be given a request to create the volume, it must create the volume and set the default protection and quota for the volume, then the volume information must be updated, the VLDB must then replicate the new data to each of its servers, then the volume must be placed on-line by the server. There is a potential for error during any of those steps.

Finally, there is a good deal of policy that must be set that have larger consequences than on the single user system. For example, decisions need to be made about the default configuration of the account, the default quota, and the default protections. Additionally, since there is not a university wide password file, a new user created on the Andrew system should not have the same user name as one which was already assigned to another person on a different system.

5.4 Summary

> The first step towards the management of disease was replacement of demon theories and humours theories by the germ theory. That very step, the beginning of hope, in itself dashed all hopes of magical solutions. It told workers that progress would be made stepwise, at great effort, and that a persistent, unremitting care would have to be paid to a disciple of cleanliness. So it is with software engineering today (Brooks, 1986).

While Brooks wrote this quote about software engineering, it applies very well to systems management. With single systems, the problems with system management were relatively manageable. Tremendous growth of distributed, heterogeneous computing has changed and expanded the problems of system management. Existing methods, at best, slow the decay, but more often the break down and create additional management problems.

System management has moved into the spotlight. Now, it is commonly agreed that distributed systems management is a pressing problem, and many claim to have a solution, or will very soon. While it may be claimed that we no longer embrace "demon and humours theories," there are so many differing "germ theories" which try to solve the problem, no single solution is capable of solving all the problems, and the different solutions do not work well together. Until more unified approaches appear and are embraced a great deal of effort will continue to be put into divergent and incompatible systems.

In essence, this chapter has only described some of the evolution of the distributed systems management problem and the most common problems encountered in managing distributed systems. In chapter 14, we will discuss strategies that offer some solutions which we hope will lower the pain to a bearable level. The real challenge in systems management is not solving the symptoms, but understanding the root problems. This chapter has defined the problem and laid the foundation for the later discussion of the solutions.

5.5 References

Brooks, F.P., Jr. 1986. No Silver Bullet: Essence and Accidents of Software Engineering. *Information Processing 86.* Elsevier Science Publishers B. V.

Feller, P.H., 1991. Configuration Management Models in Commercial Environments. CMU/SEI-91-TR-7. Mar.

Kolstad, RR., 1991. Viewpoint: What do System administrators Really Do? *Communications of the ACM* vol. 34, no 12. Dec. pp. 11–14.

Smith, S.W., and Quarterman, J.S., 1989. White Paper on System Administration for IEEE 1003.7. login:. vol. 14, no 4. Jul/Aug, pp. 17–23.

Wallace Colyer is the Andrew Systems Manager at Carnegie Mellon University. Wallace initially worked as a User Consultant running an electronic mail help system and helping with customizing workstation configurations. He went on to play an key role in designing software release and configuration management processes. Now, he is responsible for a group which oversees the day to day health and sets the architectural direction of the Andrew System, which is on the forefront of distributed computing in size, diversity, and innovation.

Walter Wong graduated from Carnegie Mellon with a B.S. in Cognitive Science. While pursuing his undergraduate degree, he became involved in system administration in a distributed computing environment. After graduation, he remained at Carnegie Mellon where he is now a System Programmer and Administrator in the Andrew Systems Group.

Chapter 6

ONC+ Distributed Computing

Written and Compiled by **Sally A. Biles**
SunSoft, Inc.

6.1 Introduction

The technologies comprising ONC™ were developed by Sun Microsystems, Inc. in the mid 1980s. ONC originally included not only the NFS® distributed file service, but also a naming service (formerly YP) and a remote procedure call (RPC) service. In 1991 SunSoft, Inc., a Sun Microsystems Company introduced ONC+™ . ONC+ is an evolved and expanded version of ONC consisting of a set of new and enhanced distributed computing services that are fully backward compatible with their ONC counterparts. ONC+ includes enhanced NFS distributed file services, the NIS+ enterprise naming service, a transport independent RPC (TI-RPC) service, developer tools, and enhanced security and administration services.

ONC is a widely implemented open, distributed computing solution with a current installed base of over 4 million systems. Over 300 organizations have licensed ONC technology including IBM, Apple, Hewlett-Packard and Novell. In addition, ONC implementations provide interoperability across all major computer hardware platforms from PCs to mainframes and across all major operating systems including VMS®, MS-DOS®, MacOS™ , UNIX®, and MVS®. The written specifications for ONC technologies are available to the public and the source code is licensable from Sun.

ONC+ is a key component of multiple standards profiles. It is a building block of the UNIX International ATLAS (UI-ATLAS™) standard for distributed computing. The recent common open systems environment (COSE) agreement between leading vendors such as HP, IBM, SunSoft, SCO, Univel and USL includes support for the ONC+ distributed computing platform. In addition, NFS is a part of the X/Open standard for internetworking among X/Open compliant systems[1].The extensive installed base of ONC together with its inclusion in

[1]See the X/Open CAE Specification "Protocols for X/Open Internetworking: XNFS,", Issue 4.

multiple standards profiles is an indication that ONC+ will continue to be supported on multiplatform systems in enterprise environments well into the future.

ONC+ is a key component of SunSoft's Solaris™ operating system. The source code for ONC+ is also licensed separately to parties interested in implementing ONC+ on their platforms. For more information on how ONC+ fits in to SunSoft's distributed computing strategy, see Chapter 13, Section 5. The following sections go into detail on the components of ONC+.

6.2 The NFS Distributed File Service

6.2.1 Introduction

NFS was one of the first distributed file services in existence, and continues to be one the most successful in the world today. In 1985, Sun Microsystems introduced NFS and demonstrated how disk and file sharing among multiple client systems on a network, can drastically reduce the per client cost of computing in a networked environment. Because of its simple design and robust architecture, NFS has been implemented on all major operating systems and hardware platforms including both open and proprietary systems.

NFS provides features that fully support user requirements for distributed file systems in enterprise environments. Foremost is the ability to provide easy, transparent access to files in a worldwide heterogeneous network. This includes allowing users to access files in a consistent way, no matter where those files may reside on the network. In addition, NFS also supports secure access to files so that proper controls can be enforced and access restricted if necessary. Near term enhancements to NFS include a new, more efficient file mounting facility, a revision to the NFS protocol offering performance enhancements and improved scalability, the ability to run NFS over wide area networks using connection oriented transports, and support for client side file caching.

6.2.2 Basic Design Principles

NFS was designed to simplify the sharing of file system resources in a network of heterogeneous machines. It provides a way of making remote files available to local application programs without requiring the developer to modify, or even relink the application and without requiring end users to know that files are not on their local disk. In addition, NFS was designed to make access to remote files comparable in speed to access to local files.

NFS original design principles include the following:

- *Transparent Access:* When using NFS, users access files on remote systems in the same way as they access local files. Applications do not need to perform special pathname parsing, use additional libraries, or be recompiled in order to access remote files. Further, application programs cannot tell whether a file is local or remote.
- *Machine and Operating System Independence:* Although originally designed on the UNIX operating system, the NFS protocols were designed to be independent of

UNIX so that an NFS server would be able to supply files to many different types of clients. The protocols are also simple enough that they can be implemented on low-end platforms such as PCs.

- *Fast Recovery:* NFS was designed to recover easily from system failures and network problems so that users have reduced interruption of service when failures occur.
- *Performance:* Access to remote files is comparable in performance to local file access, increasing user perception that all files are local to ones machine instead of shared across the network.
- *Portability:* NFS was designed to be portable to multiple operating system platforms. This is one of the reasons why NFS has been so successful over the years and enjoys such a large installed base today.
- *Security:* NFS allows the incorporation and use of multiple security mechanisms so that administrators can tailor NFS to suit the security needs of their specific environments.
- *Network Protocol Independence:* NFS was built on top of a network protocol independent remote procedure call mechanism. This gives NFS the flexibility to run on multiple transport protocols instead of being restricted to a particular one.

Although basic principles still apply, NFS has gone through an evolution to support demands of today's enterprise environments. The following sections provide details on the basic concepts and new features of NFS.

6.2.3 NFS Basic Concepts

NFS consists of three major components: the client, the server, and the protocol. These are detailed below.

6.2.4 NFS Clients and Servers

6.2.4.1 Servers and Exporting

An NFS file server shares–that is, lets other machines have access to–one or more of its file hierarchies. A server advertises the directories that it will permit other computers (clients) to access files on its disk(s) by *exporting* file hierarchies. A special file called the `dfstab` file (formerly the `exports file`) lists the directories the server wants to permit access to, which clients are allowed to access them, and any access restrictions that must be applied. A system dependent program[2] invoked at boot time looks at the `dfstab` (or equivalent) file and informs the server's kernel about the permissions applicable to each exported file hierarchy.

[2]On some systems, the *exportfs* command is used. On others a different command that provides the same function may be used. For example, on SunSoft' s Solaris 2.0 operating system, the *share* and *unshare* commands are used.

Using this same program, file hierarchies can also be explicitly exported and unexported after the server is up, or the export permissions of an exported file hierarchy can be changed.

6.2.4.2 Clients and Mounting

NFS clients access files on the server by *mounting* the server's exported directories. When a client mounts a directory, it does not make a copy of that directory. Rather, the mounting process sets up a *link* between the client's mount point and exported file system on the server that the client wants access to.

Clients and servers communicate with each other using a network-based mount protocol. The mount request sent by the client is received by a daemon process called the *mountd* on the server machine. The mountd processes the information and decides whether or not the client should have access to mount the file hierarchy. Once a client mounts a remote directory, files can be accessed as if they resided on the local machine.

The mount process can take the request from the mount command line, or it can utilize a special file called a *map file* to determine where to mount file hierarchies. A map file contains information necessary to successfully complete the mount. It defines the association or mapping of a file system on a server to a mount point in the client's file name space. A map file may be local, or it may reside and be accessed through a name service such as NIS+ (discussed in Section 6.2) in which case it is referred to as a *global map*. A global map used in conjunction with the *automounter* or *autofs*, described in the next sections, permits an administrator to easily define a consistent shared name space in an enterprise. A consistent shared namespace means files can be accessed using consistent file naming conventions no matter where they reside on the network.

A special file called the `vfstab` (formerly `fstab`), which stands for virtual file system table, can be used by the mount command to mount all desired file hierarchies. `vfstab` contains a reference to all the file systems a user wants to mount, along with any file system options.

A client can mount a directory in three ways:

- At boot time.
- By issuing a mount command.
- Using the automounter or autofs.

There are a variety of map files which help simplify file system mounting when using different mount commands. More information on maps is contained in the following sections.

6.2.4.3 Automatic Mounting

The *automounter* is a service that automatically mounts file systems upon first reference. The user no longer has to know the superuser password to mount a directory nor does he have to know how to use the mount and unmount commands. The advantage of this is that file systems are mounted and unmounted on an as needed basis. When using the automounter, NFS file systems appear to be immediately, and continuously available to users; File system mounting and unmounting is done automatically and transparently.

Whenever a user on a client machine running the automounter invokes a command that requires access to a remote file or directory, such as opening a file with an editor, the hierarchy to which that file or directory belongs is mounted and remains mounted for as long as it is needed. Whenever five minutes have elapsed without the file hierarchy being accessed, it is automatically unmounted.

The automounter is a daemon process that is started at boot time and runs in the background. It takes care of two tasks: determining which file systems need to be mounted by reading the information in map files and then mounting file systems accordingly.

The automounter uses a variety of map files to help it figure out how to mount file systems. There are three kinds of automount maps: master, direct, and indirect. The master map named auto.master, is consulted when the system starts up. It contains default mount points (e.g., /net and /home) and the names of the direct or indirect maps that the automounter consults when performing its job. (For more information on direct and indirect mounts, see Section 6.2.4.6).

6.2.4.4 Improved Automatic Mounting: Autofs

Although automounter offers many advantages over static mounting, the implementation has slight disadvantages. First of all, the automounter accomplishes file system mounts by setting up symbolic links between the client mount point and the remote file hierarchy. This requires a temporary directory to be created, typically /tmp_mnt. Thus when a user issues a command like `pwd` (print working directory) /tmp/mnt appears in the pathname of the mounted file system.

Another disadvantage is that a set of mount points to be automounted can only be specified when the automounter is initially started. If a new mount point is added to the master map, automounter must be stopped and restarted in order to utilize the new information.

To address these issues, a new automatic mounting process called *autofs* will soon be available as part of ONC+. Autofs is implemented as a virtual file system (VFS) that supports automatic mounting with some significant improvements. Autofs solves many of the shortcomings of the automounter. For example, because it is a VFS, autofs does not need to support symbolic links to mounted file systems as did the automounter. This means that a directory operation such as `pwd` will not exhibit a reference to /tmp_mnt as it did with the automounter. Another advantage is that new mount points can be added to the master map and the associated file hierarchy can then be mounted without interrupting the autofs service.

6.2.4.5 How Autofs Works

Like automounter, autofs is a client side service. When a client attempts to access a file system that is not presently mounted, the autofs file system intercepts the request and calls automountd, to mount the requested directory. The automountd locates the directory, mounts it within the autofs and replies. On receiving the reply, the autofs allows the waiting request to proceed. Subsequent references to the mount are redirected by the autofs–no further participation is required by the automountd.

There are three components that work in conjunction to accomplish automatic mounting: the automount command, the autofs file system, and the automountd. The automount command, called at system start up time, reads the master map file `auto_master` to create the initial set of autofs mounts. These autofs mounts are not file system mounts–yet. They are points under which filesystems will be mounted in the future.

Once the autofs mounts are set up, they can trigger file systems to be mounted underneath them. For example, when the autofs receives a request to access a file system that is not currently available under an autofs mount, autofs will call the automountd which will actually mount the requested file system.

Unlike automounter, in this new implementation, the automountd daemon is completely independent from the automount command. Because it is separate, it is possible to add, delete or change map information without having to stop the process first. Once the file system is mounted, further accesses do not require any action from the automountd.

After initially mounting autofs mounts, the automount command is used to keep autofs mounts synchronized with the master map. It will add, delete, modify or remount autofs mounts as necessary by comparing the list of mounts in `auto_master` with the list of mounted file systems in the mount table file `/etc/mnttab` (formerly /etc/mtab) and making the appropriate changes. This allows system administrators to change mount information in `auto_master` and have those changes implemented by the autofs processes without having to stop and restart the autofs.

6.2.4.6 How Autofs Supports Different Types of Mounts

Autofs supports both direct and indirect mounts, as well as variations on these basic mount types. The following sections go into more details.

Direct Mount: A direct mount is the simplest and most intuitive form of automatic mount. On receiving a request to access its mount point, the autofs calls the automountd, providing the mount point and a direct map name, for example:

```
/usr/man      server:/export/man
```

The automountd mounts the file system over the autofs mount point and replies. On receiving the reply, the autofs redirects the blocked request to the new mount point. When the mount is unmounted, the autofs mount is exposed again (see figure 7.1).

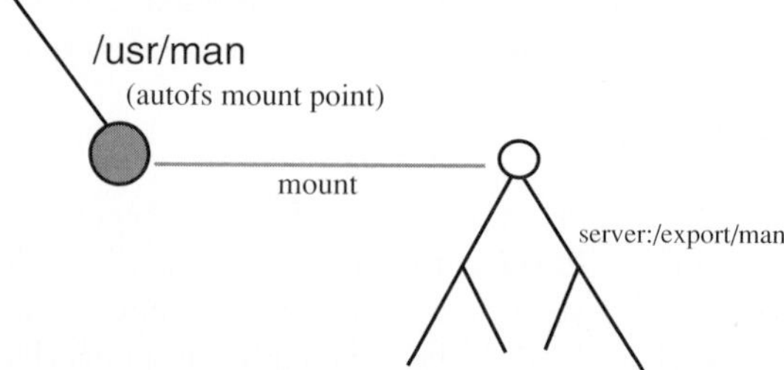

Figure 6.1 Direct mounts. The striped circle indicates the autofs mount point. A direct mount overlays the autofs mount point.

Indirect Mount: An indirect mount is simply a directory of automatic mount points. On receiving a request to look up a name in this directory, the autofs calls the automountd with the indirect map name. The daemon looks up the name in the map, mounts the corresponding file system and replies to the autofs. Once the file system is mounted, communication with the daemon is no longer required.

As an example of indirect mounts, consider the case of /home. On a local client machine, /home is a (default) mount point set up at system boot time. It is an indirect mount point that can potentially trigger autofs to call automountd to mount file systems underneath it.The file systems which can be mounted under /home are listed in the `auto_home` map file. A sample auto_home is shown below:

```
sallyb      morale:/export/home/morale2/sallyb
hagmann     diskus:/export/home/diskus1/hagmann
petera      cerritos:/export/home/cerritos3/petera
```

Consider that petera listed above wants to access a file in hagmann's home directory. If petera does a cd to /home/hagmann, autofs will look in auto_home map file for the path name to hagmann's home directory. It will then invoke automountd to mount diskus1:/export/home/diskus1/hagmann under /home/hagmann. After that point, if petera does an ls on /home, he will see hagmann listed in the directory there. Figure 6.2 graphically depicts this example:

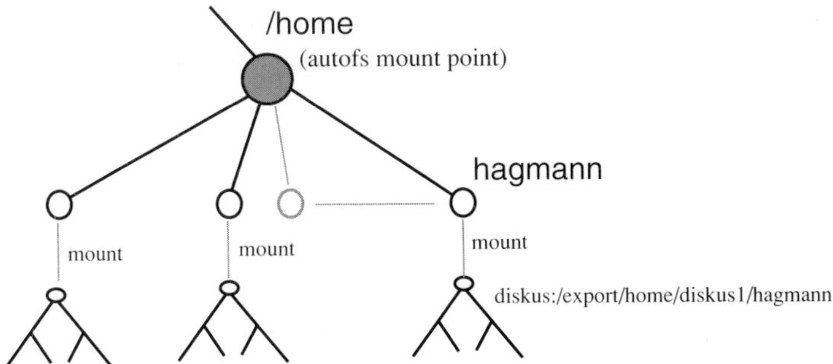

Figure 6.2 Indirect mounts. The autofs filesystem, in this case /home, is required to support a directory of mount points. A lookup request for a name (e.g. hagmann) that is not in the directory but is in the map auto_home will cause hagmann to be added to the directory when the mount is complete.

Note that petera can continue to mount additional file systems under /home transparently using autofs in conjunction with the auto_home map file.

Offset Mounts: An offset mount is a mount that is several directory levels below the direct (or indirect) mount point. In this case, the mount desired is offset by some number of directory levels from the directory that triggered the automatic mount. The autofs is required to provide as many directory levels as necessary to account for the offset.

An example of this is shown in figure 6.3. In this example, there is an autofs mount point on /host. There is also a map entry in a map file created especially for this example called `auto_hosts` that looks like the following:

server1 /usr/local/bin server1:/usr/local/bin

The user does a cd to /host/server1/usr/local/bin. The reference to /host triggers a mount on /host/server1. However, the actual mount point desired is /host/server1/usr/local/bin. This means that autofs must provide directories along the path server1/usr/local/bin before the mount can succeed.

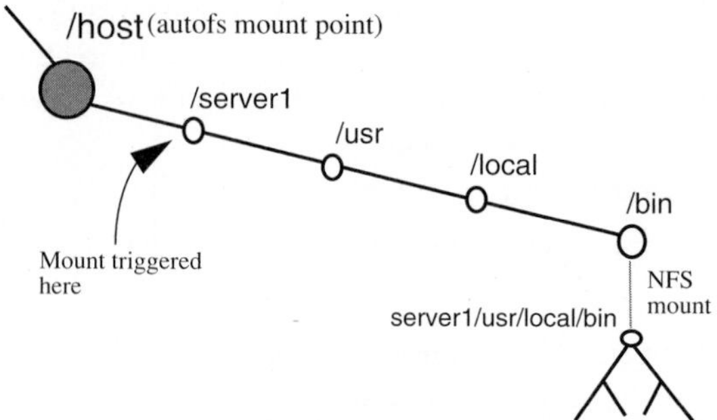

Figure 6.3 Offset mounts. An offset mount requires one or more directories be created within the autofs filesystem to create a path to the mount point.

Multiple Mounts: Sometimes mount requests require that more than one filesystem needs to be mounted at one time. An example of this can again be seen with the /net facility. The /net facility allows users to easily access exported file systems on other servers on the network. When a user requests access to /net/servername with a cd or other command, the automountd attempts to mount *all* the exported file sytems from that server. The automount daemon creates offset paths as necessary to construct mount points within the autofs filesystem (see figure 6.4).

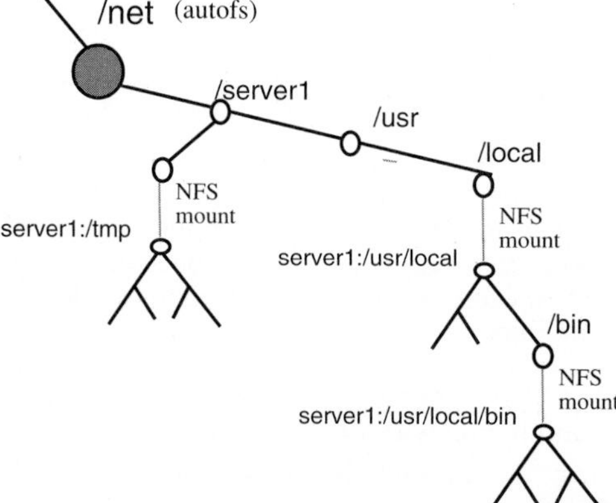

Figure 6.4 Multiple mounts. Several filesystems may need to be mounted as a hierarchy. The automount daemon creates the offset paths as necessary to construct mount points within the autofs filesystem. The daemon responds with a successful mount complete message if at least one of the file systems has been mounted. This facility is most commonly used with /net mounts that attempt to reproduce an NFS server's exported hierarchy on the client.

6.2.4.7 Auto-UnMounting

To avoid an ever increasing number of mounts, periodic unmounting is required. Filesystems that have not been referenced for five minutes are candidates for ummounting. Periodically, the autofs checks for file systems that have not been referenced for five minutes. It this is the case, the autofs sends an *unmount* request to the automountd with a list of the file system device identifiers to be unmounted. If a filesystem is busy, the automountd will not unmount it. It will respond with a failure notification and will try again later.

6.2.5 The NFS Protocol

The NFS protocol is a collection of procedures and structures that allow NFS clients and servers to communicate with each other. Simple file operations such as `read`, `write`, `rename`, `mkdir` (make directory), and so on, are part of the list of routines that allow NFS to manipulate files and directories[3]. The most common NFS procedure parameter is a special structure called a *file handle*. New file handles are returned by the server to the client when the client calls the `create`, `lookup`, and `mkdir` procedures. Subsequent procedure calls take the file handle as an argument to the procedure. Although the client never looks at the contents of the file handle, it must be used when operations are done on the file that the file handle belongs to.

NFS utilizes the Sun developed remote procedure call (RPC) mechanism[4] to communicate over the network. All of the NFS protocol procedures are actually implemented as remote procedure calls. For the same reasons that local procedure calls help simplify programs, RPC helps simplify the definition, organization and implementation of remote services. Because the NFS protocol is defined in terms of a set of procedures, arguments and results, RPC is convenient to use as RPCs behave just like familiar local procedure calls.

The NFS protocol and RPC are built on top of the Sun external data representation (XDR) specification. XDR defines the size, byte order, and alignment of basic data types such as string, integer, union, boolean and array. Complex structures can be built from the basic XDR data types. Using XDR makes the NFS protocol machine and language independent.

Because NFS is built on a transport independent RPC mechanism, it can run on new transport protocols such as ISO and XNS in addition to TCP/IP. The protocols can be *plugged in* under the RPC mechanism without affecting the NFS protocol. This also gives NFS the flexibility to support future network protocols as they emerge.

The NFS protocol is what is known as a *stateless* protocol. The parameters to each NFS procedure call contain all of the information necessary to complete the call. The server does not keep track of any past requests and does not have to reconstruct state after a crash. This makes crash recovery much less complex. If state is maintained on the server, recovery is much harder. Both client and server need to reliably detect crashes. The server needs to detect client crashes so that it can discard any state it is holding for the client, and the client must detect server crashes so that it can rebuild state on the server. Because of this, stateful distributed file systems tend to be more difficult to administer and maintain.

[3]See the Sun Network Filesystem Protocol Specification for more details.

[4]For more information ONC+ TI-RPC, see Section 6.4

6.2.5.1 A New NFS Protocol: Version 3

The NFS protocol is currently undergoing a revision from Version 2 to Version 3. The Version 3 protocol provides many new enhancements to NFS including the following:

Improved performance: NFS revision 3 provides improved performance by supporting safe asynchronous writes, provided the NFS `write` procedure is used in conjunction with the `commit` procedure. The `commit` procedure provides a way for a client to flush data from previous asynchronous write requests on the server to stable storage, and to detect whether it is necessary to retransmit the data. The facility for safe asynchronous writes means that clients do not have to block, waiting for an NFS server to write file data to disk. At the same time they are assured that their data will be safely written or they will be notified if an error occurred.

Increased server scalability: With NFS Version 3, file attributes are returned on every NFS procedure call. Previously, file attributes were requested separately. Returning file attributes on every call significantly reduces server load in that clients do not have to query the server specifically for file attributes. Thus per server client requests are reduced decreasing server load and increasing scalability.

Unlimited Transfer Size: In NFS Version 2, the data associated with a read or write request was limited to eight kilobytes. This restriction has been removed allowing the client and server to negotiate a transfer size that will utilize the available network bandwidth. This is offers a tremendous advantage when attempting to use NFS over high bandwidth networking technologies such as FDDI, ATM, or 100 Megabit Ethernet.

Improved Permissions Checking: The NFS protocol revision improves file access checking by adding support for a file access check to be done on the server. In NFS Version 2, clients were not able to know about their file access permissions until actually attempting access. With Version 3, a new procedure has been added to allow clients to determine ahead of time what kind of operations are permitted on the file. Using the `access` procedure, the client can ask the server to indicate whether or not one or more classes of operations are permitted, giving the client a better idea of what can and cannot be done.

Access checking on the server is also advantageous when there are file permission settings on the NFS server that are substantially different from UNIX style permissions. An example of this is when access control lists (ACLs) are in use by the NFS server. In this case it is insufficient for the client to attempt to deduce permissions by simply inspecting the `uid`, `gid` and `mode` fields in the file attributes. Therefore, access checking on the server gives clients a more complete picture of file permissions than the client can determine on its own.

Support for large files: NFS can now support files with 64 bit sizes and offsets. This means that multi-gigabit file systems can be accessed on NFS servers. This is particularly important to support 64 bit CPU based platforms that are emerging rapidly in the industry today.

6.2.6 Consistent File Names

Today's enterprise networks, both large and small, are comprised of multiplatform systems connected over local area networks (LANs) and worldwide, over wide area networks (WANs).

In these environments, easy and transparent access to information is of the utmost importance. Transparent access to files is significantly impaired when a user is required to use different file naming conventions to access a file depending on where the file resides on the network. Autofs working together with the NIS+ global name service and NFS provide a way to set up consistent file naming conventions for accessing files on multiplatform systems.

The name space policy is initially established when file sytems are mounted. autofs, when used in conjunction with global maps (defined within a name service, e.g. NIS+) permits the definition of a global, consistent shared name space, giving users a simple way to reference files no matter where they reside on the network. An example of this is shown in how autofs enables users to access other users home directories under /home (See Section 6.2.4.6 under "Indirect Mounts"). In the example, it is shown that users can access each other's home directories using a consistent naming scheme, for example, /home/username, that is independent of the actual location of the data. It also gives users the flexibility of having their home directory available no matter which machine they log into on the network.

6.2.7 File Caching

Under certain conditions, remote file systems may experience performance delays as a result of inherent problems or properties of the network. An example of this is using remote file system over a wide area network with high latency and reduced throughput characteristics. File caching increases performance by enabling data to be cached on local system. Once file information is cached, subsequent requests for file data go directly to the local cache, bypassing the remote file system.

An NFS client typically caches data on its local page or buffer cache. However page and buffer caches have limited size and cached data will not survive client reboots. A new feature that works in conjunction with NFS to provide improved file caching is called *CacheFS* which stands for *Cache File System*. CacheFS allows the use of high speed, high capacity disk drives on local workstations to store frequently used data from a remote file system. The larger local disk cache typically exceeds what is available in client page and buffer caches. The fact that cache is non-volatile means that data in the cache will survive system crashes and will be available when the system reboots.

CacheFS can use all or part of a local disk to store information from a remote file system. A user accessing a file does not need to know whether the file is stored in a cache or is being read from the original file system. The user opens, reads, and writes files as usual.

6.2.7.1 Terminology

In CacheFS terminology, the remote file system is referred to as the *back file system* and the files in it are *back* files. Examples of back file systems are NFS and CD ROM based file systems. The *cached file system* resides on the local disk and files in it are called *cached files*. The *cache directory* is a directory on the local disk where the data for the cached file system is stored. The file system in which the cache directory resides is called the *front file system* and its files are called *front* files.

6.2.7.2 How CacheFS Works

Figure 6.5shows how caching works for NFS. The initial request for information is directed to the (slower) remote file system. After first reference, all subsequent requests go to the cache.

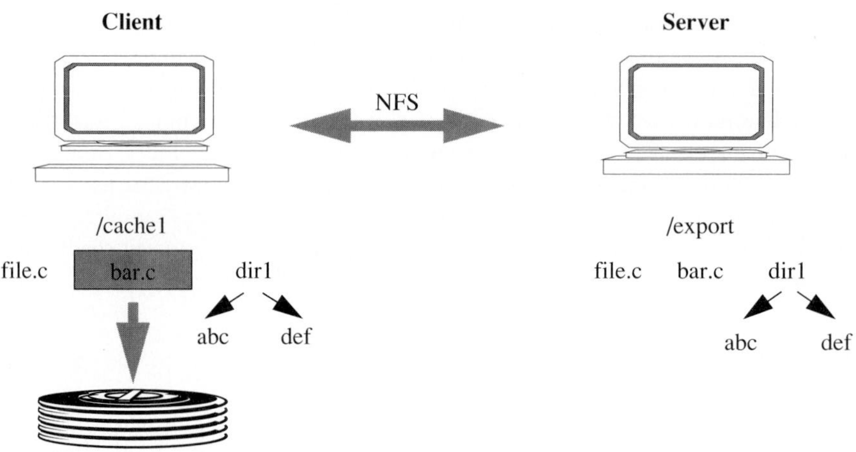

Figure 6.5 How CacheFS works for NFS. At first reference, bar.c is cached on the local system.

NFS procedure calls such as `read`, `readdir`, `readlink`, and `lookups` are virtually eliminated once the cache is populated. This reduces network traffic and per client load on the NFS server, thereby increasing performance and scalability. Performance is particularly improved when using NFS over slow links such as over wide area networks where high latency is often prevalent. Note, CacheFS works identically for other high latency file systems such as CD ROM based file systems.

6.2.7.3 Design and Implementation

CacheFS is implemented as a virtual file system (VFS). It was designed to be independent of any specific file system(s) technology so that its services can be utilized by many types of remote file sytems. This gives CacheFS flexibility and versatility in supporting new file system types as they emerge, both network and non-network based. Figure 6.6 shows CacheFS architecture and how it was integrated into the SVR4 standard *vnode/VFS* interfaces. It also shows how back and front file systems communicate with CacheFS.

The cache resides in a directory of the front file system–no special disk partitioning is required. Because of the way CacheFS has been architected, it is possible that many caches may co-exist in the same front file system. These caches may be servicing a variety of back file systems concurrently. There also may be multiple file systems per cache, which can all be managed cooperatively.

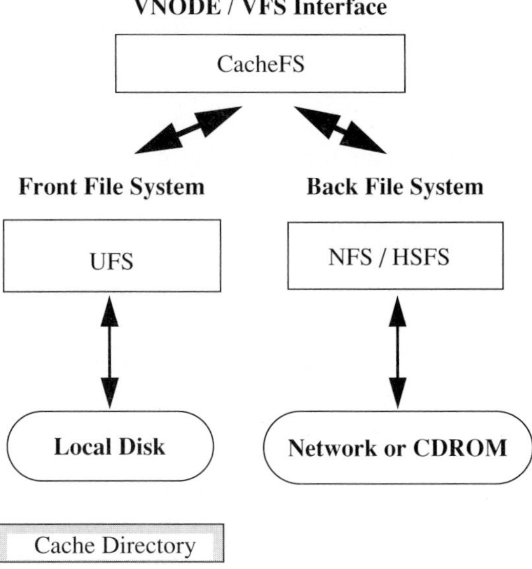

Figure 6.6 CacheFS architecture.

6.2.7.4 Cache File Allocation

CacheFS requires a *UNIX File System* (UFS) as a front file system. After the cache is created, it is then populated with directories and files upon reference. Cache directories are populated when a directory operation is performed. Front files are allocated on `open`, `create`, and `readdir` calls. They are read in to the cache in 64K byte pages. CacheFS is smart enough to anticipate future page demands by *reading ahead.*

Dedicating a file system exclusively to CacheFS allows the greatest control over caching.

6.2.7.5 Cache Administration

There are two steps to setting up a cached file system. First the cache must be created using an administration tool called *cfsadmin*. Then the file system being used as a cache must be mounted using the mount command with the *-F* flag which allows the specification of the file system type as *cachefs*. After the cache has been created, cache parameters that specify front file system resource usage can be configured or modified.

The cfsadmin command allows the cache administrator to perform a variety of cache related tasks including the following:

- Create a cache
- Delete a cache
- Set or modify cache parameters
- Display information about a cache

There are a handful of options that can be set using the cfsadmin command to customize the cache environment including the following. Values are expressed as a *percentage* of total resource available, except for maximum file size which is expressed in megabytes:

Maximum file size: Expressed in megabytes, this sets the maximum size for any file in the front file system. By default, this value is three megabytes.

Maximum number of files: Maximum number of inodes CacheFS can claim expressed as a percentage of the total number of inodes that are available.

Minimum number of files: Allows CacheFS to claim up to and established minimum as long as desired resources are available.

Maximum number of blocks: Expressed as a percentage of the total number of blocks that CacheFS is allowed to claim within the front file system.

Minimum number of blocks: Allows the cache to claim blocks or files up to the established minimum so long as the desired resources are available.

Defaults values for maximum blocks and maximum files is 90%. Default values for minimum blocks and minimum files is 0%. Unless options are specifically set at cache creation time, default values are used.

It is possible to check cache parameters at any time using the cfsadmin command with the *-l* flag. A list of cache parameters and values is the output. Also, a cached file system can be deleted after it is first unmounted using cfsadmin with the *-d* flag.

In addition, CacheFS provides a version of the file system check (fsck) command to check the integrity of cached file systems. This version of fsck automatically corrects problems it encounters without requiring administrator interaction.

6.2.7.6 Cache Semantics

CacheFS supports a modular architecture which allows different consistency mechanisms to be enabled. Cache consistency options are settable at file system mount time on a per file system basis. By default, CacheFS provides file system semantics that are compatible with NFS. However, if an administrator is confident that there will not be writing to the same file concurrently, CacheFS can make consistency assumptions for the sake of performance. For example, there is an option to disable consistency checking altogether. This option should only be used when the back file system in use is a read-only file system.

6.2.7.7 Cache Resource Management

CacheFS uses a least recently used (LRU) replacement scheme for deciding when to release data from the cache and reclaim cache disk space. Files are put on the LRU list when they become inactive. Space used by these files can be reclaimed on demand. In a situation where it is not possible to reclaim cache space, new file access will simply bypass CacheFS without causing an error condition. In this situation, an application may experience slightly degraded service but that is due to the fact that the caching mechanism is being bypassed.

6.2.8 Accessing NFS Files over Wide Area Networks

The emergence of multinational corporations with offices that are widely geographically dispersed has increased the need for information sharing over wide area networks. The requirement is for files to be accessible on server machines which reside in distant locations as easily as they can be accessed on LANs.

In its current implementation, NFS utilizes user datagram protocol (UDP) as the network transport protocol underneath RPC. UDP provides a *connectionless* datagram service which gives NFS greater speed, but which lacks reliability mechanisms that would guarantee data delivery to the recipient. This requires that reliability mechanisms must be built into the NFS layer itself in order to compensate for the absence of this capability in the underlying protocol. The reliability mechanisms built into NFS are appropriate for local area network support, but are somewhat challenged by the problems imposed by slow links, particularly the high latency often experienced on wide area network connections.

In the near future, NFS will include the ability to run over *connection oriented* or reliable protocols such as transmission control protocol (TCP). This allows NFS to take advantage of the guaranteed data delivery attributes found in connection oriented transports, such as dynamic retransmission, packet sequencing, and so on. The end result is that the NFS program is off-loaded from having to do the work necessary to ensure data is delivered to the recipient process.

6.2.9 Authentication and Permission Checking

Protecting files from illegal access is a critical requirement of today's enterprise distributed file systems. NFS offers security mechanisms that allow it to protect files from unauthorized access on the network.

NFS has the ability to support multiple authentication *flavors* at once so system administrators can choose the solutions that fit the needs of specific environments. There are three flavors currently supported by NFS including:

- UNIX style
- DES (National Bureau of Standards Data Encryption Standard)
- Kerberos™

Authentication information is passed between the client and server as a parameter to the RPC utilized by NFS for client/server communications. The NFS server does permission checking by taking on the identity of the caller (client) before servicing a remote request. For example, using the UNIX authentication flavor, the client sends the server its effective user id, effective group id, and groups on each call. The server uses this information to check access. Using user ids and group ids implies that the client and server either share the same id list or that there is a local user and group id *mapping* between client and server systems. In practice, such mapping is typically performed on the server following a static mapping scheme or a mapping scheme established by the client at mount time.

The DES and Kerberos flavors of authentication provide greater security by using data encryption and key passing mechanisms to ensure the privacy of authentication information. For example, a malicious intruder is prevented from access to encrypted authentication information if he does not have the network password or private key.

DES and Kerberos also provide additional improvements over UNIX authentication. Instead of passing uid, gid, and groups information, the client and server agree on a network-wide name which is registered with the key distribution center. This network-wide name, called a *netname*, maps to the identity of the user. Mapping from network name to a user's identity is much more operating system independent than the UNIX uid, gid, groups mechanism. It can therefore be used more easily on a variety of operating system platforms.

6.2.10 Preserving File Integrity

ONC+ supports an optional but recommended record and file locking service. This service provides UNIX style locking between cooperating client processes and the server, allowing synchronized access to shared files. A process may lock a file or part of a file for shared or exclusive access. When a file is locked for shared access, no other process will be granted exclusive access. When a file is locked for exclusive access, no other process will be granted shared access. A request for a lock may fail due to a conflict in access type. However processes may request to block until the lock is available or return an error condition.

Two cooperating daemon processes, called the *lock manager* and the *status monitor*, work together to provide stateful locking and access control capability when used in conjunction with NFS. The lock manager provides *advisory* file and record locking which means that files locks can only be detected by applications using the lock manager. The status monitor provides information on host status. Because the lock manager uses a stateful protocol, the status monitor is used to provide notification of client or server reboots. Although the status monitor is used primarily by the lock manager, it may be used by any distributed application wishing to coordinate host state changes.

NFS provides monitored locks as well as non-monitored locks. Monitored locks require that the lock manager and the status monitor are both in use by the client and server. When a client uses monitored locks, it is assured that the locks will be reinstated in the event that a server crashes and recovers. Conversely, if the client crashes with locks in place, the locks will be automatically freed by the server host. If a client uses non-monitored locks, the locks will not be reinstated if the server crashes and recovers. The client is responsible for detecting a failure on the server and re-establishing the locks.

For these reasons, monitored locks are recommended over non-monitored locks. Non-monitored locks are provided for single tasking systems which cannot support the lock manager and status monitor at the same time.

6.2.11 Diskless and Dataless Client Support

In order to allow customers to take advantage of the tremendous cost savings that can be realized by allowing multiple clients to share the same expensive disk resources, NFS servers have the ability to support diskless and dataless clients on the network. With this facility low cost, low end, diskless, and dataless clients can all share files residing on the same server disk.

6.3 The NIS+ Distributed Name Service

The last few years have seen enormous growth in client/server computing. Accompanying this growth has been a fundamental change in the nature of applications supported by such networks. For example, the recent corporate *rightsizing* trend has been accompanied by expanded use of client/server networks for personal productivity and commercial applications.

This growth in use has been accompanied by a corresponding growth in size of typical client/server networks, which today commonly consist of tens of thousands of systems across an enterprise. These trends present new requirements for efficient administration of entities, such as users, systems and printers, across enterprise networks.

NIS+, a component of the ONC+ family of distributed services, provides distributed systems management software for storage of administrative data.

6.3.1 Client/Server Computing and Naming Services

This section presents an overview of the evolution in client/server network characteristics. It also discusses how the original ONC NIS and the new ONC+ NIS+ naming services support efficient administration of such networks.

6.3.2 ONC NIS Overview

The first generation of client/server computing began in the mid-1980s. Such networks had specific characteristics, including:

- Their size seldom exceeded a few hundred multivendor client desktops and a few general-purpose servers.
- They spanned at most a few geographically remote sites.
- They had friendly, trusted, and sophisticated users–security was not an issue.
- They were administered centrally.

The original ONC NIS naming service (initially called yellow pages or YP) was designed to address the administration requirements of client/server networks in the 1980s. NIS was a vehicle for centralized administration of the first generation of heterogenous client/server networks. NIS replaced the UNIX `/etc` and corresponding configuration files for other operating environments with a central repository. (The original configuration files specified the address and other characteristics of all network-accessible entities and resided on each system on the network.) The NIS implementation had the following characteristics:

- The central database was organized in flat (i.e. not hierarchical) ASCII *maps* for different types of information; for example, host address, user password, and e-mail aliases. Each map consisted of key-value pairs with the key column being used for searches.
- The database was replicated for lookup performance and reliability. Each network supported one NIS master server and a number of slaves, depending upon the size of the network.
- The replica-updating model assumed infrequent changing of information in the database and assumed that the time delay in the propagation of changes to replicas could be handled by applications as a policy issue. Database updates could be made

only from the master server and typically took a long time to propagate over the network.

6.3.3 Enterprise-Wide Client/Server Computing

Client/server networks have undergone tremendous growth since the mid- 1980s. Enterprise-wide networks of client/server systems, typically spanning multiple sites across the globe, are now being used for corporate mission-critical applications. Such networks typically have the following characteristics:

- 100 – 10,000 multivendor client desktops and 10 – 100 specialized servers across a number of geographically dispersed sites spanning the globe.
- Frequent addition, removal, relocation, and reassignment of resources.
- Several independent groups across the enterprise requiring administrative autonomy.
- *Untrusted* connections to public networks.

The evolution of enterprise-wide client/server networks presents a new set of requirements for naming services. These include:

- Support of very small to very large networks.
- Support of a range of administration models for the enterprise networks, ranging from centralized administration of the overall network to distributed administration of smaller domains.
- Authorized access to network resources.
- Support for rapidly changing network environments.
- Easier and more consistent administrative operations.
- Increased automation of administrative operations.

The NIS+ naming service, a replacement for NIS, was designed to address the administrative requirements of enterprise networks of the 1990s. It provides a highly secure and available storage facility for administrative information for enterprise networks. The following sections present an in-depth look at NIS+ capabilities for administering enterprise networks, particularly in relation to NIS.

6.3.4 NIS+: Evolution from NIS

NIS has been widely deployed on dozens of hardware and software platforms and has an installed base exceeding two million users. Like its predecessor, NIS+ serves as a central repository for information on users, systems, printers, and other network entities. In addition, NIS+ contains several major enhancements over NIS, which are summarized in table 6.1.

Table 6.1 Comparison of NIS and NIS+ Features.

Capability	NIS Features	NIS+ Features
Namespace	Organized along *flat* lines	Organized along hierarchical lines
Database	Centralized database for each independent network domain	Partitioned into directories to support each network subset or autonomous domain
Data Storage Scheme	Multiple bi-column *maps* having key-value pairs	Multi-column *tables* with multiple searchable columns
Replication	A minimum of one replica server required per IP subnetwork	Each replica server can serve clients on multiple IP subnets
Privileges for Updating	Updates require super-user privileges on master server	Updates can be performed programmatically or through an interactive command
Update Process	Updates require using `make` files on master servers	Updates are performed through command line interface or API
Update Propagation	Administrator-initiated; Requires transfer of whole maps and takes a long time	Automatic and high-performance updating via incremental transfer
Authorization	Anyone can read all information stored in a NIS database	Fine-grained access control to NIS+ directories, table column and entries
Resource Access Across Domains	Not supported	Permitted for authorized users

NIS+ includes features allowing NIS sites to migrate to the new naming service in a phased and smooth manner. NIS sites that migrate to NIS+ will gain the following benefits:

- Distributed and remote administration of network domains by authorized users.
- Support for range of networks.
- Fast and automatic propagation of updates from master to slave servers.
- Fine-grained access to naming service information.
- Easier and more consistent administrative operations.
- Increased name service reliability and availability.

6.3.5 Distributed Administration

As corporations grow, they frequently reach a point where administration of the overall organization as a single entity becomes too difficult. At this stage, most corporations undergo reorganizations, typically involving breaking up the corporation into autonomous components to promote efficiency.

Decentralizations typically affect the use and administration of corporate information resources. Expanded use of client/server computing is one aspect of decentralization of these resources. Another aspect is decentralizing authority to administer the distributed information systems.

The original NIS was designed to support only centralized administration of information resources. NIS+ makes possible flexible system and network administration to support the growth and decentralization of corporations. It allows both centralized administration of such networks and (as requirements emerge for distributed administration) selective distribution of administrative authority across the corporation. Specifically, it provides the following capabilities for distributed system administration:

- Creation of domain hierarchies allowing administrative efficiency and autonomy.
- Distributed and secure administration of NIS+ service.

6.3.5.1 Manageable Growth through Hierarchical Domain Creation

NIS+ has been designed to allow effective utilization of system administration personnel within corporations. For smaller organizations desiring centralized administration, NIS+ allows the entire network to be treated as a single domain or administrative entity. NIS+ replicated servers provide a central, high-performance, and secure repository of configuration information, optimally addressing the administration needs of a smaller organization.

As corporations grow or reorganize, requirements emerge for decentralized administration. For example, entities such as business units, functional groups, and departments within such corporations may define their own budgets and policies for system and network administration. In addition, such entities may also desire independent system and network administration groups for control and on-going support, while relying on the corporate information resource group for training and support.

NIS+ addresses this requirement by allowing the creation of multiple *domains*, or subsets of the enterprise network, that may be administered on an *autonomous* basis. As a domain grows to consist of two or more organizational entities requiring autonomous system administration, the domain can be subdivided by authorized administrators into two or more hierarchical sub-domains. The NIS+ directory for the original domain, containing administrative information for domain-specific resources, can be partitioned into several directories, each supporting a new sub-domain. This process of creation of new domains and partitioning of directories can be continued as the network grows. NIS+ domain hierarchies provide the following features:

- NIS+ can be used as the administrative information repository for a range of networks–from very small to very large enterprise networks. NIS+ gracefully scales to support network growth so that the size of each NIS+ domain, and therefore of its directory, can be kept within manageable bounds, while the overall network can have unbounded growth.
- Information in NIS+ servers is visible to authorized users and applications across the domain hierarchy. Thus, NIS+ enables communication across the enterprise by

allowing authorized users to access resources, such as printers and servers, across domains.

- NIS+ can rapidly respond to queries from local clients for domain-specific information as directories supporting individual domains are smaller and more manageable.

As an example, figure 6.7 illustrates the process of domain creation and its benefits for a fictitious company, ACME Corporation.

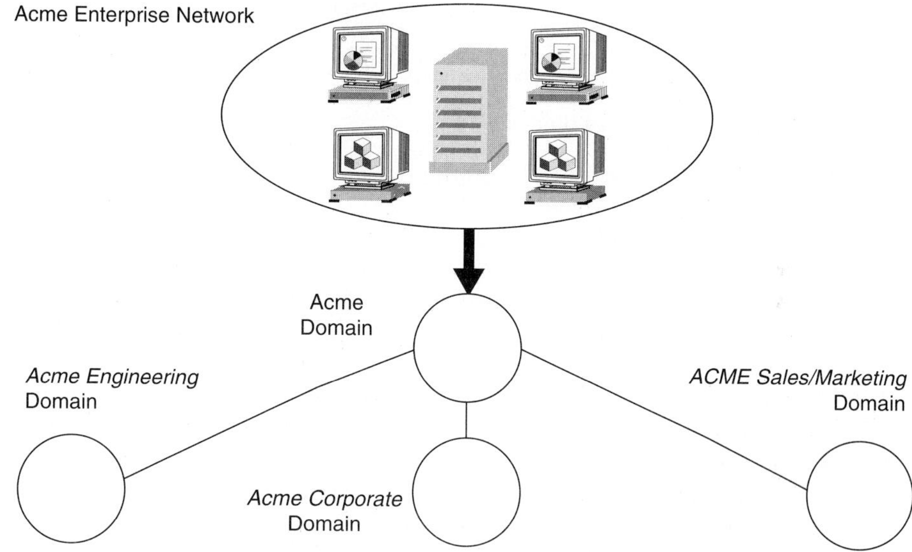

Figure 6.7 Creation of administrative domains.

Initially, NIS+ is used for centralized system and network administration of the Acme enterprise network. As Acme Corporation grows, the corresponding growth in size of its NIS+ directory, beyond supporting a few hundred systems, affects the directory's manageability and performance. Further, functional groups such as engineering and sales/marketing may choose to devote resources for autonomous administration of their networks, to off-load administration tasks from the central administration group and improve response time for such tasks as installing new users. NIS+ allows the ACME enterprise network to be subdivided into three autonomously administered domains: *Acme Corporate* domain, *Acme Engineering* domain, and the *Acme Sales/Marketing* domain. The NIS+ directory for the enterprise network can be partitioned easily into smaller directories, supporting the three new domains for increased manageability and performance.

As ACME Corporation grows and as further decentralized administration requirements emerge, the domain creation can be continued along functional group or other administratively intuitive lines. Figure 6.8 illustrates how ACME's network may be organized to promote continued administrative efficiency as it evolves.

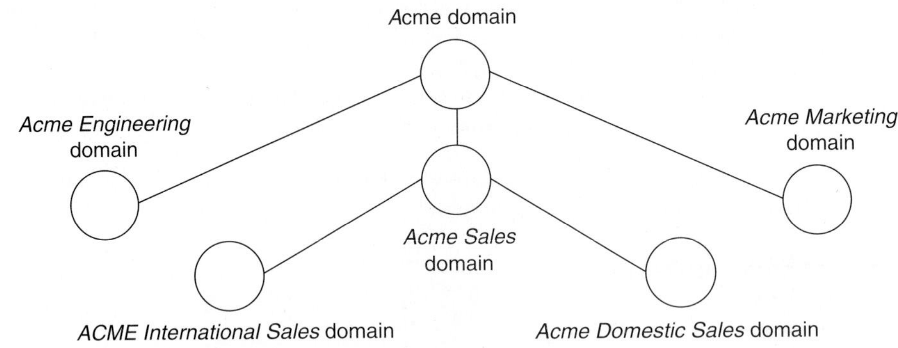

Figure 6.8 Hierarchical domains.

6.3.5.2 Highlights of Distributed Administration Model

NIS+ includes a flexible administrative interface that facilitates and automates administrative operations. Managing NIS+ servers, including creating directories and setting up domains and server replication, can be performed with ease. Information within NIS+ directories, which consists of a number of multi-column tables, can also be modified efficiently using the administrative interface.

Distributed NIS+ Server Administration: The NIS+ command-line or programmatic interface allows authorized administrators to interactively administer and add, delete, or change information in NIS+ servers, from systems across the domain or enterprise network. Administrators do not need to remotely log into or have super-user privileges on these servers in order to perform administrative functions. In addition, the interface allows the creation of scripts to automate execution of routine service administration tasks.

Distributed administration of the naming service allows efficiency, ease of growth, and setting of site-specific policies. For example, authority for specific NIS+ administration tasks for servers in different domains can be easily distributed to groups or personnel across the corporation, depending on their level of expertise and other considerations.

Distributed Access to NIS+ Information: An recent enhancement in NIS+, is that its command-line and programmatic interface allows authorized users direct read/write access to information served by NIS+. This access can further be controlled to a fine-granularity (discussed in section 6.3.8 entitled "Security in NIS+"). This makes it significantly easier and faster to change NIS+ tables and directories on servers, without requiring the creation of text files and conversion of these files into databases, as is required for updating information in NIS *maps*.

Tasks such as addition of users and systems to a particular domain only require changing information in that domain's NIS+ directory. These operations can also be performed remotely (i.e., from systems around the domain) without requiring super-user privileges or having to remotely log into NIS+ master servers.

To return to the Acme Corporation example, here is how the NIS+ hierarchical model and its information and administrative interfaces allow efficient administration of changes to the corporate network. As shown in figure 6.9, NIS+ servers in each domain of the Acme

Corp. maintain directories, consisting of multi-column tables, having administrative information on resources local to that domain. To accomplish an administration task, such as the addition of a new workstation and user within the *Acme Engineering* domain, changes need only be made to the NIS+ master server for that domain. Authorized users or administrators in the domain can use NIS+ table access utilities (either manually or programmatically) to easily add IP address, password, and aliases information to local NIS+ tables. Thus, a new user and system can be easily brought on-line in the *Acme Engineering* domain. Next, this new information is automatically transmitted to replicated servers for this domain using the NIS+ updating utility.

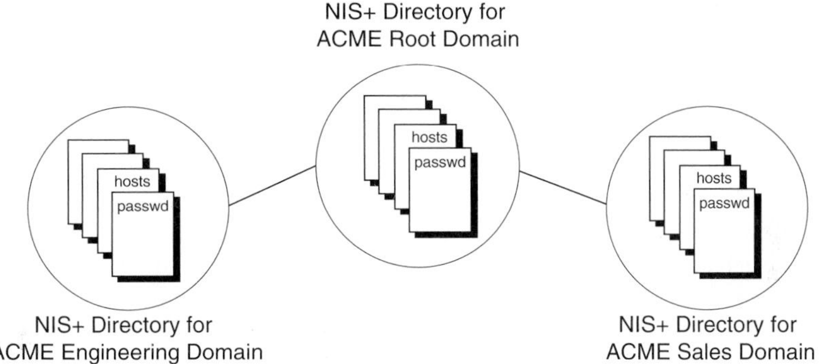

Figure 6.9 NIS+ Directories allow autonomous administration.

Through this simple set of operations, the new user and system are quickly visible to users and hosts across the *Acme* enterprise network, and network applications, such as electronic mail and remote file access, are easily enabled for the new user.

6.3.6 Table-Based Storage of Information

NIS+ directories consist of a set of tables containing domain-specific administrative information. There are 16 standard NIS+ tables for storage of different kinds of administrative information, including tables for host name and network address information, location of boot, swap, and dump partitions of diskless clients, and password information about every authorized NIS+ user or system. Tables have multiple columns and entries and each column in the table can be specified as searchable. Finally, tables can support ASCII as well as binary information.

NIS+'s multi-column tables, in conjunction with utilities allowing column-level access to this information, provide significant flexibility and ease in administering NIS+ information. Multi-column search capability of NIS+ tables also obviates the need to have reverse maps (as was required with NIS).

With NIS+, administrators can easily find the network address of a workstation by using its hostname–or vice versa. For the former task, the table search function looks through the Hostname column until it finds the hostname (*baseball,* in the example in figure 6.10), then moves along that entry to find the host's network address. NIS+ provides utilities for easy searching of tables for displaying, adding, modifying or deleting information in those tables.

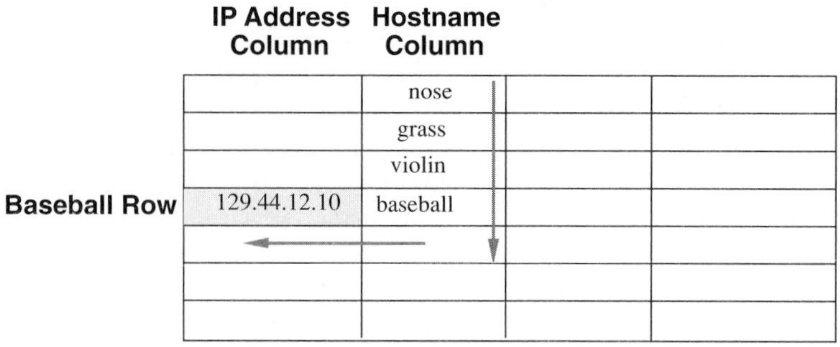

	IP Address Column	Hostname Column		
		nose		
		grass		
		violin		
Baseball Row	129.44.12.10	baseball		

Figure 6.10 NIS+ table search.

An additional area of flexibility within NIS+ is the ability to easily create new kinds of tables and store custom information in these tables. Access to these custom tables can be controlled on a selective basis (for further information on table access controls, see section 6.3.8).

NIS+ has no built-in limitations on the kind or size of information that can be stored in it. However, NIS+ is not a general-purpose distributed database or a full fledged directory service, such as OSI X.500 Directory Service, which is used to store large and complex amounts of information for inter-organizational networks. The design of NIS+ is *optimized* for storage of an enterprise network's administrative information, such as host addresses, e-mail aliases, network addresses, file system mount points, and user passwords.

There are significant practical constraints that will affect NIS+'s performance and efficiency, if used to store information that is not of this type. First and foremost is the resource constraint on NIS+ servers, which need to have adequate physical memory and disk space to support NIS+ directories. For example, if a NIS+ directory is used to store large binary files or tables having entries of bit-map image information, it would need high, possibly prohibitive, amounts of memory on an NIS+ server. Such data is better stored in NFS files, with NIS+ tables being used to store pointers to such files. Second, updating information, such as large files and bit-map images in NIS+ directories and tables, would cause degradation in update performance.

6.3.7 High -Performance Replication

The NIS+ replication model provides high performance, availability and reliability for naming service operations. This section discusses the benefits of the replication model and specific replication enhancements in NIS+ that allow improved performance and reliability for system administration.

6.3.7.1 Master and Slave Servers

NIS+ allows for a primary copy of a directory to be stored on a master server, with zero or more slave servers storing replicas of the primary copy. Updates are made only to the master server, which then propagates them to its replica servers. An NIS+ client can send lookup requests to any of the replicas and update requests to only the master server. This arrangement has two benefits: it avoids inconsistent updates between tables because only one master exists;

and it makes the NIS+ service much more reliable and available. If either master or slave is down, the other server can act as backup server for lookup requests.

Each domain in an NIS+ network has its own master server and may also have a number of slave replicated servers. The number of slave servers in a domain depends upon domain size and server capabilities, such as memory and swap space. The overall reliability of the network is enhanced when there are multiple master servers across the network, one for each domain, as opposed to a single master for an NIS network. If a master server is down, only updates for its particular domain are disabled, while updates to the rest of the network are not affected.

Finally, the NIS+ replication model allows for an improved server-to-client ratio, as the master and slave servers can serve clients on multiple IP subnets.

6.3.7.2 High-Performance Updating

One of the most significant enhancements in NIS+ is in the area of replica update performance. NIS updates, normally handled manually, usually took a day in large organizations. NIS+ master servers generally update replicated slave servers on an incremental basis (as opposed to the NIS case of whole *maps* being transferred from master to slave servers for updating). A change to a table in an NIS+ directory is automatically and instantaneously propagated by the master server to its replicas. The result is that updates are received by replica servers much more rapidly than before, allowing for rapid implementation of administration tasks, such as change of Ethernet or IP address information in NIS+ for system upgrade and relocation.

This new updating scheme has several additional benefits. It allows for efficient use of network bandwidth, since only the changes to the tables are transmitted from master to slave servers, as opposed to complete maps. In addition, slave servers are contacted only once with an aggregate update to all tables occurring within a short time interval, as opposed to separate updates for each map in the NIS case.

6.3.7.3 Reliable Updating

NIS+ updating model includes a transaction-based facility for consistent and reliable updating. It guarantees that the requested change has been made to the server's database correctly, even in face of failures. When a change is made to a table in an NIS+ directory, the NIS+ master server logs the update, waits for a few seconds for any further updates and then send its replica servers a message with the timestamp of the latest update. If replicas are out of date, they ask for updated information since their last updating.

The transaction log model provides rollback recovery and consistency of NIS+ databases, even in face of server failures during updates. NIS+ master and replica servers are able to automatically repair their databases to their state before such failures occur.

6.3.8 Security in NIS+

NIS+ is designed to protect the information in its directories and tables from unauthorized access. The goals of the security functionality in NIS+ are to not only prevent access to information in the NIS+ directories by unauthorized clients, but also to also ensure that unfriendly sources are not able to destroy or change such information. This functionality allows NIS+ to be a very secure repository of system and network administration information, without restricting the capability of changing information in NIS+ to only the super-user of the master server.

For example, an authorized user can create a table listing the home telephone number and address of members of the *Acme Engineering* domain as part of the domain's NIS+ directory, with access to this table limited to all or part of the Engineering organization. Or, a desktop application can create NIS+ tables of application-specific information which is required to have network-wide visibility. Or, finally, confidential personnel information, such as company identification number and job category for employees, can be stored in an NIS+ table granting authorized access on a very selective basis.

NIS+ controls access to servers, directories, and tables in two ways:

- *Authentication* to verify identity of a system or a user desiring access to NIS+.
- *Authorization* to control access to information stored in NIS+.

6.3.8.1 Authentication

Every request to a NIS+ server is actually made by a NIS+ *principal.* A NIS+ principal can be a user or workstation. *Authentication* is the process of identifying the principal who made a request to the NIS+ server by checking credentials, which are based on encrypted verification information stored in NIS+ tables. The purpose of authentication is to obtain the principal's name so that the principal's access rights to information in the name server can be looked up and verified. All interactions that a NIS+ principal has with a NIS+ server are authenticated.

In addition to protecting NIS+ information from access by untrusted clients, authentication provides much more flexible and secure administration of NIS+ servers. The use of authentication means that administrators do not need to have root privileges or remotely log into master servers. Authentication allows all authorized administrators to administer NIS+ servers from systems across the network.

NIS+ authentication can be turned off for sites that have minimal or no security requirements. However, this is hazardous because any NIS+ principal in such an environment could modify or destroy information in the master NIS+ directory by mistake and then have these changes quickly propagated to all slave servers in the domain.

6.3.8.2 Authorization

Once the identity of the NIS+ principal is known, *authorization* is used for granting users or systems access rights to NIS+ directories and tables, as shown in figure 6.11.

The first step in the process is a request for access to a table by an NIS+ principal to an NIS+ server. This request includes the principal's credentials for authentication purposes. The server then verifies the identity of the principal using its credentials. If the verification proceeds successfully, the NIS+ server looks up the definition of the table to verify that principal has rights (discussed in the following section) to access it, performs the principal's request and replies.

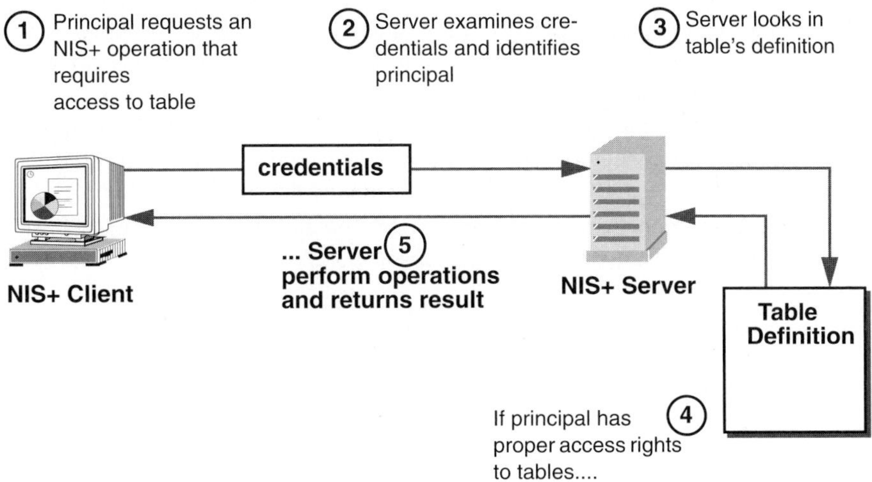

Figure 6.11 Use of authorization in controlling access to NIS+ tables.

Table and directory access rights: Access rights for tables or directories are granted not to specific NIS+ principals but to four categories of NIS+ principals: *Owner, Group, World,* and *Nobody.* The possible rights are *Read, Modify, Destroy* and *Create.*

The *Owner* is a NIS+ principal who owns that particular NIS+ directory, table or table entry. By default, a directory or table's owner is the principal who created it. A NIS+ *Group* is simply a collection of NIS+ principals, grouped together as a security convenience. The access rights granted to a NIS+ Group apply to all the principals who are members of that group. The *World* is the category of all NIS+ principals who are authenticated by NIS+. The *Nobody* class includes everybody, including all authenticated and *unauthenticated* NIS+ principals (see section 6.3.9.1 "NIS Compatibility Mode" for an explanation of unauthenticated NIS+ principals).

An NIS+ table or directory can grant one or more access rights to one or more categories of clients. For example, a directory could grant Read access to the World category, but Modify access only to the Group and Owner. NIS+ authorization supports flexible and secure administration. For example, the Group access right allows finer granularity of control for NIS+ administration. It can be used as a means of maintaining security and control as administrative authority evolves along decentralized lines. In the initial stages of NIS+ domain creation, a group consisting of only central administrative personnel could have Modify and Create access rights to directories across the network. As the domain creation evolves and administrative expertise builds up across the corporation, directories could grant such access rights to new groups consisting of local and central administrative personnel, allowing smooth transition of control.

Table column and entry security: In addition to the security assigned to the entire table, NIS+ tables provide additional levels of security allowing access to information stored in tables to be controlled at a finer granularity.

A NIS+ table itself provides two levels of security: *entry* and *column*. Access rights assigned to a table can apply to all the columns and entries in the table. In addition, individual columns and entries can assign multi-level access rights to NIS+ principals. A table may grant Read-only access rights to a group, which means that any member of the group can read the contents of the entire table but not modify it. A particular column, however, may then assign the group Modify rights. This means that although the group members can read the contents of the entire table, they can only modify the contents of that particular column.

As an example, take the case of a table containing three columns of host information for a particular domain: *Hostname*, *IP Address*, and *Ethernet Address*.

NIS+ Principal Category	Hostname	IP Address	Ethernet Address
Nobody			
Owner	Modify	Modify	Modify
Group	Modify	Modify	
World	Read	Read	Read

The table grants Read access rights to the World principal category. All authenticated users and systems will thus be able to read information in the table. Modify access for the Hostname and IP Address columns may further be given to the group allowing the domain administrative group to easily update the table as host names are changed and as hosts are moved to different subnets within the domain. The Ethernet address column, which is changed less frequently, provides Modify access only to the Owner. Thus, access rights can be flexibly controlled for each column and entry.

6.3.9 Compatibility with ONC NIS

NIS is supported on all major UNIX variants including SunSoft's Solaris® 1.0, DEC® Ultrix®, IBM® AIX™, and HP/UX™ c. In addition, PC-based products such as PC-NFS also provide client-side NIS support. NIS+ has been designed to be a replacement for environments and systems using NIS. It includes a number of capabilities that allow NIS clients and servers to not only coexist with but also migrate to NIS+. These capabilities, taken together, provide a number of options for NIS/NIS+ compatibility and migration.

NIS compatibility is included as a transition aid only, and applies primarily to support of NIS clients accessing an NIS+ server. NIS+ utilizes a completely new internal design with an advanced administrative model. The administration of NIS and NIS+ are very different for the reasons stated earlier. It is recommended that NIS+ not be run in NIS compatibility mode as a long term solution.

The specific capabilities allowing NIS/NIS+ migration and coexistence are:

- NIS+ servers running in NIS Compatibility Mode
- NIS+ for Solaris 1.0 systems

Table 6.2 Solaris NIS+/NIS Client and Server Compatibility

Client Type	*Solaris 2.x NIS+ Server*	Solaris 1.x[a] NIS+ Server	Solaris 1.x NIS Server	*ONC*[b] NIS Server
Solaris 1.*x*	Supported	Supported	Supported	Supported
Solaris 2.*x*	Supported	Supported	Supported	Supported
ONC[b] NIS	Supported	Supported	Supported	Supported

[a] There is a version of NIS+ that runs on a Solaris 1.X server.

[b] These are non-Solaris clients and servers running an operating system, such as IBM AIX, HP-UX, or DEC Ultrix, that supports NIS.

- The Name Service Switch
- Utilities allowing transfer of information from NIS maps to NIS+ tables and vice versa

6.3.9.1 NIS Compatibility Mode

NIS+ provides *an NIS Compatibility Mode*. This mode enables an NIS+ server to answer requests from NIS clients from other systems while continuing to answer requests from NIS+ clients. The NIS Compatibility Mode can be selected while setting up the NIS+ server. NIS clients require no additional setup or changes. In fact, they are not even aware that the server that is responding is not an NIS server.

An NIS+ server running in NIS Compatibility Mode has the same security requirements for both NIS+ *and* NIS clients as a normal NIS+ server. However, because NIS clients do not provide the credentials that NIS+ servers use to authenticate *all* clients, they end up classified as *unauthenticated* clients belonging to the *nobody* principal category. Therefore, to allow NIS clients to access any of the information in NIS+ tables, those tables must provide access rights to unauthenticated principals. Note, however, that an NIS client cannot update information in NIS+ tables, and that all administrative activity would have to be done from an NIS+ client.

NIS+ servers running in the NIS compatibility mode only respond to queries from NIS clients and do not exchange information with other NIS servers using the NIS server transfer protocols. However, NIS+ provides utilities (described below) that allow information in NIS+ and NIS to be synchronized and kept up-to-date.

6.3.9.2 Information Transfer Utilities

NIS+ includes utilities to transfer contents of an NIS map into an NIS+ table. The contents of the map can replace, be appended to, or be merged with, the contents of the NIS+ table. NIS maps containing both administrative and custom information can be transferred to NIS+ tables. In order for this utility to be used, the maps need to reside on or be transferred to a system running NIS+. In addition, NIS+ includes utilities allowing transfer of NIS+ tables into NIS maps on a Solaris 1.0 server. These maps can then be transferred to Solaris or non-Solaris NIS servers using NIS transfer utilities.

NIS+ information transfer utilities allow NIS+ master servers to provide up-to-date information to NIS master servers, or vice versa. In this way, NIS+ or NIS servers can effectively act as master servers for NIS or NIS+ sites respectively.

6.3.9.3 The Name Service Switch

The Name Service Switch is the means by which multiple name services can coexist, and by which administrators can set up policies for the use of such services. Although currently part of Solaris, the Switch will be made available to the ONC+ licensee community in the near future. The Switch allows systems to be clients of multiple naming services. Using the Switch, operating systems, applications and scripts can access system configuration information from the following sources:

- NIS+ tables
- NIS maps
- `DNS hosts` table
- Local `/etc` files

Once these services are set up, one can obtain system administration information from one or more of these sources, in place of, or in addition to NIS+ tables.

The Switch includes a configuration file that allows administrators to specify which name service(s) will be used for each type of configuration information, such as password and host IP address. Further, administrators can specify the order in which different naming services are used for each type of such information, and the criteria for search continuation if information is not found or if a naming service is unavailable. The Name Service Switch also allows the setting of flexible policies for naming service use. The Switch can be used to easily describe and change these policies once site requirements change.

The Switch allows systems to easily take advantage of information served by different naming services. For example, a system accessing the Switch could obtain its hosts information from an NIS+ table, its group information from NIS maps, and its password information from a local `/etc` file.

6.3.10 NIS+ and Other Naming/Directory Services

NIS+ is one among a number of naming services available for use in client/server computing environments. Directory services, a specialized form of naming services, are typically designed to support larger and more complex information about network entities.

This section presents an overview of the role of different types of naming and directory services in client/server environments, and the technologies for allowing interoperability across these services.

Each type of network entity, such as user, file, application, printer, or system, typically has its own naming system. Naming systems maintain a mapping of names with network entities, and allow applications and users to access these entities. These naming systems include:

- Enterprise or organizational naming services, such as NIS+, NIS, and OSF's DCE™ CDS (Distributed Computing Environment Cell Directory Service). These services facilitate communication within an organization or *cell* by maintaining and managing information about network entities, such as users and systems. Users and applications retrieve such information for location-independent access to these network entities.
- Naming systems that are typically integrated with application or system services. File systems used by operating systems such as UNIX and VMS have integrated naming systems defining syntax and access commands. Productivity applications such as stock quotation and personal calendar managers also typically have integrated naming systems.
- Global naming systems supporting the specific characteristics of inter-organizational communication, such as longer distances and delays, and differing levels of trust and administration policies. Global naming systems include Internet Domain Name System (DNS) and OSI X.500 Directory Services.

The properties of different network entities are sufficiently diverse to require use of a range of naming systems in client/server computing environments in the future. These properties include:

- Scalability or the size of the information base supported by a naming system. For example, a global host naming system, such as DNS, will be required to support information on hundreds of thousands of hosts, whereas a naming system supporting an enterprise network, such as NIS+, may need to have information on only tens of thousands of systems.
- Lifetime or frequency of updates on different network entities. For example, the file naming system needs to support much more rapid updating of file names and locations than NIS+ can reasonably handle. (NIS+, although able to support a much more dynamic information base than its predecessor, NIS, nonetheless assumes that changes to hostnames, passwords, etc., will be relatively infrequent.)

6.3.10.1 Interoperability Across Naming/Directory Services

The continued existence of multiple naming systems supporting different types of network entities presents a challenge for users and applications in transparently accessing resources across the heterogenous enterprise network. One strategy for such interoperability is to provide standard naming interfaces allowing applications to easily access information and resources supported by different naming systems. Two technologies supporting this goal are the Name Service Switch (described in section 6.3.9.3) and federated naming.

Name service switch: The Name Service Switch capability allows application and system software to use the UNIX/POSIX standard *getXXbyYY* naming interface to access naming information from NIS, NIS+, DNS, and `/etc` local configuration files to access resources within and beyond the enterprise. The switch design is modular, allowing it to easily accommodate other naming systems, such as CDS or X.500.

Federated naming: Federated naming is the second and more extensive solution for naming interoperability. Federated naming allows integrated and consistent support of multivendor naming systems, including global and enterprise naming services supporting high-level entities (such as hosts and users) and specialized naming systems for files, printers, spreadsheets, and personal calendars. Federated naming will create applications to consistently and easily access this diverse range of entities through a simple naming interface. In addition, the federated naming service interface will be published by SunSoft, allowing developers to easily incorporate their naming systems into the federated naming architecture.

6.4 Transport Independent Remote Procedure Calls (TI-RPC)

6.4.1 The Purpose of RPCs

The main purpose of Remote Procedure Calls (RPCs) is to help developers more easily design and implement distributed applications. Distributed applications are the next wave in empowering individuals and groups of users. They allow collaboration among groups of users at local or remote sites, through applications such as calendars, document processing and review, conferencing, and project management. They can also lessen the cost of computing by allowing expensive resources to be shared among many users on a network. Distributed application technology is currently being applied in many areas such as office automation, financial services, distributed databases, computer-aided design, and manufacturing.

RPCs make developing distributed applications easier by providing developers with a familiar local procedure call paradigm that can be applied to procedures which will execute remotely on other machines. This can greatly increase the speed and development of networked applications. Further, TI-RPC is run time transport independent, which means that one version of an application can run over multiple network transport mechanisms without modification. This reduces maintenance requirements and makes applications flexible to support new transports as they are added to the system.

Transport independent RPC (TI-RPC), developed by SunSoft (with USL), is designed to further simplify distributed application development by providing an RPC mechanism which is independent from the underlying network transport protocol. This means that developers no longer have to be network experts. They can focus on application functionality, instead of the network communication.

In addition, there are also tools available that aid in the development of TI-RPC based distributed applications. These compiler tools automate the creation of TI-RPC client and server source code routines.

In the remaining discussion, it is assumed that the reader is familiar with the concepts of BSD 4.2 sockets and UNIX System V Release 4 (SVr4) Transport Layer Interface (TLI) communication paradigms. A basic working knowledge of RPC is also assumed.

6.4.2 The Original ONC RPC Implementation

ONC RPC was originally implemented on UDP/IP and TCP/IP transports on top of the 4.2 BSD socket interface. The RPC mechanism was implemented through a library of routines to provide local procedure call semantics. The design was not based on any particular aspects of the underlying transport, but rather on the class of the transports: *connection oriented* or *connectionless*.

However, as the RPC implementation progressed, certain TCP/IP specific features (mainly naming and binding) found their way into the RPC library and the application developer had to be aware of some of the low-level details of network communication.

The reality of today's networks is that they are a collection of heterogeneous systems connected with a variety of transports. Therefore the goal of TI-RPC was to completely remove the reliance on any specific TCP/IP features, and to make the implementation generic enough so that all transports can be used with ease.

6.4.3 TI-RPC Design Principles

A main goal of the TI-RPC architecture design was to base the implementation on general transport classes rather than specific transports. As with RPC, this gives TI-RPC the flexibility to run on any transport that could be classified in either of the general classes. A further goal was to not require applications to be modified or recompiled in order to run on a new transport mechanism.

Briefly, the design goals of TI-RPC were to achieve the following:

- *Provide a simple and consistent way in which transports can be dynamically selected depending upon user preference and the availability of the transport.*
  The objective was to make developing network transparent applications easier, but also to allow knowledgable application developers to utilize network transport specific facilities if they wish.

- *Provide a uniform addressing mechanism which applications can use to address any entity on the network.*
  This means applications do not have to know about the different addressing, name binding, and resolution mechanisms for each transport.

- *Provide a generic interface to the underlying transports so that the TI-RPC library can talk to different transports in a unified fashion.*
  This makes TI-RPC more flexible to support new transport mechanisms as they are added to the system.

- *Provide the above goals without major changes to the ONC RPC interfaces or protocol.*
  This aids backward compatibility with the wide range of existing RPC-based applications and provides for a smooth transition from the earlier implementation to the new one.

6.4.4 Overall Architecture

TI-RPC design is based on three sets of interfaces: *Transport Layer Interface, Network Selection, and Name-to-Address Translatio*n as defined in the following:

- The Transport Layer Interface (TLI) module provides the mechanism through which the RPC library can communicate with any transport in a generic fashion.

- The Network Selection module provides the mechanism through which transports can be dynamically selected.
- The Name-to-Address Translation module provides the mechanism through which transport addresses can be referred to in a unified way. It is also used to translate host names to transport addresses.

In addition to these three modules, *rpcbind* (previously known as *portmap*) provides a registry of addresses of RPC services running on a machine. This eliminates the need for each RPC service to have a *well-known* transport specific address.

The TI-RPC architecture is shown in figure 6.12. More detailed information on these modules and on rpcbind is covered in the following sections.

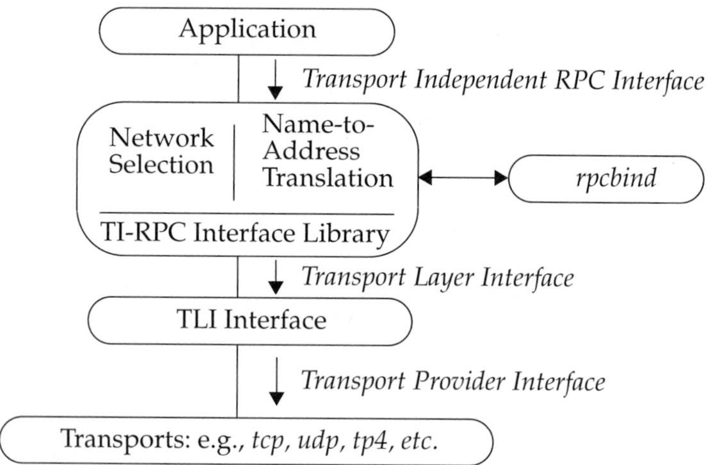

Figure 6.12 TI-RPC architecture.

6.4.4.1 Transport Layer Interface

There are two main communication paradigms through which transports can be addressed in a transport independent manner: Sockets and the Transport Layer Interface (TLI). The TLI package contains a general, flexible set of tools for development of SVr4 UNIX system communication services. The TLI standard interface enables modular and portable development of network services and their components. TLI provides a protocol independent application interface to distributed services based upon the service definitions of the OSI reference model.

TLI was utilized to support TI-RPC due to its protocol-independence, its well-defined layered model, and its better negotiating primitives. TLI divides transports into three classes: connectionless (datagram), connection-oriented (virtual circuit), and connection-oriented-with-orderly-release. The design of TI-RPC is based on this division.

6.4.4.2 Network Selection Mechanism

In many existing distributed applications, either the transport information is hard-coded in the application itself or the application is required to be linked in with special transport libraries. This approach sufficed in the past because there were very few transports and the application developer could afford to support separate applications for each transport.

With the growth in the number of available transports and the fact that the application developer can no longer assume availability of a given transport on the machine, it has become very difficult for application developers to support applications on different transports. Moreover, application users do not want to deal with the cost or complexity of having multiple copies of the same application to run on different transport types. Finally, because there are multiple network transport mechanisms to choose from, applications must be flexible to run on any new transport that may be added to their machine in the future.

The network selection mechanism provides the means to choose the transport on which an application should run at *run time*. Run time transport independence means applications do not have to be compiled separately for each transport. The network selection mechanism is based upon two inputs, the `netconfig` database (`/etc/netconfig`) and the optional environment variable *NETPATH*. The netconfig database lists the transports available on the host, including information about the transport such as its type, device name, and name to address translation module. A sample netconfig file is illustrated in figure 6.13.

```
#netidtypeflagsfamily      protocol   device address   loadable module
udptpi_cltsvinet           udp        /dev/udp         /usr/lib/tcpip.so
tcptpi_cots_ordvinet       tcp        /dev/tcp         /usr/lib/tcpip.so
tp4tpi_cotsvosi            -          /dev/tp4         /usr/lib/iso.so
ticltstpi_cltsvloopback    -          /dev/ticlts      /usr/lib/straddr.so
ticotstpi_cotsvloopback    -          /dev/ticots      /usr/lib/straddr.so
```

Figure 6.13 Sample */etc/netconfig* file.

Each transport entry in the database contains a unique identifier (*netid*) by which it is normally referred. *netid* has significance only on the local machine. The same transport on two different machines can have two different *netid*. The *type* field specifies the type of the transport (connectionless, connection-oriented, or connection-oriented-with-orderly-release). This can be one of the criteria which applications use to pick a transport. This is an important parameter because the semantics of the remote procedure call depend upon the class of the transport used. The *flags* field specifies whether this transport is available (visible) applications[5].

The *family* and the *protocol* fields identify the family name and the protocol name of the transport, respectively. These fields are used when an application is looking for a specific transport family and protocol. For example, an application may wish to run only on TP4/OSI because it uses some transport specific features. The *device address* field gives the file name of the transport device. The *loadable module* field has the name of the *name to address translation* module which does the name resolution. These dynamically loadable shared libraries are linked into the application at run time. The TI-RPC library uses this shared library to resolve host names for the chosen transport. The actual functionality of the name to address translation module is discussed in section 6.4.4.3.

---

[5]Some transports may not be available because they are being used for "experimental" reasons.

Loopback transports: The last two entries in the sample netconfig database list the loopback transports (*ticlts* and *ticots*). Loopback transports are used for registering services with the TI-RPC registration service, *rpcbind. rpcbind* also uses them to find out the actual owner of the RPC service. Loopback transports can be used for testing and development when no other transports are available on the machine.

6.4.4.3 Name-to-Address Translation Mechanism

All transports have their own specific ways of addressing network entities. For example, a TCP/IP address consists of a port number and an IP host address. The same address can be represented in different ways depending upon the machine architecture or the transport interface. For example, *sockets* and *TLI* have different address structures. Even for the same transport interface, implementations exist in which different structure information is used. For example, the length of *sockaddr_in* address structure for UDP is 8 bytes in some implementations, while in others, it is 16 bytes.

TI-RPC provides a transport independent addressing scheme that allows addresses to be exchanged between networked processes without worrying about the transport interface or the transport implementation. To make this address representation useful, it is essential that there be a universal representation of addresses for every transport family which can be understood by all implementations of that transport. For example, a universal representation of a TCP/IP address could look like *h1.h2.h3.h4.p1.p2*, where *h1...h4* denote the IP address of the host and *p1.p2* denote the port number of the transport endpoint. This address can be exchanged between clients and servers, who can then translate it to their own local representation of the transport address. If there is a mechanism to translate between the specific transport layer address and the universal representation, transport independent addressing can be achieved.

The term *universal address* refers to the concept of universal representation. A universal address is a string representation of a transport address. This representation is particularly useful in the scenarios described above because these addresses can be referred to in a uniform way. However, a universal address by itself is meaningless—it is essential to know the transport family associated with it. The universal address format for each transport family may be different. The authority for a given transport will decide the format of its universal addresses. For example, the Internet's transport authority is the *Network Information Center (NIC)*. The NIC decides the format of the universal addresses for UDP/IP and TCP/IP.

For each transport family, translation routines are provided to translate the universal address to transport specific address and vice-versa. When a client wants to know the address of a particular TI-RPC service, it inquires rpcbind, the TI-RPC registry service on the server's host. The TI-RPC service addresses are passed in universal address format to the client application by the rpcbind service. The client then calls the transport specific translation routines to convert the universal address into the local transport specific TLI address structure called *netbuf.* The client can then use this transport address to contact the server.

6.4.4.4 Rpcbind

Rpcbind (formerly *portmap*) is a daemon process running on the server machine that lets clients look up the transport addresses of registered TI-RPC services in a standard way. rpcbind maps a TI-RPC program numbers, version numbers, and *netid* of the transports supported by a TI-RPC server on a given machine to universal addresses on which the services are *listening*. A client can therefore ask rpcbind for the transport specific universal address of the TI-RPC service with which it wants to communicate.

Rpcbind is the only TI-RPC service on the host that has a well known address. Thus rpcbind eliminates the need for *each* RPC server application to have a well known transport specific universal address. Rpcbind is assigned the port number 111 for both UDP and TCP.

Each transport authority must specify a well known address for rpcbind. The well known address of rpcbind on local loopback transports is the string *rpcbind*. Other TI-RPC server processes can be assigned network addresses statically or dynamically. Dynamic addresses must be registered with rpcbind on the server machine. However, rpcbind is not required if the address is static.

6.4.4.5 New in rpcbind Version 4

In version 4 of rpcbind, some new routines were added to the rpcbind client interface library. One requiring special mention is the `rpcb_getaddrrlist` routine. With this routine, clients can determine the universal address of the server without having to know the transport protocol ahead of time as was the case with version 3. `rpcb_getaddrrlist` returns information about the server's transport, it's type, protocol, family name, and the universal address to the client. `rpcb_getaddrrlist` further increases efficiency by allowing the client to find the transport on which the server is listening without going through the process of binding to each of the transports specified in the *NETPATH*.

6.4.5 New Interfaces to TI-RPC

An application must choose an appropriate transport because the semantics of a remote procedure call depend upon the semantics of the transport. These applications can roughly be divided into three classes, depending upon the type of transport they use:

- Applications which do not worry about any particular semantics associated with the underlying transport. These applications are the ones which will be most portable.
- Applications that need at-most-once semantics associated with their remote procedure calls, or those that want to send a stream of data across the network. These applications will use connection oriented transports.
- Applications that support idempotent operations. Their remote procedure calls normally require at-least-once semantics. These applications may use connectionless transports. Their argument and result size may be limited to the maximum data size of the transport.

New TI-RPC interfaces provide the functionality required by these three classes of applications as well as providing an interface to any particular transport of the application's choice.

The main focus here is on the TI-RPC interfaces through which the application creates the client or the server handles. Most of the transport *dependent* information (such as server address, transport name) is stored in these handles. Multiple client handles can be created so that an application can use both sets of semantics (idempotent and at-most-once) in the same instance of client. The new interfaces can be divided into the following classes: client side RPC layers, server side RPC layers, and simplified interfaces.

Four layers of client and server creation routines have been provided so that application programmers can choose an appropriate layer suitable for their applications. The topmost RPC layer, which is above the network selection layer, takes a *nettype* parameter through which an application can specify the class of transports on which it wants to run. *Nettype* can take one of the following values:

- *VISIBLE*: Choose the transports which have the visible flag *v* set in the netconfig database. The entries which do not have the *v* flag set are not for normal use. *VISIBLE* should be used by applications that want to use the transports listed in the netconfig database and do not care about user preference.
- *CIRCUIT_V*: Same as *VISIBLE* except it chooses only connection-oriented (with or without orderly-release) transports.
- *DATAGRAM_V*: Same as *VISIBLE* except it chooses only connectionless (datagram) transports.
- *NETPATH*: Choose the transports which have been indicated by their *netid* in the *NETPATH* variable. If *NETPATH* is not set, it defaults to *VISIBLE*. This should be used by those applications which care about user's preference.
- *CIRCUIT_N*: Same as *NETPATH* except it chooses only connection-oriented (with or without orderly-release) transports.
- *DATAGRAM_N*: Same as *NETPATH* except it chooses only connectionless (datagram) transports.
- *udp*: This is for backward compatibility with the earlier implementation and refers to the Internet UDP transport (family = *inet* and protocol = *udp*).
- *tcp*: This is for backward compatibility with the earlier implementation and refers to the Internet TCP transport (family = *inet* and protocol = *tcp*).

6.4.6 Client Side RPC Layers

On the client side, the interface layers can be drawn as illustrated in figure 6.14.

In `clnt_create( )`, an attempt is made to create a client handle from among the transports belonging to the class *nettype*. It successively tries to bind with the server using each transport until it succeeds or the list of transports is exhausted. `clnt_create( )` is used by applications that care only about the type of transport (circuit versus datagram) and are not concerned about the actual transport over which the services are rendered. The means of specifying a particular transport is through setting the environment variable *NETPATH* or by choosing an appropriate nettype value. `clnt_create( )` is the most general interface to the underlying client side RPC layer.

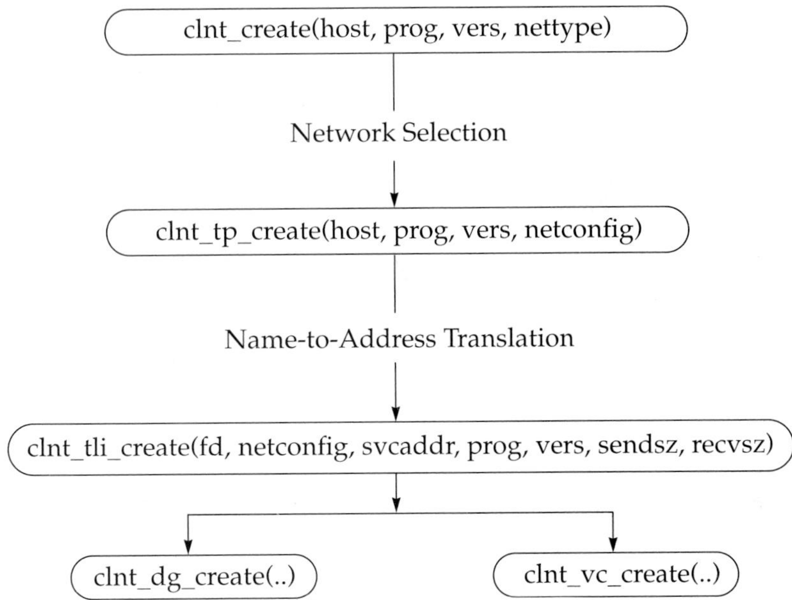

Figure 6.14 Client side interface layers.

Below the network selection layer is `clnt_tp_create( )`. Instead of the *nettype* variable, it is passed a *netconfig* structure returned by the network selection routines. It relies on rpcbind and name-to-address translation library routines to do host name and service mapping. The `clnt_tp_create( )` routine is used by applications that want to use a particular transport and are not interested in the other aspects of client connection such as server address and receive and send buffer sizes. Default buffer sizes appropriate to the transport are chosen.

At the third level is the transport-specific `clnt_tli_create( )` routine which deals with *TLI netbuf* addresses. It can be passed a *TLI* file descriptor for the connection, which may be bound and connected. If the descriptor is not open, `clnt_tli_create( )` will attempt to open and bind it, using the supplied `netconfig` structure. The `netconfig` structure contains the name of the file to be opened. Depending upon whether the transport is datagram or circuit oriented, one of the two lower level routines (`clnt_dg_create( )` or `clnt_vc_create( )`) is invoked. If the buffer size (`sendsz` or `recvsz`) is zero, an appropriate value is obtained through `t_getinfo( )`. This routine does not perform any RPC binding to the server. It is the responsibility of the caller to specify the address of the remote server. This level is used by applications which do not want to use the default parameters. For example, UDP or TCP reserved ports can be passed to this layer or the application that already knows the address of the remote server can use this layer.

clnt_dg_create( ) and clnt_vc_create( ) are the lowest level interfaces which create the client handle depending upon the class of transport. These routines are not normally used directly by the application developer.

The changes to the client side to make RPC transport-independent are limited to the client creation routines. The existing interface to make the actual RPC (clnt_call( )) remains unchanged.

6.4.7 Server Side RPC Layers

The server side layers are symmetrical to the client side RPC layers. The server side interface layers can be drawn as illustrated in figure 6.15.

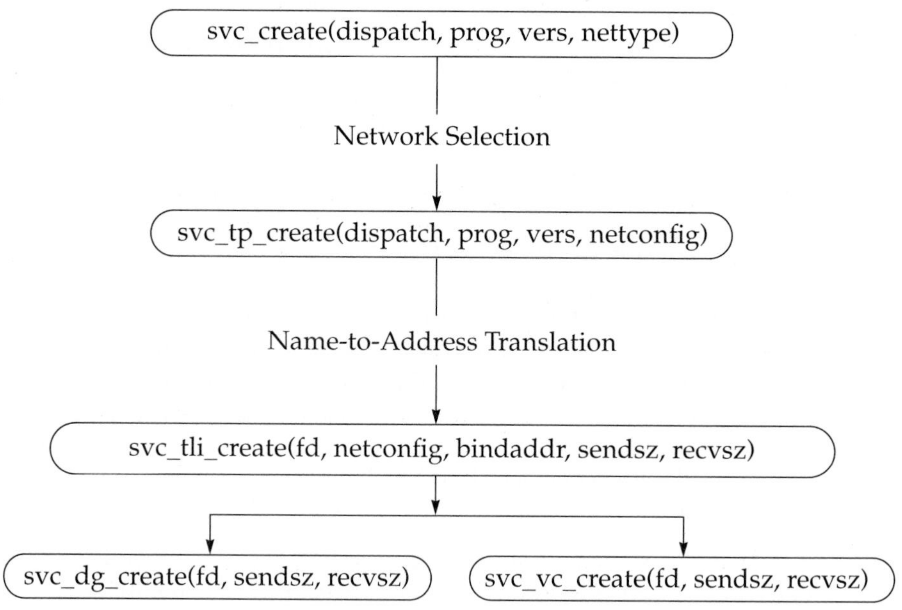

Figure 6.15 Server side interface layers.

On the topmost layer is the svc_create( ) routine. nettype takes any of the values discussed earlier. A server that uses svc_create( ) would listen for the requests on transports belonging to the given nettype. svc_create( ) also registers the service with rpcbind. svc_create( ) is used by applications which may care about the type of transport (circuit versus datagram) but are not concerned about the actual transport over which the services are offered. The way to specify a particular transport is through use of the *NETPATH* environment variable. The use of this layer provides for transport-independence.

Below the network selection layer is the `svc_tp_create( )` routine. It registers the service with rpcbind and sets up a server to listen for requests on the specified transport. `svc_tp_create( )` is used by applications which want to use a particular transport, but are not interested in selecting the other parameters such as bind address and receive and send buffer sizes. Default buffer sizes appropriate to the transport are chosen.

On the third layer is the transport-specific `svc_tli_create( )` routine. It can be passed a TLI file descriptor of the connection, which may already be bound. If the descriptor is not open, `svc_tli_create( )` will attempt to open and bind it using the *netconfig* structure obtained via the network selection routines. If `sendsz` or `recvsz` is zero, appropriate buffer values are obtained via `t_getinfo( )`. Depending upon whether the transport is datagram or circuit-oriented, one of the two lower level routines (`svc_vc_create( )` or `svc_dg_create( )`) is invoked. It is the responsibility of the user to register the service with rpcbind. This level is used by applications which do not want to use the default parameters. For example, a reserved UDP or TCP bind address can be passed to this layer.

On the lowest rung of the server-create ladder, we have `svc_vc_create( )` and `svc_dg_create( )` routines. They set up the actual server handle depending upon the class of transport. Normally, these routines are not used directly.

As on the client side, the changes to the server side to make it transport-independent are limited to the server creation routines. All the other existing interfaces for handling of the calls remain unchanged.

6.4.8 Easy-to-Use TI-RPC Interfaces

A set of routines are provided for TI-RPC usage that do not require creating handles. They make a few assumptions (such as time-out values for the RPC), but make it easier for the programmer to get the job done. The routines for the client and server side are as follows.

- *rpc_call*(host, prog, vers, proc, inproc, in, outproc, out, nettype) – client side
- *rpc_reg*(prog, vers, proc, progname, inproc, outproc, nettype) – server side

In `rpc_call( )`, the *host* parameter specifies the name of the host where the server is located; *prog*, *vers* and *proc* uniquely identify the service that the client wants. *In* and *out* are the arguments and the results of the call, respectively. *Inproc* and *outproc* are the XDR routines for the arguments and results, respectively. *Nettype* takes any of the values discussed earlier. With `rpc_reg()`, the server need not create a separate dispatch function; instead, the routine *progname* that handles the procedure is supplied.

6.4.9 Backward Compatibility

The TI-RPC protocol is backward compatible with the RPC protocol. Most of the changes made were in the routines that *created* client and server handles. No changes were made to other routines which *use* client or server handles. The routines from the earlier implementation have been implemented in terms of the newer TLI-based interface.

The earlier implementation was compatible with the notion of UDP and TCP *reserved* ports. This is a very transport and operating system specific concept and its support has been replaced by a transport independent mechanism. The root process can bind itself to a reserved port, using `netdir_options( )` and subsequently calling `clnt_tli_create( )`.

Old Interfaces		New Interfaces
clnttcp_create( ), clntudp_create( )	:	clnt_tli_create( )
svctcp_create( ), svcudp_create( )	:	svc_tli_create( )
callrpc( )	:	rpc_call( )
registerrpc( )	:	rpc_reg( )
clnt_broadcast( )	:	rpc_broadcast( )

Because backward compatibility with existing applications was desirable, applications that do not make any explicit socket system calls are source compatible with the new implementation. Applications that make socket system calls require some minor changes.

Rpcbind (version 3, 4) is backward compatible with portmap (version 2). Services that register with portmap also get registered with rpcbind and vice-versa (only for UDP and TCP).

6.4.10 Secure RPC

Secure RPC provides network authentication for TI-RPC, enabling the development of secure distributed applications and network services. Authentication involves verifying the client's identity for network operations. This is achieved by the client and server using cryptographic algorithms to demonstrate that they know a secret, for example a special key value, without actually revealing it.

There are currently three authentication *flavors* that can work in conjunction with TI-RPC:

- UNIX
- Kerberos 4.0
- DES

TI-RPC is also extensible to support new and emerging authentication mechanisms in the future. For more detailed information on the mechanisms of specific authentication flavors, refer to Chapter 4.

6.4.11 TI-RPC Developer Tools

In order to make the development of TI-RPC based applications easier, there are a variety of tools available that can automatically generate TI-RPC function calls once the interfaces have been specified. Included with ONC+ is a code generator tool called *rpcgen* which provides basic toolkit capability and is described in section 6.4.11.2. SunSoft also provides a production quality developer toolkit called the *ONC+ RPC Application Toolkit* which enables more extensive customization of TI-RPC based applications. In addition, NobleNet, Inc. offers a toolkit called EZ-RPC™ which offers similar capability[6].

6.4.11.1 The ONC+ RPC Application Toolkit

SunSoft offers an unbundled developer toolkit called the ONC+ RPC Application Toolkit. The ONC+ RPC Application Toolkit consists of a protocol compiler based upon RPC TOOL™ technology from Netwise, Inc. and a collection of supporting libraries.

The ONC version of RPC TOOL accepts an RPC specification as input and produces client or server source code files and client or server header files for an application. The RPC specification describes the RPC specific interface or relationship between the client and server application processes within an application. In the specification the programmer declares every procedure that is called by the client application across the client/server interface, listing all of the parameters and external variables that are passed to or returned from each procedure. The specification is written in Input Specification Language (C-ISL) which is based on the C language standard produced by the American National Standards Institute (ANSI). The same RPC specification file is used as input to the ONC RPC TOOL code generator twice: once to generate client RPC code and again to generate server RPC code.

The specification also contains information on communication links made between the client and server processes during remote procedure calls. These links, or RPC bindings as they are referred to, are managed by the RPC code. The developer must determine whether a binding should remain in effect for a single remote procedure call or for the duration of several remote procedure calls.

The input specification is fed in to the ONC RPC TOOL. The tool outputs source code files containing structured and tested code that handles all communication required for the remote procedure calls declared in the RPC specification. The application-specific procedures contained in the RPC source code files can be divided into two groups. One group supports network communication and is comprised of the client stubs, server stubs, and dispatcher. The stubs and dispatcher establish communication links between software components running on different networked computers, or different processes on the same computer. The other group of procedures is comprised of `pack` and `unpack` procedures. These procedures convert data structures that are passed between communicating processes into a standard format for transmission across the network. The encoded information is transferred across the network in Protocol Data Units (PDUs).

The client stubs, server stubs, and dispatcher are structured as state machines. They are built in a straight-forward manner that is easily understandable. perhaps more importantly, this structure lends itself easily to customization. A state machine is characterized by an orderly movement from one defined state to another. Each state has an associated set of instructions that performs a particular task. Completion of the instructions associated with one state signals movement to the next state and the execution of its instructions. When instructions in the final state have executed, the procedure returns.

---

[6]Note EZ-RPC is not covered in this manuscript

Client stub: Every time the RPC Code Generator encounters a remote procedure declaration within an RPC specification, it produces a client stub. Each client stub corresponds to a specific remote procedure and is designed to behave exactly like that remote procedure from the perspective of the client application code. The client stub has the same name as its corresponding remote procedure and, when called by the client application, accepts the same parameters and variables as the remote procedure. The client stub transfers values across the network to the server process. On return, the client stub receives values transferred from the remote procedure and, barring errors on the network, makes them available to the client applications's calling procedure.

After the client stubs have been linked with the client application code, the stubs act as surrogates for the procedures that execute remotely in a distributed application. The calling sequence for the client stub is the same as that of the remote procedure. This means that when a procedure is distributed to one or more remote computers, the basic mechanism for calling procedures in an application remains unchanged.

Dispatcher: Within the RPC code generated for the server process, the ONC RPC TOOL creates from the RPC specification, a single dispatcher procedure. The dispatcher is responsible for directing a request PDU received from a client process to the correct server stub. The RPC TOOL code generator automatically assigns every remote procedure an RPC number; the dispatcher determines whether a client process is requesting a valid remote procedure by checking this number.

Server stub: When the ONC RPC TOOL code generator encounters a remote procedure declaration within an RPC specification, it creates a server stub. Each server stub corresponds to a specific remote procedure.

The server stub receives values transferred from the client stub and actually calls the remote procedure, passing appropriate parameters and variables. To the remote procedure, the server stub has the appearance of and behaves exactly like the calling procedure. When the remote procedure returns, the sever stub packs and transfers the return value and any other values needed by the calling procedure.

Pack and unpack procedures: The RPC source code files also contain pack and unpack procedures. These procedures are based on information provided in the RPC specification concerning complex data types that are transferred across the network. The pack and unpack procedures ensure that the information passed between computers on the network is interpreted correctly.

The pack procedures encode information into the XDR format. The XDR format specifies that values are encoded as fixed-sized elements in the PDU. The unpack procedures decode the transmitted data into standard C structures that adhere to the format used by the machine receiving the PDU.

The code generator produces two sets of pack and unpack procedures—one used by the client stub and one used by the server stub. The pack and unpack procedures for the client stub pack the request PDU and unpack the reply PDU.

Server control libraries: The ONC+ RPC Application Toolkit also provides the RPC server control libraries for implementing basic server control capability for your server process. This library is accessible through the Standard Control Interface that consists of three procedures which start, run and stop a server process. The ONC RPC TOOL code generator can automatically generate code that calls the procedures in the Standard Control Interface.

6.4.11.2 The Rpcgen Compiler

ONC+ includes a bundled code generator compiler called *rpcgen.* In its latest release, rpcgen has been converted to use TI-RPC. Like the ONC+ RPC Application Toolkit, rpcgen reduces development time that would otherwise be spent coding and debugging low level network routines. It accepts a remote program interface definition written in a language called RPC Language which is similar to the C language. It produces C language output for RPC programs. This output includes skeleton versions of the client routines, a server skeleton, XDR filter routines for both parameters and results, a header file that contains common definitions and, optionally, dispatch tables which the server can use to check authorizations and then invoke service routines.

The client skeletons' interface with the RPC library can effectively hide the network from their callers. The server skeleton similarly hides the network from the server procedures that are to be invoked by remote clients. Rpcgen's output files can be compiled and linked in the usual way. The server code generated by rpcgen has support for `inetd` which means the server can be started via `inetd` or at the command line.

The developer writes server procedures in any language that observes system calling conventions and links them with the server skeleton produced by rpcgen to get an executable server program. To use a remote program, a programmer writes an ordinary main program that makes local procedure calls to the client skeletons. Linking this program with rpcgen's skeletons creates an executable program. Rpcgen options can be used to suppress skeleton generation and to specify the transport to be used by the server skeleton.

6.4.11.3 Rpcinfo

`Rpcinfo` is a useful tool which can be used to report information about RPC services, including whether a service is currently available or which versions of the services are supported. It can also be used to list all the services registered with `rpcbind`. It is also possible to *ping* a known RPC service by specifying its transport and universal address.

6.5 Conclusion

Today's networks are exploding in size and complexity. Enterprises are becoming increasingly global in scope. As networks grow, users need increasingly secure, transparent and easy access to information. ONC+ includes a full set of distributed services designed to meet the needs of users in today's global enterprise environments.

The NFS distributed file system, originally developed in 1985, has evolved beyond a simple file sharing service for local area networks. NFS includes autofs, a more efficient automatic mounting facility which gives users transparent and consistent access to files. A client file caching service called CacheFS improves NFS performance by caching data to the local file system and increases server scalability by reducing per client load on the server. NFS can be tailored to meet the security needs of specific environments by offering the optional use of a variety of authentication flavors. Near term enhancements to NFS include the ability to connect NFS clients and servers over wide area networks, and a revision to the NFS protocol providing performance and scalability improvements.

The Network Information Service Plus (NIS+) is an enterprise name service designed to replace the widely installed ONC Network Information Service (NIS). NIS+ is a secure and robust repository of information about network entities, such as users, servers, and printers, enabling efficient administration of enterprise client/server networks. Administration tasks such as addition, removal, or reassignment of systems and users are facilitated through efficient addition to or modification of information in NIS+. Important enhancements in NIS+ increased scalability, greater performance, flexible security. Because of it's ability to simplify administration tasks, NIS+ lowers the cost of ownership of enterprise client/server networks.

Distributed application design and implementation is greatly aided using ONC+ technology. TI-RPC provides a transport independent remote procedure call platform that allows developers to distribute application tasks across a network of multiplatform resources. Code generation tools such as rpcgen, ONC+ RPC Application Toolkit and EZ-RPC, greatly reduce the time and effort required to build networked client/server applications.

ONC+ is continuing to grow and evolve to meet the future needs and requirements of global enterprise users. It is a key component of multiple standards profiles.

Sally A. Biles is a senior marketing manager for ONC+ networking technology at SunSoft, Inc. a subsidiary of Sun Microsystems, Inc. She is an honors graduate of the University of California, Santa Cruz, and received her bachelors degree in Computer and Information Science in 1983. She has ten years experience in network engineering and marketing. She has been an employee of Sun Microsystems since 1989.

Chapter 7

The OSF Distributed Computing Environment (DCE)

David Chappell
Chappell & Associates

7.1 Introduction

Distributed applications can offer many advantages over their more traditional single-system brethren. Actually building distributed applications, however, can be quite challenging. They require supporting services, things like a protocol allowing the application's various pieces to communicate, a directory service to locate those pieces, and mechanisms for providing security. It's not uncommon today for each distributed application to use custom-built supporting services, created just for that application. Doing this makes about as much sense as writing single-system applications each with its own custom operating system, that is, in most cases, it makes no sense at all. A better approach is to factor out the common support services required for distributed applications into one common infrastructure, then build those applications on top.

Many vendors have already done this for their own environments. These proprietary solutions, while often including excellent technology, are not really appropriate for an increasingly multi-vendor world. Since no single vendor has had their complete solution accepted by all of the others, a user cannot build distributed applications that effectively span an arbitrary collection of systems. What is needed is a broadly supported infrastructure for building distributed applications.

Providing this infrastructure is exactly the goal of the Open Software Foundation's Distributed Computing Environment (DCE). With promised support from most major vendors, DCE is a vendor-neutral platform for supporting distributed applications. Among the services it provides are support for remote procedure calls (RPCs), a directory service, security services, and a distributed file system. Taken together, these services provide something analogous to an operating system for distributed applications.

7.2 How DCE Was Created

The Open Software Foundation (OSF) is a membership organization devoted to the creation of vendor-neutral software infrastructures. In general, OSF does not create technologies from scratch. Instead, it takes advantage of work already done by vendors, universities, and anyone else active in an area of interest. For DCE, as for its other technologies, OSF issued a request for technology (RFT). An RFT is a brief document describing what problems OSF wishes to solve and soliciting solutions for those problems. For DCE, the problems included a mechanism for communication between parts of a distributed application, a way for these parts to find each other, security services for the application, and several more things. The RFT was widely distributed and anyone, OSF member or not, could respond.

The response to an RFT is not just a description of a proposed solution. To be a contender, actual working code must ultimately be provided, typically from a product the submitter already sells. OSF employees and a team of outside experts evaluated the submissions for each area, then selected those that they believed provided the best solutions. The code comprising those solutions, almost entirely written in C, was then integrated into a coherent whole by OSF and made available to the world.

Anyone can license the DCE source code, but most licensees are system vendors and large software vendors. End-users will typically buy shrink-wrapped DCE products from these vendors rather than license the DCE source directly from OSF (of course, some of the money vendors receive for these DCE products is paid to OSF as royalties, and some of that money is paid as royalties to the original creators of the technologies).

DCE 1.0 was released by OSF in January 1992. Early products based on this code began to appear by the end of that year, with a larger set of more complete DCE products available in 1993. Actual distributed applications based on DCE appeared as DCE itself became available.

7.3 DCE Components: RPC

DCE is not a simple thing, comprising as it does well over one million lines of source code. It consists of several different components, each of which depend to a greater or lesser extent on the others. Perhaps the most fundamental of those components is DCE's mechanism for remote procedure call (RPC).

Traditional applications written in a high-level language almost universally are broken into a series of procedures (also called subroutines or functions). Each of these procedures generally takes some number and type of parameters, performs some function, and returns some kind of result. When making the jump to distributed applications, starting with this familiar procedural model is very attractive. A fairly obvious way to support distributed applications via this paradigm is to separate the caller of the procedure from the procedure body, to let the first execute on one machine and the second on another. To the caller, these procedures behave much the same as ordinary procedures. Their remoteness, and the fact that they may actually execute on some other system entirely, is hidden.

RPC fits very naturally into a client/server model. The process that invokes a remote procedure is the client, requesting some service, while the process that executes that procedure is the server. And despite its prominence in DCE, RPC is not a new idea; DCE's RPC component is derived from the Network Computing System developed by Apollo (now part of Hewlett-Packard).

7.3.1 Implementing RPC

While RPC is an undeniably elegant concept, actually implementing it requires some work. For example, client and server must agree on exactly how each remote procedure should be invoked. In DCE RPC, this agreement is embodied in an *interface*. Each interface contains the definitions for one or more procedures and their parameters expressed in DCE's Interface Definition Language (IDL). For a simple picture of IDL, imagine ANSI C with only function prototypes, typedefs, and constant definitions (there are in fact several important extensions, but these things constitute the bulk of the language). An example interface is shown in figure 7.1.

```
[ uuid(a01d0280-2d27-11c9-9fd3-08002b0ecef1),
  version(1.0) ]

interface math {
        const long ARRAY_SIZE=10;
        typedef long array_type[ARRAY_SIZE];
        long get_sum([in] long first,
                     [in] long second);
        void get_sums([in] array_type a,
                      [in] array_type b,
                      [out] array_type c);
}
```

Figure 7.1 An IDL interface.

The unusual 16 byte hex value shown at the beginning of figure 7.1's interface is a universal unique identifier (UUID). As their name implies, UUIDs are globally unique, and they can be generated at will by any DCE system (uniqueness is ensured by incorporating a timestamp and a unique system identifier in each UUID value). Every interface is assigned a UUID to distinguish it from all others. UUIDs are also used for various other things in DCE, including providing a unique identifier for every human user.

Following the UUID are a version number for the interface and the constants, types, and procedures that interface defines. The syntax for each of these definitions is derived from ANSI C, with the most obvious addition the [in] and [out] preceding each parameter. These attributes indicate whether values are passed into or out of the procedure (it is also possible to say [in, out]) and thus control exactly what information is copied when during the remote procedure's execution.

When a client process invokes a remote procedure, the procedure's body is (obviously) not actually present in that process. Still, the client must invoke something when it makes the call. What is actually invoked is called the client *stub*. Among other duties, this stub converts the procedure's parameters into a form suitable for transmission across the network (a process called *marshalling*) and causes one or more packets to be sent to the server. At the server, a server stub *unmarshalls* the parameters, putting them in the correct format for that system, and invokes the requested procedure. The procedure executes, then sends any results back via the same path, that is, through the stubs. Once complete, the called procedure returns from the client stub back to its caller like an ordinary procedure. Throughout this process, the applications and the stubs rely on library routines linked into both the client and server process. Known collectively as the RPC *runtime*, these routines provide a number of basic services. The path taken by an RPC is shown in figure 7.2.

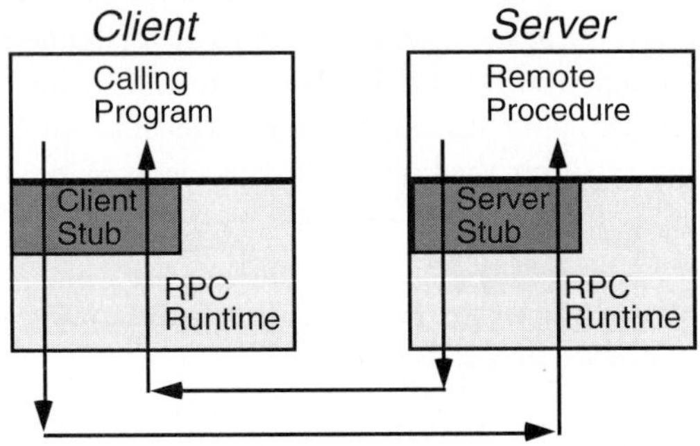

Figure 7.2 RPC operation.

While masochists might choose to write these stubs themselves, DCE provides a more convenient option with the IDL compiler. Taking an IDL-defined interface as input, the IDL compiler generates appropriate client and server stubs for that interface, along with a header file to be incorporated by the users of those stubs. The generated stub code is then linked with the user-written client and server code and the runtime library to create a complete application. This process is illustrated in figure 7.3.

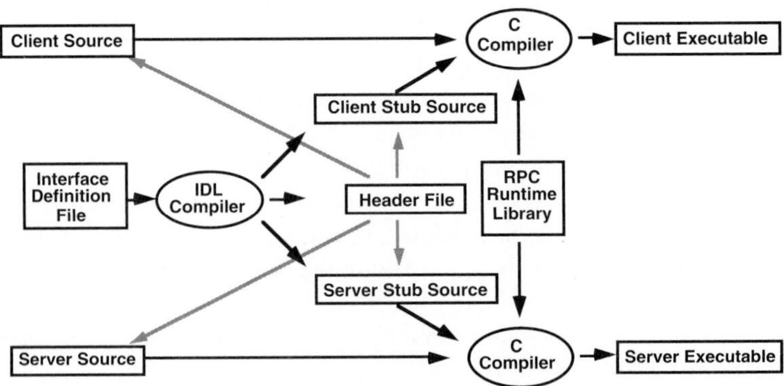

Figure 7.3 Creating an RPC application.

Creating a distributed application with DCE, then, requires specifying all interactions between clients and servers in one or more IDL interfaces. These interfaces are used to produce stubs, which in turn are combined with the actual application code. Whatever the distributed application is doing, DCE RPC can provide a foundation for interaction between its components.

7.3.2 Semantics and Transport Protocols

Remote procedure calls can sometimes behave quite differently from local calls. In particular, since two different systems are usually involved, new kinds of errors can occur. For example, a client process may issue a request to execute a remote procedure and get no response. The code that called the procedure should not be forced to deal with failures due to packets lost in the network. Still, some part of the client system (typically the RPC runtime library linked into the client process) must handle this situation. What should that library do? If the request itself was lost, then the obvious correct choice is to retransmit the lost packet. It is also possible, though, that the request was received and the remote procedure executed, but the result was lost. In this case, blind retransmission would result in a single call to an RPC causing two executions of the procedure. For some procedures, said to be idempotent, this is not a problem. For many others, however, it is unacceptable.

In DCE RPC, every remote procedure by default exhibits *at-most-once* semantics. This means that whether the request to execute a procedure is lost or the response to that request is lost, or (ideally) neither one is lost, a called remote procedure is guaranteed to be executed no more than once. If this rather strict standard of behavior is not necessary, an application developer can indicate as part of a procedure's IDL definition that it is idempotent. In this case, error recovery is done via a simple retransmission strategy rather than the more complex protocol used to implement at-most-once semantics.

An obvious question: why at *most* once rather than *exactly* once? The answer is that if a call fails to return due to a server crash, the client has no way to determine whether or not the call was executed prior to the crash. The most that can be said was that it definitely was not executed more than once. For exactly-once semantics, some kind of transaction processing approach is required. While this can readily be added on top of DCE RPC, it is not directly supported.

One other option for RPC semantics is called *broadcast*. As with idempotent, a remote procedure can be given the broadcast attribute in its defining IDL file. When a procedure with this attribute is called, it broadcasts a request to all reachable servers that are listening on the requested interface. All of those servers respond, but only the first response is returned to the caller; the others are discarded by the RPC runtime library.

RPC protocols generally execute on top of transport protocols like the transmission control protocol (TCP) or the user datagram protocol (UDP). DCE RPC can run over either of these and others, as well. But TCP and UDP offer a very different service to protocols that use them. TCP provides connection-oriented, reliable delivery of data, while UDP provides only a very simple, connectionless, unreliable delivery service. A user of DCE RPC, however, would see virtually identical behavior no matter which of these protocols was used below. At-most-once semantics or, if desired, idempotent semantics, can be provided over either TCP or UDP.

To do this, DCE actually includes two different RPC protocols. One, called DG, is used over connectionless transport protocols like UDP. It implements acknowledgments, flow control, and everything else needed to make up for UDP's deficiencies. The other RPC protocol, CN, is used when running over connection-oriented protocols like TCP. Unlike the DG protocol, it relies on TCP to provide acknowledgments, flow control, and so on. Both are available and both provide virtually identical service to an RPC user (the one difference is that not surprisingly, broadcast RPCs are not possible with CN).

7.3.3 An Aside: Cells

In a typical distributed environment, most clients perform most of their communications with only a small set of servers. This locality of reference is made explicit in DCE through the notion of a *cell*. A cell consists of some number of clients and servers (along with the machines on which they run) that do most of their communication with each other. A cell's size both in number of machines and in geographical extent is determined by the people administering the cell—there are no fixed limits. Although DCE allows communication between clients and servers in different cells, it optimizes for the more common case of intra-cell communication. A sample cell is described at the end of this chapter.

7.4 DCE Components: Threads

There's a fairly obvious limitation with RPC as a mechanism for supporting distributed applications. The limitation is this: since each call acts like an ordinary local procedure, the caller is blocked until the procedure completes. For non-remote procedures, this probably makes sense (at least on single processor systems), since caller and callee both run inside the same process on the same system. For a remote call, however, there are generally at least two CPUs involved, one at each system. Why block the entire calling process waiting for a remote server to complete? Similarly, why block other clients while a server executes a procedure for only one of them? To make effective use of the parallelism inherent in a distributed environment, some way around this problem must be found.

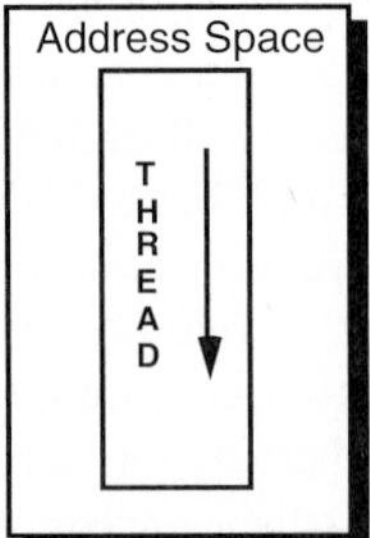

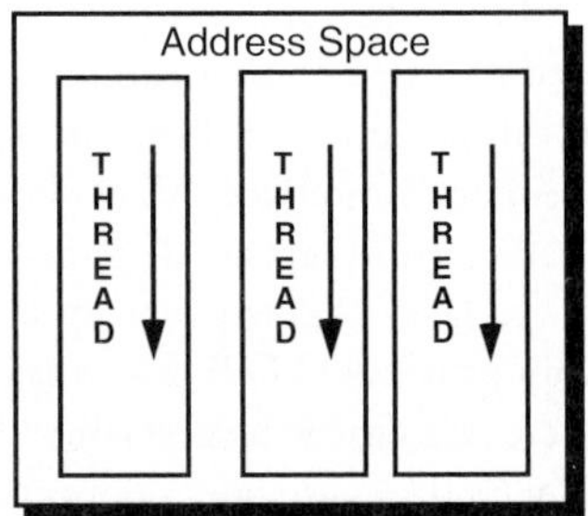

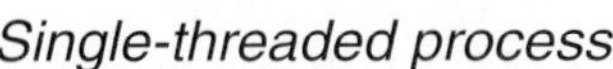

Figure 7.4 Threads.

DCE's solution is to incorporate *threads*. The basic idea is straightforward, and is illustrated in figure 7.4: allow a single process to have more than one simultaneous flow of control. For clients, this means that while each call to a remote procedure will still block, it will block only its own thread; other threads in the process are free to continue executing. For servers, support for threads means that a single server process can service requests from multiple clients at once, each in its own thread, rather than forcing one client to wait until all preceding requests have been completed.

7.4.1 The DCE Threads API

Some operating systems provide direct support for multi-threaded processes, while others (probably the majority today) do not. DCE specifies an application programming interface (API) to access thread services from applications written in C. Called *pthreads*, it is based on work done by the Institute of Electrical and Electronics Engineers (IEEE) POSIX committee. Somewhat unfortunately, this committee's work was not complete at the time DCE's design was stabilized; as a result, the threads API in DCE 1.0 may not exactly match the final output of the POSIX committee. If a system supporting DCE has operating system kernel support for threads, the pthreads interface can serve as an API to it. If a system supporting DCE has no intrinsic support for threads, the pthreads API can interface with a DCE threads library linked into the process. This library provides all of the functionality required to control threads within that process. In this situation, the operating system is unaware that the process is multi-threaded. To a programmer, however, things look very much the same whether or not kernel threads are supported.

7.4.2 Using Threads

The pthreads interface provides routines that allow a programmer to create and terminate threads, have one thread wait for another to complete, and perform various kinds of thread synchronization. In a typical client, a separate thread might be started for each remote procedure call, allowing several to be in progress at a time. If one thread needs the result of another's RPC before continuing, it can simply wait for that thread to complete, then proceed. While this style of programming adds complexity to an application developer's life, it also makes RPC (and, for that matter, other kinds of concurrent programming) much more useful.

Among the most important of the threads routines are:

- pthread_create(): creates a new thread. The routine's arguments include the name of the thread's start function and a single argument to be passed to that function. When a call to this routine returns, the start function has been invoked in its own thread, and there are now at least two threads active: the original one that called pthread_creat
- e() and the one just created via that call.
- pthread_exit(): called from within a thread, it causes the thread to terminate. A thread will also terminate when it returns from its start function.

- pthread_join(): causes the thread that calls it to block until the thread specified in this routine's argument terminates. For example, a thread might use this function to wait for another thread to complete an RPC and exit.

A pictorial example of how these calls might be used is shown in figure 7.5.

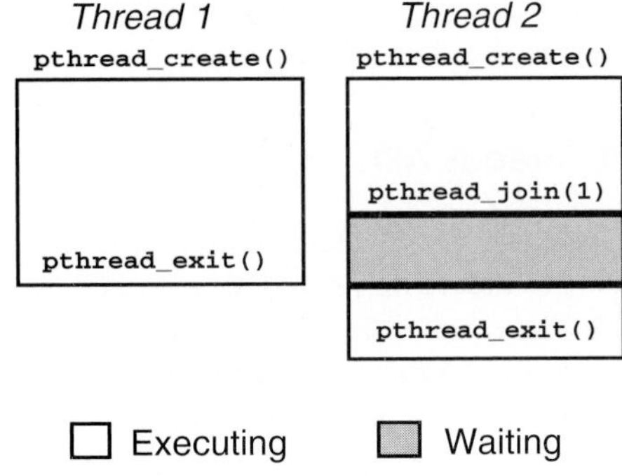

Figure 7.5 A simple threads example.

Whenever a single process has multiple threads active within it, the possibility exists for those threads to interfere with one another. For example, suppose two threads both need to increment the same global variable within the process. For this to occur safely, each thread must ensure that it has exclusive access to this variable for some period of time. This is made possible by the use of *mutexes*. A mutex looks like a variable of any other C type, and is declared just like any other variable. It is used, however, as a lock. If two threads both wish to modify the same global variable, each must first try to lock the mutex associated with that variable. Once a thread has acquired a lock on the mutex, it can modify the variable and release the lock. Any other thread that attempts to acquire a lock on the mutex will be blocked until the thread that holds the lock releases it. Some of the pthreads routines for working with mutexes are:

- pthread_mutex_lock(): locks a mutex. If the specified mutex is already locked, the thread that calls this routine is blocked until the mutex is unlocked.
- pthread_mutex_trylock(): attempts to lock a mutex. If the mutex is already locked, the call returns rather than blocking.
- pthread_mutex_unlock(): unlocks a mutex. If a thread is waiting on this mutex, that is, it has called pthread_mutex_lock() while another thread held a lock on this mutex, that thread is awakened and now holds a lock on the mutex.

An example of how these calls might be used to control access to a global variable is shown in figure 7.6. In the figure, a mutex called count_mutex is defined that will be used to control access to the global variable count. Thread 1 successfully locks the mutex, then modifies count, prints it, and unlocks the mutex. Meanwhile, assume that immediately after thread 1 acquired the mutex, thread 2 began executing (since threads are preemptively scheduled, any thread can be switched out at any time) and it, too, attempted to lock the mutex.

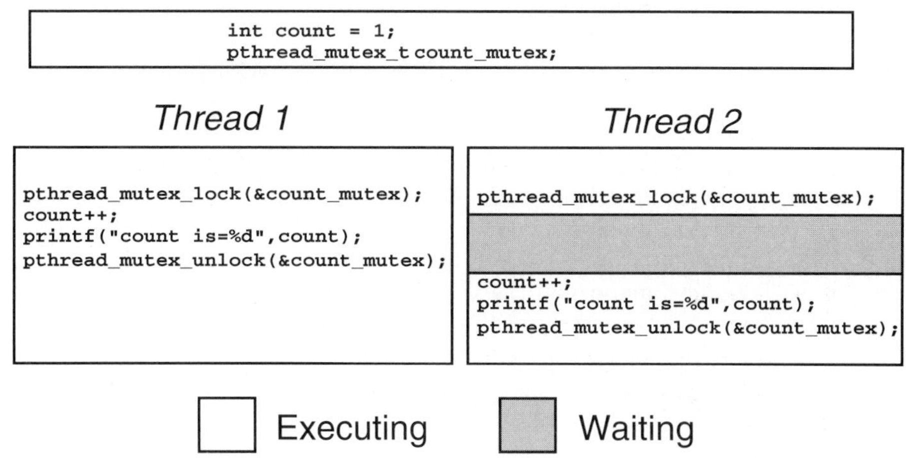

Figure 7.6 A mutex example.

Since thread 1 already held it, thread 2 was blocked. Only after thread 1 released the mutex did thread 2 wake up, this time in possession of a lock on the mutex. Thread 2 can now safely increment count, then unlock the mutex. If mutexes were not used in a case like this, the two threads might interfere with one another during the update of count. If this interference occurred at just the wrong time, count might end up containing the wrong value.

One important note: mutexes provide only advisory locks. Nothing prevents a thread from simply modifying the global variable without first attempting to acquire the mutex. It is the programmer's responsibility to make sure that all threads follow the rules.

There are cases where mutexes are not enough. Suppose, for instance, that rather than blocking other threads, a thread wishes to block itself until some condition becomes true. One example of this is when one thread in an application adds entries to a queue, while one or more other threads remove and process those entries. The processing threads must wait until an entry exists on the queue. To make this possible, yet another construction is defined called a *condition variable.* Unfortunately, condition variables are a bit too involved to describe in this short summary. Still, along with mutexes and the pthread_join() call, they are among the options pthreads provides for controlling interact ions among threads in a single process.

7.5 DCE Components: Directory Services

Dividing applications into clients and servers is all very well, but how exactly do those clients find appropriate servers? Solving this problem is the job of DCE's directory services. To access a server, a client needs to acquire that server's *binding information,* information that the server must first place into the directory. Making RPCs to that server requires only that the client learn the server's name, then use this name to look up the binding information. While the DCE directory service can be used for more general purposes, its most common application at the moment is this simple but critical function.

7.5.1 Levels of Directories

DCE's designers reasoned that most client searches for binding information would be for servers in the same cell. Intra-cell lookup, then, should be as efficient as possible. There is also some advantage in a directory service that is entirely under OSF's control, that is, one that is not a complex, rigid, standardized solution. To meet these requirements, DCE includes the cell directory service (CDS). CDS is derived from Digital Equipment Corporation's DECdns directory service, although a number of modifications were made to the original technology, including making it run over DCE RPC and using DCE security. When a server wishes to make its binding information available to clients, it *exports* that information to one of its cell's CDS servers. When a client wishes to locate a server within its own cell, it *imports* that information from the appropriate CDS server. A client actually performs this operation by calling on a CDS *clerk*, a process resident in the client's system.

Sometimes, though, clients need to access servers in foreign cells, that, in cells other than their own. For this to work, the CDS servers in all cells must somehow be linked together. An obvious protocol contender for carrying out this linkage is CDS itself. But since DCE is envisioned as eventually comprising a large number of cells scattered all over the world, this would require maintenance of a worldwide CDS directory of some sort, an unappealing task. Instead, DCE's designers chose to use an existing global directory to link cells together: the domain name system (DNS), already in very wide use on the Internet. Each cell is assigned a domain name (e.g., osf.org), and information about how to find a CDS server in that cell is stored under that name in DNS. To access a server in a foreign cell, a client gives the cell's name and the name of the desired server within that cell. A component called a global directory agent (GDA) extracts the location of the named cell's CDS server from DNS, then a query is sent directly to this foreign server. The components of the DCE directory service and how they interact are shown in figure 7.7. (One important note: DCE also allows the use of OSI's *X.500* in place of DNS. In this case, cells are given X.500-style names. Even though DCE actually includes X.500 source code, it seems unlikely that it will be used much for linking cells until there exists a worldwide directory system that runs X.500. When, or perhaps if, that happens, DCE is ready.)

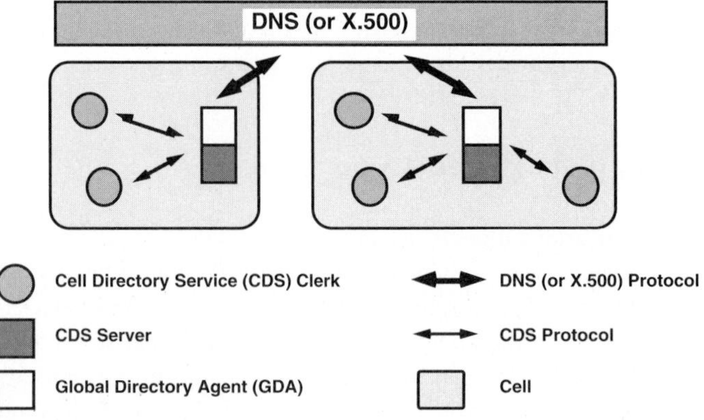

Figure 7.7 DCE directory components.

7.5.2 The DCE Namespace

While this multi-part structure makes excellent technical and administrative sense, it leads to some complexities in actually naming things. The DCE namespace is conceived as a single, worldwide structure, with a global root denoted by the symbol "/...". Below this root appears the DNS namespace, used to name each cell. If X.500 is used to name cells, its namespace also appears below the DCE global root, sitting *alongside* the DNS namespace. Finally, each cell contains its own internal namespace, starting from the cell root. An example of this structure using DNS as the global namespace appears in figure 7.8.

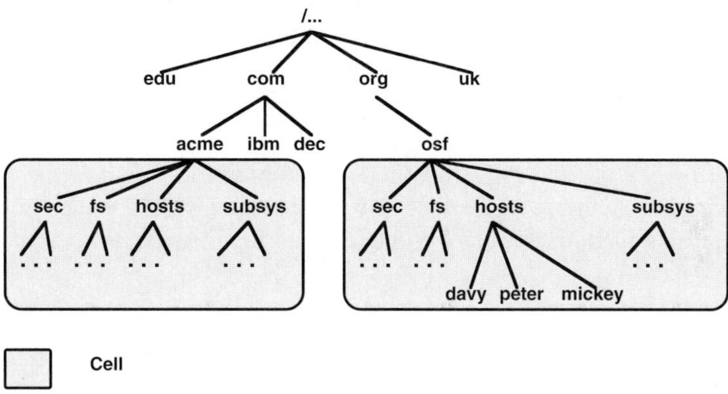

Figure 7.8 The DCE namespace.

As is shown in the figure, each cell typically contains a number of standard directories, including:

- sec: information about each user in the cell is contained here. Although part of the DCE namespace, this information is not actually maintained by CDS. Instead, it is kept in the security service and accessed via a junction, described below.
- fs: all files managed by DCE's Distributed File Service (DFS) have names below this point in the cell namespace. Once again, although these names are part of the DCE namespace, the named items (i.e., the files and directories) are not maintained by CDS. Instead, they are stored on and accessed through DFS (using another junction), as described later.
- hosts: each machine that belongs to the cell has an entry here (and this information actually *is* maintained by CDS). In the figure, the cell osf.org contains machines named davy, peter, and mickey.
- subsys: although not required, servers may export their binding information to entries stored below this directory. DCE itself stores binding information for some of its own servers here.

Each of the components in a DCE name is separated with a slash. For example, a server in the first cell shown in the figure might have the global name /.../acme.com/subsys/my_server, while /.../osf.org/hosts/mickey names a particular host in that cell. These names identify the same things from anywhere in the DCE world. To make life easier for people who may be typing these names, a shorthand form exists for use only within the server's cell. If a name begins with "/.:" rather than "/...", it is only a cell-relative name rather than a global one. A client in the same cell as the server named above could refer to it simply as /.:/subsys/my_server. The symbol "/.:" is really shorthand for *the root of the local cell.*

7.5.3 A Closer Look at CDS

Two of DCE's supported directory services, DNS and X.500, are well known standards. But the third, the cell directory service, is not. Running over DCE RPC and relying on DCE security, CDS provides a critical piece of DCE's functionality.

Each CDS server maintains one or more *clearinghouses.* Each clearinghouse contains some number of *directories,* analogous to but not the same as directories in a file system. Each directory, in turn, can logically contain other directories, *object entries,* or *soft links.* An object entry is, as the name suggests, an entry about some object, while a soft link is an alias that points to something else in CDS. The relationship between these components is illustrated in figure 7.9.

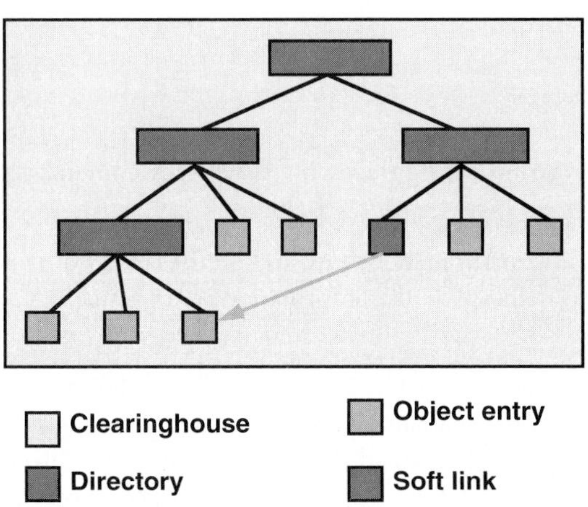

Figure 7.9 CDS components.

CDS supports replication of its information, that is, having a copy stored in more than one place. Replication is done at the directory level, so any directory and the objects it contains can be copied by a cell administrator and kept in two or more CDS servers running concurrently within a cell. Replication is a very useful feature for a directory, both for performance, since every request need no longer go to the same server, and for availability, since the crash of a single CDS server no longer stops all directory lookups. While every DCE cell must run at least one CDS server, most will choose to run two or more, with critical information replicated among them.

Object entries, the leaf nodes in CDS, come in various types. Given the primary current use of CDS in DCE, it ought not to be surprising that the commonly used types so far relate to letting clients find servers. These types are:

- server entries: a server entry typically contains binding information for a single server, put there either administratively or by the server itself when it begins executing. A server's binding information consists of things like the network address of the machine on which it is running, which protocols it is running over, for example, TCP/IP or UDP/IP, and the interface UUID(s) for the RPC interface(s) it supports.
- group entries: it is often the case in distributed environments that multiple server processes running on multiple machines may provide the same service. In a case like this, a client might not care which one it accesses. Group entries exist to support this situation. A group entry contains the names of one or more server entries and/or other group entries. These names are stored as character strings, since they are just ordinary DCE names. When a client attempts to import binding information from a group entry, the server entries referred to by this group entry are accessed, and their binding information is returned to the client. If a group entry contains other group entries, they are also dereferenced in the same way, until ultimately binding information stored in server entries is found. This entire process is transparent to the client that is looking for binding information; all it knows is that, somehow, it has found what it was looking for.
- profile entries: group entries are useful, but they are not always the right solution. When a client imports from a group, the entries within that group are returned in a random order (this can be thought of as a simple attempt at load balancing). While this is entirely appropriate for many situations, it is entirely wrong for many others. Imagine, for example, a user wishing to print a file via some DCE-based print service. If all of the print servers in her building had their binding information stored in a single group entry, she might have to search the entire building to find her output, since a printer would be chosen at random. Profile entries, the third type of object entry commonly used in CDS, provide a better solution for situations like this. Profile entries are somewhat like groups, in that they can contain the names of other server, group, or profile entries. They are unlike groups in some ways, too, since they allow defining the order in which their members are returned. In the print server example just described, all of the print servers in the building might be pointed to by a single profile entry. A client attempting to import binding information from this entry would find that it always received its results in the same order. Perhaps, for instance, the user above has defined a profile that gives the highest priority to the print servers closest to her, next highest to those next closest, and so on. Her print client will attempt to bind to and print from first the nearest print server, then, if that fails, the next nearest, and so on. While each user (or perhaps each floor) might need their own printer profile entry, profiles do provide a way around the sometimes undesirable randomness of groups.

One other feature of the DCE namespace was referred to above and is worth mentioning: *junctions*. A junction is a point at which control of the named information passes from

CDS to some other DCE service. While the DCE namespace within a cell appears to be seamless, in fact, not all of the named information is stored within CDS servers. For example, the name /.:/sec, present in all DCE cells, appears to be a normal CDS directory. In fact, it is an object entry, not a directory. More specifically, it is a group entry containing binding information for the security servers in the cell. For example, suppose a client process attempts to look up the name /.:/sec/principal/smith. This process will extract the binding information for one or more security servers from the group entry /.:/sec, then use this to bind to a security server in the cell. The remainder of the name, /principal/smith, is passed to this server for further processing. (DFS does the same thing with filenames, as is discussed below.) By using junctions, a server can provide its own structure and storage for information while still allowing that information to have an ordinary DCE name.

7.6 DCE Components: Security

Virtually no one today would use a multi-user operating system that did not include effective security measures. The same caution ought to apply to a platform for building distributed applications. With this in mind, DCE's designers have incorporated a number of security services, along with appropriate mechanisms to provide these services.

7.6.1 Security Services

DCE provides four major services critical to building secure distributed applications:

- authentication: in short, authentication means proving you are who you say you are. When a client requests some service from a server, it must not only identify itself, it must provide some information that proves that this is its true identity. When a human user logs into a computer system, she commonly types her login name and password. The password, known only to her, verifies that this is her true identity. Solving the same problem between the parts of a distributed application is substantially more complex, but no less important.
- authorization: once a server has authenticated a client, the next question to be answered is this: does this client have the right to perform the service it is requesting? The request may be to invoke a particular remote procedure or to access a certain file or to modify an entry in CDS or to perform any other service this server makes available. Whatever it is, an authorization decision must be made. Authorization is sometimes called access control, perhaps a slightly more descriptive name since access is exactly what is being controlled. Note that despite their similar names, authorization is a completely separate thing from authentication. As will be seen, DCE uses entirely separate mechanisms to provide these very different services.
- data integrity: when data is sent across a network there exists the potential for someone to modify it during transit. For example, a request from client to server to add \$100 to a checking account might be intercepted, changed to \$100,000, then sent

on its way. A data integrity service guards against this by allowing the recipient of a message to determine whether it has been tampered with.

- data privacy: this is perhaps the most obvious of the security services provided by DCE. It ensures that data sent between clients and servers cannot be read by anyone but the parties involved in the communication.

7.6.2 Security Mechanisms

Security services are actually provided by security mechanisms. In DCE, the services of authentication, data integrity, and data privacy are provided by a slightly modified version of Kerberos Version 5, created at the Massachusetts Institute of Technology (MIT). For authentication, Kerberos issues clients a series of encrypted bytes called a *ticket* that allows them to prove their identity to servers. For data integrity, a cryptographic checksum is computed for each packet sent, then encrypted using a Kerberos-supplied key known only to the client and server. Any modification to the data will be detected, since the receiver's calculation of the checksum will not match the decryption of the checksum value it received. And for data privacy, the data is simply encrypted before transmission, again using a key known only to the client and server (this randomly generated key, the same one that is used for data integrity, is provided by Kerberos along with the ticket). All of this encryption is done using an algorithm called the data encryption standard (DES).

Kerberos by design does not address the problem of authorization. DCE does, however, and it uses one common mechanism to provide this service: access control lists (ACLs). An ACL is exactly what it sounds like: a list that controls who can access some service or object. When a server receives a request, that request typically contains the privilege attribute certificate (PAC) of the requestor. This PAC identifies who made the request and what groups he belongs to (both the requester's identity and his groups are represented by UUIDs). A component of the server called the ACL manager compares the UUIDs from the PAC with the entries on the ACL of the desired object. If they match correctly, access is allowed. If not, access is denied. This process is shown in figure 7.10.

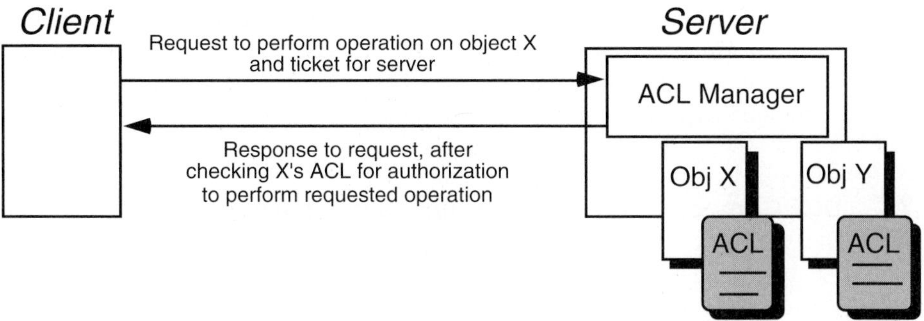

Figure 7.10 ACLs and ACL management.

Application developers can select which, if any, of these services they wish to use. For authentication, data integrity, and data privacy, the choice is made with calls to the RPC API. For authorization, the developer of a server must create an ACL manager. Since adding security can subtract from performance, DCE's designers did not wish to mandate any particular level of service. By supporting security, however, DCE becomes a candidate platform for mission-critical applications, something that likely would not be true if these services were omitted.

7.6.3 Components of Security in a Cell

Every cell runs at least one security server process. This server, which may be replicated, provides a service that is described as having three distinct parts:

- Registry service: the registry service is essentially a database along with services to maintain the information in that database. Stored in a cell's registry are entries for all of that cell's users, called principals, all of its groups, and all of its organizations. Each security server in a cell (if there is more than one) must have a complete copy of the registry database, and tools are provided to allow administrators to add and delete registry entries.
- Key distribution service: this is essentially the Kerberos authentication and ticket granting services. It provides tickets to clients and provides the other Kerberos services. It accesses the registry as needed to perform its function.
- Privilege service: the privilege service is responsible for supplying PACs. It, too, accesses the registry to acquire the necessary information, and it also interacts in some ways with the key distribution service.

All of these services, while conceptually distinct, are typically provided by a single process, the security server. This server must run on a secure machine, since the registry on which it relies contains a secret key, generated from a password, for every principal in the cell. Although these keys are encrypted while stored on disk, the key to decrypt them is also stored on the machine, since Kerberos requires access to each principal's key. Exactly what qualifies as a *secure machine* will vary from one site to another. For one, it might mean a system that sits in the cell administrator's office and runs no login daemons, while for another site it may mean a machine with only one account kept in a locked room with video cameras and motion sensors. In any case, maintaining security in a cell requires keeping security servers free from unauthorized access.

7.7 DCE Components: Distributed Time Service (DTS)

Computers typically come with built-in clocks. These clocks are not always especially accurate, and they are often set in a casual way, for example, by an administrator glancing at her watch and setting an approximate time. For an effective distributed environment, clocks on all systems must be fairly closely synchronized. In DCE, this is accomplished using the distributed time service (DTS).

Derived from a DEC-defined protocol, DTS exhibits the usual client/server structure. DTS clients, daemon processes called *clerks,* request the correct time from some number of servers (typically three), then reset their clocks as necessary to reflect this new knowledge. How often a clerk resynchronizes, and thus how accurate that system's clock will be, is configurable by the system's administrator.

There's an obvious problem with this scenario: when a server responds to a clerk's request, it checks its own clock to determine the time value to send back. By the time the packet containing this time arrives at the clerk, it is no longer correct because of the inherent delay in packet delivery. To handle this problem, the clerk attempts to compensate for the round-trip time of its request (actually an RPC) to the server. In addition, DTS does not define time as a single value. Instead, a clerk querying a server for the correct time receives in return an interval, expressed as a time plus or minus an inaccuracy. A clerk computes a new interval that is the intersection of the intervals it receives from servers, then sets its own system clock to the midpoint of this interval. This process is illustrated in figure 7.11.

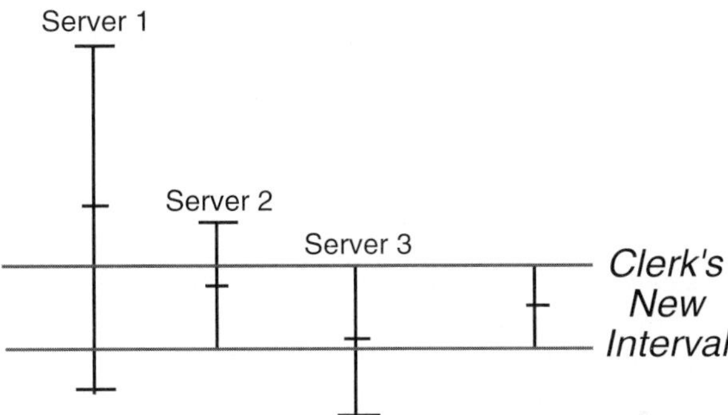

Figure 7.11 Time synchronization.

Servers synchronize with each other in a similar way. In a typical cell, one server has access to a source of high-quality time, for example, a radio listening to a continuous time broadcast or a network time protocol (NTP) connection from the Internet. If this is true, DTS will keep the machines in a cell in sync both with each other and with the true time.

7.8 DCE Components: Distributed File Service (DFS)

Everything discussed so far is part of DCE's basic platform for supporting distributed applications. DCE itself actually includes something that can be viewed as just such an application, however, one that makes use of all of the services just described. DCE's Distributed File Service (DFS) allows sharing of files among clients and servers in the same cell or in different cells. Derived from the Andrew File System (AFS), it is built on DCE RPC, uses threads to enhance parallelism, relies on the DCE directory to locate servers, and uses DCE security services to foil attackers.

DFS has a few important differences from DCE's other components. One of these is its optional nature: it is entirely possible to use the rest of DCE without DFS. This is not true of any of the components discussed above; creating a true DCE cell requires using all of them. Also, DFS is the only DCE component that is strongly biased toward Unix. Although likely to be available on a variety of operating systems, its view of files and file semantics is exactly that taken by Unix.

7.9 DFS Architecture

Like everything else in DCE, DFS relies on a client/server architecture. DFS clients, called *cache managers,* communicate with DFS servers using RPC on behalf of user applications. The slightly unusual name for clients derives from the way they work, which is heavily dependent on caching. When a file is first accessed by a user application, that system's cache manager copies the file's first *chunk* back to its local disk. The default chunk size is 64K bytes, so many (in some environments most) files will be copied in their entirety. A client is then free to read and write the data in its cache. A primary reason for taking this approach is obvious: better performance. Once a chunk is present in the cache, access to its information takes place without the delays inherent in access across a network. If multiple clients are reading and writing the same chunk of the same file, a somewhat elaborate token mechanism is used to maintain consistency among their caches, ensuring that each client sees the most current copy of the data.

DFS is designed to support a group of servers within a cell that provide file access for that cell's clients. Toward this end, DFS presents a single file namespace to its clients. As shown in figure 7.12, all of the files managed by DFS in a cell appear within the fs directory immediately below the cell root. From within a cell, a DFS file can be specified as, for example, /.:/fs/tmp/test or, using a DFS-specific shorthand notation, as just /:/tmp/test ("/:" is shorthand for "/.:/fs"). If this cell's name was acme.com, the same file could be referenced as /

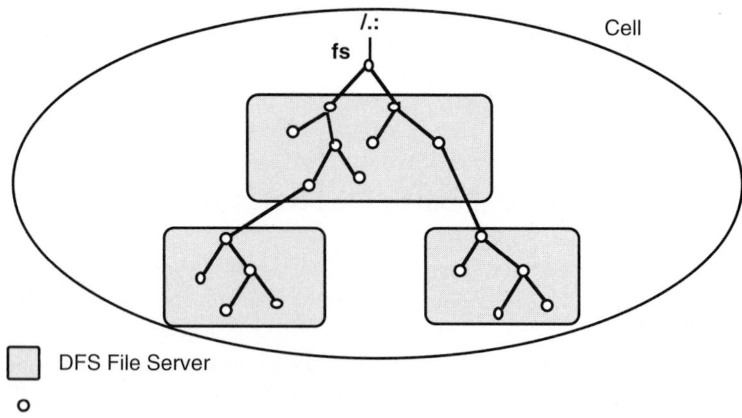

Figure 7.12 DFS file naming.

.../acme.com/fs/tmp/test, a name that uniquely identifies this file from anywhere in the world. A group of interconnected DCE cells supporting DFS can provide a global file system with files accessible to any of their clients.

To access a file, DFS clients need know only the file's name and the location of their cell's CDS server. Unlike the commonly used network file system (NFS), DFS clients do not mount files from specific remote servers. Instead, a request is made to the CDS server requesting binding information for DFS's *fileset location servers* (this information is kept in the CDS group entry/junction at /.:/fs). Once the binding information is acquired, a DFS cache manager passes the name of the desired file to one of these servers. This server checks its copy of the fileset location database and returns to the requesting client an indication of which DFS server it should communicate with to actually access the file. To prevent this process from becoming unworkably slow, a DFS client will cache the location of the fileset location server and the assigned DFS server, obviating the need for repetitive lookups. This process is pictured in figure 7.13.

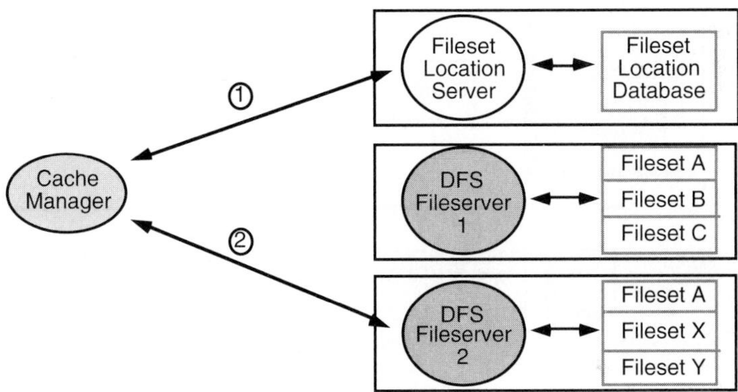

Figure 7.13 Finding files.

7.9.1 The Local File System (LFS)

DFS defines how clients talk to servers. How a server actually accesses its files is defined by the server's file system. To get the full functionality of DFS, a server can use DCE's Local File System (LFS), also known as *Episode*. DFS servers with LFS allow file replication, support standard DCE ACLs, and provide various administrative conveniences. Although DFS is certainly useful without LFS, this extra component adds significantly to the service it provides.

7.10 An Example Cell

Figure 7.14 shows a typical DCE cell, complete with each of the required servers:

- Security server: running on a physically secure machine, this server also maintains the cell's registry;

- CDS servers: the cell shown in the figure has two CDS servers. Since CDS supports replication of its information, having more than one server and replicating critical information in both can improve both performance and availability of the cell's services;
- DTS servers: the example shows three DTS servers, a reasonable number. Note that, although it is not shown in the figure, one of these servers will typically be connected to a source of high-quality time.

Although it is not required, this cell also contains a DFS server.

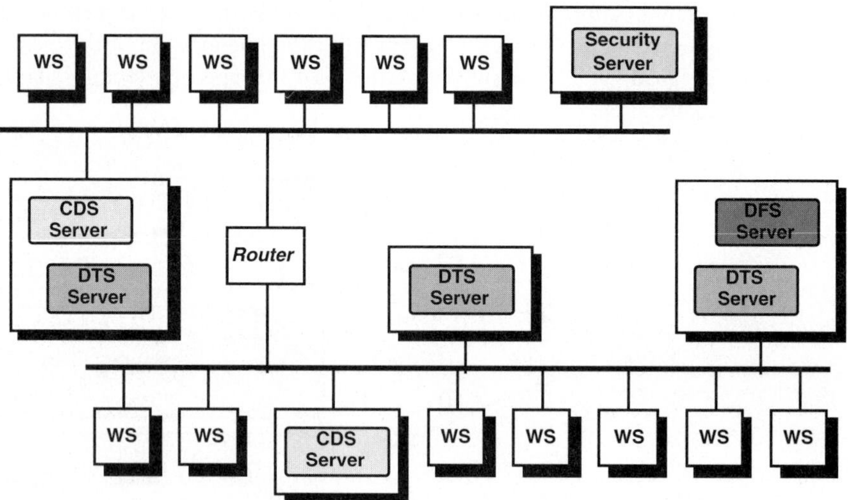

Figure 7.14 An example cell.

One important thing to note: the core components of the DCE *Executive* must run on every machine in this cell, including those running various DCE servers. The executive includes the key client pieces of DCE: RPC, threads, a CDS clerk, a security client, and a DTS clerk. Without this minimum set of services, systems cannot fully participate in the cell.

7.10.1 A Sample Distributed Application

Suppose an existing stand-alone application, one that accesses a database, is to be distributed within this example cell. The goal is to exploit the processing power of the cell's workstations while still preserving a central database. Doing this requires partitioning the database and its application into separate client and server components. The server will run on the mainframe, where the database is located, while the clients run on the workstations. Communication between the two pieces, along with other needed services, will be provided by DCE.

To actually implement the database server and its clients requires carrying out the steps described in section 7.3.1, including:

- Writing the client code that will make database requests and the server code that will actually implement those requests. Since in this example an existing application is being modified, much of the required software will probably already exist.
- specifying the RPC interface between client and server, and precisely defining its RPCs using IDL.
- Compiling this IDL interface with the IDL compiler to produce client and server stubs.
- Compiling and linking the client code and client stub to create the client executable, and the server code and server stub to create the server executable. These executables must then be installed on the appropriate systems.

Several things have been omitted from this brief list. Among the most important are:

- Discussion of the design process for distributed applications: this omission is not meant to imply that no design is required for DCE applications–far from it. Instead, design considerations for distributed applications are a large topic in their own right, and so are omitted from this short discussion.
- Performance considerations: while using available CPU cycles on workstations has the potential for performance enhancement, careful design may be required to actually realize this potential.
- Security considerations: DCE applications are not required to use security, but it is strongly recommended. In this example, it is reasonable to assume that the original non-distributed version took advantage of available system security. So, too, then, should the distributed version take advantage of DCE security. The remainder of this chapter assumes that the application uses DCE's security services.

7.10.2 Exporting Binding Information

For our example client to be able to locate its server, the server must have a name in the DCE namespace. As described above, these names are used to identify the CDS entry into which a server exports its binding information. A client that wishes to access the server will typically learn its name, then import its binding information from that CDS entry. There is no one *right* way to name a server, although one supported option was described above: using the /.:/ subsys directory present in every cell. For this example, assume this cell's owners have created a directory in CDS called /.:/servers and assigned this server a simple name like /.:/servers/ dbserver.

As part of its initialization, the database server will export its binding information to a CDS server. As shown in figure 7.15, with an application using DCE security there are actually two steps involved:

1. The database server must contact the cell's security server to acquire a ticket to CDS. Without this ticket, the database server has no effective way of proving its identity to the CDS server, that is, of authenticating itself.

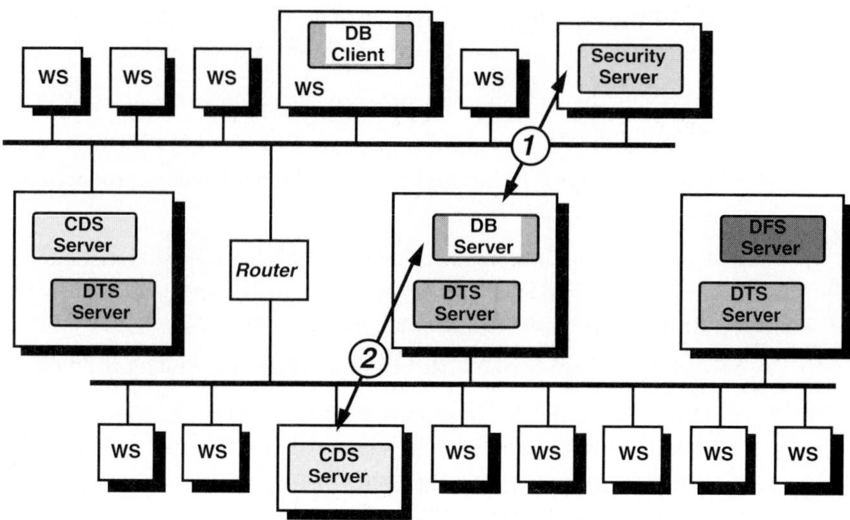

Figure 7.15 Exporting binding information.

2. Once it has a ticket, the database server can export its binding information to a CDS server. In the cell shown in the diagram, there are two CDS servers, each maintaining some part of the total cell directory information. A server exporting information to CDS is unaware of how many CDS servers there are or of which one its information is stored in. The exporting server simply gives a name, for example, /.:/servers/dbserver, and CDS stores the information in the appropriate place.

7.10.3 Importing Binding Information

Importing binding information is just the reverse of exporting it. A client that wishes to contact the database server must first learn the server's name, then query CDS for the information stored under this name. How a client learns a server's name is its problem; in some cases, a human user may type the name, while in others the name might be embedded in the client software or read from a configuration file.

Figure 7.16 shows a typical sequence of events when a client imports a server's binding information:

1. Before contacting CDS, the client must first contact the security server for a ticket (it is also possible that the client already has a ticket for CDS, gotten prior to an earlier lookup for some other server). As always, this ticket will be presented to CDS to prove that the client is who it claims to be.

2. This cell has two CDS servers. A typical client will always begin its search at the same point. In this case, that point is the nearest CDS server to the client. Unfortunately, information stored in the specified entry (again, assume the entry the client is

looking for is named /.:/servers/dbserver) is not kept in this CDS server. Instead of responding with the requested information, this CDS server responds with a referral to the other CDS server in this cell. The client's CDS clerk receives and correctly handles this referral; the client application remains blissfully unaware of this change.

3. This CDS server does contain the requested binding information, which is returned to the client.

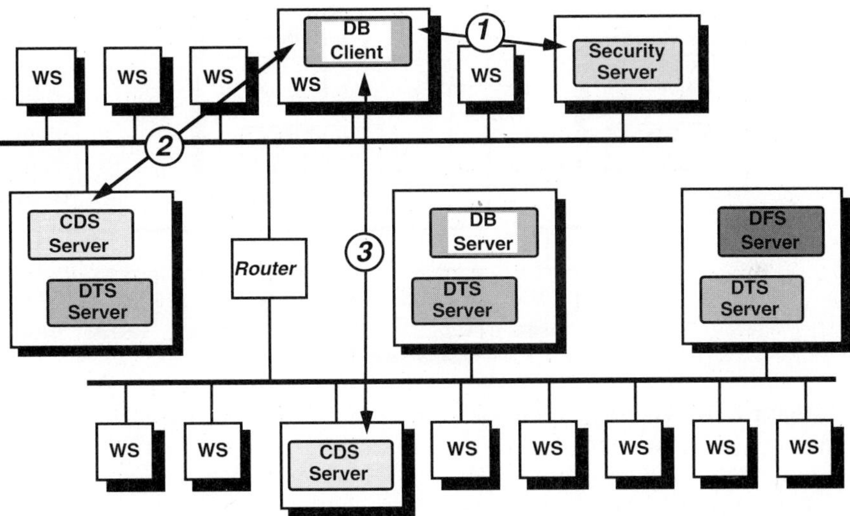

Figure 7.16 Importing binding information.

7.10.4 Accessing the Server

Finally, the goal is within sight: client access to the remote database server. Once again, there are two steps, shown in figure 7.17:

1. As before, the client must acquire a ticket from the cell's security server. Note that this request happens only the first time this client attempts to access the database server. From then on, the ticket acquired via this exchange may be used over and over to verify the client's identity (or optionally, though with less security, the ticket may be presented only on the first access).

2. The client makes the first actual RPC to the server, requesting some database-related service. This request and those that follow it are the whole point of everything up to now: remote access from client to server.

Although this process may seem somewhat complicated, most of what has just been described happens only once. A server exports binding information only at start-up, and a client imports it only when it is first invoked. Similarly, as just mentioned, the client's request for a ticket (step 1 above) occurs only the first time the client accesses the server. Once these initialization steps have been completed, access from client to server consists of a series of direct requests and responses, implemented via remote procedure calls.

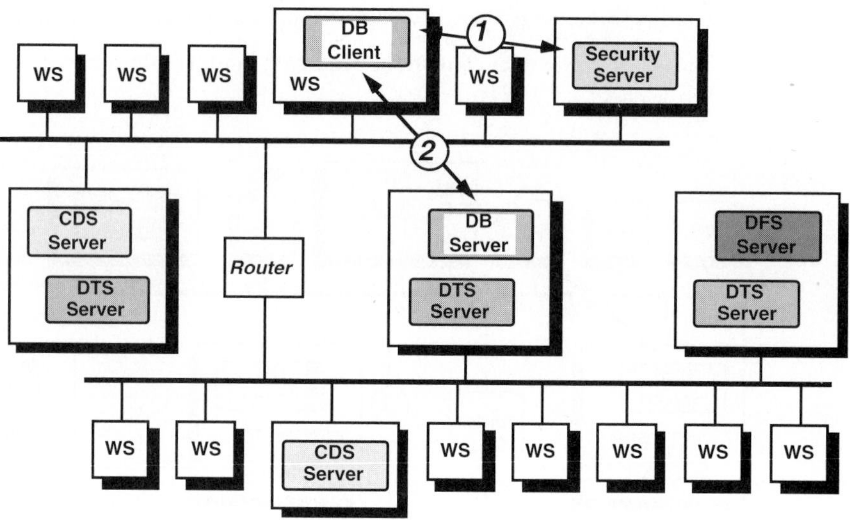

Figure 7.17 Accessing the server.

7.11 Conclusion

DCE provides a vendor-neutral infrastructure for building distributed applications. It includes the fundamental services required: RPC, threads, directory services, time synchronization, and security. It also includes an optional application, the Distributed File Service. DCE is not simple, but it is also not unusably complex. Supported by virtually every vendor, it is intended to become the standard platform for distributed applications in a multi-vendor world.

David Chappell is principal of Chappell & Associates, a training and consulting firm focused on distributed computing for open systems. He has written and taught many courses on distributed computing and related topics to clients in North America and Europe, and has served as a consultant on numerous communications projects. Among his current projects, David is a consultant to the Open Software Foundation (OSF), involved with OSF's Distributed Computing Environment (DCE) and Distributed Management Environment (DME). His previous experience includes software engineering positions with NCR Corporation and Cray Research, where he was a principal architect of Cray's original Unix-based OSI product. He also chaired the Upper Layers Special Interest Group of the National Institute of Standards and Technology (NIST) OSI Implementors Workshop from 1988 until 1990. David holds a B.S. in Economics and an M.S. in Computer Science, both from the University of Wisconsin-Madison.

Part II

Case Studies

Chapter 8

Project Andrew

John Leong
Carnegie Mellon University

The *Andrew* project of Carnegie Mellon University (CMU) is one of the most significant large scale distributed computing projects of the 80s. Given that numerous in-depth, technical papers have already been published on the various components of the project, this chapter will be tilted towards the lessons, some technical and some non-technical, learned from our five plus years of operating the system as a production service.

8.1 Introduction

Carnegie Mellon is a small university located in Pittsburgh, Pennsylvania. It has a population of approximately 4,400 undergraduates, 2,600 graduates, and 3,000 faculty and staff. As one of the world leaders in computer and related sciences, the CMU community has developed a large appetite for computing and communications services.

In the early 80s, it had become apparent that time-shared, large boxes behind glass doors mode of computing was dated. Because of the economics of the computer market place, it was expected that desktop computers, and lots of them, would be taking over the world.

While there are problems associated with general purpose, time-sharing systems such as not being cost effective, unpredictable, and often poor response time for interactive work and so on, it does provide a relatively coherent computing and information system environment to an organization. Sharing of data and programs can be accomplished easily and naturally since everything is in the same box. In contrast, unplanned scattering of desktop computers, for all their advantages, can quickly lead to fragmentation and chaos. This is particularly the case if one has a widely heterogenous collection of incompatible machines.

The challenge is to allow physical distribution of computing resources while providing logical coherency for the overall enterprise. To address this challenge, a partnership was formed between IBM and Carnegie Mellon in 1982 to create a large scale, coherent distributed computing environment for the campus. This is the Andrew project.

Andrew has been operational since 1986. The first few years were pretty dismal. It was more in line of a large scale beta test than service provisioning. It took us another three to four years of determined efforts to stabilize the system. Heterogenous, distributed computing service is not simple, and that is probably a gross understatement.

Today, Andrew is a reasonably reliable system with acceptably good performance. It is also much more manageable. Andrew is supporting over 8,000 active and relatively contented users on over 4,000 computers ranging from high power, state of the art workstations to antiquated PCs.

The Andrew project has three main components: the network infrastructure, a set of network based services and a set of workstation client software. We will discuss each one in turn.

8.2 The Network Infrastructure

The importance of good networking capabilities for distributed computing was never in question. The definition of good in this context, is high throughput, large bandwidth, reliable, maintainable and adaptable to rapidly changing technologies. Additionally, in a large scale distributed computing operation, networking should be a utility much like the telephone system.

As part of the Andrew project, a comprehensive cable plant was installed. The cable plant has two components: intra-building and inter-building.

8.2.1 Intra-building Cabling

Intra-building cable plant design and implementation is probably the least glamourous aspect of data networking. It is important, however, in that its implementation is disruptive, labor intensive and hence expensive. It is something one would prefer to do once and only once for the lifetime of the building. In contrast, networking technologies go through new development every five years or so. So, it is important for the cable plant to be adaptable.

For intra-building cabling, we selected the IBM cabling system. Every building, including all student residences were re-wired. Over 12,000 Type 2 cable outlets were installed. Type 2 cable consists of two high quality shielded twisted pairs (STP) for data and four unshielded twisted pairs (UTP) intended for voice and other telecommunication applications.

We selected the IBM Type 2 cabling system because (a) it was, and still is, a good cabling system and (b) IBM agreed to grant us all the cables, outlets, and associated equipment required for the project. We almost declined the very generous offer. Back in 1983, there was no obvious way to run Ethernet over the Type 2 cable. Ethernet's Attachment Unit Interface (AUI) called for four shielded twisted pairs and there were only two data pairs in the IBM cable. The problem was resolved when we got together with a new start-up company called SynOptics. With it, the hub based local area network industry was born. Experiencing deja-vu, we have recently been confronted by the potential wire pairs shortage issue once again.

AT&T and HP submitted a proposal for 100 Mbps Ethernet standard requiring four unshielded twisted pairs while a competing proposal called for only two data pairs. As you may have guessed, we are not a fan of AT&T and HP's approach.

Although the IBM cabling system is a well engineered product, it is relatively costly, both in term of parts as well as labor. On the other hand, we have been pleasantly surprised by the advances made in high speed data operation over UTP, particularly the class 5 data grade variety. Not only will it support 10 Mpbs Ethernet operation with ease, even 100 Mpbs does not seem to be a problem as in the case of Copper Distributed Data Interface (CDDI). As a result, the most cost effective intra-building wiring scheme today would consist of running two sets of four pairs, class 5, data grade UTP from a wiring closet to a wall outlet equipped with two RJ-45 connectors. Generally, one set would be used for telecommunications, the other for local area networking. The run length between wall outlet and wiring closet should not exceed 100 meters as this is the design parameter most local area networks are using.

What about fiber optics to the desktop? Three interesting reference points are: (a) FDDI to the desktop has not been that well received, (b) 100 Mbps over copper is possible and (c) good quality VHS video can be transmitted using today's compression technology at well under 2 Mbps. Hence fiber to the desktop is neither cost effective nor necessary today, and may not be for a while. There are of course special cases. But, then, we should treat them exactly as that, special cases.

A low cost and good hedge against media obsolescence is to put in plenty of space. Conduits, cable trays and other cable run support structures should, if possible, be installed with plenty of spare capacity. Additionally, conduits should be equipped with pull strings. That way, new cabling can be added as needed relatively easily in the future.

In a larger building, there are typically multiple wiring closets. In our cable plant, every wiring closet is directly connected to one main closet. The connectivity is done with IBM Type 1 cables for data and appropriate multiple UTP pairs bundle for telecommunications. The ratio of Type 2 to Type 1 wiring is 4:1. This takes into consideration the likely presence of data multiplexing equipment in the wiring closet plus some level of redundancy. This redundancy has served us well. When we introduce a new network technology into a building, subject to run length constraints, we will typically equip only the main wiring closet with the necessary electronics. We would then patch all the nodes through to that location for connection. Only when the demand increases to an appropriate level would we deploy electronics to the other wiring closets. Besides providing better control over our capital expenditure, it is particularly appropriate for sparsely used technologies.

The main wiring closet of a building is also called the building entrance facility (BEF). It is where the inter-building connectivity happens.

8.2.2 Inter-building Networking

Every building is interconnected with multiple 50 and 62.5 micron, multimode fiber optic cables. Over 300 pairs of cables have been installed. The 50 micron cables were installed before the 62.5 micron variety became the current standard.

The cable plant has a mostly rooted tree topology. The root of the tree is conveniently located in the computing center. This topology allows us to easily configure private subnets for a specific group of buildings on demand. As shall be seen later, the rooted tree topology contributed to the ease of network management.

Additional fibers have been installed between strategic nodes so that a ring topology network can also be formed if necessary for redundancy.

We have recently installed a few single mode fiber pairs to support research and experimentation calling for bandwidth in excess of 500 Mbps. As of today, the demand has not yet justified campus wide addition of this media to the cable plant.

8.2.3 Local Area Networks

Every building has at least one Ethernet, one Token Ring and multiple Local Talk (the original AppleTalk for the Macintoshes) networks. Together, there are over 2,000 Ethernet, 2,000 Local Talk and 500 Token Ring nodes on campus. Ethernet is the dominant, and increasingly so, network technology. Practically all the workstation vendors are shipping machines with built-in Ethernet. The Macintoshes are also moving in that direction.

This raises an interesting point. We used to spend a fair amount of time debating the merits of Ethernet versus Token Ring. On reflection, it was pretty academic. Whether a network technology is going to be successful on the desktop depends very much on the computer vendors. Hence despite the fact that Local Talk is neither a standard nor particularly wonderful, the fact that it comes free with the very popular Macintosh ensures its role in the networking Hall of Fame. On the other hand, after almost five years of existence, the number of FDDI nodes on the desktop remains very small. It will continue to be a minor niche player as long as workstation vendors keep producing machines with built-in Ethernets. The problem with FDDI is also compounded by the fact that, until the recent dramatic increase in computing power of desktop machines, its higher bandwidth could not be really be fully exploited because of protocols and other software overhead.

The two places where FDDI has potential are the attachment of high demand network services such as file servers and as the network backbone. So far, we have been able to support our servers load with multiple Ethernets. This will likely to change as newer and more powerful clients emerge. In the case of the backbone, we have explored a totally different approach which will be described in the network management section.

An interesting lesson we have learned from our early Ethernet operation is that regardless of the logical topology of the network, physically, star or rooted tree is the preferred configuration from the maintenance point of view. The original coax bus type of Ethernet quickly proved to be very difficult to manage. With the physical distribution of potential trouble spots all over the map, troubleshooting called for a lot of leg work. That translated into long down time and poor service.

Hub based, star or rooted tree topology Ethernet fares considerably better. The old standby troubleshooting method of network partitioning by trial-and-error can be accomplished orders of magnitude faster at the hub location. Additionally, hub based networks can be reconfigured much more easily and quickly.

Finally, while we have been tracking the development of the various new LAN technologies such as 100 Mbps Ethernet, Asynchronous Transfer Mode (ATM) LAN, FDDI II, fiber Channel Systems (FCS) and so on. we believe that Ethernet will be around for a long time.

Our expectation is that it will evolve from a shared media network to a low cost, commodity, point to point link in the same spirit as the venerable RS-232.

8.2.4 Communication Protocols

As you may have guessed, TCP/IP is our standard protocol. While we would like to support only one protocol, the popularity of the Macintoshes and Novell Netware dictates that AppleTalk and IPX also need to be supported.

Initially, we tried to bypass the multi-protocols problem by tunneling AppleTalk and IPX over IP. This was particularly important when our early home grown routers could only handle IP. However, protocol tunneling can introduce considerable complexity. As our old routers fade away, they are being replaced by the more effective commercial multi-protocol routers.

8.2.5 Network Management

Building a network complex is no longer that difficult a task. However, building one that is manageable is still a considerable challenge.

We would like to think that we had a grand master plan from day one for our network. The truth is that the network evolved over the years as we learned from our mistakes and took advantages of appropriate new developments. In the early days, simply getting reliable connectivity between subnets was a major feat. As the network grew, we quickly realized that our rather haphazard, initial approach of chaining subnets together would result in an unmanageable monster. So, in additional to building up our arsenal of troubleshooting tools which we shall discuss later, we took a hard look at our backbone configuration.

8.2.5.1 Backbone Evolution

When we first started building our network complex, we had a router in each of the few buildings we were linking together. The routers were daisy chained together using fiber optic Ethernet transceivers to form an ad hoc backbone. We soon found this daisy chained backbone configuration difficult to troubleshoot and manage. Applying the experience gained from Ethernet operation, we reconfigured the backbone as a star using a fiber optic Ethernet hub. This immediately reduced the average problem location time from hours, and even days, to minutes. Through simple trial and error at the hub, we could quickly identify and isolate an offending subnet so that the rest of the network could be put back in action.

With this version of the star shaped backbone, once a problem subnet had been identified and isolated, we still had to send out a technician to determine whether the problem was with the router, the subnet, a station on the subnet or some combinations of the above. Outcall is both labor intensive and time consuming. To reduce outcall, we came up with a new twist–an *inverted backbone* (see figure 8.1). It is sometimes referred to as a "collapsed backbone," a term we don't like for obvious reasons!

In this approach, instead of having a backbone reaching out to connect the subnets, we have the subnets coming back in to be connected. As a result, all the routers are pulled back from the field into the central data communications facility. This makes troubleshooting and

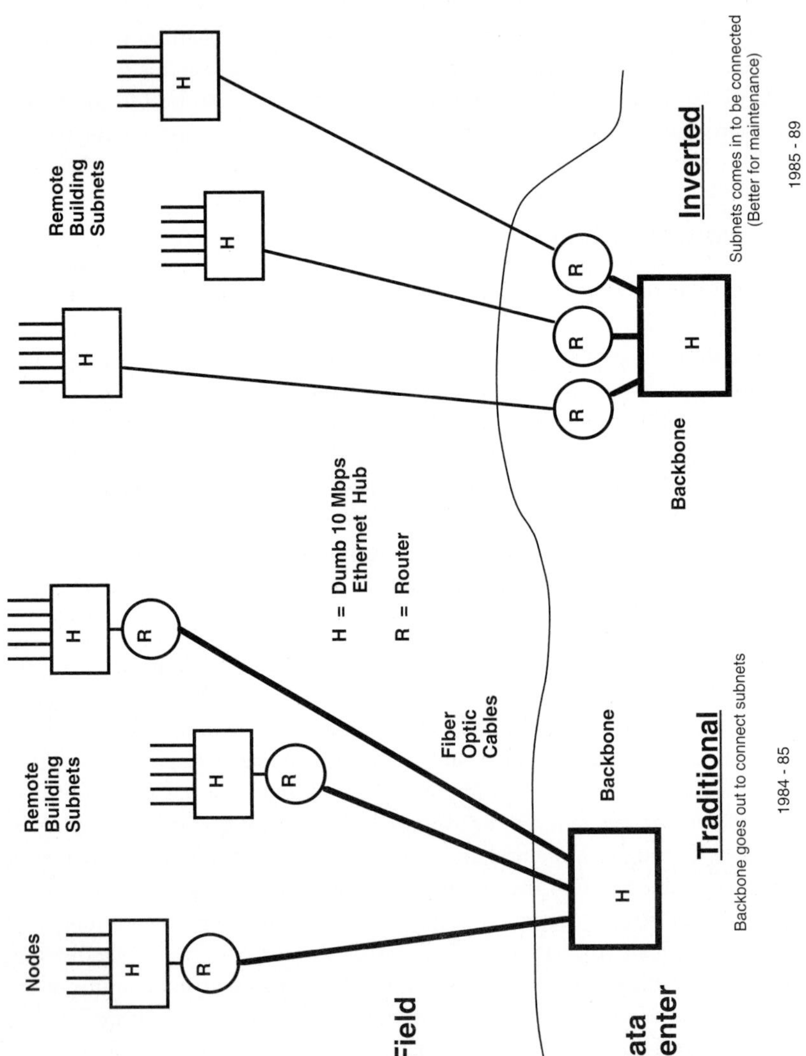

Figure 8.1 Traditional and inverted backbone networks.

repair of the routers considerably easier. All the tools, parts and expertise are close at hand. Additionally, since we now have an instance of every subnet appearing in the central location, subnet diagnosis can often be done right there instead of in the field. Subnet monitoring can also be done much easier. This was particularly useful before the dawn of the simple network management protocol (SNMP) and associated remote management capabilities.

We used this Ethernet hub based inverted backbone until the end of the 80s when it started to show signs of overload. We bought time by partitioning it into two bridged segments. We also looked at the then soon-to-be standard FDDI as a longer term solution. That was very expensive, unstable and the complex SMT specification had not yet been finalized. At the same time, it occurred to us that our backbone was really the backplane of the hub. It also occurred to us that backplane or bus, being parallel devices, can typically run considerably faster than 10 or even 100M bps.

So, we conceptually designed an inverted backbone hub with a high performance, standard or proprietary backplane which could be a bus or a switching fabric, supporting multiple standard LAN interfaces such as Ethernet, Token Ring, FDDI and so on. In order to support the mix of LAN technologies, routing and/or bridging functions were built into the unit. A colleague formed a start-up company to implement that design but fell victim to one of the many problems face by start-ups. We then learned that Cisco was producing a multi-ports router that fitted the bill almost exactly even though it was not designed as a backbone.

For the past three years, we have been using a Cisco AGS+ multi-port router, or rather, its 530 Mbps C-bus, as our backbone hub. We have hierarchically reduced the over 150 subnets to 22 primary Ethernet subnets for connection to the hub. A second AGS+ supporting a number of lightly loaded and experimental subnets functions as a hot spare. Our experience with the inverted backbone has been very positive (see figure 8.2).

Due to the recent up surge in interest in multimedia, we are planning for the next phase of our backbone evolution. We are looking closely at the *asynchronous transfer mode* (ATM) technology. Besides being reasonably well received in both the data and telecommunications worlds, it offers scalable aggregate throughput, a good range of line rates, and will support *isochronous* communication for real time transmission of synchronized video and voice data.

Note that while ATM has potential as a desktop solution, as discussed earlier, whether it will make it, and when, is likely to be a function of its acceptance by computer vendors. That remains to be seen. Our current interest is limited to using it as a next generation backbone for connecting multiple multi-ports routers and bridges together.

8.2.5.2 SNMP and All That

Running a network complex with no monitoring tools is like steering a submarine among underseas canyons with absolutely no instrumentation. Not only would you not know what problems you may be having, often, you may not even know you are having a problem until the phones ring off the hook.

We view *network management* as such an important issue that the bulk of our network development efforts have gone into this area. The main objective is to reach a state such that (a) we will know of and be able to fix problems before they affect significant number of users, and (b) network operation can, by and large, be handled by people other than network gurus.

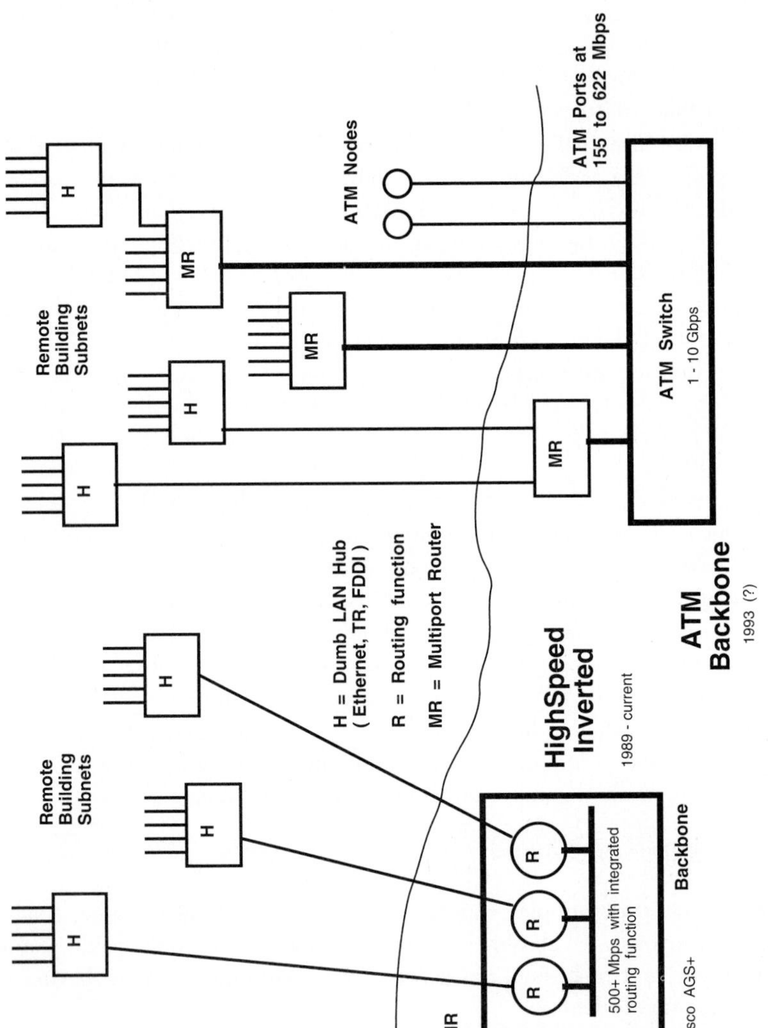

Figure 8.2 Backbone evolution.

When we started our network building exercise back in the early 80s, there were no commercially available tools. We developed our own set of monitoring and test tools. Additionally, our home grown routers were fully equipped with remote management capabilities. Not only did this permit us to remotely troubleshoot, and sometime fix, problems with the routers, it enabled the routers to function as windows into the connected subnets.

Like the router, the protocol used to interact with it was home grown. At that time, we were also deploying bridges from DEC which used a proprietary protocol for their interactions. It was clear that unless there was a well accepted standard protocol, the benefit of remote control of multi-vendor network components would be very difficult to achieve as vendors would be tempted to use proprietary protocols as a mean of locking in their customer base. So, when the *SNMP* effort got started, we backed it whole heartedly. In the process, we contributed to the development of the RMON MIB, *AppleTalk* MIB and the new and improved SNMP 2. Additionally, we have established a purchasing policy that made SNMP practically mandatory for most of our networking equipment.

While SNMP allows us to gather data, receive alarms and, to a lesser extent, remotely control network components, it provides only the basis for network management. The issue is what does one do with all the raw data and alarms? While they may be meaningful to an experienced network engineer, presenting a mountain of raw data to a less skilled operator on the graveyard shift will likely draw a blank. What is needed is a *management station* that can turn the data into useful operational information and instructions. Unfortunately, most of the management stations in the market today act mostly as relatively simplistic visualization engines. The user typically is still required to do considerable amounts of interpretations. Furthermore, problems such as routing table corruption cannot be easily deduced from graphs, charts and colored maps. We have developed a complimentary management station package that will process the data received and inform the operator, in plain English, that problems have been detected, the suspected nature of the problems and recommended remedial actions.

In conjunction with SNMP, a key component of our network management arsenal is the network information database. This crucial database contains records for all officially registered nodes on the network. Each record contains information such as the node name, IP address, Ethernet or other LAN address, system type and other system information, contact name and phone number and so on. Besides providing operational and resource management information, the database derives data used by the Domain Name System, BootP servers, host tables for workstations and so on. As with any manually maintained database, keeping it up-to-date is a continuous challenge. We developed a suite of programs that regularly audit the database content against real life data provided by various monitoring agents such as routers, bridges, and RMON devices. We also regularly purge entries from the database for devices that have not been seen for an extended period.

8.2.6 Off Campus Services

In addition to the on campus local area networking complex, we have a very popular metropolitan campus network. This is a *CO-LAN* service provided by our local telephone company, Bell of Pennsylvania. Service is available to members of the university living in areas served by three central offices. With this service, data connectivity to the campus at 19.2K asynchronous or 64K synchronous is provided simultaneously and non-intrusively to the standard voice service over the regular phone line. For the 19.2K service, we have a number of terminal servers that can also function as serial line routers for Serial Line IP (SLIP). Due to the lack of cost effective synchronous interfaces for workstations and, more importantly, the lack of serial line routers for 64K synchronous links, 64K synchronous service is very limited.

CO-LAN is a forerunner to ISDN. We will be happy to convert our CO-LAN service to ISDN if and when (a) the service is available and the price is right, (b) cost effective or built-in ISDN interfaces are available for the computers, and (c) cost-effective serial line routers for 64K and 128K links are commercially available. Although we were an early participant in the local ISDN trial, we are still waiting for it to become a practical reality.

8.3 The Andrew Client Software

When the Andrew project got started back in 1983, it was before the Macintosh and decently powered PCs. There was an assumption by the Andrew development team that UNIX workstations would take over the world. We were wrong. In any event, the main thrust of Andrew client software development has been for the UNIX workstation. The three main products were a windowing system, a multi-media tool kit and a set of messaging system front ends.

The windowing system development was somewhat of a disappointment and offered some very interesting non-technical lessons. WM, the Andrew windowing system was technically sound. It was operational at least a year or two before the X windowing system. However, attempts to widely distribute it, with source code, quickly got bogged down by corporate lawyers and managers who failed to understand the unwritten rule of the *open* world. Instead of keeping great idea to oneself, the challenge is to thrust it down everyone's throat as the standard, against all other potential alternatives. Proprietary development would quickly fade into the sunset once an incompatible, publicly available, and widely accepted standard takes hold. That was what happened to WM. Before we could extricate ourselves from the legal and bureaucratic quicksand, X established a strong beachhead. Independent software vendors started developing their wares on that platform and the rest was history. We gave up and moved over to X.

The WM experience was not totally in vain. Its failure paved up the way for the other Andrew components to be made available to the public and as candidates for standards. The most noticeable are the Andrew Tool Kit and the Andrew File System which will be discussed later.

The *Andrew Tool Kit* (ATK) was a powerful windowing system tool kit developed initially for WM. It was one of the earliest multi-media tool kit available. This tool kit has been converted to run under X and is currently being distributed by the ATK Consortium located at Carnegie Mellon. A number of utilities including a multi-media editor and a Multipurpose Internet Mail Extension (MIME) compliant multi-media messaging system front end have been developed based on the tool kit.

Another major UNIX client related development was in the area of software management and administration for distributed systems. Given that we had hundreds of differently configured workstations under our direct and indirect management, the main challenge was to devise ways such that the incremental cost of looking after an additional workstation was kept to a minimum. Specifically, we did not want to have to send people out to work on individual workstation whenever a major software release was made. Furthermore, the administrative package had to allow departmental system administrators and/or end users to carry out additional customization without affecting the effectiveness of our remote software management capability. Details of these developments, DEPOT and EMT, are described in the systems management and administration chapter (chapter 14) of this book.

Finally, as the project progressed, we realized that UNIX workstations would not be the only game in town. While there were plenty of workstations on the campus, there were a greater number of Macintoshes and PCs around. Indeed, few students bought workstations. They generally preferred Macintoshes and PCs, and for such good reasons as cost effectiveness and the availability of vast quantities of application software. We did some remedial work to include the PCs and the Macintoshes into the Andrew framework. Those developments allowed the PC and the Macintoshes to be clients of some of the Andrew network based services and will be covered in the following section.

8.4 Andrew Network Based Services

8.4.1 Andrew File System (AFS)

Besides the network, by far the most significant and successful component of the Andrew project is the file system. Andrew File System is the foundation on which practically all our other distributed services such as messaging, print servers and so on are built.

The Andrew File System differs from most other file systems in that it was designed from the ground up with scalability in mind. So while Appleshare was designed to handle the tens of users sized work group, network file System (NFS) for the hundreds of users market segment, AFS was designed to serve communities of thousands efficiently. In order to achieve scalability, the design partitions off as much work as possible to the client so that the incremental load of serving an additional client can be kept to the minimum for the server.

A means of reducing the server load is the extensive use of caching. When a file is opened, it is copied to the client. All subsequent read and write operations by that client are done to the local copy. When the file is closed, the copy in the client's cache will then be written back to the server.

Any time there is *caching*, particularly in a multi-user environment, the question of cache consistency will raise its head. In the spirit of pushing work to the client and in the attempt to keep the server stateless for simplicity, the prime responsibility of ensuring cache consistency was given to the client in the initial design. The client constantly checked with the server to see if the cached file had been changed behind its back by other users. This constant checking imposed a heavy load on the server and was quite wasteful since the vast majority of the responses would be negative. We then changed the paradigm from discovering to informing. With this, the file system kept a list of outstanding cached files and would inform the appropriate clients when their cached files had been modified by someone else. This is the *call back* approach. Note that the client's reaction to a call back depends on the application and is outside the scope of the call back algorithm.

Given the fact that AFS is designed to serve thousands of users, provisions have been made to support lots of servers. A design goal is that a user should not be required to remember on which server the files or collection of files, called volumes, are physically located. This is particularly important as we dynamically move volumes around between servers for load balancing. In order to provide file location transparency, AFS has a volume location data base (VLDB) which maps volumes to the servers. With VLDB, all the user needs to know is the path name of the file or directory. Since this data base is critical to the operation of the file system, it is designed for redundancy through replication. Replication is also useful for load sharing.

The file system was initially designed with a Kerberos-like authentication scheme. When Kerberos gained widespread acceptance, both authentication schemes were supported.

Additional to the standard UNIX file protection, AFS offers access control list (ACL) for directory. Users can explicitly specify the users and/or groups who may access his or her directories and their contents. Information associated with access control is stored in replicated protection servers (PTS) which happens to be co-located with the VLDBs. When a user contacts a server, information associated with the user such as UID, group IDs are passed to the server. The server uses this information to verify the user's access rights to its resources.

Acknowledging the political reality that some departments want to run their own file servers, AFS has the concept of *cell.* Each cell is essentially a set of file servers under one administrative domain. A cell administrator has overall control of all the resources within the cell such as volumes, VLDB, PTS and so on. At CMU, four departments besides the computing services operate their own cells. From an end user's point of view, cells are just nodes on the global AFS name space which actually span the world!

At the lower level, a file server can be configured with a small number of giant capacity disks or a greater number of moderately sized disks. Similarly, we can have a smaller number of high power servers or a greater number of more moderate servers. Given the fact that we have a high concurrent access environment, we prefer a higher degree of parallelism to reduce the probability of bottlenecking by head movement in case of disks and network access in the case of servers. Our servers are actually workstations with good bus structure and other I/O characteristics.

The performance of the file system has been very reasonable. An area we are keeping an eye on is the load on the server network. We have split the server pool onto multiple Ethernet segments. This has worked fine so far. When the need arises, we will move the servers to higher capacity networking technologies.

How did AFS measure up?

When it was first deployed in 1986, it was pretty awful. We had both stability as well as performance problems. Given the complexity of the software, we expected a few bugs. But the biggest problem turned out to be the fact that the system was simply not adequately engineered for operational management. There was a lack of comprehensive monitoring and diagnostic tools. We often had no idea that problems were occurring until users complained. Tracking down the sources of problems was difficult, frustrating and often led to finger pointing exercises with the networking group. Data communications managers take note! There is a tendency to attribute *all* unknown distributed computing problems to the network. The situation was made worse by the frequent releases of new software. Given the shortage of monitoring capabilities and the almost total lack of structured, regression test suites, those releases introduced additional instabilities.

At one stage, we spent considerable sums to upgrade our servers only to have both the performance and reliability nose dive! What we had unknowingly done, in this complex system with lots of interlocked components, was to increase the performance of one component to the extent that it drove another component to, and sometimes beyond, its limit. That was not difficult to do when one had no indications of what was happening. We were, for all practical purposes, operating in the dark.

This very unsatisfactory state of affairs was eventually brought under control when we made a determined effort to engineer a comprehensive set of tools for the monitoring of the key potential stress points of the system. Given the complexity of the system, and the fact that the tools implementation team differed from the original design team, monitors were mostly placed around but not into the core of the system for fear of unknown side effects. In spite of this shortcoming, the improvement was very significant. We now can often tell when the system is out of kilter or heading for trouble prior to it grinding to a complete halt. Furthermore, we are able to better tune the system as needed for maximum performance.

Besides monitoring tools, we also tightened up on the bug fixes and software release procedures. This was made considerably easier since we are now dealing with the original development team only at arms length. We no long accept binary patches. Software fixes and enhancements are only installed after we understand at least their functions. Furthermore, unless the problems are critical in nature, fixes and enhancements are no longer installed continuously as they become available. In the past, this could be a weekly or even daily event. We would wait until a convenient time such as in-between semesters before making major upgrades. While the above procedures may sound obvious, it was amazing how tempting quick fixes were particularly when delivered by a persuasive development team working at close quarter to the service organization.

For the past two years, the system has been operating reliably serving over 8,000 active users and 4,000 workstations, Macintoshes and PCs. What is the main lesson learned? There is a big difference between a clever system and a clever production system. Retrofitting monitoring and management capabilities into a complex system after it has been built is painful at best. They should be designed and engineered into the system right from the start. Finally, running a complex system as a service without instrumentation is definitely not recommended.

8.4.1.1 Epilogue

Learning from the window manager's failure, serious efforts were made to gain public acceptance of this technology. Most of the original developers of AFS joined a start-up company called Transarc to commercialize the product. They have been successful in getting the Open Software Foundation (OSF) to accept the next version of AFS as the standard Distributed File System (DFS) for their Distributed Computing Environment (DCE).

8.4.2 Andrew Messaging System (AMS)

The Andrew Messaging System (AMS) is another major service provided by the Andrew project. From the user's point of view, AMS differs from most of the other mail systems in that mail, bulletin boards and folders for filing messages are integrated together and are accessed through a common user interface.

The AMS client for an Andrew workstation is built on top of ATK, the multimedia tool kit. As a result, AMS is a multimedia messaging system – as long as the sending and receiving stations are both AMS equipped Andrew workstations. The later version of the software also supports the new MIME multi-media messaging standard.

AMS takes full advantage of the AFS file system. All Andrew users have AMS mail boxes in their AFS volumes. When one Andrew user sends a message to another Andrew user, the AMS workstation client directly deposits the message into the recipient's mail box in AFS. If the message is not addressed to an Andrew user, the AMS client deposits the message in a system outbox. A server machine called the Post Office and Bulletin Board (PO/BB) server regularly checks the system outbox and sends the messages along to their destinations using SMTP protocol. The PO/BB machine also handles in bound mail from outside the Andrew system and deposit messages into the recipients' mail boxes. In its role as bulletin board server, it will insert locally generated and imported bulletin board entries into the appropriate AFS directories.

The use of AFS as a message store for bulletin boards has caused significant performance problems. AFS is not that well suited to applications where heavily concurrently accessed files or directories are being changed frequently. Popular bulletin boards have these characteristics. As a result, the file server has to constantly issue *call backs* to inform the multiple clients of the changes. This is an AFS performance killer, particularly if some of the readers of the bulletin boards are off campus and connected to Andrew through slower and not very reliable links.

8.4.3 Services for PCs and Macintoshes

As mentioned previously, the project started on the assumption that UNIX workstations would take over the world. By the mid 80s, it became very apparent that would not be the case. There were a lot of PCs and Macintoshes on campus and they were not about to go away. Remedial efforts were made to integrate those machines into the Andrew environment by providing ways for them to access some or all of the network based services.

The most important service is messaging. This is the glue that holds the campus together. We started off by providing a terminal interface to the Andrew messaging system via an intermediary UNIX machine equipped with the AMS client software. Besides allowing users to access the messaging system from home, it also provided the PCs and Macintoshes with basic access to AMS since both systems had Telnet software. The down side of this approach was that it needed a pool of intermediary UNIX machines to accomplish the task. We considered moving the AMS client software into the PC and Macintoshes. We would have to port the AMS client library over to those machines. And in view of the dependency of AMS on AFS, we would also need to port the AFS client software. Given the complexity of the task and the severe system environment limitation of the PC and Macintosh at that time, we quickly purged that thought. However, we did develop a pair of more user friendly, *native* messaging interfaces for the Macintosh and the PC.

While the PC users could access AFS files by FTPing through an AFS UNIX client workstation, we wanted to provide a more natural form of integration. The result was a package that allowed the PC user to view AFS as additional PC drives. This is similar to Novell Netware except that the network file store is AFS. Again, because of the complexity of the AFS client software and the limitation of the PC, an intermediary server of AFS UNIX client workstation was still required. Besides providing access to the AFS servers, the intermediary machine also handled the mapping between AFS to the DOS file system.

For the Macintosh to AFS integration, we took a slightly different approach. Through Appleshare, the Macintosh had a built-in hook for an external file system. We intended to use the Columbia Appletalk Protocol (CAP) or similar package that equip a UNIX machine with AppleTalk capabilities including AppleShare and printer spooling features for this purpose. The UNIX server machine, in this case, would also be an AFS client. We had not gone too far with this. While the CAP package had potential, it was not sufficiently stable. Recent versions of CAP show a lot more promises and we will be revisiting the whole situation again. Meanwhile, the Mac users have to settle for FTP.

8.5 Andrew II

As mentioned earlier, a few years ago, most of the AFS team left the university and joined a start up company called Transarc to commercialize AFS. They submitted a new version of AFS to the Open Software Foundation (OSF) for consideration as the file system component of their distributed computing environment (DCE). It was well received and was accepted as OSF's standard distributed file system (DFS).

While DFS maintains most of the basic concepts of AFS, its implementation is substantially different. It uses DCE's Remote Procedure Call instead of AFS's Rx RPC. It has a new set of application programming interface (API). It even has a different file storage structure.

As described earlier, all current Andrew network based services have critical dependency on AFS. This is particularly the case with AMS. As AFS is replaced by DFS, all our Andrew applications are going to break. Our options are (a) carry out major surgery to make those applications work with DFS, or (b) take the opportunity to re-engineer the whole system based on our operating experiences as well as taking into consideration the changes in the technological market place over the past 10 years. We choose to do the latter.

The current shared file system centric architecture has a number of advantages. It simplifies the overall design in that a lot of distributed operations can be done through the shared file system instead of having to create new communication protocols. Since all the data are stored centrally in the file store rather than in disks local to the workstation, users can access their data from any Andrew workstation on campus. Software distribution and management is greatly simplified. The cost of a workstation is reduced as less disk space is required. This was particularly significant in the early 80s when disk storage was still relatively high. It is much less of an issue today.

On the flip side, the shared file system centric design created a lot of tightly interlocked components that must all be working, and working well, in order for Andrew to work acceptably. Failure of any one of those generally complex components such as the network, AFS client software, AFS server, VLDB server and so on could quickly render an Andrew workstation totally useless. It is an all or nothing scenario. Indeed, the current Andrew system has the feel of a time sharing system. In this case, instead of sharing computing cycles, the critical central resource that is being shared is the file system. The net results to the end users are pretty much the same.

With Andrew II, we are taking a different approach. In the new scenario, the DFS file system is one of many services attached to the network. Other services include printing, messaging, backup, authentication, directory services and so on. Architecturally, all services will be peered to each other and with little or no cross dependency on one another. Hence, if a server fails, the client will be denied of that, and only that, service.

The configuration of the UNIX workstation will fall into two categories – network dependent and network enhanced. Network dependent workstations will function the same way as the Andrew workstation today. They will to be the configuration of choice for public cluster workstations. Network enhanced workstations would have adequate local disk storage to support stand-alone operation if necessary. Provision will be made to allow users to move software packages from appropriate servers easily onto the local disk but, at the same time, allow for ease of software administration by system management staff. Users can have the best of the personal and network computing world.

In the Andrew II environment, users will have the option of storing data locally on their workstation or in the file servers. Remote backup and archival services will be provided for owners of workstations.

An intriguing area we will be addressing is *network undocking and docking* for notebook class of computers. When a notebook computer is to be disconnected from the network, the system will automatically ensure that a set of user and system pre-defined functionalities and data such as local message store, is available and ready on the notebook computer. When the machine is reconnected to the network, another set of activities such as off loading spooled print jobs to print servers, re-synchronization of local and central message stores, archiving of files so designated and so on will take place automatically.

While UNIX workstation support will remain a key element of this new distributed computing environment, we will be taking service provisioning for the Macintoshes and PCs into considerations from the onset. This has posted an interesting and difficult challenge. When the Andrew project first got started, distributed computing did not, for all practical purposes, exist. Our challenge was to create such an environment. Ten years later, we face a very different problem. Everyone is in the act and they are marching off to different directions, muttering the overloaded, and increasingly meaningless term *open*. Our challenge now is to figure out how to fit all the key pieces of the puzzle together since the likelihood of one *standard* emerging in the near future that will really unify all platforms is remote at best.

Due to our continued interest in UNIX and our history with AFS, we have a lot of interest in OSF's DCE. However, we are concerned about its complexity, size, and licencing cost. It is not clear to us that even though DCE is *open*, how significant its impact really will be for the millions of DOS and Macintosh machines around the world. This is particularly the case when there are strong alternatives from companies such as Apple, Microsoft, Novell and Lotus. Our default approach is to create TCP/IP, not necessary DCE, based common dominator solutions for service integration if possible and provide gatewaying capabilities to highly popular but inconsistent services if necessary.

Andrew II is a major undertaking. However, as the architecture calls for minimum cross dependencies between services, it gives us the flexibility to acquire components from various sources as needed besides doing our own development. At this time, we are still in an early stage of the project which could make for interesting reading in future editions of this or similar book.

Finally, this time around, we will be engineering plenty of monitoring and management capabilities on all service components!

8.6 Acknowledgments

I would like to thank all members of Carnegie Mellon University's Information Technology Center that created Andrew and the computing services that deployed and operated the system for the very valuable experience. I would also like to thank IBM for their major support of the initial project.

Borenstein, N., et al. 1989. Architectural Issues in the Andrew Message System. *Message Handling Systems and Distributed Applications,* E. Stefferud, O-j. Jacobsen, and P. Schicker, eds., North Holland.

Borenstein, N., et. al, 1988. A Multi-Media Messaging System for Andrew. *Proceedings of the USENIX Technical Conference,* Dallas, Feb.

Gosling, J., and Rosenthal, D.S.H., 1984. A Network Window Manager. *Proceedings of the 1984 Uniforum Conference,* Jan.

Hansen, W., 1990. Enhancing documents with Embedded Programs: How Ness extends insets in the Andrew Toolkit. *IEEE Computer Society International Conference on Computer Language.*

Howard, J., 1988. An Overview of the Andrew File System. *Proceedings of the USENIX Technical Conference,* Dallas, Feb.

Howard, J., et al., 1987. Scale and performance in a Distributed File System. *Eleventh Symposium on Operating Systems Principles,* Austin, Nov.

Kazar, M., Synchronization and Caching Issues in the Andrew File System. *Proceedings of the USENIX Technical Conference,* Dallas, Feb.

Morris, J., et. al, 1986. Andrew: A Distributed Personal Computing Environment. *Communications of the ACM,* Mar.

Neuendorffer, T., The Andrew Environment Workbench: An Overview. *Third Annual X Windows Conference.*

Palay, A., et al. 1988. The Andrew Toolkit: an Overview. *Proceedings of the USENIX Technical Conference,* Dallas, Feb.

Rosenberg, J., et al.1987. An Overview of the Andrew Message System. *Proceedings of SIGCOMM '87 Workshop, Frontiers in Computer Communications Technology,* Stowe, Vermont, Aug.

John Leong is the Technical Director of Computing Services of Carnegie Mellon University. He is responsible for system and network software development and management. Prior to joining CMU as a system designer for the Andrew project, John Leong has held various technical and management positions in Philips, Bell Northern Research and the Toronto Globe and Mail. He was tenured at the University of Liverpool as a member of its Computer Laboratory. John has a B.Sc. and a M.Sc. from University of Manchester, both in Computer Science.

Chapter 9

Lessons Learned from Project Athena

Daniel E. Geer, Jr.
Geer/Zolot Associates

9.1 Introduction

The Athena Project (1983-1991) built an enterprise-wide, mission-critical computing system "to foster long-lived innovations in education at the Massachusetts Institute of Technology."[1] Early on, we recognized that this would require a network services model of computation–only that kind of computing would meet the twin goals of location independence and sharing that we felt were essential to its adoption by the instructional side of the Institute. As the state of computing at that time did not include the necessary tools, we undertook a multi-year development effort. Grant support[2] gave Athena staff the opportunity to meet a class of problems not previously seen–in short, to confront the many facets of scale unencumbered by normal budget constraints. The lessons learned from this effort have applicability in any enterprise where the extent, demand, or intensity of computing is growing faster than traditional resources would plausibly permit.

This chapter first provides a snapshot of today's MIT Athena environment. It recounts the problem Athena was to address, including the constraints on possible solutions. It gives an overview of the Athena components and strategies and then focuses on the engineering and managerial lessons of the project. Next, it talks about the lessons learned from Project Athena, including the steps to take and those to avoid. It closes with a discussion of some interesting, representative problems, ones that illustrate the rules of thumb of large-scale development recognized over an eight-year period.

[1]Project Athena Mission Statement, revised, 1987.

[2]The primary sponsors were Digital Equipment Corporation and IBM.

9.2 Snapshot of a Moving Target

In round numbers, the Athena environment at MIT consists of 1,500 workstations on 30 subnetworks, supported by 100 Gb of spinning storage, it handles some 4,000 logins and 10,000 mail messages per day. Some 100 hosts provide various network services (including file-, name-, mail-, notification-, and print-service). The staff placed and configured the systems wherever it was most operationally convenient to do. The potential user pool is greater than 10,000, and has significant annual turnover; total Athena users represent about 90 percent penetration of that potential user community. Significant numbers of courses require the use of Athena. Some residential living groups have Athena installations in their common spaces. General availability for all the living groups is imminent (it hinges on network installations there).

Within logical limits, the Athena environment is immune to single-point failures of connectivity or service operation. There has been no downtime in years, except for general power failures. All aspects of system management, except for installation and hardware field service, are handled remotely from a centralized service management system. A software update service is also centrally controlled, and is fully automatic for those workstations configured to subscribe to that central service. Operations and user-account administration headcounts are an order of magnitude lower than workstation management on the timeshare model. The Athena environment has been implemented at a number of university and commercial sites, and at least one vendor[3] has based a commercial offering on that environment.

9.3 Major Design Considerations

With some satisfaction and the substantial benefit of hindsight, we can say that what we wanted is what we got. The major design considerations are as follows:

9.3.1 Consistency

A legacy of "every department for itself" was a mediocre user environment, occasionally consistent within departments, but wildly inconsistent between them. Thus, a user requiring the computing resources of multiple departments (in our case, enrollment in courses from multiple academic specialties) would need to learn and retain a different style of interaction for each department. Such a situation was untenable if the community's use of computing was to grow or if the various departments were to work cooperatively on interdisciplinary problems. In part, this was our major motivation for choosing to advance the development of the X Window System. In addition to its other features (such as facilitation of location independence via network transparency of the window system), X offered the chance to make the users' environment consistent across all display architectures, despite many variations both between and within vendor product lines. The consequences of our standardization on a virtual display

[3]DECathena, a service offering of Digital Equipment Corporation.

cannot be overstated: X has created an enterprise-wide computing environment in which the most visible user-level inconsistency is that no two manufacturers place the *delete* key in the same position on the keyboard. In retrospect, we do not believe that enterprise-wide, location-independent cooperative work would have been possible in the absence of this unification of the user environment on, between, and across the base computing and communications infrastructure.

9.3.2 Coherency

Of equal importance to a consistent user environment is a coherent programming environment. Not only must the user community be able to reapply its skills as it moves between and among the enterprise's computing facilities, it must also be possible for programmers to devote their energies to subject matter, and not to endless reprogramming to take advantage of new displays, new networks, and so forth. The X Window System's vendor-neutral, device-independent abstraction of display architecture was essential for a coherent application programming interface (API) on top of an otherwise incoherent display environment.

To complete a coherent programming milieu, we recognized that more than just the display environment needed a defined (and defended) level of coherency. In general, coherence can be established at one of three levels. First and most difficult is that of *common instruction set* coherence. The low-end personal computer world (DOS based) has this kind of coherence. This was impossible within Project Athena, because, from the outset, the available equipment mix would not support such an assumption.[4] The next less restrictive coherence model is that of a *common execution abstraction*, wherein different platforms can run from the same code base, subject to recompilation. Because we knew from the beginning that we would be operating on a heterogeneous hardware base, we decided to provide a coherent API by providing the same operating system on each supported platform[5]. This strategy of providing coherence at the API level was attractive, if not essential, to stimulate others to begin to develop an applications software base for the systems we were providing. Issues such as maximizing workstation availability in both number and geographic location, reusability of software across machine types, and minimization of the complexity of the overall environment for technical support staff and application writers all figured in this decision. An API based on common execution was a high-value outcome; unfortunately, it ultimately proved unaffordable.

As the grant-supported phase of Project Athena ended, its environment was to become another ordinary facility of a technical university. The cost issues became even more important. One of those costs was clearly unsupportable–the idea of a generally coherent API based on a common execution abstraction. A coherent API for the display environment is essential and–with X as a *de facto* industry standard– easy to provide (and getting easier as the standardization of higher layers shakes out to Motif). However, a coherent general API continues to elude us; the porting cost of providing a vendor-neutralized operating system is simply not

[4]From Digital, the VAXstation; from IBM, the RT/PC.

[5]We ported Berkeley Standard Distribution (BSD) UNIX to all of our equipment

feasible for any one user organization to assume. The question, then, is: Does that matter? The conclusion we came to is: It does not.

Given the commitment to a network services model of computation and the goal of maximizing supportable heterogeneity, it became clear that a source-code abstraction (the general API) was the wrong coherence layer. The correct layer is that of *protocol coherence.* In short, the correct procedure is to say to any potential participant in the network services environment: If you have connectivity and can talk my protocols, you can play ball. This is a *minimax* solution for the computing of the next decade–minimum arbitrary requirements on network entities, maximum interoperability between those entities. To put it in the terminology of the X community: minimum policy, maximum functionality. Choosing to defend a protocol coherence *contract* between the Athena environment and developers for it upholds Athena's mission to "foster long-lived innovations," yet without unduly constraining the manner in which that goal would be implemented.

9.3.3 Reliability

The reliability of the system proportionately controls the user community's willingness to become dependent on the system. In Athena's case, the issue of reliability hinged on ensuring two features of the system–immunity to single points of failure and avoiding silent failure modes.

There were limits on the immunity to single points of failure, since some forms of failure were unprotected. (This included the physical failure of an unshadowed disk surface containing a read-write volume.) This kind of failure–entity failure–cannot be wholly prevented except at great cost. However, we can prevent the environment from failing due to service failure or connectivity breaks.

Services in the Athena environment that must be highly available are replicable; those without that requirement are not. Not every service can operate with all its subcomponents replicated (though the Zephyr real-time notification system is capable of that, for example). Rather, each service with an availability requirement can be replicated or otherwise made operable in the face of component or connectivity loss. Some services reduce their functionality when component failure occurs; for instance, the Kerberos network authentication system continues to enable secure client-to-service communication as long as a single replicate is operating anywhere, but it does not permit the registration of new network entities if the failed component is the Kerberos master host. The environment may replicate other services by way of configuration, such as designating alternate fileservers for common read-only volumes; this may be an explicit feature in the fileservice itself, as in the Andrew File System (AFS), or external to it, as in the case of naming support for redundant NFS filesystems. Some services have no availability requirement (e.g., the Moira service management system), and so may represent single points of failure without affecting the user's expectation of the service environment's capabilities. Finally, some services (such as the enterprise-wide mail hub) have hot spares and stay on the air through swapout.

Failures, where they occur, are prompt and visible. Systems administrators of large installations must be protected from failures that worsen yet remain silent until the problem or pervasive. When, for example, a single disk drive in a sea of fileservers begins that gentle crescendo from isolated correctable read error to hard failure of the physical device, the earlier the error is detected, the better. An Athena strategy is to remotely log all physical device events to a central logging host, and to instrument that host with feature detection algorithms that can announce, for example "Six soft errors in sector xxx, drive yyy, server zzz in the last hour" or "All file servers in Building 66 respond to pings but fail to respond to NFS packets."

Similarly, the users know that, when a failure occurs, the effect closely follows the cause. This means that they may be able to diagnose and/or modify the cause. For example, neither print spooling nor mail transport queue on the local workstation. Instead of local queuing, the semantics of a satisfactory return value from a print or mail command states that the user's missile is in the hands of the network service itself, not merely that it is in a local spool file. Alternately, a service request failure is prompt, and means that printing or mail transport is generally unavailable. In the case of print, that would include any quota-related service denials, or a request for a nonexistent or an inoperative print device. In the case of mail, it ensures that mail routers are present, and also makes primitive sanity-checks on the mail message's format and addressing.

9.3.4 Manageability and Cost-Effectiveness

To scale up, it is necessary to change the equation of system administration cost. In traditional systems, operational costs are dominated by a component that is proportional to the number of users, the number of machines, or both. The Athena design changes that proportionality so that it is dominated by the number of network services, the number of subnetworks, or both. This makes the management costs effectively scale-independent of the principal constant factors of prior operational models and permits an order of magnitude improvement in the labor cost of running the computing plant. In other words, we have changed the useful fan-out of a system administrator (SA) from approximately 25 hosts per SA, to one where 250 hosts per SA is comfortable, and that is not the upper limit. A coherent, consistent and reliable computing plant was not caused by the plant *being* well run, but that the plant *could* be well run, and run cheaply. Coherence, consistency, and reliability were designed-in, under the ever-present constraint of scalability.

To put a slightly different spin on manageability, we now manage services, not hosts. Any host can participate in this environment if it has connectivity and is interoperable with our protocols. If the owner wants, the host's relationship can be very simple–an á la carte selection of services on an as-needed basis; or, if the owner prefers, the host can simply and reversibly subscribe to management that includes software update services. Athena central staff see no incremental workload worth measuring.

9.3.5 Macro-Configuration

Traditional UNIX is completely silent on macro-configuration of computing services. Redundancy, fail-soft and fall-back arrangements, asynchronous *flag-day free* updates to field operations, self-sequencing cold-start procedures, and computing as a commodity are not part of a traditional UNIX repertoire.

At Athena, the system is available continuously. Because of the large amount of equipment, hardware failures routinely occur; except for logical single-point entities (such as the workstation before which an individual user is sitting, or such as the private home directory of a particular user or workgroup), all services are provided redundantly. Access to services is (indirectly) through the nameservice, which makes planned service outages (and many unplanned ones) totally transparent. Important services are redundant and geographically dispersed so that no single point of failure in the entire network results in a service degradation for the typical user.

Workstations, being dataless, are easy to make whole in the event of failure– if a workstation is misbehaving, reload its software. If it still misbehaves, call in a hardware trouble report. This type of triage operation requires only treatment skills, and is suitable for many more personnel than only those with complete diagnostic skills.

Software installation, repair, and update all use the same mechanism–making the target look like a reference source. Installation media are subnet-independent and using them requires no prior administrative handshake (such as an Internet address assignment). A workstation can go from its crate to on-the-air in ten minutes. That figure can be reduced to one minute, which would make sense to do if it ever becomes desirable to make a full software reload be part of a login/start-up sequence.

A distributed environment is subject to partial outages and, occasionally, to complete failures (such as outages due to power failure). Athena has configured its hosts and service to restart in a fashion consistent with completely hands-off cold-start. Cold-start to full operation is limited only by file-system integrity check time, itself a function of disk acreage and CPU horsepower. Typical Athena timings are approximately one hour from complete power failure to complete normal operation.

Labor at Athena is spent exclusively on handling exceptions and on mechanical operations (such as hanging tapes). This is no accident, as the process of registering new users illustrates. New users are identified by a regular tape feed from the MIT Registrar's office. That tape provides two pieces of information: a name and an MIT ID number. The name serves as an identifier (the prospective user types it into a "register for a new account" client available as a button click on the faceplate of any unused workstation) and the ID number serves as a temporary authenticator (for the duration of the registration session). After answering the obligatory questions (such as picking a username and providing an office telephone number), the user is thanked and asked to return the next day. Overnight, the Moira system does everything required to instantiate a new user account, including (but not limited to): assigning a UNIX user identifier (UID) to the (user-selected) login name; finding a fileserver with low utilization and creating a home directory for the new user there (including modifying ownership and quota control); announcing these facts to/through the nameservice; assigning a mail delivery post office (similar to a home directory construction sequence); and so forth. Several hundred students per day can claim accounts, and a 2 MIPS host will still be loafing.

9.3.6 Constraints on the Solution Space

As in any engineering exercise, the solution space also had constraints orthogonal to the general engineering issues. First, we had to choose durable technical solutions; the Athena environment could not require the perpetual infusion of grant monies and equipment, nor the perpetual presence of its inventors. Recalling the axiom of "Fast, cheap, or reliable–choose two," it was our job to move from a heavily subsidized stage (where *fast* and *reliable* held sway) to a stable point where *cheap* was also a feature.

Second, there was the constraint of competition, not coercion–at no time in Athena's development was it mandatory for any unit of MIT to use Athena. (One by one those other facilities adopted the Athena model or passed out of existence.) In displacing other models and facilities, Athena had the fundamental advantage of the network services model; as departments considered converting their computing to client/server from timeshare, they naturally looked to us.

9.4 Overview of Athena Components

This section provides a rough outline of the Athena environment, though other papers provide more thorough descriptions (Champine, et. al., 1990)[6] Athena has become the prototype for high-use distributed computing. We had the advantage of hardware grants of large numbers of workstations; the fast deployment of these workstations forced us into devising solutions to problems that arise in a distributed workstation environment. We needed a system that was easy and cheap to manage centrally; one that was secure, and that enabled users to get at their environments regardless of their location on campus.

Indeed, this is now a problem many organizations are facing due to the high availability and lowering price of workstations. Computing has escaped from the shrine behind glass with white-coated operators; proliferation is upon us. Proliferation without control is a disaster, yet proliferation with control had been unattainable at the outset of Project Athena.

9.4.1 Model of Computation

Traditional timesharing assumes that all resources are local; a file's pathname and logical name are identical; security is uniquely that of the containment barrier of a user's password at login; service location is local and time-invariant; modifications in resources such as computational capacity are made unilaterally and unitarily; system management is organizationally and administratively centralized; and so forth. This is not distributed computing; this is not conducive to location-independent cooperative work; this is not Athena.

Athena is a set of system software, applications and, most importantly, a style of configuration and a practice of operation that permits an environment to scale up to large numbers of hosts, users, services, brand names, and more. We cover various aspects of this below, but the point is that converting a timeshare model to a distributed model means modifying practices (and the tools that support them) in such a way that there are no constraints on operational scale. Most brand names of equipment can already apply the Athena model. It is already being implemented piecemeal in the product lines of many companies, and is in the

[6]Project Athena Technical Plan, 1983-1987.

specifications of such standards-setters as the Open Software Foundation and UNIX International.

We contend that in using a distributed computing model, workstations become independent entities floating in a sea of services. To accomplish that end, Athena uses as its reference prototype a *public workstation,* one that is serially reusable and can be made widely available simply by cloning. There are, of course, many desirable private modifications that are variations on this theme, but the basic idea is that of a model with options. The prototypical model is that which is most supportable in large numbers and which forms the backbone of the service that Athena's customers receive. Variations on this model support privately held workstations and, perhaps more surprisingly, are the basis for server hosts as well. In short, it is possible to have a basic idea of what comprises an Athena computational engine, and to define all other entities in terms of differences to it. In doing so, it becomes possible to support large numbers of workstations in public areas with a cookie-cutter approach and to provide other environments (server or client) by reference.

9.4.2 System Libraries

Timesharing systems typically have large software libraries available to their users. Storing a copy of that system library on each workstation is prohibitively expensive, if not technically infeasible. The use of dataless workstations and network file services typically ameliorates this problem. Even so, it is natural for a large environment to need several geographically distinct copies of the software pool. In this situation, configuration control, software support, and software maintenance all become difficult if there is a requirement for multiple versions of the system library, whether to support software revision levels or heterogeneous workstation types.

In the Athena environment, there is one master copy of the system library, whose location and availability is under the control of a service management system. This master copy is replicated to the extent necessary to get adequate network performance, such as by providing one complete copy per local area network (LAN)–a strategy related to network bandwidth conservation. Athena supports partial copying, and workstation consumers can asynchronously initiate local updates. The fileservice is non-monolithic; any of several protocols serve a given filesystem, and the filesystem can mix and match these protocols according to requirements (with user transparency). The Athena solution, then, is (in effect) dataless nodes: fileservice replication as needed; naming services to provide location independence; automatic, client-initiated software updates.

9.4.3 Name Resolution

In unmodernized timesharing systems, programs generally translate object names into addresses through the use of static configuration files. As UNIX examples, the file */etc/hosts* maps machine names to network addresses, the file */etc/passwd* provides the pathname to a user's home directory, and the file */etc/printcap* contains printer capability information including service name to host name translation. At some size or rate of change, the approach of using static files on each system is impossible–and becomes impractical well before that. Making indirect data updates accurate, consistent, and timely is difficult, but necessary.

The Athena approach is to provide a replicable, hierarchical nameserver under central control. This nameserver translates logical names to service names at the time of service connection. The nameservice is itself called Hesiod (Dyer and Hesiod, 1988), but Hesiod is largely an application programming interface (API) for writing location-independent programs. A few replicated copies of the nameserver data are generally useful to meet performance constraints, availability constraints, or both.

A very useful feature of the underlying technology, the Berkeley Internet Name Domain (BIND) system, is its hierarchical delegation. By permitting a top-level nameserver to direct you to company X and then have company X's own nameserver take over from there, hierarchical delegation substantially relaxes the coordination costs of nameservice that is available between, as oppose to within, companies. In our view, naming services are data access engines, but are not themselves primary source repositories of that information, that is, they are read-only copies of management information. The contents of the nameservice, that is to say the data it can return, are controlled by the Moira service management system (see below).

9.4.4 Authentication

Open networks supersede the boundaries of traditional operating systems, since these operating systems often make unwarranted, indefensible assumptions about network security. For example, traditional UNIX stores encrypted passwords for every user on every machine. It is very difficult to maintain accurate and consistent password and group access files on 50 workstations, to say nothing of a larger number. Having a nameservice (or similar entity) provide such files is not a good idea: it does nothing for the user and, even worse, it highlights the nameservice as a target for penetration. But, more importantly, access to services on hosts other than the one to which the user is directly connected requires one of two highly insecure alternatives:

- The various remote services can simply trust that all potential clients are who they themselves claim to be
- The services can trust no one, and require a password–ensuring that users are typing their passwords through the suspect network in the clear

Neither solution is any solution at all.

The Athena approach uses a trusted third-party, private-key, key-distribution center as an authentication service. A single, isolated, defensible *trusted third-party* is a host on the network that provides tokens of proof of identity to users as required. Any two network entities can communicate as long as each trusts this key distribution center. It is rather like the ruler of old whose signet ring in sealing wax was not forgeable. *Private-key* is a description of the style of encryption which hides the secrets that are the basis for proof of identity. *Key-distribution center* indicates that the host securely distributes (encryption) keys in support of proofs of identity.

All in all, the transaction is one where you ask the ruler for a letter of introduction to the remote service; you get that letter from the ruler wrapped and stamped; you then ship it to the service you wish an introduction to. (This assumes that both you and the remote service recognize the same ruler.) Such a method provably achieves secure network authentication no less strong than the underlying encryption technology (Needham and Schroeder, 1978; Steiner, et. al., 1988).

Note that this is an authentication (who you are) system; authorization (what you can do, given who you are) is a matter for each service provider to decide, as authorization is unique to the access policy of that service provider. All services within Athena come under central management and, thereby, authorization policy control. However, other service providers besides Athena proper will eventually be players, and it is the exactly right modularization to vest identity control in the network service infrastructure. This allows the individual service provider to exercise access control appropriate to its task.

9.4.5 Spooling

(Spooling here applies to both print spooling and outgoing mail spooling. The latter is discussed later; here we discuss printing.) UNIX assumes that printers are local, both physically and informationally (i.e., capability information is local). Two major drawbacks of this approach are local queueing and local static network print addresses. Traditional operation puts the print queue on the local machine, where a line printer daemon either prints it or requeues it to a remote machine as specified in the file */etc/printcap*. Such local spooling is incompatible with commodity oriented workstation computing, where the next user of the host may well not respect files in local spool queues. *lpr* gives no indication as to whether the printer is actually accepting jobs, thus there is no guarantee that the job will ever be printed. The use of */etc/printcap* as a static configuration file is also a problem. If a printer is added, deleted, or moved in the system, every */etc/printcap* file must be changed, obviously a situation incompatible with scale.

In Athena, print spooling is done at the print-service, with appropriate error messages, and configuration files are handled by the name server. In this way, the print-service can be located independently of the print clients, reconfigured dynamically as required, and the successful completion of a print spooling command will indicate the acceptance of the print request by the printing system, per se.

9.4.6 Mail

In standard UNIX, mail is addressed point-to-point, typically "username@node." That the user can get mail at only one location has obvious drawbacks in reliability, security, reconfigurability, and location independence. In addition, it complicates mass distribution (mailing lists), as it requires all recipients be able and willing at all times to accept mail. Finally, traditional UNIX expects that all hosts have local mailer configuration information, which creates a totally unscalable problem (frequency of update rises linearly with the number of users, but the net-wide volume of information to be managed rises with the square of the number of users).

In Athena, mail goes to "username@athena.mit.edu," a mail hub analogous to a central mail sorting facility of the USPS. On that hub, mail is rerouted to any one of a number of *post offices,* mail spoolers running a version of the Rand MH system modified to require Kerberos-mediated authentication as access control on the ultimate delivery of mail to the recipient.

Recipients can obtain their mail at any workstation in the system by locating the relevant Post Office (via the nameservice); sending an authenticated request for spool file final delivery over the net, and entering the mail reading client of the user's choice.

9.4.7 Notification

A traditional operating environment had no direct method of determining the instantaneous community of interest in a particular facility. In other words, if the operations staff has to disable the computer, they have to broadcast a warning and hope everyone is awake, present, and interested. If a user wants to directly reach another, they need prior information as to where to look.

A short-list description of an electronic mail message might be describe by these five characteristics:

- Arbitrary length
- ASCII text
- Unauthenticated
- Deliver by best method when available
- Known recipients

Taking the converse of each of these:

- Single packet
- Not necessarily ASCII text
- Authenticated
- Deliver now or discard
- Unknown recipients

and you have the Athena concept of a *notice* and, hence, the Zephyr notification system (DellaFera, et. al., 1988). Such a service is easier to demonstrate than to describe, but in simple operation, it makes *read-me-now* messages available to whomever wants to read them from whomever wants to send them. The catch is rather like the question of whether an unwitnessed treefall makes a sound–messages carry type and class information that may or may not select a recipient from among the active subscriptions present at the time of message transmission. This means that conventions may develop between users about which subscriptions to use for group communications, much as CB radio users have developed conventions. However, the service itself does not care, just as the CB radio manufacturer does not provide any special equipment for channel 7.

Messages can be between any two network entities, for example (apologies to certain musicians of the 60s):

from a person to a person	Joe gets Authentic message from Jimi: I hear you shot your old lady down
from a service entity to a service entity	a sorting and filtering process gets syslog datagrams for remulticast in summary analysis form

from a person to a service	consulting service gets Message from luser: What is a compiler?
from a service to a person	Phil gets Message from aeolus: The current weather in Cambridge is...'

In summary, a *real-time* message transport system is useful for rendezvous between information sources and sinks, particularly where the sinks are inherently mobile. In practice, Zephyr has been most heavily used for group and personal communications, though its operational use of has more than justified its construction.

9.4.8 On-line Consulting

UNIX support has traditionally been little more than on-line manual pages. Many of these were not intended for nor adequate except for experts. Further, self-help is not always a workable solution, particularly where the user population has high turnover. To truly support computing independent of time and place, it is necessary to provide consulting services over the wire.

Athena supports an On-Line Consultant (OLC). The OLC system provides a rendezvous mechanism (to connect the person with a question with a consultant), a user interface (usually a two-panel typing window like *talk* from Berkeley UNIX or *phone* from VMS), and management controls (such as logging, promotion, and forwarding through an OLC server). Consultants can answer frequent questions by pulling in answers from a stock-answer directory. This directory, equipped with a browsing tool, is a useful adjunct for users wanting to help themselves but who find the man pages insufficient.

The average time to get an answer to a question is about four minutes, but if answers must be delayed they are returned through electronic mail. The volume of questions is growing by 15 percent per year, faster than that of other tools, which indicates a growing reliance on the OLC system for system navigation and use.

9.4.9 Other Network Services

In addition to those already discussed, Athena supports over twenty other services. The X Window System (Scheifler and Gettys, 1987) is the best known, and by now nearly everyone sees the benefit of a network-transparent, vendor-neutral, device-independent window system. Time-synchronization services, conferencing systems, message-of-the-day propagators, privatized versions of consulting and administrative systems, and on and on. A point of design is worth mentioning–in an Athena environment, services and their control are arranged on the assumption that, in the future, all nodes in the network will be both consumers and producers of services. Whether, as in the academic model, it is a professor constructing, testing, advertising, authenticating, timing, and scoring an electronically administered examination, or something similar in an industrial setting, the point is that what is described here as a centralized management model is, more precisely, centralizable. The hooks are there for whatever administrative structure exists; what is present today is the one that fit the inventing institution, MIT. Other institutions, universities, and industry alike have found that this technology can be easily made to reflect the administrative relationship of their departments.

9.4.10 Service Management

Service management is typically accomplished by a (team of) wizard system manager(s) with a fanout to hosts of 25 to 50 hosts per. Such a system is not scalable to real ubiquity (without which, there is no location independence) and perpetually suffers from version skew and managerial turnover. In addition, no standards exist in the remote management area, so every application is on its own. Until standard management interfaces appear and come to exist in actual vendor products, it will be necessary to adapt the management system to the service, not the other way around.

To perform comprehensive service management, Athena provides the Moira Service Management System (Rosenstein et. al., 1988). Moira has two principle responsibilities:

- Ensuring easy and accurate building of tables for the nameserver (and other system users of this information)
- Providing the tools to bring arbitrarily constructed network services under central control

Organized as a highly access-controlled, omniscient database and an omnipotent, omnipresent data propagator, Moira ensures two things:

- The integrity of a database of control information
- The (loose) consistency of the service fleet with that database's contents.

Constrained only by reliability and integrity constraints, Moira provides no service directly–but, rather, it makes certain that the service environment (eventually) conforms to its idealized (database resident) model. With such a system, Athena enjoys a system manager fanout of 300+ hosts per. Moira provides both a data entry and editing interface and, simultaneously, a guarantee that current data appears in field configuration files. This simplicity contributes to the serviceability of an Athena environment more than all the features of that environment discussed before.

9.5 Lessons Learned

9.5.1 What You Cannot Do

We had the opportunity to make many errors, for scaling up is seductively rich in garden paths. In fact, what our vendor sponsors really did was permit us to have other peoples' problems first by letting us get out on the deployment curve farther and faster than any customer with normal fiscal circumstances. And, as in most science and many arts, much of gaining mastery is learning what not to do; this is assuredly true of preparing for scale. To really scale up to enterprise computing and beyond, you first need to recognize and obey the seven **NOs**:

1. *No shoe leather:* Management by walking around is good policy for people managers, bad policy for system administrators. It is not practical to visit every node on any regular basis–even less so in synchrony with any other set of events. You must be able to manage what you have never and will never see.

2. *No broadcast:* Denying inter-subnet broadcast is to network administration what firewalls are to factory buildings. Broadcast does not scale, least of all across organizational boundaries. Further, almost never will it really be true that every user must hear a particular message and/or that they all must hear it because you have no classification rule. As systems scale ever larger, broadcast messages (shutdown notices, say) become ever more irrelevant to any randomly selected user; it is a pretty rational human behavior to tune out any channel that carries consistently uninteresting messages. Use something better anywhere you can (though some uses, such as ARP[7] at boot time, cannot be avoided).

3. *No interdependencies:* Services must not depend on each other for fundamental operation, otherwise, failures are not containable. It may well be (more than) nice for one service to build on another, as the usefulness of a fileservice may be enhanced by a coordinated name service, but there must be a fallback for when that name service is not there. Large scale operation cannot happen if the failure of one service necessarily and completely obliterates others.

4. *No synchronous administrative handshakes:* Important systems-managerial steps must be not needlessly depend the order in which they are done. Ignoring this rule can create unnecessary bottlenecks and gratuitous error conditions. For example, installing a workstation and isolating a network address for it are often order constrained (i.e., do not do the former until the latter has happened); if there is no constraint (such as by having a fallback method of obtaining a network address from a pool of free addresses), then there is no exposure to faulty communications or mismatched schedules between network and system administrators and none of the complexity and energy of procedures to make sure that the *wrong* order does not happen.

5. *No local state:* Every bit of local state is a maintenance problem, no matter who creates it. If you remove the possibility of local state, then you remove the problem of managing the client leaf nodes in the computing tree. In short, if there is nothing worth saving on the workstation, then there is no reason to spend the time and energy of expert therapists on it–any user is capable of restoring it to software correctness and no user can destroy anything of value (to him/her or to others) by doing so.

6. *No costs linear with hosts or users:* Economies of scale must come into play, or it will not be possible to grow beyond some point.

[7]Address Resolution Protocol, NIC RFC 826.

7. *No permanent development staff:* A permanent development staff (creating fundamental infrastructure for your distributed computing environment) means you have missed the point somewhere; ubiquitous computing demands an end to hand-tailoring and a reliance on configuration control executed from the center. In short, if an innovation is going to last, it cannot be reliant on the perpetual presence of the inventors.

All these **NO**s are simple and to the point. Each of these is one that the Athena designers discovered empirically (and we were stubborn sometimes). There are perhaps more waiting to be discovered; we do not yet know about several orders of magnitude that we will be exploring in this decade.

9.5.2 What You Must Do

To really scale up, there are a corresponding sets of musts, though *musts* are necessarily less crisp than **NO**s. Here is the other side of the coin.

1. *Ask "Does it scale?"* Nothing scales up gracefully by chance; in fact, most everything breaks within one or maybe two orders of magnitude beyond its scale in the inventor's shop. Give this question primacy at design reviews; remember that if the product is really good, the demand for scalability will follow.

2. *Buy bricks, make mortar:* Conserve your skill and effort for the job of configuration and interoperability. Even if you could build a more versatile database, a better tuned filesystem, or what have you, it is inconsistent with a dedication to making scale-up happen.

3. *Leave the door open for change:* Any service with a future will change. Build version numbers into everything; do protocol version negotiation at connect time and design in the ability to service multiple protocol versions at the same time. Automatically update software; make support more expensive if automatic update is not permitted. Ignore this lesson, and you get flag days or the worst kind of obsolescence–*adverse selection* of the user community (i.e., retaining only those unable to fend for themselves, and likely miles astern in the revision levels).

4. *Practice good hygiene:* You have to have a final common pathway for both local development (a source code control discipline that works and a well-known desk where the buck stops) and for installation (installation and update procedures so foolproof that reinstallation can be treated as a hardware diagnostic). It is not crucial which source code control system you use, just that you do. It is not crucial what installation procedures you use, just that they never get cool much less rusty.

5. *Replicate, replicate, replicate:* Only be so good as to call it "cost effective implementation of reliability goals". Replicate everything you can, but still establish rational fallbacks for when the world fails in more than one way.

6. *Let everybody play:* At first, your systems will be the sole providers of a very small number of services; later, you will expand the scope and reach of that service environment. Recognize, however, that your environment will someday be composed of service providers and consumers you will not be able to tell apart (without a program). Make sure that nothing in your design specifies only centrally owned and operated services can play in your environment. Understand that you are providing the core services needed to define a distributed computing environment on which new and composite services may arise. What you are not providing is a timeshare environment with Ethernet instead of terminal servers.

9.5.3 Some Interesting/Representative Problems

9.5.3.1 Filesystem Model

The design of a fileservice model was Athena's most difficult design problem. The fileservice of choice had to fly smoothly over a multi-dimensionally bumpy terrain. The physical issues included:

- Variability in compute horsepower
- Variability in local storage availability
- Incompatible varieties of removable media
- Uneven advances in storage technology
- Large geographic area
- Variability in network availability, throughput

Questions about what filesystem software was already available, or could be made available, included:

- Starting point of the UNIX filesystem (UFS)
- The mix of remote filesystems and remote disksystems

The distribution issues included:

- Initially public workstations, centrally owned resources
- Ultimately private workstations, a mix of resources
- Overall feasibility
- Heterogeneous user sophistication

Added to this terrain, our original thinking led us to four general requirements on the filesystem model: a detachability requirement, an attachability requirement, an interchangeability requirement, and an operability requirement.

Detachability requirement: The workstation must be useful when detached from the campus network:

- 15 percent of undergraduates, 80 percent of graduates are housed in off campus apartments
- If privately owned, the workstation must be useful at home during the summer
- If privately owned, the workstation must be useful after graduation
- If effectively detached, for example, connected by dialup, some level of service must be possible

Hindsight says that these detachability-related issues are desirable, but less so are their requirements. Under a model of publicly owned resources and reliable connectivity, detachability is of small import. Increasingly pervasive connectivity makes the detached state less likely to occur, while fast-dropping unit disk storage costs make detachment easier to ameliorate with copies of otherwise remote file resources.

Attachability requirement: Network attachment must substantially augment usefulness:

- Currency–keeping local data and software up to date
- Access–drawing data and software from the larger world
- Communications–send and receive electronic messages of many types
- Announcement–propagation of interchange information to subscribers
- Sharing–export private files to others, with adequate control and import private files from others, with suitable permission

We have naturally emphasized this throughout the construction and use of the Athena computing environment. In fact, the attractiveness of attachability proved so strong that it has, itself, been a primary motivator for wiring all of MIT. The first advantage for a new user of the Athena computing environment is either communications (the ability exchange messages) or file access.

Interchangeability requirement: The file storage model must make invisible the incompatibilities of file systems between various hardware platforms.

- Native byte-order must not matter
- Removable media, if relied upon, should be interchangeable
- Reduced service, but still service, for low-end machines.

Operability requirement: The file storage model must be actually operable.

- Costs consistent with having students bear them
- Tolerate brief network outages, degrade gracefully to detached state for prolonged outages
- Be a good network neighbor
- Support high client to server ratio
- Provide or permit tools for server management
- Be transparently reconfigurable.

When discussing a file system model, there are also philosophical and practical issues that remain open to discussion, including:

- What does it mean to structure data? What is the last word on choosing between hierarchic naming vs. naming networks?
- What is the desired effect of a directory listing (e.g., */bin/ls*) at a point where the tree splits 10K ways?
- Should a large scale filesystem follow globally agreed upon names or is the users' interest more consistent with some limited view constructed by the user as needed?
- Should the half-life of information be reflected in the access path to it? For example, should entities that will be used lightly and discarded have a technique of reference different than heavily used files or archival data?
- How are exporters of private filesystems to advertise them, to make them available, or to withdraw them?
- How can a scale-independent filesystem model have the least policy and the most facility?

At Project Athena, we began with a (disk) block server, the "Remote Virtual Disk" (RVD) system. This was an attractive preliminary solution for reasons of performance (server to client ratio, *i.e.* fanout), simplicity (from both server and client points of view), and availability (the Remote Virtual Disk system, known as RVD, was available from the Lab of Computer Science). It was essential in allowing us to use VAX 750 class servers on a one-per-subnet basis and achieve the per-subnet redundancy of the read-only filesystems that constituted the common basis for all workstation clients.

9.5.3.2 Diskless vs. Dataless

In addition to a filesystem decision, we needed to decide what the nature of local facilities would be on our workstations. A core decision was diskful vs. diskless– we instinctively picked diskful because we could not see using the network as a swap device and, by serendipitous historical accident, our sponsors only had diskful machines for us at that early date anyway. Once we decided on diskful, the next decision was what was on that disk. Mindful that the less there the better (from a maintenance point of view), the design decision was to include a root filesystem and a local filesystem. The root would contain only enough software to bootload the workstation and get it on the network, plus a small number of utilities (*ed, netstat, ping,* and the like) that are useful on malfunctioning workstations. Everything else about the base environment, for example, the contents of */usr,* is off-board on (largely read-only) fileservers. Configured in this way, the workstation struggles to its own feet, but does not attempt to provide a user environment on its own. This strategy assumes intermittent software update of this root filesystem (see below), but minimizes the volume of software subject to that requirement.

In addition to the (centrally managed) root filesystem, there is a local filesystem–local in the sense that its contents are purely local and cannot be recreated from remote servers. In the canonic case, this local filesystem contains only */tmp* and, where useful, an AFS filesystem cache. This layout may be modified by the workstation owner in the case of a privately owned machine, but such modification carries with it the responsibility of preserving those local modifications through update cycles to the root filesystem. (Even when the workstation is privately managed, the root filesystem remains, in effect, the responsibility of Athena Operations as the service provider.)

In short, the configuration specifies local disk for coldstart, swap, cache, and temp space, and subscribes to fileservices for the rest. It draws a line across the local disk separating ownership and responsibility into managed and unmanaged sectors. If the unmanaged sector is not encumbered with data of value, the workstation contributes no central management load whatsoever beyond intermittent update of the small managed (root) filesystem.

9.5.3.3 Private Files and Backup

However valuable the dataless model is from system administration's view, it is not necessarily consistent with the workstation owner's view. In particular, the first request for relaxation of the dataless model is generally for local file storage. Given the partition oriented nature of the UNIX File System (UFS), it is a simple matter to divide the workstation disk real estate such that the local user/owner has a partition that can be thought of as private file space. Such a division does not, in practical fact, violate the dataless model if it meets two conditions; first, that for the purposes of software maintenance, the private space is simply *off the books* (it is not the responsibility of the system administrators to take any particular pains to preserve its contents) and, second, that contents of that private space not contain primary (that is, irreplaceable) data. The former condition permits the system administrator the latitude to take corrective action consistent with the aims of dataless nodes (including the idea of treatment without diagnosis). The latter requires a service agreement with the user community that provides some global understanding of the nature of file preservation, that is backup.

Backup, canonically speaking, is the process of taking a replicate of a file or filesystem at a particular point in time such that the file or filesystem could be recreated as of that point in time. The solution we took to the backup question permitted broad latitude of user choice, consistent with the idea that the user community is best able to evaluate trade-offs when those trade-offs can be clearly laid out. Specifically, all workstations in our environment had removable media so that those faculty and students that wished to retain materials by the most portable and most conventional means could do so. In many cases, the provision of removable media devices also permitted the user community to enlarge their personal storage inventory without relying on centrally operated storage facilities to do so (i.e., they could retain more material than they had quota to support).

Beyond locally operated removable media, however, we provided a grade of filesystem oriented backup that was of little incremental cost to the central plant and yet had a low enough activation cost to the user to encourage frequent backup on the user's part. In the pool of fileservers supporting the campus, those that were read-only supported workstation operation itself (e.g., the contents of */usr*). Other filesystems were provided users or projects with private space. These were read/write, and central administration backed those up by relatively conventional means. The remainder were read/write filesystems that central administration did not backup, but which served as slush for the private workstation owner. Those workstation owners could, if they chose, copy their local and private filesystems from their workstation to these read-write fileservices and achieve backup, that is they could have a copy of their environment sufficient to recreate that environment as of the moment of backup. Central administration did not need to provide any management of these *backup servers* beyond hardware field service and quota control.

9.5.4 Not in Use *Means* Not in Use

Workstations in a university environment are generally subject to serial reuse by different individuals, and those not so subject are best managed as if they were. When a user logs out from an Athena workstation, there is a short refractory period in which a login window appears and a login causes immediate action. This accomplishes two things; first, during periods of peak usage, such as when there are waiting lines for workstations, this allows the next user to begin his/her work immediately. Second, users occasionally log out inadvertently and a setup such as this permits immediate recovery with as much of the execution environment preserved as is feasible. (For example, remotely mounted filesystems remain mounted and the contents of temporary space are not scrubbed.)

However, after this short period (two minutes, say), a process called *toehold* asserts its latent authority and performs a number of housekeeping steps. It reloads some local files from their canonic forms (*/etc/passwd*, say), breaks all remote service connections by appropriate means (unmounting NFS filesystems, say), and halts the (X) display server. Workstations that are the sole responsibility of Athena central take a further step: *toehold* updates the workstation.

This brings the workstation back to a status identical to that of a freshly installed workstation, recycling it to a ready-to-use status, but it consumes no resources for the rest of the idle period (until a user shows up). This ensures that remote service failures only matter to in-use workstations, and that only in-use workstations contribute to service load. This is also diagnostically helpful–if a workstation fails during restart for the next user, that failure is local to the workstation. Reloading that workstation's software, then, is a therapeutically complete step. If the reload cures the problem, it cures the problem. If the workstations is still inoperable, it has hardware problems.

9.5.4.1 Software Update

Under a diskful-but-dataless hardware configuration, only the root filesystem requires update. Such updates are likely to be infrequent, given the core nature of the minimal software residing there. In the case of machines for which the *unmanaged* local filesystem contains nothing of permanent value, except where contraindicated by a workstation owner's explicit configuration instructions, *toehold* starts an asynchronous, client-initiated software update process. Fine-grained nameservice support (under the control of the service management system) provides the name of a filesystem that is canonic for the workstation vendor, model, subnet, and version. The update process, running on the workstation itself, disables keyboard input and proceeds to compare that model filesystem to the local root filesystem, reconciling any mismatches. When it finishes with that reconciliation, it marks the workstation as updated both in a local logfile (*/etc/version*) and remotely to a logging host (provided by the nameservice), and, finally, reboots the workstation.

This paradigm (fast one-to-many updates initiated by the workstations themselves when idle) allows a remarkable degree of control with almost no labor. It is typical to expect a thousand workstations to be updated in a matter of hours without operational staff leaving their offices. By making the update dependent on the nameservice, the initiation of workstation updates in general can be crisply defined by operations staff. By making the update run on the workstations when and only when truly idle, the fileservice load and workstation downtime can be smeared out enough to be effectively irrelevant. By permitting workstation owners to opt out of automatic update, no version-related service losses (between common software and local conditions) can occur by surprise. As the update process is merely reconciliation of a remote, canonic filesystem with the local root, update is, in fact, directionless; privately managed workstations may request *update* to any available version number, such as to permit a workstation owner to take a recommended version update on approval, backing out if local software is shown to be disabled by it. If you are relying on users to do their own update, then you need to make sure that their resistance is minimal.

9.5.4.2 Coldstart Performance

Configuring for hands-off coldstart of a large-scale computing environment is an area where garden paths abound. For example, we once reasoned that nameservice is the highest priority service save routing, so nameservices should be instantiated only on the most reliable computers in our network. At the time, "most reliable" translated to "on 24 x 7 field-service," and, so, the nameservices were put on the small number of hosts under such service agreements. What is the garden path? Simple; we were buying 24 x 7 service for the fileservers with single-source (non-replicated) data. These exceptionally large fileservers were reliable to be sure, but when we coldstarted the entire campus they were always the very last systems to be on their feet, due to the massive filesystem self-consistency checks (*fsck*) they had to do. So, by putting the most necessary service on the most reliable server platforms, we ensured that coldstarting the campus was absolutely as slow as it could be: not good.

Needless to say, nameservices are today on stand-alone servers, and start quickly. The overall coldstart routine is:

minutes since failure	what service and when available
0	gateway boot servers (on UPS)
:30	gateway service in general
8:00	nameservice (since these are replicates, any single one establishes service)
8:01	authentication (on UPS, but now visible through nameservers)
<15:00	mail delivery, consulting, notification, etc. (dependent on above)
<30:00	read-only fileservers (basic service–one per subnet; some replication)
<90:00	read-write fileservers (typically larger and slower starting).

Power failures are usually dirty enough to damage at least some hardware, but, except for such damage, recovery of an Athena environment is nearly hands-off. The expected time to full recovery is the filesystem consistency check (*fsck*) time for the larger read-write fileservers. As in other circumstances, a great deal of remote logging records how the coldstart progressed. This logging makes detecting parts that are not recovering easier, and generally teaches us something.

9.5.4.3 Partitionability

We wanted to preserve as much function as possible in the face of network connectivity faults. Single point partitions are relatively easy to prepare for–in a linear spine network such as ours, putting replicable services at each end of the spine (minimum) and in the middle ensures that single point failures of that spine cannot eclipse any service. The inherently unique services, such the provision of a read-write filesystem, require the protection of redundant networks and routing support for them. As previously mentioned, services with a master-slave design may suffer some diminution of service where partitions isolate the master host (such as an isolated Kerberos master host causing a denial of password-changing service).

A second example of partition is isolation of a subnet from the spine network. We put the basic fileservice that provides the workstation execution environment on each subnet. In this way, isolation of a subnet does not diminish that aspect of the workstations' capabilities, and some, perhaps most, useful work can continue. Replicating the basic fileservice on each subnet spares the spine's bandwidth. We can confirm this for Athena: if the workstation is paging to a local disk and the central library of binaries is on the local subnet, then private filespace can be put on servers anywhere across the spine network without overloading spine bandwidth. Partitionability is congruent to bandwidth preservation.

9.5.4.4 Barefoot Doctors

After putting considerable effort into making the environment manageable without shoe leather, in fact without seeing what is being managed, it remains necessary for customer service to do basic quality control on the day to day operability of the workstation environment that the user sees. In short, there must be some walking around. Those who perform this activity (Athena's *cluster patrol*) are lightly trained and often part-time employees who go into areas of high workstation concentration (*clusters*) to check those aspects of the state of the world that require direct assessment.

When a workstation fails, the users in these large areas, at most, label it as broken. The cluster patrol's job is to fix it (if possible), or call for help. This requires simple triage rules, ones requiring basic diagnostic and therapeutic skills. Their instructions were to:

1. Reload the workstation's software
2. Try to use the workstation
3. If it is still failing, call it in as a hardware fault

This is a triage decision anyone can make. This barefoot doctor approach contrasts sharply with traditional approaches. If a hyperskilled technician returns triumphantly from a day in the field and announces that "a non-ECC detectable intermittently bad bit in the login binary on disk was isolated, the offending block remapped and the bit fixed on disk in stand-alone mode," you should shoot the technician's manager. It is a cost-ineffective folly, not to mention nonscalable, to diagnose beyond the level at which it makes a therapeutic difference. Workstations should be configured to have disposable software. If it breaks, get a fresh copy. If it is still broken, you know that it is the hardware. This method succeeds in the hostile environment of MIT, where every user is (potentially) that hyperskilled technician and computing resources must always be available. In short, it is unglamorous and it works.

9.5.4.5 Hostname and Network Address Assignment

When installing a computer on a network, associating that computer's hardware address with a routable network address and a symbolic representation (*i.e.* hostname) is an essential aspect of bringing the computer into operation. Unfortunately, this is hard to do well in a small environment. The problem worsens as the environment grows. From users who uncrate their own machines and "just plug them in" to well meaning sysadmins who set off duplicate IP address alarms, there are problems with making this work. Experience has shown that this is one of those situations for which "an ounce of prevention is worth a pound of cure" was coined.

The idea is simple: addresses need not be permanently assigned to workstations–they just need one when they need one. That can work without administrative handshakes and in a way that lets everyone dodge the rogue user/sysadmin who manages to install a duplicate address. At installation time, test if the workstation had an address before by looking in the usual location it would be stored (such as in some one of */etc/*.rc*). If there is such an address, ARP for it to see if it is in use. If it is not in use, this workstation can continue to use it (the preferred result). If the address is in use or, equivalently, if the workstation has no address (it is being installed for the first time), then ask for support for picking an address. This support can come from anywhere with a derivable net address, so the gateways are a simple and logical place to get it. The support is in the form of a range of addresses that are (re)assignable. The workstation (for quick dispersion) hashes its hardware address into the range and picks an address. If that address is unused, that's it; otherwise, get a new one (by adding 1) and try again.

This strategy does not require all addresses to be reassignable and, indeed, it would be a mistake to reassign server addresses in this fashion. Client addresses, however, are another matter and this strategy avoids the administrative hang-ups of getting addresses when and where you need them. Further, it treats an in-use address as a hint, not a failure indication. This strategy sidesteps problems, whatever their source. The result, as always, is remotely logged.

One aspect of this strategy is still troubling, however, as up till now, there have not been deployable nameservices that could dynamically reassociate a derived network address with a preferred hostname. In consequence, the assignment of an essentially random network address brings with it an equally random hostname. Many Athena staff have strongly held opinions that *vanity* hostnames are an administrative bother and a financial drain. By adopting this hostname assignment strategy, that question is closed–only private workstations and servers can get a stable hostname.

9.6 Other Good Ideas

9.6.1 Cooperation over Competition

If your interests are in the use of computing, making a standard can be more important than making a revenue stream. In our case, the clearest statement of this can be read in the copyright notice accompanying the publicly available source tree for the X Window System. MIT has clearly gained more that is relevant to its educational mission by taking those steps that made X a standard than it could have by attempting to derive revenue from what was, at its birth, another unknown piece of university research work. The same can be said of the Kerberos Network Authentication System, and may yet be said about other components of the Athena environment. It pays to recall what your aims are.

9.6.2 The Network is Essential

Though our design left room for preserving services in the face of a network failure, the network is essential. Our current view is that if you are interested in a distributed computing environment, do not do anything else until you have a stable, regularized network and sense of how it can be made ubiquitous. Network connectivity is about as interesting and about as necessary as electric power.

9.6.3 Winning Hearts and Minds

In getting much of this enterprise to adopt a new computing model, even one that made obsolete considerable skill and in-place investment, we found that we had the upper hand primarily due to the network services model of computation. Getting the computing users and suppliers of the entire organization to play ball does not happen all at once. Instead, each decision maker does a cost-benefit calculation using their own utilities. Parts of the cost that a potential adherent sees are inescapable, such as a network, new hardware, maintenance contracts; as a network services supplier, you cannot radically change that cost side of the equation. On the other hand, you have control over the benefit side of the equation and, owing to the nature of network services as a way to deliver computing, you can make that benefit side arbitrarily rich. In so doing, you eventually take the field because, for every cost idea a decision maker has, you can, in principle, provide a benefit level that is sufficient to make the new model a bargain by comparison.

9.7 Looking Forward

9.7.1 Migration Paths

If one organizational lesson has become clear, it is that the manner of introducing distributed computing to existing enterprise computing matters; a plan that requires sharp change at precise instants is an unworkable plan. The Athena experience indicates that it is possible to make this transition while providing service at the same time. Taking as a goal the provision of a fully distributed environment and as constraints to take the very minimum of disruptive acts, a timeline might go like this:

- *Devise an initial service agreement:* understand what is your best guess goal for distributed computing within the enterprise; be prepared to modify this as experience accumulates.
- *Regularize network connectivity:* provide good, solid, reliable connectivity, with as simple an interconnection diagram as possible.
- *Solidify and expand naming:* ensure that a nameservice exists and that it is possible to use the chosen nameservice for not only host-to-address translation, but for any lookup purpose that advances the goal of location-independent access; nameservices that support hierarchic delegation and have editable data files are preferable.
- *Introduce file service:* provide all files remotely as well as locally, even if there are few takers initially; permit early adopters to use this service as soon as they are able, making sure that the backup question is clear.
- *Establish authentication:* install an authentication system that is consistent with an open network, even if it is currently true that the local network is truly local and impeccably trustworthy; create verifiable identities for at least your system administration personnel and remove password-based superuser access to your service hosts (basing superuser function instead on the privileges associated with separately verifiable network authentication names for your sysadmin staff).
- *Bring service environment under central control:* establish a database abstraction of the correct working configuration of your entire environment and use that abstraction to manage the that environment; ensure that access control to that database is fine grained and based exclusively on authenticatable entities; turn over the management of individual server hosts to this system as you are able, and all of them eventually.
- *Expand authentication to envelope user account administration:* establish authenticatable identities for everyone in your user community by integrating the user account administration functions with a combination of the authentication system and the service management system; ensure that all users are in a position to take advantage of the service environment on the basis of well designed and well applied access control policies and their own authenticatable identity.
- *Reconfigure workstations:* make the transition the pure, dataless network service clients; establish software update mechanisms that are centrally mediated; complete the reeducation of private workstation owners to meet the needs of the service agreement that your organization can feasibly provide.
- *Integrate applications:* begin a process of adding naming, authentication, remote procedure call, and other support to the existing application base and permit those applications to take full advantage of the environment in which they now exist; pro-

vide your application development staff with a suite of libraries and design guidelines that fully integrate distribution and replication into the applications they will prepare someday.

9.8 Summary

Much has been written about Project Athena and if you are interested in the details of any specific module or how the educational applications turned out, there are articles available. This paper gives you the idea that distributed-systems design is composed of a lot of meaty problems and nonintuitive sensitivities to unseen thresholds of failure, and that macroengineering such large environments is possible. We invite you to be a part of creating a computing future that will permit each of us to partake and provide services within a globally connected computing plant.

9.9 Acknowledgments

Strictly, this is impossible to do. Athena was a long-running, heavily subsidized, exciting collaboration for which no one person (including this author) can assume credit, and many deserve a share. Numerous people's help in Athena proper was crucial, and much of that help was given. Some, even, was taken, simply by exposing our community to our half-baked code. In that regard, I am reminded of George Eliot's observation that "...the growing good of the world is due in no small part to those who lie in unmarked graves."

For the purposes of this paper, I am indebted to Kenneth C. Zolot and Joshua Q. Lubarr for editing help. Of course, opinions and errors remain mine.

9.10 References

Champine GA, Geer DE & Ruh WN: Project Athena as a Distributed Computer System. IEEE Computer, 23:9:40-51, Sept 1990; Project Athena Technical Plan, 1983-1987.

Dyer SP, Hesiod, USENIX Conference Proceedings, Winter, 1988.

Needham RM and MD Schroeder, Using Encryption for Authentication in Large Networks of Computers, CACM 21:12, 993-999, December, 1978.

Steiner JG, BC Neuman & JI Schiller, Kerberos: An Authentication Service for Open Network Systems, USENIX Conference Proceedings, Winter, 1988.

DellaFera CA, MW Eichin, RS French, DC Jedlinsky, JT Kohl & WE Sommerfeld, The Zephyr Notification System, USENIX Conference Proceedings, Winter, 1988.

Scheifler RW & J Gettys, The X Window System, ACM Transactions On Graphics 5:2 p. 79-109, April, 1987.

Rosenstein MA, DE Geer & PJ Levine, The Moira Service Management System, USENIX Conference Proceedings, Winter, 1988.

Daniel E. Geer, Jr., is President of Geer Zolot Associates, a software products company located in Cambridge, Mass. Previously, he served as Technical Director of the Innovation Technology Resource Center, Digital Equipment Corporation, Corporate Research & Architecture, and as the Manager of Systems Development, Project Athena, where he was responsible for all technical development, including X, Kerberos, Hesiod, Zephyr, Moira, and all other aspects of the Project Athena Network Services System. He holds a Bachelor of Science in Electrical Engineering and Computer Science from MIT, and a Doctor of Science in Biostatistics from Harvard University. Member of several professional societies, he is active in USENIX, serving most recently as the Chair of the Symposium on Mobile and Location Independent Computing, August, 1993.

Chapter 10

Institutional File System at the University of Michigan

Ted Hanss
University of Michigan

10.1 Introduction

Sharing of information is critical to the University of Michigan's missions of research and instruction. With the move away from central timesharing, a requirement emerged for a university-wide distributed computing infrastructure to support tens of thousands of heterogeneous desktop systems. The first application in this environment is the institutional file system (IFS).

This chapter describes the IFS as a mechanism for providing large scale, distributed file service. The following section provides an overview of the University of Michigan, to set the context within which this project's requirements were defined. Subsequent sections detail the effort's requirements and objectives, the system's architecture and features, performance analysis, and deployment experiences.

10.2 The University of Michigan

The University of Michigan is a large research university with over 35,000 students and approximately 20,000 faculty and staff on the Ann Arbor campus. Seventeen schools and colleges comprise the university, which has a budget in excess of $2 billion per year.

Despite the decentralized nature of administration, Michigan has a strong history of central computing and networking support. The Information Technology Division (ITD) provides academic, administrative, and telecommunications services. ITD supports essential central services, such as mission critical transaction processing systems, public workstation clusters, and data and voice networks. ITD offers central support for decentralized systems by providing such services as training, negotiated software licenses, and a help desk. As ITD cannot dictate hardware or software solutions for the university, it needs to operate through incentives and initiatives for open systems interoperability. ITD works closely with other service providers on campus, including those in the Medical Center, the Engineering College, and the Business School.

The university has a significant investment in information technology, currently realized through approximately 20,000 personal computers and workstations, three mainframe data centers, and ubiquitous networking. The desktop systems on campus include Apple Macintoshes, IBM PS/2s and PCs, PC clones, Suns, Apollos, IBM RS/6000s, Suns, Digital DECstations, and a smaller representation of other vendors' products.

The 20,000 systems listed above do not include the student-owned machines. Surveys indicate that approximately half of the students have computers. For those who do not own their own machines, the University provides nearly 2,000 systems in public clusters for walk-up use. ITD has forecast that each student, faculty member, and staff person will have access to a workstation by the mid-'90s, which could mean up to 50,000 networked systems.

The three IBM mainframe sites are: the University Hospital data center (ES/9000-580) and ITD's Academic Computing Center (ES/9000-720) and Administrative Data Systems Center (ES/9000-580). The Model 580s are three processor machines and the 720 has six processors. The Hospital and the Data Systems Center run the MVS/ESA operating system supporting a variety of applications, including databases and transaction processing on both and IFS development and deployment on the data systems machine. The academic system runs the Michigan Terminal System (MTS), a locally developed operating system supporting large-scale timesharing, MVS/ESA to run the library's on-line catalog system, and VM/ESA and AIX/ESA for IFS development and deployment purposes.

The university is housed in more than two hundred buildings distributed across twenty square miles. Each office and dorm room is networked via unshielded twisted-pair wiring incorporated in the phone network installation. The twisted-pairs provide Ethernet, PhoneNet (supporting AppleTalk), or asynchronous connections to the network. The campus fiber backbone is a 100 megabit per second FDDI ring based on Cisco routers. The campus connects to the Internet through a link to the T3 (45 megabit per second) NSFNET.

10.3 Needs and Motivations

The profile of campus computer users varies widely. Word processing and other personal productivity applications are the primary desktop applications, with electronic mail and conferencing also prevalent on both timesharing and LAN-based systems. In the Engineering College, programming and computer-aided design represent significant workstation use. Statistical tools and databases are data and computationally intensive applications used widely throughout the University. Beyond the horizontal applications, there are myriad specialized applications.

With a very large campus and a mobile user community, the ability to access applications and personal data from any spot on campus is important. An individual (whether student, faculty, or staff) should not be tied to a single desk, required to carry large numbers of floppy disks, or compelled to use complex file transfer procedures just to access his or her data.

With a workstation-based user population, we recognize that heterogeneity is the reality. Services made available to the campus must work across multiple desktop computers. Therefore, it is important for us to support standard protocols and not specific vendors.

Despite the movement to computing on the desktop, there still is a need for strong central provision and support of services. It is important that we provide the information sharing and support benefits of central timesharing with the ease-of-use and flexibility of desktop workstations.

In response to the above needs, we decided to address the information infrastructure requirements through an initiative called the Institutional File System Project (IFS). Although there are over 400 file servers on campus today encompassing Novell NetWare, AppleShare, Banyan Vines, and NFS, the aim is to provide a coherent enterprise-level approach for integrating these systems. IFS will serve as the glue that unifies Macintoshes, PCs, and UNIX systems.

Joining Michigan in this effort is IBM Corporation, which has a strong interest in supporting large scale client/server environments. IBM has provided critical resources, including on site participation by developers from various development laboratories. The project's base is in the university's Center for Information Technology Integration (CITI), an applied research and development center that works jointly with corporate and government partners to enhance the university's computing environment. Within CITI, the IFS project involves approximately 44 staff members, which includes full-time development staff, faculty members, graduate research assistants, undergraduate programmers, and on-site IBM representatives.

10.4 Key Objectives

The key goals of the IFS project include designing, developing, and implementing a campus-wide distributed computing infrastructure, the first user-visible application of which is the IFS. The design target is to support 30,000 active client workstations.

This work is being done in multiple phases. The initial phase, which started in 1988, focused first on file server functionality and proof of concept. We successfully demonstrated an operational IFS in October 1989 at the higher education computing conference EDUCOM, which Michigan hosted that year. We subsequently focused on scale and performance. We re-implemented using the knowledge gained from the first version. This second implementation serves users campus-wide today. In the summer of 1991, a new three year initiative began to further enhance and extend the IFS in the areas of compliance with the Open Software Foundation's Distributed Computing Environment, hierarchical storage support for distributed file systems, disconnected operation supporting laptops, and more.

The research and evaluation component of the project provides feedback from the University to IBM on products and services. Based on our deployment experiences, we are building a spreadsheet-based model to analyze the costs of offering file service from multiple configurations. The model encompasses hardware and software expenses along with operations and administration costs.

10.5 System Features

The aim of the IFS is to provide high functionality, offering more than users have today through wider file sharing, daily backup, and easy software distribution. Drawing from campus input, we established requirements for access, transparency, performance, security, availability, heterogeneity, and integrity.

Wide accessibility is important. The IFS offers access to files from any networked campus workstation. This facilitates system access by users not tied to any particular desktop. Students, for example, can access the IFS from a public cluster in the afternoon and from their dorm room in the evening. It is not necessary to carry floppy disks around, and users know that others on campus have the same access to the IFS.

The system is easy to use. The interface is natural extension of the local desktop environment. This transparency provides a native file system view to users. For Macintosh users, the IFS appears as an icon on the desktop, for DOS users it is a disk drive, and for UNIX users it is part of the inverted tree hierarchy (see figure 10.1). Users are not required to learn new ways to access files. In addition, users continue to access their favorite applications as the IFS implements its enabling code beneath the operating system interface.

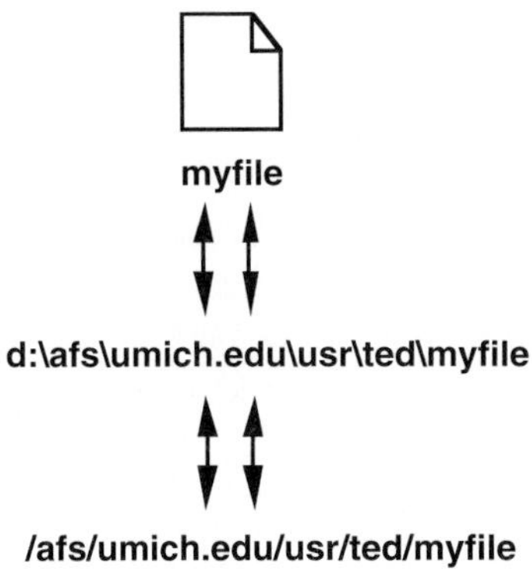

Figure 10.1 The IFS is simply an extension of the desktop environment for Macintosh, DOS, and UNIX users, respectively.

The objective is for IFS to provide performance nominally equivalent to a local hard disk (or better), even to thousands of simultaneous users. If not achieved, users will buy larger hard disks for their local systems. The university thus loses the returns to scale it hopes to attain by centralizing such services as backup and software distribution. While there are many network file server technologies available, none are suitable for addressing the needs of tens of thousands of heterogeneous client workstations while maintaining high performance.

The IFS is an open system that supports a very diverse community through multiple client workstation interfaces. Clients access the IFS primarily through networks supporting the Internet Protocol standard, though the gateways described below support other transport and file system protocols.

Security through authentication and access controls ensures privacy of data. Users only have access to information to which they have been extended permission. IFS authentication uses Kerberos, from MIT's Project Athena.

The system must be as available as local workstations. The university operates seven days per week, 24 hours per day. Therefore, users expect their files to be accessible whenever logging into a workstation or powering on a personal computer. Thus, the IFS is available even during backup operations.

Integrity through centralized storage, backup, and recovery is a key element for a campus file system. We back up the IFS on a regular basis and provide file restore services to users. Here we aim to provide benefits drawn from experiences in maintaining central timesharing services, but now provided to workstation-based users.

10.6 Architecture and Implementation

The IFS architecture provides a central point of data management augmented by the distribution of files through intermediate servers. This central support provides the ability for reliable central data management (backup, software distribution, privacy, etc.). Intermediate servers provide a platform for disk caching and protocol translation close to the client workstations. This section details the architecture and implementation of IFS.

10.6.1 Transarc AFS as a Base

The IFS uses as its base Transarc's AFS, first developed at Carnegie Mellon University as the Andrew File System. When we began the design of this effort in 1987, we surveyed the distributed file system activity underway at both commercial and research organizations. For example, among the systems we reviewed were Sun Microsystem's Network File System (NFS), AT&T's Remote File Sharing (RFS), the Locus Computing Corporation distributed system, and work underway at various universities. We found that AFS provided the closest match to our needs. We began working with Carnegie Mellon at that time and have continued to work closely with the AFS developers since the establishment of Transarc as a CMU spin-off in 1989.

As the IFS provides a superset of AFS functionality, an overview of AFS will explain the base from which we are building our system. The following describes AFS 3, the current product available from Transarc. Transarc provides a variety of AFS client and server implementations for workstations from IBM, Sun, DEC, NeXT, and HP. (As we have several hundred Apollo workstations at the University, we developed an AFS client for the Apollo Domain system.) Subsequent sections detail the Michigan extensions to AFS.

In May of 1990, the Open Software Foundation selected Transarc's follow-on to AFS as the key data-sharing component of the OSF Distributed Computing Environment (OSF/DCE). OSF shipped this technology, the DCE Distributed File System (DFS), with DCE 1.0 to vendors in early 1992. OSF delivered a more robust release in mid-1993. DFS includes many enhancements to AFS covered in Chapters 2 and 7.

The AFS design goals were to provide the amenities of a shared file system to UNIX workstation-based users. It uses TCP/IP networks as the transport for client/server connectivity. AFS allows workstation users to share both within workgroups and, through inter-organizational links, across the globe. AFS offers a homogeneous, location-independent file name space to all clients. Users access files through the same absolute path name from any AFS client workstation.

AFS addresses such scaling implications as degraded server performance and complicated administration and operation. The latter is very important to us, recent budget cutbacks at Michigan reduced the number of user support staff. Therefore, scaling administrative tools is as critical as providing high performance. AFS compensates for scaling problems, which plague other network-based file servers, by distributing the workload between the server and the client and by providing powerful administrative tools.

Communication between AFS clients and servers occurs through a remote procedure call mechanism. Each AFS client workstation runs a local process that manages an important component of AFS–high performance disk caching. Local disks on UNIX-based AFS workstations have a cache that fills with files requested from the primary servers. The client satisfies subsequent requests for the same files from the cache, providing true local disk performance. Caching reduces the network load and improves server performance. With the client disk cache, AFS satisfies between 80 percent and 92 percent of the file requests from the local disk (once the cache is filled) (Howard, et. al., 1988).

This caching technology provides the concept of a *dataless* workstation. The workstation has a local disk, but only a few required system files reside there permanently. All data files and applications reside in the cache. At Michigan, we take advantage of this dataless feature to provide essentially commodity workstations for user desks. System administrators configure UNIX workstations over the network from templates that install the necessary files to boot the system. The remaining disk space contains swap partitions (if necessary) and AFS disk cache. Therefore, we do not back up local machines. If a desktop machine fails for whatever reason, an administrator configures a new disk or machine in less than ten minutes. This greatly aids in system administration. Operations costs are driven not by the number of workstations on the network but primarily by the number of different workstation architectures supported.

A callback function provides data consistency. Callbacks are promises, delivered by the server along with a requested file, that the server will notify the AFS client process if another user stores a modified version of the file. The design point is to avoid validity checks, which occur frequently with Sun Microsystems NFS, for example. The benefit is savings in server and network performance. The client sends modified versions of a file through to the primary server, where a copy of the file always resides.

The AFS consistency semantics provide for writes to an open file to be visible immediately only to processes on that workstation. Once a user closes a file, the changes are visible to new file open requests anywhere in the network but not to already open copies of the file on other workstations. Other file operations (e.g., protection changes) are immediately visible across the network. As we find there is very little write-sharing of files outside of database applications, conflicts rarely occur. Databases, for example, enforce synchronization of data access within the application.

Off-loading tasks to workstation clients, such as pathname resolution, enhances server performance. AFS uses a low-level internal filename (FID or file identification number). UNIX directories are cached in the memory of the workstation. The client process does the pathname lookup in the directory and passes the FID to the server as part of the file request. This eliminates server CPU load for pathname resolution at no observable cost on the workstation, where there are generally excess cycles available. In addition, context switching is minimized for both client and server processes by implementing them using threads or lightweight processes. Without the server threads implementation, each client would have to be assigned a dedicated UNIX task (and all its accompanying overhead).

AFS operability objectives led to important functionality for system administrators. AFS provides simple migration of files from server to server for load balancing or system maintenance reasons. As AFS file hierarchy is independent of a server's physical location, these operations are transparent to users. In addition, AFS offers space quotas for users, replication of seldom-changed system files, on-the-fly backups, and simple restoration of lost or damaged data.

One of our favorite features of AFS allows users to access the previous day's backups, which are mounted within an individual's home directory under the name OldFiles. If someone accidentally deletes a file, he or she can simply use the standard copy command on the local workstation to fetch the version from yesterday's backup. By putting this backup image on-line, AFS essentially eliminates the operator requests for backup tape mounts. This feature uses a copy-on-write mechanism and thus does not require twice the disk space. Our experience at Michigan is that we need less than ten percent additional capacity.

Volumes are the key administrative unit for AFS. A volume is a collection of files forming a partial subtree of the file name space. Mount points are the connections between volumes. Volumes are the units by which the system administrator handles backups, load balancing, and other management tasks. System administrators only deal with volumes; individual files are transparent to the administrator. Users, on the other hand, are generally not aware of the volume organization. The notable exception is that volumes are the units upon which AFS maintains space quotas. Thus users must contact system administrators to expand their volumes when requiring additional storage space.

In investigating possible solutions for Michigan's information sharing needs, we determined it was not feasible to develop our own file system from scratch. (Although Michigan does have a history of developing its own operating systems and network protocols.) Therefore, we decided to base our work on previous efforts and selected AFS. We did not consider NFS a viable base for several reasons. The AFS protocol is well suited for long haul networks, which is important to our cross-site collaboration. Dozens of sites around the world participate in the global AFS file system and we interact with many of them. NFS time-outs are a problem for even a campus network, much less a world-wide system. The AFS caching model provides high performance. By pushing CPU-intensive tasks to workstations, AFS allows an order of magnitude higher client-to-server ratios than NFS. We also believe AFS has better authentication and richer protections than NFS. AFS protections use access control lists (ACLs) based on directories. These ACLs include read, write, lookup, insert, delete, lock, and administer permissions. These permissions may be extended to groups, which are user maintained, as well as individuals.

10.6.2 Server Extensions to AFS

The following describes the IFS server extensions to AFS. Subsequent subsections cover intermediate file servers, support for mobile computing, and proposed mass storage extensions.

When identifying the attributes we desired in our ideal file server platform, we listed high input/output capability (tens of megabytes per second both to disk and to the network), disk capacity in the hundreds of gigabytes and eventually terabytes, large amounts of RAM to cache files in memory, utilities to back-up and administer the system, and a very reliable platform.

We realized that we had described features that apply to mainframes. The academic mainframe, for example, has 128 I/O channels, each capable of communicating at ten megabytes per second, it is straightforward to attach terabytes of disk, we have gigabytes of memory installed, it is a very reliable platform (very few hardware or software failures), and there are extensive administration utilities. The machine is well balanced for data-intensive uses.

The university's use of timesharing is destined to decrease, but we will continue to support mainframe platforms for some time due to the investment in major mission-critical applications. Could we find a new role for these systems that exploits their advantages? The growth in data storage needs is increasing dramatically. By providing a centrally managed system we may offer economic operations advantages over managing myriad distributed servers. We therefore decided to investigate supporting file service using extra capacity on the mainframes. We would first see whether it could be done technically, then we would examine the economic issues. We hoped to identify the bottlenecks to scaling and address them in a way applicable to any future server platforms.

Development work and production file service occur on the academic and administrative computing IBM ES/9000s, which continue to run other production services as well (e.g., on-line library catalog system, timesharing systems, database and transaction services, etc.).

We decided to implement IFS on three of IBM's mainframe operating systems: MVS/ESA, AIX/ESA, and VM/ESA. We picked all three for two reasons. We did not know which one would offer the best performance, so we built all three to compare. We also had a marketing-related reason, in case IBM decided to make an offering based on IFS. We thought it would be easier to walk into a customer's MVS facility with an MVS application rather than ask them to install UNIX to provide file service.

The IFS Central Process, based on AFS 3, consists of approximately 80,000 lines of C code (with some assembly language) laced with UNIX system calls. To remain 100 percent compatible with Transarc's AFS product, we aimed to minimize changes to this code base. We concentrated our development effort on the System Platform Adapter, where we exploit hardware and software features of the underlying platform and mask operating system differences (see figure 10.2).

As MVS/ESA does not provide a UNIX interface, we developed a UNIX File System Simulator as part of the system platform adapter. This simulator is about 20,000 lines of C and assembler that takes UNIX operations, such as read, write, open, and close, and maps them to the local equivalent. We measured very little overhead on the file server due to this layer of code.

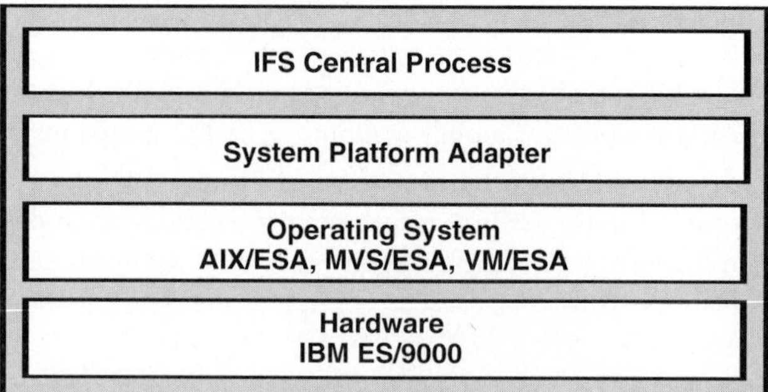

Figure 10.2 The IFS server consists of the Central Process, based on Transarc's AFS code, and the System Platform Adapter, which provides a UNIX emulation layer and exploit mainframe services. It runs on three of IBM's operating systems.

Re-implementing threads was relatively straightforward using the MVS subtasking facility. As UNIX signals do not have an MVS equivalent, we replaced their functions with RPC calls. To avoid the long pathlength in opening and closing MVS files, we map a UNIX file system partition to a single MVS file (a virtual sequential access method linear data set, or VSAM/LDS, which can be up to two gigabytes). Each VSAM/LDS holds several AFS volumes. The IFS supports many of these linear data sets, giving us the large capacity on the server. An extension unique to the MVS server is the ability to bring new partitions on-line while the server is operational. Thus, we can add additional capacity without taking the system down, as required by standard Transarc AFS servers.

By not providing a one-to-one mapping between client files and server files, we do not offer either workstation access to host-based data or host-based applications to use workstation-created files. Our aim was to provide the highest performing server to workstation users. To provide host data access would have compromised both performance and transparency (due such issues as ASCII/EBCDIC conversion, which we can avoid as all clients store ASCII files).

The system platform adapter is also where we introduce code to exploit system features. For example, Carnegie Mellon developed AFS on workstations with only a few megabytes of RAM. We have gigabytes of expanded storage memory on the mainframe. Thus, using MVS/ESA's data-in-virtual feature, we built a memory-mapped file system that further optimizes system performance.

One of the difficult tasks in porting AFS to MVS was dealing with ASCII/EBCDIC issues. The IFS stores data in ASCII, which is generally opaque to the MVS operating system. The RPC headers, however, contain ASCII strings sent by clients to the MVS server application, which expects EBCDIC. The AFS RPC uses Sun's external data representation (XDR) for parameter conversion. Unfortunately, that version of XDR did not support EBCDIC, so we had the time-consuming task of rewriting the parameter handling routines in the server.

We developed systems management utilities that data center operators access from IBM 3270 terminals. As the operators were trained to provide MVS support, we made the IFS look like a typical MVS application for such tasks as bringing up the system, doing backups, and so on. The UNIX-based tools that Transarc provides are still available. Staff with UNIX skills manage the IFS using workstation-based utilities, unaware of the underlying MVS operating system on the server. Through multiple management interfaces, we provide portability of staff skills as we move from timesharing to client/server systems.

We ported the file system simulator to VM/ESA as well, but we do provide a one-to-one mapping between client files and host files on VM. In talking with a large number of potential IFS customers, however, we have not found a good application that would justify sharing with mainframe applications. In most organizations, interactive applications that are on the mainframe have moved or are being moved to workstations. Many of the applications remaining on mainframes are databases, whose clients use SQL calls to access data. In our data storage model, databases and distributed file systems are kept separate. That is, there is no benefit in storing databases in the distributed file system as the database applications mediate sharing.

The MVS/ESA platform offers production services on campus today. We run the VM/ESA server internally for evaluation purposes and have no plans to move it into production. We are now focusing our development activities on OSF/DCE (see figure 10.3). We are porting the DCE distributed file system (DFS) to MVS/ESA and plan to offer pilot file service in late 1993. As with Phase I, MVS/ESA development comes first. Any work with VM/ESA will follow once we complete the MVS platform.

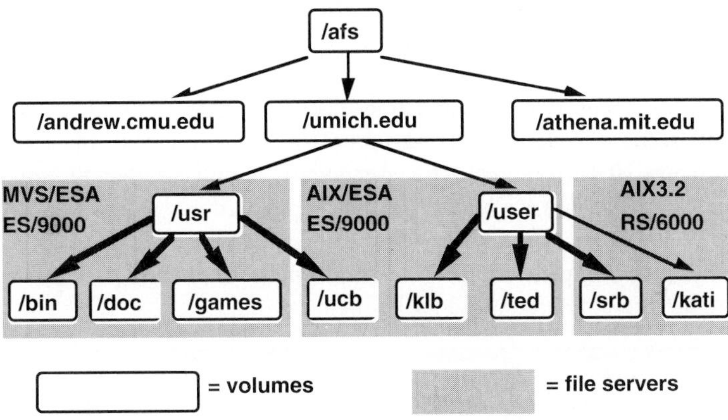

Figure 10.3 The location transparent nature of the IFS allows us to offer file service from multiple platforms. Directory links can cross systems without user awareness of the underlying operating systems. Management tools support moving data from one server to another in real-time, while users interact with the system.

Porting AFS to UNIX on the mainframe was a good deal more straightforward. In Phase I of the project, we focused on porting AFS 3 to AIX/370, which used a Locus Computing kernel. Some incompatibilities with BSD UNIX led us to make significant changes to the kernel inode library to facilitate porting. In Phase II, we moved our development base to AIX/ESA, which has an OSF/1 kernel, and found it a better development platform than AIX/370 and much more reliable. We ported AFS 3 server code to AIX/ESA and currently offer production service from this platform. As part of our new focus, we also ported all the components of OSF/DCE including DFS to AIX/ESA and intend to offer pilot use in 1993.

As noted earlier, AFS requires TCP/IP connectivity. The MVS/ESA file server has an Ethernet connection to the campus backbone. The AIX/ESA server connects directly to the

FDDI backbone. We work very closely with IBM's TCP/IP development organization to improve the code's performance. For example, we developed enhancements that both improve throughput and reduce CPU consumption of IBM's MVS TCP/IP. We provided those modifications to IBM, which has added them to the base product.

IBM announced in April 1993 an offering of the AFS-based MVS/ESA and AIX/ESA IFS file servers. The IBM subsidiary AdStaR provides this as a program request for price quotation (PRPQ). This is essentially an as-is offering of the code run in production at Michigan to meet the requests of organizations interested in running AFS file service from mainframes.

10.6.3 Intermediate Servers

An important component in the IFS is the intermediate file server, which addresses scaling issues at Michigan (Howe, 1992). The intermediate server performs two functions–providing an intermediate disk cache and acting as a protocol gateway platform. These servers run on UNIX workstations, currently IBM RS/6000s with about one gigabyte of disk space, which we place on the local area network-side of the FDDI backbone routers. Placed on the LAN, intermediates support the needs of workgroups within a building. The assumption is that there exists locality of reference for sharing within a department that would benefit from the intermediate caching function.

The intermediate provides an extension of the local disk cache for a native AFS client workstation or as a remote cache for a non-disk caching AFS clients, such as Macintoshes. The pure AFS scenario is designated "AFS protocol pass-through" in the accompanying illustration (see figure 10.4). Our trace-driven simulations indicate that the intermediate server provides benefit when there is a high degree of sharing within a workgroup (Muntz and Honeyman, 1991). Otherwise, AFS clients should directly access the primary servers. For non-caching clients, the intermediate provides performance benefit for the client and reduced workload on the primary servers and backbone network.

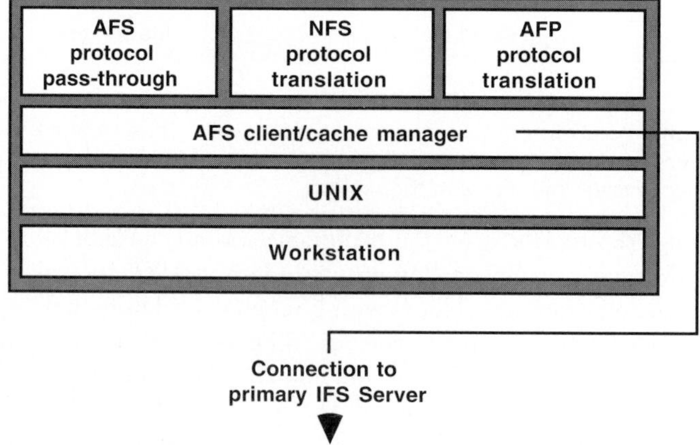

Figure 10.4 The intermediate server is an AFS client that presents multiple server interfaces to its own set of clients. Files are cached on the intermediate to speed subsequent references. Modified files have their changes sent to the primary IFS server.

The following describes how the intermediate works. When a user requests a file for the first time, the IFS processes retrieve the file from the primary server, cache it on the intermediate, and deliver it to the client. Re-references to that file can come from the initial requester or another client on the LAN authorized for sharing. The IFS satisfies subsequent requests from the cache on the intermediate, therefore not requiring access to the primary server. Despite the capacity of both the servers and the backbone, potentially tens of thousands of clients can produce an overwhelming work load. This approach keeps the backbone traffic to a minimum and blunts the peak demands on the file servers.

As the intermediate is essentially a disk cache, it requires little administration. The IFS sends modified files through to the primary server, thus we do not back up the intermediates. As with client workstations, the system configurations are identical, installed from a standard template.

Many file system protocols other than AFS are in use at the University. We have several NFS servers and over one hundred each of AppleShare, Novell Netware, and Banyan Vines servers. We do not expect these local servers to go away, but we do wish to permit their clients access to the campus-wide file system. As a protocol gateway, the intermediate provides an entry into the IFS for non-AFS clients.

Each intermediate server is an AFS client itself, but provides a server interface to its own set of clients. Through the intermediate, we provide access to systems running Sun Microsystem's Network File System (NFS) and Apple Computer's AppleTalk Filing Protocol (AFP), also known as AppleShare. NFS and AFP clients see the intermediate as a native NFS or AFP server. Inside the intermediate, however, a connection is made to the IFS.

Several issues must be resolved and trade-offs examined when implementing a protocol translator for an intermediate server. Some of these issues include:

- User authentication
- Permission mapping (ACLs)
- File naming
- Semantic content of files
- Navigation
- Availability of AFS commands
- Migration

One of the most important features of a large scale file system is security of user data. In the standard AFS implementation, Kerberos handles authentication issues. The issue of authentication becomes problematic, however, for clients that cannot or do not support Kerberos. Therefore, Kerberos support must be developed for those systems. In addition, the Kerberos model of mutual authentication between systems on untrusted networks does not address our intermediate server. That is, how does a client give its identity and authorizations to the intermediate, which goes and requests files on the client's behalf? And can we avoid introducing security loopholes into the system? To meet this requirement, we made extensions to the Kerberos Version 4 authentication exchange to support proxy authentication (Doster and Rees, 1992). This is not a change to the Kerberos protocol itself but in the transaction steps. It does not require modifications to the primary server, thus permitting client access to AFS servers outside the university.

Another issue related to security is file permission mapping. AFS uses access control lists (ACLs) attached to directories, and allows a user to specify the following permissions: Read, Write, Lookup, Insert, Delete, Lock, and Administer. The permissions Read, Write, and Lock apply to files in the directory. Lookup, Insert, Delete, and Administer apply to the directory itself. In most cases, the file server protocol being exported, for example AFP, does not have permissions that map to ACLs on a one-to-one basis.

A third issue concerns the naming of files. Certain characteristics of filenames may differ between the client and AFS. Some of the problems encountered in file names include maximum length, allowable characters, and directory separators. When differences occur between what the client allows for a file name and what the server allows, the IFS must correct for incompatibilities.

A fourth issue concerns the semantic content of a file. DOS text files, for example, use a carriage-return/line-feed combination to end each line, whereas UNIX does not. This difference makes editing the same file on the two different systems problematic. Also, AFS stores files as a byte stream with no support for record orientation. This can cause problems if the client operating system assumes some form of record-oriented support. For example, some applications may assume that the ability to lock records exists. How is this handled if the file system does not support records?

A fifth issue concerns file system navigation. How does the user access various files? The navigation methods should match those of the native client interface. A Macintosh user should be able to manipulate folders, and an NFS user should be able to use file and path names.

A sixth issue concerns the availability of AFS commands to the end user. AFS provides several commands that allow a user to view various characteristics of the file system. For example, commands exist that indicate the status of the available file servers. Another command returns file space usage information. It may be possible to integrate some of this information into the client environment without special commands (or even the user's knowledge). The question becomes how many of the AFS-specific commands to make available, and in what manner.

Finally, there is the issue of migration. How do users who are currently not using the distributed file system migrate to the new file system? How are their databases and individual files moved to the new system without disrupting their work?

When confronted with the issues described above, it is necessary to examine the trade-offs to achieve a high degree of compatibility between AFS and the client protocol. The biggest area for trade-offs concerns modifications of the client. Modifications fall into one of three types:

- No modifications to the client are necessary.
- Client requires modifications that are not visible to the user.
- Client requires user-visible modifications.

Client modifications can range from adding and requiring the use of new programs to changing the operating system itself. The goal is to create a seamless appearance for the user.

The AFP to AFS protocol translator runs in the kernel of an intermediate server. The protocol translator looks like an AFP server to a Macintosh client. No changes were made to the AFP protocol or to existing software running on the client. However, we install additional utilities on the client.

Accessing an AppleShare volume stored in AFS is no different from accessing a normal AppleShare volume. (Despite using the same term, there is generally not a one-to-one correspondence between AppleShare volumes and AFS volumes.) The user opens the Chooser dialog box and selects the file server to access. After selecting a file server, the system prompts the user for authentication information. After authentication, the user views a list of volumes available from the file server. Selecting one or more volumes results in those volumes appearing on the desktop. Users manipulate these volumes as they would any other AppleShare volume.

An AppleShare volume exported by an AFS server is simply a portion of the AFS tree. Usually a user has a choice between mounting the entire AFS tree and mounting just the user's home directory. A user can create a configuration file stored in a home directory, called AppleVolumes, which will let the user define the volumes presented for selection. The configuration file maps from a volume name to the corresponding portion of the AFS file tree.

Authentication occurs through a new Macintosh program module that works in conjunction with the Chooser dialog. The new module implements the Kerberos authentication mechanism. To make use of this module, the user simply stores a copy of the program in the AppleShare folder on the local disk. After that, whenever accessing an AFS file server from the Chooser, the system gives the user the option of using either the standard AFP authentication method or the Kerberos authentication method.

To connect to the AFS server, the user must select Kerberos authentication. From that point on, authentication looks identical to the user. A dialog asks for the user's ID and password. Assuming the ID and password are acceptable to Kerberos, the Mac presents the user with a list of available AFS volumes.

The toughest part of authentication is providing a mechanism by which the intermediate operates as if it were the user. Because the intermediate makes file requests of the primary server, the intermediate must possess the credentials necessary to access files desired by the user. In the Macintosh environment, the requests are approved through a moderately complicated series of conversations among the client, intermediate, and authentication servers. The intermediate runs an additional service that mediates a Kerberos authentication conversation. The conversation is managed so the intermediate obtains usable credentials, while still providing the same high level of security.

AFS supports most allowable characters in MacOS and vice-versa. File name length presents a problem. The Macintosh Finder imposes a maximum name length of 31 characters. File names in AFS that are longer than 31 characters are displayed on the Macintosh with characters truncated starting at the 32nd character. Most Finder operations and applications are unable to process these files. Long file names that map to the same truncated name will display with the same name, but with different icons. The Macintosh file system provides for a file tree through the use of folders. In general, users have no need to think of folder separator characters when manipulating folders through the Finder.

Occasionally, however, users do want to refer to a complete path name when accessing a file. On the Macintosh, the character used to delimit folder names is a ":". The AFS/AFP translator simply translates this character into the AFS equivalent ("/"). Unfortunately, most Finder operations or application programs cannot process AFS files that contain a ":" in the filename.

After mounting an AFS volume, an icon representing that volume appears on the user's desktop. Double-clicking on the volume causes the volume to open. Inside the volume, files appear exactly as the user would expect. The user manipulates the directory hierarchy by opening and closing folders. Users start applications by double-clicking on the application or a data file that is associated with the application. In other words, the user manipulates AFS files in exactly the same manner as regular Macintosh files.

In the Macintosh environment, only authentication and ACL manipulation commands are currently available. The user does not use the AFS command itself, but a Macintosh program that fits the Macintosh paradigm and presents an equivalent capability. Instead of issuing a UNIX style command, the user makes choices and fills in values on a dialog box (see figure 10.5).

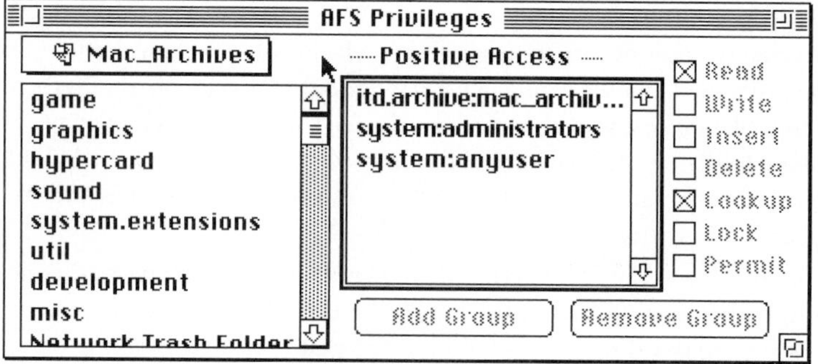

Figure 10.5 Macintosh users install a desk accessory (DA) that permits graphical manipulation of AFS access control lists.

The NFS/AFS translator runs in the kernel of the intermediate file server. The IFS project developed an NFS/AFS translator because no other translator was available. Transarc subsequently produced an NFS translator with minor performance and authentication differences. (While this section describes our work, we switched to Transarc's code for production use due to its vendor support.) The NFS client requires no changes; the intermediate appears to the user as a standard NFS server. Additional programs are installed in the intermediate kernel, which manage authentication and file access control. Access to the server is through the NFS mount command.

Authentication in the NFS environment requires an additional login program to authenticate to the intermediate server. The intermediate runs a service that takes end-client identifiers and performs authentication mapping. Performing authentication in this manner creates a shared secret between the client and the NFS translator. This mechanism allows the translator to act on behalf of the client without possessing a copy of the user's password. Permissions are handled with the standard AFS commands. File naming and navigation are also essentially identical in both NFS and AFS.

An intermediate server is not strictly required. We could build protocol translators on the primary server. However, running translators on intermediates does provide advantages. For example, off-loading translation from the primary server isolates its more resource-intensive services. Thus translation activity does not impact native AFS client performance. The system also benefits from the distributed caching described above, which would not be available if the translators ran on the primary servers.

By remaining 100 percent protocol compatible with AFS, the intermediate servers can interact with any off-the-shelf Transarc server. By providing the multiple server interfaces, we meet our objective of supporting protocols and not vendors.

An advantage of the IFS architecture is that it provides a suitable base for adding additional client support. Our future plans include porting the current translators to OSF/DCE and expanding the number of interfaces. For example, we are currently researching support for Novell Netware clients. While waiting for a Novell interface, the IFS deployment group is releasing a DOS client that uses a very simple protocol running over TCP/IP called SNAP. This client, which does not provide a local disk cache, draws on code developed at Carnegie Mellon and uses the translator functionality of the intermediate server. It allows DOS users to access the IFS as a logical disk drive (see figure 10.6).

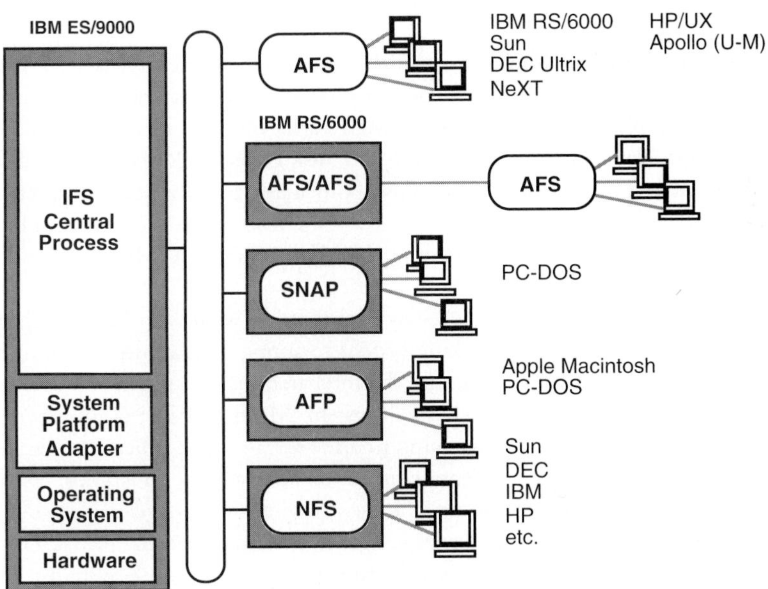

Figure 10.6 The IFS components are the primary servers, the intermediate servers, and the various client platforms. Connecting native AFS clients directly or through the intermediate server is a policy decision based on degree of data sharing within a workgroup.

10.6.4 Mobile Computing with AFS

We anticipate that the term *desktop computing* will become an anachronism later in this decade as the majority of computing will be done not at a desk but accessed ubiquitously. Cost and miniaturization are driving the opportunity as vendors provide high powered microprocessor systems in laptop, notebook, and palmtop systems. Software, however, has not kept pace with the progress of hardware. Therefore, there is little support for distributed computing in a mobile environment.

As an extension of the IFS activity, CITI undertook in 1991 an effort to support mobile computing as part of our campus distributed computing infrastructure. Much of the commercial mobile computing activity today is limited to electronic mail. The applications we sought to support were all those used in the office today, but with freedom of movement. While mobile, therefore, users will want to access file servers for their data and applications, email servers, directory services, and so on.

One problem in mobile computing is TCP/IP routing. That is, how does one determine the IP address of a system once it moves away from the office Ethernet? The concern is supporting end systems with frequently changing addresses. The Internet Engineering Task Force has a Mobile IP working group looking at routing issues. While we intend to benefit from whatever they develop, our focus is on reconfigurable services that are not tied to a specific IP address for the client system. Reconfigurability is a benefit of AFS, the challenge/response nature of AFS lends itself to throwing away a connection and re-establishing a new client/server link. We believe software developers will modify other services over time to support dynamic reconfiguration.

Various mobile platforms are available to us. There are tablets with pen input, voice (phone) interfaces, and built-in networking such as the Eo system. Enhanced hand-held systems include Apple's Newton and the Hewlett Packard 95LX. Many of these systems support PCMCIA slots, for which there are solid-state disk cards, 100 megabyte hard disks, Ethernet cards, and wireless network interfaces. Given our desire to provide a full function workstation and to concentrate on the software issues, we targeted off-the-shelf parts to build our laptop system (specifically an IBM laptop with a 20 MHz 386SX, 60 MB drive, and 10 MB memory).

In choosing the right operating environment, we went with Carnegie Mellon University's Mach as we needed a multitasking system to support distributed computing. Mach provides a close match to UNIX, it runs on the Intel architecture, it uses resources efficiently, and we have source. By being a relatively small system, Mach does not occupy as much disk space as other operating systems. By swapping to a file versus a pre-allocated disk partition, it also economizes on disk use. To compensate for the smaller screens on laptops, compared with the 19-inch displays on desktops, we use the tvtwm window manager with the X Window System. Tvtwm establishes a virtual screen several times larger than the physical display.

A distributed file system is essential to support these mobile systems. Laptops provide limited permanent storage. Using a distributed file system allows centralized administration (e.g., backup and software distribution). As with the workstations in the offices described above, we configure the mobile system as a dataless entity. Through use of the local disk cache, we minimize network traffic. This is extremely important due to the cost and congested nature of networks available to mobile systems. Before going mobile, the workstation is *warmed up* on the local network. That is, the user plugs the system into the Ethernet and works for a couple of hours. The assumption is that the applications and data accessed (and thus cached) will be those desired later.

The networking choices available for mobile computing include wireless and dial-up. Wireless options encompass spread-spectrum, which can be limited in range, and satellite, which may have bandwidth constraints. Dial-up links include cellular, which is truly mobile, and land-based (i.e., standard phone wall jacks), which is more affordable but limits mobility while computing. In evaluating the costs of various services, we found that on a per-byte cost, cellular can be an order of magnitude less expensive than commercial satellite or radio networks.

We targeted cellular and land-based dial-up for our networking. We currently run serial line IP (SLIP), but are moving to the point-to-point protocol (PPP). Our first cellular link was through a package called an Outback, consisting of a 3W Motorola cellular phone, a Telebit Cellblazer modem, and a battery pack. Unfortunately, this setup is roughly the size and weight of a car battery, which constrains mobility. Our second configuration uses a Telebit Q-Blazer modem and an OKI 900 cellular phone, with a total weight of approximately one pound. (In the spirit of investigation, we have also used acoustic couplers and GTE Airphones at 30,000 feet to connect, but with severe performance constraints.)

In performance studies conducted while mobile, we measured data rates of up to 1600 characters per second (compressed) for both land-based and cellular. This throughput allows quite reasonable use. As the local disk caches applications, generally only small files must be fetched from a server over the link. Achieving these rates required a fair amount of work on the AFS remote procedure call, including header compression and congestion avoidance and control based on Van Jacobson's work with TCP/IP (Van Jacobson, 1990).

As noted above, cellular can be much cheaper on a cost per byte basis than other wireless options. That assumes, however, that the data rate is sustained continually. As analog cellular service is not measured per byte but per minute, time spent in local processing still generates connection charges (which get expensive very quickly). We thus sought a method of limiting the connect time. A manual process of explicitly downloading and uploading files would destroy the commodity aspect of the local disk. We therefore decided to again take advantage of the local cache by implementing disconnected operations through optimistic replica control.

In this method, the system's standard state is no network attachment. The client logs write/modification activity on the local disk. After a missed read from the cache, the user has the choice of canceling the operation or establishing a network link (e.g., by establishing a cellular modem link). If the user connects to the network, the laptop fetches requested data from the file server and replays the write log back to the server. Conflicts at the server are resolved by user interaction. If someone else had modified the same file while the user was disconnected, the client software renames the disconnected file and notifies the user (the other version is not overwritten). This approach is similar to that of Coda at Carnegie Mellon, except our implementation requires no modification of the file server code or operations (Satyanarayanan, et. al., 1989).

Future work includes investigations into higher speed internal modems, hibernation, power management, caching strategies, and user interface issues (e.g., for conflict resolution).

As most UNIX systems are not turned off, quick shutdown and restart has not been a priority. Hibernation is similar to what the DOS and Macintosh laptops provide by closing the lid and going to *sleep*. With UNIX, hibernation requires swapping out all processes to disk and pushing the kernel data spaces out to a file. The disk-based information is read back into memory upon power-up. Power management is difficult to approach in a standard way. PC laptop systems typically implement proprietary mechanisms. Our hope is that the industry develops a widely used standard set of interfaces for spinning down disks, scaling back memory requirements, and so on. The Microsoft/Intel Advanced Power Management specification is one effort in this area.

AFS currently uses a least-recently used algorithm for cache management. We have found this works well, travel with a disconnected client has shown that missing one to three files per day from the cache can be typical. Thus we do not find it intrusive. However, there are files that due to their size should always remain in the cache as fetching them over a phone line could take a very long time (e.g., the X Window server). Therefore, we will research ways to ensure the cache is filled with the right mix of applications and data.

The result of these efforts has been a good approximation of the office environment when on the road. While laptops are not as powerful as our desktop workstations, measured in MIPS, the functionality is all there. We have used the system in hotel rooms and airport lounges throughout the U.S. Truly mobile trials have included both car trips and Amtrak journeys cross-country.

10.6.5 Mass Storage

We have discovered that most file systems are *write once, read never*. That is, people create data files but never remove them as there will always be that day when the information is needed again. Given this situation, it does not make sense to keep all file system data on expensive disk drives. The university simply does not have the money to buy them or the floor place on which to store them. Therefore, we would like to extend AFS to allow us to store data on higher density, lower cost media such as tape robot systems or optical jukeboxes. This requirement will also become more important as data file sizes change dramatically as we proliferate applications using digital video and digital audio.

The majority of such mass storage systems operate through an explicit download/upload mechanism for archiving data. Given our goal of transparency, we would like the system to continue to appear as a giant hard drive with all files remaining as part of the users' file system directories. Therefore, we would like AFS to automatically migrate files based on pre-established criteria, such as date last read, size of file, use count, and so on.

Transparency extends beyond keeping the appearance of using the directory structure to keep tape-based data appearing *on-line*. There is the concern with access latency when fetching a file through a robot system, for example. The delay in accessing the file, if it has been staged to tape, will become apparent to the user. Also, the distributed file system itself cannot cope with delays and the remote procedure call request may time out and fail.

To cope with these requirements, we have outlined complex caching strategies to provide data quickly to the client application. We also see this effort as making the mass storage system the entire file system, not an appendage to the disk-based file system. This more tightly integrated approach is similar to the Plan 9 file system developed by Bell Labs (Presotto, et.

al., 1991). In mid-1993, we have a design outlined for a mass storage extension to AFS and are doing simulation studies to test the effectiveness of the design, but have not started code development (Antonelli and Honeyman, 1993).

10.7 Performance Analysis, Modeling, and Testing

Due to the complexity of large scale distributed environments, we have a team analyzing the IFS and the campus network. They are collecting data of actual usage patterns and using the numbers to construct a model that will help anticipate scale and performance bottlenecks and aid in configuring the network topology. One study collected several weeks of trace data from the IFS servers by logging every call made to the file server. This study helped us to better understand workload characteristics (Subramanian, 1992).

Through these performance studies, we achieved a better appreciation for how AFS works. For example, delays we had attributed to either network or server bottlenecks were actually due to AFS's slow read performance in fetching files from the local disk cache. We intuitively expected there would be some overhead with managing the local cache, but not that read performance of AFS cached files would be half the performance of the local file system. Through optimization of the AFS client code, we reduced that overhead so that reads of locally cached files perform within 10 percent of the local file system (Stolarchuk, 1993). We made our enhancements available to Transarc.

NetMod is an analytic modeling tool we developed at CITI. We use NetMod to evaluate complex networks. It applies queuing models to calculate component utilization, throughput, and packet delays. NetMod represents various network components as icons, including Ethernet networks, routers, bridges, individual or clusters of workstations, and so on. Each component contains its performance characteristics or, in the case of users, their workload profiles. By constructing a model, we can identify where bottlenecks may occur (see figure 10.7).

Functionality testing of our IFS file servers and OSF/DCE environment relies on a testing framework we have developed using the scripting language expect (Libes, 1992), which comes from Don Libes at the National Institute of Standards and Technology and Tcl , the tool command language, created by John Ousterhout at UC Berkeley (Ousterhout, 1990). As we are building a heterogeneous environment for both our server and client platforms, we conduct extensive tests to validate consistent and equivalent functionality on all systems.

To provide user and administrative experiences from outside Michigan, we conducted a field test of the IFS servers at various universities (e.g., Cornell and Rensselaer Polytechnic Institute) and within IBM. The external exposure has been very valuable. We incorporated comments from those sites into system improvements.

10.8 Deployment Experience

Responsibility for IFS campus deployment falls outside CITI in the Research Systems production department of the Information Technology Division. CITI established this group as a spin-off, thus carrying with them experience and knowledge of the system. As CITI concentrates on research and development, offering production services is outside our scope.

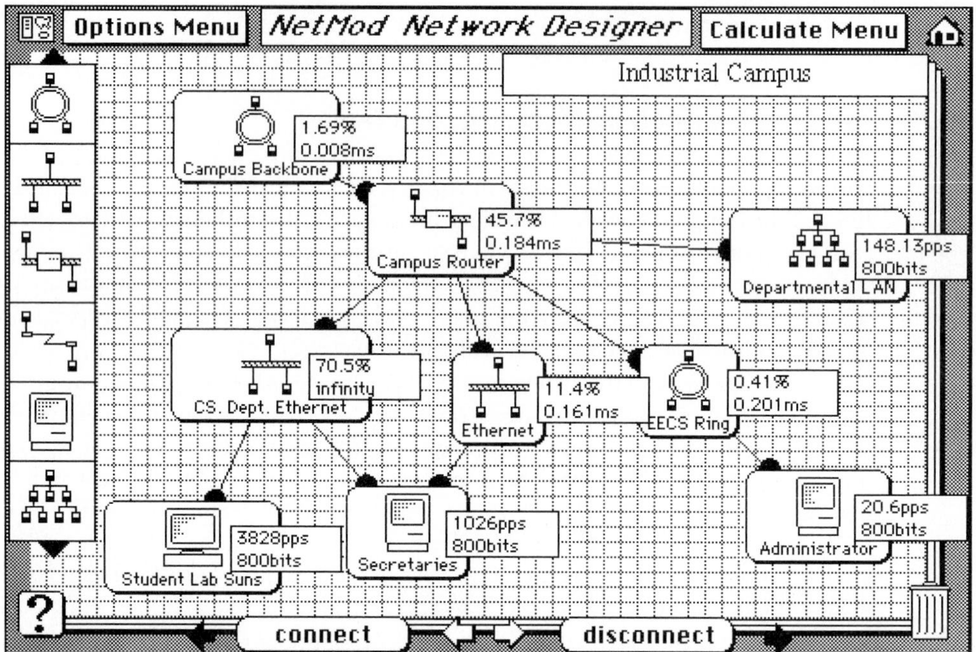

Figure 10.7 NetMod supports designing a network and identifying workload balance and system bottlenecks. User and system profiles are built in to the tool. It runs on Macintosh (shown), Microsoft Windows, and UNIX.

The Information Technology Division has a great deal of experience deploying and supporting desktop computers and mainframes, but the institutional file system was the first distributed application. This had an impact, therefore, in areas ranging from account management, help desk support, management tools, and so on.

The first task addressed was establishing a campus-wide name space for user logins. With the various islands of computing on campus, we were sure user name conflicts existed that would cause problem when deploying campus-wide services. That is, how could you be sure of the identity of the person behind the login name? Our solution was to establish a new network-based server called Uniqname, which provides a Kerberos-based registry for logins and UNIX UIDs. System administrators around campus register their users in Uniqname, guaranteeing them a consistent login for all campus services. Users select their top three choices for the three to eight character logins. Most select initials or some combination of initials and last name. We have had very few problems with people wanting to register conflicting names. Uniqname is linked to the campus X.500 directory service, which provides both standard X.500 and UNIX finger interfaces and a email-forwarding service. Thus campus users can verify to whom a login belongs by querying the X.500 directory. We currently have over 35,000 individuals registered in Uniqname.

One problem with a large number of users is the UNIX UID space, which many systems limit to approximately 32,000 identities. As Kerberos does not use UIDs for authentication, UID conflicts do not cause problems with services like AFS. However, utilities such as the UNIX directory command, ls, do use UIDs to fill the owner field in detailed file name lists. While this does not grant rights to someone (AFS access control lists manage rights), it can be confusing for UNIX users. While we wait for the vendors to support larger name spaces, we maintain a unique UID space for UNIX users and distribute overlapping UIDs to Macintosh users, from whom any conflicts will be hidden from view.

AFS, and thus IFS, organizes clients and servers under common administration into an organizational entity called a cell. AFS performs user authentication, for example, on a per-cell basis. Cell administrators may have different policies for directory naming (e.g., where applications are stored and how user directories are named). To provide a coherent environment at the University, we would like to limit the number of cells to as few as possible. At this time, we have two major cells: the campus-wide cell managed by the Information Technology Division and a cell within the Engineering College. These two organizations jointly operate some public workstation clusters and many people use services provided by both organizations. Therefore, we desired a coherent file system environment despite having two cells. The system administrators worked out a common naming scheme so that users can keep their home directory in only one cell, but still easily access applications and data in either cell.

Another issue was funding IFS deployment. Many University central services work on a re-charge basis. With mainframes this is much more straightforward than distributed systems. In addition, what to measure must change. In the timesharing world, we charge users for network connect time. In the client/server world, one is *connected* all the time. Therefore, we had to introduce an accounting and billing system for distributed application, with IFS again being the first. The accounting code uses software we wrote initially for logging file system activity (targeted at performance analysis). The accounting system collects statistics on disk space usage of each user, from which the system generates a monthly bill.

To establish the charges for IFS service, we had to determine its costs. As it was the first distributed application, it drove the infrastructure requirements of the accounting and billing system, campus-wide authentication, the Uniqname service, directory services, management tools, and so on. As these will be used by a range of future services, IFS users should not bear the whole cost. Otherwise, distributed file service would be too expensive. We do not have an easy answer as to how costs should be allocated, and thus will frequently review the pricing model over the coming years as we introduce new services.

The deployment team based IFS fees on amortizing hardware over several years and on the actual staff costs per year. For the '93 – '94 school year, the deployment group charges are $1.25 per megabyte per year for students, faculty, and staff. Additional quota requested but not used costs $.25 per megabyte per year. That is, if someone requests a 100 megabyte quota but only averages 80 megabytes of storage, the charge will be 80 times $1.25 and 20 times $.25. Students have a free allocation of three megabytes to start. Faculty and staff pay a yearly fee of $75.00 to cover user services, such as the help desk.

There are additional fees for replicated data on multiple servers and restoring data from backup tapes. The backup policy for IFS is to provide daily incremental backups (rotating the tapes every week) and weekly full saves (rotating the tapes every four months). At the end of each term, we permanently archive the last full backup.

As of mid-1993, we have several thousand users and 100 gigabytes of disk in the IFS. The University expects to deploy approximately one dozen translator servers for the '93 – '94 school year.

Automated management of the IFS occurs through a suite of tools called Big Brother that monitor the network 7 days per week, 24 hours per day. When detecting a server outage, Big Brother notifies an on-call person about the problem specifics through special codes sent to a staff member's pager.

Example uses of the IFS include placing our public domain and shareware archives in the IFS. Volunteers verify files before placing them in the IFS, where the can be accessed by both people on campus and AFS users around the world. Users easily access these files in their standard format, running them directly out of the IFS. Macintosh users simply browse the three gigabytes of Mac archives by opening folders and launching applications by double-clicking. There no longer is the need to use a transfer protocol to download the file from a bulletin board system and go through the steps of converting from some intermediate format (e.g., BinHex) to an executable.

Another use is by the Population Studies Center, who have placed gigabytes of U.S. census data files in the IFS for statistical analysis by workstation clients. Before using the IFS, the data resided on a mainframe and researchers had to mount several reels of tape, feeding the data into a batch process. By storing the data on the IFS and using powerful workstation clients, they have greatly reduced the time it takes to run an analysis. They have found the quality of their research is improving as they use the data much more, and thus better understand it. The center also shares data both within the University and with researchers at other universities who access our IFS servers transparently over the Internet.

In the future, one of the deployment concerns we face is moving users from AFS to the OSF/DCE distributed file system, DFS. Outside of editing access control lists, for which we hope to provide graphical interfaces, we expect the user visible changes to be minimal. On the administrative side, however, we face moving user account information and data from AFS to DFS as DFS uses a new and different underlying storage architecture. Transarc will provide tools to assist with this effort, but it will still require substantial effort. In addition, we must time this move well. As AFS and DFS do not interoperate, we do not want to move to DFS and find ourselves isolated from the AFS world. While we are targeting 1994 for DFS deployment, we expect that many other sites will run AFS for several more years. One proposed mechanism is to have dual protocol clients (i.e., run both AFS and DFS cache managers). However, the processor, disk, and memory requirements for that configuration are beyond most of our workstations. We are considering building AFS/DFS and DFS/AFS translator servers that would allow bridging between both data sharing worlds.

10.9 Summary

The aim of the IFS is to provide a coherent, widely accessed distributed system to support heterogeneous clients. Phase one began in 1988 with the initial goal of proof-of-concept followed by campus-wide deployment of a production-level file service based on AFS. The second phase began in the summer of 1991 and is a three year effort to enhance IFS functionality while still improving performance and scalability. Major work items include bringing the IFS to full OSF/DCE compliance on all platforms, implementing protocol translators to support popular personal computer LAN environments (notably Novell Netware), providing a hierarchical storage interface, and researching mobile laptops in a distributed computing environment.

In 1988 we began building our distributed environment on AFS, Kerberos authentication, the remote procedure call client/server paradigm, and so on. We feel that OSF's selection of these technologies as the basis for DCE validated our work. By moving to OSF/DCE compliance we will build an industry-standard infrastructure to support interoperability both within the university and with other organizations. We are now sharing with our hardware and software suppliers our need for DCE support in their products.

Use of the Internet has been critical to our success. IFS developers working closely with Carnegie Mellon and Transarc had instant access to source code changes through *global AFS* links. Rather than waiting for tapes to be cut and mailed or files placed for ftp access, source code and other data were simply on-line as part of the file system. This collaboration environment has likely saved months of staff time. And, as noted above, campus users now exploit the Internet for sharing data (see figure 10.8).

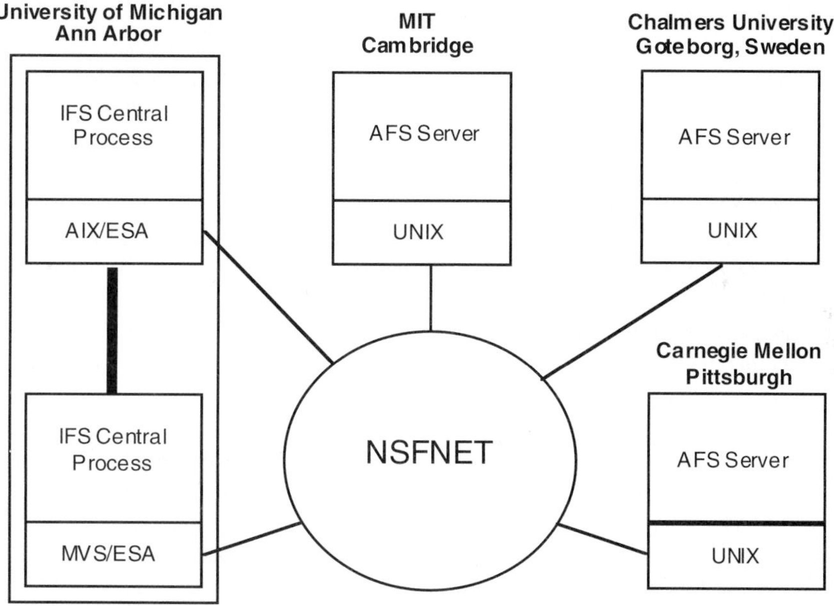

Figure 10.8 NSFNET provides access to dozens of other AFS sites around the world. NSFNET links to all continents provide the basis for a truly global file system. By remaining compatible with the AFS protocol, IFS users at Michigan can share with others or access their own files when away from the university.

Our approach will scale well to support thousands of heterogeneous systems. We have found that it is feasible to provide central management of data and applications while allowing distributed decision making on access. Separating those responsibilities fits the model of the university well–control of the data remains in the users' hands. Through wide availability, the IFS facilitates increased sharing of information. The user experiences with IFS reinforce this point.

Future directions include offering many more services incorporated into this distributed environment. Plans include replacing all functionality of the academic timesharing system with workstation and client/server solutions by September 1994. Services under development include electronic mail and conferencing, statistical computing, enhanced directory services, distributed printing, and much more. Deploying the IFS provided important insight into the issues of rolling out new systems in a large scale environment.

IFS development and deployment resulted from the contributions of a very talented group of university and IBM people. All credit for what has been achieved goes to them. IFS development has been supported by IBM Corporation. The mobile computing efforts have been supported in part by both IBM and Telebit Corporation.

10.10 References

Antonelli, C.J., and Honeyman, P., 1993. Integrating Mass Storage and File Systems. *CITI Technical Report 93-2,* Center for Information Technology Integration, The University of Michigan, Ann Arbor.

Doster, B., and Rees, J. 1992, Third-Party Authentication in the Institutional File System. *CITI Technical Report 92-1,* Center for Information Technology Integration, The University of Michigan, Ann Arbor.

Howard, J., et. al., 1988. Scale and Performance in a Distributed File System. *ACM Transactions on Computer Systems,* vol. 6, no. 1.

Howe, J., 1992. Intermediate File Servers in a Distributed File System Environment. *CITI Technical Report 92-4,* Center for Information Technology Integration, The University of Michigan, Ann Arbor.

Jacobson, V., 1990. Compressing TCP/IP Headers for Low-Speed Serial Links. *Internet Request for Comments,* no. 1145.

Libes, D., 1992. Regression Testing and Conformance Testing Interactive Programs. *Proceedings of the Summer 1992 USENIX Conference,* San Antonio, Texas, Jun.

Muntz, D., and Honeyman, P., 1991. Multi-level Caching in Distributed File Systems. *CITI Technical Report 91-3,* Center for Information Technology Integration, The University of Michigan, Ann Arbor.

Ousterhout, J., 1990. Tcl: An Embeddable Command Language. *Proceedings of the Winter 1990 USENIX Conference,* Washington, D.C., Jan.

Presotto, D., et. al., 1991. Plan 9: A Distributed System. *Proceedings of the Spring 1991 EurOpen Conference,* Tromso, Norway.

Satyanarayanan, M., et. al., 1989. Coda: A Highly Available File System for a Distributed Workstation Environment. *Computer Science Technical Report CMU-CS-89-165,* Carnegie Mellon University, Pittsburgh.

Subramanian R., 1992. Workload Characterization of AFS File Servers. *CITI Technical Report 92-6,* Center for Information Technology Integration, The University of Michigan, Ann Arbor.

Stolarchuk, M.T., 1993. Faster AFS. *Proceedings of the Winter 1993 USENIX Conference,* San Diego, pp. 67–75.

Ted Hanss directs the Center for Information Technology Integration at the University of Michigan. At CITI, Ted oversees projects developing a multi-vendor, multi-protocol distributed computing environment for the University. He is a frequent speaker on distributed computing trends and directions. Ted chairs the Open Software Foundation End User Steering Committee, which facilitates end user involvement in OSF processes. Ted received his Bachelor of Science degree from Boston College and will receive his Masters of Business Administration from the University of Michigan in 1993.

Chapter 11

Hewlett-Packard's Migration to Client/Server Architecture

Wallace A. "Skip" Ross
Hewlett-Packard Company

11.1 Introduction

Hewlett-Packard has annual revenues exceeding $16 billion and employs more than 90,000 people worldwide. It is a global company, with most of its business outside North America. Information technology is used pervasively throughout the company. HP has one of the largest private Internet networks in the world, interconnecting its many field and factory locations with high speed data communications. Most of HP's information systems employ Hewlett-Packard computers–HP 3000s, HP 9000s, PCs and Unix workstations. The applications are highly integrated, moving data among themselves and to users. The present suite of applications was developed during the 1980s, and the architecture laid out at the beginning of that decade is fully deployed.

HP is now moving to a client/server architecture for its internal business applications. This chapter will:

- Summarize the reasons for making this change.
- Describe the client/server architecture adopted within HP.
- Discuss various methods of migrating from our legacy architecture
- Review the results to date in HP's Worldwide Customer Support Operations' move to client/server, beginning in early 1989.
- Identify some issues and challenges for organizations contemplating migration.
- Review the benefits of the client/server architecture.

11.2 Reasons for Change

The move to client/server at HP was very much driven by business imperatives, not technology. Toward the end of the 1980s a number of issues were facing HP's information technology organizations. It was clear that the traditional systems approaches would not suffice to address these issues. Something had to change.

11.2.1 Dynamic Business Change Requires Rapid System Development

The rate of change of the business environment is accelerating. Information technology plays a critical role in HP's Customer Support business. To accommodate the rapid business change, new business systems must be developed, released and implemented more and more rapidly. Our traditional terminal-host development methods and implementation architecture were proving inadequate. We needed something new.

11.2.2 Management Needs Access To Operational Data

HP's Customer Support management needs real time access to information about the status of the business. This information is needed by all levels of management, from first-line operations to corporate headquarters. Our legacy systems have the data embedded within the application. It is distributed across the organization for ready access by front-line managers. This makes headquarters access to cross-functional data very difficult to obtain. A new architecture was needed to satisfy the needs of both sets of managers.

11.2.3 Global Business with Local Adaptability Requires Local Clients

HP is a global company. Increasingly our key customers are global as well. These global customers expect HP to look and act the same anywhere in the world. At the same time, HP managers in different countries have to deal with local competition, legal requirements, and customer practices. We need to be able simultaneously to provide both a global context and local control of processes.

11.2.4 Partnerships Require Electronic Integration Between Companies

Information technology allows more efficient relationships between suppliers and customers. Electronic communication can eliminate redundant activities in the combined value chains of the two partners. A way to implement this is to allow HP's customers and partners to have clients which access servers used within HP.

11.2.5 Data Integrity Must Be Protected

While providing all the flexibility of locally specified or developed clients, and partner access to servers, HP's core business data must maintain high integrity. This means that the business rules which govern changes to that data must be clearly defined and centrally managed.

All of the above requirements can be addressed by the client/server technology. These were the business drivers that led HP to pursue implementation of that technology.

11.3 Description of the Architecture

11.3.1 Some Popular Interpretations of Client/Server

Client/server is a ubiquitous term. It seems to be applied to almost every computer architecture by the popular press and product vendors. Some of the more common configurations referred to as client/server are the following.

11.3.1.1 Windows Integration of Traditional Application User Environment

A PC or workstation can, with windows, perform a very useful terminal emulation function. Multiple application screens, each in its own window, can be open and accessible to the user. In fact, this is a quick way to make significant productivity gains for users of traditional terminal-minicomputer/mainframe applications. The rapid context switching and simple addition of ancillary tools have been shown at HP to yield 10 to 15 percent gains in a typical administrative user's productivity without any changes to the core applications.

11.3.1.2 Graphical User Interface Replacing Terminal Screens

Software exists for PCs and workstations to convert traditional terminal screens to equivalent graphical user interface (GUI) windows. This provides the benefits of terminal emulation with the additional ease of use and context standardization of the GUI.

11.3.1.3 SQL Calls to Remote DBMS

An application can be written so that the logic resides on a PC or workstation client and the database on a server–another PC/workstation, a minicomputer or a mainframe. Communication between the client and server is via Structured Query Language (SQL). The client can thereby remotely perform reads and writes, through SQL calls, on the server database. SQL provides a fair, though not complete, measure of standardization among database vendors. This configuration provides the benefits of off-loading the application from the central computer. It also yields portability across vendors' products, to the extent that there is adherence to industry standard SQL constructs.

11.3.1.4 Remote Procedure Calls

Remote procedure calls are similar to local procedure calls but executable over a network. They allow an application to be split between a desktop client and a remote file server. This facilitates optimum partitioning of the computing resources. It also can reduce network traffic by executing some of the application logic at the server rather than passing elementary data from server to client.

11.3.2 HP Client/Server Architecture

HP has defined an architecture to use for all its internal information technology client/server applications. The technical architecture comprises five major components. These are interconnected through message-based interfaces which allow physical separation if needed (see figure 11.1).

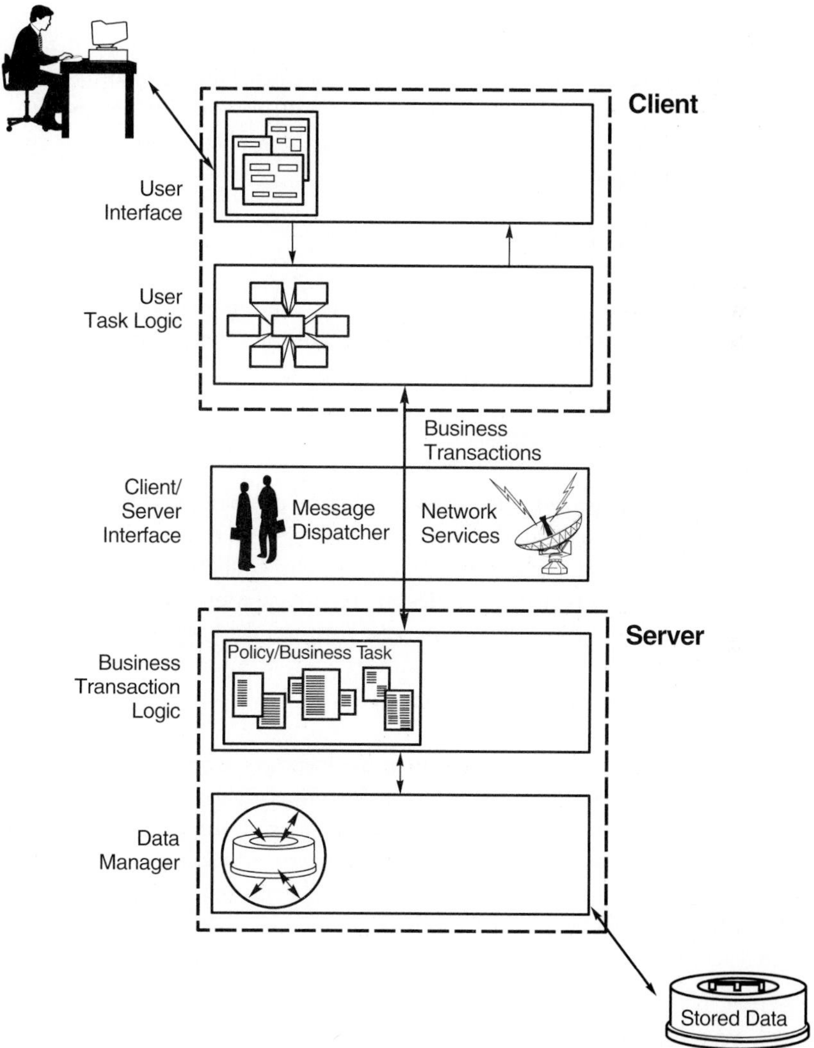

Figure 11.1 Technical architecture model.

11.3.2.1 User Interface

The *user interface* presents data and functions to the user, and collects the required data and function selections from him or her. The most common implementations of the interface will be X-Windows/Motif and/or Windows.

11.3.2.2 User Task Logic

User task logic controls the user choices and interactions, and creates business transactions to pass to the server. There may also be some local edits. This logic normally resides in the workstation. The workstation thereby off-loads from the central CPU much of the transaction processing. Typically the combination of user interface and application logic constitutes the client part of the system.

11.3.2.3 Business Transaction Logic

Business transaction logic is applied to the transactions passed between the client and the database. This business transaction logic is the set of rules that enforces business policy and manages database integrity.

11.3.2.4 Data Manager

The *data manager* provides access to the physical database(s), with a standard language (SQL) independent of what vendor's database is used. Note that there may be more than one *physical* database operating as a single *logical* database. This could be for reasons of capacity or physical distribution. The data manager hides any such separation. Typically the combination of business transaction logic and data manager constitutes the server part of the system.

11.3.2.5 Message Dispatcher

The above components communicate using messages, which are business transactions defined by the data models. In our technical architecture, a *message dispatcher* manages the message traffic between client and server. It includes a network directory to all clients and servers. The message dispatcher relieves the other components of needing any knowledge of the physical source or destination of the messages they use. In this way, the applications can be designed to be independent of the physical implementation– centralized on a single computer or distributed across a network.

11.3.3 Client/Server Application Model

Figure 11.2 shows how an application is designed using this architecture. It is very specific, and very different from traditional application designs. In fact, the whole concept of an application changes in very important ways.

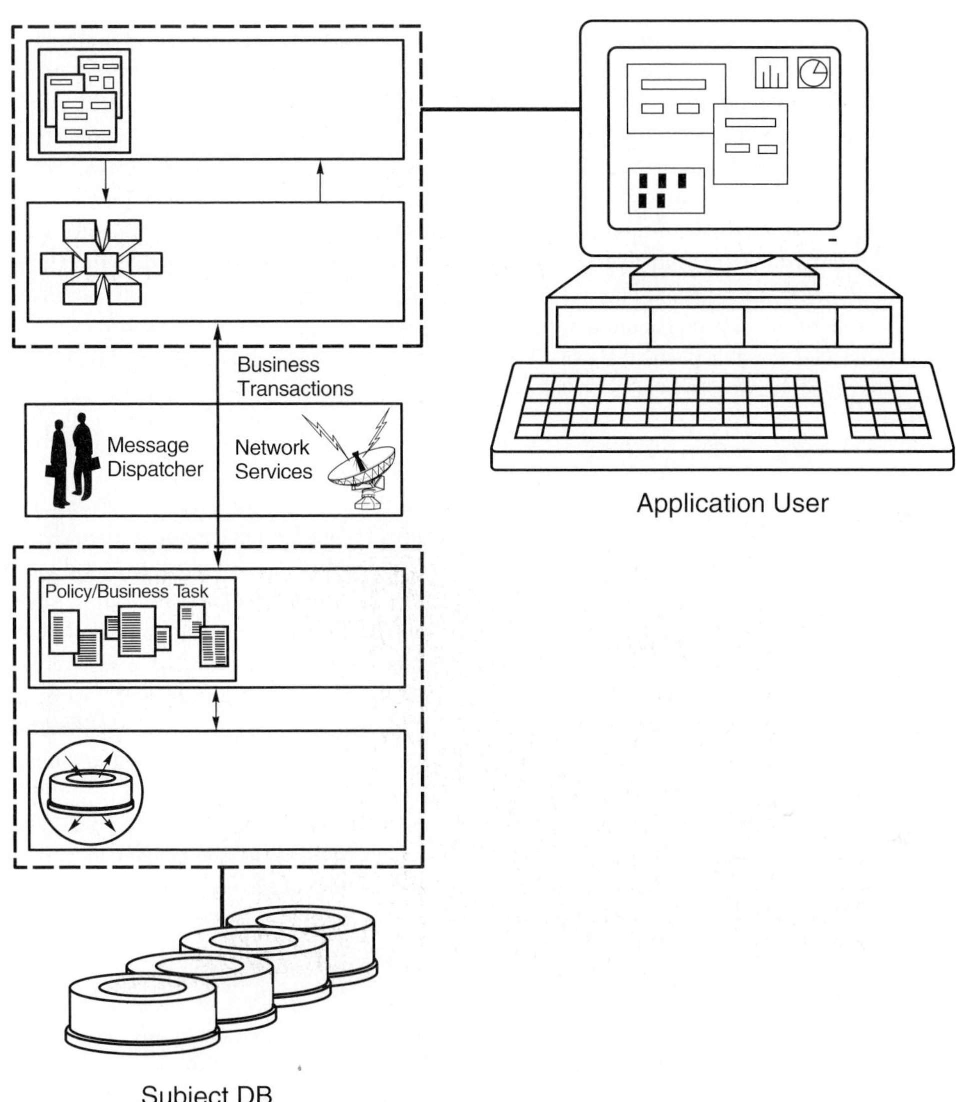

Figure 11.2 Client/server application.

11.3.3.1 Process/Task Clients

The client contains the logic that makes an application perform the functions that a user needs to accomplish a given process or task. It is very specific to that process or task. This is quite different from a traditional minicomputer/mainframe application, in which the user often performs his/her whole job using one application. The traditional application performs a variety of often unrelated tasks, which leads to overlapping functions across applications. An example is order management. Order management is a process done by people in many roles, as a part of their jobs. Therefore, order management functions are built into many applications, which are built around the different jobs. In the client/server paradigm, there would be an order management client. Anyone needing to manage an order could have that client available on his/her workstation. On the same workstation, there would also be the other clients needed for that particular user. There would be no requirement that any two users have the same collection of clients–that would depend on their job responsibilities.

11.3.3.2 Data Servers

A data server provides the clients with access to one or more databases. A database (ideally) contains only a single data subject. A data subject contains a collection of data elements which are all closely related. Some examples of data subjects are: order, customer, product. Any client might access multiple data subjects, and each data subject will serve multiple types of client. This is in definite contrast to applications which have dedicated databases. These databases typically contain data belonging to many data subjects. For example, a service call management application contains data about customers, products, orders, and so on. With these kinds of databases, there is redundant data, the data is sometimes defined differently by each application, and there is no single place to find all of a given type of data. This problem is solved with subject data servers.

Within the server are all of the business rules governing the server's data, and the logic to enforce them. This means that no client can modify the server data in violation of the rules–the offending transaction would be rejected. Therefore, clients can be written anywhere, any time, by anyone and not jeopardize the integrity of the data in the servers.

11.3.3.3 Business Transactions

In the HP client/server architecture, communication between client and server is via business transactions. These transactions are defined in the business data models, and managed in the data dictionary. This provides isolation between the designs of the clients and servers. Any client can communicate with any server (aside from security restrictions) using the business transactions defined for it, and only using these transactions. The design of either client or server can change without affecting the other, as long as the business transactions are preserved. Given a server, new clients can easily be added by simply producing and reading the relevant transactions. These transactions are driven by business models, not technology.

A business transaction will typically span multiple data subjects. This isolates the client design from the data architecture, that is, how the data is partitioned into subjects. The data servers responsible for a given business transaction, therefore, must resolve it into data subject transactions and pass some of these on to any other servers required.

Business transactions are objects, to use the parlance of object oriented design. HP's client/server architecture is, in essence, *object oriented in the large.*

11.3.4 Enterprise Architecture Using Client/Server Applications

The application architecture for an enterprise or company is very conceptually simple when it consists of only client/server applications of the type defined in the HP architecture. Figure 11.3 portrays this. The entire enterprise is interconnected by a global LAN (a contradiction in terms if taken literally, but conceptually useful and not difficult to implement). All clients and servers are connected to this LAN. Each server has a (logical) single database, containing only a single data subject, (administered by a single owner). The implementation might employ multiple distributed databases, but they would be logically single per subject–DBMS technology would resolve the interconnections and intercommunications. Each client supports a single process or task. Workstations contain whatever combination of clients each user needs.

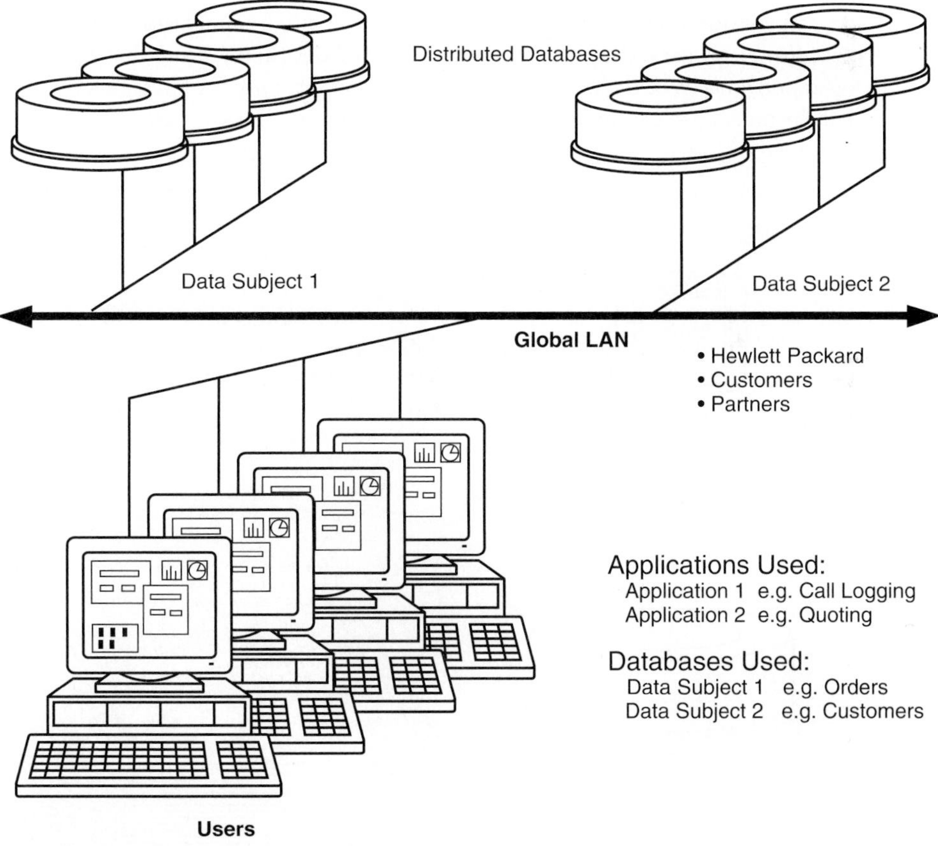

Figure 11.3 Client/server architecture.

Not shown on this diagram, but typically present, are specialized non-database servers. They perform, for example, input/output, batch processing, and so on.

This architecture can easily be extended beyond an enterprise's boundaries to provide Electronic Data Access (EDA) to the company's servers for its customers and business partners. This requires a gateway between the company LAN and that of the partner/customer to provide security for limiting access. The gateway can be selective to whatever level of data is needed–specific instances of specific elements in specific servers. Providing this level of interconnection between companies allows far more robust interchange than EDI. It allows elimination of redundant portions of the combined value chains of the company pairs.

11.4 Migration Methods

HP, like most corporations, has a large installed base of legacy applications. These range all the way from being robust and meeting current business needs to being old and nearly obsolete. In general, however, they share the problem of being difficult to evolve rapidly. This provides the impetus for migrating them to client/server. Migration can take two fundamentally different forms: leverage and design from scratch. For modern applications that are still meeting the operational needs of the business, there is often opportunity for leveraging the existing code. For the more obsolete applications, it is better to throw them away and start with a clean sheet of paper.

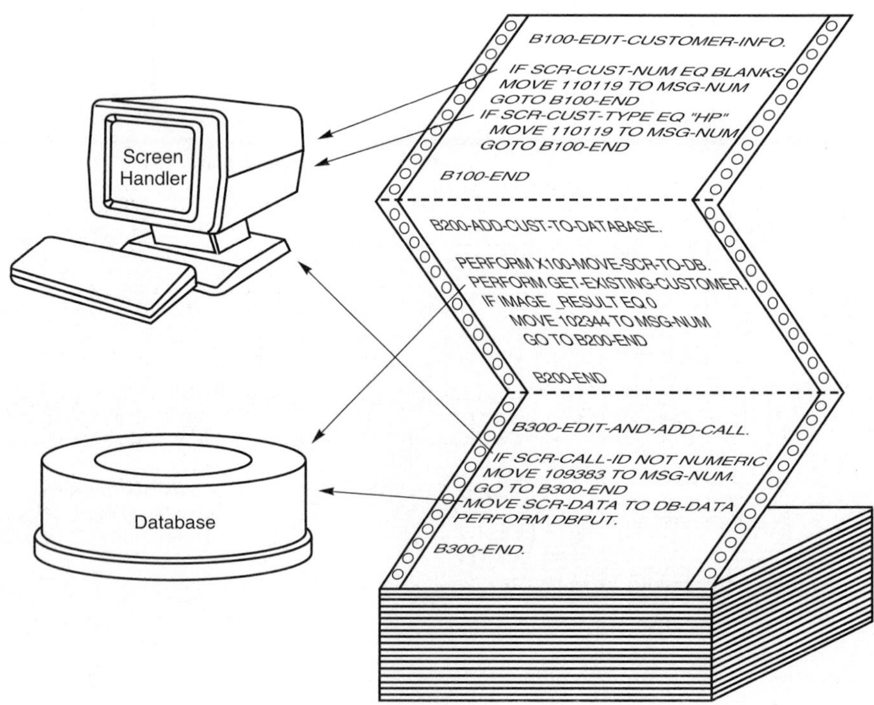

Figure 11.4 Existing application architecture.

11.4.1 Leveraging Existing Applications

Figure 11.4 portrays a legacy terminal-host application. These typically have several hundred thousand lines of COBOL code which incorporates the program logic, the screen handling and the database access calls. While not necessarily poorly structured, they tend to be large monolithic applications. This is what makes them hard to evolve rapidly. Making a change often requires people with a good knowledge of the code and how it is structured, as well as the impact any code change might have on other parts of the same application or interfacing applications.

A technique we have used at HP for migrating these monolithic but still useful applications to client/server is portrayed in figure 11.5. Here we retain the existing database but put a server around it. We create the server by going into the existing monolithic application and literally cutting out useful portions of code. These are then organized appropriately for the server business transaction logic. Our experience has been that we can reuse up to 60 percent of the resulting server code from the prior application. The client, since it is GUI-based, must

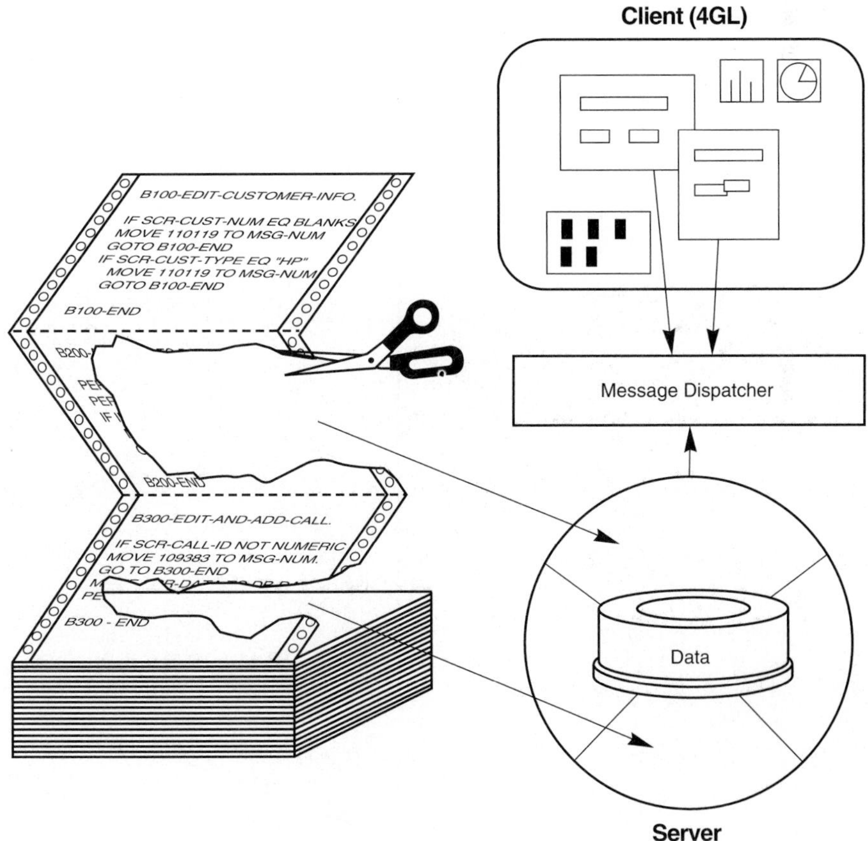

Figure 11.5 Migration of existing applications.

be designed from scratch. A typical client, though, is about 30 percent of the code in the resulting client/server application, so this is numerically the small part of the job. Also, client design should be done by iterative prototyping with user involvement, to ensure that the end result has high usability and meets user needs. The server, by contrast, is driven from the enterprise data models in a more linear fashion.

11.4.2 Design from Scratch

When there is no opportunity for leveraging an existing application, the new client/server application is designed from scratch. HP has selected the *information engineering* methodology for such development.

11.4.2.1 Information Engineering

Information engineering is the name for a methodology for designing information systems. As shown in figure 11.6, it can be visualized as a pyramid, where the sides represent data, process and technology (Martin, 1986). The pyramid has four layers which are, from the top down:

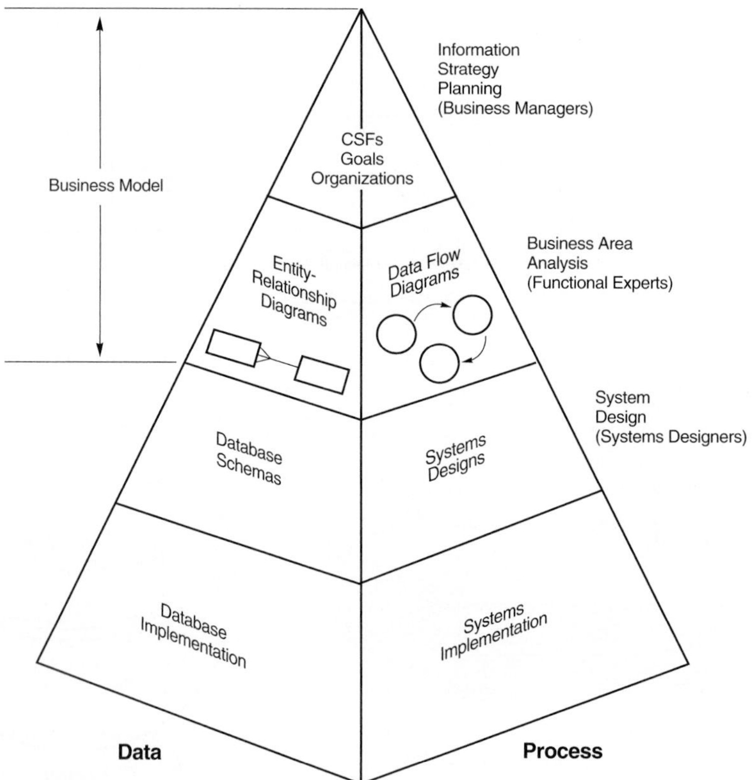

Figure 11.6 Systems design methodology.

1. Information strategy planning (ISP)
2. Business area analysis (BAA)
3. System design
4. System construction

The premises for the information engineering methodology are.

- The design for data and process are separate, though linked.
- Design proceeds top down, starting with an ISP based on the goals of the business.

This approach yields designs in which the business information needs of the enterprise are better met, because they are explicitly examined. The business goals of the enterprise are better met, because they drive the designs in very tangible ways. Information engineering is ideally suited to the design of HP client/server applications. The separation of data and process corresponds to the separation of server and client. Business area analysis divides all the enterprise data into data subjects, as required for server partitioning. It also separates and decomposes processes, yielding proper partitioning for clients.

Information engineering is a data-intensive methodology. It requires a CASE tool to manage all of the data used in the analysis and design processes. Early in our move to the client/server architecture we did a CASE gap analysis. It compared the capabilities of existing integrated CASE tools with the requirements of the client/server architecture we have chosen. No CASE tool at the time fully met our needs. We listed and prioritized the gaps between the tool capabilities and what we needed. The most important missing element was the ability to develop the application program interfaces (APIs) between the client and the network and the server and the network. To bridge this gap until the CASE manufacturers filled it, we developed an API generator. It automatically builds these application program interfaces to connect the client and the server to the network. The specifications used by the API generator come from the data models and business transaction definitions for the application. By combining this API generator with a commercially available integrated CASE tool, we are now able to build fully generated servers from our data and process models. We expect that by sometime in 1994, we will also be able to use the tool to generate the clients. In the interim, we will continue to use fourth generation language tools to build our GUI clients.

11.4.2.2 Development Environment

The HP client/server architecture can be the basis for all of the business applications for the company. If implemented properly, all the applications will intercommunicate without imposing on the development teams that design them a need for intimate joint project planning. The structure provides the coordination required. To enable multiple independent teams to develop clients and servers which can participate in the company-wide architecture, a common development process and common environment must be employed. The following discussion supports that assertion.

As shown in figure 11.7, elements of the client/server architecture implement corresponding elements of the information engineered models.

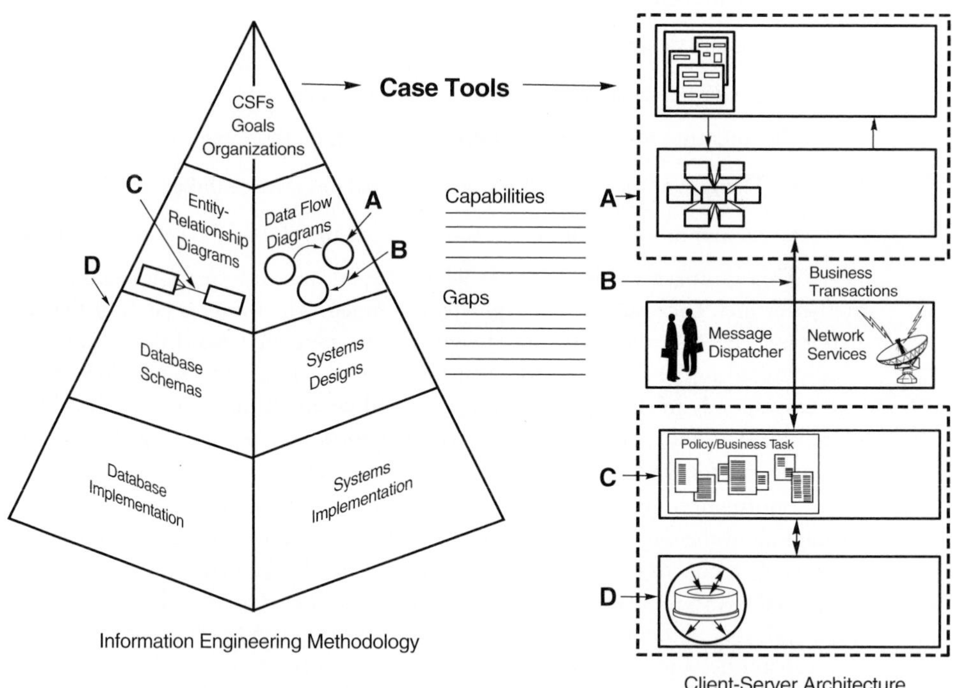

Figure 11.7 New client/server application.

1. The client application logic automates processes from the data flow diagrams. (A)
2. The business transactions are the data flows in the data flow diagrams. (B)
3. The business transaction logic, or business rules, in the server capture the data relationships from the entity relationship diagrams. (C)
4. The data manager is constructed using the database schemas derived from the data models. (D)

Figures 11.8 through 11.10 indicate how a succession of projects across the company over time would be developed in a common information engineering/CASE environment. To maximize the possibilities for sharing and reuse of models and designs, a corporate repository is essential. It must be capable of storing all of the deliverables produced at the various stages of the life cycle. All the CASE tools must interface to it, ideally with real time, version-managed interchange among all users. Figure 11.11 portrays this in terms of the information engineering pyramid.

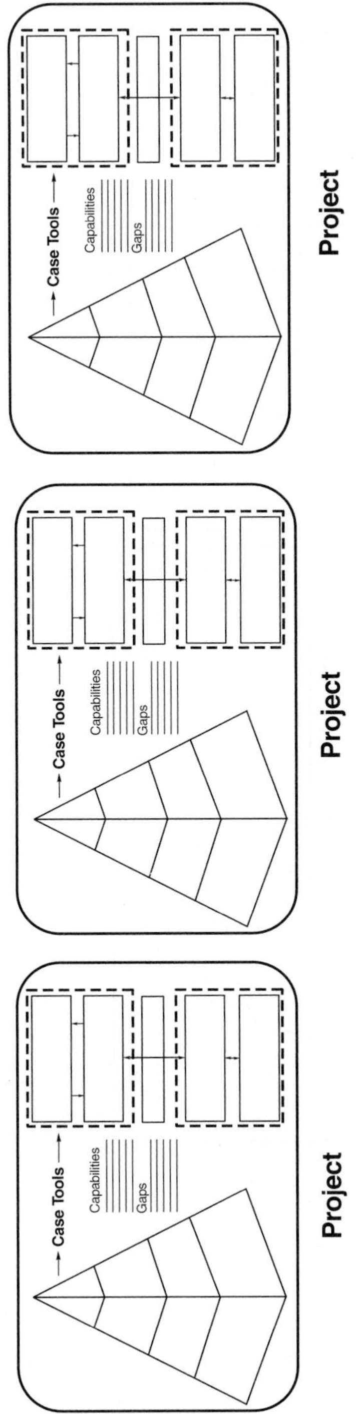

Figure 11.8 Enterprise development projects.

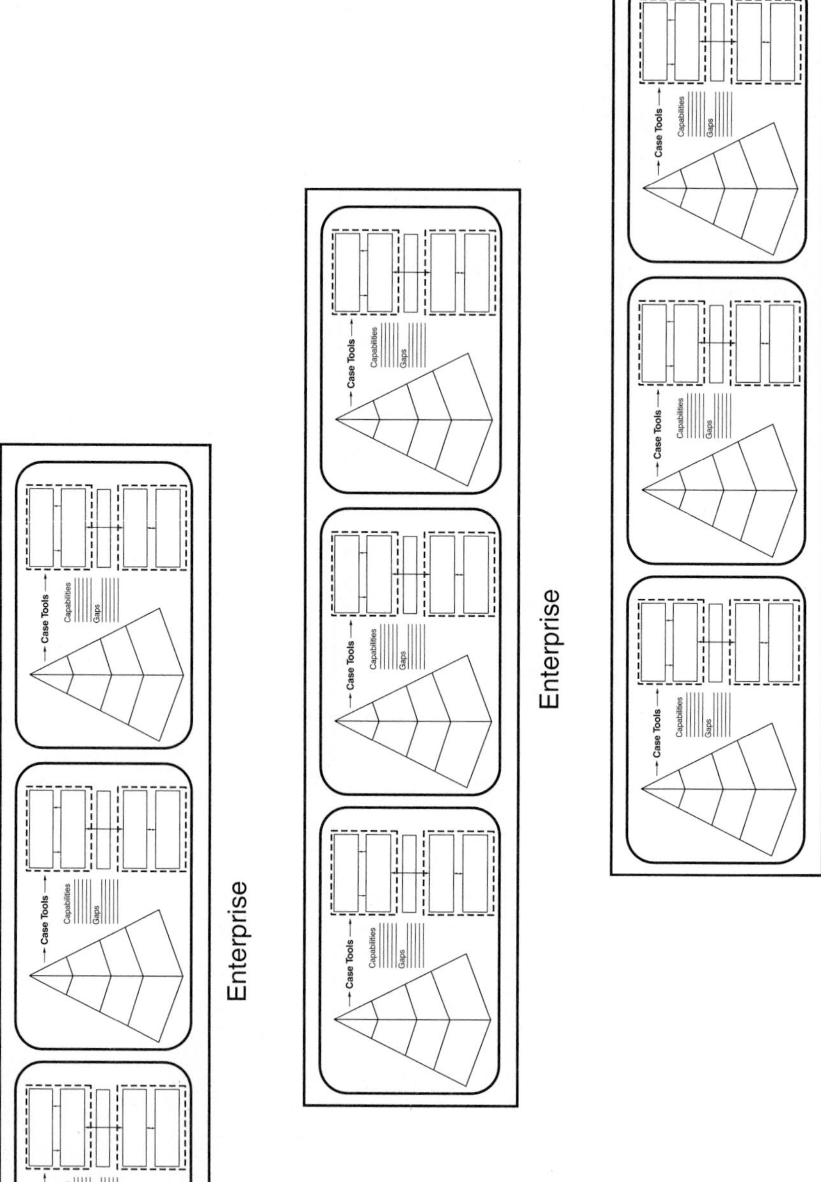

Figure 11.9 HP development projects.

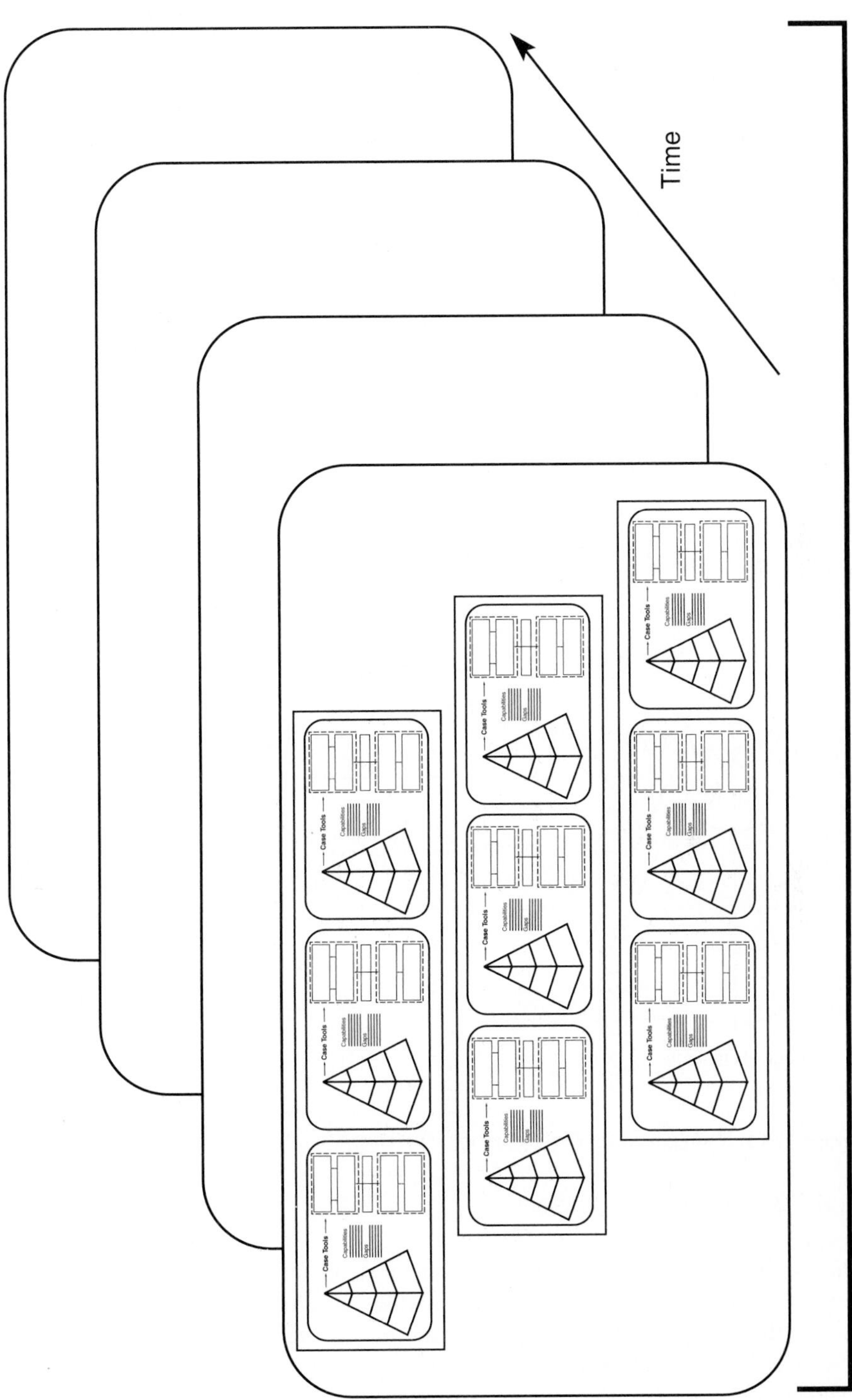

Figure 11.10 Development projects over time.

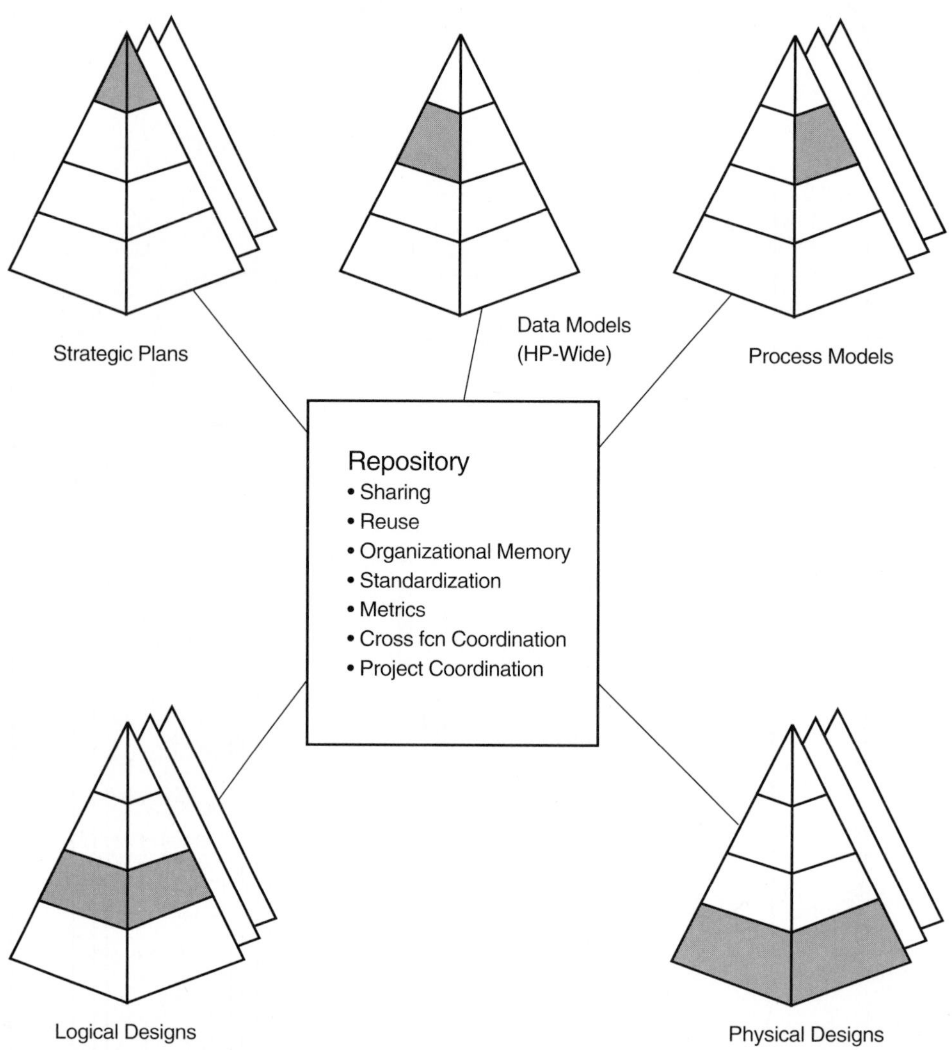

Figure 11.11 Corporate-wide repository.

11.4.2.3 Usability Engineering

The user interaction in client/server applications occurs in the client. X Windows/Motif is an example of a standard user environment which already has usability engineered into it. Beyond this, any particular client presents one or more screens to the user within the X Windows/Motif standard. To maximize the user productivity with the client, these screens should be designed using the tools and methods of usability engineering. This involves having users interact with prototypes in a controlled environment. Human factors experts observe the users as they use the prototype and the design is iteratively tuned to make it as usable as possible.

11.4.2.4 Performance Engineering

Designing for high performance in a client/server environment is complicated by the subdivision of the application between client, server, and network. Each of these elements affects the performance of the application. For this reason, design teams must employ the modeling and analysis techniques of performance engineering to ensure that the application will meet its performance goals in all target environments. This can be done early in the project for critical transactions.

11.5 Results

For an organization contemplating the move to client/server architecture, it may be instructive to understand some of the steps we took at HP.

11.5.1 Unstructured Experimentation

In early 1989, we knew very little about what client/server was or how to go about designing for it. We assigned a team of six people to work together for six weeks in a mode of exploration and discovery. They were not responsible for producing any deliverables; rather, their goal was to increase their understanding of this topic.

11.5.2 Development of Logical Architecture

When the experimentation was over, we formed a task force of ten people (part time) for six months. The objective of the task force was to develop, on paper, a logical model of a client/server architecture. Figure 11.1 resulted from this task force. The task force produced a paper which they shared with a number of people around HP for criticism and feedback. By the fall of 1989, they were satisfied with the result.

11.5.3 Structured Pilot

The next step, beginning in October of 1989, was to use the logical model designed by the task force to pilot some clients and servers to test it. Another group of six people was put together on a full-time basis for six weeks to conduct these pilot tests. They developed three clients and three servers of different types: PC, UNIX work-station, relational and non-relational databases. Their experiences were very positive. Specifically, they found that the work could be divided into small, one- or two-person tasks. The task teams could meet at the beginning, agree on transaction definitions for communication between client and server, and then independently work on their own piece, be it a client or a server. When the client and the server were complete, they found that integrating them was very rapid because of the fully specified business transaction definitions.

11.5.4 Major Leveraged Migration

The next step, in February 1990, was to migrate an existing and still very useful application from terminal-host to client/server. Eight months were allocated for the project. Three teams were formed: a client team, a server team, and a network services team. The network services team was necessary because at the time the network tools required were not commercially available. As in the pilot, the work was divided up into small tasks organized around the business transactions. Meetings were held early in the project to agree on the transaction definitions and then the teams were able to work quite independently of each other. On October 1, 1990, the project was delivered, on time. This confirmed results of the earlier pilot and validated our logical client/server architecture.

11.5.5 Small Application from Scratch

In the summer of 1990, an important new business program for HP was launched. The deadline for completion was February of 1991. It required the development of a completely new tool in a six month period. The lab manager responsible for the development of this tool recognized that traditional design methods had very little chance of completing the project on time. Aware of the very positive results of the client/server project underway at the time, he chose this new platform as the basis for the tool. Using the same architecture, designing both the client and the two servers from scratch, his team was able to produce a very high quality product in six months.

11.5.6 HP Standardization on Architecture

By the spring of 1991, there was sufficient positive experience with the client/server architecture to propose it as the standard for HP to use company-wide for information technology programs. A corporate-sponsored team was formed to review and refine the architecture. It was subsequently adopted as the corporate standard. Under corporate leadership, work has proceeded on defining standards for this architecture and documenting its use for widespread development throughout the company.

11.5.7 Small Application with Significant Client and Server Reuse

In May of 1992, HP launched a major support offering for introduction November 1. This required a new client accessing three separate servers. All the software had to be implemented worldwide (in approximately 40 sites) by the end of October. The development schedule was very tight, allowing about five weeks for all code and test. Fortunately the team was able to reuse significant amounts of the application described in section 11.5.5. Although the function performed by the client was very different, much of the user task logic and many of the business transactions were reusable. Two of the three servers were the same, so only one of the three servers had to be designed. This project began to demonstrate the real payback of the client/server architecture in reusability.

11.6 Issues and Challenges

There are a number of issues and challenges that we encountered in migrating to a client/server architecture. None of these were major impediments, but it is valuable to recognize them up front and develop a plan to deal with them.

11.6.1 Investment

Investments in several areas will be required to migrate.

11.6.1.1 Hardware and Software

Unless the client/server architecture is implemented on the existing platform, which is possible, hardware and software for the new platform must be purchased. This will include workstations or PCs for the clients, computers for the servers, and whatever software licenses are required for the DBMS, the network services, and so on.

11.6.1.2 Telecommunications

The client/server architecture envisions and enables distribution of the computing power across a high speed network. Unless this network is already in place this will represent a cost for the new traffic.

11.6.1.3 Training

To the extent that development and implementation of a client/server architecture involves skills not already existing in an organization, training will be required to develop these skills.

11.6.2 Skill Requirements

New skills are required, both for development people and the operations people, to implement a client/server architecture. The exact nature of the skills will depend on the platform hardware and software chosen. In HP we found needs for the following:

11.6.2.1 Development

The majority of our client/server applications use UNIX workstations and relational databases. They communicate over Internet. The new applications are developed using information engineering and integrated CASE tools. None of these attributes characterized our legacy systems, so we needed to train our developers in them. This was not difficult, as training is readily available, but we had to plan for both the investment and time.

11.6.2.2 Data Center Operations

The client/server architecture introduced into HP's multiple data centers worldwide the need to deal with UNIX systems and networks. These skills were not common at the time we moved to client/server, and training was not readily available. We used what training we could, provided mentoring from skilled engineers in our service organization, and worked with both internal and external training vendors to have needed classes developed.

11.6.3 Standards and Guidelines

To realize all the desired benefits of migrating to a client/server architecture, and do so cost effectively, requires the implementation of certain standards and guidelines throughout the organization.

11.6.3.1 Development Methodology

The client/server architecture that we selected at HP is heavily driven by the enterprise business models. This requires that the development organizations use an information engineering methodology to produce those models and generate code from them. By using a common methodology, CASE tools and repository, we maximize the reusability of the designs and design products throughout the company.

11.6.3.2 Platform

Provision for client/server within an enterprise requires high speed connectivity throughout the enterprise between servers and clients. For this to be achieved, certain standards must be developed for the elements of the architecture. In addition, the network must be standardized across the enterprise. An important benefit of this standardization is to relieve the many development teams of any need to investigate platform alternatives as part of the design project. This enables a much faster development time–one of the objectives of moving to client/server architecture.

11.7 Summary of Benefits

The HP client/server architecture provides many business and technical advantages over the traditional application design. Applications today tend to be self-contained, multi-function systems. Because of this, they contain redundant data. Moving this redundant data among applications requires complex interfaces. Each application has embedded business rules for its own data, and these can be inconsistent among applications. Users have suboptimal access to data not a part of the core application, because the application is their window on the world.

With the HP client/server architecture, these shortcomings are eliminated. Data and application are separated. Data subjects are unique and self contained in single (logical) servers, providing the foundation for better information management. Redundant data is eliminated. Access to data is simple, shared across clients rather than interfaced among applications. Explicit, dictionary-driven business rules are with the data, and not duplicated, avoiding possible inconsistency. The business rules are managed by the data subject owner for the entire enterprise, allowing timely response to business changes. Processes within the enterprise can be changed without changing the servers.

11.7.1 Business Benefits of the Architecture

Our experience to date with the client/server architecture has demonstrated a number of very important business benefits.

11.7.1.1 Responsiveness to Business Change

A key driver for HP to move to client/server was to increase our ability for information technology (IT) to respond to rapid business change. We can attribute very significant improvements and responsiveness to this migration. We have already had several key business programs with short fixed deadlines. By providing the needed systems in the client/server architecture we were able to meet these deadlines. Traditional approaches, we are convinced, would not have done so. As business changes demand rapid deployment of new processes, these may be automated by adding clients to the LAN. Because the data is protected and accessible through defined transactions, clients may be written wherever most expedient, including within the user organization.

11.7.1.2 Local Adaptability in a Global Environment

The client/server structure allows optimum combination of global and local processes and policies. Local clients can meet local needs. Control of server business rules can be centralized or delegated as needed. Even early in our move to a client/server architecture, we have had special clients developed in the end-user community to meet specific local needs. These communicated with centrally developed servers and their global business rules, so data integrity was not jeopardized.

11.7.1.3 Scalability

The technology underlying the client/server platforms is quite scalable, from a single workstation to a collection of workstations and servers serving many users. Each component of the logical model can be split or scaled to a hardware platform or technology. Transition to new hardware and software technologies can be implemented easily.

11.7.1.4 Integration on the Desktop

With this architecture, a user can tailor the set of windows on his or her desktop for the set of tasks to be performed. This makes all the tools available for ready access and eliminates unnecessary clutter. The result is higher user productivity and ease of learning the job.

11.7.1.5 Foundation for Information Management

Our legacy systems contain the data within the application. The client/server architecture we have defined separates these. Further, it segments the data by data subject and provides one logical subject data server for the entire enterprise. When this architecture is fully implemented, the elimination of redundant data and logical structuring of data will greatly simplify access for management decision support.

11.7.1.6 Staged Migration from Existing Architecture

It is essential that the migration be stageable as very few organizations could afford the time or the investment to replace all their legacy systems at once. This architecture greatly facilitates staged migration. Given a windowed workstation user environment, it is possible to mix legacy terminal screens with terminal emulation and new client graphical user interfaces. In fact, in leveraging an existing application a server can be partially migrated. Terminal access can continue to the database while clients access the same database through a partial server shell. Later replacement of the database with properly designed subject databases is possible without replacement of the clients. In this manner, the migration can be driven according to business priorities and not technology.

11.7.2 Development Benefits of the Architecture

This architecture provides many benefits to the system development organization.

11.7.2.1 Rapid Development

Given that a key driver for moving to the client/server architecture was responsiveness to business change, it is essential that this architecture facilitate rapid system development and deployment. This has in fact been shown to be the case. We expect this to improve still further as we get all of our developers standardized on a common methodology and using the best available CASE tools. To date, we have not done any projects using CASE generated code, but our experimentation with the tools that provide this capability indicate that this will dramatically shorten our development cycles.

11.7.2.2 High Quality Development

The client/server architecture has improved the quality of our products for two very different reasons: one is that the products are structured in very explicit ways and divided into small understandable components. Thus, a designer tends to not introduce quality problems due to complexity. A second contributor to quality, at least on the server side, derives from the use of very explicitly defined business transactions for communicating between client and server. Given that all of the inputs and outputs to a server are defined in advance, we were able to develop a testing *client* which fully exercises our servers whenever they are developed or changed. For example, the first project on which this was used automatically executes 2500 independent tests in about two hours.

11.7.2.3 Partitioned Development for Small Teams

The logical architecture we have chosen inherently divides the application up into very well defined parts. In fact, the processing of each business transaction by the server can be treated as a separate sub project. Small teams then can be assigned a set of small well-defined tasks where the interfaces are all clearly specified. This has allowed us to rapidly form project teams for complex projects with very large numbers of people, without suffering the very high communications overhead that typically dooms this kind of an approach. Both high quality and short development cycles result.

11.7.2.4 Simplified Maintenance

Unlike our legacy applications, where we have large monolithic structures, a client/server application is broken down into many small pieces, each well defined. This greatly simplifies maintenance and goes a long way toward eliminating the need for people who are experts in the application on the maintenance team.

11.7.2.5 Lower Development Cost

While we have not collected metrics to compare the development cost in this architecture to our legacy costs, all of the attributes of the client/server architecture contribute to a lowering of cost for development. The small team, simplified communication, automated testing, well structured code, use of common methodologies, and availability of CASE tools and code generation all remove cost from the equation. Also, because of the high degree of modularization, there can be maximum reuse of both designs and code. In fact, we can look forward to almost completely eliminating new code development, relying on CASE generated code and reuse for most of any design.

11.8 Summary

At HP we now have about four years of experience with defining and migrating to the client/server architecture. Even with all that experience, we are still learning very rapidly, evolving our methods and our approaches. Although it was somewhat painful for us to start as early as we did, when there was very little guidance and very little tool or platform support, starting early was the right thing to do. The benefits of this architecture have given us pay-back on our investment from the very beginning of its use. We have developed a body of knowledge and experience which positions us well to move rapidly as the tools and infrastructure evolve and mature.

Migration from a legacy architecture to a new architecture is, for any organization, a many-year process. The sooner one starts, the sooner he finishes. It would be a mistake, I think, for an organization to wait until every last piece is in place to begin moving to a client/server architecture. One should start small, expect to change direction as you learn, and possibly even to replace some of the earlier work as your plans and approaches become more firm. But this will be true no matter how long you wait to start. The technology is evolving so rapidly that there may never be a time when all the answers are known. So take that first small step. You, too, may find the journey irresistible.

11.9 References

Martin, J., 1986. Information Engineering vol 2: Strategies & Analysis, Carnforth, Lancashire, England: Savant Institute.

Skip Ross joined Hewlett Packard in 1963 as a Development Engineer, responsible for the design of electronic instrumentation. He spent five years, from 1971-1976, in manufacturing, managing production engineering and special systems engineering. From 1976 through 1980 he served as R&D Manager for the Santa Clara Digital Signal Analysis/Laser Division. He joined Worldwide Customer Support Operations (WCSO) in 1980, responsible for development of information systems for customer support worldwide. In 1990 he was appointed Group Information Technology Manager, expanding his role to include all the information technology activities for WCSO.

Skip holds a BSEE and MSEE from Stanford University, and an MBA from the University of Santa Clara.

Chapter 12

Eastman Kodak's Distributed Computing

Gary E. Sterling
Eastman Kodak Company

12.1 Introduction

The rapid change of pace in today's computing world is abandoning the old philosophies of monolithic computers in centralized data centers providing mainframe computing power to dumb terminals and local islands of automation and replacing them with the new concepts of distributed computing, interoperability, and client/server configurations. Integrated computing is replacing the dream of yesterday with the realities of today while providing environments rich in opportunities for economies of scale and significant productivity gains through advanced sets of system management tools applied in non-centric administration schemes. Environments are increasing in the number of workstations requiring support while it is not cost effective to add system support people in a linear trend with workstation growth. Quality support can be provided in a distributed architecture without negatively impacting an individual user's ability to perform job functions independent of others by providing scalable and extensible environments through the use of distributed support supplied in a centralized manner. Increasing the ratio of workstations to support personnel through the use of improved system administration tools and support services will minimize the need for additional personnel while providing existing personnel with satisfying challenges and opportunities in the new world of distributed computing.

In 1990, Eastman Kodak Company completed a vision study describing the mid-range computing environment necessary to serve the future computing needs of the company. Two components were studied, the computing environment and the support structures. Technologies needed to bring this vision to reality were identified and their state of maturity was assessed in pilot projects designed to help develop the functional specifications and requirements of the distributed computing environment essential for the 1990s.

The pilot programs were developed to identify and define a distributed computing utility mapped into a client/server structure. Procedures, policies, and tools were to be designed to support the distributed environment in an efficient fashion geared towards clarity and ease of use for the less sophisticated users. End-users are no longer necessarily engineers, or others trained in computer use, but frequently highly skilled individuals who do not want to become computer experts, they simply want to use the tools to enhance their unique abilities to perform in today's complex business environment. It was necessary to compile an inventory of today's needs, a list of future needs, and develop the methods and models by which change could be applied in a directed, organized, efficient manner to move from today's confused and tortured environment to tomorrow's distributed computing paradise.

DECathena was chosen as a pilot project to test the mid-range computing vision. Rochester Distributed Computing Services (RDCS), a division of Eastman Kodak's Information Systems Group, was responsible for implementing and testing Athena on a small group of DEC workstations originally running under the ULTRIX operating system as a group of stand-alone systems. It was their responsibility to effect a small implementation of the distributed computing vision in a *sandbox* environment using DECathena and the DECstations to prove or disprove the value of the vision. If modifications were necessary, this pilot would detail the changes to be made and implement them in the sandbox. Success would be rated on the ability of the vision to fill the mid-range computing needs of Kodak, not on whether DECathena was the proper implementation tool. The first pilot proved the validity of many of the first concepts of distributed computing as envisioned by the mid-range computing environment study. Several deficiencies were noted that could not be blamed on the immaturity of the beta Athena code, but on misconceptions of the mid-range vision.

The successes of the first pilot encouraged a second pilot to determine if DECathena was indeed an appropriate tool for implementing the mid-range computing vision. The second pilot was to delve more deeply into interoperability between dissimilar platforms, including non-DEC platforms. The use of SUN workstations was also growing with no tools for managing a distributed computing environment. It was imperative that the mid-range architecture support machines from several vendors, rather than select a vendor-of-choice and require that all new hardware purchases be made from that vendor.

12.2 Methodology to Develop the Architecture

Based on the previous mid-range computing studies conducted at Eastman Kodak it was decided to base the distributed computing architecture of this project on a client/server model utilizing distributed workstations and centrally provided services as a prudently dispensed commodity comparable to services provided by telephone companies. The architecture must allow for both public and private workstations, distributed laboratories, access to traditional monolithic computers and acceptance of desktop personal computing devices. Network shared services such as printers, tape drives, CD-ROM readers and distributed file servers were to be an integral part of the design. Client management was to be provided with a minimum number of system administrators and a minimal amount of travel around the campus, administrators should be able to remotely manage client workstations.

12.2.1 Reason for Study

The vision was developed to present a picture of a future state of distributed computing. From the vision, the necessary changes and strategies could be mapped to move from the vision to the reality of a distributed environment. The significant features of the vision would be detailed into an architecture describing the hardware and software components as well as the standards, policies, and procedures necessary to support the environment in a consistent, seamless manner.

The study was approached initially as a high level abstraction to enable management to get a feeling of the scope of the endeavor. Then current trends in mid-range computing were studied and a broad overview theoretical approach to mapping into the as yet largely unknown problem set was attempted to encourage management support of an undertaking that could so vastly change the philosophy of mid-range computing across the company.

12.2.2 Survey Current Problems

An initial project was outlined to survey the end-users and computer professionals within the company to determine the current problem set facing them, from this an initial state could be determined. Problems were to be outlined and used as a basis for a minimal solution set. Additional wants and needs would be added to serve as the foundation from which the distributed model would be developed.

12.2.2.1 Administrative

System administrators were in dire need of a system to provide scalability to their existing environment. In some places a form of distributed architecture had already been implemented in an ad hoc basis by progressive system administrators with an eye to the future. However, with a ratio of one system administrator for every 30 to 40 workstations, increases in end-users and workstations meant a linear increase in the number of system administrators. It was important to find tools that would provide the system administrators with methods to increase the ratio and manage costs by being more efficient. Only about 40 percent of the average system administrators job consisted of those activities normally associated with system administration. The rest of their job consisted of end-user education and problem resolution, as well as the ever present need to generate reports of system utilization for management. As more users were added to an environment more time was necessary for user assistance, and management requests, and less time was available for actual system administration. Administration tasks were assumed by workers of lower skill sets that had traditionally been handling tasks such as backups. End-user satisfaction was slipping because of the downward spiral of services being provided by a support staff that was overwhelmed by the amount of work needing to be done, while time for training to bring the newer support staff personnel up to a skill level necessary to provide the services desired did not exist.

Each workstation group had different requirements and therefore different hardware and software configurations. System administrators were unable to backfill for each other in times of crisis because of the disparity in configurations of different groups. As the mid-range environment grew dramatically, time and staff were not available to adequately plan either strategic or tactical solutions to an ever growing amount of problems caused by the increased workload. Do-it-yourself system administration was escalating because workstations were viewed as just another PC that the end-user could maintain in his spare time. In several work groups, a number of people exhibited a talent for system administration and became either lead users in that group or assumed the actual title of system administrator. In these cases the work group configurations seemed to diverge even further because of individual preferences in how things should be done.

When computing was accomplished only by using a terminal to execute commands on a mainframe computer, control was maintained by limiting physical access to the terminals and computers. As mid-range computers were introduced and networking became available systems became harder to control. Large security holes existed in systems that grew up overnight with a need to coexist with other dissimilar systems. Often these holes could be exploited and security arrangements defeated by talented individuals that may not have had the system's best interests in mind. Distributing computing power to workstations throughout the network gave rise to the existence of the *trusted host* concept to allow software and applications to run on a variety of machines across the enterprise. Frequently however, the host could not be trusted and security holes existed. The issue of distributed computing brings serious security concerns to the table for many system administrators.

12.2.2.2 End-user

End-users who had either recently moved from working with terminals connected to mainframes or stand-alone personal computers on their desktops were frustrated with the increased complexity of workstations. In the past they had either simply turned their computer on in the morning, or logged into an account on the mainframe. Now they had to log into an account on their personal workstation, and depending on how their environment had been set up, they may have to log onto or connect to several other machines in order to do their job. The simple task of password maintenance had become a burden, while file version control had become a nightmare. Overworked system administrators took too long to answer simple questions while changes to systems or environments were less than timely.

Backups were inconsistent and unreliable, especially when work was moved between platforms. File control was almost impossible given the state the environment was in. Users complained they had to do certain tasks more than once because direct communications between many machines did not exist. Moving files between platforms required several translations, there was no seamless method. There also was no ability to interchange graphics between various tools on different platforms. Working on multiple platforms was time consuming, cumbersome, and counter-productive. In short, end-users wanted their PCs back.

System administrators that tried to plug security holes inherent in traditional UNIX systems and networks frequently made tasks more difficult for users, thereby masking any benefits provided by workstations in a distributed environment. Since, in most instances, workstations reside on a particular user's desktop the feeling of ownership of the workstation is strong. With PCs, the user owned it and was the only user of the PC. However, workstations by nature of their multi-user architecture provide opportunities for sharing a single workstation between several users in different locations. This frequently leads to system administrator resentment because the *owning* user feels that their needs are not adequately responded to while other users access of their machines cause a degradation in service to them.

This feeling may take a long time to pass, and a distributed computing environment implementation of any kind may not adequately address problems of this nature.

12.2.2.3 General

Since each work group was largely responsible for it's own capital and expense budgets for information services, there was not ample opportunity to document similarities with other groups and form an effective organization to take advantage of quantity discounting for hardware, software, and licensing costs. In general, islands of technology developed in several locations around the company independently of others with each island developing it's own technologies to fit the particular needs of it's work group. Developing standards that could be applied across the board for all work groups did not take place because of the nature of individual organization interaction in large companies. People expense was skyrocketing, both for administering the new systems as they were purchased, and for training end-users in new applications as they were developed or purchased. Corporate information system expenses were climbing at a rate that was causing concern, but no mechanism existed to check the trend. This type of growth is more common in larger companies where individual groups have the autonomy to fend for themselves; smaller companies have an advantage in that protection of financial resources usually requires a closer company-wide look at information system costs and computing costs in general. At Eastman Kodak the growth accelerated faster than the company expected. Individual work groups adopted the technology necessary to perform their functions in as efficient a way as possible in order to complete their business functions.

Network access to mid-range computers allows multiple users of each workstation. Different requirements of multiple users may cause problems that actually dilute the benefit of distributed computing by overloading some machines and under utilizing others. Mid-range computing provides powerful tools at the desktop, but the costs are not trivial. When problems in system administration and end-user access occur, improper utilization may result, thereby increasing costs beyond acceptable limits. Because costs are not as easily discernible as in timesharing environments, cost may remain hidden and what appears to be an effective, cost attractive computing environment may actually cost much more than intended or acceptable.

12.2.3 Develop Distributed Model

The distributed model was developed in a team effort over a period of several weeks. Encompassing several factors, the model was not intended to be exhaustive, but cover the minimal requirements necessary to support mid-range distributed computing given the unique circumstances faced. Given that equipment was purchased from several vendors it is necessary that any solution be heterogeneous providing a common user interface. Compatibility at any of various levels is a factor with protocol compatibility being a burning issue. In an effort to sever physical implementation of a function from the logical support of that function a vigorous naming service is required. Reliability of the implementation through redundancy of system components is paramount to a successful distributed computing environment. To minimize the amount of labor support necessary scalability must provide a major pay back. System administration tools must allow modification of active configurations provided by service management tools that behave similarly across all platforms in the environment. Lastly, security must provide both authentication of users and authorization to use services.

UNIX was selected as the operating system of choice because of its versatility over a wide range of platforms. The virtual machine interface for applications is virtually identical on all hardware platforms. The X Window system was selected to provide a heterogeneous feel to the user interface, with Motif being the preferred interface manipulation tool.

Compatibility was imperative at the protocol level, important at the execution level, and desirable at the binary level. Execution of the same binaries across all platforms is an aspiration of the model to simplify binary configuration and control, however, this is not a firm requirement because different vendors rarely agree on hardware compatibility. Significant compatibility at the execution level is beneficial so that source code can be compiled and properly executed on each of the platforms without requiring code modifications. The most important form of compatibility requires that all platforms support a standard set of protocols for fundamental system services. Services such as file access and security. The network file system (NFS) was chosen to provide compatibility of filesystem access to allow different workstations to cooperate in filesystem perception.

Eastman Kodak's inter-machine communication takes place in a fairly complex network of local area networks (LANs) and Ethernet subnets. As a result a dynamic name service, such as Berkeley's BIND, is required because of the need to dynamically resolve names and link them to their physical objects. Static name linking is not feasible in a distributed environment considering the difficult task of reloading static configuration files across a wide area. The domain name system (DNS), of which BIND is an implementation, is a distributed database of network information allowing dynamic name resolution. Local control of each segment is maintained while data in local segments is available across the entire network. An effective client/server application provides sufficient performance through caching and replication.

Redundant system components are required to provide reliability of necessary system services. Sufficient failover techniques must be built into the systems to provide reliable uninterrupted service. However, it is expected that failure of file servers providing private home directories would cause acceptable service interruptions. As a precaution against severe network interruptions no workstations will be directly connected to the network backbone, routers must be used to provide protection from network outage caused by improper workstation configuration.

To provide for control of labor costs it is necessary that any implementation of a distributed computing environment be scalable. Dataless workstations with identical software configurations on each workstation operating as interchangeable elements across the environment provide location independence for the user and minimize system administration labor requirements. Paging and swapping will be handled on the local hard disk to prevent network traffic overload, but all necessary data files and applications will reside on centrally located file servers and NFS mounted at logon. Configuration files that are normally replicated on each workstation should be centrally stored to reduce the overall community storage requirements.

System administration tools must reduce the amount of intensive labor required to support many workstations in a distributed environment by automating the routine management tasks and requiring human intervention in occasional special or unique cases. Tools should be automated and intuitive, with much of the responsibility for maintenance resting on the shoulders of lower skilled personnel to provide more time for higher skilled personnel to devote to critical or technically more difficult problems. Configuration management should be similar for divergent hardware platforms with data access tools providing capabilities for updating and manipulating stored information. A centralized management tool should be furnished for each of the major services provided by the distributed computing environment.

In the eyes of the end-user two subsystems of the environment are more critical than all others, those being user account management and electronic mail delivery. User account generation and management should be simple and timely. Mail tools should be easy to use and secure. A simple interface to send mail should be provided to ease the system administrators through the cumbersome tasks of maintaining an electronic mail system.

Filesystem management tools must be similar for all platforms. Use should be straightforward and robust to permit users the flexibility required in a distributed environment. File servers must be centrally located and secure both physically and logically. Easy interfaces for file management such as backups and disk quotas must be provided.

Network print services must be provided to allow users to print to whatever printer is closest to the workstation they happen to be using. Support of specialty printers is also required. Interfaces for adding, modifying, and deleting printers from the environment should be simple and easy to use.

Name service interfaces must be provided to maintain and manage data objects within the distributed computing environment. Tracking of changes in data objects is preferred so that reports of activity can be generated in a timely manner. A simple interface to DNS/Bind is favored to reduce the amount of labor required to support this subsystem.

The security portion of the distributed computing environment must have two features designed into the structure; authentication and authorization. Authentication must be done in such a way that clear text passwords are not transmitted across the network. Security must be maintained in such a way that no sensitive data is exposed to risk. Service authorization must be controlled to prevent risk of data exposure by ensuring that not only are users authentic, but have a need and privilege to access the service being requested (see figure 12-1).

12.3 Description of Architecture

The mid-range computing architecture includes all the computing needs exclusive of mainframe and personal computing. It encompasses engineering, manufacturing, application development, and general computing support. The systems involved range from UNIX workstations and servers to DEC VAX mid-range machines. It is also necessary to tie in personal compute devices such as PCs, but the mid-range architecture does not exclusively answer all needs of personal computing, generally only the interaction of personal computers with mid-range computers. These constituent parts are viewed together as one total system conforming to published industry and Kodak standards as defined by various standards bodies within and outside the company.

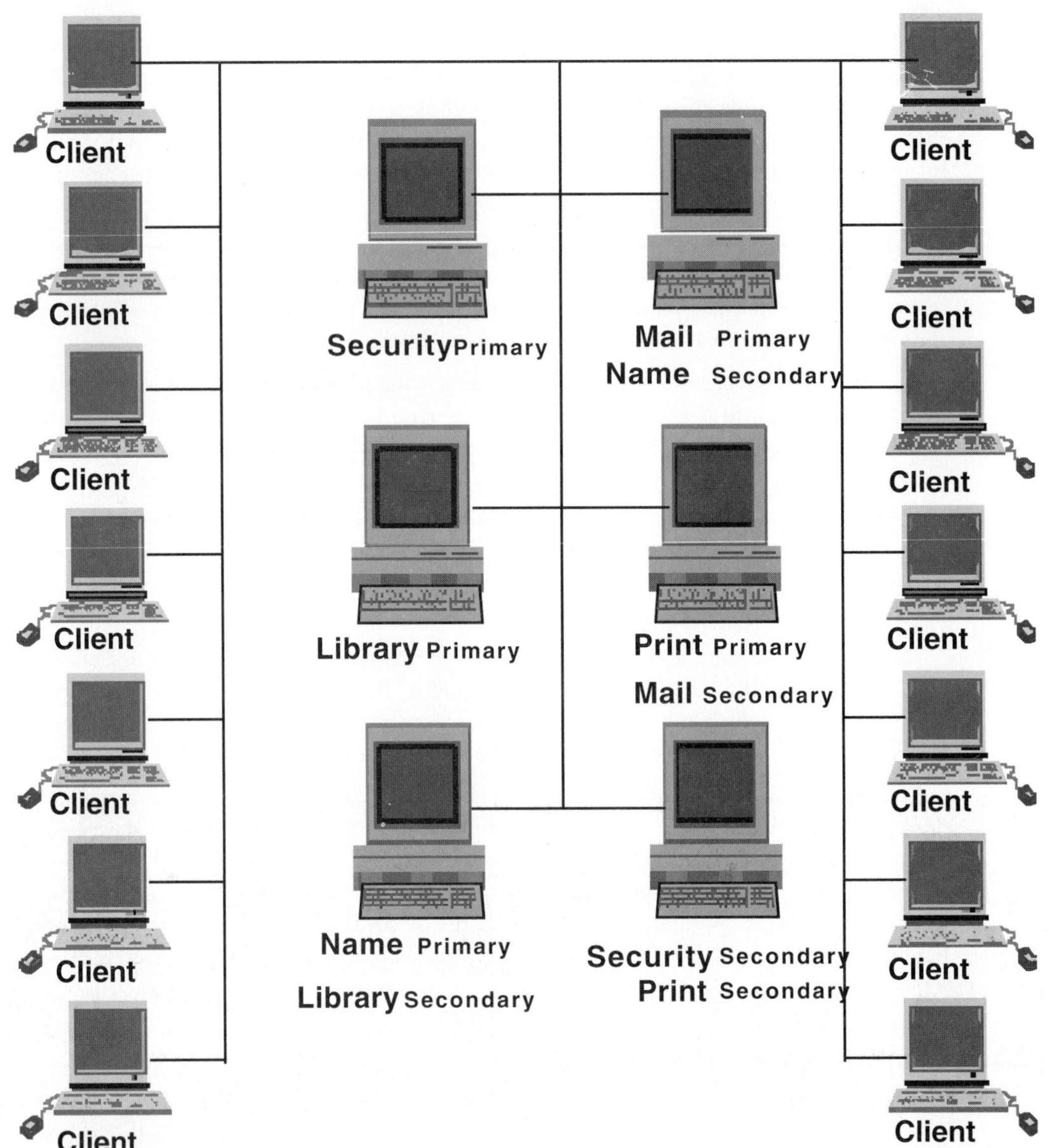

Figure 12.1 Distributed model.

The overall architecture is viewed as a collection of individual devices and services identified as integral parts of the whole. Included are users, devices, services, work groups and the network. Distributed local client/server groups will develop their own self-contained services, applications, servers, and other peripheral equipment bound by prevailing standards. They will be able to define who and what is authorized for access and may independently maintain their own local environment. In order to take advantage of additional services throughout the mid-range environment they will be authorized access as required, but must comply with all policies, procedures and standards defined for using the environment.

Three basic component parts will make up the total architecture. The first is the compute infrastructure itself. The second is the administrative support necessary to maintain the compute environment and keep it functioning in a reliable and efficient manner. The third component is the end-user, the people or processes that use the mid-range computing environment. This consists of all the physical devices used to provide compute services. Included in this list are the network backbone, the work group LANs, compute servers, file servers, print servers, data storage archives, and the distributed computing environment itself.

12.3.1 Infrastructure

The compute infrastructure can be viewed as all those physical devices necessary to support the distributed computing environment. The foundation by which all computing is supported. The most important of the structures is the network backbone. Of necessity, no computing device will connect directly to the backbone, but will be connected through a routing device. This limits the number of events that can impact the entire network while protecting users from disturbances created in other sub-nets. The infrastructure should also provide mechanisms for support of resource management and delivery of significant administrative services including but not limited to monitoring, managing, diagnostics and support.

The infrastructure services should provide a toolbox of components to ensure that basic services are maintained. These are the building blocks by which infrastructure maintains it's performance and reliability. Performance management is critical to a sound infrastructure. Tools will be provided that monitor performance and sound alarms if intervention is needed. Workload distribution and capacity planning are integral parts of this subsystem of the infrastructure. Configuration management is vital to the overall success of infrastructure administration. The physical and logical relationships maintained by configuration databases provide information as to where physical connections are made and what logical dependencies exist. To ensure that all corporate security standards are maintained and prevent disclosure of sensitive data to unauthorized access, it is necessary to include security management. Tools to accomplish this task are essential to a secure infrastructure. Finally, daily operation of the infrastructure must be accomplished using tools that automate procedures as highly as possible. Remote administration of key infrastructure components is a fundamental element of infrastructure operation.

12.3.2 Policies for Administration

The availability of different technologies to provide answers to different problems has increased the productivity and efficiency of end-users. However, just because technologies are available, it does not mean they will cooperate or even coexist together. Compatibility and interoperability can be assisted by proper application of policy. Policy in and of itself will solve no problems and could encourage increased uncertainty in a complex environment. But carefully constructed policies that build on technologies, rather than inhibit them, will serve to instill behavior patterns that are consistent with long term goals. Policy is a difficult tool to apply and must be exacting in its creation so the resulting behavior patterns produce the needed outcomes. Policy can be implemented by a variety of means. Backups can be automated to result in suitable protection of data. Passwords can be set to expire at time intervals that require change appropriate to security requirements. Policy implementation should be used as a last resort to ensuring compliance to stated goals. Overuse of policy tends to erode the users confidence in their abilities and that of their organization. Environments that must rely heavily on policy implementation are perhaps poorly designed and should be revisited with a fresh view of purpose.

12.3.3 Applications

Applications provided in a distributed architecture should be those necessary to conduct the business practices desired. Of course, applications to support the infrastructure and environment are critical and essential. Then there are those applications directly related to the business practice of the user or work group. These also must be maintained, however, they should be available from a distributed server, rather than residing locally on an end-users workstation. License management servers can provide the needed technology to minimize the number of licenses required while maximizing the utilization of those licenses and providing improved productivity on the part of the end-user by maintaining proper application availability. The organizations involved and supported by the distributed computing environment can best determine what applications are demanded by the business practices of their end-users. Other applications necessary to support the end-users may be transparent to them and work subsequently to or separately from applications they knowingly use on a daily basis.

Examples of applications that are necessary for end-user support are electronic mail and messaging systems, file control systems, configuration systems, and maintenance components. Electronic mail is the most widely used application in computing environments today, however, many organizations do not adequately consider the impact of the mail system used and whether a better, more efficient, and more cost-effective system is available to them. Most end-users and organizations alike take electronic mail for granted, careful consideration should be given to how mail is handled. File control is frequently better handled than mail. The choice of file systems is often better studied and more knowledgeably selected. Frequently the configuration management scheme is not versatile and may not be capable of being replaced with other configuration schemes. Care should be taken to configuration, determination of alternatives created, reviewed, and acted upon.

The maintenance tools available to system administrators are becoming more dynamic and rapidly increasing in number. When considering maintenance tools it is recommended that proper care be taken to determine the actual current needs of an organization and the probable short term needs. The best tools available in a cost-effective manner should be obtained to service these needs. Long term needs should be recognized, but tools should not necessarily be acquired to satisfy long term goals as superior tools may be available before the need actually materializes.

Applications used in a distributed computing environment should be chosen with prudence as to their ability to coexist with other applications and the infrastructure itself. The applications ability to meet the current need as well as it's ability to grow into recognizable and probable future needs should be determined before the application is procured. Application selection should not be treated as an inconsequential circumstance of system, environment, or infrastructure administration, but should be given all the attention necessary for the size of the aggregate corporate expenditure for software and applications.

12.4 Views of Distributed Architecture

There are three basic components to the integrated distributed computing architecture, the end-user, the system administrator, and the computing infrastructure itself. The two views of the architecture we are concerned with are the views of the end-user and that of the service provider or system administration. The infrastructure is the physical and logical networks, servers, applications, and configuration databases. When the end-user has access to the infrastructure in an unrestrained fashion, productivity increases. If the infrastructure were to remain static there would be no need for system administrators, however, the only static systems in existence are those that have the power permanently removed. In a properly designed and integrated environment, the system administrator is inconspicuous to the end-user and only becomes apparent when the end-user has a request. In actuality the system administrators are always busy behind the scenes resolving problems and improving performance, hopefully in a manner that prevents the end-user from knowing that such work is on-going. The end-user should be able to continue working in an uninhibited manner expecting efficient, reliable performance without worry of system obstacles.

12.4.1 Administrative

The system administration view of the distributed computing environment of necessity must be all-encompassing and ever-present. Day-to-day support services to maintain the infrastructure is the first routine task of system administrators, reliability and stability should be the keywords for this function. Tools must be provided to integrate service delivery and maintain a proactive stance on infrastructure support; process and procedures must be well defined and easily used. Three aspects of system administration are the centerpieces of service delivery, day-to-day operational support, resolution of problems, and new or modified service requests. Daily operations should be handled by tools that are intuitive and automated in order to free as much of the system administrators time as possible for managing problem resolution and handling request for service additions and modifications.

Routine tasks that should be automated include configuration and security management, server control and management, mail and name service management, and software and application management. Tools should be available to maintain the distributed computing infrastructure without restricting user access and flexibility. System administrators should not have to spend the majority of their time servicing requests that are routine and repetitive in nature, intelligent tools will help save time from these tasks for the more intricate tasks distributed computing in a client/server environment supplies. The ability to monitor the performance of the network, servers, and infrastructure equipment in order to guarantee the functioning of these elements and safeguard the productivity of the end-users is required.

Functions must be provided for remote file system management, network administration, ability to perform remote and local backups and restores, remote software installation capability, and single point of authentication and authorization. Server management from a central location is desirable so as to minimize the amount of time system administrators are traveling about the workplace rather than performing administration tasks.

Dynamic management of environment-wide support services by remote access will reduce the growth rate of system administration personnel. It is essential that the linear expansion of system administration ranks be reduced, it is necessary to increase the ratio of systems to administrators by providing better, intelligent, easier tools, rather than increasing the workload on each system administrator and expecting them to work longer and harder.

12.4.2 End-user

Several different communities provide the end-users of the distributed computing environment. End-users, as defined here, will include not only people, but processes that reside outside of the realm of control of the environment that have access to the computing environment. Services must be provided to application development, business, engineering, manufacturing, and research and development. These communities require both similar and dissimilar computing functions. All need mail services and various business reporting services, however each has unique demands of the environment from application development and analysis tools to graphics and word processing tools. Each community of end-users may have several sub-classes of users or work groups that have unique requirements different from both their parent group and their sibling groups. The environment must present the flexibility necessary to support the diverse needs expected by the disparate end-user community. The end-user, once appropriately authorized for access, will use the environment for various business and technical needs.

Figure 13-2 displays the end-user view and the administrative view of the Eastman Kodak's model of distributed computing. The end-users may or may not have all applications available to them, depending on their access rights.

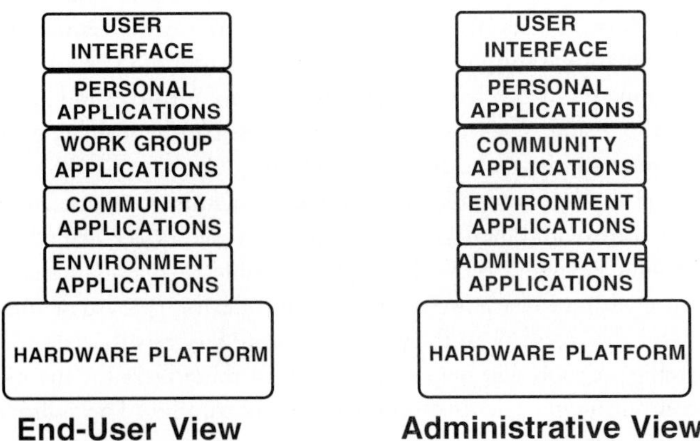

Figure 12.2 Architecture Views

12.5 Development of the Environment

In November 1990, RDCS chose DECathena as the tool to prove their distributed computing environment concepts. Additionally, DECathena was under testing also as the possible implementation answer for Kodak's distributed computing environment. The original lab environment consisted of several DECstation 3100s as clients and a collection of DECstation 5000/200s and DECstation 3100s as servers. Several SUN SPARCstations were used as system library and boot servers for the SUN SPARC workstation clients. The environment was developed by first installing the MIT version of Athena and exploring different aspects of distributed computing. Many of the functions of this code were unworkable in this environment due to inexperience of the team, and attempts to force an academic package into a commercial environment. After three weeks of working with the MIT code the systems were flushed and the beta version of DECathena was introduced. This improved code allowed quicker development and refinement of the distributed computing environment. After several weeks of working with DECathena, the original model was revisited. It was necessary to modify some aspects of the model and add others. Some of the elements of the model were not yet technically feasible to implement, however, as a whole the model survived the testing with DECathena in a rewarding manner.

12.5.1 Testing the Distributed Computing Architecture

Although the environment was not large enough to prove the scalability of DECathena, it did prove many of the original concepts designed into the environment, as well as some deficiencies and elements not previously conceived of as being important to the environment. The original software brought into Kodak was MIT code. Modifying the MIT code to fit into the Kodak business environment proved to be a complex task taking about three weeks of full time work by four people. Implementing this code proved to be beneficial in that it laid a groundwork of understanding of the Athena concepts. Due to the fact that DEC had already modified and improved the MIT code to a degree of refinement, the implementation team felt that bringing the DEC beta code in first might have been inhibitive to a firm grasp of the concepts needed to thoroughly understand distributed computing in a client/server environment. The architecture developed for this pilot was based on the distributed computing model completed prior to the implementation, however, concessions were made due to limitations in the model, restrictions of the Athena implementation available, and misconceptions designed into the model.

Using DECathena in its beta version proved to be challenging and rewarding. Beta software by its very nature tends to require considerable attention to detail that one would not expect to be required by production ready products. Several of the modules within the code either did not work as planned, or did not work as required. DEC engineers were extremely helpful in chasing bugs, as were the developers committed to realizing modifications and enhanced features requested by the pilot implementation.

Several areas of deficiency in the model were noted during the first pilot. The complexity of mail handling in a distributed environment had been grossly underestimated. Athena's implementation of electronic mail using the post office protocol (POP) proved to be one of the strong points of the Athena vision. Although the model called for location independence, the perception of mail handling was flawed to a point. Users would have had their mail tied to a particular system, instead of being independent of systems. Another area of deficiency noted was in actual system administration itself. Other than logging into each affected system and using write to all users (wall), the UNIX tool that blasts real time messages to all users on a particular system, notification of users in real time was not provided for. Mail or message of the day (MOTD) would have been used. Enter Zephyrgrams, probably the most visible and widely used tool within Athena. Volumes could be written on the value and foresight of Zephyr, suffice it to say that anytime any user or system administrator wants to send a message to any other user, they have the capability of real-time messaging in a pop-up window that grabs the attention of the user and does not require the system administrator to log on to each of various systems in the environment. Bulletin boards and on-line help systems had been discussed during the design phase of the distributed computing model, but were not deemed as absolutely necessary to a functioning distributed computing environment. However, DECathena provides an excellent bulletin board system with Discuss and a good on-line help system with on-line consulting (OLC).

Discuss is a bulletin board or electronic conferencing system available across the network. Participants can either reply to meetings or topics, or begin a new topic. Discuss is helpful for documenting on-going discussions within an organization, as well as keeping people informed as to what is occurring within their environment.

On-line consulting provides access to a stock answer database covering frequently asked questions that can be updated by consultants as needed. It also provides the capability to talk on-line with a consultant who is an expert in a particular subject. Technical experts are made available to end-users without the user being required to leave their workstation looking for one. Using Zephyrgrams for real time communications, and mail for delayed communication, OLC provide the backbone to an exceptional on-line help system.

Print services in a distributed environment are convoluted procedures that are not intuitive or self-evident. The original Athena code tested did not adequately address the complexities of distributed print serving. The tools were available, but the intricate details of putting printers into service were not easily handled. It was expected that future versions would probably address this issue more fully.

File management under Athena is much easier to use than expected. File systems are easily mounted by the end-user using the attach command. Users are unable to mount filesystems under the UNIX operating system without assuming super-user status. With Athena, system administrators prepare filesystems with easy-to-use tools that will allow users to attach filesystems as necessary. Adding Hesiod to the mix allows the user to merely specify the filesystem by name, Hesiod resolves the hardware address and passes the information to Attach, which then mounts the filesystem.

Security with Athena is much improved over typical UNIX systems. Kerberos is the authentication server that maintains user passwords and creates tickets allowing access to network resources. This system provides trusted third-party authentication for the Athena environment requiring that both users ad services authenticate themselves to one another, users cannot impersonate other users and client machines cannot assume the identities of servers. This eliminates the need for each workstation to be secure since the user, not the machine, is being authenticated. Kerberos transactions are transparent to the user with the exception of expired tickets. When tickets expire, users are denied access to Athena environment services and must renew them.

To supply centralized management of environment-wide data DECathena provides Moira as the service management system. This menu-driven front-end to a relational database provides the tools to access and modify the data, and distribute the information to the necessary servers. Moira is an inspired combination of tools supplying management of most of the other Athena subsystems and distributed computing environment information, refer to table 12.1.

Table 12.1 Moira Service Management System

Clusters	Machines	Subnets
DNS Zones	MX records	CNAME records
Lists	Physical file systems	Logical file systems
DCM services	User accounts	Server-hosts
	Printcap	

To provide name service for objects in the distributed computing environment DECathena supplies Hesiod. Hesiod does not replace, but cooperates with the Internet Domain Name Service (DNS) to provide hostname-to-IP-address translations. The Hesiod server may reside on the same machine providing Internet DNS, or it may reside on another machine. Traditionally, Internet Domain name service has been provided by a set of manually maintained data files that are predisposed to error because of the nature of their maintenance. Most versions of NAMED do not provide syntax error messages, they use the data *as is* which may cause corrupt or inaccessible databases. DECathena allows Moira to maintain Internet Domain name service data, providing validity checking for hand input data. Hesiod name service provides information about specific objects within the distributed computing architecture. Hesiod name servers get their information from Moira, therefore all Hesiod servers are primary name servers. This allows secondary name servers to also be primary name servers and vice versa, providing an enhanced degree of redundancy in name service. Hesinfo is the user tool to look up data in the Hesiod name server. Consisting of two parts, Hesinfo queries expect the HesiodName and HesiodNameType to be supplied and return the physical information requested. Nslookup is provided to supply Internet Domain name service resolution.

12.5.2 Results of the Pilot

Findings from the pilot proved that the original concepts of a distributed computing environment were by and large generally correct. Several misconceptions and deficiencies were discovered and modifications made to the model to address these issues. The distributed computing environment model must remain a living model subject to change as technology advances become available and academic theory progresses.

System administration is simplified using DECathena. The service management system provided by Moira allows intuitive and timely dynamic updates of environment and system data. User accounts are easily created and maintained allowing control of personal filesystems, mail addresses, group and mailing lists. Kerberos mappings are accessible from within Moira, thus one collection of tools basically does it all for service management. All DECathena subsystems are manageable from within Moira. Subnets, machines, machine addresses, clusters, lists, groups, physical and logical file systems, and server-host pairs are easily maintained from within Moira. Managing these objects in a typical UNIX environment is generally a group of complex, time consuming and unforgiving operations requiring the use of cryptic procedures and requiring hand editing of configuration files. Moira manages BIND information, including SOA and MX records in an encouraging manner that allows access to, and management of, Internet Domain name service databases without being an expert in DNS. It is still not a trivial matter, however, it is not the painful task that system administrators have faced in the past.

It is important that the distributed computing environment be well designed and the implementation well planned before actual installation. Insufficient planning due to inexperience in distributed environments caused most of the problems with the pilot installation. Some problems were caused by product immaturity, however, DEC cooperated fully in attempting to solve these problems in a timely manner. When issues could not be resolved in the short term they were referred to development engineers who in turn worked on solutions for subsequent code releases. All-in-all, Digital Equipment Corporation was a good partner for this type of pilot, always showing a willingness to cooperate and technical capabilities second to none.

Server installation was non-trivial and time consuming. It is important that all aspects of a servers use be well thought out before setting up the server. In the original version of Athena tested in this pilot, server configuration was extremely difficult and not generally user installable. Engineers from DEC came with the software in order to install the servers. To be fair, subsequent releases of the software have greatly improved on the server installation and made it a more palatable task that is less time consuming and requires much less intensity.

Client installs, on the other hand, were straightforward and with few exceptions, trivial. Problems in the server setup caused by incomplete planning were propagated to the clients which in turn had to be hand corrected. Repairing the problem at the server allowed subsequent client installs to complete correctly with no human intervention required.

Security provided by the Athena systems is far and above much better than typical UNIX security. The chance of unauthorized access to data under DECathena control is minimized by the Kerberos subsystem. To many system administrators, this feature alone is worth the price of admission.

Location independence is a key benefit to the distributed nature of DECathena and the model as designed. Since user files and applications are stored on centrally managed servers, logging on to any of the available client workstations allowed easy, transparent access to the users *expected* environment. Minor differences between the presentations of SUN workstations and DEC workstations did not seem to trouble the users or cause undue problems of software control.

Mail service using the post office protocol and RAND MH as the sendmail agent was transparent to the user and allowed total location independence. Some problems existed with SUN mail in the beginning, but were resolved as the pilot progressed. Several mail tools are available for use with Athena, satisfying the needs and wants of the users. Each message is stored as a separate file which can then be accessed through the XMH mail tool or as a typical UNIX file. MX records are maintained via Moira, as is the MH user profile for each user. DECathena mail allows distributing the mail load over several mail servers and also allows mail queues to be moved when hosts are unavailable to process mail.

There are two options at this time to providing system library service for SUN workstation clients. One option allows a DEC server to be used as the syslib server, the other option requires the use of a SUN server as the syslib server. Both options were tried with success. When the DEC machine was used as a syslib server, full functionality was provided, but there appeared to be hesitations in image activations that were barely perceptible and generally acceptable. When a SUN machine was used as the server there was no hesitation, the server responded as expected. Implementation of syslib servers for SUN clients is recommended to be done on SUN machines due to the faster response time and intrinsic sensibilities.

On-line consulting worked as advertised and provided functions necessary to help users understand their environment and allowed them to access a stock answer database to build their confidence in solving some of their own problems. The original character cell interface was less than inspired and proved to be the only bad feature of OLC. This has recently been replaced by an X interface that seems to work quite smoothly and fills the needs of the users and on-line consultants. Although not fully implemented during the pilot it is highly recommended that OLC be used from the first day of any Athena installation in order to build a stock answer database that more accurately reflects the individual distributed computing environment being implemented. DEC provides a stock answer database with Athena that answers many of the often asked questions users have, but it cannot answer questions that may be unique to the particular environment into which it is being installed.

Discuss seems to be a more than adequate bulletin board system that provides access for all users within the distributed computing environment. This feature was also not fully tested during the pilot, but comes highly recommended to be used from the beginning of any DECathena installation. Using Discuss, documentation of environment, system, and tool setup can be automatic and precise. Discussions of topics of interest can be maintained from the beginning, allowing input from individuals who may have good ideas, but inadequate access otherwise to share or express their ideas and concerns.

Zephyr provides an excellent way of real-time contact with other individuals on the system. It can be customized to inform of system and environment events as well as allow social event notifications. Subscription lists allow tailoring of service to fit nearly any need. No task that was attempted with Zephyr failed during the pilot, and many inspirational uses were conceived of, if not actually tried. This subsystem is probably the most widely useful part of Athena.

12.6 Migration Process

Originally RDCS intended only to use DECathena as a means of testing the validity of the distributed computing environment as designed in the model. With the success of the pilot projects it became apparent that DECathena was a viable tool to implement the distributed computing environment and solve some of the problems that led to creating the vision of distributed computing at Eastman Kodak. The first migration effort was centered around a work group comprised of SUN workstations. Work group *M* was located about twenty-five miles from the central DECathena servers in an area that was extremely interested in adopting distributed computing and using a tool such as DECathena in an effort to slow the growing costs of system administration. RDCS would provide the Athena servers and central services while work group *M* would provide client stations. The process did not go as well as expected due to problems detailed later. The new area consisted of many SUN workstations, the plan was to roll out a few at a time to prevent a large influx of end-users to an environment that was not, as yet, stable enough to support production type end-users. When the first systems were introduced unforeseen problems occurred that took several weeks to resolve. Name service problems were the most severe and most difficult to overcome. Because all of the workstations in work group *M's* environment could not be converted to Athena clients at once, it was necessary for the converted clients to not only reside within the DECathena realm, but also in the pre-existing network information service (NIS) domain. NIS does not allow traversal of the name space, only lookup of data about hosts and users in the local NIS domain. DNS implementations allow full traversal of the name space, but use different databases than NIS. Cooperation between the two systems is limited but can be accomplished if built together. However, the existence of a current NIS domain complicates implementation to the point that child domains have to be created in an attempt to override the limitations enforced by mixing the two non-interchangeable name services. Eventually clients were built at work group *M* that functioned properly and seemed fairly easy to maintain.

It was recommended that subsequent implementations be installed at locations with fewer clients that could all be converted at one time, until sufficient expertise exists at Eastman Kodak to properly support larger operations. Business pressures affecting all large corporations to gain more from their information systems with less expense is one of the demands requiring more investment in time and personnel to distributed computing strategies like DECathena. This urgency to do more with less is the driving force behind implementing distributed computing environments around client/server applications.

To properly implement DECathena requires a full understanding of the concepts involved and an appreciation of the tools available. Planning is a key ingredient to success, however, the most important aspect to success in distributed computing and client/server applications is a CLEAN network. The physical network is the most important characteristic of a successful roll out.

The second most important element is good quality name service. Plans must be made in advance of implementation as to how name service is going to be affected and maintained. Once installed DECathena manages name service marvelously, but if being installed in a pre-existing environment, it must be clean first. Other areas that cause concern are mail handling and daily operations. Again, once installed DECathena does a good job of mail handling. However, if problems already exist, Athena may not be the tool to fix them, only manage them after being repaired.

Daily operations like backups are not addressed by DECathena and procedures to handle these requirements should already be in place or installed separately. DECathena does not provide these services, but it also does not impede them. The subject of backup procedures could fill pages but is outside the scope of this discussion.

Migrating from a traditional UNIX environment to a distributed computing environment by using DECathena is not a trivial task. But given the proper amount of planning and foresight it is not as difficult as one might think. The important elements are planning, preparation and diligence in implementation.

12.7 Experiences

In November 1990 Digital Equipment Corporation provided a copy of Athena developed at the Massachusetts Institute of Technology for trial use at Eastman Kodak. The code worked very well at MIT, but was not as suitable for use at Kodak. Designed around an academic environment, Athena contained many procedures that worked only for that environment. When installed in a commercial venture, it did not fill the needs as anticipated. However, MIT Athena provided a learning experience that encouraged developing a beta test site for the first, and subsequent, version of DECathena.

The beta version of DECathena was laden with problems, but it also provided learning experiences to help understand the world of distributed computing. DEC was very responsive to requests for enhancements and suggestions for changes that made DECathena a robust product that is able to fill the requirements of a distributed computing environment. Each new release of DECathena provided improvement in an almost exponential fashion.

Today, DECathena is a dynamic distributed computing environment that supports multi-vendor platforms in a manner consistent and compliant with developed standards of distributed computing. Currently it is supporting DEC, SUN, and Hewlett-Packard workstations in a seamless distributed environment.

The various machines involved are able to interoperate in a manner only imagined a few years ago, providing a powerful tool with which users and system administrators can work.

The early days of Athena at Eastman Kodak provided trials for the pilot evaluation team. Every conceivable problem imaginable, and some not imagined, occurred. Network, administration, and software problems occurred on a daily basis. RDCS developed a laboratory Athena realm comprised of primarily DEC workstations. A SUN server was installed to act as the system library server and the boot server for SUN workstations, each hardware platform within an Athena environment requires a system library server and boot server of like kind. Several SUN workstations were added to the mix to test interoperability. Work group *M* is a production area comprised of mainly SUN workstations.

One of the features of DECathena is that system administrators do not have to go to each client workstation to load software. The software is stored on the system library server and boot server to be downloaded by booting across the network. The network boot provides the necessary software to the client workstation and then builds the boot kernel in place. From that point on, the machine is booted locally, network boots are only needed to download new operating system software. Application software resides on the system library server rather than the local workstation, thereby maintaining the dataless workstation architecture required. The necessary filesystems are attached during user login, and detached upon user logout. In the original RDCS lab environment, the software loads were smooth and fast, usually under ten minutes. However, when work group *M* was rolled into the environment download problems occurred. The network backbone was unable to pass boot request protocols through the routers, thus when bootp, a UDP Datagram protocol, was used to request software downloads, communication did not take place.

To solve the problems it was determined to place a boot server locally to each installation that would require download boots. This solved the problem and provided the opportunity to make each of the boot servers a local system library server also. By placing a system library server locally the network backbone traffic was decreased and response time was improved. This setup also provided the opportunity to place replicated servers for the various Athena components locally to provide redundant services, thus system interruption and downtime was reduced to a minimum. Replicated servers were set up for Kerberos authentication service, Hesiod naming service, and Zephyr notification service. In the event that remote work groups were separated by network problems from the main servers they would be able to operate until the connection was reestablished, without inconveniencing the users. Of course, if they needed an application or service that was only provided from outside their local group they would not be able to use it until the network link was repaired.

Name service and name resolution became a problem when trying to roll Athena out in an existing domain comprised mostly of SUN workstations. Athena's Hesiod provided naming service for data objects and services within the distributed environment, no local Network Information Service was created for the SUN workstations. Hesiod is based on Berkeley's BIND implementation of the Domain Name System. The SUN and DEC workstations performed well in this environment and users were able to work on either platform intuitively. DECathena structures the users working directory in such a manner that the DEC and SUN binaries are maintained separately and activation is dependent upon which platform is being used.

A name service problem developed when work group *M* was introduced into the environment a few machines and users at a time. The users were familiar with NIS and had no previous knowledge or need of DNS. As the first group of SUN workstations became Athena clients, they lost their ability to communicate with members of their work group remaining in the old environment. New installations begun from the ground up were able to accommodate a mix of platforms, however, existing installations did not cooperate as well. Had the entire work group been moved into the Athena environment at one time, the move would have been a smooth transition from NIS to Hesiod, which would provide the ability to navigate the entire name space. The inability of NIS to navigate beyond local boundaries caused communication problems between disparate work groups that Hesiod would eliminate, thus providing increased service and easier communication between machines in different domains of the name space.

To solve the problem, it was necessary to create a new local NIS that could communicate upward in the hierarchy to the hosts in the parent NIS domain. This NIS domain was a child of work group *M's* original NIS and provided the transparent access to the parent domain the users required. A child DNS domain was also created for the purpose of maintaining symmetry for support people. It was not technically necessary to create the new DNS domain, but made support easier from a human viewpoint (see figure 12.3).

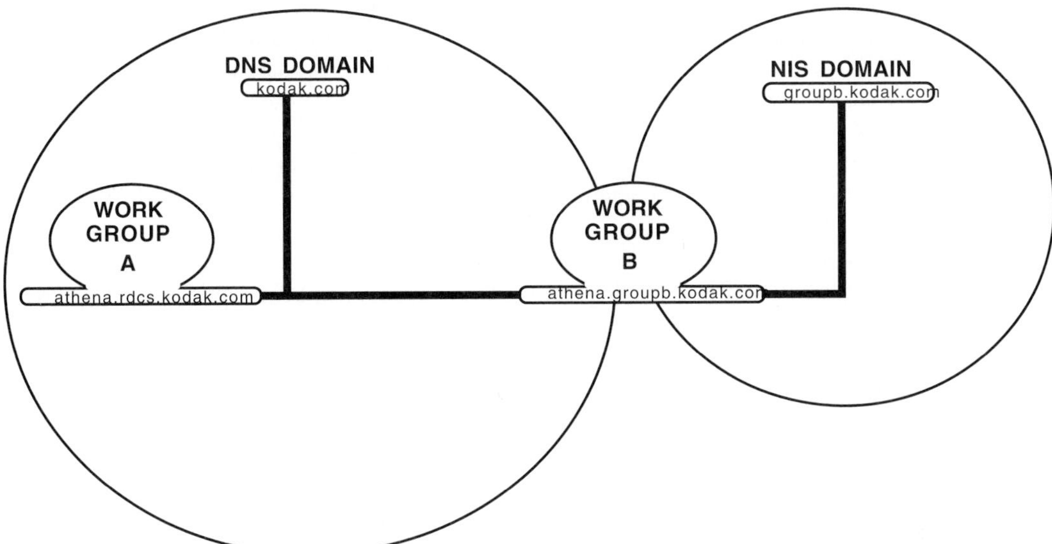

Figure 12.3 DNS/NIS domains.

12.8 Summary

As technology races into complexity it is important to note that no system as yet developed can sustain itself without human intervention. All computing environments are created for the express purpose of making humans more efficient and productive, we should not lose sight of the human needs by embracing technology for technology's sake, but insure that technological improvements serve in ways that improve the human existence. The rapid change from monolithic to distributed systems provides opportunities to explore avenues that will provide significant productivity gains while making jobs rewarding and satisfying.

The vision that created Kodak's distributed computing environment did not happen overnight, and neither will implementation. But steady movement in the right direction is being provided with tools such as DECathena. Many benefits of distributed computing in general, and DECathena in particular, were discovered through the pilot programs and installations. The reduction of labor required for each new workstation purchased will help create a ratio of system administrators to workstations that is acceptable and desirable. Security over traditional UNIX environments is enhanced thereby protecting a company's valuable data from accidental or intentional exposure to those not authorized.

DECathena, when installed properly, puts little measurable increased load on networks, much of the network traffic required already exists in one form or another; Athena codifies it into a reliable entity that rides rather than fights the network. DECathena code largely functions as advertised, and when discrepancies are identified DEC is quick to take the proper steps. The installation is not trivial, but then anything worthwhile does have it's price. The service management system configuration is straight-forward and easy to use, as is the client installation. System administrators have tools that are greatly improved over those available in typical UNIX installations, and in many cases tools are provided by DECathena that exist nowhere else. The system administrator can manage the infrastructure and all aspects of the Athena environment transparently to the end-users without limiting any of the UNIX capabilities the users have come to enjoy prior to Athena. Centralized support is provided without requiring centralization of the end-users. Effective mechanisms for distributed system administration provide an increase in administration productivity over traditional methods.

A single point of logon exists for the user thus simplifying the procedures necessary to perform useful tasks. With the addition of on-line consulting and discuss meetings, the users have increased flexibility to finding answers and improved performance and productivity. Zephyrgrams provide a degree of flexibility in personal communication not heretofore available in UNIX environments. Location independence, while being of limited value in many commercial environments, is provided and encouraged. This location independence does require dataless workstations, a fact that greatly improves security of corporate data from accidental disclosure and aids in the reduction of unnecessary disk space being used at individual workstations. The storage requirements are greater in central locations where backups of disk servers may be more efficiently implemented thus decreasing the risk that work and time may be lost when data files have not been properly protected by adequate backup measures. Access to a users personal environment can be accomplished from any workstation in the Athena environment, consequently roving personnel can easily work from any location in the distributed computing environment. Reduction of redundant software requirements can be affected by placing licensed software on compute servers that restrict the number of users for that software to the number of licenses available. Reduction in the number of licenses purchased will reduce the cost of computing without reducing the productivity of users. No one can lock the disks in their desk before they go on vacation causing others to be unable to perform their tasks because of inability to access scarce resources. The resources will be on compute servers, to be used when needed. The use of the X-window system reduces the need for multiple machines in one office while providing a multi-windowed view of the computing universe.

Distributed computing environments provide the avenues to reduction in corporate computing costs while providing an alternative to the traditional monolithic approach to information services. Distributed computing in client/server environments more closely approximates the way organizations perform work and is intrinsically better able to accommodate the computing needs of today. Service can be maintained in a centralized manner, as proven to be successful in monolithic computing, while service use is distributed to the sites needing it. Flexibility in modifying environments and moving users from one location to another is enhanced by distributed computing while control can be firmly maintained to protect corporate data from accidental and intentional exposure. A few years ago distributed computing had not been envisioned and mainframe computers were the end-all of computing. Monolithic mainframe use is decreasing as distributed computing is on the rise, it would be foolish nevertheless to believe that distributed computing is the ultimate advance in computing from which all other steps will be mere improvements to the consummate system of distributed computing. The future of corporate computing is not clear, however, suffice it to say that distributed computing will be a part of our environment for quite some time... and then will be replaced by environments of which we can only dream.

Gary Sterling works with developing technologies at Eastman Kodak Company, Rochester, New York. He is currently working on Kodak's distributed computing strategy and is responsible for implementing DECathena at Eastman Kodak. Kodak is a beta test site for DECathena. Previously he provided engineering support developing human interfaces for mid-range computing.

Sterling holds a BS in computer science from State University of New York and studied computer science at Penn State University.

Part III

Implementation and Management Strategies

Chapter 13

Vendor Strategies

Sally A. Biles
SunSoft, Inc.
Raman Khanna
Stanford University
Michael J. Mathews
Hewlett-Packard Company
Robert J. McCann
IBM Corporation
Mark Ryland
Microsoft Corporation

13.1 Introduction

Information technology environments at large organizations are evolving rapidly. Many organizations have decided to implement distributed computing environments and migrate mission-critical applications from mainframes to specialized servers. Early adopters of distributed computing are realizing that supporting mutli-vendor distributed computing environments is very complex. Although most vendors are trying to comply with standards, there are so many standards that selection of one vendor's system might preclude an organization from buying systems from other vendors. Every week, users hear about the formation of a new consortium in response to the formation of some other consortium. People have realized that there are disadvantages to creating heterogenous environments with systems from a large number of vendors. As a result, many organizations are planning to work with two or three strategic vendors who have resolved interoperability problems among themselves. Before entering into a long-term relationship with a vendor, organizations must understand the vendor's distributed computing strategy. To meet the need of user organizations, every systems vendor is going through its own transition, and it is important for users to understand the distributed computing strategies of leading vendors.

I thought that it would be useful to ask key vendors to provide summaries of their distributed computing strategies so that readers can compare them. I invited eight vendors to submit their strategies and received five submissions. The following sections describe the distributed computing strategies of the Hewlett-Packard Company, IBM Corporation, Microsoft Corporation, and SunSoft, Inc. Apple's Open Collaboration Environment is discussed in Appendix C.

13.2 Hewlett-Packard Company's Distributed Computing Strategy

Distributed computing is the key component of Hewlett-Packard's strategy to help customers develop, manage, and use applications across enterprise wide networks of varying brands and models of computers. Based on open systems and industry standards, HP's Distributed Computing offering is being implemented using HP's expertise and products in distributed computing, software engineering, and user interface technology. The new environment provides a clear *road map* and migration path to distributed object computing that works with legacy applications and data.

The primary goal of HP's distributed computing strategy is to develop and market a distributed object computing environment for heterogeneous networked systems. Fully supporting the Object Management Group's (OMG) Common Request Broker Architecture (CORBA) standard, this environment will be designed to deliver the benefits of object technology without requiring users to adopt a brand new operating environment.

As one of the core services for DOCP, HP has identified the Open Software Foundation's Distributed Computing Environment (DCE) as a critical strategic framework for delivering open, distributed computing solutions. Since DCE is poised to become a *de facto* industry standard for combining multi-vendor system components into a cohesive distributed computing environment, HP is committed to provide DCE on all of its platforms.

By providing and building on this environment, HP's Distributed Computing Strategy aims to facilitate the interaction of people, applications, and systems in heterogeneous networked environments. For end-users, the environment will make it intuitively easy to access information and use applications that are distributed around the world. It will also enable developers to create new applications faster by leveraging existing applications and objects.

13.2.1 Distributed Computing

HP believes distributed computing is important for several key reasons. First of all, large, monolithic machines are being increasingly replaced by computational clusters of networked systems, servers, and workstations. Also, with the proliferation of personal computers (PCs), individuals desire more computing power at the desktop but with easier access to information distributed around the environment.

Secondly, with host computers, mid-range and open systems platforms, and PCs being tied into enterprise networks, applications now need to span many different operating environments and protocols. Information stored in databases may now physically reside on computers located throughout the enterprise. The only effective way to develop, manage, and deploy these new distributed applications is through a standards-based, open, distributed computing strategy.

HP's distributed objects strategy is designed to give customers integrated, desktop *client* access to enterprise-wide *server* information and resources in a distributed heterogeneous systems environment. Through both peer-to-peer networking technologies and client/server, HP is removing the technical barriers of location dependency and multi-vendor incompatibility to enable greater levels of interaction and access for users and applications enterprise-wide.

Figure 13.1 shows HP's distributed open systems model. While only HP products are shown, HP has designed it as a *plug and play* environment that can include standards-based products from other vendors. This environment provides standards-based products to support applications development (C++ SoftBench), to display and manage applications in a distributed environment (OpenView), and to integrate applications and data (OpenODB). It also includes a graphical user interface (HP VUE) so that users experience a common *look and feel* throughout an enterprise. Customers may also use HP Distributed Smalltalk with ParcPlace's VisualWorks object-development environment as an alternative choice for Smalltalk-based application development.

HP believes that a distributed computing environment must support five fundamental requirements:

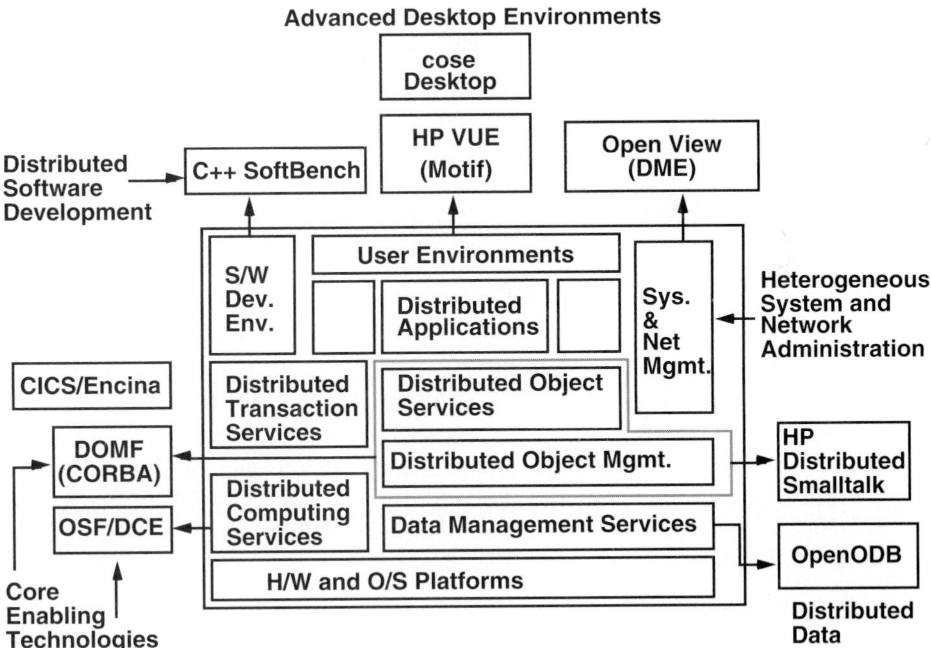

Figure 13.1 Hewlett-Packard's distributed open systems model.

1. *Object Interaction (application and user):* The ability of objects to communicate through a central messaging mechanism to request and deliver services, exchange data, and perform other functions in a cooperative and dynamic manner.
2. *End-User Access:* All end-users need consistent access to the environment so they can use any resource necessary to perform a task. As tasks or resources on the network change, the *window* to the environment for the end-user should remain the same.
3. *Information Access:* All types of enterprise-wide data must be accessible (with appropriate security controls) to all users and objects in the environment. A consistent access model should be available regardless of where the data resides or how it is stored.
4. *Application Development:* Developers need the ability to build new applications quickly using existing and new components. Languages of choice supported by powerful tools must be available. The development framework should work as part of the larger enterprise-wide environment.
5. *Resource Management:* Network and system administrators must be able to deploy and manage all of the resources of the environment (users and applications, systems and networks) in a dynamic and flexible manner across all types of platforms.

13.2.2 HP's Distributed Computing Strategy

HP has been working with distributed and object technology since 1981 which could be one reason its software now underlies many key standards in distributed computing. This software includes the OSF's Motif graphical user interface, HP's Network Computing System (NCS) as the remote procedure call service for DCE, a component of the Distributed Management Environment (DME), and the OMG's CORBA specification.

13.2.2.1 HP's DCE Products

HP uses the DCE distributed services as the core of its distributed computing strategy. To provide access to these services, HP offers HP DCE/9000 products consisting of DCE Core Services HP DCE products DCE Core Services and the DCE Application Development tools.

The DCE Core Services are a set of application programming interfaces (APIs) used by application developers to write DCE-based applications. HP's DCE Core Services have been tested for interoperability to ensure compatibility with OSF's DCE reference platforms. HP's DCE Core Services components include:

- *Remote Procedure Call:* Provides efficient communication over LANs and WANs.
- *Threads:* Provides multiple, simultaneous flows of control in an application, yielding improved performance.
- *Distributed Directory Service:* Provides a single naming model throughout the distributed environment.

- *Security Service:* Provides a secure means communication that ensures both data integrity and privacy, preventing unauthorized access to the distributed environment.
- *Time Service:* Synchronizes all system clocks on a network.
- *Distributed File System:* Provides transparent access to a global file system anywhere on the network.

The DCE Application Development tools from HP allow developers to design and debug DCE-based applications easily. These advanced programming tools specifically address the needs of the DCE developer by providing logging and analysis tools to ease application design, development, and troubleshooting. The tools also include an instrumented interface definition language (IDL) compiler that provides additional insight into DCE application activity and sample DCE applications to initiate development.

13.2.2.2 HP's Distributed Computing Products

In order to provide interoperability with a broad range of operating environments, tools, and systems, HP is integrating DCE with the following components into its distributed computing offering:

- *User Interface:* HP VUE, providing a consistent *look and feel* throughout the enterprise, based on OSF's Motif.
- *Application Development:* HP's DCE Application Development tools, HP's C++ SoftBench. HP's Distributed Smalltalk is the first product available from this work. ParcPlace Systems, Inc.'s VisualWorks object-based application development environment.
- *Multi-Platform Distributed Application Support:* HP's implementation of CORBA, known as the Distributed Object Management Facility (DOMF), allows the development of distributed, object-oriented applications that run on computer systems of different vendors, regardless of operating system, graphical user interface, or networking protocol. DOMF is part of HP's Distributed Application Architecture (DAA) which is a framework for distributed applications.
- *Transactional Environments:* HP will build on its DCE foundation to offer distributed on-line transaction processing capabilities through Transarc's Encina suite of transaction products and monitors. This will provide transaction integration across multivendor platforms and remote database management systems. For installed IBM environments, HP will offer its implementation of IBM's Customer Information Control System (CICS), so that CICS applications can easily be migrated over to HP platforms.
- *Database Integration:* HP's OpenODB database combines object and relational technologies in providing client/server or gateway access to HP databases and outside data sources.
- *Integrated Network and Systems Management:* HP's OpenView, allowing applications to be displayed and managed in a distributed environment, and OSF's DME.

- *Operating System Environment:* OSF's DCE technologies and other DOCP technologies will be available across all operating systems including HP-UX and HP MPE/iX. HP is also participating in a initiative to create a common Unix environment called Common Operating System Environment (COSE) which will be supported by OSF's DCE and HP's DOCP.
- *Hardware Platforms:* All HP PA-RISC based computers.

A critical aspect of HP's strategy is how well it complements HP's client/server strategy. HP's distributed object computing strategy calls for the implementation of a common messaging infrastructure over which diverse client-based objects will be able to interact. These objects will either be operating system independent or based on the leading desktop operating environments. HP will support the leading client environments and a wide range of client-based applications to work with its scalable servers and services.

By providing better integration of client technology with its servers, access to server-based functions, and network and system services, HP is extending the benefits of client/server to the distributed object computing environment.

At the same time, HP is continually building on its distributed computing offering to tie into its framework all relevant HP and industry standard distributed computing products. In addition, HP will continue to drive evolving object standards vital for the development, management, and deployment of distributed applications.

13.2.3 Security

As large customers adopt open systems and client/server on a global scale, the job of securing an organization's information assets from unauthorized access becomes more complicated. Organizations are evolving their computing infrastructure to more distributed or cooperative computing paradigms to achieve lower cost of operations, increased productivity, and competitive advantage.

HP is committed to delivering security solutions that address the complex security challenges associated with implementing a distributed computing environment. HP's security must be complementary and not incongruous with these objectives. For example, to help companies protect a competitive advantage, HP envisions a security perimeter that can be extended to both customer and supplier system interfaces, essentially removing the security obstacles inherent in entering or developing new markets such as home banking, electronic data interchange (EDI), information and multimedia services, and portable/mobile computing telecommunications services.

HP has developed an information security development model for global, distributed computing environments called *secure open computing.* With its commitment to DCE, HP will continue to be a leader in implementing and evolving the basic DCE security features. However, HP will also invest in local system capabilities which compliment the level of security service provided by DCE such as encryption/integrity hardware for performance and smart card support for safe key distribution/storage and two-factor authentication. HP was a technology provider to OSF for DCE security in release 1.0 and is currently working on security for DCE version 1.1.

13.2.4 Enterprise Data Management and Legacy Systems

Although distributed computing brings many benefits, there are many difficult challenges that need to be overcome in order to implement and support critical on-line transaction processing (OLTP) applications.

As was discussed in the section above, a distributed system needs to ensure adequate security services such as identity authentication and data encryption for OLTP applications. Additionally, sharing work and computing resources over an enterprise network requires the ability to extend programs to support remote procedure calls that allow multiple processes to work together over the network to perform a common task.

In order to achieve interoperability in a distributed OLTP environment, it is also necessary to adhere to standards such as X/OPEN's DTP model with XA and OSI/TP. Finally, for distributed OLTP, there needs to be a way to maintain application data integrity and develop applications in a heterogeneous network environment. This requirement becomes even more challenging when it is necessary to integrate new distributed OLTP applications with legacy data stored in IBM CICS or DB2 environments.

HP is relying on the DCE services to offer the necessary communication and resource sharing capabilities to build secure, distributed applications. Even though DCE addresses most of the complexities of distributed computing, there are additional services or extensions required for developing and running mission critical, distributed OLTP applications. To build on its DCE platform, HP has added in support for Transarc Corporation's Encina OLTP technology.

Encina provides a set of standards-based distributed services for simplifying the construction of reliable, distributed OLTP systems with guaranteed data integrity. Encina expands on the DCE framework to include services that offer full data integrity with a transactional two phase commit protocol, a high level API with simplified transaction semantics, and additional transactional semantics required achieving deterministic results with RPCs.

In addition to these services, Encina offers a rich environment for application development, extended administration features, and interoperability with IBM CICS and DB2 environments. Encina's XA interface allows it to work with XA compliant relational database management systems such as Oracle Corp.'s Oracle Server, Sybase, Inc.'s SQL Server, and other leading databases.

In addition to Encina, another leading transaction processing environment is IBM's CICS, used by more than 20,000 customers in more than 90 countries worldwide. In order to directly support CICS applications on HP's open platforms, HP offers a full implementation of IBM's CICS on HP's scalable PA-RISC-based computers.

HP's CICS offering will be implemented on top of the DCE and Encina technology. By providing consistent application programming interfaces, CICS on HP platforms increases platform choices available to users building OLTP applications for open environments.

13.2.5 Integrated Network and System Management

HP OpenView with the newly introduced Operations Center delivers integrated network and systems management for multivendor distributed computing environments. HP OpenView solutions comprise a broad portfolio of management applications running on an industry standard platform as well as test-and-measurement products and support tools. Over 170 HP OpenView applications and solutions are available from HP and third-parties for a variety of platforms including the HP 9000 and HP 3000 business systems, servers and workstations, Sun workstations, and Windows-based PCs.

HP OpenView has become the strategic platform in the marketplace for independent software developers, network equipment providers, and system integrators. HP and these partners build applications using HP OpenView to provide customers with the system and application management solutions they need for today and in the future.

The OpenView technologies have been adopted by the Open Software Foundation and incorporated into DME framework for management of distributed computing environments.

In addition, the HP OpenView platform has been licensed by IBM and Group Bull for incorporation into their management products.

13.2.6 Distributed Application Architecture and OpenODB Database

To help foster the development of distributed, object-based applications that can operate across a heterogeneous collection of computers, HP developed the Distributed Application Architecture (DAA).

The purpose of the DAA is to allow users of a computer network to access information, applications, and services through a single, consistent user environment. DAA allows developers of all kinds to create new information, applications, and services rapidly by taking advantage of existing system or application components. This is possible because DAA's object-oriented approach enables both users and programmers to focus on the information used and the operations performed rather than the underlying hardware or software specifications.

Applications written to DAA will interoperate across different operating systems implementing the architecture. A distinctive feature of DAA is that these connections typically can be made by end-users or system integrators, not just by developers.

The core components of the DAA infrastructure is the Distributed Object Management Facility (DOMF) which manages object interactions. The concepts embodied in OMG's Common Object Request Broker Architecture standard are derived from the DOMF specifications submitted to OMG.

HP's commercial grade object-oriented database, OpenODB, is designed to support complex applications and large numbers of users. OpenODB offers customers data-center security and maintenance, a query language, 24-hour availability, and simultaneous back-up capability.

HP's database approach allows users to progress naturally to object-oriented technology while still accessing and using relational database applications. This is because OpenODB's object-oriented structured query language (OSQL) allows users to retrieve information regardless of where or how it is stored.

13.2.7 Application Development Tools

In terms of application development for the DOCP, HP offers several alternatives ranging from structured to object programming environments. One of the most widely used HP developer tools is the C++ SoftBench development environment which can tie legacy and object applications together.

The SoftBench framework for computer-aided software engineering provides a common graphical user interface and communication services for a wide selection of development tools.

The framework supports distributed software development in a multi-vendor environment. SoftBench technology underlies the National Institute of Standards and Technology and European Computer Manufacturers Association standards, and has been licensed by multiple companies.

HP's Distributed Smalltalk is an implementation of the CORBA specification for distributed computing. HP Distributed Smalltalk adds features and services on top of CORBA and the Smalltalk programming language to provide a rapid development environment for portable applications shared by workgroups. HP's technology includes a full set of object services and many sample applications, so developers can build new application objects quickly. These objects can link to information stored anywhere in the enterprise using HP's object-oriented database, OpenODB.

Customers may also use HP's CORBA implementation of ParcPlace's VisualWorks object-oriented development environment which is also based on Smalltalk. VisualWorks enables developers to create graphical, client/server applications that are completely portable.

HP offers the complete range of hardware, software, and services to support distributed computing applications through its commitment to open systems and industry standards. HP believes that distributed computing will facilitate the convergence of the telecommunications, computing, entertainment, and mass media industries, fostering the emergence of the *information utility,* a global network of networks offering a wide range of new information services to businesses, education, and consumers. HP is at the forefront of this information revolution, creating the framework that will allow the seamless integration of distributed computing technologies in the decades to come.

13.3 IBM's Open Distributed Systems Strategy

For a distributed processing environment to be effective, a user needs to have access to the required information resources regardless of their location, characteristics or systems platform. This ability, called *interoperability,* is enabled by the use of open standards–consistent ways to access system resources. These open standards are mutually agreed to, published, and usable by any provider of computing resources.

The goal of IBM's open distributed systems strategy is to ensure that customers have the greatest choice of products available to help them access and share the information they require. It addresses their multivendor, multiprotocol environments and encompasses configurations ranging from a simple LAN to a complex distributed environment with multiple LANs and hosts.

IBM is accomplishing this by:

- Delivering a broad range of quality products that allow different types and brands of computers to work together easily;

- Adopting, promoting, and contributing to industry-wide hardware and software standards;
- Working with the industry, through partnerships, alliances, and licensing agreements, to develop and deliver leading-edge technology that adheres to such standards;
- Providing comprehensive services and support to help customers integrate their applications to meet their business requirements.

13.3.1 Open Distributed Systems Structure

Supporting the strategy, the open distributed systems structure (figure 13.2) describes a target structure for implementing distributed systems and applications across both IBM and non-IBM systems. The structure describes a set of resource managers; each a service program which manages and provides access to a processing resource such as a file of data, an application, or a presentation device. The open distributed systems structure helps manage the consistency of the interfaces, protocols, and functions of the various resource managers it defines. The usage, by resource managers, of open interfaces and protocols enables interoperability across the network.

Figure 13.2 provides an overview of the open distributed systems structure. The boxes indicate convenient groupings of resource managers based upon similarity of function, and are not intended to indicate a *layered* structure. In fact, not all the resource managers or services are necessary at each node or system in a distributed network.

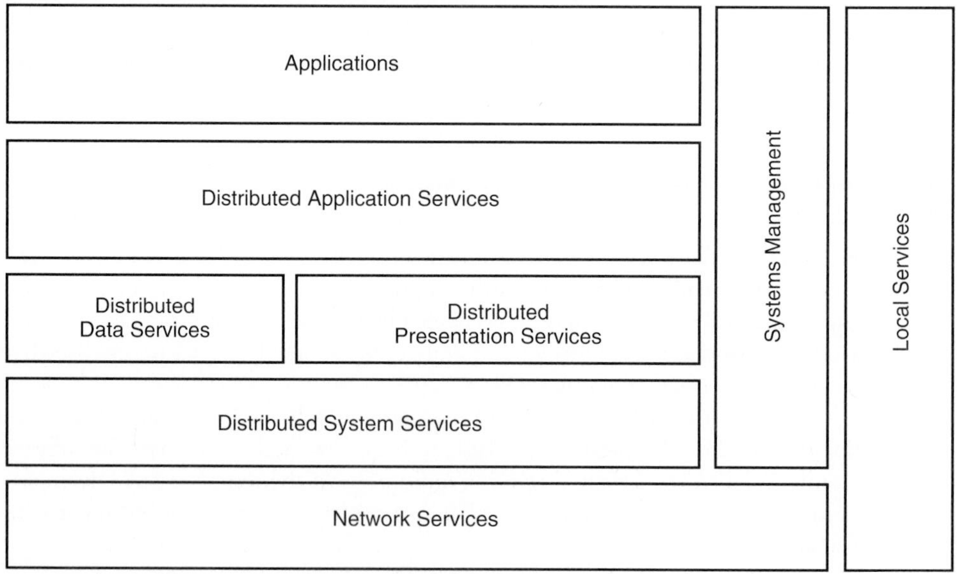

Figure 13.2 Open distributed systems structure–overview.

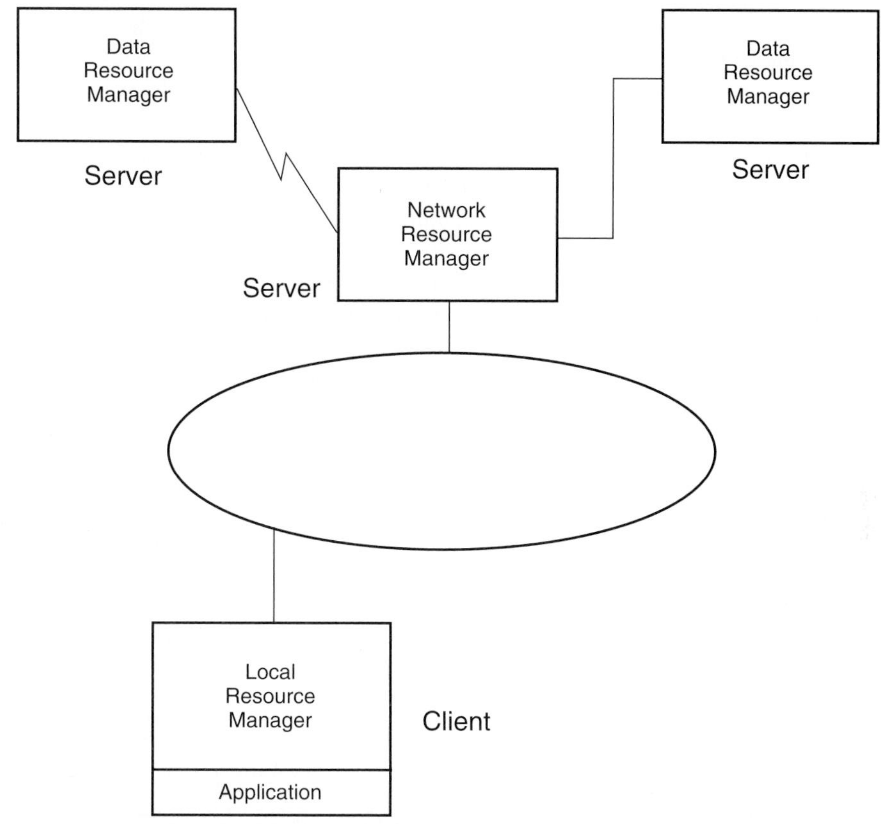

Figure 13.3 Distributed resource management.

The functional groupings are:

- *Distributed Application Services:* Facilities which extend the application by providing common functions and support for processing consistency.
- *Distributed Presentation Services:* Capabilities to provide an effective and consistent user interaction for both display and printed interfaces.
- *Distributed Data Services:* Functions which allow an application to use both local and remote data that is in a wide variety of formats.
- *Distributed System Services:* Mechanisms used to support application-to-application interaction in a networked environment.
- *Network Services:* Facilities which support the transport of data between a point in one system and the end point in another system.
- *System Management Services:* A suite of capabilities, including frameworks and applications, that allow management of all system resources, both local and distributed.

In the open distributed systems structure there are two basic kinds of services, local and distributed. A local service operates within the confines of a single system or platform. An example of a local service is memory management.

In a distributed environment, a particular service may involve functions in multiple systems within the network. For example, to accomplish a request for data from a workstation (client) application, the client or local portion of a distributed data service may be used to locate the data (directory service). Then, remote network and data resource managers would be invoked to gain access to the actual information which is located elsewhere in the network (see figure 13.3).

The way an application or a user accesses these services is independent of the particular operating system platform. When the interfaces and functions are based upon broadly accepted (i.e., open) standards, any vendor's system can participate as either a client or a server. In addition, an application which was constructed using standards, may be relocated to a different platform in support of changing business conditions.

13.3.2 Distributed Systems Structure Components

IBM provides a variety of operating systems including IBM defined environments of MVS/ESA, VM/ESA, OS/400 and OS/2, and UNIX environments of AIX/ESA, AIX/6000 and AIX PS/2. All these systems participate in the implementation of IBM's distributed capabilities. A detailed diagram of the open distributed systems structure (figure 13.4) identifies the specific components it contains.

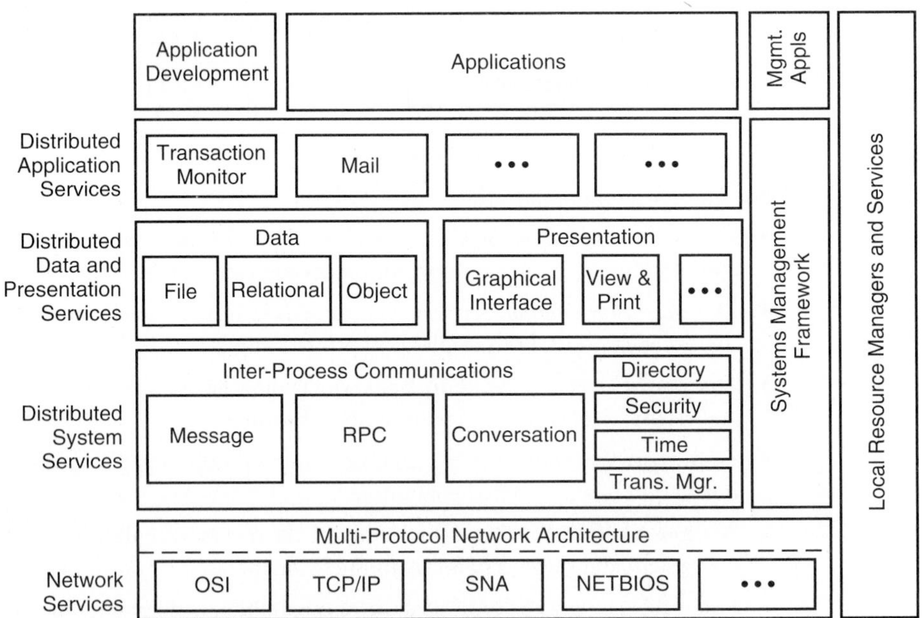

Figure 13.4 Open distributed systems structure.

13.3.2.1 Distributed Application Services

13.3.2.1.1 Transaction Monitor

Transaction processing systems require two components: a transaction manager which coordinates and synchronizes resources, and a transaction monitor which maintains the transaction processing environment that is accessed through application programming interfaces (APIs).

IBM offers three monitors that support distributed transaction processing: the CICS family, Encina, and the IMS family.

- *CICS (Customer Information Control System) Family:* IBM's CICS family provides a widely used transaction processing environment which has had, for some time, the capability to support a distributed implementation. CICS provides both transaction manager and monitor functions and is available for the OS/2 and AIX/6000 platforms, as well as the OS/400 and MVS/ESA host or server systems. The CICS APIs are available to the industry, and Hewlett-Packard has announced its intention to implement CICS on their systems.

CICS on the AIX/6000 platform uses the transaction management functions of Transarc's Encina and the RPC (Remote Procedure Call) facility of OSF's DCE.

- *Encina:* For the UNIX environment, IBM also offers a complete implementation of Encina. IBM's Encina capability on the AIX/6000, provides both transaction monitor and management functions in a modular structure that may be customized to the needs of a particular customer. Functions provided include Transactional RPC, Transactional C and a two-phase commit facility. Communications over both SNA and TCP/IP networks are supported.

- *IMS (Information Management System) Family:* IMS is another widely used complete transaction processing environment developed by IBM. Functions of an established application can be easily distributed by using the IMS Client Server/2 product from IBM or the IMS Production Option from Micro Focus. These products execute in an OS/2 environment on IBM and compatible hardware platforms.

13.3.2.1.2 Mail

IBM and its business partners support several protocols for multivendor mail, including simple mail transport protocol (SMTP) and X.400, as implemented by Lotus Notes and CC:Mail and the IBM OfficeVision product family. Interfaces and gateways are available to link LAN and host based environments using different mail systems and protocols.

In addition, IBM is an active participant in the Vendor Independent Messaging consortium which is focusing on the definition and implementation of a common mail API. This interface allows consistent application access to mail systems from multiple vendors.

13.3.2.2 Distributed Presentation Services

13.3.2.2.1 Graphical User Interface

The focus for the delivery of presentation services at the workstation is on a graphical user interface (GUI). OSF/Motif provides an accepted GUI capability that has been implemented, or is a stated direction, on all IBM platforms. IBM's Common User Access (CUA) was an input to OSF's definition of Motif and also provides a consistent *look and feel* for distributed OS/2 applications.

13.3.2.2.2 View and Print

IBM's direction is to migrate its host based printing capabilities, advanced function printing (AFP), to support an open distributed environment. Implementation has begun by providing a standard font (Adobe Type I) across all platforms, and by supporting a LAN based print server that delivers AFP output.

The Print Services Facility, available in the OS/2 and AIX/6000 environments, handles AFP and other data streams and provides server support for most generally available types of printers.

Development and use of print applications can be simplified by using the AFP workbench. The workbench allows AFP data streams to be viewed, as a full page, at a workstation prior to printing.

13.3.2.3 Distributed Data Services

IBM's strategy addresses both relational and non-relational data.

13.3.2.3.1 Non-Relational

IBM supports both byte and record level file structures.

For byte files, IBM supports Sun's network file system (NFS) on all its major platforms. In addition, implementation of the DCE Distributed File System (DFS) has begun with availability on the AIX/6000 platform. The direction is to provide DFS function across all key platforms while continuing to support the NFS alternative.

Consistent record level files are provided through IBM's Distributed Data Management (DDM) architecture. DDM has been implemented on the MVS, OS/400, OS/2 and PC/DOS platforms, and published specifications are available for implementation by other vendors.

13.3.2.3.2 Relational

The functions of SQL-89 are available on all IBM platforms except AIX/ESA (announced direction) through the DB2 (Database 2) family of products. In addition, functions of the SQL 2 standard have been announced for the MVS environment.

To support a heterogeneous data environment, IBM has defined the Information Warehouse framework as an architectural approach for the access and utilization of data across an organization. It is based on the standard SQL APIs for data access. The framework includes tools and architectures supporting the use and management of information from IBM and non-IBM data management systems, in both relational and non-relational formats. A key component in this framework is the Distributed Relational Database Architecture (DRDA).

DRDA defines a set of interface protocols between a client application and a remote relational or non-relational database, which may be in a dissimilar operating environment. More than a dozen vendors, including leading database suppliers, have announced plans to deliver products which use DRDA.

The latest level of DRDA supports a *distributed unit of work* or multisite update capability in which a single transaction can initiate updates to multiple remote databases.

13.3.2.3.3 Object

Object database is a key emerging technology for information management. As part of its activity in this area, IBM and Object Design, Inc. have initiated a technology, development and usage agreement involving Object Design's ObjectStore database management system.

13.3.2.4 Distributed System Services

IBM is implementing the following systems services defined by OSF/DCE to enable distributed computing across its major hardware/software environments:

- Directory
- Security
- Time

X/Open's Transaction Processing Model outlines a set of standard based functions and APIs that allow an application to manage a wide variety of systems resources with capabilities such as two-phase commit and resource recovery. Transarc's Encina has begun implementation of this model. IBM is an active supporter of this direction for the transaction manager function and is providing an Encina manager on the AIX/6000 platform.

Distributed system services will be integrated with the corresponding local components. For example, distributed authentication services provided by DCE (security) will be integrated with local authentication services available on each platform (e.g., the Resource Access Control Facility (RACF) on MVS).

The open distributed systems structure identifies multiple ways to implement communications between distributed applications. In addition to the DCE Remote Procedure Call, IBM provides a conversational interface (CPI-C) through the Advanced Program to Program Communication (APPC or LU 6.2) facility of SNA.

DCE/RPC is available on the AIX/6000 platform and is an announced direction for other key platforms. APPC is available (or stated direction) on all platforms except the AIX/ESA environment.

CPI-C and APPC have been adopted by X/Open and the ISO, respectively, in their specification for a conversational application interface.

IBM has introduced a Message Queue Interface (MQI) as an asynchronous application communication alternative. It supports protocol independence, work flow based processing and the enabling of compound transactions. The MQSeries, developed through an alliance with Systems Strategies, Inc., provides MQI products for both IBM and other vendor systems. In addition, MQI has been submitted as a proposed standard.

13.3.2.5 Network Services

IBM supports a variety of wide area and local networking protocols including OSI, TCP/IP, SNA and NETBIOS, and has begun to implement a multiprotocol transport networking architecture (MPTN). This architecture provides application independence from lower level network protocols. It allows the network protocol decision and the application interface processing decision to be independently determined. This means that an application originally designed for implementation in SNA using CPI-C, could interoperate under TCP/IP without restructure or use of external gateways.

MPTN provides a transport layer gateway which functions by converting an envelop of data from one network to the format of another. AnyNet/MVS is the initial implementation of MPTN providing TCP/IP sockets over SNA and SNA (APPC) over TCP/IP for both the MVS and OS/2 platforms.

13.3.2.6 Systems Management Frameworks and Applications

To assist the delivery and implementation of systems management functions in a multivendor environment, IBM has established the SystemView framework. This framework aids the management task by supporting applications and functions which are structured to allow data sharing, product integration and use of a consistent user interface. SystemView follows the ISO systems management model including the specifications for managed objects and manager/agent interaction. It addresses the disciplines of change, configuration, performance, operations, problem and business management. Products are available to support either centralized or distributed management control.

Through capabilities available in the NetView family of products, the network management protocols of CMIS/CMIP, SNMP and SNA-MS (SNA - Management Services) are supported. All these protocols can be integrated into a common network management approach.

IBM has actively supported the development of OSF's Distributed Management Environment (DME) and intends to integrate DME functions into its systems management offerings. As part of this, the X/Open XMP API has been incorporated into SystemView and is available on the OS/2 and AIX/6000 environments. In addition, OSF and the Object Management Group are defining an object oriented framework based on the CORBA standard, which is expected to coexist with XMP.

Other vendors of systems management products including CANDLE Corporation, Information Retrieval Companies and PLATINUM technology, are participating in the delivery of SystemView products through alliances and development partnerships.

13.3.2.7 Local Services

For consistent access to local operating system facilities such as basic task oriented services, IBM has begun delivery of the POSIX standards (IEEE 1003.1, 1003.2 and 1003.4a) on its platforms. The direction is to implement other POSIX services, as they become defined, to meet user requirements.

13.3.2.8 Application Development

IBM's capability for application development begins with standards conforming tools such as the ANSI compilers for C, COBOL, FORTRAN, and Pascal. For IBM defined platforms, the AD/Cycle framework provides a compilation of integrated tools to facilitate host-based and distributed development. For the UNIX environment, a commensurate set of development tools are provided by AIX Case. Both AD/Cycle and AIX Case are structured for the integration of products and tools from multiple vendors.

The need for a consistent application development environment that supports multiplatform, multivendor applications is well understood. To facilitate this, IBM is using the European Computer Manufactures Association PCTE (Portable Common Tool Environment) model as a base for development of an integrated case solution. In addition, work has begun with Hewlett-Packard for the design of a common framework based on HP's SoftBench integration services. Today, IBM products can assist the management of software development configurations on HP and Sun, as well as IBM, workstations.

13.3.3 Implementing Distributed Solutions

The key to successfully implementing distributed systems in an open, multivendor environment, is balancing an organization's needs for business improvement, protection of investments and new technology. An information technology (IT) plan which aligns with the business' direction and objectives provides a strong foundation. Using this plan, an assessment of the appropriate technologies and standards can be made, and available products from the marketplace can be interrogated. Projects can then be structured that migrate the current environment to address specific areas of improvement.

It is recommended that this be an iterative process which maintains a long term view. The IT plan can be regularly revised through feedback from short or limited term projects. From these, the effect of new technology and the resultant improvements or impacts to the business processes can be determined. Results can be used to stimulate enhanced business objectives and a more integrated and accurately targeted IT plan.

IBM offers a variety of support alternatives to assist in the development and implementation of an open distributed systems environment. Beginning with planning, the IBM Consulting Group has experienced people that can help construct business restructuring plans and define information technology architectures. IBM's Open Systems Centers are staffed with individuals experienced on multiple vendor platforms. The centers can use their installed systems from most leading vendors, to outline, design and prototype a specific solution. In addition, services are available to implement, manage and operate an open, multivendor, distributed environment, from both local and other IBM service organizations.

13.3.4 Meeting Future Requirements

IBM is an active participant and contributor in many standards and industry organizations such as the Object Management Group, the Open Software Foundation, the ODA Consortium, X/Open, as well as ANSI and the ISO. Today's products meet many profiles and specifications, including XPG3 and FIPS 151, and IBM's intent is to meet other requirements being requested by its users, such as XPG4.

A summary of the key standards and technologies that are included in the open distributed systems structure are presented in figure 13.5. This is just a portion of the available capabilities. IBM offers many other products for the distributed environment addressing functions such as LAN data backup and support for DecNet and Novell's IPX.

The unspecified areas in the structure diagram (figure 13.4) indicate capabilities and technologies that are under investigation. Key technologies that are expected to emerge include, calendar services, multimedia presentation services and distributed object management.

IBM is continuing to work with other vendors to facilitate new technology and function. For example, IBM has joined with Hewlett-Packard, The Santa Cruz Operation, Sun Microsystems, Univel and UNIX Systems Laboratories to develop a common open software environment (COSE). The six companies have decided to adopt common products and jointly define or endorse specifications supporting a common, multivendor, desktop environment. The common desktop will incorporate elements from IBM's CUA model and Workplace Shell, OSF/Motif and components and specification from the other vendors. This alliance will also focus on the areas of networking, graphics, multimedia, object technology, and systems management.

IBM's open distributed systems strategy and the supporting structure provide a foundation on which organizations can gain the benefits of open distributed computing today, while supporting growth to new technologies. IBM is committed to helping its customers use open technology in a distributed, multivendor environment, and will continue to evolve its products and services to meet their changing business requirements.

IBM Platform	AIX PS/2	AIX/ 6000	AIX/ ESA	OS/2	OS/ 400	VM/ ESA	MVS/ ESA
Application Services							
Encina	–	AV	–	–	–	–	–
CICS	–	AN	–	AV	AN	–	AV
X.400	SOD	AV	–	–	AV	AV	AV
SMTP	AV	AV	AV	AV	AV	AV	AV
Presentation Services							
OSF/MOTIF	AV	AV	AV	SOD	SOD	AV	AV
X-Windows	AV	AV	AV	AV	SOD	AV	AV
Legend:	AV – Available AN – Announced			SOD – Statement of Direction – Not Announced			
Source:	Open Enterprise Produce Guide – 8th Edition, April 1993						

Figure 13.5 Availability of key standards and protocols.

Data and Systems Services							
SQL	AV	AV	SOD	AV	AV	AV	AV
NFS	AV	AV	AV	AV	AN	AV	AV
OSFDCE	–	AV	SOD	SOD	AN	SOD	SOD
POSIX 1003.1	AV	AV	AV	–	SOD	SOD	AN
POSIX Draft 1003.2	–	AV	AV	–	SOD	–	AN
POSIX Draft 1003.4	–	AV	AV	–	SOD	SOD	AN
X.500	–	SOD	SOD	AV	AV	AV	AV
Network Services							
OSI	SOD	AV	SOD	AV	AV	AV	AV
TCP/IP	AV	AV	AV	AV	AV	AV	AV
Sockets	–	AV	AV	AV	SOD	AV	AV
SNA (LU 6.2)	SOD	AV	–	AV	AV	AV	AV
Management Services							
CMIS/CMIP							
Manager	–	–	–	AV	AV	AV	AV
Agent	SOD	SOD	SOD	AV	AV	AV	AV
SNMP							
Agent	SOD	AV	AV	AV	SOD	AV	AV
Monitor	–	AV	–	–	–	AV	AV
SNA/MS	–	AV	–	AV	AV	AV	AV
Application Development							
C and FORTRAN	AV	AV	AV	AV	AV	AV	AV
COBOL	AV	AV	SOD	AV	AV	AV	AV
Pascal	AV	AV	–	AV	AV	AV	AV

Legend: AV – Available; AN – Announced; SOD – Statement of Direction; – Not Announced

Source: Open Enterprise Produce Guide – 8th Edition, April 1993

Figure 13.5 Availability of key standards and protocols. (Continued)

13.4 Microsoft's Distributed Computing Strategy

13.4.1 IAAYF, or Information Ain't At Your Fingertips–Yet

Computers are still far, far too hard for people to use. Networked computers and distributed systems are even worse. Humans are forced to adapt to computer systems instead of the other way around. Users of distributed systems must navigate their way through a variety of tools that tend to solve and re-solve and solve again very similar naming, querying, and storage problems. In Editor Raman Khanna's example on page 2, the hypothetical user must first find and use the query tool for a financial database, then a human resources database (which could be a directory service if the directory is queryable), then a mail system (which could use the same directory but typically does not), then a *groupware* database, then a *document manage-*

ment system, then a *network operating system* or distributed file system.[1] To put it bluntly, distributed systems today are nightmares for most users.

Fundamentally, the user's nightmare derives from the developer's nightmare. First, programmers today are forced to grovel in all these *differences* between distributed systems–different file and print sharing protocols, different directory services, different security services, different mail services, different systems management services, different software licensing services, different SQL database programming models, different *groupware* or unstructured replicated database services. Second, even if these services and their programming models were separately standardized, they would still all be totally *different from each other!* The programming model for querying a SQL database would have no resemblance to querying the file system or the directory service or the groupware database or the message store–although all are, in fact, databases! Is it any wonder that application developers almost always preserve and present the gory details of all these differences to users rather than hiding them like they should?

The problem is evident. The question is, how are we going to *fix* it?

At the Comdex tradeshow in the Fall of 1990 Bill Gates gave Microsoft and the industry a vision of a solution to the problems of distributed computing. He called his vision "Information At Your Fingertips." (In good reductionist computing fashion this vision is now a slogan and the slogan has become the acronym "IAYF.") Gates envisioned a distributed system where heterogeneous back-end data sources are hidden by a single object system model with a single, extensible browsing and querying interface. Users become information consumers rather than computer jockeys; micro-computers become *information appliances* rather than specialized business tools.

Visions are great. They tell us where we need to go. But they do not tell us how to get there. The industry needs to move from the "IAAYF" (Information Ain't At Your Fingertips) of today to the IAYF of tomorrow. The remainder of this paper will discuss some short-term steps that Microsoft is taking to ease these problems and a longer-term solution based on a distributed object architecture.

13.4.2 First Moves: Crawl Before Walking

There is a lot of talk in the industry today about the challenge of bringing forward into modern computing architectures *legacy systems,* by which people typically mean proprietary mainframes and minicomputers. There is a seldom-noticed flip-side to this problem, however,

[1]Today's most sophisticated corporate user would use something like the following set of tools for that scenario: (1) custom applications specific to Oracle or Sybase or CICS back-ends to query and browse financial data; (2) another custom HR database application, or, in a progressive organization, perhaps a network directory service with its unique browsing and querying utilities (although many directories are not fully queryable!); (3) in some cases, the same tool as for (2), but not, for example, with Novell NetWare 4.0 which uses a non-integrated mail directory; (4) a Microsoft Access database application or Lotus Notes; (5) a document management system such as Saros File-Share, or perhaps the document management add-on for Lotus Notes; (6) network-specific file management and administration utilities for UNIX, NetWare, Microsoft LAN Manager, or Banyan VINES.
That is the good news. The bad news is that the average user in the average a company is simply unable to get these kind of basic services from his computer systems.

which is the vast installed base of open architecture IBM-compatible PCs running MS-DOS. Millions of these machines are insufficiently powerful to run modern graphical applications, much less participate fully in a distributed system. Even the more powerful 32-bit PCs often have limited amounts of volatile and persistent storage and run only older applications.

For tens of millions of users the Microsoft Windows (TM) operating system 3.x has been the bridge that allowed them to move from out-moded applications and computing styles to innovative GUI applications while maintaining compatibility with a vast range of MS-DOS-based applications and device drivers. Windows has also done a good job of unifying the client-side user and programming models for basic file and print services in the traditional *network operating system* business.

So now Windows is the interface between a huge number of users and the distributed systems that everyone is eager to build. Microsoft is working hard to make Windows a tremendous asset rather than a liability in a distributed computing environment. These efforts have three main thrusts: 1) continue to improve the functionality of the base Windows on MS-DOS platform while adding a high-end version of Windows (Windows NT (TM) version 3.1) with much richer capabilities; 2) in partnership with ISVs, develop common call-level programming interfaces for heterogeneous back-end services such as messaging and relational databases; and 3) in partnership with ISVs and other vendors, develop an object architecture that solves more fundamentally the problems of heterogeneity in distributed systems. Let us look at these issues in turn.

Improvements to the Windows base platforms: The Windows 3.1 platform is limited in two rather important respects from the perspective of building distributed systems: 1) the lack of preemptive multi-tasking and threading, which simplifies distributed programming considerably; and 2) the lack of a complete 32-bit programming model. (While the Win32s libraries for Windows 3.1 address the latter problem by retro-fitting a subset of the full Win32 API onto Windows 3.1, they cannot solve the former problem.) The next major of release of Windows on the MS-DOS platform will, among other major improvements, provide a large subset of the full 32-bit Win32 API available in Windows NT, including preemption, threading, file mapping, asynchronous I/O, and other advanced operating system features.

Of course, the Windows NT product itself is available, providing a Windows user interface and a vastly extended 32-bit Windows programming model on top of a new network-ready portable operating system base. Windows NT provides to the mass market a version of Windows with capabilities never before available in a high volume platform such as support for RISC architectures and excellent performance scaling on tightly-coupled multiprocessing machines.

Finally, Microsoft is rapidly solving the low-level networking issues. It is building in basic file and print services using industry-standard protocols such as SMB and the Internet suite. Microsoft is moving rapidly to use TCP/IP as its standard network protocol, with IETF-approved extensions to make administration of TCP/IP networks as easy as NetBEUI or IPX/SPX. Microsoft is also working to ensure complete functionality of its operating systems and networking technology on Novell NetWare protocols for those users who prefer them to TCP/IP.

Windows universal client APIs: WOSA: In conjunction with third parties, Microsoft is providing today a number of important call-level programming interfaces designed to hide differences in communications implementations and back-end services. These *universal client* APIs are grouped together loosely in a *market-tecture* called the Windows Open Services APIs (WOSA).[2] Among these first-generation APIs for distributed computing are:

- Open Database Connectivity (ODBC), a call-level interface for SQL-based data access. Dozens of vendors are selling or demonstrating tools based on ODBC, and it will be available on the Macintosh, UNIX, and a number of other operating systems thanks to the efforts of third parties. ODBC works around the lowest common denominator problem by specifying levels of driver/back-end compliance that is determinable by applications at run-time.
- Messaging API (MAPI), a set of rich programming interfaces for developing back-end independent mail applications for Windows, as well as front-end-independent messaging service providers through the MAPI SPI (Service Provider Interface). A subset of MAPI known as Simple MAPI is also available to applications that need only minimal send and receive services.[3]
- Windows Sockets, a standardized programming interface for network IPC based on the Berkeley Sockets model with extensions for non-preemptive environments and for use on other network transports besides TCP/IP.
- Microsoft RPC, an OSF DCE-compatible implementation of RPC for MS-DOS, Windows, and Windows NT that meets the harsh size, performance, and cost requirements of the PC marketplace.
- Desktop Management Interface (DMI), a set of programming and reporting interfaces for managing PCs in a heterogeneous environment. DMI was defined in conjunction with all leading PC and workstation vendors as the output of a group called the Desktop Management Task Force.
- Licensing API (LSAPI), providing a standard policy-neutral mechanism for desktop applications to access software licensing servers from any vendor.

Starting to walk with Windows Objects: OLE 2.0: The primary focus of Microsoft's recently-released Object Linking and Embedding 2.0 specification and runtime libraries (OLE 2.0) is to enable office automation applications for Windows to create, manage, and store compound documents in powerful new ways.[4] Over the next year hundreds of Windows-based applications will emerge using OLE 2.0's rich services for application integration, external programmability, and compound document storage. OLE 2.0 will also be ported to other platforms by Microsoft's partners. But do not be mislead by its name and initial focus:

[2]All of the WOSA APIs listed are available in source-compatible 16-bit and 32-bit implementations, with the exception of full MAPI which is 32-bit only.

[3]Microsoft will also support the XAPIA's Common Mail Calls on all platforms when those are defined and available.

[4]The OLE 2.0 Development Kit is available from Microsoft for less than $100. It includes a license to distribute the run-time DLLs for free. The kit is also included in the Microsoft Developer Network service (less than $50 per year) on its quarterly CD-ROMs.

OLE 2.0 lays the groundwork for a full-blown but upward-compatible distributed system object model that will emerge in Cairo.

13.4.3 Microsoft Cairo–Implementing IAYF

Within the Microsoft Systems Division for more than two years a core group of designers and engineers have been building Microsoft's first truly distributed operating system–a product code named *Cairo.* Drawing on work done by the team working on Windows NT, the LAN Manager team, the OLE 2.0 team, and other sources inside and outside the company, this group has made significant strides towards solving some the hard problems that confront any attempt to build a distributed system that makes significant strides toward the IAYF vision.[5] Figure 13.6 shows a functional block diagram of Cairo.

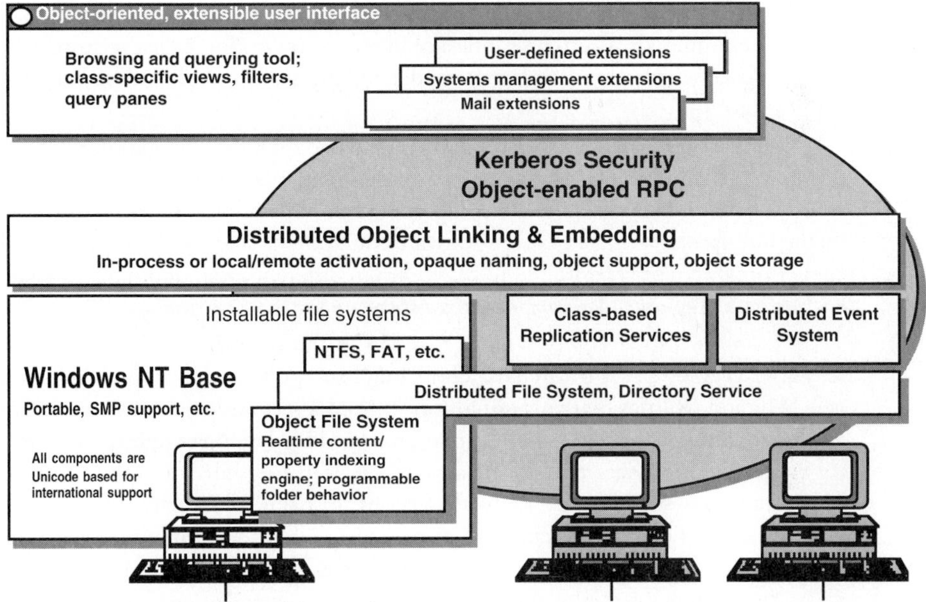

Figure 13.6 Cairo block diagram.

Software objects–fact or fiction? Before taking a very brief tour of the Cairo system, let's deal with an important issue. Why all the focus on *objects?* Isn't *object orientation* just the latest and greatest meaningless buzzword to laden the sentences of industry FUD-masters? Well, yes, as matter of fact is that–but not *just* that.

[5]Indeed, the Cairo team has already provided significant output to help other Microsoft products move towards a distributed object-based system. For example, the Microsoft RPC used to build Windows NT 3.1 itself and also distributed for MS-DOS and 16-bit Windows as part of the Windows NT developer's kit was developed in the Cairo group, as was the implementation of structured storage for a standard filesystem found in OLE.2.0.

Object technology does a number of important things for distributed system software.

It provides both the technology and an opportunity to re-unify today's over-complex systems around a manageable set of common operations–in other words, to treat like things alike. By using object abstractions, for example, the programming technique used for enumeration of things within a container can be the same for windows on a screen, files in a directory, rows in a database table, threads in a process, and so on. To take a higher level example, generic database operations can be performed on any object that wants to act like a database, whether the object represents a file system, SQL database, message store, directory service, configuration data, or any other persistent store.

It blurs and eventually eliminates the distinction between systems and applications. All software simply becomes either a provider or consumer (or both) of a set of defined services. The system implementation of a service can readily be replace or augmented by an application (third-party software). Conversely, the system now calls application software to perform class or object-type specific system operations on data maintained or manipulated by the application. For example, the Cairo user interface binds to application code executing within its own address space[6] to display, print, and render on the system clipboard objects owned by the application.

Similarly, the dream of building software based on reusable components finally becomes possible. Unlike object-oriented programming languages, which typically require a tight *de facto* integration between software components, an object-based system must rigorously specify the interface or *contract* between software components since those components are likely to come from different vendors and to be written in different programming languages. This rigor enables true plug-and-play *componentized* software for the first time.

Cairo–an introduction: What is Cairo? On the one hand, it is simply the next major release of Windows NT. It will have all the bug fixes, performance improvements, and general new bells and whistles that you would expect from a second major version of a popular operating system. On the other hand, Cairo is an incredibly broad yet tightly integrated set of distributed system services that taken as a whole leap-frog current technologies by unifying important areas such as core network services, distributed security, directory services, and groupware functionality via replicated object store. All of these functional areas are based on a single model for distributed storage, management, and invocation of software objects. The Cairo distributed object model is in turn based on an extended, extensible, and upward-compatible version of the OLE 2.0 component object model.

Cairo is a broad and deep product. What follows is a very short and incomplete summary of its approach and capabilities.

Distributed object model: Cairo extends the OLE 2.0 component object model (COM) along a number of important dimensions. First, it provides transparent local and remote object binding via Microsoft RPC.[7] Second, it provides a mechanism for objects implemented

---

[6]As noted below, Cairo also supports out-of-process invocation of objects (whether locally or remotely) for better security and reliability but lower performance.

[7]While OLE 2.0 uses RPC semantics for its communication mechanism, it does not use real RPC and–at least initially–is local only.

in dynamic link libraries (DLLs) to be invoked either in-process (for performance) or out-of-process (including across the network) using a surrogate process and RPC stubs.[8] In-process invocation must be acceptable to both client and server; either can veto it for reasons of security or robustness. Third, it provides an extension mechanism: interfaces and interface implementations can be added to objects at runtime either by the object itself or by other objects. Fourth, it provides system-level support for the OLE 2.0 structured storage model; OLE containers and storages are implemented natively in the file system.

Object support services.: Cairo provides additional support for objects beyond the relatively bare-bones approach of OLE 2.0, services like persistent connections, multi-client support, and multicasting services for one-way connections. It also provides an enhanced version of *monikers,* OLE's opaque naming mechanism, that among other things supports object links that automatically *track down* an object as it moves around the network. Cairo also provides a distributed registration mechanism so that the code that implements an object can be found and loaded when the dormant object (object data, actually) is invoked from storage.

Distributed services infrastructure.: Cairo provides a new file system called the Object File System (OFS). OFS provides very efficient storage of both very small files (even on very large media), multi-streamed files, native storage of OLE 2.0 structured files, and native storage of extensible property sets. Moreover, OFS optionally provides content and property-based indices of all data (optionally calling application-supplied code for indexing of object data on a per-class basis), enabling applications to access their objects by any property at speeds identical to the system indices.

Cairo's distributed file system (DFS) is built on OFS; it provides a global logical "file" namespace for an entire organization, as well as domain-relative and machine-relative naming. The Cairo directory service is simply a well-known OFS folder maintained on one or more domain controllers that is replicated by the standard multi-master replication services available for any data on any OFS volume. Cairo uses Kerberos security at the RPC and SMB levels to maintain two-way authentication and discretionary access controls on all system services, as well as encryption and digital signature services either at the RPC or application level.

Systems Management. Cairo provides a distributed sink-source event system compatible with the OLE 2.0 local event model upon which management tools and applications are easily layered. The system management tools provided as part of the Cairo product are simple extensions of the native browsing and querying tools to minimize the learning curve for system administrators and maximize usability. The management model and interfaces are totally open and extensible and third parties will provide many of the more specialized functions that certain administrators may desire.

Development. While Cairo does not attempt to wrap the entire Win32 API with object semantics, it will provide development tools that implement (and allow arbitrary extensions to) an object-based forms technology that reifies the standard window manager objects (windows, buttons, list boxes, scroll bars, etc.) as true light-weight software components. The

[8] Objects implemented in stand-alone executables (EXEs) always execute in their own process and must be invoked out-of-process, of course.

develop tools will also provide for the visualization and manipulation of arbitrary non-visible software objects. Because the forms technology is based on entirely on COM, it provides language-independent binding and is completely compatibility with the *medium-weight* and *heavy-weight* objects provided by OLE and Cairo. Higher-level tools will also be available for user programming of folder and object behavior.

User interface enhancements. Cairo embodies a vast range of enhancements and extensions to the Windows user interface. For purposes of this paper, it is sufficient to note that the main interface application is a browsing and querying tool that is completely malleable and extensible to the objects that it operates on. Moreover, in addition to per volume content and property indexing, OFS/DFS provides an indexed flat-file database called a *catalog* on a per volume basis and, as defined by administrators, a global catalog that summarize the contents of an arbitrary number of volumes in the enterprise and is fully browseable and queryable.

This is Cairo in an over-flowing nutshell. Keep in mind that Cairo is not a special-purpose distributed operating system. It is simply the second major version of Windows NT.

What about interoperability? Emerging standards for distributed systems in the UNIX and large system market space—products such as OSF's DCE/DME and projects such as the Object Management Group's CORBA—are clearly good for the industry. From Microsoft's perspective, in some cases these technologies are appropriate for PC products and Microsoft will use them. Even to the extent that other technologies are more appropriate to the PC space, distributed system standards are quite useful because they bound potentially nightmarish interoperability problems into a well-defined space.

Microsoft is using technology that is compatible with much of OSF's DCE technology, including RPC, Kerberos, and the specification of SMB-based file and print connectivity.[9] In addition, Microsoft is working with its industry partners such as Digital Equipment Corporation, Hewlett-Packard, Inc., and Siemens-Nixdorf Inc. who are building OFS-based DCE products to make sure that its implementations are fully interoperable. In cooperation with its industry partners, Microsoft will also provide a seamless gateway from the Cairo directory to the CDS/X.500 directory components of DCE.

Compared to DCE, DME is much less mature at this point. Depending on customer demand and industry acceptance, Microsoft will provide interoperability layers or gateways between the system management tools it builds and those provided on DME systems. Third parties will provide the DME suite itself on Microsoft's platforms.

As for OMG, the issue of *CORBA compliance* is generally misunderstood. The OMG object request broker (ORB) is designed to be a gateway between incompatible object systems. As the standard solidifies to the point where interoperability testing becomes possible, and as the market for OMG technology becomes real, Microsoft will make sure that it has the software in place to meet customer demand for interoperability between Cairo objects and OMG-style ORBs.

---

[9]Note, however, that Microsoft has written its own implementations of these technologies and is not–for reasons of licensing cost, size, and speed–using OSF's source code product.

13.4.4 On to IAYF

Microsoft is committed to carrying forward the huge investment of its customers and partners in MS-DOS and Windows technology. The components of WOSA will help solve many of the immediate problems facing customers. The Windows component object model has already emerged in the OLE 2.0 environment and will be extended in the future by the Windows Cairo environment. Cairo, combined with a set of compatibility and interoperability layers for other distributed systems, will for the first time begin to provide Microsoft customers with Information At Your [Their] Fingertips. It's about time.

13.5 SunSoft's Distributed Computing Strategy

13.5.1 A Vision for the 90s and Beyond

The last ten years have seen a revolution in information technology. Users who formerly shared a mini or mainframe computer with hundreds of other users are now accustomed to controlling the same power on their desktops. In just a few years, most enterprises have become complex webs of computers of various sizes, attempting (and often failing) to interoperate through a web of networking technologies. Information technology vendors are quick to offer solutions for the sort of global distributed computing that users require. They have been slower to address the more difficult problem of making all of these solutions work together well on one network.

SunSoft, Inc. is well positioned to meet the challenges of distributed computing in the next decade. As part of Sun Microsystems, Inc., SunSoft pioneered interoperability in mixed-vendor networks and is widely regarded as a leader in open systems. Sun's Open Network Computing (ONC™) Network File Service (NFS ®) distributed file system technology has won industry-wide acceptance as a de facto standard for file sharing in heterogeneous environments, with an installed base exceeding four million nodes in early 1993. Now, SunSoft is dedicated to evolving its Solaris® operating environment to meet the distributed computing needs of information processing users in the 1990s.

The SunSoft vision of distributed computing for the 90s is to make computing with its UNIX® System V Release 4 (SVr4) based Solaris operating system global, mobile, and simple:

- *Global:* Users have transparent access to information and computing resources, such as information repositories, applications, files, printers, and servers without regard to the location of the resource.
- *Mobile:* As users move from location to location they maintain consistent access to the computing resources available to them. The computers they use can move about, disconnecting from the network and easily reconnecting, or they can simply use the closest available computer as if it were their own desktop.
- *Simple:* Administrator resources are utilized efficiently through the use of automated system and network administration. Cost of ownership is further improved through

reducing costs associated with incorporating new technologies as they become available and minimizing end-user training. Key components of SunSoft's Global, Mobile, and Simple distributed computing solution include Federated Services and ONC+™ . These technologies are supported by an underlying framework that provides maximum interoperability and insulates network services from underlying communication protocols. The next sections go into more detail on these technologies.

13.5.2 Solaris Federated Services Overview

Today's demanding business climate frequently requires responses in the fastest possible manner. Likewise, the pace of technological change offers more and more alternatives which solve a specific need for an organization, but which may be different than the technology currently in use. While an organization cannot permit unchecked incompatibility, it is unwise to force one type of computing solution on every problem.

What is required is a way to balance the needs of the larger organization–cost control, maintainability, ease of use–with the needs of the particular user. SunSoft's response has been to design a set of mechanisms we call Federated Services. Figure 13.7 shows how the Federated Services architecture provides Solaris with the ability to support multiple autonomous distributed services in *plug and play* fashion, allowing these services to coexist and cooperate on the network in a manageable, consistent way. Federated Services has the following benefits for Solaris end-users, application developers and administrators:

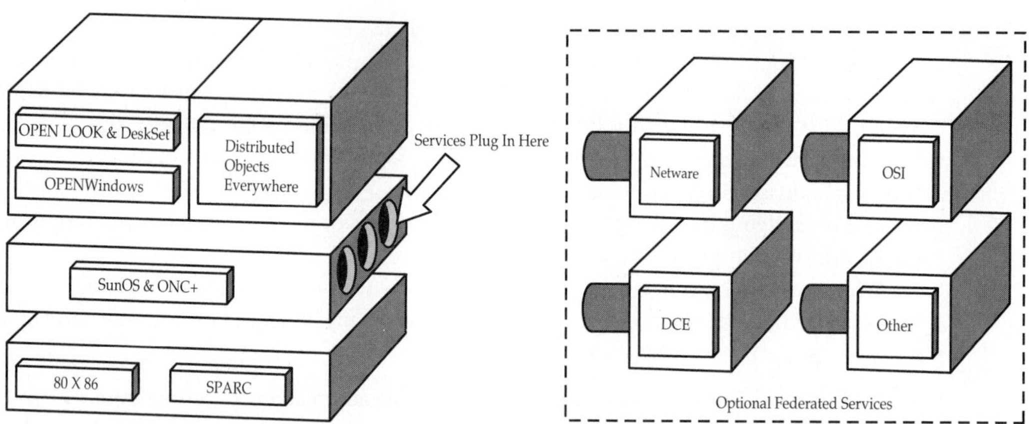

Figure 13.7 Solaris Federated Services architecture allows integrated and manageable support of multi-vendor distributed services.

- Users are empowered by being able to transparently access resources, such as files, servers, and applications, across multivendor global networks.
- Developers build applications that are shielded from the distributed services they use and transparently operate in heterogenous network environments, allowing portability and extension of scope.

- Administrators easily add or replace distributed services, like distributed file systems, without requiring modification of applications, allowing simplified support of heterogenous environments and migration to new technologies.
- Solaris Federated Services Architecture Allows Integrated and Manageable Support of Multivendor Distributed Services
- Federated Services is based on some key assumptions:
- Heterogenous computing is the rule. No single distributed service (for example, file service or naming system) will predominate. Users must use a variety of protocols and services across the enterprise.
- Even if a particular service is *best* today, something better may come along tomorrow. Users will require an operating environment that lets them adopt innovative technologies quickly and easily.

The Solaris Federated Services architecture insures that users will be able to choose the best solutions for their environments today, as well as being able to migrate easily to new and emerging technologies in the future.

13.5.3 The SunSoft Transition to Federation

Federation is a logical extension of the SunSoft distributed computing philosophy. Figure 13.8 illustrates Sun's evolution from NFS, to ONC, ONC+, Federated Services, and ultimately to Distributed Objects Everywhere (DOE).

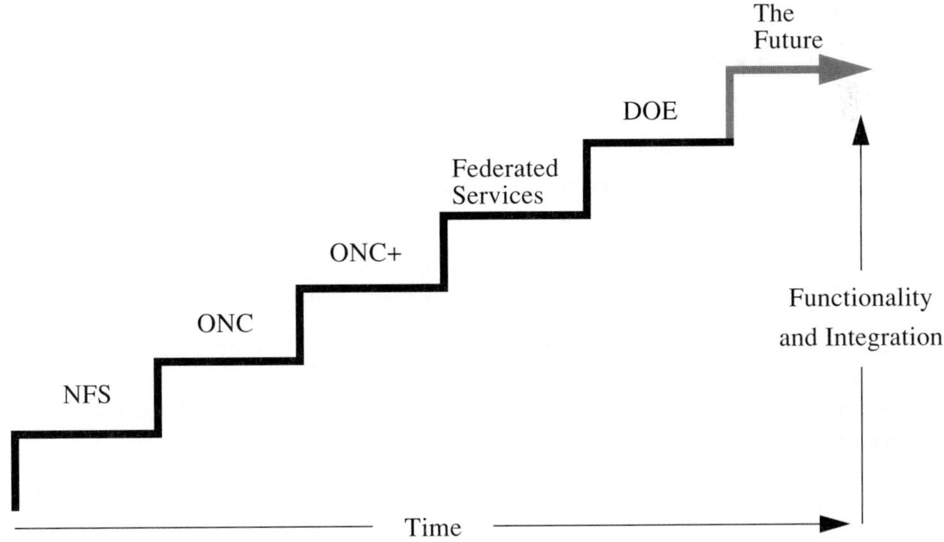

Figure 13.8 The SunSoft evolution to federated services and beyond.

The evolutionary process starts with the ability of NFS to perform filing tasks for heterogenous systems. ONC provided more services including naming and RPC services in this heterogenous environment. ONC+ expanded the scope of ONC, providing services to the heterogenous network from LANs to WANs while improving robustness and power. As Federated Services mature, more services for the heterogenous network are being integrated into the Solaris operating environment.

DOE is a logical extension of federation. DOE benefits from underlying federation technologies that enable it to operate in a wider range of distributed computing environments. More importantly, the DOE focus on interface definition technology for objects brings the power of federation to applications.

13.5.4 Federated Services Defined

- *Definition of Federation:* A federation of services uses interfaces and implementation techniques to enable transparent coexistence or cooperation of those services within systems on a network.
- *Terminology:* Federation is typically accomplished by layering interfaces. Specific vendor specific service types (e.g. Novell NetWare®, OSF DCE™ , Banyan VINES®) are integrated into a federation through FSIs (Federated Service Interfaces). The Federation Interface (FI) abstracts the *essence* of the service type that most (if not all) users of the interface will find appropriate and adequate.

The Solaris Federated Services architecture enables the federation of a variety of distributed computing service *classes* such as those listed below:

- Filing
- Naming
- Security
- Communication

In the following section, the approach to file service federation is discussed as an example[10].

13.5.5 File Services: An Example of Federation

The UNIX operating system uses the file system and file system APIs as a fundamental abstraction mechanism: many things appear as part of the file system. For example, devices and interprocess communication mechanisms are treated as files. Federated file services preserves this aspect of the UNIX operating system.

Originally, the UNIX file system implementation was so much a part of the kernel that only one file system *type* was feasible. In the second half of the 1980s, the vnode and VFS interfaces began to emerge as *de facto* standards for incorporating new file systems types into

[10]For more detailed information on the mechanisms of federation, contact SunSoft, Inc.

the UNIX operating system, based on the success of NFS in both UNIX and non-UNIX operating systems. Many of the non-UNIX implementations of NFS either adapted to interfaces that played a role similar to that of the vnode and VFS interfaces in the host operating system, or modified the host operating system to add analogous interfaces.

The vnode and VFS interfaces provide federation of file systems by permitting *coexistence*. However, to be transparent, a minimal form of *cooperation* is required: the file tree must appear to be a single, large file system to applications and users. Since the UNIX system originally used the concept of *mounting* as a means to construct a single file tree from file trees residing on multiple disk drives, extending the machinery to enable mount points leading to a different file system type was straightforward. Thus, in the execution of *open,* the kernel may access a number of different file system types before it obtains the vnode for the file being opened. Subsequent *read, write,* operations go directly to the service type for the file itself. This is a case where cooperation is a useful illusion: the file system types do not communicate directly, but are administered so the kernel can unify them.

Figure 13.9 illustrates the Solaris SVr4 implementation of the vnode and VFS interfaces.

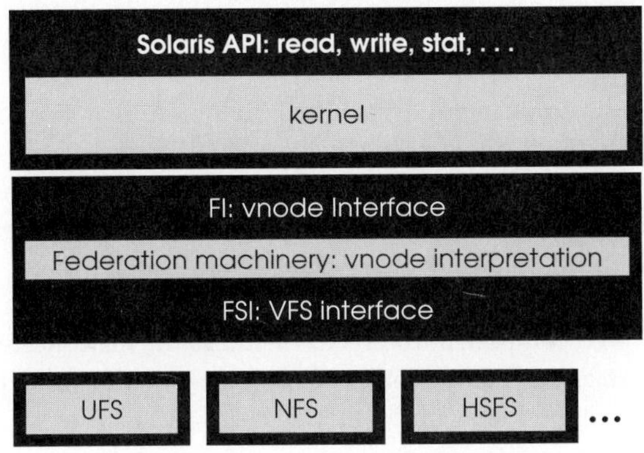

Figure 13.9 Solaris SVr4 Implementation of the vnode interface.

Direct cooperation between file system types is both possible and useful with the vnode and VFS interfaces: file systems can be layered, much in the spirit of STREAMS but without dynamic stacking and unstacking. This means that new features can be provided ubiquitously without having to change existing file system services.

The current vnode and VFS interfaces have proven themselves in service and have enabled value-added specialized file system types from system software vendors, successful businesses for NFS vendors, and businesses in other value-added file system types. Based on this usage, several areas for improvement of the interfaces have been identified, and a UNIX International working group is developing requirements for further evolution of the interfaces.

SunSoft recognizes that federation interfaces must be industry standards to achieve their fullest value. The federation architecture is consistent with the UNIX International ATLAS™ model for distributed computing. SunSoft federation activities include leveraging existing standards when possible and working with standards bodies to develop appropriate solutions where none exists.

13.5.6 Solaris Core Distributed Service: ONC+

In addition to the Federated Services architecture, Solaris includes a set of core distributed computing services called Open Network Computing Plus (ONC+). ONC+ is a family of networking protocols and distributed services which provide the foundation for distributed computing within Solaris. ONC+ is fully compatible with widely installed ONC and includes new capabilities for filing, naming, security, administration, and distributed application development. SunSoft is dedicated to evolving ONC+ to support global, mobile and simple computing.

ONC+ became available in Solaris in July of 1992. ONC+ has been embraced by the UNIX International standards body as a part of the UI-ATLAS model for distributed computing. It is also a component of the Common Open Systems Environment (COSE) being spearheaded by leading UNIX vendors in the industry today.

13.5.7 ONC+ Components in Solaris

13.5.7.1 The NFS Distributed File Service

NFS is an industry-standard distributed file system that provides transparent access to remote files and directories across the network. The NFS protocols have been widely adopted in the industry. Users can access files using NFS on PCs, workstations, minicomputers, mainframes, and supercomputers, independent of the underlying operating systems being run. In addition, NFS is currently installed on over four million systems today. It is a truly heterogeneous distributed file service.

The NFS component of ONC+ includes the major features summarized below:

- *Security:* NFS optionally incorporates several authentication mechanisms including the Diffie-Hellman Public Key based mechanism, or the Kerberos™ system from MIT's Project Athena. Through the use of this capability, NFS protects against fraudulent access.
- *Performance:* NFS includes many performance enhancements such as improved write throughput and a multi-threading capability. Multithreading improves performance by allowing NFS to perform multiple tasks in parallel, instead of one at a time.
- *Scalability:* The NFS distributed file system can support groups of users on small local area networks, departmental workgroups, and enterprise environments with thousands of users.
- *Uniform File Names Across the Enterprise:* This feature ensures that files can be accessed uniformly no matter where they reside on the global network. File names do not have to change just because a file is moved to a new location.
- *Supports Wide Area Network Connections:* With this feature, NFS clients will be able to access files on NFS servers over wide area networks in the same way they access files on local NFS servers.

- *File Caching:* A client file caching service is provided to improve the perceived performance of repeated access to the same files. A client request for data is cached on the local disk for more efficient subsequent access.
- *File Locking:* NFS provides a file locking mechanism that preserves file integrity. Locking insures that files are protected from concurrent updates by multiple users.
- *Diskless Client Support:* NFS supports diskless clients. The benefit of this is that diskless clients can share multiple server disks instead of having to support expensive local disks of their own.

Together, these features enable the NFS distributed file service to fully support small to large enterprise computing environments.

13.5.7.2 The NIS+ Enterprise Naming Service

The Network Information Service Plus (NIS+) enterprise naming service is a replacement for widely-installed ONC NIS. ONC NIS has been deployed on dozens of hardware and software platforms and has an installed base exceeding two million users. Like its predecessor, NIS+ serves as a central repository for information on users, systems, printers, and other network entities. Some of the major features of NIS+ include:

- *Hierarchical domain creation:* For organizations desiring centralized administration, NIS+ allows the entire network to be treated as a single domain or administrative entity.
- *Automated administration operations:* NIS+ includes a flexible administrative interface that facilitates and automates administrative operations including creating directories and setting up domains and server replication.
- *Distributed server administration:* The NIS+ command-line or programmatic interface allows authorized administrators to interactively administer and add, delete, or change information in NIS+ servers, from systems across the domain or enterprise network.
- *Distributed access to NIS+ information:* The NIS+ command-line and programmatic interface also allows authorized users direct read/write access to information served by NIS+. This makes it significantly easier and faster to change NIS+ tables and directories on servers.
- *High performance replication:* The NIS+ replication model provides high performance, availability and reliability for naming service operations.
- *Security:* NIS+ is designed to protect the information in its directories and tables from unauthorized access. NIS+ includes mechanisms for authentication and authorization of clients.
- *Compatibility with NIS:* NIS+ has been designed to be a replacement for environments and systems using NIS. It includes a number of capabilities that allow NIS clients and servers to coexist with and easily migrate to NIS+. These capabilities, taken together, provide a number of options for NIS/NIS+ compatibility and migration.

13.5.7.3 Transport Independent Remote Procedure Calls

Remote Procedure Calls or RPCs, are viewed as building blocks for distributed applications. In many implementations, RPC mechanisms are intimately tied to the underlying network transport protocol. ONC+ includes a *transport independent* RPC mechanism called transport independent RPC (TI-RPC). TI-RPC was co-developed by UNIX Systems Laboratories and SunSoft and is part of the UNIX System V Interface Definition (SVID) Issue 3.

TI-RPC is backward compatible with ONC RPC, SunSoft's initial RPC technology. Considered a *de facto* standard, ONC RPC currently enjoys an installed base of over three million systems. TI-RPC also has growing industry support. The source code is available on the Internet via anonymous FTP.

TI-RPC provides *run time* transport independence. What this means is that an application can select whatever transport mechanism is available on the system at run time. With other RPC implementations, applications must be compiled specifically for *each* transport that will be used. The result is that several versions of the same application must be made available for use on different types of networks. The fact that TI-RPC is run time transport independent means that only one version of the application must be provided. This has the obvious benefit of reducing complexities imposed by maintaining multiple versions of the same application.

TI-RPC achieves its transport protocol independence through its use of the Transport Layer Interface (TLI). TLI is the standard UNIX System V networking interface.

Exchanging data between multivendor systems poses problems arising from dissimilar architectures and hardware configurations. *EXternal Data Representation* or XDR, another component of the TI-RPC technology set, is an architecture-independent method of representing data, resolving differences in data byte ordering, data type size, and so on.

13.5.7.3.1 Secure RPC

Secure RPC provides network authentication for RPC, enabling secure distributed applications and network services. Secure RPC can be configured to use either the Diffie-Hellman or Kerberos 4.0 authentication mechanisms.

13.5.7.3.2 Distributed Application Developer Tools

A number of developer tools are available from SunSoft as well as third parties to assist developers in using TI-RPC to build distributed applications. rpcgen is a TI-RPC code generator compiler that is included in ONC+. It comes bundled with Solaris, ONC+ source and TI-RPC source from SunSoft. In addition, several third parties have developed their own RPC code generator compilers that support TI-RPC. For example Netwise, Inc. offers a product called the RPC TOOL™ and Noblenet, Inc. offers a product called EZ-RPC™ . The ONC+ RPC Application Toolkit is also available as an unbundled product from SunSoft.

These tools make it easier to develop client/server distributed applications that benefit from the communication facilities provided by TI-RPC. Instead of programming directly to the TI-RPC interface, the developer creates what is called an *interface specification* that is written in an specific *interface specification language.* The developer describes the interfaces to the client and server programs using the interface specification language. The specification is then fed into the code generator compiler. The compiler output is the C language client and server routines. These routines are then compiled in to the client and server components of the application using a standard C compiler.

13.5.8 Insulation from Low-Level Protocols

In addition to Federated Services and ONC+, the Solaris Distributed Computing Framework supports multiple protocol stacks for maximum interoperability and insulates network services from underlying communication protocols. A particular stack of protocols can be selected at runtime to match the services available on another system. This is true both at the remote procedure call (RPC) level and for the underlying network transport protocols.

13.5.8.1 Modularity at Protocol Level

Traditionally, distributed applications, whether using RPCs or the older Berkeley sockets, have been dependent on a specific network transport. The Solaris architecture again uses a standardized interface to shield applications from the underlying low-level protocols. This interface is the System V Transport Layer Interface (TLI), equivalent to the X/Open Transport Interface (XTI).

TLI provides a common means of accessing connection-oriented or connectionless transport services. Addressing is opaque, so applications do not depend on any of the properties of a particular addressing scheme, such as Internet protocol port numbers. This vastly simplifies the implementation of networked applications.

13.5.8.2 Kernel Interfaces

A number of standard interfaces and frameworks in the Solaris kernel facilitate the development of new device drivers and protocols. The reduced development costs ensure that a large selection of connectivity products will be available for Solaris.

Developers can gain access to low level protocols through the Transport Provider Interface (TPI) and the Data Link Provider Interface (DLPI). Developers can also provide alternative implementations of these low-level protocols. A protocol implementation offers its services to the system through one of these provider interfaces.

The STREAMS framework provides a consistent and powerful set of basic mechanisms for implementing protocol stacks and device drivers. While Solaris also supports the Berkeley Sockets mechanism, STREAMS are the native facilities of UNIX SVr4 and of Solaris 2.X.

Solaris supports the UNIX SVr4 standards for interfaces between device drivers and the system kernel. Device Driver Interface (DDI) and Device Kernel Interface (DKI) provide longevity and portability to conforming drivers.

13.5.9 New Models of Distributed Computing–Distributed Objects

Project DOE–Distributed Objects Everywhere is a major SunSoft initiative to bring the leverage of open systems to the application arena. DOE extends the Solaris model with the full range of capabilities, services and partnerships required by an enterprise-ready, distributed object environment. Distributed object computing will provide significant and far reaching advantages over the traditional monolithic computing model of today.

DOE enables developer innovation, making it possible to build and sustain new, highly functional applications, and to easily construct successive generations of those applications on the foundations that precede them. DOE provides a software framework for a wide spectrum of solutions and supports standards-based interoperability within computing environments.

DOE is being developed according to standards defined by the Object Management Group (OMG).

13.5.9.1 DOE Features

DOE includes a broad set of features providing for the support and integration of object-based applications in a distributed, client-server computing environment. Among those capabilities and services are:

- *A Distributed, object-oriented computation model:* Provides the flexibility to support object-oriented facilities across heterogeneous distributed networks
- *Location independence:* Protocol and network transport transparency enables complete freedom for object location
- *Scalability:* Computing platforms and networks can range in scale from small work-groups to enterprise networks
- *Support for full interoperability between applications:* 100 percent compliance with the OMG standard for complete object and application interoperability
- *Standard interfaces which allow interchangeability:* Leverages the object-oriented benefit of information hiding and extensibility to permit graceful evolution of objects and applications
- *Full range of services:* Security, persistence and naming
- Framework: A sound architecture based upon the Object Management Group Object Request Broker (ORB) standard for distributed object management
- *Tools:* Allow migration, application development, and system management

Figure 13.10 illustrates the architecture of how DOE services are layered.

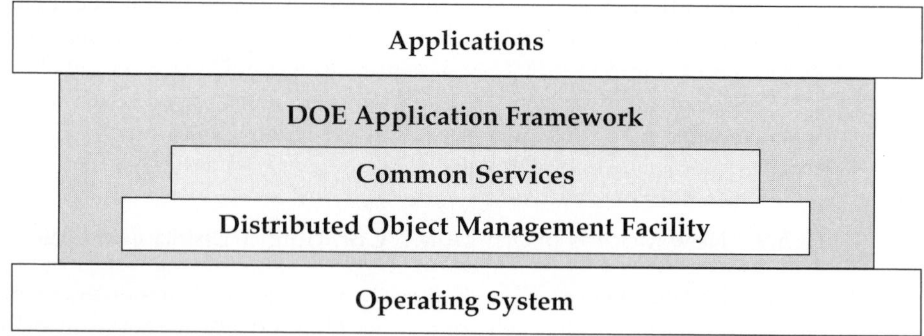

Figure 13.10 DOE architecture.

Through Project DOE, SunSoft and Sun Microsystems have defined a path to the future of objects. By providing a framework for distributed object solutions Project DOE will enable greater interoperability between systems and simplify application architectures.

The last ten years have seen a revolution in information technology. The 90s will likely see even more dramatic changes as networks grow in size and complexity and as the industry moves towards new paradigms in computing. With Federated Services, ONC+, and DOE, Solaris will be ready for the future with an architecture that easily and transparently supports rapid change, allowing users to quickly benefit from innovation in technology.

13.6 Conclusions

The previous four sections illustrate that vendors are aware of the problems users are facing in developing distributed applications and implementing distributed computing infrastructures. Vendors are planning to develop distributed services infrastructures, application development tools, and systems management tools. It is clear that systems vendors have to worry about their installed base and provide a migration path from the installed base to future technologies. It is very encouraging to see that these vendors are working with each other so ensure compatibility with industry standards. HP, IBM, and Sun are three major players behind the common open software environment (cose); Microsoft is working with HP and using technology that is compatible with much of OSF's DCE; SunSoft's Solaris Federated Services architecture will include support for OSF/DCE and Novell Netware; and HP, IBM, and SunSoft are all members of OMG. Object technology is a key element in the distributed computing strategy of all of these vendors.

We hope that one day organizations will be able to buy components from different vendors to create distributed computing environments that meet their business needs. The consumer electronics industry seems to have solved this problem. After all, most of us buys components like amplifiers, Television sets, CD players, and so on from different vendors to create our personal entertainment systems at home.

Imagine

Imagine there is no incompatibility
It's easy if you comply
Software without walls
Accessible through GUIs

Imagine business applications
Implemented in a day

You may say I'm a dreamer
But I'm not the only one
I hope someday information systems
Will be plug and play

Imagine no inter-vendor squabbles
It isn't hard to do

No API wars
And interoperability will rule

Imagine all the information
At our fingertips night and day

You may say I'm a dreamer
But I'm not the only one
I hope someday all vendors
Will provide interoperable solutions

Sally A. Biles is a senior marketing manager for ONC+ networking technology at SunSoft, Inc. a subsidiary of Sun Microsystems, Inc. She is an honors graduate of the University of California, Santa Cruz, and received her bachelors degree in Computer and Information Science in 1983. She has ten years experience in network engineering and marketing. She has been an employee of Sun Microsystems since 1989.

Raman Khanna is the director of Networking Systems at Stanford University. He is responsible for the design, implementation, and management of a campus-wide data communication network, distributed computing infrastructure, and academic computing environment on Stanford campus. Raman has special interest in the integration of personal workstations in distributed computing environments.

Raman holds a BS in Electrical Engineering, an MS in Computer Science, and an MBA in High Technology Management. He has been working, consulting, and lecturing in computing and data communication fields since 1980. Raman is contributing editor of a recent book on FDDI published by John Wiley and one of the contributors to the Internet System Handbook published by Addison Wesley. Raman also teaches courses on Computer Networks and Distributed Computing at the UC Berkeley Extension program.

Mike Mathews is the Product Marketing Manager in the Distributed Computing Program of HP's Open Systems Software Division (OSDD), part of the Standard Technology Group located in Cupertino, California. He is responsible for the product management of higher level (object and application) services designed to work with HP's implementations of the OSF/DCE and OMG/CORBA standards. In addition, he manages internal HP partnerships, external alliances and standards activities relevant to HP's Distributed Computing Program.

Robert J. McCann is a Program Manager in Software Marketing for IBM in the US. Based in Atlanta, he has been actively involved in the introduction and marketing of IBM's open systems strategies and capabilities. He is now focusing on the distributed transaction processing environment.

Mark Ryland is a Senior Program Manager in the Advanced Systems Division of Microsoft. He is part of the Windows Cairo design team. He focuses on issues related to integration with outside technologies and technical communication with key vendors and customers that will be most affected by the Cairo project. Before joining the Cairo team Ryland worked as a Senior Architectural Engineer in Microsoft Federal Systems.

Ryland claims to know nothing about computers beside what little he has learned from goofing around with them. He is actually a reformed lawyer with a B.A. in philosophy from the University of San Diego and a J.D. from U.C. Berkeley (Boalt Hall).

Chapter 14

Systems Management Strategies

Wallace Colyer
Walter Wong
Carnegie Mellon University

14.1 Introduction

This chapter builds on Chapter 5 on Distributed System Management by examining strategies used in managing distributed systems. The discussion of the strategies is organized by the management categories formulated in the earlier chapter. A discussion of the various system management models follows. Finally, an extensive case study of the management strategies implemented in the Andrew System is included. Although there is already a chapter on the Andrew project, this section complements that chapter and provides an example of good and bad things to do in distributed management systems.

As with the previous distributed systems management chapter, network management is included mainly for completeness and the reader interested specifically in network management should refer to Appendix D. Further discussion of distributed management strategies can also be found in Chapter 9 on Project Athena.

14.2 Strategies

In the process of examining and evaluating strategies for system management, there are several, sometimes interrelated, sometimes divergent, themes that stand out. These themes are automation, recovery, scalability, passivity, and simplicity.

The computing industry has developed around a need to eliminate humans performing repetitive steps that require a great deal of precision. In managing these computing systems, it is not good to create a system which again requires a human to perform repetitive tasks which would be much better suited for automation. Instead, it would be a great time savings to automate tasks and delegate tasks to tools. Additionally, automation reduces the chance of simple errors, such as incorrectly typed data. Automated systems can perform extensive error checking and greatly help to reduce the chance of human error. Also, if a mistake is made by an automated task, usually that error can be more fixed easier. The procedures which introduced the error are well known and it is usually just as simple to reverse the error. Finally, automated systems help to smooth the transition of system managers. Well developed automated tasks should continue to run without intervention for a considerable period of time. They need to be documented and understandable to speed the learning process and reduce the magic needed to run a system. Automation is a necessary component of any scalable management system.

Scalability is commonly mentioned in the context of distributed computing. In fact, one of the benefits being sought by acquiring distributed systems is the ability to scale. This is because many distributed systems are designed so that low cost units can be easily added to create larger systems. In distributed systems management, the need for scalability applies to all aspects of the system, and considerable over design of system management system to shield against future growth is a good idea. Any methodologies or tools really need to be scalable enough to handle not only the load that exist today, but it also has to be able to handle considerably more than the expected future load. It it not uncommon for distributed systems to grow an order of magnitude or more than the expected growth of the system. Management systems must be scalable enough so that they do not detract from their application's scalability.

The "undo" command which has become very popular in applications today is also an important aspect of distributed management systems. Recoverability is important because no matter how rigorous testing is, there will eventually be a case where a catastrophic problem is not detected until after a system is put into production. When that happens, it is essential to be able to restore the system to a previously working state and do it in a quick and efficient manner. In general, it is almost always best to undo the harmful change, however, given the scale of distributed systems, it may not always be practical. Implementation of the undo procedure can take many forms. For example, it can be done by rolling the system back to a previous state from backups, or by playing back a record of the changes in reverse. In a system where changes are layered upon each other, undo can occur by removing the new layers. It is a reality of many large systems that changes are constantly occurring. It is not always possible to replace the system with a complete image from a previous period or roll the changes back out through a reply attempt. Layered systems which keep all the changes made in a period and document them well provide the greatest amount of flexibility, but they use considerably more resources.

The necessity of doing work constantly is the enemy of the system manager. The more management work which needs to be done, the more problems that a system will have in scaling. If the work is to be distributed to all the clients, it must not interfere with the work the computers are actually there for. Passive management systems encourage keeping day-to-day work down to a minimum. Passive management requires that a more initial work be done so that systems can be left to run themselves. For passive management to be successful, the manager needs to plan out what is necessary to keep things running smoothly and automate the necessary tasks. Ideally, once the automatic tasks start running, the manager can concentrate on handling any unforeseen emergency that has arisen or use the time to plan for the future. Passive system management significantly improves scalability since adding another machine to the management environment should not be a high cost endeavor.

Keeping things simple eases the task of explaining and understanding a system. Simple solutions are the easy ones to port. They tend to end up being the systems which are actually used because they can be implemented and adjusted to changing conditions. Commonly, there is less room for error in a simple system. Furthermore, with the extremely diverse computing facilities which exist, the simple solutions can most easily be adopted from platform to platform. Unfortunately, simplicity often conflicts with the details necessary to achieve the scalability or even automation. Sometimes simplicity is sacrificed, but that should only be after careful examination.

14.2.1 User Management

The types of facilities made available for helping users vary greatly. The most common forms include the following:

- help desks where users can come in person or call for help
- electronic mail addresses where users can send questions
- on-line help systems
- central documentation depositories
- on-line and personal training, training through video tapes
- vendor help hot-lines
- handouts
- bulletin boards and distribution lists for discussion and announcement of official information
- consultants on call to help with problems
- hypertext information depositories
- expert systems

Most sites use a variety of these techniques to help their users.

With user management, a good rule of thumb to follow is "help the users help themselves." This can be implemented in a number of different ways. First, there is the use of a user contributed environment where users may submit software to be available publicly. Examples of these include the bbn-public at BBN (Schaefer, 1992), and /usr/contributed on the Andrew System. These environments help expand the amount of application software environment available and usually can be done with relatively little central support. This method also provides a testing ground of software. When it becomes apparent that software in the contributed environment is important to the organization, that software can migrate from the contributed environment to the fully supported one.

Another example of getting users to help themselves is through the use of electronic bulletin boards or newsgroups. Users send queries to these locations and any users who know the answer are free to reply. Some sites use the Zephyr notification service to achieve a *real-time* user supported question and answer system. These mechanisms often encourage the creation of frequently asked questions (FAQ) summaries.

By automating normal request channels, users can perform more actions on their own. Rather than having users send mail or call a system manager when a change in a system attribute regarding them is desired, systems can be built which use the same decision making process that the human at the other end uses to automate the process. The user gets the change done in a much shorter period and the system administrator did not have to field a call or respond to mail. Some systems, such as the system at the University of Pittsburgh, go so far as to allow users to create their own accounts and the different computer systems they use. The University of Michigan and MIT both have systems which create accounts for the users and allow them to choose their own user id. Of course, if systems are built for users to use directly, they must have simple, understandable user interfaces and be well documented. Allowing the users to do more of the tasks that are normally left to system managers can lift a great deal of the burden off of a system administration staff and the users will often appreciate the increased flexibility and response time.

Often in trying to create simple interfaces, the need for automation and use by the more sophisticated systems managers are forgotten. Early interfaces to user management systems would only allow one user to be added at a time through their interfaces. While this is useful if there is only a small number of users to be added, it becomes extremely tedious if a thousand people need to be entered at one time, as many universities do for incoming students. While some systems support creating multiple accounts in batch, there are those that forget about removing accounts en-masse.

14.2.2 Task Management

Task management has two major categories: process management and monitoring. Process management controls the process of starting, stopping, and controlling jobs while monitoring ensures that the jobs are running properly and that there are adequate resources for them to keep running.

A simple implementation of a process management system is the UNIX cron facility. It starts jobs at specified intervals and then forgets about them. Another trivial process management system implementation consists of a script that continually loops and restarts any process that exit.

Often, a more complex task management system is required, especially in distributed systems. While a good deal of research has been done investigating how user processes can be scheduled, load balanced and run in a distributed environment, little work has been done in the configuration and *baby-sitting* of system level processes in a distributed system. The distributed task management system should not only start jobs and restart jobs that abnormally exit, but should also be able to notify someone when jobs fail. Waiting for an operator or one of the users to notice that a process has stopped running and take action to restart can create long and unnecessary service disruptions. An authenticated network interface for reconfiguring and rescheduling is also necessary for a distributed environment. With hundreds of servers running on many machines it is not feasible to have to login to every machine to make a simple change.

Good monitoring facilities is an extremely important part of task management. Monitoring facilities can actually automate the recovery process in the event of failure. For many fault conditions the solutions are easily automated. When a disk fills up beyond some specified level, data can be automatically moved to other disks or unnecessary data can be removed to clear up space. When a server dies, it can be restarted. Any automated monitoring system should also have a notification service to inform secondary systems and finally humans in the event of a failure that could not be corrected automatically. It is important that records be kept of fault conditions which were corrected automatically so the process can be reviewed in case of unexpected problems.

14.2.3 Software Management

There is a division in the software management area between application software management and workstation administration. At the core, the same problem exists and many of the distribution and configuration issues are the same, however, workstation administration tends to be more complex as a greater amount of customization is required in addition to having to handle the initial operating system bootstrap process.

14.2.3.1 Workstation Administration

The simplest approach to workstation administration is cloning. Cloning is simply setting up a single machine and then copying that configuration to any number of other machines, and as such can be done without any additional tools or infrastructure. Cloning is simple and effective as long as configurability of the cloned hosts is not an issue. There has been work done to customize cloned UNIX workstations (Jones, 1991), but as the clone deviates from the original, the benefits gained from cloning decrease. To continue using the cloning system and also do customization requires that many master images be kept around to copy for each configuration option. When cloning becomes impractical, a system is developed which applies customizations directly from the vendor distribution. This makes it easier to identify and apply changes with future operating system upgrades.

Managing diskless workstations is really a specialized category of the cloning process since many workstations are simultaneously working on a copy of the same operating system image. In essence, they are a simple extension of single system management. Although workstations may be distributed widely, the management is still done centrally and works around many of the distributed systems problems, namely distribution and synchronization. Similarly, many see X terminals as another way of being able to centralize almost all of the management tasks. Both these approaches effectively make the remote machine the equivalent to a terminal.

In order to address the failings of diskless and X terminals, more sophisticated approaches have been developed. Most of these approaches are generally file based.There is generally a configuration file which lists what files should be copied from what location. Modification of the destination file is generally not performed and, if modification is at all allowed, it is done through *scripts* that execute native commands. An example of this approach is package (Yount, 1986), which will be discussed in the Andrew case study section, later in this chapter.

A common simplification is the *dataless* workstation. The underlying concept is that the workstation has a local disk, however, the information on that local disk can be reconstructed either from some cloning process or a more sophisticated configuration management system. There is no information kept on the workstation which is not also housed in some central location which can then be replaced in case of a disk or other catastrophic failure. There is no user data stored directly on a dataless workstation. The users use distributed filesystems to store their data. Data which is moved to local storage is done for performance reasons. Applications and portions of the operating system which are used often are on the local disk of the workstation while less used ones are kept on distributed filesystems. Some maintenance tools are also kept in local storage to help with troubleshooting. A dataless workstation can be obtained by cloning, but this does not have to be the case. Sophisticated configuration management systems can be used to permit a great deal of customization, but copies of the configuration files must be stored centrally.

Finally, one of the major failings of workstation administration is the lack of standards for the initial operating system load. Many operating systems, especially the PC[1] ones, do not have the capability of being installed over the network. Even the UNIX machines that have procedures, rarely specify the methods used and provide methods for customization. Often, even different models of the same vendors product will have drastically different procedures for network loads. There also tends to be an assumption that the operating system will be installed on the machine that the distribution media is read from. The whole concept of remote installation is still in its infancy. Ideally, one would be able to set aside any class of machine that could act as a download server for any class of machine and the operating system could be loaded onto its disk.

14.2.3.2 Application Software Management

Application software is usually easier to manage than operating system software. The diversity of configurations is less of an issue. Application software has more general configuration parameters for site specific changes. For example, an application software package may want to know a list of available printers or allow for a system wide default font. Any further customization to the software is generally done through user *preferences* which are stored in a per user configuration area. It is unusual for there to be machine by machine differences for the same application software in a common distributed environment, but the capacity for dealing with this issue should not be ignored. It is best for the application to deal with those differences at run time because many sites produce common application environments on distributed filesystems and leave no room for customization of those packages on a per machine basis.

Many application software installation procedures make assumptions that the location the package is installed into will be the location it is run from. Taking into consideration that there may be separate installation and run-time areas allows for much flexibility. It is common that software is not installed directly on each machine, but is distributed by a separate distribution system. The installation systems which are provided often work very well for the manager of a single system, but they quickly fall apart in distributed systems. Due to the lack of standardization of installation procedures, information about the machine the software was initially installed on may get exported to other machines. This often causes unexpected behavior on the other machines. As a result, the installation must be manually done and the installation process must be picked apart to find out what it is doing. The more complex the installation, the more time it takes. The installer now has to go through and find out what the

[1]This includes the Macintosh and DOS/Windows operating systems.

installation procedure would be doing under different circumstances and try to repeat it in a more machine independent manner.

14.2.3.3 Compartmentalization

Compartmentalization is an important concept in software management. Compartmentalization consists of two parts: categorization and separation. All the components of software packages are categorized together, and therefore, all the components (e.g. files and directories) of a package can be associated with the package. In addition, different applications are separated and local customizations are kept separate. Where local customizations become separated from vendor packages, the system often becomes layered. In a layered system management approach, each layer of customization must be distinct from the other, but they build on top of each other to represent a consistent image.

The real point behind compartmentalization is the localization of changes and different aspects of the system in such a way that upgrades will not automatically undo all the work that has been done in building the custom environment. The categorization lets all the packages and their changes be identified to help speed the process of integration in future versions. There are often large numbers of these modifications. In large systems, the number of individual files which comprise the installed software and configuration information number in the thousands. Keeping track of the modifications and additions, why they were made, and all the different files which were changed is very difficult. This is especially the case since a single application may install files all over the file system. When the files are all managed individually even if accurate records it can be next to impossible to manage the system.

A very common method of managing these files is to compartmentalize or break them up into discrete objects. The objects contain sets of related files. Each object is a manageable unit and the method the objects are introduced to the environment, how they are laid out, and other requirements are well specified. Preferably each of the objects is independent of each other, but if not the relationship between objects should be identified and there should be a mechanism for describing the relationships. In the ideal situation each object is self-contained within a portion of the file system and does not interact with any other objects, but that is rarely the case.

In addition to the preservation of changes, compartmentalization provides a way of distributing the management tasks. As the objects remain independent of (or at least non-conflicting with) each other, multiple people or groups of people can work on a problem, each in a different object, without interfering with each other. As with other object oriented approaches this approach when well specified and documented allows the work of other people to be built upon and increase productivity.

14.2.3.4 Distribution Methods: Push versus Pull

There are two fundamental methods of network distribution of software and configuration information. They are push and pull. The push method of distribution has a central service actively distributing changes out to distributed locations. The central location has knowledge of the workstations to distribute to, what needs to be distributed, and on what schedule. In the push model, the distributed workstations are passive while the central service is active. On the other hand, in the pull method, the distributed workstations are active and it is the servers that are active. The pull model has each workstation polling the central service to pick up modifications. The distributed workstation is responsible for scheduling, distribution, and selection. The conflict between push versus pull is representative of the conflict between centralized and decentralized management which is addressed over and over in discussions of management issues in distributed systems.

These two methods address fundamentally different approaches. Push and pull systems are often suitable to different situations as they have different advantages. Pull systems tend to be more scalable and lend to greater flexibility and customization by the individual workstations. Push systems offer greater control for the central administrators, but tend to be less scalable.

The most robust systems are built utilizing a combination of both methods to take advantage of each of their strengths.

14.2.3.4.1 Push

The push method of distribution has the central administrative authority *pushing* all the changes out to the distributed workstations. Scheduling and configuration management is handled by the central authority.

In the typical push model, a central machine or set of machines keep track of the configuration of a set of workstations. Either all workstations they manage are configured identically or the central authority maintains a database of the different configurations of each machine. The central authority will determine on what schedule which machines will be updated and maintains information about which machines have been updated successfully and what failures have occurred. These systems will then either retry updates which have failed or will flag them for an administrator to take care of.

In most of these systems, only the central authority can modify configuration information for individual machines. Some more complicated systems allow some degree of customization by the users or owners of workstations. They allow certain information in the central database to be modified directly by authorized individuals.

Push systems offer the greatest amount of control for central administrators, but as systems grow they tend not to scale very well because they require an active central system to scale with the system. They work well in tightly managed workstation environments where it is very important to maintain consistent and operational workstations. In these environments the ratio of system managers to machines is generally high.

The central machines which manage remote configurations are often designed with small numbers of workstations in mind. As the number of workstations increases and the number of custom configurations increase the load on both the central configuration management servers and the system administrators grows substantially.

Often the load on the system administrator is lessened by creating a standard set of customizations and not allowing custom configurations for each new workstation. Unfortunately, this often does not meet the specialized needs of many workstation users.

14.2.3.4.2 Pull

Individual workstations are responsible for updating their own software and configuration information with the pull method of distribution. The scheduling and configuration management tasks are handled by the target workstation rather than a central service.

The typical pull model has each workstation maintain a schedule to poll the central service looking for changes. The schedule may be hourly, daily, weekly, on reboot, or only manually started by the workstation user or owner. The workstation contacts the remote configuration service to get updates. Generally the individual workstation maintains its own configuration information, though this information may be stored on a central service or there may be some set of local information for the workstation and a set for the central service.

The workstation will use the configuration information it either stored locally or pulled from a central service along with information about the state of the central service to determine what needs to be updated. After determining what needs to be updated, the workstation will begin to update its configuration using files and information from the central service.

In the event of an error the workstation may reschedule the updates, leave notice for the user or workstation owner to take care of the problem or send notice to the central system managers.

Often the central service is only a distributed filesystem with configuration files and software. The workstation will check configuration information on the filesystem to determine if there have been any changes since it last updated then copy any files which have changed.

Pull systems generally allow a great deal of configurability and customization for each machine. Since each workstation is making the determination of what to do, a great deal of the load on the central machines is reduced. These systems tend to be much more scalable, though if the scheduling is not done well it is possible to overload the central service through a storm of configuration requests.

If each workstation is scheduling updates independently of the other workstations or of the central service, it is possible for a large number of the workstations to request updates at the same time and overload the service. Consider updates that occur on reboot. It is not uncommon for a power failure to cause large numbers of workstations to reboot simultaneously. In a pull system which updates on reboot, a major power failure can easily cause the central facility to be overloaded. The failure conditions in these circumstances have been known to lead to critical overload of the systems which can not be corrected without manual intervention.

If the critical overload problem is solved through planning to ensure either the load of a massive update can be tolerated or to prevent this type of occurrence, pull systems can be very successful. They are ideal for systems where the ratio of system managers to workstations is very low. In these environments, it is important to keep the incremental cost of each new additional workstation very low. Often there is a central organization which maintains the workstations, but ownership is distributed and there are extremely diverse needs for the use of the workstations requiring different configurations.

14.2.3.4.3 Push and Pull

The push system is very good at maintaining control centrally, but because it tends to require the central service to do the majority of the work it does not scale very well. On the other hand, pull systems scale very well when used properly, but the central system maintains very little control.

You want to have a greater degree of control over the servers in a distributed system as their failure has a much greater impact on the system as a whole. In this case, the push system seems like a much more reasonable approach. It gives control and helps to ensure that the servers are running with the proper configuration.

A much better system can be created with a combination of the push and pull models. A typical combined model has a central system which maintains configuration information and manages the scheduling. The distributed machines are either activated by the central machines or the negotiate and follow scheduling information with the central service. The central service is then queried for configuration information and the distributed machines use that information to determine whether they need to be updated. Any files which need to be updated are then pulled over by the workstations.

This gives much of the control gained in a typical push system, but a great deal of the work is actually done by the distributed workstations which in the end use a pull model to update their software adding scalability and configurability.

14.2.4 Hardware Management

Some of the strategies used in software management can also be used for hardware management. Distributed systems deal with larger numbers of machines, many of which are identical. When possible, it is important to keep these machine as similar as possible. When one looks at a set of software objects which can be installed across the network on any machine and a set of similar machines each of which can house any of those objects it makes for a much more flexible environment. This often calls for careful examination of the initial configuration process. Unwise choices early on can lead to different hardware configurations which will limit flexibility down the road. These choices need to be made in the components to add to the machines such as disk drives and monitors and the configuration of those devices.

For hardware management, it is important to note the distinction between servers and clients. In a distributed environment, a heterogenous mix of various clients with different hardware configurations is inevitable. However, identical configurations for servers that provide the same service is very useful. Not only does this reduce the cost of having spare parts around, but it also provides a way of *cannibalizing* machines in order to keep some level of service going.

It would be useful if all hardware came bar coded in a standard fashion such that all the manager would have to do is scan a light pen across the code and the data would be automatically added. This is a prime example where automation would save many hours and reduce the potential for data entry error.

14.3 Management Roles

In single systems and even in small distributed systems, the staff of system managers that perform the tasks necessary to keep the system running is very small. In larger sites, it is necessary to divide and delegate the management problems. In many cases, the breakdown falls into the management categories that were given. In other cases, it breaks down into *system support* and *user support.* Regardless, of the actual division of labor, there are several inter-related roles, as shown in figure 14.1, that a system manager may fill.

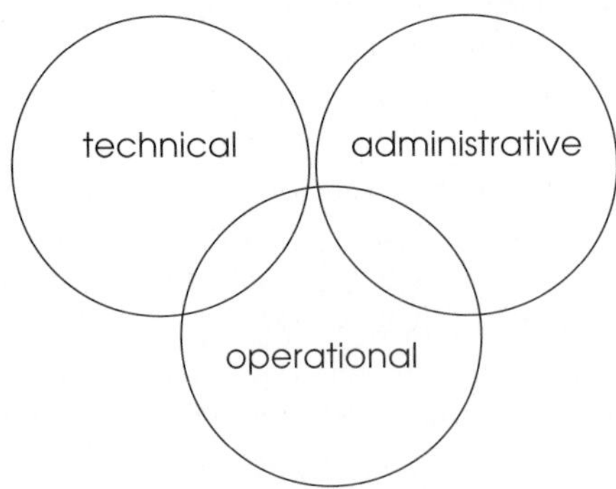

Figure 14.1 Management roles.

First, there is the technical role. The technical system manager performs the tasks that requires a larger degree of technical skills. This usually requires a systems programmer with strong detailed knowledge of the implementation and design of the system. The tasks performed by the technical system manager deal with development of new system management tools, maintaining the existing tools, and fixing critical problems in the system. This position may also install new applications software, though in some sites that is an operational issue, except for the more complicated installs.

The administrative role takes care of all of the paperwork, such as managing licensing and planning budgets. This is also the area that manages user accounts. They decide which users should have accounts, managing the process of creating and deleting accounts, and what resources the accounts should have access to.

The operational role is for more day to day activities, such as mounting tapes.The operational role also provides a means of training future technical people. In larger organizations, once the technical issues are solved and the process is automated, the operational role takes on those duties.

The goal should be to reduce all the technical and administrative tasks to operational ones. Then through automation the amount of actual work which needs to be done can be kept to a minimum.

14.4 System Management Models

Methods of managing computer systems has been a widely debated topic. At first, the debate was between centralized versus decentralized computing. The argument was over, whether computing should be managed by a single department[2] or distributed among each department (King, 1983). With distributed systems it becomes more difficult for separate departments to be totally isolated, as to have a distributed computing system, there needs to be a network connection. While each department may maintain their own internal network, there still needs to be central services that provide inter-department connectivity and, possibly even,

[2]We refer to a department as any organization unit large enough to have some grouping of computers.

connectivity to the rest of the world. In addition, when one department or the central service puts up a service on the network that is useful to the other departments there is a great deal of pressure to make it possible to use that service.

Some form of central organization of computing services are crucial for any effective organization. However, the amount of control that the central services have is more a factor of the organization. This statement is justified by looking at the management models of computing through an examination of them in political terms and then propose a model for distributed systems management.

14.4.1 Model Classifications

14.4.1.1 Totalitarian

Computing began in a *totalitarian* environment. The mainframes were controlled by the MIS department and those that wanted computing services had to go through them. The MIS department controlled the configuration and the access to the computer. In many ways, one had no choice but to take whatever the MIS department provided. It was simply the case that there was no way individual departments could purchase a computer. Even if they could, they would have to spend large amounts of money maintaining the system, as well as spending more money hiring qualified people to run and program the machines.

14.4.1.2 Confederacy

The introduction of the minicomputer was the first step in significantly changing the management paradigm. The cost of ownership and maintenance had reached a level where individual departments could actually justify the expense. Many departments that could take advantage of this fact, did, and split away from the central facilities. This still required a sizable investment as staff was still necessary to maintain the computers and even provide programming support. However, the focus of the computing staff was now tuned to the departmental level and not to the organizational level so the users enjoyed a more suitable environment. In many ways, though, the environment is still a totalitarian environment, it is just that the users do not mind as much because the environment is probably less restrictive in some ways but just as restrictive in other ways they had not yet noticed. We enter the age of the *confederacy*. There were still organizational bindings, but each computing facility was generally independent of each other.

14.4.1.3 Warring States of Greece

The workstation and the personal computers created another shift in management. Today, the cost of obtaining computers and software is at a level where most people can afford to purchase. Users no longer have to be at the whim of their department or any central computing facility. They can go out and purchase their own computers, and finally, do whatever they want– no more restrictions on CPU time, disk space, or user id naming–the machine is all theirs. Unfortunately, the cost of ownership has many subtle aspects. Ownership of a computer is similar to owning a house. They can no longer expect someone else to fix the problems that arise. It becomes the owner's responsibility for fixing the problem or paying for the repairs, and for the new owner, most of the problems that do arise are unfamiliar and generally require assistance. This situation describes a management environment best described by Peg Schaefer as the "Warring States of Greece" (Schaefer, 1992). This environment is characterized by a lack of central support. Some central facilities may exist, but it is really up to each individual department or person to provide their own computing support. Cooperation may occur but competition is more common. This extreme state of *decentralization* generally results in a large degree of duplicated work. The quality of the computing environment for each department is almost solely dependent on the quality of their system manager.

In reaction to the anarchy of the "Warring States of Greece," there is often a shift back towards totalitarianism. The management problems of ownership became so great that the loss of *computing freedom* was seen to be the lesser of the evils. Then there are the organizations that never allowed their users this degree of freedom. but rather followed the dispersion model where central control remains, but the actual computing hardware is spread out. In this totalitarian environment, the central administration designates a supported environment and everyone must strictly follow the environment in order to obtain any support. These edicts often consist of specific machine and software configurations. Consistency is maintained in the environment by making the machines identical through a process of cloning. It should be noted that this is usually the easiest environment to manage. For many organizations, this lack of freedom is a small price to pay for systems that are properly managed. Unfortunately, this environment may not be sufficient for other organizations. If this is the case, and if a department sees an opportunity to break away, they will. Some may flourish independently, but many end up reverting to the "Warring States of Greece," and be forced to return to the central services.

14.4.1.4 Laissez-Faire

An intermediate option, the *laissez-faire* model, exists. In the *laissez-faire* model, central management creates specific services in order to address the problems in each management category. It is up to each department to take and use these services and customize them, or to provide solutions on their own. An example would be that the central management provides a default password file and manages the authenticate for each user in that password file. Each department could take that user authentication method and allow anyone in the organization to authenticate on their machines, or they could customize it such that only members of their department may authenticate on their machines, or they could simply use their own authentication mechanism. The central department also publishes APIs for using the management and other services so that they can be used from *unsupported* platforms. These published APIs usually come with some level of commitment to maintain the APIs over a period of time.

The laissez-faire environment is a balancing act between flexibility and manageability. The administrator that ends up controlling manageability too much finds himself in a totalitarian environment. The user that demands too much flexibility ends up in the "Warring States of Greece" scenario by overwhelming the management.

In some organizations, only one of these models may exist or there may be a confederation of differently managed environments. The next section provides some implementation strategies including implementation strategies for totalitarian and laissez-faire environments.

14.4.2 Model Implementation

14.4.2.1 Totalitarian

There are numerous ways of implementing a totalitarian system. The easiest is to proclaim what configurations are allowed. This can be done by allowing only certain configurations to be present in the management environment. The configuration limitation encompasses all hardware and software. In general, the management problem is made easier by limiting the scope of the system. This is very successful in environments where one group has total control and the authority to place limits. For distributed systems with limited applications and in a closed environment, totalitarianism makes sense. Often the groups making the decisions in these cases also buy the machines, receive and install them. They control the group which helps their users with the machines. A good example of an area where a totalitarian system makes sense would be for a bank or video tape rental system. In these areas, the amount of customization and configurability needed is rather small. In the case of the bank, the total control of a totalitarian system is necessary. A video tape rental system has a very limited domain so configurability is not an important issue.

14.4.2.2 Laissez-Faire

The laissez-faire system is more resource intensive than the totalitarian system because it allows for a much larger degree of freedom in configuration. A single central department will be very hard pressed to understand, let alone perform, the myriad of customization tasks that may be required for various diverse departments in any large organization.

In order to bridge the gap between the central department and all the other departments, a layered system management approach can be taken. Peg Schaefer describes a two layered approach, comprised of the central layer, the central system administrator, the outer layer, and the local system administrator. The central system administrator (CSA) has the tasks that are at an organizational level, including:

- Network Management
- E-mail
- Printing
- Security
- Backup and archive
- Software Licensing
- Obtaining software of interest to the organization
- Information gathering and dispersal (such as vendor product information, policy, training.

As you can see, the CSA has the most diverse set of tasks and provides the services that would generally be of use to the organization as a whole. On the other hand, the local systems administrator (LSA) responsibility is at the departmental level. The LSA acts as *front-line sup-*

port for the departmental users but he can call upon the CSA for assistance. By virtue of having detailed knowledge of the department, the LSA also acts as a technical liaison between the CSA and the department. In this manner, the departmental users have someone nearby that reports directly to them. The LSA is able to concentrate more fully on the users needs by not having to replicate all the tasks already performed by the CSA (Schaefer, 1992).

14.5 Andrew: A Case Study

This section will describe in detail the management structure of the Andrew System. We will begin by describing the early management system and show how it progressed to what exists today. Then, we shall identify some key problems in the current scheme, examine some commercial products that are available, and then discuss the system management areas being dealt with in the Andrew II project to some extent.

14.5.1 The Beginning

To summarize John Leong's discussion in Chapter 8, the Andrew System was initially built around a central distributed file system, known today as AFS (Satyanarayanan, 1985). While hindsight may suggest that using the filesystem as the transport and synchronization layer is a bad idea, there are some benefits to doing so, as long as the assumption that the network and file system are reliable is correct. AFS has a number of features which make it particularly suitable to distributed environments. It has access control lists for which their administration can be delegated which eases the delegation of duties. AFS makes good use of the concept of volumes, which allow the administrator to easily balance partitions and manage quotas by creating containers of files and directories which can be transparently moved. These volumes can be replicated which reduces the dependencies that clients have on a single server and allow for load sharing. Perhaps the best benefit of AFS is that it gives an ubiquitous view of the filesystem. The path to a file in AFS is the same no matter where the file is accessed, whether that is across the room or across the world. The concept of server transparency introduced by AFS was also quite helpful. The ubiquitous AFS path names contain or a cell or site name, but there are no machine names needed. A volume directory service (volume location database or VLDB) at each site (or cell) is used to lookup locations behind without any need for user intervention. Finally, though the backup system supplied with AFS still needs considerable work, facilities for network based backups are an integral part of the AFS design.

Although central management was desired, Andrew client machines were never to be diskless. Andrew workstations have always had a local disk in order to locally cache AFS files to increase performance and scalability. The use of the local disk created the side effect of having to manage the files kept on the local disk. Most files and directories were symbolic links to an appropriate location on AFS. Those files could be managed centrally, but there were still the files that were needed to boot the system and start AFS, not to mention the symbolic links themselves. On some systems there were several hundred symbolic links which needed to be maintained.

To address this problem, a tool called *package* was written. The package process is a configuration file that describes all the files, symbolic links, directories, and devices that should exist on the local disk of a workstation. It contains information about the UNIX owner, group, and mode bits of the files. If given a source path, package will check the dates of the source files and make any needed updates to files on the destination path with those from the source path. Any files or directories not specified by the configuration file and which exist under a directory marked to be kept clean by package in the configuration file are deleted. Package is run on every reboot to keep the local workstation in sync with AFS. By doing this, full operating system upgrades could be done just by running package. The significantly harder task of distribution was left to the filesystem which already did an excellent job.

In many ways, workstation management was the only management issue addressed in the early Andrew days. Users were created through the use of simple scripts. Their quotas were adjusted by anyone who had the necessary rights and felt like doing so. Task management was considered a non-issue as each person would have their own workstation. Software management for release control aspect was nonexistent. Software was released by directly installing files into the release environment. The release environment was made of thousands of files and no records were kept of where those files came from. There were often problems when software was released because of these lax processes.

Many of these issues were simply not important given that Andrew was still an experimental system with critical bugs that had to be fixed. The majority of the effort was put into building manageable development environments and little was done to improve the release environments. Package made it possible for many workstations to be added to the system with little effort from the development team.

14.5.2 The Present–1993

The Andrew System is now the major central computing environment supported by the university. Several departments maintain their own computing environments, quite separate from Andrew. Others use parts of what is provided by Andrew and integrate that with their own environment. Today relatively few departmental facilities do not use some of the technologies generated by the original Andrew project.

Many items have changed since the early experimental days. In general, Andrew is still relatively totalitarian, though some areas have become laissez-faire. For this discussion, the system will be discussed in terms of the management categories described in the first section.

14.5.2.1 User Management

Information about the users is still kept on a VAX/VMS system. It is stored in the Computer Resource Information System (CRIS), which is based on an Ingres database. The user information is obtained from the human resources department and the registrar's office. All students are given an account at the beginning of their freshmen year. CRIS sends requests to another component, the Andrew Account Management System (AAMS), in order to actually modify and create users accounts on Andrew. AAMS adds, suspends and deletes accounts as well as changes passwords and disk quotas. A third system, the Andrew Resource Information

Service (ARIS), collects data about resource usage and verifies user information consistency. ARIS ships data to the CRIS system for long term storage and analysis. ARIS also generates reports and posts them to bulletin boards of the weekly usage of system resources. Unfortunately, there is no consistent format for the storage and location of resource usage information. Thus, the ARIS system must gather the information from a wide variety of locations and formats and process the information for some level of consistency.

Users on Andrew have a restricted AFS quota. Currently students can request up to a maximum of 6 megabytes of storage, and faculty and staff can request to 12 megabytes. This quota is for personal use, in the event additional space is required for "university sponsored" activities, a project volume can be requested by faculty and staff (students may be given project volumes if sponsored by faculty or staff). Project volumes provide many benefits over extending an individual's quota. First, it stores the work in a specific location; there is no need to go looking for the work in an individual's personal area. Second, it solves many privacy issues; for example, in the event an individual leaves the university, the department can get at his work without having to go through the paperwork necessary in getting access to the directories. Third, it provides some sort of tracking mechanism for what resources various groups are consuming. Finally, it is a way to keep the quota on user accounts from continually growing, as it is very hard to take away disk space from individual accounts.

One of the major impacts of the move from time-shared systems to the Andrew distributed system was a move towards use of the computing system by a much larger segment of the community. Not everyone is using the computing facilities were doing traditional computing, such as programming or number crunching. Now, many an increasing number of people were only reading mail, using the word processor, and using other application software packages. These non-traditional computing users tend to need more assistance in general and the consulting has moved largely away from being technical in nature and has tended to based on using the system and applications.

Electronic mail help services have been a major component of services provided for users. The largest is a service called advisor which is a single mail addressed answered by a group of full-time staff members and students. The advisor service is backed up by a large number of subject specific bulletin boards read by staff members who are experts in different areas. These bulletin boards are used to assist the advisors in answering questions. There are also specific mail addresses for data communications problems, the computer store, workstation administration help, and a variety of other services.

A telephone help desk is manned by full-time staff members during normal working hours. Also, many public computer facilities are staffed by students who can provide a *front-line* answer service. In addition to all of this, there is a board "andrew.hints" where users may post questions that other users may be able to answer. There is a zephyr instance that performs a similar task.

One major distributed system component missing in the Andrew System is a general purpose directory service. Traditionally when directory services have been needed files have been stored in AFS which are then fetched when the workstation needs them. Even the user directory services, the white pages, are stored as files in AFS. This has proven to be an adequate directory service for some purposes. Since AFS is only directly accessible from UNIX workstations, and at that the limited subset of UNIX workstations to which AFS has been ported, it has proven a major barrier to providing robust disturbed services. The yellow pages or NIS solution from SUN Microsystems, though simple and easy setup has major scalability problems and does not incorporate any real security. MIT's Hesiod is better suited, but as use of directory services sometimes require extensive modifications to existing and future programs, it is not desirable to use a system that is unlikely to last. Hesiod, while an effective and imaginative solution, is really just a hack on DNS and does not have many of the features a general purpose naming system needs like good pattern matching, and well defined and flexible fields.

Many sacrifices have been made on Andrew because of the lack of a user directory service. On each Andrew workstation, there exists a complete password file of every Andrew user. As of this writing, there are 10,830 entries in the password file. This file must be distributed to each workstation. The process used to do this, package, is explained in the software management section. Not every workstation owner wants all 10,830 users to have access to their workstation. To restrict access, there is a file, /etc/user.permits. If the file exists, only users listed in that file can log in to the workstation. AFS groups are also used so that members of groups listed in /etc/user.permits can log in to the workstation. This tact is preferable to removing users from the password file as one may want to use the "~" shortcut to access a person's directory even though one may not want him to use their workstation. The workstation owner also has the option of changing the root password.[3]

14.5.2.2 Task Management

Task management has only been considered critical on the AFS file servers and to address that need, a program called "bos" which is supplied with the AFS distribution from Transarc is used. Bos allows for server processes to be added to a list of processes to be started automatically and restarted upon failure. When a server crashes and produces a core file it will copy the core file to an appropriate location with an special name. These processes can be started, stopped, added, and removed remotely. Information about the state of running processes, when they started, and whether any core files exist is available remotely.

More and more software today is following a client/server paradigm and so it is becoming increasingly important that the server processes keep running. With a few modifications to remove dependencies on AFS, bos would be sufficient for those purposes, however it would be better to be able to *define* tasks and have the machine start to perform them. In addition, it is important to define groups of users who can manage these tasks. Bos only has the concept of a super-user which can do everything.

One of the problems with the Andrew workstation management system is that it is file based. There is no easy way to create a single file from a number of locations. Bos, like many other utilities, has a single configuration file which describes the tasks to be performed. Since the Andrew workstation management system is all file based, that requires a different configuration, with possibly duplicate entries, for every different set of configurations. With modifications to make it possible to separate different groupings of processes into different files it

[3]We do not care if local workstation owners have root access because AFS does not trust the *root* uid and one still needs to obtain authentication for any administrative task.

would make management easier. In the long run the workstation management system needs to handle these situations better.

A great deal of the task management issues are addressed through monitoring. The CMU computing services group has a machine room which is manned 24 hours a day seven days a week. Though, the manned machine room is largely a hold over from the days of large timesharing systems, it has become increasingly important as the usage and dependence on the central distributed computing system increases. Machines that are necessary for service to be provided are monitored by the operators. In the event of a failure condition, there are people on-call.

Monitoring was mostly an afterthought in the development of tools for managing the distributed services. Unfortunately, there is a tendency industry wide to include monitoring as an afterthought rather than an integral part of the system from the beginning. For monitoring to be truly effective the objects being monitored must be well instrumented. Since many of the Andrew services were not instrumented, external indicators were used. The mail system was monitored by examining the response time of clients. The low level RPC used by AFS had some debugging tools which were used to build tools to identify bottlenecks and problems with the system.

14.5.2.3 Software Management

A great deal of attention has been paid to software management on the Andrew System. This is due to a great deal of initial problems caused by earlier inadequate systems. Instead of dividing the domain as we did before into operating system management and application software management, we now divide software management into: workstation administration, or administering the software necessary to get the machine to run; and application software administrator.

14.5.2.3.1 Workstation Administration

Workstation administration is still being performed using package. As the number of different configurations increased, the more difficult it was to maintain all the static configuration files. Even though the various configurations contain much of the same information, the static configuration file approach requires that a different configuration file be generated and used for each configuration, no matter how small the difference. To help solve this problem a simple macro pre-processor, *mpp*, was developed to build the configuration files and a set of relatively complicated libraries using mpp have developed over time to build the configuration file.

Mpp builds the package configuration file based on a prototype file, /etc/package.proto. When the workstation boots, the system defines a few extra variables before *mpp* is run which describes the architecture, operating system, and components of the hardware configuration. Then *mpp* and *package* are run. By running the configuration file through *mpp* at boot time, the workstation picks up the most recent configuration information from the central package libraries. On the other hand, any errors made in the central package libraries also take effect immediately.

A sample /etc/package.proto file looks like this:

```
%define doesanonftp
%define dept acs
%define deptadmin
%define beta
%define betalocal

%include /afs/andrew.cmu.edu/wsadmin/public/src/public.proto
```

The first definition, *doesanonftp,* tells the central libraries to add the configuration lines to setup an anonymous ftp service on the machine. The final two definitions change some of the central variables used to find the base path of software to a beta location for software testing. For software moved from the central /usr/local tree to the local machine the variable ${local} would be used in place of any references in the package libraries. The beta and betalocal definitions would cause the ${local} variable to point to a different path.

By defining deptadmin, mpp will incorporate another file into the final package configuration file. The location of the file is determined by the dept definition. In this example, the department is *acs.* In this departmental configuration file, actual package definitions can be given or more mpp variables may be defined. In this manner, changes that apply to the entire department can be made in a single location, rather than in the package.proto for all the machines in the department.

Both the configuration libraries for package and the actual files themselves are clearly separated. That is, the local package configuration libraries are stored in a separate file from the operating system configuration files and that the files that are referenced by the local package configuration files are stored in a different directory hierarchy in AFS. For example, figure 14.2 shows the possible ways for package to obtain /etc/inetd.conf and the separation that occurs in the system. In the figure, the first path given is the path of the configuration file. The second is the location of the actual file. As you can see, the workstation owner has the option to override any other definition. He may choose to override the departmental option. The departmental administration may choose to override the Andrew definition. The Andrew administration has the option of overriding the vendor definitions. The vendor definition given in the example is for the DEC MIPS machines running Ultrix 4 which has a system tag of pmax_ul4. For other vendors, the only difference would be with the system tag. As with all the overrides, the location of the real file is different. The benefits of this separation are discussed in more detail in the compartmentalization section.

Mpp with *package* provides a great deal of flexibility. The local workstation administrator can make rather complicated configuration changes through simple variables in a local configuration file. The construction and maintenance of the central libraries and the files those libraries point to can be delegated to the central services. Also, full operating system updates can be done (and have been done) with minimal changes to the departmental configuration files.

One limitation of package is that it has no concept of hierarchy. If there are any conflicts in the configuration file it will exit with an error. Any flexibility on the installation of files which override default system files from the central package libraries needs to be built into the package libraries. This requires the workstation administrator to interact with the central administrators who maintain the package libraries to make changes in these files.

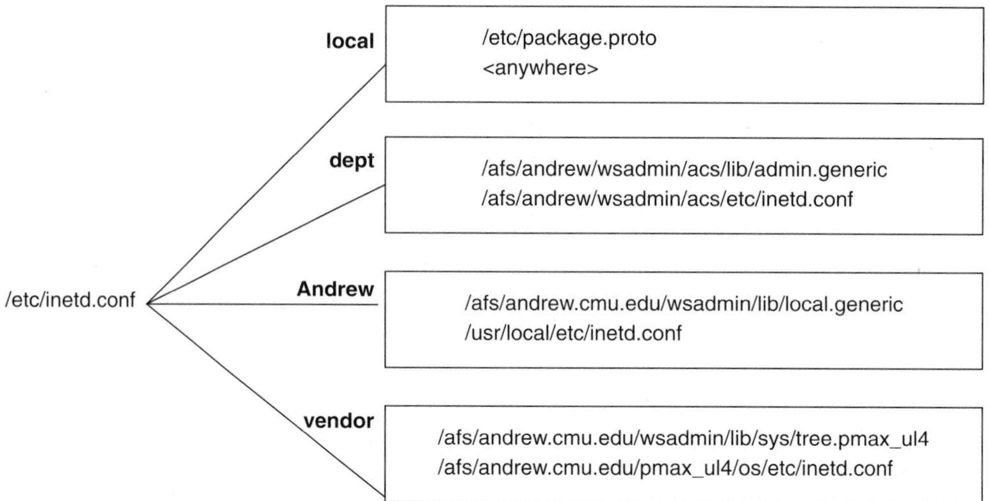

Figure 14.2 Separation of configuration and actual files.

14.5.2.3.2 Application Software Management

All supported application software is accessible to the user in the /usr/local tree on every Andrew workstation. Andrew specific customizations and configurations are pulled to the local disk from a /usr/local tree which lives in AFS. In addition to /usr/local, there is also a /usr/contributed which houses software submitted and supported by users. The application base for the PCs and Macintoshes is made available on Novell servers and no special tools are used to manage that software at the present time.

This differs from other sites in that software is not installed on a per machine basis. Software is installed into /usr/local on AFS and then each machine picks up the installed software simply by accessing it through /usr/local. The /usr/local tree seen on a workstation is either a symbolic link to a directory in AFS or it is a collection of files and directories which are linked or copied from AFS.

Application software is managed by depot. It provides a simple, flexible, mechanism for maintaining third party and locally developed software in large heterogeneous computing environments of UNIX workstations. The depot framework partitions software into separately maintained software objects, known as collections. Depot facilitates the introduction, update, and removal of these collections into an environment, the directory hierarchy representing the union of all the software objects. With depot, custom environments and complete test environments can be created for individual machines or for sets of machines. Individual collections or files can be moved from remote file systems to the local disks of workstations without worrying if the files become stale.

The collection object is best represented as a small file system containing the files and directories belonging to that object. The files and directories are in the exact format in which they will eventually be integrated into the software environment. Files placed in the bin directory in the objects file system will appear in the bin directory of the final environment. This reduces the amount of knowledge of the system needed to create new objects. The directory hierarchy of the objects file system is the exact image of the final installation.

With each invocation, depot processes a single software environment. The software environment starts with a specified directory hierarchy and encompasses everything within it, including subdirectories. Depot defines the environment as the union of a set of collection objects. System administrators have the benefit of separation and the users the benefit of integration. A software environment like /usr/local which in many environments consists of thousands of files becomes manageable by using depot. The abstraction of collection objects and the simplicity of their use make this possible.

The environment is customized through a set of configuration options. These options determine which collections will be integrated into the environment and how they will be integrated. Conflicts between collections can be resolved either by specifying that one collection overrides another or by using configuration options to move files or directory hierarchies.

There are currently two ways a collection can be integrated: copying or linking. For collections that are linked, symbolic links are made from the environment to their location in the collections specific directory. To reduce the overhead of the links, they are made at directory level wherever possible. With the copy option, every file and directory is copied into the target environment.

In many cases, multiple collections need to install files into a common directory. Index files are often kept of the contents of the directory, such as fonts.dir in the case of X11 font directories. Through configuration options, automated procedures for updating these index files can be created. A command can be run whenever a collection or directory has changed.

Today, even with multiple environments, software can be easily installed and removed from the system. Much of depot's success can be attributed to four factors: independence, integration, mobility, and simplicity. The concept of combining independence and integration provided the manageability we needed without sacrificing the consistency that users demand. Mobility gives us flexibility in configuration and testing. Finally, the simplicity has made it popular with developers and allows us to integrate depot with other tools, rather than trying to make depot a *kitchen sink* tool. Depot has proved to be a flexible mechanism for maintaining our software environment.

While depot provides the architecture, there are still many tedious tasks that need to be performed. In order to manage the process of collection creation, release, replication and deletion a tool was created called the environment maintenance tool (EMT) which automates those processes.

In the Andrew environment which each collection has an AFS volume created for sources and each system type being supported, there are at least nine steps needed in the creation of a new version of a collection. There can be problems and type errors in any of those steps. In order to perform the steps, a great deal of system privileges are needed.

EMT automates those steps so that all that is needed is that the name of the collections be specified, whether to copy the contents of the sources from an earlier version, the version number and the system types to be supported need to specified. All the steps will be taken care of. The privileges can be granted per person or on an environment or collection level. No one needs to have full system administrative privileges to create, release or delete software.

14.5.2.4 Hardware Management

The Andrew System replaced four timesharing machines. There are now over 100 servers providing a large number of varied services. The major servers break down into PC/Mac servers (17), UNIX timesharing servers (12), fileservers (22), post office machines (12), operating system download servers (2), compilation machines (4), print servers (8), administrative servers (2), Zephyr servers (3), and a variety of miscellaneous servers. This does not even include the machines needed to support the network, though some services currently co-exist on the same machine, such as the Zephyr and download services. Though the failure rate of the system is much lower, with the massive increase in components problems are not uncommon. A full time hardware staff is on call 24 hours a day to fix problems with critical production machines.

The numbers of clients are equally impressive. There are two classifications of UNIX clients which use the Andrew services. The first, an Andrew workstation, is fully configured in the Andrew environment. It has the Andrew password file, users log in to their home directory in Andrew's AFS space, and the software on the machine is configured using the Andrew workstation administration tools. The central group takes little responsibility for these machines. They are owned and managed by different people through campus. Their software is supported and the tools to manage the software are controlled centrally. The next section will describe how those tools work. The hardware is the responsibly of the owner. Today there are about 470 Andrew workstations. UNIX workstations run by other campus groups use Andrew facilities. There are around another 500 of these machines which actively use Andrew facilities in a week. The vast majority are Macintoshes and DOS machines. As described in Chapter 8 on the Andrew System, they use translator services to access Andrew facilities. There are over 2000 active Macintoshes and 800 DOS machines.

To avoid the problems of adding new hardware, we try to make things as generic as possible. For example, the kernels that are distributed are compiled for all reasonable architecture variations for that operating system release. The presence of new disks is detected by changes in the fstab. The configuration management system will probably detect possible differences in display types and other hardware components and automatically reconfigure the machine on reboot to take advantage of the change.

14.5.3 Network Management

Network management is not part of the Andrew System. Rather, there is a parallel network development and operational group. Regardless, it is worth noting that the network management at CMU takes a laissez-faire approach. Many of the larger computing organizations manage their own internal networks, including assigning IP addresses and actually maintaining the wiring within their own areas. All the central support does is provide inter-connectivity.

A good description of the CMU network and its evolution is provided in the chapter on Andrew Project.

14.5.4 Summary

In the Andrew environment, it would be unthinkable to return to the previous state of software management. Installations were lengthy, error prone processes. Often the installation of a new application would break previous applications. There was no smooth way to restore the environment to a previous state. Even though numerous man hours were put into maintaining the environment, the system was essentially in a state of anarchy. As a result of a strong software management system, not only can resources be allocated to other work on other projects, but now the delegation and distribution of tasks is a much easier process.

In terms of the management model, Andrew is slowly leaving the totalitarian model. The Andrew management model is similar to the BBN model with two exceptions. First, the local system administration (LSA) is not a required component. For those without an LSA to customize the environment, a default environment and configuration is provided. Those with an LSA enjoy added benefits which are similar to the benefits at BBN. The LSA acts as the liaison with the Central System Administrator (CSA). The LSA is the one who understands the local environment enough to *add value* by customizing what the CSA provides. The second difference is that the Andrew model encourages multiple layers by allowing for multiple avenues of customization. Generally, there is only an additional layer of customization applied where the workstation owner adds a layer of customization to what the CSA applied. Some arbitrary restrictions exist because of the difficulty to coerce the system to provide these layers. Future work will concentrate on making the system more laissez-faire by providing modular services with this sort of distributed management philosophy. The following section on Andrew 2 discusses this in more detail.

14.6 Andrew 2–The Future

The problems with the tight dependency between AFS and the Andrew services is highlighted by the emergence of OSF's DFS. It is expected that AFS will be replaced entirely by the DFS. Before commercial support for AFS disappears, either existing Andrew services will have to be ported to DFS or the Andrew group will have to pick up support for AFS. Since continuing to port AFS to new environments would be extremely costly and it is anticipated that a great deal of work will be done with the DFS, it was decided to plan on a conversion to the DFS. This has provided a good excuse to re-engineer many aspects of the system to use current technology and to learn from past mistakes. This new effort has been named Andrew 2. John Leong provides a general overview of Andrew 2 in his chapter on Andrew. This section will describe the activity going on in the management side of things.

14.6.1 The Problems

Before trying to solve a problem, it is generally a good idea to determine what the problem is. The key problems of the current Andrew management environment are as follows:

Mpp/package has been used for over six years now and has proven to be very flexible over time. There have been several major changes in the way that it has been used. However, the mpp/package is reaching the end of its life cycle. This combination does not provide enough flexibility and it has become too complex for many system managers to use effectively. People do not deal well with configuration files that go off and make magical things happen. Local software installation is difficult. Central software installation is not much better. There is a steep learning curve, a lack of documentation, and the configuration files can be confusing. The complication comes from having to deal with all the files on the workstation individually. The configuration files do not allow for groups of files or layering of changes on top of each other. There is no hierarchy. A more natural method of dealing with files and directories combined with the object orient approach that depot uses proves to be a much better tool to give to people.

There is a poor integration of non-UNIX platforms. DOS machines and Macintoshes have to go through translators. Currently none of the software management systems even begin to deal with these platforms. The entire Andrew management system is built around AFS. Since the DOS and Macintosh clients do not have native access to AFS, they are left out of most of the solutions.

There is a lack of cohesion among the services provided. There are a variety of support services which serve different areas and in some cases overlap. There has been no concerted effort to develop a unified support system and to share information and expertise between services. This had led to the typical situation where the right hand does not know what the left hand is doing. Development was separated from support so that development could get done but technical expertise and in depth of knowledge was left solely in the development groups.

Though there are a good set of tools for getting tasks done, there is no general cohesive frame which it all works together in. Utilities do not have a good way of talking to each other when it becomes necessary. Reports and monitors do not try correlating data with each other. There is no central repository for data about system usage and no defined formats for storing usage and performance data.

Partially because of the lack of central data storage and format standards much of the data collection is for real time fault analysis and used to produce short term reports. There are no unified tools for trends analysis. When a report is requested on usage or performance trends a great deal of work is put into tracking down and formatting the data.

14.6.2 Vendor Products

The computing world has changed dramatically since the inception of Andrew. It is no longer necessary to build everything from scratch. One of the goals of the next generation Andrew 2 project is to reduce the amount of software developed or extensively modified in house. The use of *shrink-wrapped* software is encouraged not only to avoid the development costs, but to reduce the sky rocketing support and maintenance costs of maintaining locally developed software.

Finding vendor system management products that can replace the existing tools is very difficult. This is largely due to the lack of tools which can scale to the level needed and which are available on the variety of platforms needed. Evaluation of these packages is difficult and often requires actually installing and putting the systems into production.

The overhead of installing and customizing the products is often a problem. For example, the Andrew System has a user database of over 10,000 users. Any user management system has to work with our existing AFS protection, file, volume location and authentication servers.

Many management systems are built for corporate IS environments where there are large numbers of bodies to take care of the tasks of the system. These systems still require that machines be visited to install software and modify many configuration files. They do not generalize the workstation to the level where there is a low incremental cost per additional workstation in manpower.

Outside of the framework area where the Andrew System has a clear need for a system which will help to create a cohesive and comprehensive system, there is little existing vendor software which can meet the needs for scale, automation, out heterogeneity.

14.6.3 Vendor Frameworks

Work done in developing vendor frameworks appears to be promising. Frameworks are infrastructures around which a management environment can be built. For example, frameworks often consist of the user interface stubs and the communications layers which tie management systems together into something that appears cohesive and homogeneous. They are the building blocks of a management system, though there is *some assembly required.* These systems often require more work to setup but, as a result, they can provide the flexibly that many large sites need which would otherwise be unavailable.

Most frameworks provide the base tools for abstracting network services, and for tools which have been integrated into the management system there are communications stubs for managing the services. These systems usually define their own communications protocol as well as using industry standards such as CMIP and SNMP. In addition, they allow new interfaces to be created with little effort to talk to services which do not use these standard interfaces.

Tivoli's Management Environment (TME) is one such management framework which is rapidly being adopted across the distributed UNIX market.

14.6.4 Directions

Much of the current Andrew management structure will remain the same for the foreseeable future. The Depot and EMT combination will remain, though EMT will likely have to learn to manage other areas such as the DFS instead of AFS as that migration nears.

The simpler to use, object oriented depot management tool is targeted to replaced package and mpp in the workstation management arena. Currently a new version is being worked on which addresses some of the problems which limited depot to managing software environments and not workstations. The tool should be more generalized and able to manage the disks of workstations when that is done.

A management framework needs to be found and integrated to help make the management system have a consistent interface and help tie together divergent management structures. As vendors tie management into their applications and services, it will be important to choose a management framework which will work well with those systems.

The most challenging aspect of the future will be the Macintosh and PC integration. Even though these machines are becoming more and more powerful, there is still exists a need to be able to support, to a certain extent, older configurations with less memory and less powerful operating system. Coming from a single user, stand-alone environment, many of the design philosophies and methodologies for these machines need to be changed to so that they may operate optimally in a distributed environment. While this is slowly changing, it is hard to say if the PC environment is really learning from the experiences in the UNIX world. The application to watch for appears to be Microsoft's Hermes, though it appears that Hermes is targeted only for the high end Windows market and it is unclear how well it will deal with the emerging heterogenous market which will appear with the Window/NT. It will be very interesting to see exactly what issues it addresses and what problems it suffers from.

14.7 Summary

More and more people have an increasing number of machines that are to be interconnected. They are demanding that the computer be working and ready for them to use their desired applications. The increase in system managers is not keeping up with those increases. As a result, strategies for managing distributed systems are becoming increasingly important.

However, many strategies are not applicable from organization to organization. This is especially true in organizations where the infrastructure has been built up over time. To replace it would impose a significant cost that management is unwilling to spend. There often are not replacements which will fit the needs of the organization, even if they were willing to spend the resources to convert. As a result, if a system manager goes from one organization to another, his core skill is still useful, but a tremendous amount of training may still be required to learn a completely different management system in the new location. The end results are often similar, but the means of achieving them vary greatly. They are all trying to produce that working system.

As a result, many vendors and many standards organizations are describing the benefits of their system, but the inter-operability between competing systems and the actually adaptability of the systems to large scale heterogenous distributed systems is yet to be seen. As a result, most organizations are required to muddle through with mostly homegrown utilities.

Distributed systems management is still a relatively new field where a considerable amount of research and effort still needs to be invested. There are many other strategies that were not mentioned in this chapter not only for the lack of space, but due to the lack of ready information in this field.

There is some hope on the horizon that common management frameworks will come out and help to tie the currently divergent and noncooperative management systems out there together. There will probably always be systems which do not cooperate and they will have to be dealt with specially if the applications those systems perform are essential.

The strategies presented and referred to in this chapter are nothing more than a weak guideline that may help steer the direction of distributed systems management. Hopefully, producers of software packages will pick up on some of the lessons learned here to make their installation and customization processes fit better into distributed environments. Hardware and operating system vendors need to get together and develop standards and methods of downloading software onto machines in a scalable and configurable manner which works in heterogeneous distributed computing environments. At a minimum what is needed is an awareness of the issues which must be dealt with.

As of yet, because of the diversity of the organizations, the diversity of the machines, the diversity of the users, and the diversity of software there are no champion distributed system solutions which will make all of our lives easier. When they emerge the winners will be the users who will see a more consistent environment with better response time and more flexibility.

14.8 References

Colyer, W., and Wong, W., 1992. Depot: A Tool for Managing Software Environments. *LISA VI Proceedings. Usenix Association,* Oct.

Jones, G.M., and Romig, S.M., 1991. Cloning Customized Hosts (or Customizing Cloned Hosts). *LISA V Proceedings. Usenix Association,* Sep.

King, J.L., 1983. Centralized versus Decentralized Computing: Organizational Considerations and Management Options. *ACM Computing Surveys,* vol 15, no 4, Dec, pp. 319–349.

Satyanarayanan, M., Howard, J. H., Nichols, D. A., Sidebotham, N., and Spector, A. Z., 1985. The ITC Distributed Filesystem: Principals and Design. *Proceedings of the 10th ACM Symposium on Operating System Principals.*

Schaefer, P., 1992. bbn-public–Contributions from the User Community. *LISA VI Conference Proceedings. Usenix Association,* Oct.

Schaefer, P., 1992. Is Centralized System Administration the Answer? *LISA VI Conference Proceedings. Usenix Association,* Oct.

Yount, R., 1986. Package. Academic Services. Carnegie Mellon University.

14.9 Additional Reading

On Andrew:

Andrew 2 Requirements Documents. Computing Services. Carnegie Mellon University. Available via anonymous to export.acs.cmu.edu in /pub/Andrew2.

Colyer, W., Held, M., Markley, D., and Wong, W., 1992. Software Management in the Andrew System. *AFS User's Group Proceedings,* Jun.

Wong, W., 1992. The Andrew Workstation. Computing Services. Carnegie Mellon University.

It is well worth examining the LISA conference proceedings, as the papers presented within offer many different implementation strategies on almost all aspects of systems management.

Wallace Colyer is the Andrew Systems Manager at Carnegie Mellon University. Wallace initially worked as a User Consultant running an electronic mail help system and helping with customizing workstation configurations. He went on to play an key role in designing software release and configuration management processes. Now, he is responsible for a group which oversees the day to day health and sets the architectural direction of the Andrew System, which is on the forefront of distributed computing in size, diversity, and innovation.

Walter Wong graduated from Carnegie Mellon with a B.S. in Cognitive Science. While pursuing his undergraduate degree, he became involved in system administration in a distributed computing environment. After graduation, he remained at Carnegie Mellon where he is now a System Programmer and Administrator in the Andrew Systems Group.

Chapter 15

Migration Strategies

R.L. "Bob" Morgan
Roland Schemers
Stanford University

15.1 Introduction–Migration from Distributed to Integrated

Distributed computing solutions, such as OSF's Distributed Computing Environment (DCE), are a response to the challenges faced by today's large, information-intensive organizations. These organizations are already running large, distributed computing systems, though they might not call them that; they are all too aware how difficult this is. In most cases *distributed* is a synonym for *disorganized.* The office worker who has to log in separately to five different systems to get his work done is faced with the reality of distributed computing, as is the administrative manager who wonders whether the network is secure enough to support her department's application.

The appeal of technologies like DCE is in offering an integrated solution to the most fundamental problems faced by these organizations, such as providing global information access; writing correct, efficient, flexible distributed programs; and providing scalable, secure, manageable services. DCE's complexity is a challenge in itself, however. It is likely that only organizations that are already hip-deep in the distributed computing swamp will be able to appreciate the benefits offered by an integrated (but still complex) environment. Yet these organizations are the ones that have the most investment in existing distributed computing technology.

At most sites, then, making use of advanced distributed system technology will not be a matter of building new systems from scratch, but of migrating from the systems and practices that are in use today. In this chapter, we look at some of the technical issues and strategies involved in this migration. These will be illustrated in the context of Stanford University's computing environment.

The analysis in this chapter is *bottom up*. First we present an analysis of Stanford's current computing situation, focusing on problem areas. This allows us to build up a picture of *integrated distributed computing* by considering the problems it has to solve. Then we analyze how OSF's DCE, today's leading contender, might help us to solve those problems, and also how it may give us additional headaches. Lastly we describe how we might get from here to there, with an emphasis on problems of managing DCE itself. See Chapter 16 for a more top-down approach to many of these same issues.

Each organization's existing computing infrastructure is different, and so each will see different trade-offs in adopting integrated distributed computing solutions such as DCE, and will have a different idea of how best to migrate to it (or whether to do it at all). We hope that our assessments will be generic enough to offer some guidance. Note that DCE, and especially the state of its availability in real products, is a moving target; all observations here are as of this writing in May 1993.

15.2 Networked Computing at Stanford

The networked computing environment at Stanford is typical of those at other large research universities. Many large government and corporate networks have been adopting similar methods. At Stanford *distributed computing* has been the rule for many years for reasons that are at least as much organizational as technical.

Unlike some sister institutions, Stanford has never had a major *project* to introduce a new generation of distributed computing technology to the campus. Such projects often have the advantage of building a new environment on a substantial amount of new hardware. But at most sites the reality is that bringing in enough new hardware to make a difference is no longer feasible. New systems must be built on the current computing base; this is what we examine in this section.

15.2.1 SUNet

The Stanford University Network (SUNet) is made up of a campus-wide backbone network (including both Ethernet and FDDI segments) to which departmental subnetworks are attached through routers. The backbone network and the routers are managed by a part of the central computing support organization. Each department or other group is responsible for managing the network and computers that serve their area.

SUNet includes about 150 IP subnets, with over 11,000 active IP nodes. There are also over 500 AppleTalk networks. There are on the order of 6000 networked Macintoshes, 2000 UNIX-based workstations, and 3000 IBM-compatible PCs. After increasing by 50 percent per year for several years, the growth in Stanford's networked computer population has slowed to *only* 30 percent over the last year (May 1992 to May 1993). We expect these growth trends to continue.

As shown in figure 15.1, SUNet is made up of a large number of independent *islands*. These islands rely on the SUNet backbone for transport, and some core SUNet services (e.g., the Internet Domain Name System) but for the most part they provide their own infrastructure: cabling, computers, file servers, user accounts, and so on.

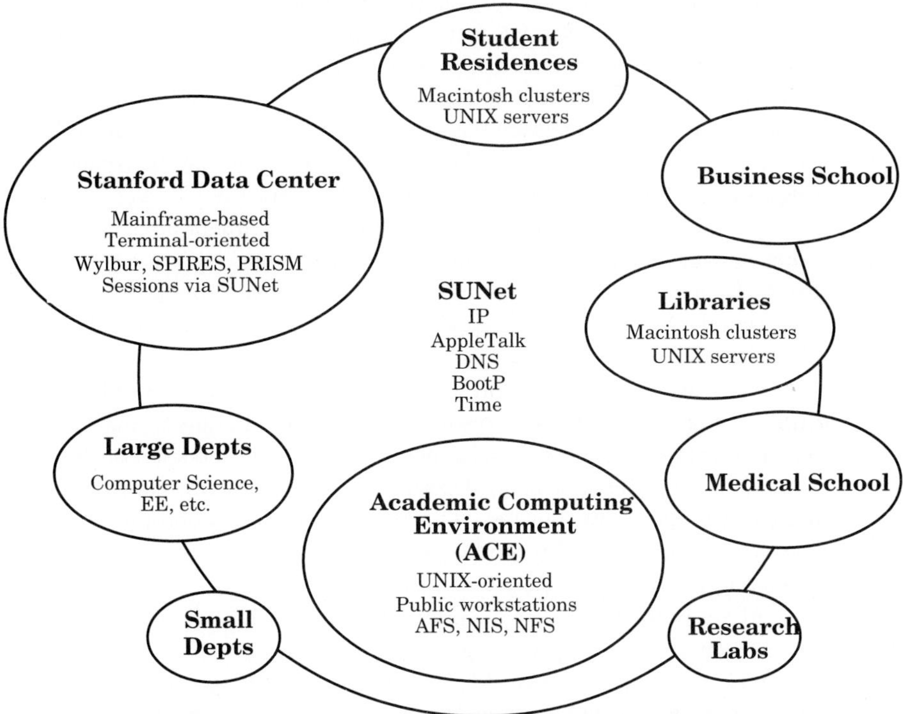

Figure 15.1 Stanford University Network (SUNet) environment.

15.2.1.1 Academic Computing Environment

The academic computing environment (ACE) is Stanford's primary resource for instructional computing. It offers electronic mail, timesharing, file storage, software, and workstation access to 17,000 users, primarily students and faculty. ACE hardware includes over 100 UNIX workstations (Digital, IBM, NeXT, and Sun) for general use by students; several large UNIX-based file servers with over 100 gigabytes of storage; several UNIX-based timeshare computers. ACE provides access to large data sets for the humanities and social sciences, commercial and university-ware application software, and Stanford-developed courseware.

Within its workstation environment, ACE provides *location independence.* A user can sit at any workstation and have all their personal resources available: home directory, email, applications, window system, and so on. The workstations are operated in the *dataless* mode (as described in Chapters 9 and 14); their local disks store only operating system executables, all applications and user data being supplied from file servers.

ACE is in the midst of its own distributed computing migration. It has traditionally used Sun's NIS to distribute password, group, and home directory information among the workstations, and NFS for file service. Over the last two years, Transarc's AFS (see Chapter

10) has been slowly replacing NFS. Almost all application software and libraries are now supplied via AFS, as are the home directories of about 15 percent of the users.

The change to AFS has some important benefits. File server performance is improved due to client caching of files. File system mounting on the workstations is much simpler since the entire AFS tree is mounted in only one location, while each NFS filesystem must be mounted separately. AFS volume management is much more flexible and transparent. AFS ACLs provide much more flexible control over directory access. AFS use of Kerberos authentication provides improved security. The AFS file service can easily be expanded to be a campus-wide service, not just supporting the ACE workstations.

On the other hand, this transition has not been without problems. AFS ACLs are confusing to many, especially those who just learned about UNIX permission modes. The fact that ACLs apply only to directories, not files, has been a source of complaint. AFS, being more complex and not directly supported by system vendors, has suffered from a lack of robustness, though recent versions are much improved.

Over 200 departmental workstations also make use of the AFS file service, primarily for access to pre-compiled application software (e.g. X-based utilities, emacs). This use of AFS to provide a campus-wide file system has been successful on a modest scale despite very little central support simply because many departmental system administrators see immediate benefits in their own operations. But the AFS system's mission is supporting the core ACE facility; there are occasions when this conflicts with departmental use (e.g., a version of a program for use in a class differs from that desired by a department).

AFS uses the Kerberos authentication system. We have encouraged the growth of the Kerberos database (now up to about 12,000 users) as an important building block in establishing an integrated campus-wide distributed computing infrastructure. As we describe below, we are now beginning to use this database to authenticate functions other than AFS.

15.2.1.2 Stanford Data Center

The Stanford Data Center provides a large-scale mainframe-oriented environment for the operation of Stanford's mission-critical institutional applications. It operates an IBM ES/9000, using both the Stanford-developed Wylbur timesharing system and IBM's MVS/ESA. This system provides electronic mail service for over 10,000 campus users, mostly administrative staff and faculty.

Most large data center applications are based on the Stanford-developed SPIRES database management system, and the associated PRISM interface for end-user transactions. Applications development is divided between data center staff and programmers in the various client departments.

The Folio system provides public access to a wide variety of large university databases and other information sources, including the Socrates catalog of the Stanford University Libraries, faculty/staff and student directories, course and degree information, event and job listings, and so on. Folio is based on SPIRES and PRISM.

The data center is facing the usual challenges of large mainframe-based facilities in the 1990s. Its strategy for meeting these challenges is based on moving toward open, non-proprietary client/server systems, as described in detail in Chapter 16.

The data center recognizes that certain information resources should be able to be accessed in an authenticated way by all members of the campus community. For example, everyone should be able to update their own directory entry interactively. Similarly, a recently introduced system is used by all students to prepare their list of courses on line, which are then approved on line by their advisors. Users access these sorts of operations using their University ID numbers as their identity, and a bank-style PIN as a sort of password. PINs are assigned to all students automatically, and to faculty and staff upon request.

15.2.2 Core SUNet Services

There are a number of core services that support the SUNet environment. All the services in this section are centrally operated, and are available to all departments without charge.

15.2.2.1 Routing

Routing of data packets from one network or subnetwork to another is the most fundamental of services, the basis of internetworking. Behind this seemingly straightforward service is a complex process of router configuration. A substantial amount of its complexity is driven by fairly high-level user requirements: forwarding of particular flavors of packets, static routes to user-provided gateways, multiple subnets for multiple organizations, and so on. Our backbone routers currently route only Internet Protocol (IP) packets, but there is much user pressure to support other protocols (e.g., Novell's IPX) to meet the needs of particular applications.

AppleTalk protocols are also used on most Stanford Ethernets and over 300 LocalTalk networks. Encapsulation of AppleTalk in IP is used to support cross-campus AppleTalk internetworking. Configuration information for over 300 department-owned AppleTalk gateways is supplied from a central system. This information is managed using a Stanford-developed registration database application, NetDB (see section 15.2.4), which allows access to departmental managers.

We continue to focus our efforts on providing high-quality global IP connectivity. Applications that run over IP have the inherent advantage that they fit in with our campus-wide routing infrastructure. Distributed computing solutions that are based on other network protocols face an uphill battle. To the extent that the IP-based DCE provides a rallying point for system vendors of all kinds, we can hope that the need to support special protocols and special configurations of all kinds can be reduced.

The routing service provides us with a perspective on providing other higher-level services: that of the campus-wide utility. SUNet's service definition says that any part of campus that wants IP connectivity can get it, eventually. Similarly, other centrally-provided services must at least potentially be usable by any member of the campus community. This is an key design constraint for many services, as seen below.

15.2.2.2 Name Service

The Internet Domain Name System (DNS) provides a naming service whose primary function is mapping names of computers to their IP addresses. The configuration files and servers for the "Stanford.EDU" domain are maintained by the central computing support organization. The DNS database is managed by departmental managers using the NetDB database (see section 15.2.4). The distributed management capability of NetDB has allowed us to avoid supporting sub-domains (e.g., `somehost.somedepartment.stanford.edu`) for this purpose (with one exception). We believe this improves the robustness and usability of our DNS system. We will return to this theme later in the chapter.

As we describe below, there is an increasing need for a more general naming or directory service to provide information such as the user mailbox names, locations of home directories, server attributes, encryption keys, and so on. Some efforts have been made to extend DNS to store generic information, notably Project Athena's Hesiod at MIT. Among the problems that stand in the way of this approach are UDP packet size limitations and lack of authentication. In addition, the more that DNS is extended to support generic naming features, the more we question whether it will meet the reliability and performance requirements that we have of the service in its current form. It seems that a new approach to directory service is needed, onto which we can map current DNS functions as appropriate.

15.2.2.3 Bootstrap Service

Another centrally-provided service is based on the bootstrap protocol (BootP) and the trivial file transfer protocol (TFTP). This service provides a way for systems to find their IP address and other low-level configuration information at start-up time, and to load start-up files. By using BootP, IP addresses can be assigned and changed in the BootP database without having to change configuration files on clients. This is intended to make management of network devices easier and more flexible. As with DNS, the BootP database is maintained using NetDB.

Over 1000 SUNet clients use the service. They are almost entirely of two types, either low-level network devices such as bridges and network monitors, or desktop computers (i.e., PCs and Macintoshes).

BootP illustrates the difficulties of making network device management easier. If generation of BootP entries is more difficult than configuring nodes by hand, local administrators will not use it, even if it promises a desirable flexibility. If the BootP service is at all unreliable, they will avoid it like the plague. If some required configuration information has to be entered manually via some other means because BootP is unable to supply it, administrators will not bother to use BootP at all. The ideal service must be very comprehensive, very easy to use, and very robust, which is a difficult standard to meet.

15.2.2.4 Time Service

It is important for computers in a distributed system to keep their clocks synchronized not only to each other but to the global time standard. Among other uses, security protocols generally depend on accurate timestamps to prevent attacks involving resending captured packets. The central support group participates in the Internet distribution of network time protocol (NTP) time service by synchronizing our reference hosts with off-campus sites and with radio-based signals.

Further distribution of NTP service on campus is not as effective as it should be, however. The large number of potential NTP clients, combined with the relatively small number of clients that a single NTP server can support, creates a substantial configuration problem. We could solve part of the problem by generating configurations centrally for each NTP client host. The fundamental problem, however, is that configuration items such as this are entered by hand for all hosts by their administrators.

What is needed is a method of centrally generating configuration information for large numbers of nodes so that the global configuration is optimized. Then, a method of installing this configuration information onto these nodes is needed. Such facilities exist (such as CMU's "package," see Chapter 14), but are not yet part of our general infrastructure. Also, they are not available for the Macs and PCs that make up most of our population.

15.2.2.5 Dial-in Service

Stanford currently has three types of centrally-provided dial-in service. One is traditional terminal-oriented dial-in, via SUNet-attached terminal servers which can initiate telnet or rlogin sessions to other systems on campus. These terminal servers also support the Xremote protocol for running X-windows over a serial line. A second dial-in service provides remote IP access to SUNet using serial line internet protocol (SLIP). This service will be extended to include the point-to-point protocol (PPP) as industry support for this protocol increases. A third service provides higher-speed access over Integrated Services Digital Network (ISDN) links. This service uses a dedicated Ethernet-ISDN bridge at each end of a link to provide transparent access to SUNet for the home user.

Dial-in network access raises a number of interesting questions. The first is access control. Dial-in facilities have traditionally been entry points for network *crackers.* For our terminal-oriented service we have not restricted who can dial in, but have adopted the time-honored practice of restricting connections from the terminal servers to within SUNet (thus unfortunately concentrating the crackers's attacks on our facilities). This approach still leaves open many avenues of attack; terminal service users strongly resist any more restrictive measures, however.

SLIP (or IP-over-PPP) connections are a more obvious threat, since the caller can transmit any kind of IP datagram; it is "like being directly attached to the net." There is a definite need to authenticate users of this service, yet the potential user community is very large and very diverse, including all segments of the campus. Taking advantage of a central authentication system is an obvious solution. We have done this using the Kerberos authentication database underlying the ACE environment, using some locally-developed software (i.e., kludges). Yet the ACE database currently only covers about half the campus population, since it is used primarily to support academic computing. Extending it to include all potential dial-in users raises problems of its own (see section 15.5.1).

A second issue with dial-in is support. At Stanford users of computers on departmental networks are supported by their departments. When those same users dial in from home to use departmental computers through central facilities the support question becomes more difficult.

15.2.3 SUNet Application Services

We now turn to network-based applications that take advantage of one or more of the core services. We assume the reader is familiar with these applications since they appear at many other sites in similar forms. Our purpose is to highlight the problems these applications pose in meeting the increasingly sophisticated needs of an increasingly broad user population. Though a common thread of issues and problems runs throughout, each service has its unique requirements that contribute to the overall requirements for the distributed system. Note that unlike the core services, the services that are described here are run by many different groups across campus.

15.2.3.1 Remote Login

The most popular network application continues to be remote login to departmental servers, ACE systems, or the Data Center's administrative mainframe. TCP/IP-based clients are available for virtually every computer attached to SUNet.

Remote login continues to be a gaping security hole. Using telnet, thousands of passwords are sent over the network in the clear every day. The alternative, BSD rlogin, does not send passwords but has its own notorious security problems. (The data center provides encrypted connections to users of their locally-developed PC- or Mac-based login clients.)

In addition, a user with accounts on systems in several different departments is likely to have several different usernames, user id numbers, and so on. As the number of service-providing hosts increases, a user is often obliged to log in to several different systems to accomplish a single task.

15.2.3.2 File Service

Among the network-based services, file service is perhaps the most varied in its forms, functions, and appearances. It may be invisible to the casual user, who only knows that the files show up where they are expected. It may be explicitly invoked after browsing a large list of possible servers. It provides access to personal file storage and to files shared by large communities. In many PC-based systems *the network* and *the file server* are indistinguishable.

In its traditional form a single file server provides service to a small group of clients in a department. At Stanford such a server might be a Unix server using the NFS protocol, a Macintosh server using the Apple Filing Protocol, or a NetWare server using the NetWare protocols. In this traditional form, the client and server are usually the same hardware/software platform.

From this simple start file service has evolved in all directions. More and more servers are now able to provide file service via multiple protocols: both Unix and NetWare servers often provide AFP service these days. The AFS system, supported at Stanford by the ACE facility (see section 15.1.2 and Chapter 10), allows a large collection of servers to appear as a single unified file system supporting thousands of users and hundreds of gigabytes of storage. The ability of the average UNIX workstation to be both NFS server and client has increased both the flexibility and the fragility of NFS use in typical departments, which often discover their workstations enmeshed in a thicket of cross-mounted file systems. The appearance of

Macintosh *personal filesharing* has prompted an explosion of AFP servers. Over 1,300 now appear among the Stanford AppleTalk zones: perhaps as many as one out of three networked Macintoshes is acting as a file server.

These services present a wide spectrum. To the user, a centrally-managed, large-scale service offers all the institutional benefits: security, consistency, well-managed backups, technical support, vast storage resources, global access, and so on. It also presents the traditional institutional obstacles: bureaucracy, high start-up costs, lack of end-user control, complexity, contention over shared resources, and so on. A completely distributed approach (e.g., a sea of Macintosh workstation/file servers) presents the opposite balance: ease of setup and individual control are maximized, but security, backups, support, and scalability are sacrificed.

It is clear that these extremes each have their place in the file service marketplace. A successful integrated solution should draw as many benefits as possible from each end of the spectrum. We foresee a system that offers a global filesystem view but that has a place for both large-scale centrally-maintained stable institutional file servers and low-overhead casually-offered servers.

The AFS system provides us with our closest current approach to location-independent integrated distributed computing. Its use of Kerberos keeps passwords from being sent across the network in the clear (as long as the user is sitting at the AFS client workstation). Its global file-system view allows users to get to their personal files, to shared data files and to applications from any client machine. Replicated read-only files allow uninterrupted service despite file server outages.

The current AFS system also has some shortcomings as a complete distributed computing solution. In its standard configuration AFS does not allow the client workstation to use its Kerberos credentials for other purposes (there are workarounds that do permit this). AFS offers no direct support for Macintoshes and IBM-compatible PCs (see Chapter 10 for an approach to providing this support). Lastly, AFS assumes that all servers in a cell are under a single administration. This presents obstacles to distributing the operation of servers among different organizations within the campus. Departments cannot merge their local disk resources into the overall system without simply donating them to the central organization, which they are not inclined to do.

15.2.3.3 Electronic Mail

Almost all campus computer users take advantage of electronic mail (email). Email at Stanford is almost entirely IP-based, using SMTP for transmission. Due to early efforts that promoted the use of email on mainframes and departmental host computers, users became accustomed to Internet-style email addresses (user@somehost.somedomain), and to the global connectivity that Internet mail provides. This relative homogeneity is in contrast to many large organizations, where islands of proprietary mail systems are connected via gateways (usually using SMTP).

Stanford email users employ a bewildering variety of mail user agents (MUAs) to read, compose, and manipulate their mail. Many log in to hosts and use terminal-oriented MUAs (e.g. ELM). Many microcomputer users use MUAs (e.g. Eudora) based on the post office protocol (POP) to retrieve mail from mailboxes on central hosts. Workstation users generally use graphical MUAs (e.g. xmh). Use of MUAs with interactive mail access protocol (IMAP) capability is increasingly popular for reading mail that is maintained on central mail servers.

While IP-based mail has been important common denominator, it has also been a least common denominator for many. IP-based mail (actually RFC 822-based) is ASCII only. Inclusion of formatted files (e.g. word processor documents or graphics) has been obscure and error-prone, as has been support for non-English characters. A campus-wide directory service is available (Whois, described below), but it is not integrated with MUAs, so lookup and copying of addresses is done separately from message composition.

Unlike many sites, Stanford does not offer a central mail-forwarding scheme; in general mail sent to user@stanford.edu will not go anywhere. The wide distribution of hosts currently handling IP-based mail is the main obstacle to such a scheme: hundreds of currently non-coordinated machines would need to have their mail software configured consistently. Users are very familiar with the "user@somehost.Stanford.EDU" form of addresses; yet determining which "somehost" to use can be a challenge (see the Directory Service section below). Within their communities, the ACE and administrative computing environments do provide centralized email service.

Like most other services, email currently suffers from a complete lack of security. It is trivial for mail to be intercepted or spoofed. Remote mailbox access generally involves sending passwords across the network in the clear. As more important business is done using email every day, these risks becomes more prominent.

15.2.3.4 Printing

Networked printing, at Stanford as elsewhere, was revolutionized a few years ago by the appearance of the Apple LaserWriter, which not only provided easy access to shared printing, but helped to establish Adobe's PostScript as a standard page description language. Almost 1,000 LaserWriters or equivalents are available on SUNet. A large number of campus UNIX systems print to these printers as well, primarily using the publicly-available Columbia AppleTalk Package (CAP). UNIX systems, and many PCs, also use the BSD lpr/lpd protocol to transfer print jobs between systems. Even much printing from the administrative mainframe uses a combination of lpr/lpd and AppleTalk to deliver print jobs to local printers.

As with other systems printing often suffers from difficulty of setup and inconsistency in use. A printer may be known by one name when printing from a Macintosh, another when printing from a UNIX system. CAP configuration provides excellent job insurance for UNIX gurus. Capabilities of networked printers have become more varied (e.g., color, high resolution, double-sided pages, binding, fax transmission), but information about these capabilities is not easily accessible to users.

The major problem facing print service suppliers, especially in more public areas, is accounting and access control. LaserWriters and equivalents are wonderfully accessible but hard to control. Spooling through UNIX servers improves the situation, but the mesh of servers and printers makes managing of user accounts and quotas difficult. For student printing, making use of the ACE accounts database (and therefore its underlying authentication system) is an obvious choice. There has been some success with this approach, but software to apply this to the printing problem has had to be written from scratch.

15.2.3.5 Directory Service

The domain name system, described above, provides a low-level naming service for host names and IP addresses. The central computing organization offers a separate directory service, based on the Whois protocol, which provides a higher-level white pages style directory for the campus. This directory includes listings for all Stanford people, and all networked computers (all those that have IP addresses, at least). Figure 15.2 shows the output from a query on "schemers." Other types of queries include information on hosts "Slapshot.Stanford.EDU", and IP addresses "36.5.0.10."

```
% whois schemers
    Stanford University Whois Service
         name: Schemers, Roland
       e-mail: schemers@Jessica
 organization: University
   department: Networking/Communication Sys
     position: Systems Programmer
      address: G16 Redwood Hall
        phone: (415) 723-0000
          fax: (415) 723-0010
    mail-code: 4122
       handle: rschemers
%  whois slapshot
                Stanford University Whois Service
Gretzky, Gordy J.    <ggretzky>  (415) 498-0000 slapshot@Leland
  Engineering: General, Junior
Slapshot                <slapshot.stanford.edu>    36.5.0.112
  Networking & Communication Systems, DEC-5000/240 ULTRIX (4.2a)
```

Figure 15.2 Output for Whois directory queries.

The Whois service is very popular, receiving several thousand queries an hour at peak periods. Whois data about people is assembled from various official university sources. Whois data about computers is supplied by NetDB (see section 15.2.4).

Whois illustrates a variety of issues. Its popularity shows that there is a great demand for on-line directories. The difficulty of assembling the data and keeping it current and consistent shows the difficulty of providing a service that covers the whole institution evenly. At a technical level, the Whois protocol is the simplest possible one, which allows us to easily provide clients on all platforms. However, it provides no support for redundant service, structured queries, programmatic access, authenticated access control, distribution of authority or data, and so on.

Directory service is coming to be seen as the cornerstone of distributed, location-independent computing. As we hear from different vendors about their plans for file service, or electronic mail, or printing, they always start with "First, put all this information into our directory service." Of course each vendor's directory (even though many are "X.500-like") has a different structure and different access protocols. We know from experience that maintaining even a single campus-wide directory is difficult; maintaining several would be impossible.

15.2.3.6 Software Distribution and Licensing

Currently licensed software distribution is performed by various methods. There are a number of anonymous ftp servers on campus that only accept connections from computers located on SUNet. Other software distribution uses NFS; in this case access is restricted to specific machines, which increases both security and administrative overhead. There also have been AppleTalk file servers which use the "Guest" account for access to licensed Macintosh software.

As off-campus dial-in becomes more and more common place it becomes harder and harder to define what is part of the Stanford network and what is not; thus controlling access based on network address becomes less appropriate. Of course, breaches in security in this application could lead to not just exposed or lost files but to lawsuits for copyright violation. The use of AppleShare Guest access for this purpose has been mostly abandoned, for example, because innovations in AppleTalk tunneling permit, at least in theory, anyone in the Internet to access Stanford AppleTalk networks.

This is another application for campus-wide authentication. We are experimenting with modified ftp and AppleTalk servers that use the ACE Kerberos database for authentication. This works reasonably well to provide low-overhead access control, but suffers from the ACE database not being truly campus-wide, and the fact that the unmodified FTP and AppleShare clients continue to send the user's password over the network in the clear.

Software licensing presents related problems. Many modern software packages incorporate their own license server which checks out licenses to authorized users as needed. This is good in being an improvement over buying a separate copy of the software for each potential user, but running a separate server for each application is cumbersome at best. In some cases, the burden of license server administration is so onerous that users buy separate copies of the software anyway. Clearly a unified approach to license service, based on a standard authentication scheme, would make this approach much more generally useful.

15.2.3.7 Information Access and Conferencing

The tremendous growth in the quantity and diversity of information via campus networks and via the Internet as a whole in the early 90s provides ample evidence of the emergence of the network as an information utility. Campus wide information systems (CWIS) in various forms have evolved to both deliver information to users and provide a structure for them to locate it.

Campus-wide conferencing is available to almost all SUNet users via the Usenet News system. Many classes on campus use the news system to discuss course related topics. Campus organizations of all kinds use newsgroups as an electronic meeting place. Support of users of various campus computing services is delivered via newsgroups, both by official support people and by volunteers. Unlike many campuses that have had large investments in mainframe-based single-host conferencing systems, Stanford has supported multi-system *bulletin boards* for many years. These locally-developed systems have gradually been absorbed into the more general Usenet structure.

Usenet, true to its UNIX roots, is an administrator-intensive system. Groups are created centrally, as are policies about access, article expiration, and so on. The central computing group provides both the news servers used by most of the campus and the administration of the service.

The Internet Gopher is a CWIS developed at the University of Minnesota. It is a relatively new service on campus and is part of the current crop of campus wide information systems (CWIS) available on the Internet. The central computing group supports a root Gopher server which provides links to several other Gopher servers on campus. It also provides access to other sources of information (e.g., the archie archive service) via gateways. One particularly interesting experimental gateway has been set up by the data center to provide access to its vast Folio information resource. This offers an opportunity to reshape this venerable terminal-oriented service for the 90s.

The growth of Gopher has been a phenomenon all across the Internet; Stanford has enjoyed its success too. Its attraction is in the way it distributes control along with information. At Stanford no organization could provide an integrated CWIS if it had to gather and manage information from a vast number of sources. Gopher allows us to provide a central service that hands off control to other local services as appropriate. Here again we observe that the model of distributed control with central coordination, mirroring the design of the Internet as a whole, is a key organizing principle of a successful integrated distributed computing system.

15.2.4 Distributed Management

Any central computing organization is obliged to make decisions about how much of the computing environment to control centrally, and how much to distribute to its client organizations (in some cases these decisions are made for them, of course). At Stanford the reality is that management of most of the network and its computing resources is distributed to the various departments. We have adapted to this situation by: 1) continuing to manage those resources that can only be successfully managed centrally (e.g., the backbone network), and 2) developing and providing tools to departments to promote the effective management of their local resources. This section describes the latter approach in more detail, and considers the impact of DCE on this strategy.

15.2.4.1 Local Network Administrators

Each department or other organization whose local network is attached to SUNet is required (at least in theory) to appoint a person (or group) as its local network administrator (LNA). The LNA is a single point of contact both for departmental network users and for central support. The central computing organization provides the LNA with training, documentation, and access to tools such as NetDB (see the next section). The goal is that the LNA be able to resolve most installation, configuration, and troubleshooting issues without involving central support personnel.

In different areas the LNA function takes different forms. In some departments there really is just one LNA who handles all networking needs, and probably has responsibility for other computing functions too. In larger departments a computing support staff may take on the LNA role. In many small departments, the LNA role may be only partly filled by someone who is not well trained or has little time for it; in others there is no LNA at all. The central support people are obliged to provide some load-levelling by leaving the more well-staffed areas to take care of themselves while extending more help to those that need it. This is not always effective.

In all areas as the networked computing system increases in scale and complexity the tension between users, local support, and central support grows. Users need more support from LNAs, who turn for more help to the central support groups. In turn central support is always trying to push more functions out into the departments. A large integrated distributed computing system will put these relationships to the test even more as the focus of coordination shifts from IP addresses and DNS servers to authentication, directories, and distributed file systems. A system that requires LNAs to understand all its intricacies will fail, but one that makes their lives easier will be much more likely to succeed.

15.2.4.2 NetDB

The central computing organization provides a registration service for all IP-based network nodes. A model of important network entities such as networks, hosts, and routers is implemented in a database. LNAs are given access via a terminal-oriented front end program that allows them to examine, add, delete, and modify network elements. The system prevents basic mistakes: duplicate names or addresses, addresses on non-existent networks, and so on. The information in the database is extracted regularly to generate domain name system tables, bootstrap protocol tables, AppleTalk routing tables, and so on. It also provides for the entry of other helpful information like the node's location, type, user, administrator, and so on. Over 150 LNAs use the system currently.

This system is similar in concept to other service management systems such as Project Athena's Moira. Its differences are that it is more limited in scope yet more suitable for concurrent access by a large number of users. It has been remarkably successful at pushing the day-to-day tasks of name and address management out to departments. Departmental users appreciate the local control; central support staff appreciate having someone else do the work. Everyone appreciates that the system does a reasonably good job at ensuring the integrity of the overall network configuration.

The price, of course, is in the development and maintenance of the NetDB system. It is under constant pressure to support new kinds of objects (e.g., NetWare servers and IPX addresses), and new capabilities for existing objects (e.g., variable length subnet masks). Everyone would like a better user interface. As we look at the evolution into a more comprehensive distributed system, we see that NetDB's network model needs to be extended in many directions to include users, services, dial-in lines, and so on. As we look at other configuration management systems, including commercial products, we are faced with the usual build-or-buy crisis. It is clear that whatever features it may be desirable to add, the distributed access feature can never go away; we and our users depend on it.

15.2.4.3 Network Management

Stanford's network management effort includes many components. A commercial network management system (NMS) is used to maintain a network map, to monitor the status of our critical hardware resources (principally backbone routers), to collect data on network traffic and produce reports, and to generate trouble tickets. Other locally-developed tools check on the status of our core services. Devices such as network analyzers are used to debug particular problems.

Recently, due to both the increased stability of the SUNet backbone and the increased importance and complexity of network services, the focus of network management has shifted upwards. Integrating service management into network management is desirable because our NMSs are good at the tricky problem of getting trouble information to the right people quickly. But higher-level services generally do not provide interfaces for remote, automated management; also, each is different, so the start-up cost of managing them in this way is high. Also, the NMS is better at answering "is it up?" than at determining whether a web of complex service components are healthy.

Every advanced distributed system involves a level of complex service interaction far exceeding what we have now. If such a system is to be reliable enough to be successful, it simply must be designed from the start to be manageable.

15.2.5 Integrated Distributed Computing

In the previous sections, we have tried to describe the broad class of problems faced by Stanford's existing network services. These can be summarized as follows:

- There is a tremendous upward pressure as more users use more systems to work and communicate in a wider variety of ways every day.
- There is a corresponding downward pressure as systems grow harder to understand, less interoperable, and more costly to support.

We believe the only approach to dealing with these twin pressures is to develop an integrated distributed computing system. Integration has (at least) two aspects: integration of services via a common architecture that reduces overall system complexity by abstracting and standardizing common elements (e.g. security); and integration of deployed systems so that they are able to cooperate across campus at a higher level than they do now.

From the preceding descriptions we can derive the key features of any distributed system technology that would solve these problems. These include:

- *A comprehensive array of high-level services:* A system must support most of the services described in the previous parts of this section (as well as others not mentioned, such as backup) to be viable. In particular, support for universal data access via a campus-wide file system is a crucial component.
- *Building on our existing operational bedrock:* In particular, this means Internet Protocol-based communication and UNIX-based servers.
- *Directory service:* A comprehensive, flexible directory provides numerous benefits including location independence, service reconfiguration, network navigation, and so on. It allows the configuration aspects of applications to be extracted from them and managed in a centralized, coherent fashion. An ideal directory should include support for both low-level objects such as machines and IP addresses and higher level objects such as services and users.

- *Security service:* In general this means the ability to provide system resources with appropriate protection independent of the particular applications that use them. Similar to the directory, the security service allows the authentication and access control aspects of applications to be distilled from them and managed in a consistent way.
- *Vendor-independence:* This provides safeguards against both the success and the failure of individual vendors.
- *Support for program and service development:* All aspects of the system must have published APIs, libraries, and development tools. This support is important for both building bridges to our existing systems and services as well as building wonderful new services.
- *Support for automated configuration of all components:* This includes generation of start-up files for workstations and servers, configuration of services, generation of new user accounts, and so on. This support should extend to handling distribution and configuration of licensed resources such as software packages (see Chapters 5 and 14).
- *Support for users of Macintoshes and IBM-compatible PCs:* This is perhaps the greatest integration challenge, as these systems have the most investment in non-IP technology and are the least amenable to central coordination.
- *Support for coordinated distributed management:* We return again to our theme of coordination. By "coordinated distributed management" we mean the ability to assign responsibility and control to central support groups or departments as appropriate. The system must permit us to make these assignments in response to organizational and technical needs, and to change them over time. One site refers to their approach as "centralized upkeep; distributed control" to emphasize that the central support group provides the mechanism through which the departments can implement their policy.

We have identified OSF/DCE as being the technology with the closest current fit to these requirements. In the next section, we consider some high-level aspects of DCE.

15.3 Assessing DCE

In this section, we take a look at the distributed computing environment (DCE) technology from the Open Software Foundation (OSF) to assess how well it meets our criteria for an integrated computing environment. DCE is described in more detail in Chapter 7.

15.3.1 What is DCE?

DCE is a set of services that provides a coherent vendor and operating system independent distributed environment. Since DCE is technology supplied by OSF and not a single vendor, it is a much more attractive solution then a proprietary single vendor solution. DCE is not an operating system, nor is it an application. It consists of a core set of services that together provide the framework for creating a distributed environment. You can picture DCE as being layered upon existing operating system technologies, and new distributed applications being built upon this layer:

DCE Applications

DCE

Operating System Interface

15.3.2 What Does DCE Give You?

DCE provides the tools to build and operate distributed applications. By providing these tools, DCE also gives you an environment that is portable across heterogeneous systems running DCE. DCE supports a client-server model of interaction and promotes data sharing through the use of CDS, specialized servers, and the distributed file system, DFS. One of the most important features of DCE is that it promotes a global distributed computing environment in which organizations all over the world can participate.

The DCE core services are:

- synchronized time
- authentication/authorization
- client-to-server communication
- a naming service
- a distributed file system

The DCE Distributed Time Service (DTS) provides synchronized time to computers on the network. The DCE Security service provides the tools needed for authentication and authorization. The DCE Remote Procedure Call (RPC) provides the primary method for client-server communications. The DCE Cell Directory Service (CDS), Global Directory Service (GDS), and the Global Directory Agent (GDA) provide the naming services. The DCE Distributed File System (DFS) is not a core DCE service, but rather an application built on top of the other DCE core services. Another service that DCE provides is DCE Threads. Threads are basically light weight processes that share the same address space. This allows a single server to efficiently handle multiple requests at the same time, or any application to continue working while waiting for a response from a server.

15.3.3 DCE is an All or Nothing Venture

The DCE core services are very tightly integrated. This means you cannot really pick and choose which parts of DCE you want to use (nor would you want to). For example, the time service DTS uses DCE RPC for communication, DCE Security for authentication and authorization, and CDS for finding DTS Server locations. The following table lists which services depend on which other services.

Core Service	Other Core Services Used
Threads	None
RPC	Threads, CDS, Security
DTS	Threads, RPC, CDS, Security
CDS	Threads, RPC, DTS, Security
Security	Threads, RPC, DTS, CDS
DFS	Threads, RPC, DTS, CDS, Security

15.3.4 DCE is a Framework, Not a Complete Solution

An important thing to remember is that DCE provides a framework for creating a distributed environment. Although it provides a number of useful functions, they are only the beginning.

DCE facilities can be thought of as being a distributed version of the core services provided by most modern operating systems. A full computer system includes much more: user utilities, system management utilities, programming tools, third-party applications. The single-system versions of these programs may need to be retooled or replaced for the distributed environment.

As a simple example, consider the UNIX "`ls`" command.

```
% ls -lFg
-rw-r--r-- 1 morgan network 2108 May 9 01:53 rlm.doc
```

The content of the owner field ("`morgan`") is determined by mapping the file's numeric ID to a user name via the contents of the /etc/passwd file. The mode bits and group name ("`staff`") display attributes of the UNIX file protection scheme. If this directory entry were in a DFS file system, a DFS-aware `ls` would have to use CDS and Registry facilities to determine the file's owner. The group and mode bits may be misleading, since protection is done via the much more flexible access control list (ACL) mechanism (though there is a definition of restricted ACLs that map directly to the traditional protections). Some new way must be found to convey the richer protection information that is available. The traditional `ls` command may be obsolete on such a system.

It is up to system vendors to do this low-level integration when they incorporate DCE into their systems. Application vendors must provide packages that are DCE-aware. And as system integrators, both central computing organizations and departments must decide on how best to make use of DCE capabilities. We have spent many years developing conventions and standard practices on our existing systems; this is one of the necessary early tasks with DCE.

15.4 Migration Issues and Plans

In this section, we consider some specific concerns about bringing DCE into our existing computing environment.

15.4.1 General Issues

15.4.1.1 Platform Support

DCE's availability from many different vendors is one of its most attractive features. There are a number of vendors offering DCE, including all major UNIX vendors. On smaller machines and non-UNIX machines it's likely that only DCE client software will be available or appropriate. Apple has announced DCE support for its PowerPC platforms in conjunction with the Apple Open Collaboration Environment. We are hopeful that Apple (or some third party) will also support DCE (at least DCE clients) on the existing Macintosh platform. IBM has a version of DCE for OS/2. Gradient has DCE available for PCs running DOS and Windows. Even Windows NT will support DCE's RPC, although it is unclear how it will interact with other parts of DCE. Digital is also supporting DCE on its OpenVMS platform.

Licensing costs are a real concern, especially if the DCE supplier is different from the system vendor. If a technology that is to spread across a large percentage of the campus's 11,000 systems costs several hundred dollars per node, this is a large institutional obstacle.

15.4.1.2 Operating System Integration

In order to take full advantage of DCE, vendors will have to integrate DCE into their operating system utilities. For example, the login program should be modified so when you login to a workstation it contacts the registry service to get your account information and uses the DCE login facility to authenticate you.

Digital's OSF/1 operating system is one OS that is taking steps in the right direction. DEC OSF/1 provides something known as the Security Integration Architecture, or SIA. All security sensitive programs (for example: login, passwd, su) use the SIA interface for security related calls. A configuration file allows you to pick which security mechanism you wish to use. Figure 15.3 gives an overview of SIA.

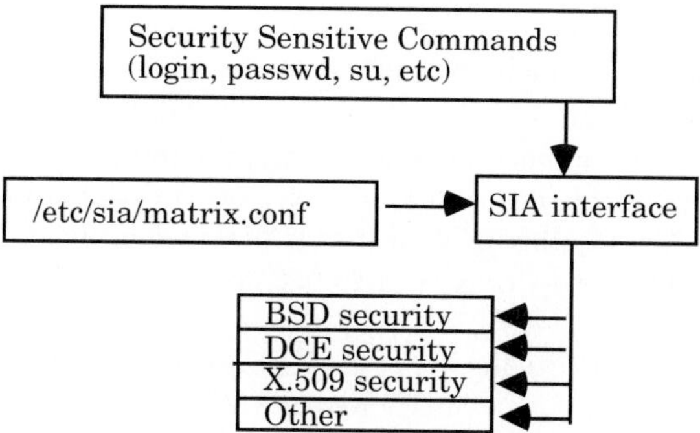

Figure 15.3 DEC OSF/1 Security Integration Architecture.

Sun also provides the same type of integration with their "Federated Services" model. The nice thing about this model is that it can be applied to different classes of distributed computing services, such as filing, naming, and security.

Models such as SIA and Federation Services are a big step forward. They allow new services to be integrated into operating systems without the need for modifying the operating system or any utilities directly. On the other hand, they represent yet another set of configuration variables that must be set correctly before a system will operate in a particular environment.

15.4.1.3 Vendor Compatibility

Even though DCE was designed to work in a multi-vendor environment, you still need to be aware of which version of DCE a vendor is shipping. For example, as of this writing the current version of DCE is 1.0.2. The next major release is DCE 1.1, which is to include many new features. To fully take advantage of these improvements you need to make sure all your DCE clients are based on DCE 1.1. If one vendor takes six months to move to a new release of DCE and another takes 12 months you have to take that into account while planning upgrades. In an integrated distributed system with hundreds or thousands of nodes, the necessity of interoperation of different versions must be acknowledged.

15.4.2 Migration of Existing Services

In this section, we consider issues related to migrating the core services described earlier to the DCE.

15.4.2.1 Authentication

Stanford does not currently have a single authentication service for the entire campus. There a number of issues that need to be solved. One of the biggest problems is deciding who is and is not a member of the "Stanford" community. This problem will be addressed in the "User Registration" section. Although Stanford does not have a single authentication server on campus, there are two major authentication camps on campus; the Administrative Computing Environment (ADMIN) and the Academic Computing Environment (ACE).

The administrative computing environment at Stanford currently uses an ID/PIN scheme for authenticating users in their mainframe environment. The ID is a unique numeric value consisting of eight digits. The PIN is also numeric and must be at least five digits long. This scheme is identical to the one banks use for ATM cards. IDs and PINs are fine for a mainframe environment but one of the glaring problems in a networked environment is that the PIN consists of only digits, making it very easy to crack. Also, the use of a numeric ID does not map well to other uses, such as UNIX account names and email addresses. The ADMIN PIN/ID database consists of 23,000 accounts, of which approximately 15,000 are active.

ACE is currently making use of the Kerberos server included with AFS. The Kerberos server included with AFS is essentially Kerberos V4, although there are a few differences. The ACE Kerberos database contains roughly 12,000 accounts.

The authentication service in DCE is essentially Kerberos Version 5, although it is not clear if standard V5 clients will work the DCE Security service. The main issues involved with migrating from Kerberos V4 to V5 are the migration of the Kerberos database, and supporting Kerberos V4 clients.

The reason that migrating the Kerberos database is not as simple as dumping the database in one format and reloading it in another is that users's passwords are stored in a hashed form in the Kerberos V4 database. This is created by taking information (such as the user's clear-text password) and running it through a string-to-key function which produces a 64-bit DES key. [see Chapter 4] The string-to-key function is a hashing function that cannot be reversed. Kerberos V4 and V5 (DCE) use different string-to-key functions, so the old database is of no use. One way of automating the conversion is to install a special **passwd** program. When a user changes their current Kerberos V4 password, the passwd program can contact a special server (using Kerberos for authentication) that has access to the Kerberos V5 database. This server would then set the user's V5 password for them automatically.

Supporting Kerberos V4 clients is also an issue. One solution is to run a V4 server in parallel with V5. This has the burden of maintaining two databases. Another solution would be for DCE vendors to modify their V5 server to handle V4 requests. The MIT V5 implementation supports a V4 compatibility mode, although its not clear at this point if vendors will enable this feature.

Another issue is supporting existing passwd files and NIS services. DCE comes with two utilities, called **passwd_import** and **passwd_export** that are used to import and export **passwd** style files. Since the DCE Security Service uses a different method then UNIX to encrypt passwords, the **passwd_import** cannot import existing passwords. New passwords need to be issued. The **passwd_export** program is used to export passwd style information from the registry database. There are a number of options available for the account information that is exported. See OSF DCE, 1991 for more information.

15.4.2.2 Time Service

DTS and NTP can coexist. Sites that already have an NTP infrastructure in place can continue to use NTP for non-DCE clients. There are number of ways DTS and NTP can coexist. The first way is to have one or more DTS servers get their time via NTP. This can done by using the DTS time-provider interface. You can use the supplied null time-provider, and run a NTP server on the same machine as the DTS server, or you can use the NTP time-provider and have the DTS server get its time directly from NTP. Another option is to use another time provider such as a radio transmission (WWV, WWVB, etc.) or from a Satellite (GPS, GOES, etc.). See OSF DCE, 1991 or Rosenberry, et. al., 1992 for more information on time providers. The other option is to export your time from DTS servers to your NTP servers, which then distribute the time to NTP clients. See OSF DCE, 1991 for more information.

15.4.2.3 Name Service

CDS does NOT replace DNS. DNS is used to provide inter-cell communication. For example, if you are in the cell **/.../stanford.edu** and try to access a DFS file such as **/.../athena.mit.edu/fs/README** then the CDS clerk (a process which runs on each DCE client) will recognize that the cellname "athena.mit.edu" is a DNS style name. The CDS clerk will then contact a CDS server and ask for the location of a global directory agent (GDA). The GDA is responsible for resolving global cell names. The GDA will contact a DNS server which then returns the information associated with the **athena.mit.edu** cell entry. The GDA will then return this information back to the CDS server, which passes it back to the CDS clerk. The CDS clerk then knows how to contact a CDS server in the **athena.mit.edu** cell. Yikes! A picture might help, see figure 15.4.

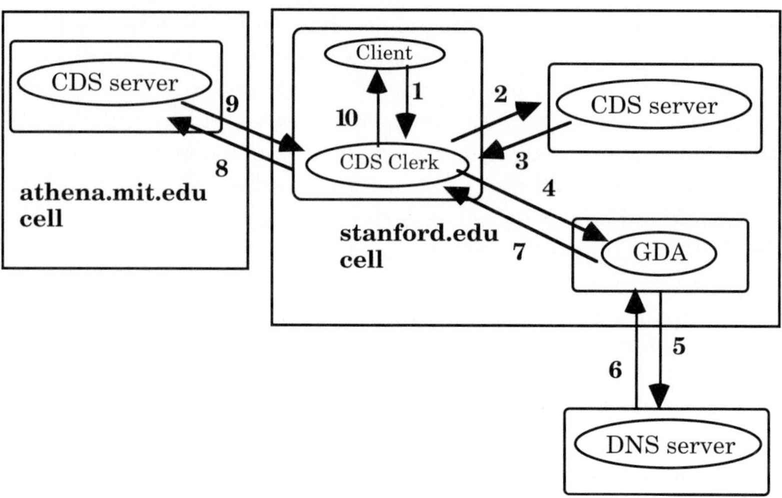

Figure 15.4 DCE interaction with DNS.

The DCE global directory service (GDS), is essentially X.500. It is based on the international standard CCITT X.500/ISO 9594 (1988). In order to work within existing TCP/IP networks, GDS can use TCP/IP as its transport, and it uses the protocol defined in RFC1006 to do so. If you currently have an existing X.500 server, you may decide to migrate to DCE's X.500 implementation. At this point its not clear if it would be worth the effort to migrate to GDS. The main reason is its not tightly integrated with DCE. For example, it does not use the DCE Security Service for security, instead it maintains its own password database. Future versions of DCE will better integrate GDS into the DCE environment though, thus at some point using GDS should be an administrative win.

15.4.2.4 AFS/DFS Migration

Stanford has a large AFS environment. We have some 12,000 accounts and 60 gigabytes of disk space in our AFS environment. Migrating from AFS to DFS is not going to be a simple task. Thankfully Transarc has been working on a migration strategy for AFS to DFS. Even more thankfully is it has been an iterative process, and they have be receptive to customer concerns.

The following information is based on a DRAFT version of the "AFS to DCE DFS Migration Toolkit Administration Guide," which was distributed at the Winter, '93 AFS users group meeting. In order to use this toolkit, you must be using AFS version 3.3, which should be shipping soon after this book is published.

Transarc's AFS to DCE DFS Migration Toolkit consists of two separate packages, **ADMIT** and **ADAPT. ADMIT** (AFS/DFS: Migration Import Tools) is used for moving accounts, groups, and passwords from AFS to the DCE security Service. **ADMIT** is also used to migrate AFS volumes to DFS filesets.

ADAPT (AFS/DFS: A Protocol Translator) is used to provide access to DFS filesets from AFS client machines. Using ADMIT and ADAPT allows you to incrementally move data from AFS to DFS, while still maintaining access to the data from AFS clients. Of course data moved into DFS will be accessible from DFS clients. The other choice is to run both the AFS and DFS client software on client machines. This will only work for machines that support both clients.

The major user-visible differences between AFS and DFS are:

- **Pathnames** — Fully qualified AFS pathnames begin with the prefix **/afs/cellname** while DFS pathnames begin with **/.../cellname/fs.**
- **ACLs** — In AFS, only directories may have an ACL, and they apply to every file in the directory. DFS (when used with LFS) allows ACLs on both files and directories. Access rights on files and directories also differs between AFS and DFS.
- **Command Set** — Many commands used to interact with DFS are different from AFS. These include commands used for authentication, changing ACLs, managing groups, and cache manage administration.
- **UNIX File Semantics** — DFS allows hard links to files in different directories within the same DFS fileset while AFS only allows hardlinks within the same directory. DFS also allows locking on byte ranges and changes made on a DFS client are immediately visible from other DFS clients.

15.5 DCE Management Issues

One of the key goals of integrated distributed computing is reducing the complexity of managing the large-scale environment. If management functions are clumsy, not automatable, or not distributable, all the other benefits of the system may be moot since the system just will not work correctly. In this section, we consider issues related to managing DCE. We find that this is an area where much work still needs to be done.

15.5.1 User Registration

In order for users to take full advantage of DCE they need to be registered in your cell's registry database. When a person is registered they get what is called a principal. A principal is similar to a UNIX login name. Users use their principal along with their secret key (generated from their password) to authenticate with DCE services. After creating the principal, you may also need to authorize users. This is done by adding them to various groups in the registry database, and adding their principal to ACLs.

Along with adding new users, you will have to remove users when they leave your cell. Removing users involves more then just removing their principal from the registry database. You will also have to remove them from any groups and ACLs. You also have to decide on a policy for removing users. You may want to disable their account for some period of time before actually removing them from your cell. That way if they return (in the case of a student at the university for example) there is less work involved in adding them back to the cell. You might also want to delay removing them so any DFS files or ACLs that might be owned by them will clearly be identified. This will help the person in charge of transferring responsibility from one principal to another.

Getting registered in a cell gives a user certain rights within your cell. You can set things up so all users do not have to be registered. This is done by giving access to unauthenticated users. You can decide on how much access an unauthenticated user has to your cell by setting up ACLs on various parts of the DCE namespace (CDS, DFS, etc.). Most likely you will want to limit the amount of access you give to unauthenticated users and give more access to authenticated users. The reason being that you have more trust in the identity of an authenticated user (one who is registered with your cell) then any random user who stumbles upon your cell. Depending on the security of your cell, you will also have to decide who is allowed to get registered in your cell. For example, the Stanford community is made up of a large number of groups. There are faculty, staff, the Medical School, the Stanford Hospital, the Stanford Linear Accelerator (SLAC), and even students (at least that is what we have heard). Determining which users in these group will participate in the cell, and even identifying which group a user fits into will be a major problem. The only solution might be to have multiple DCE cells and some sort of inter-cell authorization policies. That way the Stanford Hospital can decide if they want to register a temporary resident or not in their cell.

All of these issues add up to a lot of work for large cells, and to a moderate amount of work for small cells. For an academic site like Stanford, we also have to worry about registering several thousand new accounts each semester, and removing (or disabling) roughly the same amount. ACE currently handles this by getting data from the registrar's office (essentially a name and Stanford ID) and loading it into an accounts database. Users can then login to a special account and ask for an ACE account. They user their student ID as a temporary password to authenticate their identity to the registration program (see also chapter 9). At this point users pick their own account name and initial password. The registration program has access to all the assigned names so the user must pick a unique name (see also Chapter 10). We found that allowing users to pick their own account name is better then forcing one on them. Once the user picks a unique name it is marked as reserved in the database. Account requests are batched up and created once a night.

We envision using a similar process with registering new DCE accounts. One way to migrate the registration of current ACE accounts to DCE accounts is to install a modified passwd program. The modified passwd program would then contact (using Kerberos for authentication) a server which checks to see if a user has been registered in DCE or not. If the user is not registered, the program would then register them in the DCE registry by using their current account and new passwd for their DCE account.

15.5.2 Managing CDS

There are a number of issues involved with managing the CDS namespace. The CDS administrator will have to create directories for users and applications to use. They will also have to manage the ACLs on directories. Some of this work can be delegated to other users and groups via ACLs. For example, the CDS administrator could create the CDS directory **/.:/group/chem** and then give authorization (via an ACL) to a user in the chemistry department. Then that person could create subdirectories and manage ACLs in the chemistry directory. Besides delegating authorization you can also delegate the management of a directory by creating a clearinghouse on another CDS server and moving that directory to the new clearinghouse. Administration of the CDS can also be delegated by adding a user to the group **/.:sec/subsys/dce/cds-admin**, which gives them full permission to administer the CDS namespace (if you follow the default cell configuration).

Your average DCE user may or may not need write access to any directories in CDS depending on how you set up your cell and your policies for administering the CDS namespace. If a user wants to write their own DCE application, then most likely they will want access to a CDS directory in which they can register their application. One way to do this is give users a *home* directory in CDS in which they can have their application servers register (e.g., **/.:/users/smith**).

The CDS administrator must also handle replicating directories and backing up the CDS database. You should try and replicate every directory in the CDS namespace if possible. That way if one of the CDS servers is unavailable then one containing the replicate will be able to continue handling requests. You can backup your CDS servers by using replication, or by using operating system backups. If you decide to use operating system backups then you need to make sure to disable a server with the "**cdscp disable server**" command before performing the backup. This will ensure the data you are backingup is not changing.

Another task in CDS management is capacity planning and load balancing. The **cdscp** command can be used to monitor counters on servers in order to determine the type and volume of CDS traffic on a server.

15.5.3 Managing the Security Service

Some of the administrative tasks for the security service were mentioned in the User Registration section. Along with registering users, you also need to register both servers and machines in DCE. For example, the principal:

/.:/sec/principal/hosts/*hostname*/self

is the principal used by the host ***hostname***. The security client daemon uses this principal. You can also use this principal for other processes on a host that normally would run as *root,* which has no meaning in a distributed computing environment. Another example is the principal used by cds-servers. The cds-server running on *hostname* would have the principal:

/.:/sec/principals/*hostname*/cds-server

It would also be a member of the group:

/.:/sec/principal/subsys/dce/cds-server

Administration of the security service can be delegated by adding a user to the group **/.:sec/subsys/dce/sec-admin**, which gives them full permission to administer the security database, by using the **/.:/sec/group/acc-admin** group, or by putting ACLs on various directories in the **/.:/sec** namespace.

The security service administrator must also handle issues such as replication, and backing up the security database.

Since the DCE security service maintains the integrity of security for your entire DCE cell, it must be kept secure. You will most likely want to keep it physically secure by placing it in a secure machine room. You should also not run any other services on the system that is running the security service. This includes limiting the number of people who can log in to that system. The tools to manage the Security Service (such as **acl_edit** and **rgy_edit**) do not have to be run on the security server host. They are DCE applications and can be run from any DCE client machine.

15.5.4 Managing DTS

Managing DTS involves setting up and maintaining DTS servers, and ensuring DTS clerks (clients) are configured correctly. There are three types of DTS servers: global, local, and courier. Global servers are used to distribute the time to other DTS servers within a cell. They should be the systems with the most accurate clocks in the cell. They can do this by getting their time via an external source such as an radio-based signals, or an NTP server. Local servers synchronize their time with other local servers on the same LAN. Courier servers are just local servers that also contact global servers.

As with the other DCE services DTS has a special group (**dts-admin**) for performing DTS administration.

15.5.5 Managing DFS

DFS is actually a DCE application, it uses all the core DCE services in order to provide a distributed file system. The DFS administrator will have their hands full in managing DFS. DFS administrator procedures include maintaining and replicating volumes, setting up backup procedures, and managing ACLs.

DFS administration can be delegated using DFS administrative domains and DFS administrative lists. A DFS administrative domain is a collection of DFS server machines in the same cell that are configured for administration as a single unit. Administrative lists are used to determine which principals are allowed to issue DFS administrative commands.

15.5.6 Managing ACLs

In general you should try not to go overboard with ACLs. You should decide at the time your cell is being initially configured your policies on access to your DCE namespace. That way as new directories are created in CDS, DFS, and so on, the default ACLs are propagated to the new directories. Another thing to consider is when placing ACLs on various objects to delegate authorization you are probably better off creating groups and placing groups on ACLs instead of individual users. For example if you want to delegate control of **/.:/group/chem** to

LNAs in the chemistry department then you should create a group called **chem-admin**, give that group access to the directory, and then add users to that group. That way you (or chemistry) can easily manage who has access to that directory. You can also use the **chem-admin** group for other uses such as DFS.

By default, the principal **cell_admin** has access perform any operation in CDS, DTS, the Security Service, and DFS. The **cell_admin** account is conceptually equivalent to the **root** account on a UNIX system. You should guard the **cell_admin** account with your life. It should only be used in emergencies as you can delegate access to DCE services by using ACLs with groups.

15.5.7 Maintaining the Consistency and Integrity of a Cell

Maintaining consistency in any distributed environment is a key issue. We envision either expanding NetDB or creating a new DCE application which will model our DCE cell using a database.

15.5.8 Education

One important thing to remember is that although DCE provides a unified distributed computing environment it is new technology and thus getting your users, programmers, and administrators to effectively use DCE is going to require some amount of training. Users will need to understand how to log in to DCE, how to manage ACLs, find their way around the DCE namespace, and so on. Programmers will have to understand how to write DCE applications utilizing the various components of DCE. Programmers who already have experience with other thread and RPC libraries will have a jump on programmers starting from ground zero. System administrators are going to have their hands full with planning, installation, and day to day management of DCE.

15.5.9 Overview of Cell configuration

We now give a brief overview of a DCE cell and cell configuration issues. Cell configuration focuses all of the distributed management issues we have raised earlier. The boundaries of the cell determine with whom you can (and are obliged to) cooperate easily; the design of the cell determines how that cooperation is accomplished.

15.5.9.1 What is a Cell?

All computers and users that participate in the DCE environment must belong to a *cell.* A cell is a way of grouping computers, users, and resources that share a common set of DCE services, such as a security server, DTS server, and CDS server. Typical cells will probably exist on the same local area network, but this is not a requirement. A cell can consist of one system or thousands of systems. Systems in a DCE cell can be in the same room, the same building, or half way around the world. A DCE cell might look like figure 15.5.

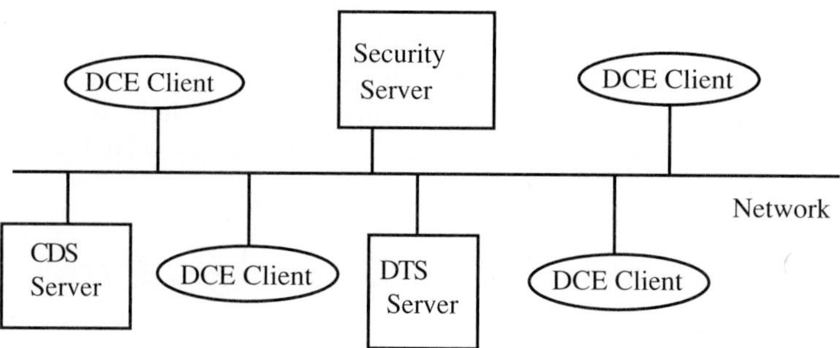

Figure 15.5 Sample DCE cell.

15.5.9.2 Why Do We Need a Cell?

A cell identifies the administrative domain of an object within the DCE environment. It helps breakdown the global distributed environment into smaller, manageable pieces. For example, it would be impractical for one DCE security to server to register every single computer that wanted to communicate in the DCE environment. This is the same problem that the Internet faced when there existed a global *hosts.txt* file. The solution was the Internet Domain Name Service (DNS). This allowed individual organizations to manage and control their own DNS, yet still be part of the global namespace.

15.5.9.3 Single Cell or Multiple Cells?

One of the things you have to decide on while setting up DCE is whether or not to setup one cell, or multiple cells. The answer depends upon your environment, and more often then not may depend on political reasons more then technical. One factor is the size of your organization. Small organizations will probably only have single cells. Larger ones will most likely have multiple cells whose boundaries are based departments or physical locations. There is also the old "You do it your way, we'll do it ours" attitude that exists among rival factions within an organization.

Even if you have multiple cells, all is not lost. DCE would not be much of a *global* distributed environment if cells could not talk to each other. Cells can determine the amount of information they want to share with other cells.

15.5.9.4 What's in a Name?

All DCE cells must have a name. The DCE Directory service provides a way to uniquely identify all resources in a DCE cell, such as a person, system, file, server, and so on. The cell name is used to identify which cell a resource belongs to. It also provides a way for local cells to access resources in remote cells. There are currently two ways to name your cell. You can either name it using a DNS-style name such as foo.bar.com, or an X.500-style name such as /C=US/O=BAR/OU=FOO. Due to the current design of DCE, you must pick one or the other. This is because all of the DCE routines that deal with cell names expect one unique cell name, and cannot deal with multiple cell names or aliases. The name of your cell also determines how remote cells will access your cell. If you choose DNS then remote cells will use your DNS server to locate your cell. If you choose X.500, then remote cells will use GDS (X.500) to contact your cell.

One thing to keep in mind is that cell names are hard to change, so unless you are setting up a test cell, choose your name wisely.

15.5.9.5 What's Needed to Set Up a Cell?

When setting up a cell, you will need to designate which machines the core DCE servers will run on. The core servers need are:

- Security Server
- CDS Server
- DTS Server

You will most likely want to setup a test cell to learn about DCE and to *play* on. Even once you have a production cell you might want to have a test cell so you can test new applications and management tools.

You can run all three core servers on one system. You can even use this system as a DCE client and thus your whole cell will reside on one machine. Setting up the entire cell one machine allows you to try out DCE without investing a lot of resources initially. In order to get a good feel for DCE's distributed nature, you will probably want to set up a least one DCE client.

This is a good way to setup a test cell, but probably not the best way to run a production cell. Why not? There are a number of reasons. First, if this machine is unavailable then your whole cell is down! Having a single point of failure in a distributed system is not good. Second, as your cell grows, then so do the resources imposed on the system these server are running on. The DCE Security Server and CDS Servers are resource intensive. They keep a lot of information in memory, so the larger your cell (in terms of users and DCE clients) the more memory these servers will need.

In order to ensure your cell does not have a single point of failure, you will want to replicate the core servers. Ideally you should have at least two security servers, two CDS servers, and three DTS time servers. If you have DFS in your cell, then you should also have multiple DFS servers. By having multiple servers, you increase the reliability of the service. If one server is unavailable, then a DCE client will be able to use another server. Having more then one server also helps distribute the load as your cell increases in size.

15.5.9.6 DCE Client Configuration

Now that we have given an overview on what servers are needed in a DCE environment, we can address what is needed to configure a DCE client. A DCE client machine will typically have the following configuration:

Security Service Client

Directory Service Client

DTS client

DFS client (optional)

DCE RPC and Threads support

Each one of these DCE service clients equates to at least one extra process on your system. In the current implementation, each user on a multi-user machine will also have its own CDS client (also refereed to as a clerk). Both CDS and DFS clients also cache information locally, and thus impose additional memory and disk requirements on the client.

Even though DCE is a distributed environment, there are still some static configuration files that must be maintained. These include files that configure what cell the DCE client belongs to, and the DCE client's hostname in the DCE namespace. Hopefully future versions of DCE will get rid of the need for DCE clients to have any local configuration files and instead get this information dynamically at start-up time.

15.6 Summary

In this chapter we have presented a bottom-up view of the problems of distributed computing today, and have defined the characteristics of a solution based on integrated distributed computing. The successful integrated system, we believe, has the potential to overcome the limitations of both the traditional centralized systems of the past and the chaotic distributed systems of the present. It does this by providing support for centralized coordination of the system, while allowing distributed resources to cooperate more effectively.

We have examined the potential of OSF/DCE as a winning integrated distributed computing technology. We find that DCE provides a useful framework but that many questions remain to be resolved in practice. Management of DCE, in particular configuration of DCE cells, is a crucial element in determining DCE's success. Better management tools must be provided, and organizations must develop management practices appropriate to the scale of the new environment. These tools and practices will find their first application in managing the transition from our existing services.

15.7 References

Champine, G., 1991. *MIT Project Athena A Model for Distributed Computing,* Digital Press.

Dyer, S.P., 1988. The Hesiod Name Service, *USENIX Association Winter Conference 1988 Proceedings,* pp. 79–109 Feb.

Hodges, J., and chemers, R., 1993. *A Comparison of NetDB and Project Athena's Moira,* Stanford University.

Levine, P., Gretzinger, M.R., Rosenstein, M.A., Diaz, J.M., Sommerfeld, B., and Raeburn, K., 1990. Section E.1: Moira, the Athena Service management System. *Project Athena Technical Plan,* M.I.T., Cambridge, Massachusetts May.

Maas, A., Zhang, J., Schemers, R., and Hodges, J., 1993. *DECathena: Macintosh Client Interim Report,* Stanford University.

Miller, S.P., Neuman, B. C., Schiller, J. I., and Saltzer, J. H., 1987. Section E.2.1: Kerberos Authentication and Authorization System. *Project Athena Technical Plan,* M.I.T., Cambridge, Massachusetts Apr.

NetDB Users Guide, Stanford University

Open Software Foundation, 1991. *OSF DCE 1.0 Documentation Set.*

Rosenberry, W., Kenny, D., and Fisher, G., 1992. *Understanding DCE,* O'Reilly & Associates, Inc.

Rosenstein, M., 1991. *Moira User's Manual.* M.I.T. Project Athena, Cambridge, Massachusetts Feb.

Rosenstein, M.A., Geer, D.E., and Levine, P.J., 1988. The Athena Service Management System, *USENIX Conference Proceedings,* pp. 203–212 Dallas, Texas Feb.

Schemers, R., 1993. *Using Kerberos V4 as an Interim Solution for SUNet Authentication,* Stanford University.

Shirley, J., 1992. *Guide to Writing DCE Applications,* O'Reilly & Associates, Inc.

Bob Morgan is a member of the Distributed Computing Group in Stanford University's Networking Systems Department. He is responsible for development of network management tools and for Stanford's extensive AppleTalk internetwork. He also contributes to planning Stanford's distributed computing architecture. Bob received his A.B. in English from Harvard University. He is a member of the ACM, is active in the Internet Engineering Task Force, and is a past President of the Bay Area Sea Kayakers.

Roland Schemers received his M.S degree in Computer Science from Oakland University in Rochester, Michigan. He is a member of the Distributed Computing Group at Stanford University. Since joining Stanford he has been investigating emerging industry standards in distributed computing, such as the OSF's DCE/DME. His interests are object oriented programming, distributed computing, and operating systems.

Chapter 16

Organizational Issues

John Sack
Stanford University

16.1 Introduction

This chapter is not about the *technology* of distributed systems so much as it is about the *implications* of such systems for the large organizations that want to move from a host-oriented base to a distributed set of systems. Other chapters have covered the *how* of such systems; here we will cover the *who, why, when, what* of the management and organizational processes that are a part of this large-scale change for a complex organization. In this chapter, we will try to answer the question, "What–other than the right technology–do we need to have a success with distributed systems?"

Managers and staff who survived earlier shifts from one computing model to another will recognize that this shift has many things in common with those earlier shifts. Indeed, many of the organizational issues and technical issues have their counterparts in previous technology shifts, allowing us to build on previous experiences. For example, the shift from file-oriented processing to database management systems in the early 80s involved significant risks, retraining, pilots, software selection, networking issues, and so on.

What is different about the move to distributed systems? Several things distinguish this era's change from what has come before:

- In most cases, previous shifts involved changing from one *technology* to another, but keeping other critical factors such as vendors and architecture relatively constant. In the previous case, the shift provides the opportunity to change all three factors at once: technology, vendors, and architecture. It is an attractive and unprecedented opportunity, one that gives no limit to the amount of variety–and chaos–you can introduce, like fighting a war on several fronts simultaneously.

- The very source of the benefits of the open systems approach distinguishes it: its flexibility. The much-hyped *plug-and-play* benefit of interoperability is the source of much of our pain–and the focus for much of our management effort–in this transition. A structure in which every element is independently articulated is very flexible, but both complicated and fragile. (Imagine your arm having a dozen elbows instead of one. It would be very flexible, but unwieldy!) There are so many *degrees of freedom*–points at which independent choices must be made–in architecting open systems that much of the management challenge is to set some elements solidly in policy or practice while others continue to change.

- A third distinguishing characteristic of this transition is the novelty of the discussion of *architecture*. In earlier generations of computing approaches, architecture–at least of application-level components–was a given, and was implicit in your choice of tools or vendor. Now, architecture as a type of computing *life-style choice* (if you will) is being made explicit. Parts of our organizations are discussing computing architecture which before had not heard of the concept, and are unfamiliar with the concept's meaning and implications applied to information systems. Suddenly everyone who has used a spreadsheet is an expert on architecture, just as everyone who has gone to school thinks of himself an expert on education. Our debates on the fine points of systems and architecture used to be with our vendors; now they are with our users!

- The process is not entirely a rational and technical one; information is power, and the new architecture redistributes both information and power in an organization. Some authors compare information systems architecture to the architecture of a house, and liken rearchitecting to remodeling.

It is best if we do not think of rearchitecting information systems for a distributed model as a home remodeling project. It really is more akin to re-development of a major portion of a city. That is, it is not entirely about bricks and mortar, but about power, politics and process.

- A final notable difference is the confluence of this change with other changes going on in large organizations and in the economy generally: the decentralization or distribution of power, the rise of the *networked* organization, the *downsized* corporation –all of these phrases appear now in management literature having nothing at all to do with information systems. It is not clear whether these metaphors were borrowed from the computing field and applied to organizations as a whole, or whether the cultural forces that caused a rethinking of computing architectures also drove a rethinking of organizational architectures. In either event, because the nature and focus of power, influence and decision-making in organizations is shifting just as many new technical decisions are made, we have a great deal of difficulty separating the politics from the technology. This does, however, provide an opportunity for us to form new relationships, and to re-negotiate existing ones. We will return to this topic later in the section on "paradigm shifts."

Many authors have contributed to the discussion of the non-technical issues arising from a large organization's move into distributed computing. A literature search shows that few seem to have written about it at length. Many seem to have a favorite short list of "how to" points. Every list seems to begin with *top management support,* but they vary after that point is made.

This chapter will be no different, really –it will include top management support in its list. But is notable that authors–including this one–reaching for wisdom on this topic are like so many blind people describing an elephant. At this stage of real organizations' practice and accomplishment in implementing distributed systems, it is too early for a complete picture to have emerged of the critical success factors in our failures or our successes, and thus it is too early to declare more than a partial and provisional list of standard *best practices* in managing such a transition.

We will begin the chapter by looking at definitions. A lot can go wrong when people think they have a shared vision, but it turns out they are using the same words to mean different things. Words like "open" and "portable" and "standard" and "object oriented" seem to have replaced "relational" and "distributed" as the Alice-in-Wonderland words of the decade. Agreeing with your colleagues and vendors what you are talking about is an important first step in intelligent communication.

16.2 Definitions

Open, distributed, compatible, object-oriented, client/server...Since everybody seems to be using the same words these days, isn't there surely a common meaning? To paraphrase Socrates, "the unexamined architecture is not worth implementing." If you query your colleagues about definitions you will undoubtedly find that what your users say they want, what you say you are buying, and what the vendor says its selling are all described by the word "open"–but the users means "cheap," you mean "interoperable," and the vendor means "It runs on UNIX".

As an experiment, put a strawman set of alternative definitions in front of your colleagues. You can then see how much agreement you really have among those you work with -- your user, your staff, and your vendors.

CCA Consulting reported in December 1992 that it had surveyed higher education on the definition of "open" and "client/server:"

Defining *Open*

Transportable Software	62%
Interoperability	61%
Open Network Protocols	57%
Standards	38%
Transparent Mail	38%
Proprietary, But Open OS	31%

UNIX	28%
LAN Network Operating Systems	26%
Public Domain Software	11%
De facto Market Leader	3%

While the concept of *freedom of movement* seems to dominate the highest ranking responses note that no single response gained more than 62 percent agreement. CCA found that among the client/server definitions, 40 percent of those surveyed did not agree with *any* of the definitions!

It is not essential that the industry as a whole agree on definitions, but it is important that any one organization agree on its internal definitions before moving ahead. Stanford has agreed on the definitions of several important terms:

Standard Definitions for Standard Systems

Open vs. Closed	*Open:* Possible for other programs to connect to it; defined interfaces *Closed:* Other programs must talk to it in a terminal style.
Standard vs. Proprietary	*Standard:* The interfaces are in the public domain and are set by standard groups. *Proprietary:* Vendor controls the specs to its advantage; may be published or not
Client/Server vs. Vertically Integrated	*Client/Server:* Open programs that separate user-interface processing–usually on a micro–from other processing–usually on a mini or mainframe *Vertically Integrated:* No separation, closed, or the separation is not done in a standard place

Note that at Stanford we defined terms and their opposites, so that people could use a definition to understand what something *was,* and what it was *not.*

It also has been important to encourage the interest of non-technical managers in the topic of *architecture.* So, we had to agree on a *definition* of architecture in the broadest sense. We did this in two ways. First, by depicting architecture as a way of fitting together some very important pieces of the technology puzzle (see figure 16.1):

Secondly, we showed what the functions are of architecture in the organization's environment:

Functions of Architecture

Definition:	• A way to organize and connect components of a system–and systems themselves
Implications for:	• The way applications, data, tools, and equipment work with each other • The skills needed by technical and office staff • How systems are developed

Functions of Architecture

Responsive to:
- The business opportunities, needs, and strategy
- The marketplace of business and technology suppliers and partners

Business Goal:
- University framework for planning and linking disparate systems and data, to gain flexibility and responsiveness

Technical Goal:
- Productivity enhancement for users and system developers
- Definition of risks, allow actions to limit risk

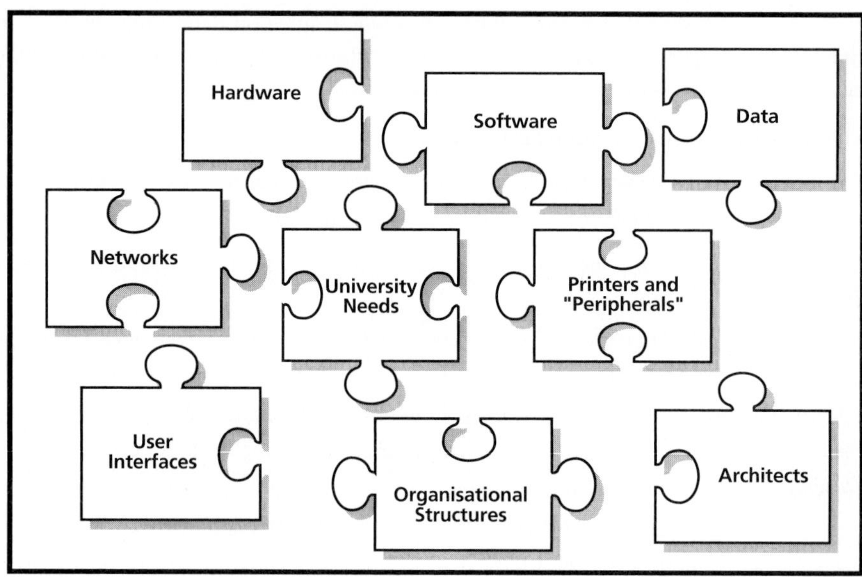

Figure 16.1 Architecture is about. . .

What other issues of definition and agreement must be discussed before you move ahead? There are several: the organization must agree on the key problems it wants to resolve, and/or the key benefits it wants to achieve from moving in a new technical direction, and the organization must agree on the assumptions, conditions or constraints that will pertain during the shift. These topics will be covered as part of the section on "Communicate with the Business," under Roadmaps.

16.3 Roadmaps

In the past a roadmap was something you got from the American Automobile Association, which had your vacation route plainly marked with a yellow highlighter, showing detours and sight-seeing opportunities. But the *maps* available today charting the path to distributed systems are more like what Columbus might have had, or Lewis and Clark; and the course has more detours and "roads under construction" than it has scenic vistas! For now, pioneering organizations must chart their own course, matching it to both their needs and abilities. But there appears to be a common set of landmarks all organizations seems to pass on the way. These common markers are the basis for the next several sections:

Educate and Get Educated

Communicate with the Business

Account for Time

Get Acceptance

Build Pilots

Know Thyself

Update your Methodology

Shift Paradigms

16.3.1 Educate and Get Educated

Learn about open systems and standards, and client /server technologies: Begin by listening to experts talk or write about the topics. Take note of what confuses or concerns you in you early encounters with the new jargon, because your own colleagues will have many of the same reactions when you begin to talk to them about the changes coming.

Beg, barrow and learn from those who have gone before you: Very credible and well-documented work on implementation of new architectures has been done by the internal MIS organizations of HP, Apple, and DEC. Each has its own distinctive approach (Apple, for example, focuses on effective desktop integration, while DEC emphasizes the system infrastructure). Each of these vendors has a set of publications describing its internal approach to IS which they will provide: to those who ask. These are far more than marketing fluff. DEC's Technical Architecture 2 (TA2) is over 100 pages; TA3 is in the works, TA1 was the basis from which Apple's "Virtual Integration Technical Architecture Lifecycle" (VITAL), described in several hundred pages of documentation now being released by Apple's Enterprise Systems Division (ESD)–sprang. Each of these vendors has a consulting service to refer you to for implementation assistance.

Get advice; find a trustworthy advisor: You do not need to rely on vendors for information. There are several consulting companies that specialize in *industry watch* services that provide excellent written materials on a very large variety of management and technical topics relevant to a migration to distributed computing models. Gartner Group and New Science Associates are two of these services. Gartner, for example has added a *client/server* and *open systems* service, along with their application development and management service, and system management services. Several non-advertising-supported publications provide in depth analysis on open systems industry trends (e.g. Nina Lytton's Open Systems Advisor) and new technologies (e.g. Judith Hurwitz's Client/Server Toolwatch and Patty Seybold's Distributed Computing Monitor). Among publications accepting advertising, Open Systems Today, Software magazine, DBMS, and Data Base Programming and Design regularly have articles, features, and reviews that are significant sources of information.

To deal with the information overload problem, consider using some on-line databases that index and abstract industry trade press and journals. Using on-line retrieval systems–instead of saving clippings of every potentially interesting article you spot–can let you do your own *re-engineering* from *just-in-case* information storage to *just-in-time* information retrieval. Most of these on-line sources can be used through your public or university library, and several of them are available on CD-ROM: Computer Select contains full-text of articles from more than a dozen industry trade press sources: INSPEC contains abstracts from hundreds of sources; ABI/Inform has company financial-statement information allowing you to check the financial stability of vendors; and "GG On-line" has full-text of all Gartner Group research reports and publications.

Prepare your staff to serve as system integrators: Especially if your staff are used to building their own software tools, this will be a time of adjustment. The shift is from being the handyman and carpenter to being the architect and general contractor; you are an integrator, assembling components and diagnosing failures. In the monolithic host systems this role was often played by the hardware vendor or the software vendor; often in the past Information Systems groups had to ingrate these two.

But the problem of integration is now an order of magnitude larger with the primitive *plug and play* state of the distributed systems vendors. For example, a distributed, client/server document/image system installed at Stanford had 37 different software and hardware components that had to be successfully integrated. This integration added months to the project, and subtracted months from our lives. The greatest number of problems arose with independent vendor releases of supposedly upward compatible software and networking components. For example, a *faster* version of an Ethernet card might be too fast for the current version of the scanner vendor's software; we then had to call supply houses searching for the old version of the Ethernet card! To gain the skills to accomplish system integration, staff will need incentives and time to dig into the standards and marketplace. Not all system-programming staff will find the system-integration challenge a welcome change.

Buy and build the right skills: Demonstrate to your current staff a commitment to train them in new skills and to give them real project opportunities to use these skills. But do not let the staff be entirely self-taught, especially if they begin from a character-based, integrated-host world; the paradigms for user interface and for application/data interaction are different with distributed systems. Create teams on the *buddy system* in which one of you current staff teaches a new staffer the business of the organization, while the new team member transfers skills and paradigms for using the new technology. (We will return to this topic later.)

Pay continuous attention to technology transfer issues: Remember that you are not just doing old work with new tools. You are enabling an *organization* to learn and to achieve new things with these new tools. Without organizational learning, you will have continuing chaos as new tools and techniques are introduced, and as new projects and staff start up. At least for the next few years, new tools and techniques will be available for every project, every few months! Attention to institutionalizing your gains will let you learn incrementally from your successes and failures, allowing you to build new *standard practices* as you learn what works and does not what from your pilot projects.

16.3.2 Communicate with the Business

Draft a vision: It can be as long or as short as you want, but it should describe how people will use–and feel about–the organization's information systems three to five years in the future. The time aspect is important: pick a date in the future and put a stake in the ground describing the systems of that time. The vision-creation process is at least as valuable as the resulting vision itself; in this case at least, "the journey is the reward." During the vision-creation process you will find the organization's business leaders talking to you about something other than the usual day-to-day firefighting–and you talking to them about possibilities. They also will be talking to each other while you listen and learn. Their conversations with each other will tell you about the inter-unit gaps that today's information systems do not fill, and that your future system will have to.

At Stanford, we developed a vision statement not only to describe an *end-point scenario* we wanted to aim for, but to inform the users of our information systems about the great amount of change that would affect them. This became a way of getting community discussion and senior management involvement.

The vision itself was only one part of a longer document that spelled out principles, objectives, challenges and actions. The outline of the document follows:

Vision for Administrative Information Systems

I. The Vision

II. Context

III. Challenges

IV. Principles for Administrative Information Systems (AIS)

V. Actions

VI. Implementation Approaches

Here is the vision in a little more detail:

Vision for Administrative Information Systems

I. The Vision

A. Allows individuals to do their best work for Stanford

B. Respected by internal and external constituents for quantity and quality of information

C. Used for day-to-day and long-range decisions, internal and external reporting

II. Context

A. Information-System Design Criteria

1. Flexibility to support an evolving management plan

2. Support the administrative goals and reflect academic objectives
3. Recognize the integrity of the records of account
4. Tailored management information tools
5. Regularly report on resource utilization for cost management

B. Characteristics of the Stanford Environment

1. Increased reliance on decentralized decision making
2. Accountability structures to assure compliance
3. Professionally-qualified managers

III. Challenges

A. Information Systems are not now fully integrated with each other

B. Operating managers lack meaningful information

C. Senior managers are unable to evaluate alternative policies

D. Senior managers are unable to establish accountability

E. Systems are antiquated or cumbersome, and do not provide timely output

IV. Principles for Administrative Information Systems (AIS)

A. AIS is one part of an overall strategy

1. Guided by the strategic objectives of the university, not objectives of systems
2. Supports change, improves management processes and identified accountability
3. Change in systems is part of integrated approach to business change

B. AIS allows for organizational diversity

1. Supports an evolving organizational structure
2. Supports the different needs of individual schools and VP areas

C. AIS provides for accountability and control at all levels

1. Provides information to enable decision making close to level of the activity
2. Establishes accountability and control as described in Andersen and C&L reports

D. AIS provides for management information

1. Improves the quality and timing of reports to the board and external audiences
2. Identifies and integrates across systems key business resources used in planning

E. AIS respects the business information architecture
   1. Complies with the Interim Information Systems Architecture policy
   2. Complies with university standards for desktop, communication and data storage
   3. Feeds and uses the University Data Warehouse

V. Actions

A. Develop a decision support system
B. Develop a program for management development and evaluation
C. Develop a core financial transaction system
D. Develop tools to achieve Human Resource objectives
E. Assess and change business practices
F. Develop a University-Data Warehouse
G. Integrate systems with the administrative activities of faculty, students, schools, departments
H. Provide an environment in which marketplace tools can meet central and departmental needs
I. Create the infrastructure for the migration to open systems

VI. Implementation Approaches

A. End-user departments will play a role in systems implementation
B. The university will add infrastructure support in schools where it is not now adequate to the plan
C. The Cabinet and Council will approve and periodically review these activities
D. The Task Force on Information Systems will have immediate oversight over these activities
E. Implementation of the vision will be under the general direction of the VP-Information Resources
F. Specific components will be directed by the cognizant vice president

Present the Business Case: The purpose of shifting to a new architecture is to fix business problems or create new business opportunities. You will need to present a business case for investment in new technological capabilities. It is best if you can focus on a single critical need understood throughout the business as the motivation for investment, and build the case from there. In some organizations, the case can be built on the need to serve customers in a way not feasible with current systems, or on the needs for new management and decision-support tools. Rarely can the case be made solely on technological grounds, such as "modernize our technical infrastructure."

Identify key business and technology driving forces and factors: These factors will allow the organization an opportunity to focus and agree on the few very significant forces that should influence specific technical directions. At Stanford, our key business forces were identified as the following:

Business Factors Influencing Our Direction

Cost Containment	• Funding will be limited and uncertain over time • Continuous improvement in productivity is necessary
Link Businesses	• Recognition of the academic line as driver of university business • Decentralization of function into schools and departments • Consolidated corporate management information
Flexibility to Respond	• Adaptability to rapid and continuous change within the university • Flexibility and rapid responses to our external business partners • Growth in external regulation and scrutiny • Reallocation of people resources to changing university goals • Work force issues: high turnover, low entry skills, residence distance, family-driven work schedules

Technical Needs Influencing Our Direction

Cost Containment	• Lower, more predictable unit costs; costs scale well as use grows • Guide and manage diversity and influx of technology on campus
Link Businesses Systems	• New function that is decentralized and distributed • Analytic tools and linked central data needed for management information • Electronic communication with the non-Stanford world
Flexibility to Respond	• Systems adapt quickly to organizational and work-process change • Faster implementations • Larger and more available pool of technical, professional, and support staff, flexibility in work locations and schedules
Rely on the Marketplace	• Reduced technical risk and increased currency relative to marketplace • Exploit innovative technology in the marketplace

Note that the business factors summarize to three categories. The dozen needs summarize to four categories remarkably similar to the business categories. The commonality of business and technical factors here lets us develop objectives and principles that are not in conflict with each other.

Craft a set of Principles for Application Development: These principles are a set of design and application-behavior agreements that are necessary to meet the business and technical needs described above. In mature application development environments, such as our host world, you would usually find the principles codified as a set of programming standards. But for distributed computing too much is yet to be learned and too little is ready to be set in such concrete. As examples, let us sample some of the principles Apple uses for its own application developers:

- Support heterogeneous transaction platforms with interface to structured query language (SQL) compliant database management systems (DBMSs). Therefore, SQL-compliant relational DBMSs should be used unless economically inappropriate.
- Validate data at the time and point of capture or as closely thereafter as economically feasible.
- Business rules that are used for validating data must be applied consistently across applications.
- Transaction-management platforms must assure posting integrity in a multi-user environment by providing adequate security, recording locking, rollback, and recovery logic.
- Separate the environments of transaction update from cross functional shared data analysis and reporting.
- All information has an identified business owner.
- Shared data exists in a series of subject-related data warehouses (databases), and is propagated to local servers based on the economics of usage and security authorization.
- Data warehouses contain the official values, in a standardized format, for information shared by business operating units.

Link standards to the principles: It needs to be clear–as you select one marketplace standard or product over alternatives–what organizationally-ratified set of principles motivates your choice. This will reduce (but not eliminate!) religious arguments over competing alternatives. It also provides you with an opportunity to be seen as an educator to the business rather that just the person who decrees certain standards.

Keep technology in perspective: The technology is only one part of the business, and by itself cannot do anything for an organization. Not only must your technology direction be aligned with an organization's strategy for the business, but it must be aligned–or be brought into alignment–with the external environment at large (e.g., the regional and national economy), and synchronized with the technology limitations and the directions in the marketplace and with the individual people and the overall culture in the organization. Because alignment is something achieved among several continuously changing worlds, you must yourself keep an *open* mind, not closing yourself off from input after decisions have been made, and continuing to listen to client and vendor concerns as you move into implementation.

Define the architecture explicitly: As obvious as it may seem, this step can easily be overlooked because it is on the one hand *obvious* and on the other hand difficult. Failure to take this step will lead to slippery discussions down the road as vendors and project implementors claim *compliance* without reference to any specific architecture document. An implicit distributed systems architecture definition is probably about as helpful as a Supreme Court Justice's famous "I know it when I see it" definition of pornography. An architecture defined only in terms of buzzwords like *open* and *distributed* plays into the hands of vendors whose marketing literature is the primary source of product specifications. And an implicit architecture offers no real help to technical staff who are looking for guidelines.

In this particular context an architecture is a set of technologies layered from the physical network and hardware at the base to applications and data models at the top. For each layer, the definition prescribes approved or acceptable tools or techniques, and the standard method used to call on lower layers for services (i.e., the API).

The Gartner Group[1] offers an excellent description and depiction of the layers (see figure 16.2):

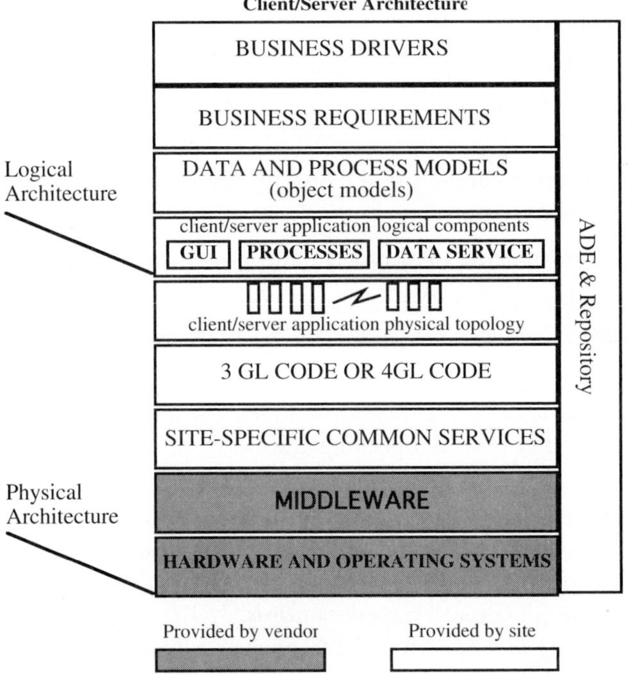

Figure 16.2 Architecture layers.

Provide a roadmap evolving to the new model over time: Having described an end point scenario and defined an architecture does not suddenly transport the organization to the endpoint in a single step. Most large organizations will have to evolve their technical sophistication and infrastructure over time. How you get there depends on where you start (see the sec-

[1]Used with permission of Gartner Group. Originally published in the Gartner Group Applications Development & Management Strategies series, March 1993.

tion on "Readiness" below), but the roadmap must be specific to your organization because it will define to the business a program for change and investment.

Stanford' s roadmap is partially shown in the vision outline cited above. Digital's internal IS organization has the following roadmap:

1. Connect the Enterprise
2. Implement Email
3. Distribute Data for General Access
4. Distribute Common Application Code
5. Distribute Data Collection and Validation
6. Develop Interactive Linkages Between Systems
7. Establish Distributed Database Architecture
8. Implement Full Distributed Systems

DEC's roadmap communicates more than a sequence of steps, however. It is actually presented as a matrix, whose rows are the eight steps above, and whose columns describe technical requirements for each of the eight phases, and management issues. Here are the different columns for row 3, "Distribute Data for General Access:"

Column Title	**Sample Column Contents**
A. Step Name	"Distributed Data for General Access (No. 3 above)
B. Characteristics	"One-Way File Transfers"
C. Typical Applications	"Information Centers"
D. Key Technologies:	
1. Networks	"Synchronous Computer-to-Computer"
2. Data Bases	"Data Dictionary"
3. Processes	"Activity Logging"
E. Management Issues	"Common Data Definitions"

16.3.3 Account for Time

Acknowledge the installed base: This admonition does not just refer to the hardware or applications installed in the data center. Here we are especially referring to the set of user equipment and skills found in the clients who will be affected by change. If someone has been doing purchase order entry on a 3270 for ten years, he or she will not adapt overnight using to a GUI via TCP/IP! You must recognize that users see their current skills and venerable procedures as a valuable investment, and new technology has the potential to wipe out that investment. Not only will they need training and support, you will need to provide incentives for change that the users value (believe it or not, an incentive of a *new computer* is not something office workers look forward to).

Prepare policy that will let you evolve toward your target architecture: For several aspects of your architecture's product standards, there will be no suitable choice in the marketplace when you initially specify the architecture and its compliant products. Yet you have confidence that a particular standard or product direction is *promising* and will likely evolve into suitable product(s). At Stanford we recognized that the primitive state of the marketplace several years ago prevented us from defining supported products in some key product categories, and yet we did wish to guide development groups toward a narrower range of choices than the totality of what the marketplace had to offer.

Our solution was to formulate a policy on *Interim Architecture* that mandated that systems be developed in one of two ways:

Over the next three to five years, the university will make a transition to a new information systems architecture based on open, client/server standards. During this interim period, Information systems or major components of systems that are newly developed, substantially enhanced, or purchased by central offices, schools, or Departments, and that fall within the scope of this policy, must follow one of the two development and operation paths:

1. They must conform to the current systems architecture; that is, reside on the Forsythe mainframe computer, use SPIRES (Stanford's mainframe DBMS) as their database management system, use Prism as their interface for end-user access and transactions, and follow other standards of the current architecture as specified in Administrative Guide Memo 61, or

2. They must conform to an evolving *narrow path* of approved hardware, software, and networking products that adhere to emerging open, client/server standards of the new Stanford architecture.

Use of products and standards not on the *approved* list–which was very short at the early stage–triggered a *variance request* process, much like a zoning variance for building permits. The variance process has been quite educational for all parties, and it explicitly recognizes that exceptions are part of the rules.

Prepare migration alternatives: It is not only the evolutionary state of the external marketplace that causes the move to distributed systems to take time. The complexity of an organization's internal systems will in many cases be the factor limiting the speed of a migration.

The complexity–especially of interrelationships between systems–may make it very difficult to shift one part of a system while leaving another in place. If the migration is not instantaneous, then some of an organization's systems will be in one technology while other systems will be in another technology. It is wise to plan ahead for the construction (if necessary) and support of interoperability between systems in the current and those in the target architecture and message and data propagation services between applications in these different environments.

Determine a suitable distributed-systems portfolio over time: Risk assessment is nothing new for major systems projects; a *portfolio* approach that balances your application project suite across various risk levels is now common (just as it is in the stock market). And it is obvious–if you look beyond the hype–that some kinds of distributed systems are high risk, and some are medium risk (unfortunately, almost none are low risk).

Ensure that high-risk projects do not dominate your pilot suite. A high-risk project would be an enterprise-wide, non-stop, mission-critical, transaction-processing system delivered on multiple client OS platforms, and running across multiple database servers. Distributed transaction processing, use of multiple DBMS, or use of multiple servers all increase risk as well.

Support the pioneers: Technical managers faced with the overwhelming novelty of their first distributed systems projects will be tempted to focus narrowly on what appears to be most different: the technical challenges of application software development. This is necessary, but certainly not sufficient, especially when the inevitable surprises arise. Surprises come from many different directions:

- The development tools are more primitive and later-intensive than you expected
- Vendor software is in alpha test that you thought would be production
- Components do not work with each other in the users environment, which does not match the vendors' environments
- Performance is not what you expected
- System operations functions ca not apparently be automated
- Users assumed that many *standard* capabilities of their host system (e.g., automatically receiving new versions of software; printing to *the usual* printers) would *of course* be included in the newer, more advanced technology; but they are not, and have to be tacked on.

Managers need to be prepared for these surprises, and they need to prepare others–such as the technical and operations staff, and the systems' users and user management. They may also need to prepare vendors for working with the other vendors involved in project.

Preparations of these different project participants are needed in several categories, at least the following:

- *Staffing:* What skills are needed, by when, and for how much time? Which of these skills are best acquired from the marketplace, and which are best developed in existing staff? Then train, or hire, as appropriate.
- *Training and/or Hiring:* Do not believe that *smart people will learn on their own* or that time allocated explicitly for training activities will not be needed. If staff are not given time to master new tools and techniques, you will find they will use the new tools just like the old tools, without understanding how they are different.
- *Support:* Have a process for decision-making and acting when things go wrong, especially once a system is in the hands of its users. Early pilot systems probably will not be tied well into your organization's standard user-support channels, yet users might expect that they will have the standard support infrastructure available to them.

- *Operations:* The operational characteristics of new distributed systems are going to be unfamiliar to your organization's data center operations staff. They will need to be brought into this new area, or else the application developers will end up spending their time on daily, traditional operations activities.

16.3.4 Gain Acceptance

Except at trade shows–where preaching to the choir is the norm–the technology cannot be sold on features; it must be sold on its benefits and its ability to aid in meeting the business' objectives. Information systems must appeal directly to users' interest: faster delivery, better functionality, flexibility for the user. The case must be credible and specific, not patent-medicine snake oil. But the users and corporate management are not the only ones to be sold on the costs, benefits and risk.

You must also *sell* to your information systems (IS) organization. Any assumption that all the individuals in IS who have chosen technology careers are interested in leaping into the unknown with you will cause trouble. Technical staff need to be sold on benefits that make sense to them; they must also believe that the risks are worth the reward and that management is not foolishly or randomly targeting *insurmountable opportunities.*

The audit department and controller who define, acceptable standards of compliance and risk in the business, must be part of the buy-in process. Do not ignore the acceptance by these non-technical standards-setters in the organization.

Acceptance does not result from salesmanship alone. The conceptual structure of the argument for distributed computing must be buttressed with early, successful pilot experiences with the technologies in the real business context. Selecting these opportunities and taking advantage of them is our next topic.

16.3.5 Build Pilots

In large organizations, a single pilot project will not be sufficient to build support and to prepare for a large scale migration effort. A series of pilots will be needed to build momentum and readiness. While the pilot series will largely depend on the needs of the business, some general observations and caveats can be made:

- Choose pilots with real payoff, but small enough to be accomplished in six to twelve months by a small team.
- Early pilots should address business problems that ca not readily be addressed within your current technical environment, e.g., decision support or document image processing.
- Early pilots should be localized in both the technical and user organizations so broad organizational and technical change is not required. Do not attempt large-scale implementations.
- Early pilots should take advantage of the technology that is most mature and avoid aspects that are less robust. For example, distributed transaction processing is probably too advanced for many of us to take on at this time.

- Pilots should not be *lone wolf* projects undertaken by a single individual. They will too easily be dismissed by others as not indicative of the organization's abilities.
- Later pilots can attempt to spread involvement and skill growth throughout the organization, but early pilot efforts should be well-focused within a team.
- Pilots should include explicit time for training.
- Pilots should not be crash, "bet the business" projects.
- Recognize–and prepare your customers for–the corollary to avoiding "bet the business" pilots: pilot technical projects will usually not be the most important business priorities you have received from your clients. These would likely be too high risk and too complicated.
- Pilots should not count on technical *and* political miracles for their success. Do not, for example, take on a pilot that requires an enterprise-wide data model, if the organization has not ever before agreed to the need for one, much less signed up for the effort involved. Do not rely on the technology to solve organizational problems that have existed for years; if you do, you may have a technically successful pilot that fails to bring about organizational change, and thus is not acknowledged as a success by the business.
- Pilot teams should be honest about their successes and failures, and report them to the organization.
- Pilots should, whenever possible, explicitly deliver or evaluate at least one part of the architecture for the organization. For example, a decision-support pilot might develop strategy and practice for data warehousing; a transaction-processing pilot might evaluate network reliability and problem diagnosis procedures.
- Pilots may want to use a *double team* approach in which a *project team* implements the product, and one or two other people, an *architecture team*, carry the knowledge gained from implementation back into the architecture per se. These folks ensure the learning is institutionalized by writing it down and updating the organization's architecture.
- Pilots should, where possible, be cumulative and incremental. You should determine what aspects of the technology change will be the greatest stretch for your organization and attempt to arrange a series of pilots that, one by one, engage these areas. No single pilot should take on many areas simultaneously; conversely, pilots should not repeatedly be targeted at the same technology aspect of the architecture.
- Pilots should be scalable to full production, unless the users are explicitly prepared otherwise. Many times a pilot will not use *production worthy* engineering techniques in some areas to save time and to concentrate resources and learning in other areas. But users may not understand that the difference between a successful pilot and production can be a factor of two-to-five in additional effort. Distributed systems are fragile in some ways, and they can be difficult to bring to *industrial strength* levels of robustness.

16.3.6 Know Thyself

Before setting your own expectations for an organizational transition into distributed computing, it will be wise to align 1) the style of the business organization, and 2) the readiness of your technical organization, with your goals for adoption. The Gartner Group provides a useful and simple framework for doing both of these, noting that the limiting factors in the rate of change can come from the enterprise culture or the basic IS culture and foundation. We will look at organization style first, then IS readiness.

16.3.6.1 Organization Styles

Gartner analyses organization styles into three types, and maps appropriate IS *aggressiveness* onto these types (see figure 16.3):[2]

Enterprise Styles

	Type A Pioneers	*Type B Moderates*	*Type C Followers*
Approach	Aggressive (High Risk)	Balanced (Low-Risk)	Cautious (Risk-Averse)
Senior Mgmt. IS Vision	Change Agent Competitive Edge	Productivity	Cost Efficiency
IS Technology Sophistication	High	Moderate to High	Low to Moderate
Available Funding	Flexible	Variable	Constrained

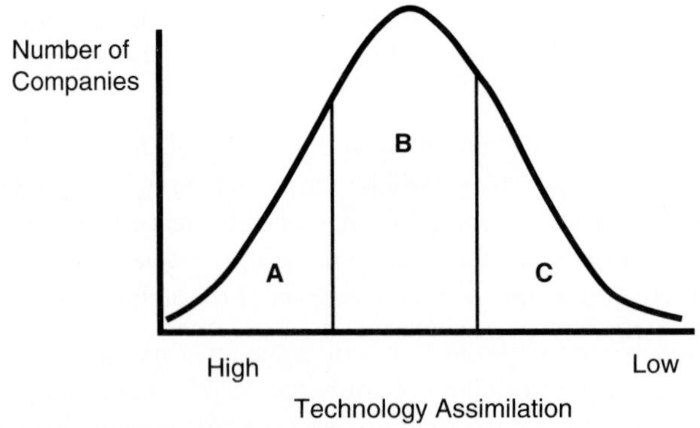

Figure 16.3 IS aggressiveness.

[2]Used with permission from Gartner Group. Published in IT Management SPA's reader notes for conference presentation, December 1991.

As Gartner suggests, "Aggressiveness in the adoption of new technology should be aligned with the organization culture."

Clearly, it would be high risk to attempt rapid migration in a type C organization. It is likely to be a *career-limiting* risk for the IS manager to hold back a migration in type A organizations; such organizations require technology aggressiveness to meet business goals.

It is worth noting that large organizations–especially diverse ones such as universities and holding companies–may well have subunits which exhibit very different styles. For such enterprises, aggressive projects that are contained within a unit's boundaries could successfully be mounted if they are aligned to the subunit's culture.

16.3.6.2 IS Readiness

Gartner notes that IS organizations themselves have styles and capabilities that can be analyzed by looking at the organization's history:

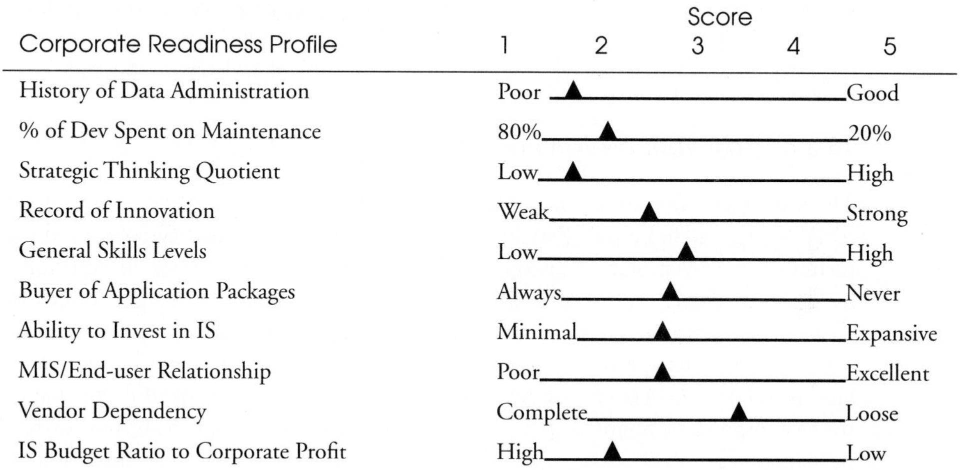

Corporate Readiness Profile	Score 1	2	3	4	5
History of Data Administration	Poor	▲			Good
% of Dev Spent on Maintenance	80%	▲			20%
Strategic Thinking Quotient	Low	▲			High
Record of Innovation	Weak		▲		Strong
General Skills Levels	Low		▲		High
Buyer of Application Packages	Always		▲		Never
Ability to Invest in IS	Minimal		▲		Expansive
MIS/End-user Relationship	Poor		▲		Excellent
Vendor Dependency	Complete		▲		Loose
IS Budget Ratio to Corporate Profit	High	▲			Low

Note: ^indicates assumed averages. The higher the score, the more ready the organization is to capitalize on new methods and technologies.

Gartner concludes that "client/server adoption will be slowed by the same limitations that hamper the adoption of other modern computing initiatives."

Particularly noteworthy in this list is the "History of Data Administration" as a bellwether for a successful transition into distributed computing. Not only are the computing hardware and software more distributed in the future, but so is enterprise definition and use of data, and control over it. Centralized data systems of the past have allowed us to avoid some issues that now must be surfaced before the data moves outward towards users' new styles and purposes of use.

16.3.7 Update Your Development Methodology

Most large IS organizations implemented development methodologies during the 1980s, at a time when projects based on mainframe computers and attached terminals were the norm. You may find the methodology of the 80s has gradually grown out of synchronization with the business targets, analytical style, programming and delivery techniques, and toolsets that are to be used for your early pilot projects. While this is somewhat expected for your *pathfinder* projects, you should not allow the situation to continue unchecked. If the methodology is increasingly irrelevant or wrong-headed for the projects the staff are doing, it will be ignored and eventually abandoned. Reinstituting the discipline of methodology far down the road will be very expensive, and probably contentious. It is best to revise methodology incrementally.

The methodology should explicitly be made an issue for the pilot project teams and the architecture teams, asking them to contribute their findings and recommendations on *best practices* to an ongoing revision cycle as results come in from pilots. Some areas likely to require modification in the typical methodology are: the lifecycle itself, which needs to take advantage of the increased opportunities for iteration and user feedback that new technology provides; integration of CASE tools with the development tools and object libraries in use; integration of dictionary tools with the RDBMS catalog(s); separation of the data capture (transaction processing) environment from the data access (data warehouse) environment; GUI design standards; testing procedures; version control and version upgrade rules.

16.3.8 Shift Your Design Paradigms

The implementation of the new technology paradigm of distributed computing will cause the replacement and renewal of many components in the business systems of the enterprise–including organizational, individual and work–process components–in addition to replacement of hardware, software and networks. This technology change–unlike some of the changes in the two decades past which substituted one computer language for another or one vendor for another–cannot be accomplished by substitution of one technology for another. In fact, few of the real benefits or an expensive migration can be derived if the change is limited to the computer components per se. Localizing change will avoid chaos, but it will also restrict payback.

The ways in which your organization designs, builds and uses its computer systems should be examined to see if an opportunity exists to time a paradigm shift with the shift in technologies. While taking advantage of such an opportunity will likely add to the complexity and uncertainty of your early distributed computing projects, the non-technical paradigm shifts may offer great early benefit, and may gain the most visible support of your user and user-management community.

There are undoubtedly dozens of paradigms you can consider shifting. The greatest opportunities–and, in some cases, necessities–may be found among the following:

User-centered rather than process-centered design: Fewer and fewer people in organizations these days use a single computer system to perform a single business process throughout the day. Yet most of our systems were designed with the workflow of a single *process*–rather than a single *user*–at the center. New technologies–such as windowed, event-driven, GUI, object-oriented tools and interfaces–let us design with the user's perspective at the center (even the desktop is an outmoded metaphor in the mobile computing world). This perspective is *multi-tasking* and *interrupt-driven* in the non-technical sense of those words: users work on multiple tasks using multiple systems simultaneously. Our system designs should take advantage of the technology to support the user's real world.

Re-engineer, rather than automate incrementally: In the 70s and 80s we would *harden* our manual business processes into systems that would *automate* the manual function. We made the business more efficient. But in the 90s–now that most of our manual systems have been automated–the message is that we can save the institution the most money by rethinking–or re-engineering–the business process into an effective one before turning it into an efficient process in software.

Separate reporting from transaction capture, rather than have reporting integrated in transaction applications: Back in the days when most reporting was from one internal organization to another, and when the reporting requirements were relatively stable, we structured our transaction applications and data to produce a set of reports regularly and efficiently. And each application had its own reporting mechanism, which understood the typical uses of data in the application.

But now, as reporting requirements mushroom because of external demands and because we are using our systems for problem solving and decision support as well as control, we need to separate our reporting mechanisms and data from the transactions mechanisms. This is not only a matter of efficiency and performance; but it is also a way of separating things that are very dynamic–like reporting requirements–from things that are relatively more stable–like the transaction processes, controls and data itself. In something like a client/server sense, reporting becomes more flexible and scalable when it is separated from the stable base of operational systems and data. And, in the new client/server technologies, the tools for reporting seem to be more mature than those for large scale transactions processing.

Provide for electronic retrieval from document repositories, rather than paper distribution from desktop publishing: Since the Macintosh created the desktop publishing market place, we have been able to very efficiently create tons of paper documents. And, having all these pretty paper documents, our distributed publishers had a lot of pride in seeing that everyone had a copy. Our campuses are awash in newsletters and flyers, reporting whatever people have need to tell anyone who has an interdepartmental mailbox to receive the document.

There is now more than enough information to go around. Several organizations are working on a concept I shall call "document repositories," which store textual information until someone asks for it. Then the repository effectively delivers a document to the person who needs to know about it, when he or she needs it. This electronic retrieval and distribution controlled by the end-user is a type of *just in time* delivery-on-demand. But the publishing process itself is still just in time from the publisher's point of view and the technology of the document repository allows the same kind of time-shifting between a document's author and its readers that we are familiar with the VCR providing between television broadcasters and viewers.

Build training-free incremental systems,rather than train users in powerful systems: In the 80s we held training classes and wrote large manuals for our *all things to all people* systems. In the 90s we should design and target subsets–or increments–of system function to users whose needs and abilities match the function and interface style of the subset; users can thus control when they are ready to take on more and more advanced subsets of system function and complexity. The better the match, the less the training burden; in many cases the system itself can deliver whatever training is needed at the point in time and place where it is needed.

For example, only the fields relevant to the user's task should appear on a screen; different fields are needed in a personnel system to hire someone than to terminate someone; yet today we typically use the same paper forms and on-line screens to do both, confusing the user who is focused on a particular task.

Data liberation, rather than vertically-integrated packages: In the 80s, we looked for packages that provided a complete set of technical functions. Packages had to have their own data entry and validation screens, data dictionaries, a built in database, and retrieval language, and a report generating system. These were what I have called "vertically integrated" packages. Now we see what kinds of costs such packages have; they hold the data they contain–which is usually structured for internal processing efficiency and integrity–captive to the manipulation routines that the package vendor has thought to provide. So, when the organization that selected the package to suit its needs has changed and finds its needs have changed, the package no longer fits as well as it once did. But the data is locked up in a black box, and can only be moved in and out through relatively manual processes. Now we are all looking for packages that at least give us the flexibility of gaining access to the data store through standard DMBS query tools and other tools that are part of a more open environment. Data is *liberated* from a type of software vendor *lock in.* We should take care that we do not just trade hardware-vendor lock-in in closed systems for software-vendor lock-in in supposedly *open* systems.

Interoperable, cellular functions rather than integrated, omnibus packages: In the 80s, the big word–even before everything was relational–was that everything was *integrated.* Every business function you needed was tied together by a single vendor into a single package, usually around an *integrated* database. This phenomenon was as true of microcomputer software as of mainframe computer software, if you recall; every vendor was trying to one-up the integrated Lotus 1-2-3 with more function integrated into a single shell. Most of these products failed in the marketplace because they compromised the ability of each of us to assemble our own suite of products from among those we considered *best of breed* for each of the functions we valued. By trying to be *jack of all trades* these products were master of none. The newer vendors of large-scale business packages seem to realize that their old *protectionism* approach, which locked the client into their product suite, really was a barrier to trade and thus a barrier to the overall expansion of the market; an enlarged market, like a rising tide, raises all boats and provides new opportunity for all vendors, especially the most aggressively *open* and *interoperable* among them.

I have used the *cellular* metaphor to suggest an amazing expectation I have for openness: I would like to see different vendor's modules hand off data as it moves from one business process to another in completing a multi-process task. Simply having all the packages using an SQL-compliant DBMS will not accomplish this.

Virtual Integration intersystem EDI, rather than point-to-point intersystem bridges: Many of us have worked wonders building two or three bridges and gateways from one package to two or three others; and we have also driven ourselves nearly crazy because a different home-brew gateway is needed between any two packages. If the phone system worked like this, you would need a different wire to connect your phone to every other telephone you would like to talk to; our systems are starting to look like rats nest's–or a neophyte networker's wiring closet. Scott McNealy of SUN Microsystems calls these *hairball systems.*

Vendors have this problem too. You can see it every time you look at how one email vendor would try and connect a LAN-based mail system to dissimilar email systems in an organization; each additional different system increases the problem geometrically.

Matching Tools to Tasks

Category	Focus On	Orientation To	Who? e.g.	Tools	Supported By
Back Office	Internal Questions	Batch Processes	Accounting Clerks	Main-frames; Process-Oriented Data	Internal & External EDI Process Re-Engineering Distributed Electronic Forms Scalable Servers Interoperable Servers & Databases Legacy system Encapsulation Outsourcing
Front Office	Customers & Suppliers	Transactions	Departmental Admins-trators	Client/ Server Systems; Cross-Functional Data	Internal & External EDI Windowing, Multi-System Views Data Warehousing Common User Interface GUI Integration, Screen Scraping Fax Machines, Email Integrated Data/Image Distributed Electronic Forms Scalable Servers Searchable Document Repositories Open, Client/Server Systems
Knowledge-Develop-ment	Business Solutions	Projects	Managers Professionals Faculty Students	Desktop Tools; External Data; Enterprise Data	Decision Support System Multi-media Email BBoards & Electronic Conferences Collaborative Tools Computer-Assisted Meeting Video-Conferencing Data Analysis Tools Mobile Computing Scalable Clients Training-free ATM-Like Interfaces Network Navigators Current-Awareness Agents Open Client Tools

Derived in part from "How I.T. Can Drive White Collar Productivity" by the Gartner Group.

Figure 16.4 Matching tools to tasks.

Similarly, the DBMS vendors, in trying to prove their openness, had to build gateways to each other system in the market; so they–well, all except IBM–architected their way out by forming the SQL Access Group, which goes well beyond standardizing on a SQL dialect. These new forms of links are not point-to-point links, they are the result of vendors agreeing on a common interchange approach and format. I have called this *virtual* integration, because it makes it seem like you have an integrated system, but you have some of the flexibility that the *interchangeable parts* paradigm shift brought to the early automotive industry.

Informate; rather than automate: This distinction was best clarified by Shoshana Zuboff, in her book *In the Age of the Smart Machine: The Future of Work and Power.* It is a brilliant but somewhat turgid book. Her basic point is that our computer systems not only take over the work of the blue-collar worker when they automate some factory or clerical process, but in doing that, they also collect information about or *instrument* the work itself. This information about the work is grist for the knowledge-worker's mill, as he or she takes on the task of trying to improve the basic work processes. Zuboff refers to this an "informating" process. Our task is to ensure that our systems can deliver this kind of basic process information to knowledge workers, rather than hiding such information from them.

Match tools to tasks, rather than one-size-fits-all solutions: In the 80s we provided very generalized tools and solutions to the masses–often encumbering tools with *featuritis,* or else providing lowest common denominator tools that met no one's needs in particular. Markets of the 90s appear to be much more specialized and focused that those of the 80s; you hear less about mass marketing than you do about products that are well-targeted to a specific market niche and then take that niche over.

What is the equivalent of this in the information systems world? I think we can reasonably talk about market segmentation among the different types of knowledge workers in our institutions, based on what they do, what tasks they focus on, who they work for, and what tools and data they use in accomplishing all of this. Some specific technologies that the market place wants to provide to us are appropriate only for one or two segments of the knowledge worker *market.* If you have received the challenge from your institution to provide better support for knowledge workers, I would suggest you figure out who they mean first, and then decide whether the solution is video-conferencing, or electronic forms, or email, or fax machines, collaboration tools. Some specific examples are shown in figure 16.4:

16.4 The Planning Process

An important activity in any large organization is to gain an understanding of your planning process–what it is, and what it is not–and then to be sure that understanding is shared by others. Some people will assume that the plan is something you can create in a matter of days containing what is in reality only a sketch of one possible strategy; others will not believe something is the plan unless it contains detailed task and resource estimates, timelines and dependencies, stretching out over multiple years. Both of these extremes are plans of a sort, and may be appropriate at different parts of a planning cycle in different organizations. The key is to set expectations for what the planning cycle is, and what the goals and deliverables are for each step in the planning process. A planning process must fit the style of the organization it is for. The process also must be communicated to the organization if it is to have a chance of success; being clear about the process may be as critical a success factor as the specifics of the process itself.

The development of a plan is usually preceded by stages in which 1) the organization assesses where is it and where it wants to go, and 2) the organization develops a high-level strategy to get from where it is to where it wants to be, looking at options before deciding on the best direction. After these two stages, the plan per se can be developed. Deloitte and Touche, a consulting company with experience in information systems strategy consulting, recommends a three-phase planning approach (see figure 16.5).

16.5 A Reality Check on Costs and Benefits

16.5.1 Faster? Cheaper? Better?

A traditional justification for moving from host-based architectures to *downsized* and distributed architectures is that the new approach saves money. The source of the savings is the less expensive, more scalable hardware. Managers of enterprise environments must look at all the costs of delivering and supporting information systems, not just hardware cost, however.

In a large-scale environment; let us assume 30 percent is frequently the case that hardware will represent only 20 to 40 percent of the total cost of IS. Of the portion that is hardware, the CPU itself may be only half (50 percent) of the cost, with peripherals such as storage and communications interfaces taking the remainder. If the hardware savings are as large as 50 percent on the CPU, the savings from CPU hardware might represent as little as 15 percent of the total cost of the IS environment (i.e., 50 percent of the 30 percent).

A corollary is that any change that raises costs in the remaining (non-hardware) parts of the IS environment could wipe out the savings from hardware. For example, if staff, hardware and software were each about one-third (33 percent) of the cost of the total environment, a technology change that raised staff costs and software costs by only 20 percent (e.g., a 20 percent increase, from 33 to 40 percent) each (e.g., from 66 to 80 percent, a 14 percent difference) could wipe out 50 percent of savings in CPU hardware. Pioneering organizations in distributed computing have certainly found potential increases of 20 percent each in staff costs and software. Figure 16.6 illustrates this point.

Software increases: The source of software increases is easy to find: many more copies of a piece of software are needed to support a workstation-based environment than the centralized, mainframe environment; vendors are increasingly shifting to *per seat* pricing, which exacerbates this problem. Additionally, open systems often require more pieces of software to be purchased and integrated in order to provide function (e.g., word processing software may require scanner software, fonts, printer drivers, etc., to provide full function). While workstation and server hardware may be scalable, software costs may not be.

Staffing increases: The sources of increased cost in the staffing component of IS costs are more subtle, and it is not clear how many of these costs are permanent aspects of distributed environments, and which are really *start-up* or *transition* costs associated with the newness of the environment and the immaturity of the technology. Most of these costs are attributable to

	Assessment →	Strategy Development →	Plan Development
	Information Systems Strategy Review	**Information Systems Strategy Direction**	**Information Systems Master Plan**
Questions	• Where are we? • Where is our competition heading? • Where do we want to go? • What are the issues?	• What are our options? • What are the costs/benefits and trade-offs? • What is the *best* direction?	• What are the priorities? • What resources are required? • When will it be done? • How do we manage it?
Considerations	• Business direction/needs • Internal capability/position • Industry/competitive trends	• Business objectives/goals • Information needs • Broad alternatives Applications Data management Technical Organization • Business impacts/risks	• Organizational capabilities • Resource constraints • Financial implications • Measure of success • Responsibilities • Risks
Activities	• Review business • Determine user needs/satisfaction • Review MIS plans, organization and management • Assess competitive IS direction • Review technology trends • Define key IS strategy issues	• Develop preliminary objectives • Define potential business/functional IS needs (business model) management model • Develop information/data management model (data architecture) • Develop organization strategy/plan (organization architecture) • Select IS strategic direction	• Develop specific plan priorities • Develop financial plan • Develop implementation plan/assign responsibilities • Identify major milestone • Develop control reporting process • Establish management monitoring control and update responsibilities
End Products	• Application profile • Technology profile • Competitive position assessment • IS strategic planning issues	• IS objectives, goals and strategies • Information plan • Application portfolio • Technology architecture • IS organization strategy • Preliminary costs/benefits	• Master plan priority assumptions • Detailed implementation plan • Success/performance measures • Financial budget/plan • Plan monitoring/control process

Deloitte & Touche, *CAUSE Professional Paper Series,#4.* June, 1990.

Figure 16.5 Three-phase development plan.

what we can call the *cost of complexity.* Because distributed environments are more flexible, they are often more complex than host environments. There are more pieces of hardware, software and networks involved; these components are the source of the flexibility and the complexity. There are more staff needed to deal with more pieces of software, even though each piece may be simpler in some sense than its counterpart in the host environments. Each piece of software requires someone on the staff to be the *resident expert,* taking time from project assignments to be a liaison with the vendor, to keep up to date on new software releases and vendor changes to answer questions from other staff, and so on. Since there are more pieces of software than before, more people than before are acting as resident experts. There are more vendors involved than before, and that adds a further burden on staff to provide integration, to make the (software) ends meet.

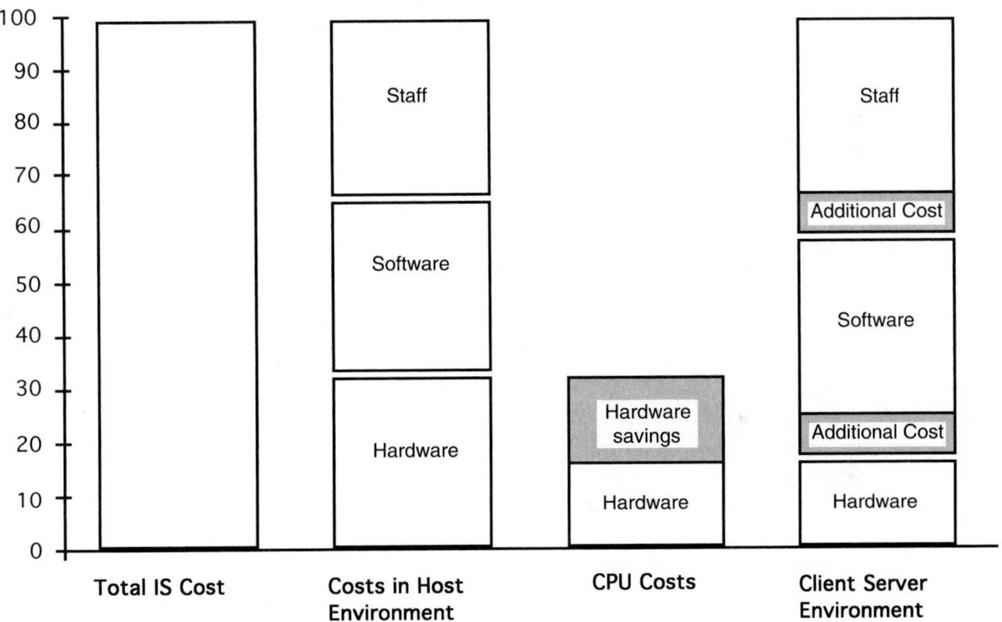

Figure 16.6 Cost comparison.

16.5.1.1 Cost Shifts

A major issue in larger corporate and institutional environments is shifts of costs from one unit's budget to another. This is especially sensitive if the savings from new technology occur in one unit, but the costs fall in another. For example, if hardware savings for servers accrue to the IS department, but end-user departments incur new costs for desktop hardware and software, strategies must be found to shift savings (from IS) to fund budgets (in end-user departments) which incur new costs.

Distributed computing is a paradigm change. With any such change it is important to expect costs to shift across components of expenses (e.g., hardware and software) and across units of the enterprise (e.g., IS and end-users). It is also important that your customer community share this expectation. One approach for analyzing and sharing this expectation is based on a matrix that lists components of expenses along the side, and organizational units in which expense is incurred along the top. The matrix is then filled in, not with specific dollar amounts, but with an indicator of whether the cost at a particular cell increases (indicated by a "+") or decreases (indicated by a "-") with a change in technology paradigm. Large changes in cost can be indicated (by a "++" and "--"); no significant net change is indicated also (by a "0"). A completed matrix for a shift from host-based to distributed computing may look like figure 16.7:

Components of Client Server Technology and their Relative Impact on Costs
(Compared with Mainframe Technology)

Component	End User	Application Custodian	Networking	Data Center
Application Support				
Development	O	—	O	O
Maintenace	O	—	O	O
Documentation (3)	O	O	+	O
Training (3)	O	+	O	O
Hardware				
LANs	+	O	O	O
Workstations	+	O	O	O
Servers	O	O	O	—
Networking Backbone	O	O	+	O
Environmentals	+	O	O	—
Systems Support				
Data Integrity (1)	O	+	+	+
Standards	—	—	—	—
Systems Software	O	O	O	+
Staffing				
Staffing Levels	—	+	+	O
Local Expertise	+	O	O	O
Transition Costs (1 time)	+	+	+	+

Figure 16.7 Host-based to distributed computing.

It is tempting to draw row and column totals for this matrix, but this must be done with great care.

16.5.1.2 If it is not Cheaper, How is it Better?

Many large organizations will discover from the above cost-shift analysis that total *cost of ownership* over the lifecycle of typical application is higher for a distributed environment, than it is for the simpler, more constrained host environment. Yet many of these organizations go ahead with delivery of services into this higher-cost environment. Why is this?

It is very important to be realistic about the benefits that open computing environments, typically client/server environments, can provide, and to whom those benefits accrue and when in time it is realistic to expect to obtain these benefits. All new technologies follow an *S* curve relating capability to cost (see figure 16.8).

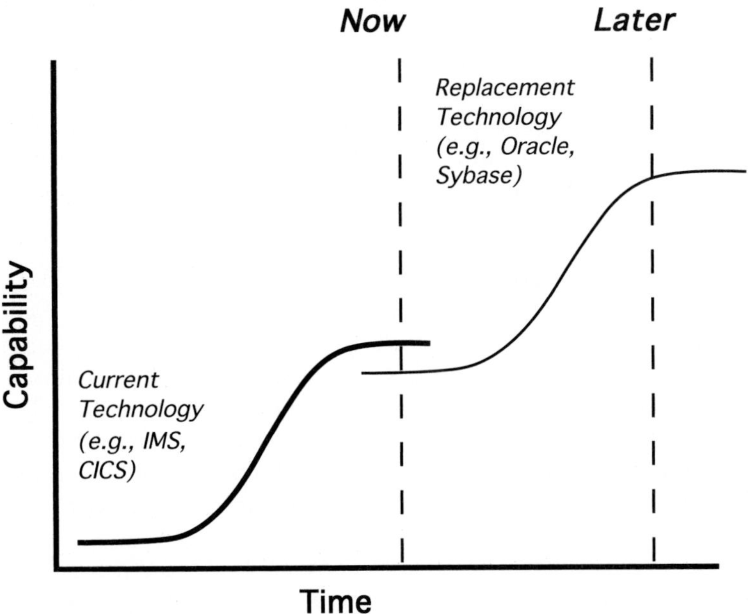

Figure 16.8 Capability vs. cost.

If you time your entry in a new technology too early, you may have a difficult time; the benefits you seek would need to be substantial. The *S* curve arises from at least four interacting factors: cost and complexity of the technology, which decrease over time; and functionality and availability, which increase over time.

Industry analysts have written a great deal on the sources of benefits. Typically the results show these benefits:

Potential Business Benefits	Potential Technical Benefits
Improved end-user productivity	Portability
Reduced end-user training time	Scalability
Improved customer service	Vendor Independence
Application-function enrichment	Investment protection
Responsiveness to change	Faster solutions
Local adaptability	Improved system integration
Desktop integration of information	Lower costs

The Gartner Group concludes that payback will occur in the end-user departments rather than in I/S and that this end-user payback is more highly leveraged than I/T costs because there are many more end-users. But by the same token, the end-user benefits are more highly diffused and thus harder to predict, document, and capture. In particular, cost savings do not seem to appear in the near term because of the start-up investments necessary.

Success in early pilots will come when the benefits that the new technology brings are well aligned with the needs the business wants to satisfy through the pilot project. For example, a pilot that needed to deliver quick results based on vastly improved programmer productivity would likely not produce the hoped-for results if it was an organization's an organization's first foray into client/server tools. At the least, there is a learning curve with new tools; and, in general, the tools today are relatively primitive, especially for projects involving teams of programmers.

16.6 Is it Open, or Is it Client/Server?

Organizations need to look at the business and technical problems they want to solve to determine where to place the emphasis in the architecture, where to be flexible in your principles, and where to be more rigorous. Because not all open systems are necessarily client/server, and not all client/server systems are necessarily open, it may be important for an organization to decide what its priorities are. If interoperability delivers the most benefit to the organization's highest priority needs, then client/server principles might be sacrificed in some cases to obtain the benefits of open systems.

If, for example, the organization's greatest need is for end-user productivity, or to support a great amount of growth in end-user access, then client/server may be a very high priority. If, on the other hand, an organization's key issues are in the area of integration of *islands of automation* to share dissimilar information within the business, or to enable *plug and play* kinds of modularity, then open (or, more precisely, interoperable, systems characteristics may be most important.

16.7 Use of Technical Consultants

Large organizations want to find ways to move quickly when a new and important idea arises that will provide substantial benefits. But large organizations also have a lot of solid history: the installed base of hardware and software, and the installed base of staff and staff skills, and the *installed base* of projects in progress, projects planned and projects in the backlog. All of these combine to direct the discussion of new ideas and opportunities towards today's architecture, rather than tomorrow's architecture.

Many organizations will take advantage of technical consultants with skills experience in distributed computing who are available in the marketplace. This can be fast and efficient for building quick prototypes. But is will precipitate a number of organizational and professional issues. Essentially, staff who are working in current technologies may feel that their knowledge base of existing systems and data has been bypassed, and their needs for professional change and growth have been ignored. Staff may see their own jobs as threatened, or their own worth devalued. And is some cases staff will see the high-value, high-motivation, most enjoyable work being *outsourced.* Consultants may be taking good ideas from the staff and implementing them; the consultants may get–or take–the credit for the implementation *and* the ideas. Finally, when the consultants leave, the staff in place may find they have inherited a new maintenance burden, and yet they have had no preparation for this responsibility.

Managers must proactively manage these issues, and must do so with more than soothing words about future training and project opportunities. Staff–not just consultants–should always be involved in these *breakthrough* projects, and their roles should be substantial rather than pro forma. Enough time must be allocated for staff to shift time to these new opportunities and to focus on the new work to be done. The newness of the distributed environment requires substantial dedicated, *quality time* for staff to understand and appreciate; without this focused time apart from their other responsibilities, the staff will produce designs and implementations that will look–and function–like a port of mainframe applications to a new environments. Interface design will be of relatively mediocre quality–looking more like mainframe screens than GUI windows–and code reusability will be low.

Consider forming small teams–perhaps using the *buddy system:* pairing a staff member with a consultant, locating consultants and staff together so there is frequent interaction, and so both implicit as well as explicit technology transfer occurs. Is some cases the staff member may serve as the functional *business-area expert* or mentor to the consultant, while the consultant acts as a technical mentor to the staff member. Evaluate your consultants to ensure that they can work effectively in this kind of environment, rather than the *Lone Ranger* environment many have the most experience with. Ensure that technology transfer to your staff is an explicit part of the work plans and deliverables of your consultants.

16.8 Conclusions

Just as the technology is evolving rapidly, so too are the management practices associated with its delivery into the organization. This chapter can only be a partial report on those practices. An understanding of best practices in terms of managing the move to distributed computing should begin to build now, as larger organizations begin to commit enterprise-wide–rather than departmental-level–systems to this technology. For smaller companies, the technology issues dominate the implementation agenda. But in large companies, management issues–especially those of people, policy and process–will tend to outgrow the already-daunting technology agenda. Management conferences, consulting firms, management-oriented periodical publications, and books like this one will increasingly contribute to the manager's shared knowledge of what does not work, and ultimately, of what works best.

John Sack is the director of Stanford Data Center. He is responsible for operation of institutional information systems at Stanford, including central administrative systems and library systems, and for the architecture and technical infrastructure of institutional-information systems on campus. John received his M.A. in English from Stanford University and a B.A. in English from University of Virginia.

Appendix A

The OSF Distributed Management Environment

David Chappell
Chappell and Associates

A.1 Introduction

Distributed environments, whatever their purpose, are not especially useful unless they can be managed. Effective management requires solving a myriad of different problems, ranging from managing network components like bridges and routers to remote administration of the systems on the network. In fact, one common division made in distributed management is exactly this distinction between network management and systems management. While the problems involved can be quite different, both areas must be addressed for a complete solution.

Other problems exist, too, which do not really fall within either of these categories. For example, a common way to distribute and install software on systems in a distributed environment can save a great deal of time and effort, yet it is not clear whether a solution like this falls into either of the above categories. Similarly, other kinds of distributed services could play a useful part in managing a complex environment.

The Distributed Management Environment (DME) created by the Open Software Foundation (OSF) takes aim at all of these problems. It includes components targeted at network management, at systems management, and at providing key distributed services. Contrary to what one might expect, DME itself does not include much in the way of traditional management applications. Instead, it provides common platforms for developing those applications.

Much (but not all) of DME relies on an earlier OSF technology, the Distributed Computing Environment (DCE). This appendix assumes some knowledge of DCE, such as that gained by reading the DCE chapter earlier in this volume.

A.2 How DME was Created

OSF exists to create vendor-neutral enabling technology, common software infrastructures for solving common problems. The process used to create these infrastructures was described earlier in the DCE chapter. That process, beginning with dissemination of a Request for Technology (RFT) and ending with release of source code, is exactly what was done for DME. The DME RFT was released in July 1990, and many organizations submitted technologies intended to address one or more of the problem areas it spelled out. OSF evaluated these submissions and announced its choices just over a year later in September 1991. As was done with DCE, the selected technologies were then integrated together and made available for licensing by anyone (see figure A.1).

One important note: this appendix was written prior to the final release of DME by OSF. As a result, some details may have changed in the final version of the technologies described here.

A.3 DME's Components

The nature of the problems addressed by DME is quite different than those addressed by DCE. Accordingly, the solutions are also quite different. In particular, DME consists of a number of components, most of which are quite independent of the others. The tight level of integration found in DCE just is not present in DME. Given the disparate nature of the problems to be solved, this should not be too surprising.

DME's components match the problems as originally described above. For network management, DME includes the network management option (NMO), a platform that supports traditional network management applications. For systems management (and perhaps other things, as well), DME provides the object management framework (OMF), an object-oriented platform for distributed peer-to-peer applications. And finally, DME includes a number of distributed services, including:

- Event services (EVS), a common mechanism for describing and forwarding events;
- Print services (PRS), a distributed printing service;
- Software distribution services (SDS), a scheme for distributing and installing software in a distributed environment;
- License management services (LMS), a common mechanism for supporting distributed software licensing; and
- A few other technologies providing simple management-related services.

Figure A.1 shows a taxonomy of DME and its components. Of the various parts of DME, all except the network management option rely on DCE. While NMO can stand alone, everything else is defined to exist within the context of one or more DCE cells.

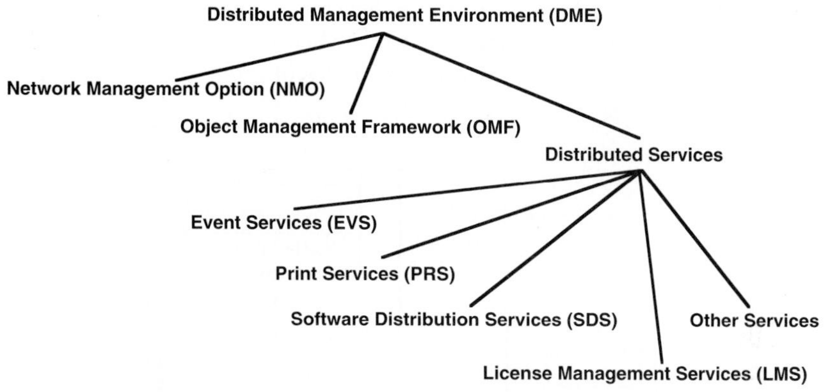

Figure A.1 A DME taxonomy.

A.4 DME Components: Network Management Option (NMO)

Network management typically refers to managing components of the network itself, including things like routers, bridges, and the lower layers of protocol software on various systems attached to networks. The established protocol for carrying out this type of management today in a multi-vendor environment is the Simple Network Management Protocol (SNMP). Created in the late 1980s under the auspices of the Internet Engineering Task Force (IETF), it has become ubiquitous.

Another contender for a network management protocol is the Common Management Information Protocol (CMIP). Developed by the International Organization for Standardization (ISO), it is not yet widely used. Some industry segments, however, particularly the telephone companies, have settled on CMIP as the best protocol for managing their networks.

Each of these protocols provides its own way of defining managed objects, abstract representations of the things being managed. SNMP uses something called an OBJECT-TYPE macro to define its various management information bases (MIBs), defined sets of managed objects. A MIB defined using this notation is said to be in Concise MIB format. For CMIP, a more complex and potentially more powerful notation referred to as Guidelines for the Definition of Managed Objects (GDMO) is used to define managed objects. Along with their distinct notations, SNMP and CMIP also assume a somewhat different structure for managed objects and provide different ways to name those objects.

Both SNMP and CMIP use a manager/agent model. One system acts as a manager, and management applications typically run on that system. Those applications communicate via the protocol with agents on other systems, such as bridges and routers. These agents, in turn, allow access to the managed objects, letting applications read or modify them.

DME's NMO includes both SNMP and CMIP, as shown in figure A.2. It also assumes that both protocols' conventions are used for defining managed objects. An application can be written that accesses either or both of them through the same application programming interface (API). Known as XMP, this rather complex API is implemented as a library linked into the application itself (note that despite the use of a common interface, an application developer must still behave somewhat differently when accessing SNMP or CMIP; the substantial differences in the way these two protocols describe and name managed objects made this unavoidable).

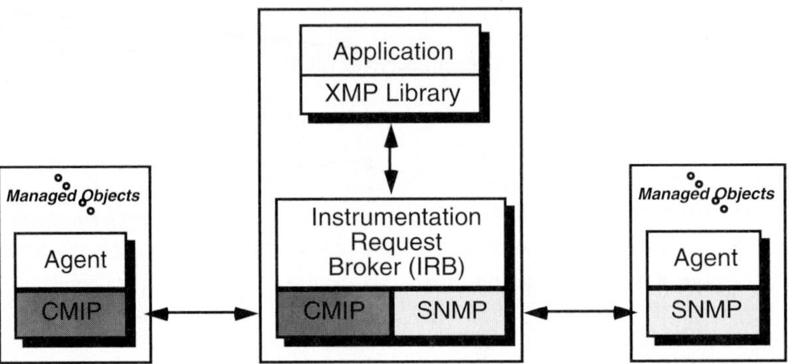

Figure A.2 The network management option.

The XMP API is used together with something called XOM. XOM allows the creation of packages, sets of C code that define the structure of managed objects. To make the creation of packages easier, NMO includes a Package Development Kit (PDK) containing a PDK compiler. This compiler automatically produces equivalent XOM packages from managed object definitions expressed in GDMO. Although no equivalent tool for SNMP's Concise MIB definitions is included in the first release of NMO, one will likely appear in the future.

With DME's NMO, an application using XMP communicates with an Instrumentation Request Broker (IRB), running as a separate process. The IRB acts as a switch, routing the application's request to SNMP or CMIP as needed. For messages received from agents, the IRB routes them back to the appropriate application. In addition, the IRB provides services for filtering events and mapping from names to system addresses.

NMO provides a common approach for manager/agent applications using SNMP, CMIP, or both. By defining a single API for both protocols in a multi-vendor setting, it is intended to become the standard platform used by network management applications in a variety of environments.

A.5 DME Components: Object Management Framework (OMF)

There exist applications for which a manager/agent approach might not be appropriate. For example, while it is obvious who plays which role when a Unix workstation is managing a bridge, it's somewhat less obvious for the case where one workstation is managing another, or for other types of systems management. While a manager/agent approach might be usable even in this situation, there are other possibilities as well. In particular, a peer-to-peer approach presents itself as an alternative. In this scheme, a management application consists of various components, each running on some system in the network. No single component is the manager and none are really agents. Instead, each provides some part of the complete service, and each plays a more or less equal role in carrying out the application's functions.

DME's OMF provides a platform on which to build this type of application. It supports the creation of object-oriented distributed applications, where no one component need necessarily act as a manager or as an agent. By providing direct support for an object-oriented approach, OMF brings with it the advantages this entails, including encapsulation of function and reusability of already implemented objects. Ideally, implementing a new application will require only the creation of those objects that add new functionality; much of the required software will already exist in reusable objects distributed around the network.

OMF is targeted particularly at systems management applications. As is described below, OMF depends on DCE, and DCE is unlikely to be present on bridges and routers any time in the near future. Accordingly, OMF-based applications run on workstations and other full-fledged computer systems.

A.5.1 OMF and CORBA

Standards for distributed object computing are already appearing. The leading organization in their creation is the Object Management Group (OMG), a consortium of vendors and users active in this area. Among the first of OMG's results is a specification for a Common Object Request Broker Architecture (CORBA). CORBA defines an interface to an Object Request Broker (ORB) and provides a language, called the Interface Definition Language (IDL), for defining the interface to the objects themselves (despite having the same name, CORBA's IDL is not the same as the IDL used in DCE). In the CORBA world, objects are defined by the interface they present to other objects. When an object wishes to request a service from another object, it does not make its request directly to that object. Instead, the request is sent to an ORB, which locates the desired object and passes the request on to it, perhaps via other ORBs. The destination object receives this request, carries it out by executing the appropriate method, then sends its response back, again via one or more ORBs. The process is in many ways similar to RPC, but the level of indirection provided by the ORBs frees objects from having to discover the location of other objects. Instead, the ORBs handle this transparently. Also, the granularity of objects in the CORBA environment is expected to be somewhat smaller than that of RPC servers; an application can thus more easily make use of exactly those services it needs from other objects in the distributed environment.

DME's OMF is an implementation of CORBA. The ORB is rechristened a Management Request Broker (MRB), but its function is just the same. In the OMF, an MRB is a process running on each system in the environment. Each object, which itself may well be a process, communicates with its local MRB to make requests of other objects. If the destination object is on the same system, the MRB simply passes the request to it. If the object is on another system, however, the MRB passes the request to that system's MRB. MRB-to-MRB communication is done via DCE RPC. A single OMF-based application typically consists of a number of objects spread among two or more systems. This situation is illustrated in figure A.3.

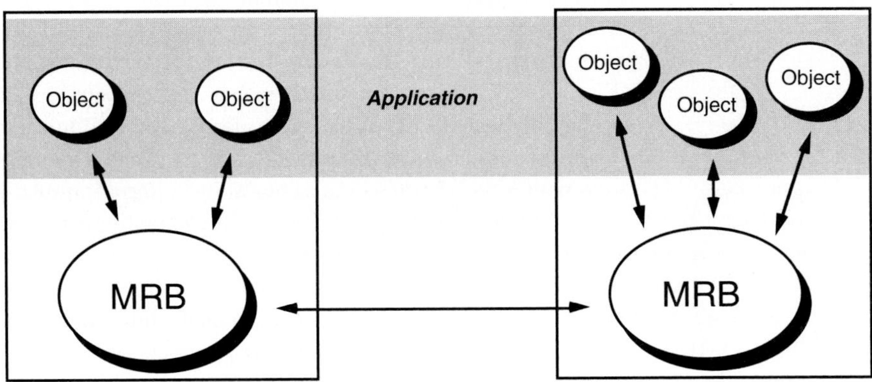

Figure A.3 An OMF application.

A.5.2 OMF Additions to CORBA

OMF supports CORBA's IDL for defining the interface to objects. Several extensions are added, however, to create a superset language called I4DL. I4DL allows specifying further information about objects, including extra detail about their implementation.

OMF also includes a component called the Management User Interface (MUI). The MUI incorporates a display server, an object intended to allow a common user interface for different OMF-based applications. The display server communicates with a user via the X Window system, and is itself an X client application. Other objects communicate with the display server both to receive operations from it (e.g., receiving a request made by a human user) and to request operations of it (e.g., asking the display server to change something on the screen).

The MUI includes a Dialogue Specification Language (DSL), a variation of the OSF Motif User Interface Language (UIL). An application developer can statically define her desired user interface using DSL and compile this definition using the MUI's DSL compiler. While the application is actually running, then, it can send this compiled DSL specification to the display server and cause the structures it defines to appear on the screen. One process, the display server, appearing as just another object to other OMF objects, can in fact provide a common portal to human users for all of them.

One more important thing to understand about OMF is this: virtually nothing in it is specific to management applications. Just as CORBA is intended to define a framework for creating all types of object-oriented applications, so too is OMF suitable for this wider role. Its inclusion in DME led to some terminology changes–MRB instead of ORB, for example–but its potential applicability is by no means limited to management applications.

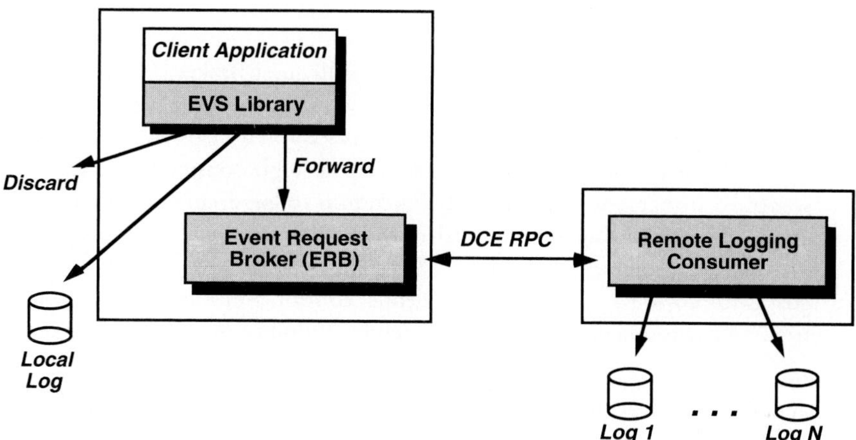

Figure A.4 Main components of EVS.

A.6 DME Components: Distributed Services

NMO and OMF both provide platforms on which to build management applications. Neither, however, includes much in the way of actual applications. Instead, their acceptance in the industry is intended to provide a common infrastructure that encourages competition among application developers.

DME does include some real applications, though. Somewhat surprisingly, these applications do not run on top of either NMO or OMF. Instead, they are based on DCE, making use of its RPC, directory services, security, and other services. Much like DCE's Distributed File Service (DFS), DME's Distributed Services are purely DCE applications, independent both from the other parts of DME and from each other.

A.6.1 Event Services (EVS)

Many applications, management related and otherwise, have a need to send events. In a distributed environment, it is often useful to have these events go to a central place rather than requiring someone to manually check many different systems. For example, security violations may occur on various systems around the network. Ideally, though, a security administrator should need to check only a single log to learn about any of these violations.

DME's EVS, whose main components are shown in figure A.4, is a generalized event handling scheme that provides tools for solving this kind of problem. Application developers can use EVS's Event Definition Language (EDL) to define particular events and the information which should be sent with them. An EDL compiler then reads this definition and produces a stub to link into the application. To send the event, the application simply calls the appropriate function.

What happens next depends on the event controllers (ECs) in effect on the system at which the event was generated. ECs are filters, and based on their values, an event may be discarded, logged locally, or forwarded on to a waiting Consumer. Events that are forwarded are first passed to another process called an Event Request Broker (ERB) on the system that generates the event. Remote consumers register with ERBs on the systems from which they wish to receive events. Forwarded events are then passed on to registered consumers via DCE RPC.

The first release of DME includes only a single consumer, the Remote Logging Consumer. As its name suggests, its only function is to log events that it receives. A log viewer is also included, allowing more user-friendly access to the logs this consumer creates.

Like so much else in DME, EVS is really a framework rather than a true application. Its goal is to provide a common way to define, control, and forward events of all types in a distributed environment. As such, it is a useful addition to the DCE world.

A.6.2 Print Services (PRS)

While most people would admit that a network print service is very useful, probably very few would expect such a service to be part of something like DME. Nevertheless, PRS is an important piece of the various technologies that comprise DME. What PRS does is exactly what one would expect: it allows users and applications to submit jobs to be printed at remote printers. Like the other distributed services in DME, PRS relies on DCE for communication between its parts.

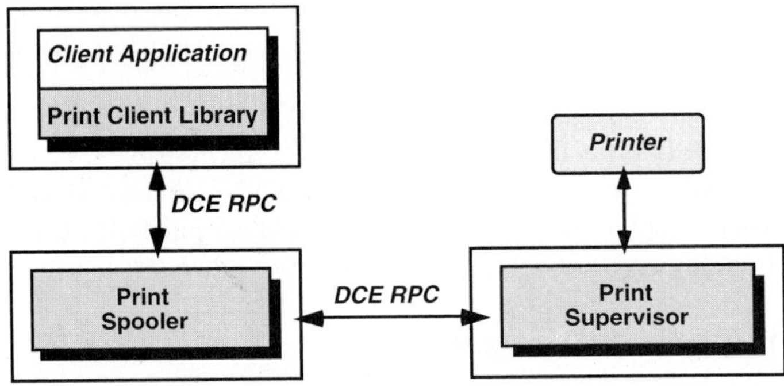

Figure A.5 Main components of PRS.

The main components of PRS are illustrated in figure A.5. As the figure shows, a user or application submits a print job via DCE RPC to a print spooler. The spooler maintains queues that map between the logical printers seen by users and the physical printers that actually print the jobs. The spoolers, in turn, submit jobs to print supervisors, which send the jobs to physical printers. The first release of PRS will include supervisors that support PostScript printers, simple ASCII printers, and a gateway to the commonly used lpd protocol.

PRS is based in large part on ISO 10175, a standard for document printing applications. Although changes were made, such as running over DCE services rather than those defined by ISO, the way in which print jobs are defined has been largely retained. In PRS, print jobs are assigned attributes indicating a job name, a job identifier, how many copies of the job should be printed, the document format (e.g., PostScript), and other things.

From a user's point of view, PRS supports familiar Unix print commands like lpr and lpq. To fully access its features, however, a user must use PRS's own commands. These commands are expected to conform to the emerging POSIX standard in this area.

While printing is perhaps not the most obvious thing to include in a set of tools for management, DME's PRS fills an important niche. For organizations using DCE, it is the natural choice for a distributed print service.

A.6.3 Software Distribution Services (SDS)

One of the most time consuming tasks of system administrators in many distributed environments is installing new software and new releases of software on the systems in those networks. The goal of SDS is to make this task easier, faster, and less error prone.

The main components of SDS are shown in figure A.6. Software to be installed is stored on a source system. This software must previously have been packaged into an SDS-defined format (this format and SDS in general is aligned with the emerging POSIX standard in this area). The software stored on the source system need not be capable of actually executing there; it is simply stored as binary information on that system's disk. A user at the manager system can communicate with a source via DCE RPC to examine the software available for installation. Once the desired components have been selected, the manager communicates with one or more target systems. Once again, this communication takes place via DCE RPC. The targets then go directly to the source, copy the specified software, and install it.

Each Target maintains a record of the software that has been installed. A manager can examine this record to decide whether a particular update needs to be done. Targets support various other features, as well, including checks for dependencies before installation and kernel build and reboot.

SDS solves a problem traditionally associated with managing distributed environments, and so it's a natural part of DME. Since like the other distributed services it requires only DCE to operate, however, it is useful in any DCE environment.

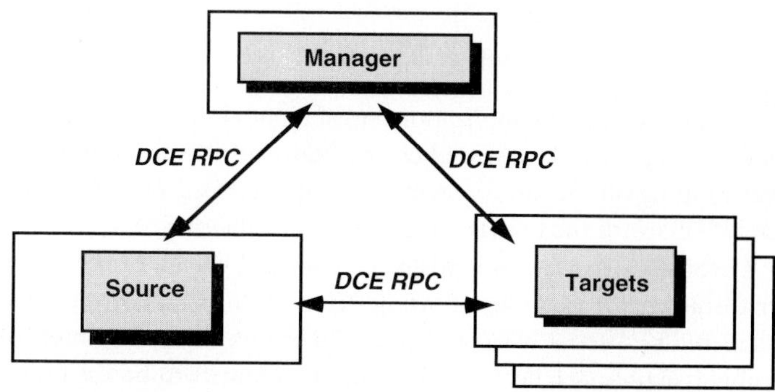

Figure A.6 Main components of SDS.

A.6.4 License Management Services (LMS)

Software licensing in the age of distributed computing has been difficult. A user might buy a single system license for some software product, but how can the vendor be sure that this one product isn't placed on a file server accessible to many clients? Alternatively, a user might buy an expensive site license for the product when only some relatively small number of people need to use it. To solve this problem, one can use some distributed licensing technology, as is done by many products today. Ideally, though, products from multiple vendors would all rely on the same licensing technology, obviating the need to support multiple license management schemes from multiple vendors.

DME's LMS, whose components are shown in figure A.7, is intended to play exactly this role. Relying on DCE like the other distributed services, it requires one or more license servers to exist in a DCE cell. Each license server maintains a license database, indicating what licenses are available and which are in use for products that use LMS. An administrator can examine or modify license databases via a license manager, a remote process that accesses the license server via DCE RPC.

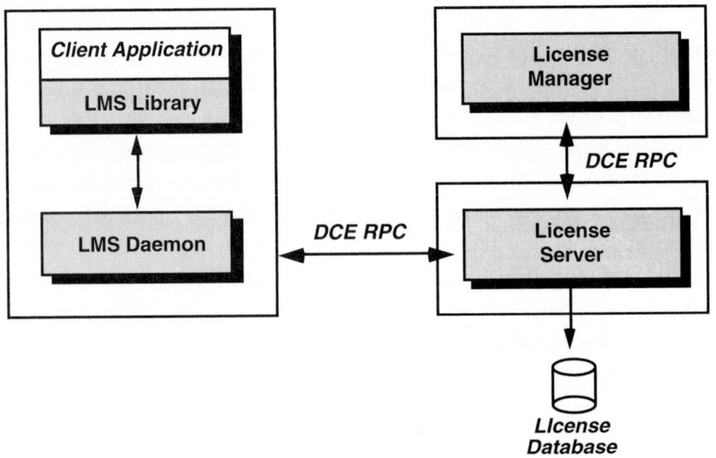

Figure A.7 Main components of LMS.

To use LMS, client applications must be modified to include an LMS library. Once this is done, starting an LMS-aware client will cause it to communicate with an LMS Daemon, a process running on the same system as the application. This daemon, in turn, communicates via DCE RPC with the license server to acquire a license.

LMS supports various kinds of licenses and license features. A user might buy 15 concurrent licenses, for example, allowing up to 15 instances of the licensed product to be used simultaneously. Alternatively, a vendor might give away demonstration copies of a product with only five use-once licenses, allowing the product to be used only five times. The license manager also allows users to queue for licenses, with some users having a higher priority than others, and permits an administrator to include or exclude specific users from a license.

Distributed license management is an example of both an important administrative function and a niche that can greatly benefit from a standard solution. DME's LMS, by providing a standard, vendor-neutral approach, is a good example of the enabling technology that OSF exists to create.

A.6.5 Other Distributed Services

DME's Distributed Services include a few other useful tools. One of them, called the Subsystem Management Service (SMS), is essentially a process whose job is to keep other process running. The SMS daemon can monitor groups of processes that should always be running, detect any failures, and restart as needed. There is really nothing distributed about SMS; it runs and monitors processes on only a single system. Nevertheless, it is included in DME's Distributed Services.

Another included set of services is called PC Services (PCS). These services allow personal computers running MS-DOS to participate in some parts of DME. In particular, PCS includes an MS-DOS client for DME's LMS and a simple remote monitoring system for the PC. Both of these PC applications communicate via a simple UDP-based protocol (not through DCE RPC) with an ally server running on a nearby machine. This Ally Server, in turn, provides a gateway into the larger world.

A.7 Conclusion

DME targets a large set of problems. Accordingly, it offers a large set of solutions, each targeted at same particular facet of management. In some environments, only some of these solutions may be useful, while other organizations may elect to use most or all of them. Whatever the case may be, the diverse technologies in DME provide vendor-neutral solutions to a broad range of management and administrative problems.

David Chappell is principal of Chappell & Associates, a training and consulting firm focused on distributed computing for open systems. He has written and taught many courses on distributed computing and related topics to clients in North America and Europe, and has served as a consultant on numerous communications projects. Among his current projects, David is a consultant to the Open Software Foundation (OSF), involved with OSF's Distributed Computing Environment (DCE) and Distributed Management Environment (DME). His previous experience includes software engineering positions with NCR Corporation and Cray Research, where he was a principal architect of Cray's original Unix-based OSI product. He also chaired the Upper Layers Special Interest Group of the National Institute of Standards and Technology (NIST) OSI Implementors Workshop from 1988 until 1990. David holds a B.S. in Economics and an M.S. in Computer Science, both from the University of Wisconsin-Madison.

Appendix B

Role of Object Technology in Distributed Systems

Richard Mark Soley
Object Management Group, Inc.

The Object Management Group, Inc. (OMG) is a not-for-profit consortium dedicated to solving problems of interoperability in distributed environments, using a novel approach based on consensus creation of *de facto* standards based on commercially available object technology. The initial basis of a suite of object-oriented standardized languages, interfaces and protocols is a communication specification called Common Object Request Broker Architecture *(CORBA)*. The CORBA architecture is dedicated to providing interoperability at the application level between systems executing under the stresses of diverse operating systems, languages, network protocols and hardware architectures. The future plans of the OMG include building on this strong foundation with services and facilities to support the application programmer.

B.1 Introduction

Any business traveler that covers the world, carrying electrical devices such as computers, shavers, irons and the like, knows the complexity of arranging power for those devices in foreign hotels. Although most of the world's electrical outlets offer 220 volts at 50 hertz, much of the world (including the United States, for example) operates at 110 volts, and 60 hertz. These standards are not that close, actually, particularly for devices that expect a consistent input frequency. And the wildly fluctuating standards across national boundaries (and sometimes *within* national boundaries) can be cumbersome to track. Worse, the *physical* power connectors differ from country to country, even within large areas that offer the same power characteristics (*e.g.,* Western Europe operates with a single 220 volt, 50 hertz power standard, but two different physical connection plugs).

By and large, however, coping with the differences in power connection between countries has become rather simple for the business traveler. Traveling accessories from irons to computers are now generally impervious to the whims of local power generation standards, accepting from 100 to 250 volts and any frequency; furthermore, experienced business travelers can easily carry in one hand converters for all of the world's power connectors.

Unfortunately, there exist few standards for such interoperability for the wildly differing standards in computer applications, operating systems, networking systems and hardware. What few standards (either *de facto* or *de jure*) that do exist concentrate on low-level interoperability: cables, plus, networking levels. Only ad hoc solutions (such as shared file formats and batch-mode format conversion programs) currently exist for true application-to-application interoperability in heterogeneous networks.

What computing users need is a *global information appliance,* with the ability to access a world of computing services from anywhere in the world, in a seamless, natural way, just as the traveler today can access the global telephone network to communicate.

B.2 The Object Management Group

The Object Management Group, Inc. (OMG) is a not-for-profit industry consortium that was created to attack this problem and provide solutions for interoperability. Besides the obvious benefits for end-users of technical solutions, a generalized solution to application interoperability offers lower-cost market introduction strategies to vendors of technical solutions as well. The primary mission of the OMG is the creation of a suite of standard languages, interfaces and protocols to support interoperability between applications in the face of heterogeneity. Unlike groups that have attempted to create homogeneity at various computing levels (hardware, operating system, application interface), the OMG takes as a given the long-term heterogeneity of computing (due to competitive as well as needs-based forces); OMG's suite of interfaces will build on, rather than replace, existing interfaces.

A key enabling technology for application interoperability is *object technology.* Offering well-structure modularity and clearly-defined interfaces, as well as a rigorous approach to the reuse of existing software (the *inheritance* mechanism), object-orientation is the perfect choice for defining services in a heterogeneous environment. Furthermore, OMG took an early decision to rely only on *commercially available* technology, in an effort to create a widely-available marketplace for "off the shelf" compatible products. The two key concepts of object technology and commercial availability form the foundation of the OMG process (see figure B.1).

Figure B.1 Foundation of OMG process.

B.3 The Object Management Architecture

The OMG is taking a "bottom-up" approach to *de facto* standards creation, starting from the viewpoint of the network and working up to application interfaces. The first step taken in the adoption of standard by the OMG was an agreement on terminology and architecture. This early agreement on direction, structure and objectives was made in mid-1990, and published as the *Object Management Architecture Guide* [OMAG]. A reference model, or architecture, formed the basis for selection of technology in a structured way (see figure B.2).

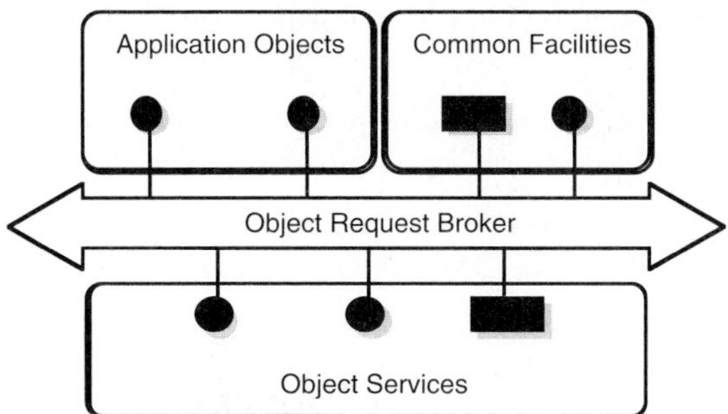

Figure B.2 Object management architecture.

To fill out the Object Management Architecture (OMA) reference model, four areas of standardization have been identified:

- the Object Request Broker (ORB), or key communications element, for handling distribution of messages between application objects in a highly interoperable manner;
- the Object Model, or single design-portability abstract model for communicating with OMG-conformant object-oriented systems;
- the Object Services, which will provide the main functions for realizing basic object functionality using the Object Request Broker–the logical modeling and physical storage of objects; and
- the Common Facilities will comprise facilities which are useful in many application domains and which will be made available through OMA compliant class interfaces.

The Application Facilities outlined in the model is a place holder for objects which belong in the realm of the application developer (independent software vendor or value-added reseller). The OMG will not adopt standards in this competitive arena.

It is important to realize that the Object Services, Common Facilities and Application Objects names are simply *categories* of objects. In the OMA model, every piece of software is represented as an object, communicating with other objects via the Object Request Broker. The OMG groups objects into these three broad categories based on relative importance in the standardization process.

The open OMG adoption process includes requests for information and proposals, requesting detailed technical and commercial availability information from OMG members about existing products to fill particular parts of the reference model architecture. After passage by technical and business committees to review these responses, the OMG Board of Directors makes a final determination for technology adoption. Adopted specifications are available on a fee-free basis to members and non-members alike.

The general outline of the adoption process, which usually consumes between 16 and 18 months from conception to completion, appears as follows:

- *Request for Information (RFI):* This step, involving a survey of the computer industry, establishes the range of commercially available software which addresses the need of a particular part of the Object Management Architecture.
- *Request for Proposals (RFP):* Once the range of commercially available solutions is known, a specific request listing requirements (as opposed to objectives) is issued, to establish the software for which specifications are available for adoption.
- *Competitive Selection Process:* Based on the overall objectives of the OMA and the available software, the OMG chooses a single interface for adoption as a standard.
- *Promulgation of Interface Specification:* Once the choice is made, the OMG makes the interface specification as broadly available as possible, and simultaneously begins revision and enhancement processes to keep the specification up to date with current technology and trends.

Recent selection process have resulted in two major OMG technologies: a baseline communication (messaging) agent for the Object Request Broker layer (called *CORBA,* for Common Object Request Broker Architecture [CORBA]); and a standard, extensible Core Object Model. Underway are selection processes for Object Services as delineated above, as well as revisions to the ORB interface to increase interoperability.

B.4 CORBA Overview

Distributed systems are not a new idea, and approaches abound to solving the everyday programming problems of integrating communications into an application service. The most popular today is the *remote procedure call* (RPC), which simplifies the task of reintegrating a program once parts have been distributed to various processors (or even address spaces).

The typical approach to using an RPC mechanism involves choosing a procedure call boundary across which to split the program (by hand!), and then rigorously specifying the interface between the calling program and the called routine to be distributed. A semi-automated compilation sequence then inserts the communications "overhead" code to perform the remote execution of the call.

While this clearly abstracts away the details of the communications channel between the two address spaces, it has several drawbacks:

- The need for the call and the details of the procedure call must be known at compile time.
- The details of the data structures (representation, extent, lifetime, etc.) passed from caller to callee must be known at compile time.

- The interface must either be specified in all programming languages from which the callee might be called, or must be mappable to all such languages (see figure B.3).

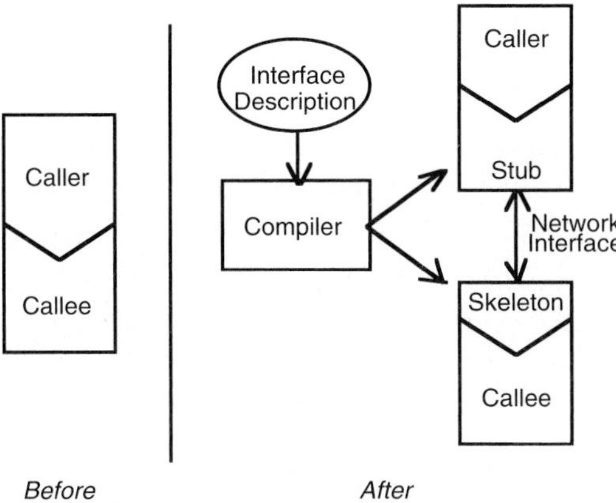

Figure B.3 Remote procedure call.

The OMG approach to distribution is embodied in the first OMG adopted technology specification, named CORBA (*Common Object Request Broker Architecture Specification*). This approach employs a similar abstraction as RPC, with a few twists that should simplify the life of a programmer (and thus lower maintenance costs and increase extensibility of products):

- A single specification language, called *OMG IDL* (for OMG Interface Definition Language), is used to specify interface independent of execution (programming) language. While IDL is not itself a programming language, it provides language independence for programmers who do not know *a priori* the likely user language of callers. The IDL is also *object-oriented,* allowing abstraction of interface representation (encapsulation), polymorphic messaging (function calls), and inheritance of interface.

- A fully dynamic representation of available interfaces in an *interface repository* (IR) representing the interfaces (or classes) of all objects available in the distributed computing system.

- A fully dynamic calling extension allowing run-time discovery of objects, discovery of available interface from an IR, construction of message requests, and sending of those requests.

- A *context* extension allowing passing of optional named (rather than order-based) parameters, for explicit control over execution.

- An abstraction mechanism (*object adapter*) for removing the details of object implementation from the messaging substrate.

Throughout the design of CORBA, the need to maintain language, operating system, hardware and network independence is paramount.

B.5 CORBA Details

The basic service provided by CORBA (or any calling distribution service) is delivery of messages (requests) from one piece of code to another, and delivery of a response (return or exception) to the caller. It is convenient to call these two objects the *client* and the *server* in such a transaction, although in the CORBA structure any object can be either a client, a server, or both. In fact, it is expected that most objects (i.e., applications) will be both clients and servers of requests over their lifetimes (see figure B.4).

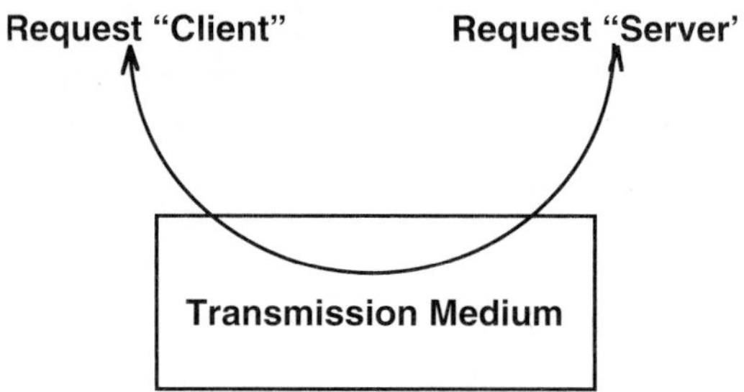

Figure B.4 Client/server requests.

The job of the transmission medium, then, is to invisibly provide transport of those communications.

CORBA compliant distribution systems can perform this duty in two totally different, but compatible ways:

- In the *dynamic* scheme, the client can discover available servers at run time (based, e.g., on location and facility), discover the interfaces of those servers, construct a request for use of the service, send the request (optionally multiple times), and retrieve the response. This is all possible without any *a priori* knowledge of the available servers or interfaces available at compile time.
- In the *static* scheme, the client must know the interface of the server to be accessed at compile time, though the discovery of available servers can be determined at run time.

Why two approaches? Quite simply, there are sound engineering reasons for using a static approach at times, even though a dynamic approach is far more convenient (or even necessary) for some applications. It seems obvious that (at least theoretically) a static scheme can yield better performance; since all the details of the implementation language, operating system, and communications channel are known at compile time, various optimization techniques can lower the run-time overhead of using the communications channel.

Nevertheless, there are important applications for which a dynamic messaging scheme are necessary. The best example is a browser; it would be nearly impossible to deliver a system browser for dynamic debugging in the distributed environment, in which new servers and interfaces may be added at run-time.

The CORBA solution, to have both static and dynamic messaging support, is made possible by the Interface Definition Language. The same language source used to compile stubs and skeletons (just as in RPC distribution) is made available to clients at run-time to aid in client discovery of interface and construction of requests (see figure B.5).

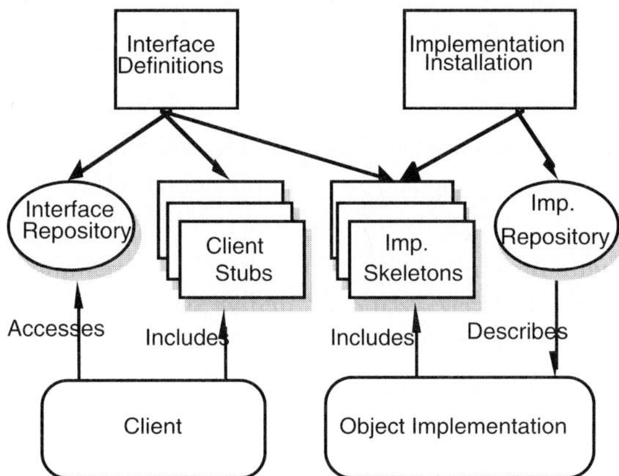

Figure B.5 Interface definition language.

This two-way choice of both static and dynamic interface allows programmers of client and server software to choose either the static or dynamic approach, based on the requirements of the software under development. Better yet, it allows application software to use *both* the static and dynamic schemes *within a single code.* Wherever the programmer knows entirely the well-defined interface at compile time, he or she can use the static interface; for other requests, the dynamic interface may be used.

Besides the static and dynamic interfaces between client/server codes and the ORB, CORBA provides generic ORB interface calls for management of the communications substrate itself. An important extension of the ORB core communications substrate is the *object adapter,* which adapts from the generic ORB model of objects to the vagaries of implementation details of objects in various different schemes. For example, objects may be implemented as application codes within operating system processes; they may be represented as objects in object-oriented databases; or they may represent programming-language level objects (e.g., *C++* or *Smalltalk*) communicating within a single address space (see figure B.6).

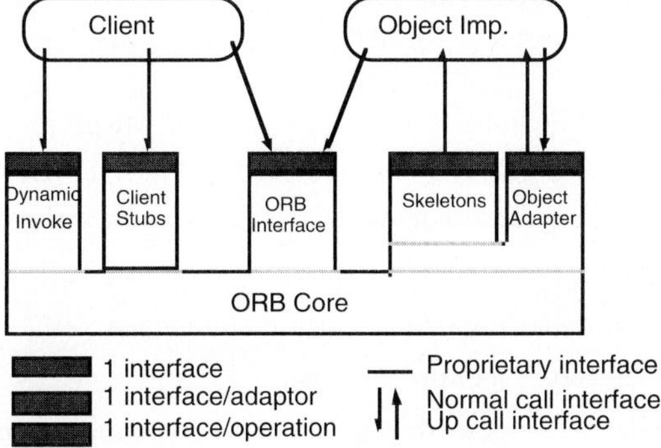

Figure B.6 ORB interface calls.

In fact, one of the greatest difficulties uncovered in reaching the CORBA standard was the many different ways that object implementation was viewed by the competing vendors. Everyone that uses objects has a different idea of what an object embodies/represents, how *large* an object is (e.g., in bytes), and how often objects need to interact. C++ programming language objects, for example, have little in common with managed objects in usual sense, except for some similarities in abstraction.

The CORBA specification therefore includes a single object model which is embodied in the Interface Definition Language itself; implementations of CORBA must then map this generic model into the implementation language(s) used by clients and servers.

The CORBA object model provides a rich, extensible set of types to the user, including:

- 16- and 32-bit signed and unsigned integers;
- single and double precision floating point numbers;
- ISO Latin-1 (ISO 8859.1) characters;
- Boolean values;
- eight bit opaque data type (octets);
- variable length arrays of characters (strings);
- enumerated types; and
- a general type (any).

In addition, this set of types may be extended by several constructed types:

- records of ordered (name, type) pairs (structures);
- discriminated unions of types;
- variable or fixed-length sequences of a type;
- fixed-length arrays of a type; and
- interfaces, which specify type operations.

In addition, there is a type representation for object references (or *handles*) which may be used to send requests, or as general parameters.

It is of course not enough to agree on a set of types; the CORBA standard also includes an application programming interface (API). This API is specified in IDL, so that its use may be mapped to whichever implementation language the user may choose. As much as possible, the various constructs accessed by this API are represented as objects as well, to allow a consistent, simple interface.

The CORBA API includes interfaces in five basic categories, including:

- Synchronous dynamic request invocation and receipt requests;
- Deferred synchronous dynamic request invocation and receipt requests;
- Memory management and housekeeping requests;
- Context (name-based parameter) list maintenance; and
- Interface repository lookup requests.

Static invocation of requests through an ORB are managed entirely during the compilation process, and therefore do not show up in the CORBA API.

B.6 Current and Future Directions

Like any technology, the CORBA interface is never *finished.* In particular, though the CORBA document defines enough of the IDL language and the CORBA API to allow creation of both CORBA-compliant ORB implementations and applications codes to take advantage of them, CORBA 1.1 is silent on federation and interoperability issues which arise in some large-network real-world situations. To rectify this lack, the OMG currently has underway an effort to select (by early 1994) an upward-compatible 2.0 revision to address primarily ORB-to-ORB communications standards, so that any two CORBA-compliant ORB implementations, though separately developed, would be guaranteed to interoperate and share namespaces. Other issues, such as native transaction and security protocols, and quality-of-service control and multicast extensions, are also being sought in the next round of ORB standardization.

In the meantime, at this writing about 100 companies (including IBM, Hewlett-Packard, Olivetti, NEC, Sun Microsystems and many smaller vendors) and about a dozen industrial consortia (including the Open Software Foundation, Unix International, the International Multimedia Association, X/Open Company, etc.) have expressed support for the CORBA standard and are including implementations of the CORBA API in upcoming products. This immediately raises the issue of layered interface specifications needed above the transmission-centered CORBA interface.

B.7 Object Services and Common Facilities

To begin to fill in these layered services, the OMG is in the midst of several related selection processes. At this writing, the OMG is a scant few months from selection of IDL-based services to support:

- Object Lifecycle Services: creation, deletion, garbage collection;
- Persistence Services: database-like long-term storage of object state;
- Naming Services: mapping of textual (and standards-based) names to object references; and
- Event Notification Services: low-quality high-volume notification messaging support.

Even as these baseline services are selected, request cycles are underway to select the next battery of services:

- Relationship/Association Services: for managing associative links between objects;
- Transaction/Concurrency Control: for controlling commitment and rollback of series of CORBA messages in the face of parallelism in the distributed system;
- Time Services: for agreement on global time values for synchronization in the distributed enterprise; and
- Externalization/Internalization Services: for managing the export and import of object state for portability.

The OMG is also actively seeking liaison with many outside groups that are in the midst of construction of standard interfaces or implementations of other layered services, both low-level (other object services such as security/authentication and interface trading, for example) and high-level (common facilities such as electronic mail and other application-level services). Wherever possible the OMG leverages existing work to increase portability, interoperability and reusability, and as the level of interface standardization grows within OMG this will become even more evident.

B.8 References

Object Management Group, Inc., 1992. *The Common Object Request Broker: Architecture and Specification*, Framingham, MA, U.S.A., Jan.

Object Management Group, Inc.,1992. R.M. Soley, (ed.), *Object Management Architecture Guide, Second Edition,* Framingham, MA, U.S.A., Sep.

Richard Mark Soley, Ph.D., is Vice President and Technical Director of the Object Management Group, Inc. (OMG), responsible for overseeing the 300-member industrial consortium's strategic and technical directions. In this position, Dr. Soley oversees the 400+ representative Technical Committee of the leading industry consortium detailing and publicizing standards in object-oriented development and execution environments. Dr. Soley was previously a founder of A. I. Architects, Inc. and a consultant to IBM, PictureTel, Symbolics, Texas Instruments and others. A native of Baltimore, Maryland, U.S.A., Dr. Soley holds the bachelor's, master's and doctoral degrees in Computer Science and Engineering from the Massachusetts Institute of Technology.

Appendix C

Apple Open Collaboration Environment (AOCE)

Gursharan S. Sidhu
Apple Computer, Inc.

C.1 Introduction

> Collaborate: "To work jointly with others, especially in an inteilectual endeavor."

Evolving personal communications needs, coupled with organizational trends, have fueled demand for a new class of applications: *collaborative applications,* which enable individuals to communicate and work together with others more effectively. Personal and organizational communication needs are rapidly becoming crucial:

- Organizational trends indicate that decision-making responsibilities are increasingly pushed downward and decentralized.
- Ad hoc teams form quickly to complete specific jobs, and then disband just as quickly.
- Whether at home, at school, in the office, or on the road, individuals must be able to exchange ideas and information with colleagues or clients–no matter where they are located.

To establish a foundation for developing such applications, Apple Computer has developed an integrated set of capabilities called Apple Open Collaboration Environment (AOCE™) technology. A series of products based on AOCE technology will be introduced for the leading personal computing platforms, starting with Macintosh® and PowerBook® computers.

Today, people in all walks of life are working together more closely. And they want their computers to facilitate their interpersonal communications, whether they involve coworkers down the hall or colleagues around the world. But most applications are still not designed to streamline the communications process.

Consider, for example, a basic project management application designed for use by a single individual. Typically, a team leader working with such a program receives schedule and task information from each team member manually and publishes a time line at periodic intervals. This process is time consuming and team schedules become quickly out-of-date because the leader and members must proactively initiate each update effort. But a truly collaborative project management application would automatically remind team members of upcoming deadlines, regularly request status and dependency information, enable routing and approval of project change requests, and interact behind the scenes with their calendaring, authoring, document management, and other collaborative applications–thus facilitating efficient and effective interpersonal communications.

Although many current applications simply offer no collaborative capabilities whatsoever, others make the attempt. However, because these capabilities are implemented at the application level rather than at the system level, they utilize different conventions and require varying user input, and necessitate extensive and time-consuming developmental effort. To truly facilitate collaboration among computer users, a common, system-level communications infrastructure is required–which is exactly what is provided by AOCE technology.

C.2 AOCE Technology: A Framework for Collaboration

C2.1 The Apple Open Collaboration Environment Technology at a Glance

AOCE software offers the following capabilities:

- *Messaging:* Allows applications to exchange information.
- *Electronic mail:* Enables users to exchange letters and documents.
- *Catalogs:* Provides an information store required for collaboration between applications and between users.
- *Authentication/privacy:* Ensures users that all communications are kept secure and private.
- *Digital signatures:* Allows users to attach reliable approval signatures to documents.

AOCE technology offers a flexible, scalable environment that addresses the communications needs of individuals, teams, and organizations–now, and as they change over time. AOCE software, in combination with collaborative applications that make use of it, is designed to empower not only end users, but also systems managers and developers:

Users: Users can achieve substantial productivity gains from integrated electronic-mail capabilities within productivity tools such as word processing and spreadsheet programs, use digital-signature technology to vastly reduce the time they spend shuffling paper for approvals and other repetitive processes, and take advantage of advanced messaging capabilities to help them work effectively in teams–no matter what their location.

Systems managers: Systems managers benefit from the flexibility and scalability of the underlying AOCE architecture, which offers "plug-and-play" interoperability with existing and emerging messaging, catalog/directory and authentication systems, as well as supporting a smooth migration from peer-to-peer to client/server systems. In addition, the catalog/directory system architecture vastly streamlines the process of administration for collaborative applications, by enabling them all to use the *same* messaging and catalog/directory servers.

Developers: Both in-house and commercial developers benefit from the business and market opportunities afforded by creating new collaborative applications or enhancing existing ones. Because AOCE technology provides the tools they need to speed development of such applications, developers will have more time to focus on building user value.

C.3 Solutions for Individuals to Enterprises

The flexibility and scalability of the AOCE technology enables it to provide solutions for a wide variety of users, from individuals whose connection with their coworkers is via modem and phone line to organizations with vast–and varied–enterprise-wide networks.

C3.1 Individuals

Stand-alone users at home or on the road can collaborate with others using a data modem and a telephone line. AOCE software includes a built-in dial-up service that enables users to communicate with one another in a peer-to-peer fashion. Users in this environment have a desktop mailbox and personal catalog/directory for receiving messages and storing information about other users locally on their hard disk. Equipped with the appropriate *service access modules* (plug-in software modules that add functionality), they can send and receive fax documents from their Macintosh desktop. Or those with subscriptions to public mail services such as MCI Mail, AppleLink, or CompuServe, and the appropriate service access modules, can use AOCE technology as a consistent environment to easily collaborate with others through these public services. In addition, stand-alone users can access their organization's networking system to retrieve and send messages using AppleTalk Remote Access software (see figure C.1).

C3.2 Teams

At the most basic level, a small team of users on a network without a server can collaborate in a similar peer-to-peer fashion: AOCE software includes built-in AppleTalk support, which allows users to communicate on a network without using a server (see figure C.2).

C3.3 Servers for Team Productivity

Servers added to the AOCE framework allow people to communicate even if their computers are not simultaneously available, as well as allow network administrators to manage gateways to other messaging systems centrally. The flexible AOCE architecture enables a full range of server-based options. For example, if an organization wishes to phase in AOCE servers gradually, server-based service access modules allow AOCE and non-AOCE servers to coexist and interoperate (see figure C.3).

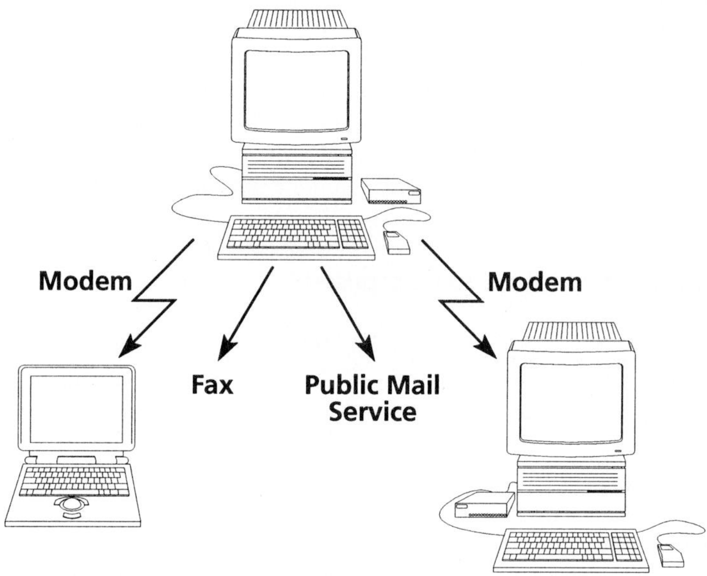

Figure C.1 Dial-up user environment.

For users who wish to take full advantage of AOCE technology, Apple will offer AOCE servers, which can provide centralized management of messaging, catalog/directory, and authentication services–even to organizations consisting of thousands of users. Such AOCE servers will act as the common infrastructure for collaborative applications such as calendaring, project management, and business-forms-routing programs, streamlining their administrative needs through the creation and use of common catalogs/directories.

The flexible, open AOCE architecture lets users choose the best server strategy to meet their needs. Migration from non-AOCE servers to AOCE servers is both easy and nondisruptive. Users who need only basic electronic-mail capabilities can take advantage of any popular mail server, such as Microsoft Mail or QuickMail, for simple storage, routing, and addressing of messages with the appropriate service access module.

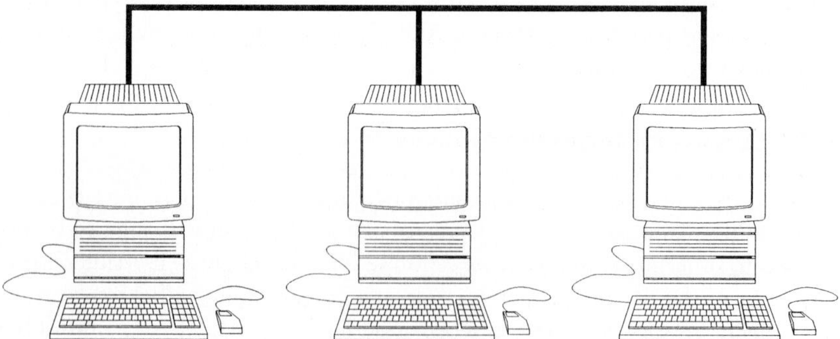

Figure C.2 Peer-to-peer environment.

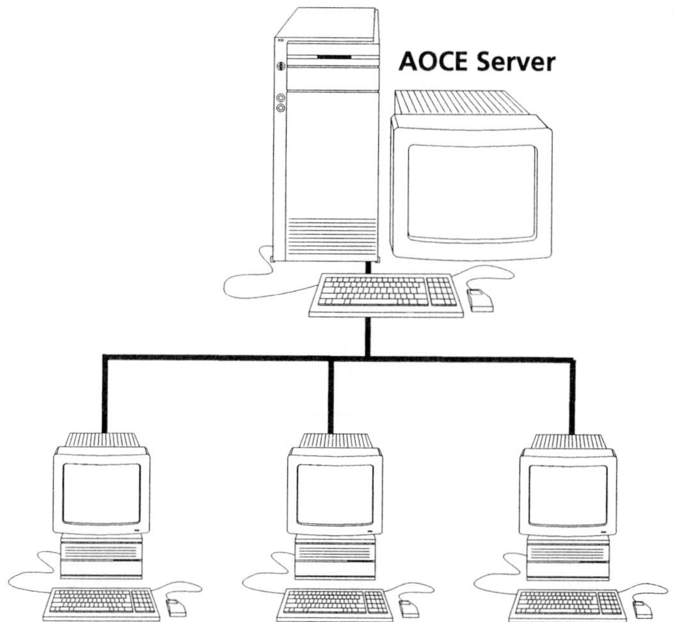

Figure C.3 Server-based user environment.

C3.4 Enterprisewide Networks

In addition to supporting a variety of electronic mail and messaging technologies, AOCE is also designed to extend across computing platforms to accommodate enterprises' heterogeneous computing environments.

Apple is committed to responding to the growing need to integrate desktop computers into enterprise system environments. AOCE technology is a key component of VITAL, the Virtually Integrated Technical Architecture Lifecycle model that represents Apple's response to this need. The AOCE architecture provides the framework necessary for developers to create collaborative applications that will meet the needs of today's organizations and their increasingly complex computing systems (see figure C.4).

Enterprisewide information systems often include a variety of networking environments, as well as many different messaging and directory technologies. AOCE software protects organizations' existing investments--and facilitates client/server migration–by providing a practical way to integrate and interoperate with both current and future mail, messaging, and directory systems. It supports connectivity with X.400, SMTP, MHS, PROFS, ALL-IN-1, and other such technologies. Users with such systems can interoperate with AOCE systems by means of service access modules. For example, organizations that adopt the OSF DCE specification (Open Software Foundation's Distributed Computing Environment) will be able to interoperate with the AOCE catalog services through use of X.500 service access modules.

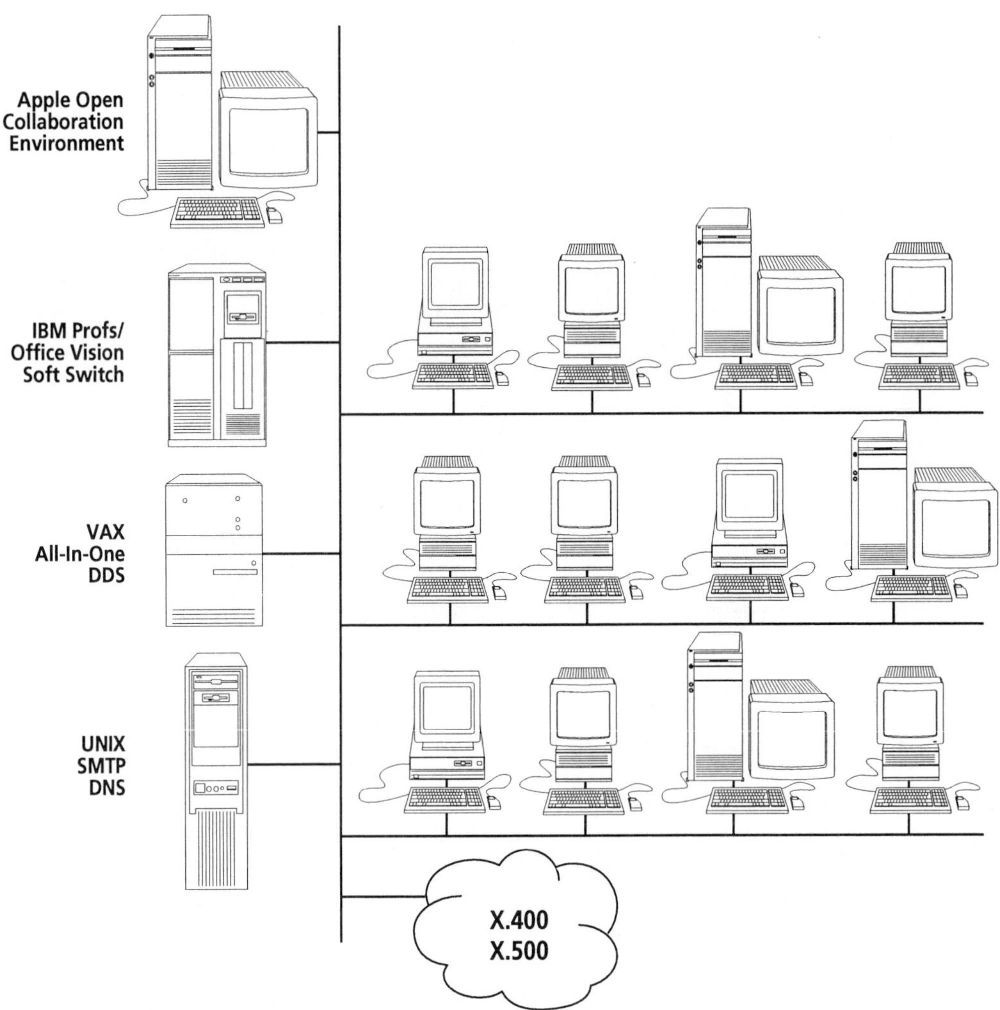

Figure C.4 Multiple vendor user environment.

C.4 Building on the Framework: A New Generation of Collaborative Applications

Previously, developers who wished to create collaborative tools found that it required two or more years just to build the underlying messaging, directory, and security infrastructures–all of this before the user-value components could start taking shape. But by providing a collaborative computing foundation in its system software, Apple is enabling the easy development of innovative collaborative applications.

AOCE capabilities are accessible to developers via easy-to-use "packages" that provide standard user and programmatic interfaces for accessing mail, messaging, catalog/directory, authentication, and digital signature systems. For example, the Standard Mail Package provides programmatic interfaces to a standard user-interface that enables any application to send messages, enclose documents, and sign letters–with minimal time investment on the part of the developer. In addition, these capabilities are accessible through low-level application interfaces. (For more details on this and other packages, see the Technology Behind AOCE Software section.)

Collaborative applications represents a significant new business opportunity. According to International Data Corporation (IDC), an independent market research organization, the market for collaborative applications, or *groupware,* is expected to grow at a 50 percent annual rate over the next five years, following the growth of LAN systems. Clearly, this emerging market holds major promise for software developers.

C.5 The Impact of AOCE Technology: A Few Scenarios

Solutions created using AOCE capabilities can be divided into three main areas: integrated personal communications, team productivity applications, and workflow automation.

C5.1 Integrated Personal Communications

Many people feel that they spend too much of their day retrieving, managing, and replying to correspondence via electronic-mail, fax, and voice messages. These technologies require various actions, such as creating messages and addressing and sending them. Yet each requires users to follow different, and often repetitive, procedures.

AOCE software offers users a desktop mailbox that provides them with a completely integrated vehicle to use any kind of interpersonal communications systems or technologies. Thus, they can receive electronic documents, faxes, or voice messages in a single location. The integrated mailbox makes use of the specific service access modules installed to allow seamless information exchange among users.

In addition, through AOCE technology, every application can become "mail-capable," and the send command in the Macintosh File menu will become as ubiquitous as the print command is today. Currently, users who want to send a document to others must exit the creating application, launch a separate electronic-mail application, address a message, and then attach the document using complex, multistep actions. But with AOCE-based applications, users create documents with their favorite word processing or desktop publishing program, add attachments, and then simply sign them and send them to others as easily as they print documents today. This can be done regardless of the mode of transmission for each addressee–e-mail, fax, and so on.

C.5.1.1 Scenario 1

A self-employed executive recruiter needs to communicate with many different clients using a wide variety of common communications technologies. Daily, she receives numerous faxed resumes, dozens of phone calls, and electronic mail via several commercial services (MCI Mail and AT&T) from potential clients, all of which require different–and sometimes relatively complex–procedures to forward on to the appropriate hiring managers.

Using AOCE-based service access modules for fax, voice-mail, and commercial electronic mail services, that same recruiter receives and manages all of these communications from her Macintosh desktop in a single, standard way–no matter what the medium. And, for example, an electronically received fax document is easily forwarded to multiple locations.

AOCE-based applications, called *software agents,* also help users by automatically gathering relevant information and by handling the growing volume of interpersonal communication by diverting, forwarding, or otherwise acting automatically on users' correspondence. Mail-handling agents take actions based on the subject of a letter, the sender, and other criteria, applying rules established by the user. For example, a financial analyst can use a mail-handling agent to automatically check subject areas of incoming electronic mail for the word *budget* or *financials* and then automatically move them to his monthly budget preparation folder (see figure C.5). A news software agent can automatically scan newswire services (such as AP or Reuters) for articles that match a user's criteria, and channel those articles into the user's desktop mailbox. Another agent might automatically forward appropriate incoming items to a user's associates when that user is on vacation, or reply to clients, telling them when the user will return to the office.

C5.2 Team Productivity Applications

Individuals who work in teams want improved group communications capabilities for collaborating across time zones and geographies. But today's collaborative applications have several disadvantages, such as requiring users to maintain multiple directories and "in-baskets." For example, calendaring applications enable users to propose meetings with others and electronic-mail applications enable users to send letters to others. However, each application requires the user to select an address from a separate directory catalog in a separate way. Similarly, recipients of meeting proposals must access and open these items from the in-basket of their scheduling application, using different steps than are required by their electronic-mail system.

With AOCE technology, scheduling, calendaring, group authoring, and other collaborative applications can share the same catalog/directory and message storage/routing facility. Users benefit from accessing catalog/directory information in one easy-to-use, consistent way, as well as receiving all their correspondence from the same in-basket. And the use of the same catalog/directory and messaging servers simplifies management for network administrators, who no longer need to support separate servers for each application.

C.5.2.1 Scenario 2

A small team of graphic designers working for an electronics company needs to get comments from a variety of groups quickly–yet these groups are located in various buildings around the world, and it's difficult to get in touch with all of the key players in the first place, let alone to find a mutually agreeable meeting place and time.

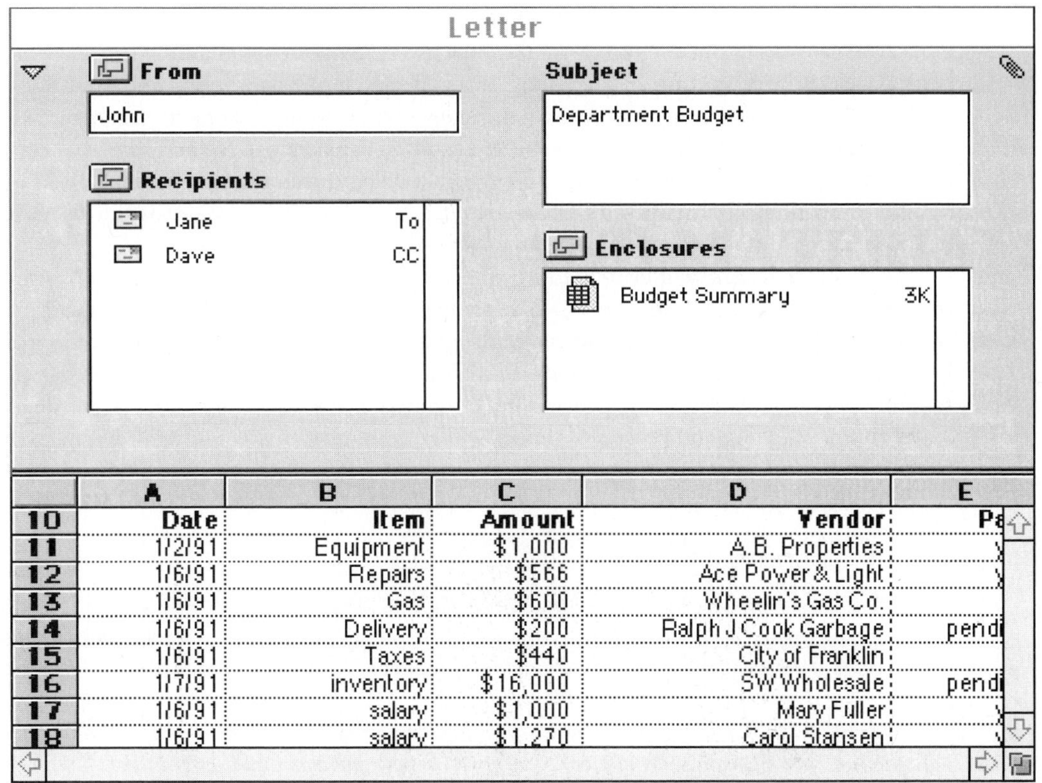

Figure C.5 Example of a mail-capable spreadsheet application. (© 1991-1993 Apple Computer, Inc. All rights reserved.)

With AOCE technology, a team member uses a calendaring application to propose a meeting to a list of appropriate meeting participants, regardless of whether the individuals are available at that time to receive the message. While waiting for meeting confirmations, he forwards (directly from his AOCE-based desktop publishing application) the packaging copy and graphics to the meeting participants. At the agreed-upon meeting time, the team leader launches his AOCE-based conferencing application, which automatically places a conference call to each participant, so the group can discuss the packaging proposal, without having to be in the same physical location. Each participant offers feedback, then passes the baton to the next speaker. The meeting concludes with the participants approving the document by signing it with their digital signatures.

C5.3 Workflow Automation

On an enterprisewide level, AOCE software will enable information systems managers to improve the efficiency and productivity of organizations, by providing organizations with extended authenticated connections and privacy capabilities to make AppleTalk networks appropriate for workflow automation solutions. The AOCE digital signature technology provides approval capabilities that can be used with any network.

Workflow solutions increase organizational productivity by streamlining processes and costs associated with routing and handling paper. For example, the routing and approval of purchase orders is done almost completely manually today, because they require manual, written signatures. With AOCE technology, purchase orders can be processed and approved completely electronically, using AOCE messaging, catalog/directory, and verifiable digital signature capabilities. Bypassing in-house manual mail distribution systems and approval methods saves users and organizations substantial costs as well as time.

Systems managers will be able to implement mission-critical workflow solutions using off-the-shelf hardware and software as a base for creating customized solutions at a fraction of the cost involved today. And individuals can simply use off-the-shelf AOCE applications to implement their own workflow solutions. In addition, with AppleScript, Apple's system-wide scripting system, AOCE technology will offer customers extensive opportunities to personally automate the sequence and process of their work. For example, an accounting program could be customized to generate a letter to a department head whenever that department is approaching budget overruns.

C.5.3.1 Scenario 3

A corporate salesperson for an office supply company needs to complete and process her sales orders rapidly to meet the needs of her clients, as well as her management. But it's difficult to make contact with the right people in a timely manner, let alone to track the progress of the requisite paperwork as it moves through the organization.

But with an AOCE-based electronic-forms application, a Macintosh PowerBook computer, a data modem, and AppleTalk Remote Access software, she completes her sales order at the client location, signs it with her digital signature, and forwards the order directly to the corporate office network for further approvals and routing. The district sales manager can track incoming orders at any point, discovering whether the proper authorizations have come in from the ordering company, whether sufficient product stock is on hand or must be ordered, and other key process issues.

To sum up, through AOCE-based applications, customers will have more and lower-cost options for automating administrative tasks, for creating secure networks, and for implementing mission-critical workflow solutions using readily available hardware and software.

C.6 The Technology Behind AOCE Software

This section takes a detailed look at all of the components of AOCE technology (see figure C.6).

AOCE system software consists of a number of components, arranged in three architectural layers:

System software managers and interfaces: These low-level system components and APIs provide developers with a rich set of services for collaboration, which can be tightly integrated into their applications. They provide programmatic hooks that allow developers to pick and choose the specific capabilities that they wish to furnish to their users. No standard user-interface capabilities are provided by these managers and APIs.

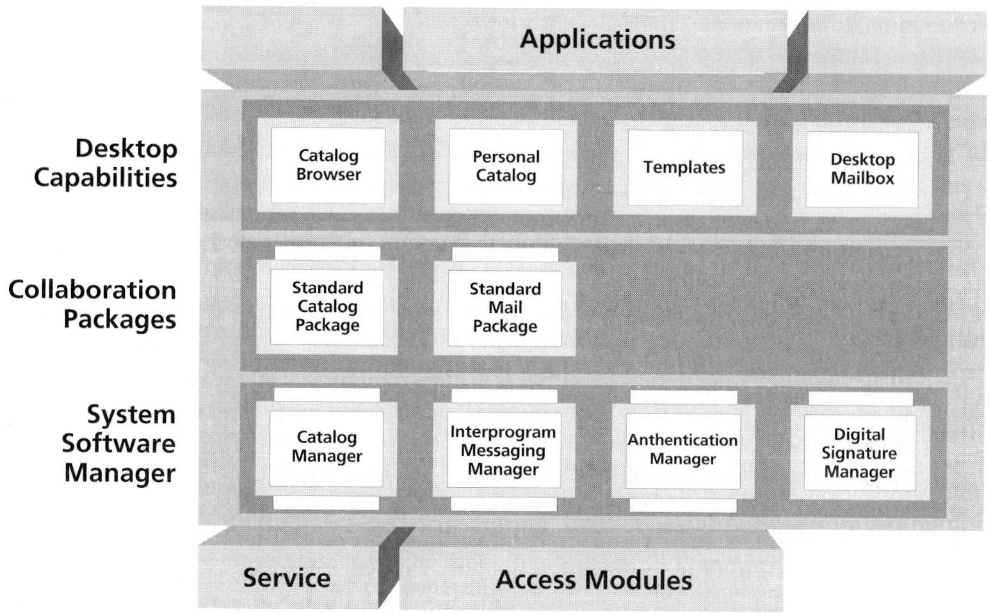

Figure C.6 The AOCE technology framework.

Collaboration packages: These are predefined higher-level collaborative functions and user-interface capabilities that can be incorporated into existing applications with minimal development effort. For example, standard dialog boxes and other user-interface elements are provided to allow users to select addresses, add attachments, and approve documents in a consistent, intuitive way from within any application.

Desktop capabilities: These provide users with simplified methods for browsing, sending, receiving, and managing information and communications conveniently from the Macintosh desktop.

In addition to the client services, Apple will provide two software servers for users of AppleTalk network systems.

C6.1 System Software Managers and Interfaces

The AOCE core is its system software managers. Four main capabilities are provided: catalogs, messaging, network-based authentication and privacy, and digital signatures. Developers can add any of these capabilities directly to their applications through standard application programming interfaces (APIs). Any application can also fit into many different messaging and catalog/directory environments by taking advantage of AOCE technology's interoperability capabilities. For example, a calendaring application today may include its own messaging and address list capabilities, but limits sharing of schedules to members of both the same server and computing platform. A calendaring application built on AOCE technology's catalog and messaging capabilities would not only take much less time to produce, but with the appropriate service access modules it could also exchange information with a calendaring application on another computing platform.

The catalog manager: This module offers application developers access to any kind of catalog/directory system regardless of the storage format. For example, today's electronic mail applications use a directory to keep track of users' addresses. In this case, a directory serves a function similar to that of a telephone directory. However, in general, catalogs can contain other kinds of information needed to make collaborative systems work well, such as position titles and hierarchy information, spending authorization limits, or pictures. The Catalog Manager makes all of this information available to applications via standard programmatic interfaces.

The interprogram messaging (IPM) manager: On the Macintosh family of computers this component complements the System 7 interapplication communications (IAC) architecture, which currently provides real-time program-to-program communications. IPM provides store-and-forward message delivery between applications, allowing messages to be stored for delivery whenever the recipient is ready to receive them. Messages can be exchanged between applications on one computer or across a network, regardless of whether the sender and receiver are available at the same time. In addition, one message can be sent to multiple destinations. With the addition of appropriate messaging service access modules, messages can be sent over any type of message transport, such as SMTP, MHS, cc:Mail, or X.400.

The authentication and privacy manager: This component enables applications in an AOCE server-based environment to ensure that the people or programs at the ends of a network connection are who or what they claim to be. Developers can take advantage of the authentication capabilities to improve overall security for their users and to simplify security administration, so that users need only one password to authenticate themselves to the system and gain access to all of its services. The AOCE catalog server grants authentication credentials by acting as the trusted third party. An application can use the authentication manager API to handle the entire authentication process to validate the identity of the collaborating entities (people, servers, or programs). With the addition of plug-in service access modules, the AOCE architecture will, in future versions, provide support for interoperability with non-AOCE authentication systems such as Kerberos. The Authentication Manager also provides the tools for applications to establish encrypted AppleTalk data stream connections using a secure extension of the AppleTalk Data Stream Protocol. This privacy capability protects information that programs or users have sent against loss through wire-tapping. The data is encrypted using the RC4 encryption algorithm licensed to Apple by RSA Data Security, Inc.

The digital signature manager: This component offers a means for attaching electronic approval signatures to computer documents, eliminating the need for time-consuming printing and circulation of paper for hand-signed approvals. The digital signature capability can be used from within any application, not only to positively identify the approver, but also to detect whether a document has been altered since it was signed. This ability to attest to the unaltered state of the document makes digital signatures more secure than hand-signatures on paper. AOCE software's digital signature capability is based on public-key encryption technology, which is also licensed to Apple by RSA Data Security, Inc. Users sign files with a special kind of Macintosh file called a Signer. The AOCE software includes a utility program for users to create a digital signature request form, which can then be given to an appropriate digital signature certificate issuing authority. Once the digital signature request has been approved, users can begin using their own unique signer to approve documents.

Service access module interfaces: In addition to the system software managers providing applications programming interfaces (APIs) to developers, they also provide service access module interfaces, which enable developers to build plug-in modules for connecting AOCE-based computers to any messaging, catalog/directory, or authentication systems. Architecturally, these interfaces form back-end hooks into the interprogram messaging, directory, and authentication managers. The architecture supports the development of three types of service access modules: messaging, catalog/directory, and authentication.

Messaging service access modules: These plug-in modules connect the AOCE InterProgram Messaging Manager to any messaging system, enabling users to consolidate and display messages from diverse messaging systems in a single, consistent manner. AOCE comes with built-in messaging service access modules for peer-to-peer dial-up, peer-to-peer AppleTalk LAN, and AOCE server messaging. Other vendors will provide messaging service access modules for other popular messaging systems, such as MHS, X.400, and PROFS, and for public messaging networks, such as CompuServe and MCI Mail.

Catalog service access modules: These plug-in modules permit users to access and browse through any catalog/directory. Users benefit from a consistent user-interface to these catalogs/directories through the catalog browser icon. AOCE software comes with built-in catalog service access modules for AppleTalk networks and AOCE catalog servers. The AppleTalk catalog service access module provides users with access to addresses for individual computers on an AppleTalk network as well as for AppleTalk services such as AppleShare servers and File-sharing. The AOCE catalog server access module allows users to access any entity records (users, groups, descriptive information, and so on) residing on one or more AOCE catalog servers.

In-house and commercial developers can build catalog service access modules to provide access to directories and catalogs, such as X.500 catalogs/directories or to private corporate directories residing on host-based systems. In addition, catalog service access modules can provide users with access to information databases such as a telephone directory on a CD-ROM or a host-based system.

Authentication service access modules: These modules will, in future versions, provide users with interoperability with non-AOCE authentication systems, such as Kerberos.

C6.2 Collaboration Packages

AOCE collaboration packages provide application developers with a set of standard dialog boxes, and other user-interface elements, as well as the tools they need to provide user access to AOCE technology's electronic-mail, digital signature, and catalog/directory browsing capabilities. They are ideal for developers of personal productivity applications such as word processing or spreadsheet programs, because they enable them to offer collaborative functions to their users extremely rapidly.

The standard mail package: This component makes *every* application an electronic-mail application. It provides a standard user-interface called the *mailer,* and other functions for making electronic-mail and digital signature capabilities available in all applications. When users click on recipients, a standard panel is displayed, allowing them to browse among various personal and shared catalogs/directories to locate address information. The subject field allows users to annotate the information they are sending. Using the mailer's Enclosures field, users can enclose other documents and entire folders of items in AOCE letters. Double-clicking on any attached document will automatically launch the application that created it; double-clicking on an attached folder will open an appropriate Finder window, even while these documents and folders are inside the mailer. Users can also use the mailer to sign letters and to verify digital signatures affixed to letters (see figure C.7).

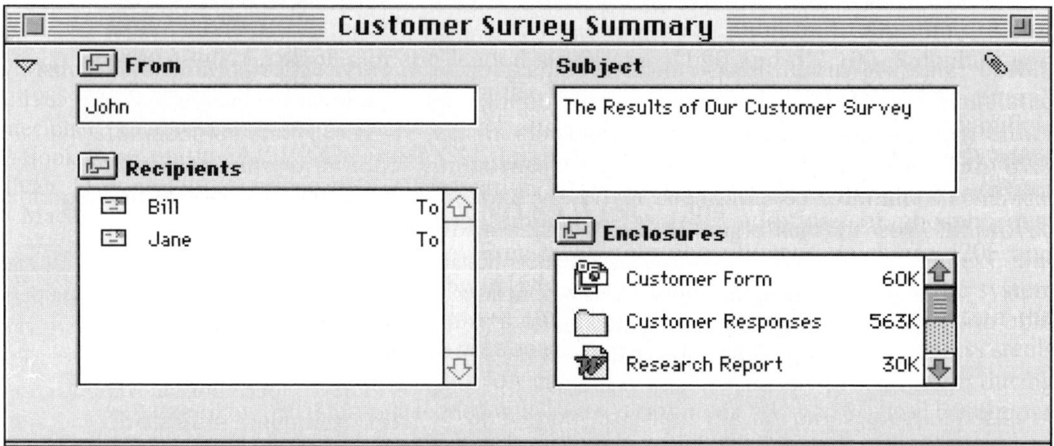

Figure C.7 One of the user-interface elements provided by the Standard Mail Package. (© 1991-1993 Apple Computer, Inc. All rights reserved.)

The standard catalog package: This component provides application developers with standard user interface elements for browsing, finding, and selecting catalog/directory records from within application programs. In the same way that users can browse their hard disk for files and folders, they will now be able to browse their catalogs to quickly access catalog information. The standard catalog package also provides the user-interface elements for applications to prompt users to provide name and password authentication information. Developers will use the package in conjunction with the AOCE catalog manager to refer to a particular entity (for example, person, group, or server) in a catalog (see figure C.8).

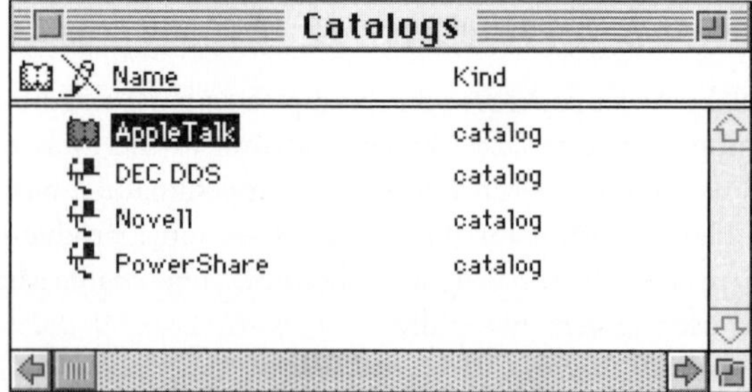

Figure C.8 The user-interface provided by the standard catalog package. (© 1991-1993 Apple Computer, Inc. All rights reserved.)

C6.3 Desktop Capabilities

At the desktop level, AOCE software provides users with immediate benefits through a desktop mailbox icon, a catalogs browser icon, one or more personal catalogs, and templates. These desktop capabilities give users consistent access to electronic mail and catalog/directory systems (see figure C.9).

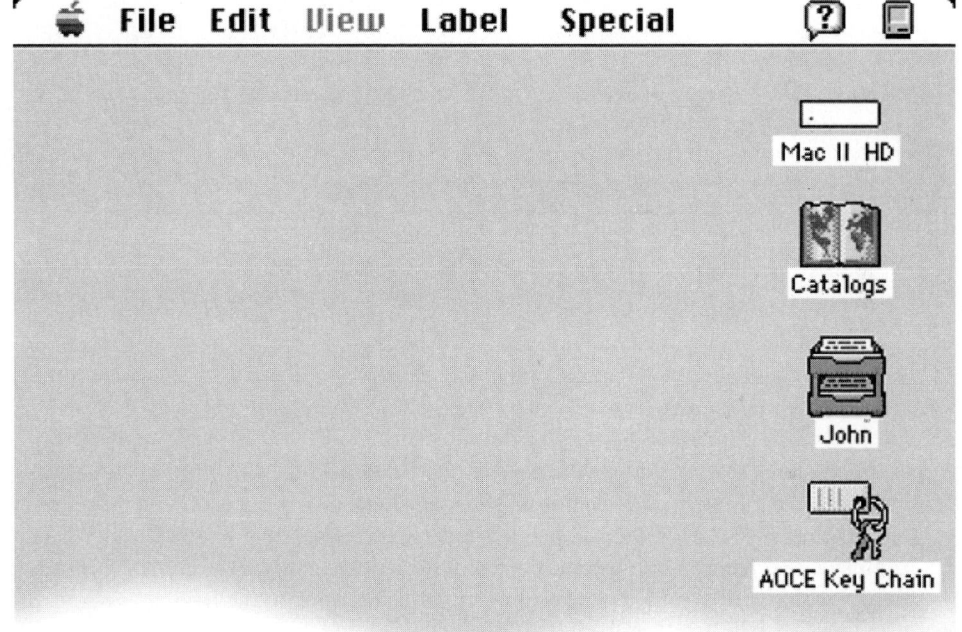

Figure C.9 The AOCE user's desktop with mailbox and catalog browser icons. (© 1991-1993 Apple Computer, Inc. All rights reserved.)

The desktop mailbox icon: All of the user's correspondence–messages/letters from multiple electronic-mail systems, voice messages, faxes, paging notifications, documents created in any application, and even QuickTime movies–arrives in a single desktop mailbox icon. Users can sort and view their correspondence, by sender, date, and name, for example, using new enhancements to the Macintosh Finder (see figure C.10).

The catalogs browser icon: This provides users with a consistent way to search for information required by collaborative systems, including identifying or descriptive information and network-based resources such as servers and commonly used electronic forms such as travel authorizations. Users browse shared catalog/directory information residing on any system through this icon in a consistent, intuitive manner. In addition, the AOCE desktop capabilities allow users to search the content of any available catalog in a consistent manner (see figure C.11).

In Tray for John

6 items

✓	Subject	Sender	Date Sent
	FAX 3/3 9.56AM	Fax Gateway	3/03/93, 4:40 PM
	meeting	Susan	2/27/93, 6:28 PM
	Phone Message	Barbara	2/23/93, 1:27 PM
	Purchase Order	Dave	2/27/93, 6:58 PM
	New ads movie	Bill	2/23/93, 1:25 PM
	SSW Forum Developers	Michael	2/27/93, 4:43 PM

MAC II HD

John

Catalogs

AOCE Key Chain

Figure C.10 The AOCE in basket which receives e-mail, voice messages, faxes, and documents. (© 1991-1993 Apple Computer, Inc. All rights reserved.)

Users can copy records located in any catalog to their personal (local) catalog or to the desktop. When such records are dragged to the desktop, a copy of the catalog record, or *information card* is made. Information cards can be sent to and shared with others in much the same way we use paper business cards today. Documents or folders of items can be dragged to information cards representing users, computers, or groups for automatic sending. This is one of several quick ways to address and deliver information with AOCE technology.

Personal catalogs: These reside on the user's hard disk and are local repositories for catalog information, which can be added to or otherwise altered by the user. Personal catalogs are completely portable. When users need key information, such as fax numbers, client information, postal addresses, or telephone numbers, while they are on the road or at home, they can take their personal catalogs along with them. This provides them with a copy of information that would normally be available only at the office.

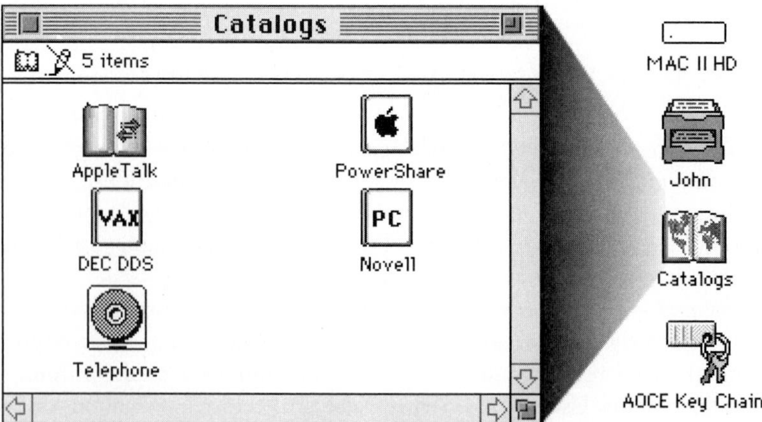

Figure C.11 AOCE catalogs browser window provides access to any catalog/directory system with the appropriate service access modules. (© 1991-1993 Apple Computer, Inc. All rights reserved.)

Templates: These control the way catalog records and their contents are displayed on the Macintosh desktop. AOCE software comes with several built-in templates, and in-house or commercial developers can also create new templates to provide users with an alternate view of catalog/directory information. For example, salespeople may want to acquire a sales leads tracking template that allows them to fill in specific client information, such as action items, purchasing plans, and order fulfillment dates. Because templates are system software extensions, users can add new ones by simply dropping them into the System Folder (see figure C.12).

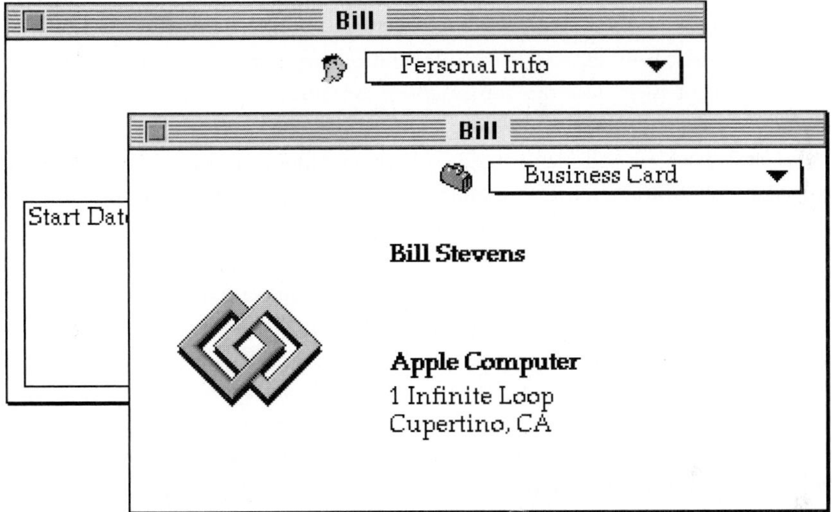

Figure C.12 Examples of catalog templates, which enable users to browse catalog information. (© 1991-1993 Apple Computer, Inc. All rights reserved.)

This extensible user-interface allows commercial or in-house developers to provide access to additional pieces of catalog/directory information. They determine which records are browsed, which information is visible, and how individual information items are displayed and edited. Organizations, for example, can build their own templates, providing users with access to specific information residing in various catalogs.

C6.4 Some Other AOCE Technology Components and Optional Servers

Server software: Two AppleTalk server-based software systems will be available from Apple: a catalog server and a mail and messaging server.

The catalog server: This server provides a full-function catalog of hierarchical containers [catalog folders] that hold records associated with entities (users, groups, servers, and other resources). The server can be used to store information needed to manage workflow processes and to communicate important information between applications. For example, applications might use the server to store information on job functions and signature-authority hierarchies. When a user signs a form and sends it, the application can then determine the next approving party based on the information contained in the catalog server; the user need never specify this information. Some developers plan to use the catalog to store common user profile information. For example, users who track the solar-power industry could be identified by their profile information, causing collaborative applications to automatically send real-time news, articles, and other special-interest information concerning that topic to their mailboxes.

The AOCE catalog server grants authentication credentials by acting as the trusted third-party, managing all session requests. Catalog servers can be located anywhere on an AppleTalk internet, and the various catalog folders can be distributed among one or more catalog servers. Copies of any folder can be placed on multiple servers and kept automatically synchronized via a built-in replication and distribution mechanism.

Users view, browse, and select information from any catalog from within the catalogs browser icon on their desktop. Information contained within catalog records is visible and browsable by users through templates.

Catalog servers will play a major role in enabling team productivity applications, making it easier for administrators to manage those applications and build more convenient access control and automation mechanisms.

The mail and messaging server: The mail and messaging server accepts mail and messages from users' computers, then delivers copies to appropriate destination servers and message queues, using a store-and-forward mechanism. The server forwards correspondence between these mail and messaging servers and enables AOCE-based computers to connect to any messaging system with the use of server-based messaging service access modules [mail gateways]. Users can have mailboxes on the mail and messaging server, allowing them to receive correspondence at all times, regardless of whether their Macintosh is switched on. The mail and messaging server also conserves users' local hard disk space by storing correspondence on the server's storage disk.

AOCE servers come with an application for remote administration over a network. Both types of AOCE servers can reside on the same Macintosh computer. Administrators also have the flexibility to install them on the same computers that contain their AppleShare or other servers, or on different computers.

C.7 The Promise of AOCE Technology

In designing its solutions, Apple has always focused first on individuals. With AOCE technology, the power and versatility of the individual's Macintosh-based solution is extended to empower groups of individuals and entire organizations.

Even as the architecture of the Macintosh computer has grown to encompass new capabilities, enhancements have always been elegant extensions of the already familiar–and AOCE technology is no exception. The same "plug-and-play" approach that characterized Apple's original collaborative tool–the AppleTalk network system–as well as later enhancements such as System 7 interapplication communications and file sharing, has been applied to AOCE technology.

AOCE technology is a major expansion of the Apple computing environment. Yet users will not have to learn new ways of working. Systems managers will not have to replace hardware and software resources. And developers will find that their job is made not more complex, but rather simpler–and more exciting.

As an open environment, the AOCE framework supports interoperability with existing and emerging messaging, catalog/directory, and authentication systems. With AOCE technology, the loose strands of voice-mail, fax, electronic mail, and remote paging will be woven into an integrated communications fabric, so that the sending and receiving of messages through diverse media will become as integral a part of applications as printing is today. In short, with AOCE technology, Macintosh and other personal computers will become the most easily networked, and most collaboration-ready, personal computers in the industry.

C.8 Trademarks

Gursharan S. Sidhu joined Apple Computer, Inc. in 1982, where he currently oversees the area of collaborative systems. He has been responsible for several product families, from idea to final shipment. These include the AppleTalk network system, LaserWriter print server, AppleShare file server, AppleTalk Remote Access, and the Macintosh hierarchical file system. He is most widely known for designing and leading the implementation of the AppleTalk network system and associated products, peripherals and servers. He also led the design and implementation of the Macintosh hierarchical file system.

Before coming to Apple, Dr. Sidhu served as senior consultant to the Mexican government in relation to that country's acquisition and installation of a nationwide public packet-switched network. He was also the program leader for an international team of scientists and engineers on an Organization of American States networking project, REDLAC, in Mexico and Brazil. He has held teaching and research positions at Stanford University, the State University of New York, and the Universidad Nacional Autónoma de México.

He has a BS in mechanical engineering from the Indian Institute of Technology, an MS in mechanical engineering, as well as an MS and a PhD in electrical engineering from Stanford.

Appendix D

SNMP and Distributed Systems Management

Steven Waldbusser
Carnegie Mellon University

The Simple Network Management Protocol (SNMP) has established itself as the basis for interoperable network management of heterogeneous devices in local and wide area networks. The Simple Network Management Protocol version 2 (SNMPv2) is the next generation of this network management framework. SNMPv1 and SNMPv2 are well-suited to managing distributed systems. This appendix describes SNMPv1 and SNMPv2 and discusses how they are useful for managing a distributed systems environment.

D.1 Introduction

The Simple Network Management Protocol (SNMP) and Framework was introduced in 1988, and has since established itself as the basis for integrated network management of heterogeneous devices in local and wide area networks. The Simple Network Management Protocol version 2 (SNMPv2) is the next generation in the *Internet-standard Network Management Framework* and provides an evolutionary–not revolutionary–advance in the state of the art.

While the SNMP architecture was originally developed to solve network management problems, it is becoming increasingly applicable to systems management tasks. The recent introduction of SNMPv2 is accelerating that trend. This appendix describes SNMPv1 and SNMPv2 and discusses how they are useful for managing a distributed systems environment.

D.2 History of the Internet-standard Network Management Framework

SNMP was introduced as the Internet-standard Network Management Framework in early 1988, when it was created to solve the pressing network management needs of the rapidly growing Internet. Since then, SNMP has enjoyed wide commercial success and provided stable and effective network management of the Internet.

SNMP has been successful for many reasons. The most recognized and important of these reasons is SNMP's simplicity. The simplicity inherent in SNMP lowers the cost of entry into SNMP network management. This allows SNMP to be *ubiquitously* implemented on a wide variety of platforms, even those with little resources to devote to network management functions. The effects of this have been seen quite clearly as SNMP has been implemented on products ranging from small embedded controllers to supercomputers.

Another reason for SNMP's success has been its stability. Many enhancements have been added to the SNMP framework through expansion of the management information base (MIB) with new MIB objects. However, until recently, the SNMP community, embodied in the Internet Engineering Task Force (IETF), chose to preserve the stability of the SNMP framework by resisting any changes or improvements to the protocol. It was felt that changes to the framework would slow the continued acceptance of SNMP and would put the installed base at risk.

In the midst of this stable environment, there was much activity. The SNMP community was gaining experience with the framework and was beginning to perceive a need for improvements to SNMP. As SNMP was applied in more new situations and more experience was gained, the pressure for changes to SNMP increased. In addition, the SNMP Security working group was working on much-needed security enhancements to the Internet-standard Network Management Framework.

The Spring of 1992 brought the conclusion of the Secure SNMP standardization effort, and with it came the first major change to the SNMP framework beyond the addition of new MIB objects. This long-awaited effort specified a new administrative model for SNMP that provided authentication, access control, and privacy.

In addition, the SNMP community succumbed to the pressures to change SNMP. In March of 1992, it issued a call for proposals to address perceived deficiencies of the SNMP framework.

These two imminent changes to the SNMP framework in the spring of 1992 threatened the stability of SNMP by introducing two transitions into the future of the Internet-standard Network Management Framework. The first transition, to SNMP Security, was to begin very soon, in the summer of that year, while the second transition would be expected to begin after a year of standardization activities. The second transition might well begin immediately after the dust settled from the first transition. The network management industry was likely to be distracted from making progress in applications and other important areas of network management for up to three years.

This environment motivated four individuals who had made key contributions to the SNMP framework to form a team and to conceive, document, and implement a successor to SNMP, which included SNMP Security. They called this proposal the *Simple Management Protocol (SMP) and Framework.* This name was chosen in part to emphasize that SMP was useful beyond network management to systems management. The release of SMP was timed so that implementors and vendors could produce one set of highly desirable changes, that is, to carry out other changes at the same time as SNMP Security is added to products. In addition, the effort was intended to be *evolutionary* in nature to minimize the impact of the transition. Users and vendors would benefit from this single smooth transition.

In July 1992, the four SMP authors presented their results at a session of the Internet Engineering Task Force. At the end of the session, the consensus of the room was that work on a second version of SNMP should begin immediately and should use the SMP proposal as a starting point. It was felt that this work should progress quickly, and a goal of a March 1993, publication date was later agreed upon. Further, the consensus was that due to the improvements that SMP made to SNMP Security, that the community should not undergo an interim transition to the (just-released) SNMP Security specifications, but should implement the security features of this second version of SNMP.

This work was later named SNMP version 2, or SNMPv2 for short. The SNMP Security working group was reconvened to discuss and standardize the security changes. In addition, the SNMPv2 working group was chartered to standardize the bulk of the new framework.

The groups performed their work during many days of meetings and via electronic mail. Many clarifications and improvements were made as a result of this effort. The results of this effort were standardized and published in 12 documents, RFC1441-RFC1452.

D.3 Design Principles

The SNMPv2 design process was guided by the same architectural principles that were key to the design of the original SNMP framework. The most important goals were thus:

- To minimize the cost and complexity of network management agents.
- To foster operational robustness by centralizing control of network management operations in management stations.
- To protect the existing investment and achieve an orderly transition by keeping the changes evolutionary.

Because there are many more agents than management stations on a network, it is important to lower the memory and CPU requirements of the agents. The function of a bridge is to forward packets, and as more resources are devoted to network management, fewer resources are avail-able to forward packets. In addition, when the burden is shifted from the many agents to the few management stations, the total cost of network management in an enterprise is lowered without overburdening the management stations. Finally, a simple, consistent design ensures that both management stations and agents may be as cost-effective as possible.

The second design principle was to increase the robustness of the network management system by retaining control in the management stations. These management stations are typically under the direct control of network management personnel and enjoy enough resources to act intelligently. These factors reduce the likelihood of failures of the network management system, or worse, failures of the network caused by the network management system. Putting too much control in agents could result in a loss of control over management resources which in turn could cause these failures. For example, if many agents on an Ethernet were to notify a management station of a high collision rate, the notifications would collide with each other, potentially causing the collision rate to spiral until a network operator intervenes.

The third design principle is to protect the significant investment in SNMP management stations and agents. In addition, a smooth transition would guarantee the continued progress of state-of-the-art SNMP network management. Careful engineering of the SNMPv2 framework was necessary to preserve the highest degree of interoperability possible with products already deployed in existing networks. *Fundamental* to the design of SNMPv2 was a plan for the periods of coexistence and transition undeniably necessary for SNMPv2's success.

It is worth noting that the second principle of retaining the control and intelligence in the management station goes hand in hand with the first principle of pushing the burden of network management into the management station. Similarly, the continued simplicity and consistency of the architecture help to guarantee that a viable transition plan from SNMPv1 to SNMPv2 is available. Finally, *a ruthless commitment to solid engineering principles* helps to achieve these goals and to ensure that the specification is implementable.

D.4 Models

The SNMP framework defines a model with several basic entities that describe the various components of an SNMP management system. These entities are the agent, the management station, the protocol, and management information.

An SNMP *agent* is a software entity that resides on a managed system such as a host, router, file server or hub. This piece of software is responsible for receiving management requests, interpreting them, executing them on the managed system, and replying with the appropriate response. In addition, the agent will at times respond to important events on the managed system by sending notification messages to a management station.

An SNMP *management station* is a software entity that performs management tasks by issuing management requests to agents. One or more network management applications exist on the management station, often providing a user interface for network management personnel in a network operations center.

The *management protocol,* SNMP, is used to transfer information between SNMP entities. SNMP uses a “remote debugging” paradigm in which a management station may inspect or alter variables on a managed system. The protocol provides security, sequencing, error notification, and information transfer. SNMP runs on top of a connection-less transport protocol such as IP/UDP because it has been shown that connection-oriented transport protocols are less robust in the face of network failures.

The fourth piece of the SNMP architecture is the *management information.* This consists of managed objects that exist on the managed system and are retrieved or altered by the protocol. Managed objects are specified and published so that management stations and agents from different vendors can interoperate by sharing the same naming and semantics.

D.5 Management Information

D.5.1 Structure of Management Information

The *Structure of Management Information* (SMI) document describes common characteristics of SNMP managed objects, how they are named, and how they are specified.

The SMI defines the data types allowed in the SNMP framework. SNMP uses the ISO ASN.1 as a specification language and as a mechanism for encoding (serializing) SNMP messages to be sent on a network. ASN.1 defines a rich set of data types ranging from integers to floating point to graphical character sets. The SNMP SMI chose a subset of these available data types to simplify the protocol engine required to build and parse SNMP messages. The SNMPv1 SMI allows the use of INTEGER, OCTET STRING, OBJECT IDENTIFIER, and NULL. The SNMPv2 SMI added the BIT STRING data type. The SMI also defines some new data types as subtypes of these base ASN.1 types. The SNMPv1 SMI added types such as Counter, Gauge, IpAddress and TimeTicks. The SNMPv2 SMI expanded this list further by adding an NsapAddress type for OSI addresses, a 64 bit counter for counting events that happen very frequently, as well as a type specifically for unsigned integers.

In order for a management operation to identify one or more variables to act upon, variables must have their names registered. ASN.1 OBJECT IDENTIFIERS are used to name variables. An OBJECT IDENTIFIER is a sequence of tagged integers, sub-identifiers, which specify a path through a registration tree. The SMI specifies that the basic structure of this registration tree is as shown in figure D.1.

To identify the object which is the number of errors received on a network interface, ifInErrors, the path from the root of the tree is:

iso.org.dod.internet.mgmt.mib-2.interfaces.ifTable.ifEntry.ifInErrors

Or more concisely:

1.3.6.1.2.1.2.2.1.14

This sequence of integers (without the "dot" separators) is what is actually sent in SNMP packets and used to uniquely identify a variable. The sequence of tags above is intended for convenience and is most likely to be seen in an SNMP user interface.

Many managed objects have more than one instance on a particular managed device. An instance of an object is specified by appending one or more sub-identifiers to the name of the object. For example, there is an instance of ifInErrors for each interface on the system. An instance of the ifInErrors object is identified by appending to the name a single sub-identifier indicating the index of a particular interface. Thus, to identify the error count for the fourth interface, the identifier is:

iso.org.dod.internet.mgmt.mib-2.interfaces.ifTable.ifEntry.ifInErrors.4

Different objects have different requirements for uniquely identifying a particular instance of each object, but all objects that make up a table will share the same instance identification mechanism. The nth instance of each object in a table effectively describes a row in that table. For those objects that have only one instance on a system and are therefore not parts of a table, a single sub-identifier with the value zero is appended. For example, the description of the system is named "mib-2.system.sysDescr.0."

The registration tree has three subtrees specified for naming different classes of objects. The mib-2 subtree is used to name objects that have been standardized by the Internet Engineering Task Force (IETF). The experimental subtree is used for standards that are still in the development process and for other experiments. Finally, the enterprises subtree is used to register proprietary, vendor-specific objects. Each interested organization will have a subtree of the enterprises subtree allocated to them. The organization can allocate objects under their subtree as they see fit.

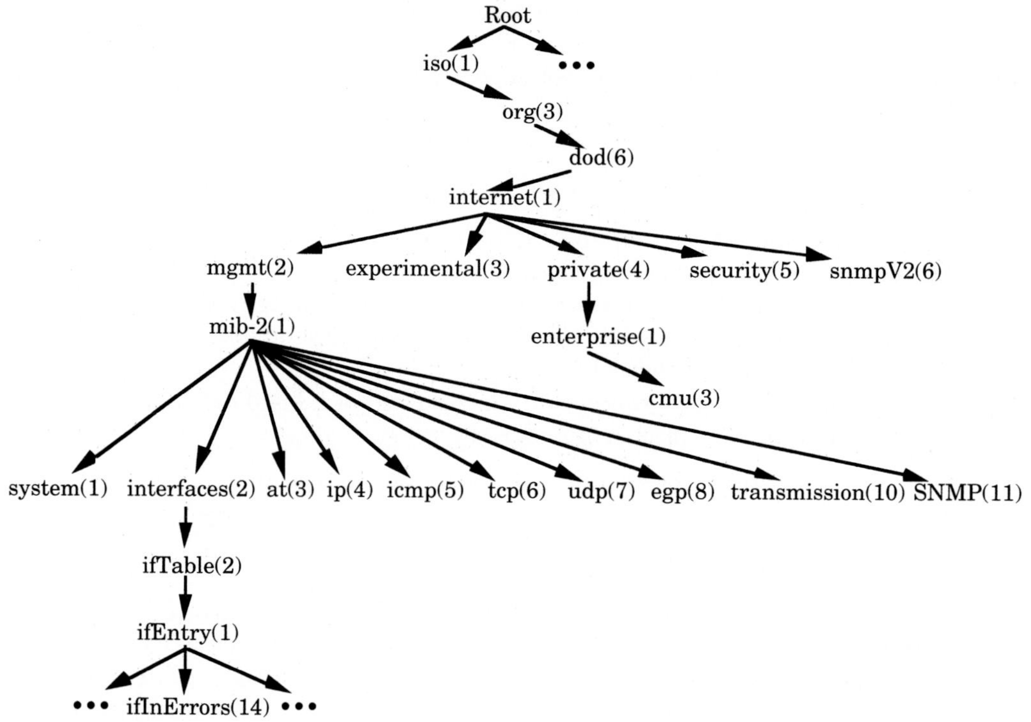

Figure D.1 Registration tree.

D.5.2 MIBs

In order for management station and agent software developers to produce products that interoperate, managed objects need to be specified and published. A Management Information Base (MIB) is the name of a document that specifies managed objects for a particular class of products or features, or a particular technology.

The SMI specifies the format in which a MIB shall define managed objects. An example of that format is shown in figure D.2.

```
ifInErrors OBJECT-TYPE
  SYNTAX Counter
  ACCESS read-only
  STATUS mandatory
  DESCRIPTION
   "The number of inbound packets that contained
   errors preventing them from being deliverable
   to a higher-layer protocol."
   ::= { ifEntry 14 }
```

Figure D.2 Example of managed objects definition.

Figure D.2 defines an object named ifInErrors whose type is Counter because it counts error events. It is read-only and it is mandatory to implement ifInErrors to claim conformance to the MIB it is a part of (MIB-2). The description clause tells the reader the semantics of the MIB object. Finally, "{ ifEntry 14 }" tells us that this object is registered in the tree as the fourteenth child of "ifEntry."

SNMPv2 changed this format somewhat by changing the ACCESS clause to MAX-ACCESS to indicate that the access specified is the most that "makes sense" for that object. In addition, a new clause called UNITS was added to indicate the units of the object (e.g., *seconds*, *errors*, or *packets*).

As a convenience, any MIB may create a TEXTUAL-CONVENTION that creates a sub-type of a pre-existing type for explanatory purposes. This sub-type is just an alias and does not change what goes inside an SNMP message. For example, the DisplayString textual-convention specifies an OCTET STRING that only contains ASCII data, and the TruthValue textual-convention specifies an INTEGER that contains either a true value or a false value.

SNMPv2 provides many more standard ways to describe the contents of a MIB. The NOTIFIFICATION-TYPE macro is used to define new interesting events that an SNMP entity might be notified of. The OBJECT-GROUP macro is used to group related objects together and to specify that every single object in the group must be implemented to claim conformance with that group. The OBJECT-IDENTITY macro enhances the ability to use OBJECT IDENTIFIERS to register other things such as hardware or software versions. The MODULE-COMPLIANCE macro defines the minimum requirements for an implementation of the MIB to claim that it conforms to the standard. Finally, the AGENT-CAPABILITIES macro is used by an agent developer to concisely describe how a particular agent behaves with respect to a standard MIB.

D.5.3 Standard MIBs

One of the strengths of the SNMP architecture is that many MIBs have already been standardized and implemented. MIB-2 is the second version of the *core* standard MIB for SNMP. This MIB defines basic objects for TCP/IP network management, and is implemented on virtually every SNMP management system in use today.

Many other MIBs exist today for managing various types of media (e.g., Ethernet, Token Ring, T1/T3); various network protocols (e.g., TCP/IP, AppleTalk, DECNet, OSI); and various types of devices (e.g., hubs, routers, network management probes).

An increasingly important area is *manager-to-manager communications.* There is a demand for hierarchical management systems that can be met easily with some of the new features in SNMPv2. Previously, with SNMPv1, hierarchical management systems could be built with specialized MIBs such as the Remote Network Monitoring MIB (RMON MIB). A device implementing this MIB performed remote network analysis, packet capture, and alarm processing, and communicated the results of these operations to a higher layer management station, typically for presentation to a human. SNMPv2 defines a similar MIB, the M2M MIB, that makes use of some of SNMPv2's built in manager-to-manager communications techniques. This MIB is the first in a series of MIBs that can be written to take advantage of these new features.

An upcoming MIB that is particularly relevant for managing distributed systems is the Host MIB. The Host MIB is oriented to general purpose computers such as workstations and PCs. With the Host MIB, a network manager will be able to find out the hardware and software configuration of the computer. This information ranges from the amount and configuration of memory and disk drives to the software that is installed or currently running on the system.

D.6 Protocol

Having covered the SNMP information model, it is time to visit the protocol that is used to perform operations on managed objects.

SNMP messages are sent over a connection-less transport protocol, usually IP/UDP. This reduces the complexity of the managed system and increases the reliability of the management protocol during times of network stress. Standards for running SNMP over other transport protocols such as OSI, AppleTalk, and IPX have been developed in recent years. SNMPv2 was designed with this capability from the start, so it is more tightly integrated.

Each SNMP message contains security information, error and sequencing information, an operation code, and a list of variable name/value pairs upon which the operation will be performed. This information is encoded into a packet using ASN.1's Basic Encoding Rules.

D.6.1 Protocol Operations

The SNMP protocol allows the following operations:

- Get

- GetNext
- Set
- Trap
- GetBulk (new in SNMPv2)
- Inform (new in SNMPv2)

The Get and Set operations inspect and alter, respectively, each of the variable name operands in the SNMP message. SNMPv2 vastly improved the capabilities of the previously underused Set operator. Most of this improvement came as a result of the definition of many additional error codes, the clarification of some of the details of Set processing, and the creation of a standard mechanism for creating and deleting rows in MIB tables.

The GetNext operator deserves special attention because it exploits the power of the SNMP approach to object naming. The GetNext operator takes one or more variable name operands, and for each returns the name and value of the object instance immediately following. This exploits the flat name-space that SNMP provides and provides a mechanism for a management station to discover objects and object instances on a remote agent.

For example, a download of a table can be started by invoking the GetNext operator with the names of the objects of interest, for example,

```
GetNext(ipRouteIfIndex, ipRouteNextHop)
```

which will return the instances of these objects that correspond to the "first" row in the IP routing table, for example,

```
GetResponse(ipRouteIfIndex.0.0.0.0, ipRouteNextHop.0.0.0.0)
```

Note here that although the request did not identify a particular object instance by name, it succeeded in returning the name of the next available object instance (and the corresponding values that are not shown above). In this case, "0.0.0.0" represents the default route in the routing table. We can use the returned names from this query as operands for the next query, for example,

```
GetNext(ipRouteIfIndex.0.0.0.0, ipRouteNextHop.0.0.0.0)
```

returning,

```
GetResponse(ipRouteIfIndex.128.2.10.2, ipRouteNextHop.128.2.10.2)
```

At this point it should be noted that this operator recognizes no boundaries between rows or tables or objects – it is truly a flat namespace. Thus, if we continue, for example,

```
GetNext(ipRouteIfIndex.128.2.10.2, ipRouteNextHop.128.2.10.2)
```

returning,

```
GetResponse(ipRouteMetric1.0.0.0.0, ipRouteType.0.0.0.0)
```

Note that the object instances returned are first instances in the next columns of the table (other examples might return information in completely different tables). This is an indication that there are no more instances of the requested objects.

A new addition to SNMPv2 is the GetBulk operator. This allows the management station to request the agent to effectively iterate a GetNext operation a specified number of times and return the result. For example, the management station might request three iterations in the following request,

```
GetBulk(ipRouteIfIndex, ipRouteNextHop)
```

returning,

```
GetResponse(ipRouteIfIndex.0.0.0.0, ipRouteNextHop.0.0.0.0
            ipRouteIfIndex.128.2.10.2, ipRouteNextHop.128.2.10.2
            ipRouteMetric1.0.0.0.0, ipRouteType.0.0.0.0)
```

A management station can typically request up to 60 iterations in a single transaction, vastly speeding up the retrieval of large quantities of data.

The Trap operation is issued by an agent that wishes to notify a management station of an important event. This notification is not acknowledged by the management station in the interest of simplicity and low cost. The SNMP architecture expects management stations to poll agents to retrieve interesting information, so the Trap operation is little used.

Finally, another new operation, the Inform operator, is used to enable manager to manager communication. This operation is used to send information from one manager to another and is acknowledged with a confirmation message. This can be used to send alarm information or any other data. This is a key element in building hierarchical management systems.

D.6.2 Coexistence

A major design goal for SNMPv2 was backward compatibility with SNMPv1 whenever reasonably possible. Great care has been taken to ensure compatibility with the installed base and to facilitate the period of coexistence that must occur while the industry transitions to SNMPv2. It was felt that this subject was so important that an entire specification was devoted to it.

There are two suggested coexistence strategies. The preferred mechanism is to create bilingual management stations, that is, they speak both SNMPv1 and SNMPv2. Such a management station can communicate with new SNMPv2 devices as well as old SNMPv1 devices. The other strategy is to use proxy agents that translate SNMPv2 requests from managers into SNMPv1 requests to agents, as well as the opposite transformation for the response packets. While this is a straightforward operation, it is still more complex than a bilingual manager. One or both of these strategies may be implemented in a particular management system.

D.7 Administrative Model

The administrative model of SNMP is used to provide security, proxy, and other administrative services. There are two models, the community model used in SNMPv1 and the party model used in SNMPv2.

There are four threats that a security mechanism can protect against. The most understood protection is against *masquerade*–in other words, to ensure that the requester is who he says he is. We also need to protect against message *replay* such as capturing a reboot command with a network analyzer and continuously re-sending it to a file server. Another protection is against message *modification*–for example, to ensure that someone doesn't capture an innocent but otherwise valid request packet and turn it into a command to reboot the system. Finally, a mechanism is sometimes needed to ensure *privacy* by protecting against *disclosure* of the message.

The community model was the first security mechanism specified for SNMP. When using the community model, a value called the "community string" is placed in a field in the beginning of the SNMP message and is used to identify both the sender and the receiver of the message. For most non-secure use, the string "public" is used. A small measure of security is gained by restricting operations to messages that contain a secret community string. The problem with this is that anyone can capture the SNMP packet with a protocol analyzer and read the secret string out of the packet and use it later. In any event, the community model provides no protection against replay, modification, or disclosure.

The party model is used to provide security to SNMPv2 and is a much more robust mechanism. A party is an identifier of one end of an SNMP communication. Thus, a pair of parties will be specified in each SNMPv2 message. In addition, the context of the message is explicitly identified in every SNMP message. The context will differentiate between different proxied systems and/or different local subsystems on a managed system.

Parties are pre-configured on each participating system to contain shared secrets, synchronized clocks, and other security information. Luckily, this configuration can be done remotely via SNMP with a MIB called the Party MIB. Two participating SNMP entities can communicate with no authentication; with authentication (protection from masquerade, replay, and modification); or with authentication and privacy.

Once an SNMP message is authenticated one can be sure who sent the request. However another step, authorization, is required to ensure that party has access to perform particular operations on particular variables. The party model defines how this authorization is to be performed and defines MIB tables that can be used to remotely configure this information.

D.8 Distributed Systems Management with SNMP

Networking management and computing management are moving closer and closer together and are increasingly being done by the same people. This creates a need for a standard for systems management that interworks with our SNMP standard for network management. Such a standard is also an opportunity to developers because it uses technology that is well understood and proven to be tractable. The key barriers to performing system management with SNMP were the lack of security, the lack of experience and robustness in the Set operator, and the lack of MIBs oriented towards systems.

Systems management places more emphasis on configuration management of user account and password management, queues, quotas, and so on. This increasingly requires remote configuration (SETs). Widespread use of SETs requires security and a more robust notion of how to perform creates and deletes and how to recover from errors.

Despite the fact that some specific needs were not met well with SNMPv1, many system vendors provided SNMP system management utilities. Systems managers could monitor system resource utilization, remotely inspect user account information, or determine what software was loaded. Novell file servers are well instrumented with SNMP, mostly to provide network protocol information. The large Unix vendors such as Hewlett-Packard, SUN and Digital Equipment each had SNMP agents that provided system management information, in some cases providing extensive user information, queue monitoring, and software status.

At Carnegie Mellon University SNMP is starting to play a role in the monitoring of distributed systems. Nearly all of the distributed system servers are being continuously monitored with the same fault management system that monitors the networking equipment. This allows the computing managers to use the same interface as the networking managers, and places this information in a single database. This facilitates the further integration of these two job functions.

The systems to date have made a lot of information available, but have not provided other necessary features such as remote configuration. In order to move further with systems management, the barriers mentioned before have to be erased. The introduction of SNMPv2 goes a long way by providing security and robust SET functions. This still left the need for standard MIBs for system management functions to augment the good work the vendors had put into proprietary MIBs.

In parallel with the creation of SNMPv2, this final barrier was being solved. The Host MIB is a soon-to-be standard systems management MIB for SNMP. The Host MIB is to systems management what MIB-2 is to network management – it is a core MIB, around which future MIBs will be built to address specific problems in printer management, mail management, software management and so on.

Other IETF working groups are currently working on MIBs for applications management and mail management. It is likely that standard MIBs for printers and other types of devices will follow. The creation of system oriented MIBs should increase further because of the better environment that SNMPv2 creates for them.

D.9 Conclusions

The Simple Network Management Protocol has established itself as the basis for integrated network management of heterogeneous devices in local and wide area networks. The recent introduction of the SNMPv2 Framework provided better documentation, better security, and improved protocol operations. This resulted in a faster and more efficient protocol, as well as a protocol that can take on manager to manager and systems management tasks.

These developments along with the development of the Host MIB move SNMP into a position to tackle standardized distributed systems management. Users will benefit from the sharing of applications and expertise when they use the same protocol for both network and systems management. Similarly, vendors will find it easier to deliver standards-based systems management products based on SNMP because they are familiar with the technology as well as the standards process.

Steven Waldbusser has been at Carnegie Mellon University for six years where he is the manager of Network Development, a small, high-profile group of software developers supporting CMU's large multi-protocol internet. He also serves as the chief architect for this leading-edge network. Steven has had personal design and coding experience with network management tools and applications for multi-protocol (particularly TCP/IP) networks. In addition, he designed and wrote the CMU public domain SNMP implementation, the most widely used SNMP implementation.

Steven also co-authored the IETF's Simple Network Management Protocol version 2 (SNMPv2), co-authored the host MIB, and authored the Remote Network Monitoring MIB (RMON MIB, RFC-1271) and the AppleTalk MIB (RFC-1243). He was also appointed to the IETF Network Management Directorate, tasked with overseeing SNMP network management standards development and chair of the IETF Host Resources MIB Working group.

Glossary

ACL	Access Control List
AFP	AppleTalk Filing Protocol (Apple)
AFS	Andrew File System
AFP	Advanced Function Printing (IBM)
ANDF	Architecture Neutral Distribution Format
ANSI	American National Standards Institute
AOCE	Apple Open Collaboration Environment
API	Application Programming Interface
APPC	Advanced Program to Program Communication (IBM)
ARA	AppleTalk Remote Access
ASN.1	Abstract Syntax Notation One
ATM	Asynchronous Transfer Mode
BIND	Berkeley Internet Name Domain
BOA	Basic Object Adapter
CAP	Columbia AppleTalk Package
CCITT	International Telegraph and Telephone Consultative Committee
CDS	Cell Directory Service
CICS	Customer Information Control System (IBM)
CITI	Center for Information Technology Integration at the University of Michigan
CM-API	Consolidated Management API
CMIP	Common Management Information Protocol
CMIS/CMIP	Common Management Information Services
CMU	Carnegie Mellon University
CORBA	Common Object Request Broker Architecture
COSE	Common Open Software Environment
CRC	Cyclic Redundancy Check
CUA	Common User Access–a graphical user interface (IBM)
DAA	Distributed Application Architecture (HP)
DBMS	Database Management System
DCE	Distributed Computing Environment (OSF)
DDL	Data Definition Language
DDM	Distributed Data Management (IBM)
DES	Data Encryption Standard
DFS	Distributed File System–a component of OSF/DCE
DII	Dynamic Invocation Interface
DLL	Dynamic Link Libraries
DME	Distributed Management Environment (OSF)
DoD	US Department of Defense
DNS	Domain Name System
DOE	Distributed Objects Everywhere (Sun)
DOMF	Distributed Object Management Facility (HP)
DPA	Document Printing Application
DRDA	Distributed Relational Database Architecture (IBM)
DSL	Dialog Specification Language
DTS	Distributed Time Service
EC	Event Controller
ECL	Event Controller Language
EDI	Electronic Data Interchange
EDL	Event Definition Language
ERB	Event Request Broker
EVS	Event Services
FDDI	Fiber Distributed Data Interface
FIFO	First In, First Out
FIPS	Federal Information Processing Standard
FTAM	File Transfer and Access Model (OSI)
FTP	File Transfer Protocol (TCP/IP)
GDA	Global Directory Agent
GDMO	Guidelines for the Definition of Managed Objects
GOSIP	Government OSI Profile
GSSAPI	Generic Security Services API
GUI	Graphical User Interface
HAL	Hardware Abstraction Layer
HMA	Host Management Application
HUGS	Host/User/Group/Subnet
I18N	Internationalization
I4DL	Interface, Inheritance, Implementation, Installation Definition Language
IDL	Interface Definition Language
IEEE	Institute of Electrical and Electronics Engineers
IETF	Internet Engineering Task Force
IFS	Institutional File System at University of Michigan
IMAP	Interactive Main Access Protocol
IP	Internet Protocol
IPC	Interprocess Communication
IPD	Installed Product Database
IRB	Instrumentation Request Broker
ISDN	Integrated Services Digital Network
ISO	International Organization for Standardization
ISV	Independent Software Vendor
IT	Information Technology
LAN	Local Area Network

LMS	License Management Services
LRU	Least Recently Used
MAC	Media Access Control
MAPI	Messaging API (Microsoft)
MIB	Management Information Base
MIT	Massachusetts Institute of Technology
MOA	Management Object Adaptor
MOTD	Message of the Day
Motif	A Graphical User Interface (OSF)
MPTN	Multi-protocol Transport Networking
MQI	Message Queue Interface (IBM)
MRB	Management Request Broker
MRM	Motif Resource Manager
MTS	Michigan Terminal System
MUA	Mail User Agent
MUI	Management User Interface
NBS	National Bureau of Standards
NDIS	Network Driver Interface Specification
NETBIOS	LAN-based Communications Protocol
NFS	Network File System (Sun)
NIS	Network Information Service (Sun)
NIST	National Institute of Standards and Technology
NMF	Network Management Forum
NMO	Network Management Option
NOS	Network Operating System
NT	New Technology (Microsoft)
NTP	Network Time Protocol
NSA	National Security Agency
NSFNet	National Science Foundation Network
ODA	Open Document Architecture
ODBC	Open Database Connectivity (Microsoft)
OIW	Open Systems Environment Implementors Workshop
OLE	Object Linking and Embedding (Microsoft)
OMF	Object Management Framework
ONC	Open Network Computing (Sun)
OLC	On-line Consultant (Project Athena)
OLTP	On-line Transaction Processing
OMG	Object Management Group
ORB	Object Request Broker
OSF	Open Software Foundation
OSI	Open Systems Interconnection
PCS	Personal Computer Services
PCTE	Portable Common Tools Environment (European Computer Manufacturers Association)
PEM	Privacy Enhanced Mail
PDK	Package Development Kit
PIN	Personal Identification Number
POSIX	Portable Operating System Interface for Computer Environments (IEEE)
POP	Post Office Protocol
PPP	Point-to-Point Protocol
PRS	Print Services
PSF	Product Specification File
RACF	Resource Access Control Facility (IBM)
RDBMS	Relational Database Management System
RFC	Request for Comment
RFP	Request for Proposal
RFS	Remote File Sharing
RFT	Request for Technology
ROSE	Remote Operations Service Element
RPC	Remote Procedure Call
RSA	The Rivest, Shamir, and Adleman public key encryption algorithm
SDS	Software Distribution Services
SLIP	Serial Line IP
SMB	Server Message Block
SMI	Structure of Management Information
SMP	Symmetric Multiprocessing
SMS	Subsystem Management Service
SMTP	Simple Mail Transfer Protocol (TCP/IP)
SNA	Systems Network Architecture (IBM)
SNA-MS	SNA Management Services (IBM)
SNMP	Simple Network Management Protocol
SQL	Structured Query Language
SVID	UNIX System V Interface Definition
TCP/IP	Transmission Control Protocol/Internet Protocol
TFTP	Trivial File Transfer Protocol
TI-RPC	Transport Independent RPC
TLA	Three Letter Acronym
TLI	Transport Layer Interface
TME	Tivoli's Management Environment
TSR	Terminate and Stay Resident
UDP	User Datagram Protocol
UFS	UNIX File System
UID	User Interface Definition
UIL	User Interface Language
UUID	Universal Unique Identifier
VFS	Virtual File System
VITAL	Virtual Integration Technical Architecture Lifecycle (Apple)
VLDB	Volume Location Database
WAN	Wide Area Network
WOSA	Windows Open Services Architecture (Microsoft)
X.400	ISO standard for message handling
X.500	ISO standard for an open system directory
XDR	External Data Representation (Sun)
X/Open	Independent open systems organization
XMP	X/Open Management Protocol
XPG	X/Open Portability Guide

Index

D

E

F

G

H

A NOTE ABOUT THE AUTHOR

Philip Ziegler, whose previous historical works include *Omdurman* (1974) and *The Black Death* (1970), was born in Hampshire, England, and was educated at Eton and New College, Oxford.

Before entering the University, he was commissioned in the Royal Artillery and served in North Africa. In 1951, after graduation from Oxford, he joined the British Diplomatic Service and was dispatched first to Vientiane, as Chargé d'Affaires, and then to Paris, Pretoria and Bogotá. Mr. Ziegler is currently an editorial director of Collins Publishers, Ltd., the British firm.

A NOTE ON THE TYPE

This book was set on the Monotype in a type face called Garamond. Jean Janson has been identified as the designer of this face, which is based on Claude Garamond's original models but is much lighter and more open. The italic is taken from a font of Granjon, which appeared in the repertory of the Imprimerie Royale and was probably cut in the middle of the sixteenth century.

Printed and bound by The Book Press,
Brattleboro, Vermont.